STATE OF GEORGIA

VERSUS

Clevon Jamel Jenkins

The Tragically Sad and True Account of
How Ambitious Prosecutors, Inept Lawyers,
and Incompetent Judges Sent a Black Teenager to
Prison for Life Without Any Possibility of Parole
for a Heinous Murder He Did Not Commit

Robert Michael Kelly, Esq.

Copyright © 2025 by Robert Michael Kelly

All rights reserved.

No part of this publication may be reproduced or distributed in any form or by any means without the written permission of the copyright owner.

ISBN: 978-1-969633-00-3

Library of Congress Control Number: 2025947037

Published by RMK Legal Publishing
150 Wrenn Drive
P.O. Box 1020
Cary, North Carolina 27512

Printed in the United States of America

First Edition

10 9 8 7 6 5 4 3 2 1

TABLE OF CONTENTS

INTRODUCTION 1

Chapter 1. A HEINOUS MURDER IN RICEBORO, GEORGIA 8

Chapter 2. A MUCH SAFER PLACE TO LIVE 24

Chapter 3. MEET ATTORNEY ROBERT MICHAEL KELLY 35

Chapter 4. MOTION FOR A NEW TRIAL 49

Chapter 5. ENUMERATION OF THE ERRORS 55

Chapter 6. JUDGE HARVEY DENIES THE MOTION 148

Chapter 7. APPEAL TO THE GEORGIA SUPREME COURT 198

Chapter 8. PETITION TO THE U.S. SUPREME COURT 249

Chapter 9. MEET FEDERAL JUDGE JOHN NANGLE 254

Chapter 10. PETITION FOR A WRIT OF HABEAS CORPUS 262

Chapter 11. JUDGE NANGLE RETURNS TO THE STAGE 353

Chapter 12. APPEAL TO THE ELEVENTH CIRCUIT U.S.
 COURT OF APPEALS...361

Chapter 13. PETITIONS FOR REHEARING AND CERTIORARI 376

Chapter 14. A WHOLE NEW LAWSUIT IN BROOKLYN.........................380

Chapter 15. APPEAL TO THE SECOND CIRCUIT
U.S. COURT OF APPEALS 419

Chapter 16. COMPARING THE FOUR DECISIONS THAT
DENIED JENKINS HIS LIBERTY 426

Chapter 17. SOME SIGNIFICANT CHANGES IN
THE LAW SINCE 1995 454

Chapter 18. AN APPLICATION FOR CLEMENCY OR PAROLE..........472

Chapter 19. WHY DID I FAIL? 493

Chapter 20. WHAT HAPPENED TO JENKINS' ALLEGED
CO-CONSPIRATORS?..510

Appendix A. List of the Cases and Proceedings Filed on
Behalf of Mr. Jenkins...515

Appendix B. Decision of Judge Harvey Denying Jenkins'
Motion for a New Trial 517

Appendix C. Decision of the Eleventh Circuit Denying Jenkins'
Habeas Appeal..534

Appendix D. Decision of Judge Garaufis Dismissing the
Declaratory Judgment Complaint 540

AUTHOR BIOGRAPHY 545

INTRODUCTION

Friday, October 8, 1993, was an unusually hot and humid day in Midway, Georgia. In the afternoon, after school had finished, Clevon Jamel Jenkins was "walking along the side of the road" with his new girlfriend Entwindle Williams. Jamel, as he was usually known, was an affable, chubby, seventeen-year-old black man who loved singing and composing rap music. He was not a particularly good student, not eager or ambitious, and he had a very low IQ, although not so low as to be considered mentally retarded. He was very large for his age, but he was also very gentle and somewhat submissive. Born and raised in Brooklyn, in the crime-ridden neighborhood of Bedford-Stuyvesant, Jamel had only recently relocated to Georgia to stay with his maternal Grandmother, Essie Mae Bacon, in Midway.

Jamel's mother, Dorothy Donaldson, was a hard-working decent Christian woman who did everything in her power to raise Jamel right and protect him from harm. She had reluctantly agreed in July to let Jamel stay year-round with his grandmother. Jamel, of course, wanted to stay close to his girlfriend, but Dorothy saw this as a great opportunity to avoid trouble for her son and get him away from the "mean streets" of Brooklyn. Being born and raised in Brooklyn myself, I fully empathize with Dorothy's concern.

Apart from Entwindle, Jamel did not have many friends. He was amiable and easy to get along with, but he was also somewhat reticent and shy and, as noted, he had only recently moved to Georgia from Brooklyn. For the most part, he was considered an "outsider" and a "New Yorker" by the "good old boys" of Midway. Four boys who Jamel did know were Cedric Brown and his brother Shawn, and Maurice Fleming and his half-brother Terry Roberts. Jamel knew them from school and from the neighborhood, and he would socialize with them occasionally, but they were not "bosom buddies" by any means. At this time, Roberts was 21, Cedric and Maurice were 19, Jamel was 17, and Shawn was 16.

As Jamel and Entwindle were walking along Bill Carter Road in Midway, Roberts, Cedric, and Maurice drove up alongside them in Roberts' car, and Cedric yelled out, "Hey, Jamel, get in." There was no discussion about where they were going, or what they would do, but Jamel obediently got in the car as requested.

After driving around aimlessly for a while, Roberts went to Cedric's house where they picked up Cedric's brother Shawn. Roberts then turned onto Route 84 heading towards Riceboro, but they stopped at a place called The Corner Store where Cedric got out of the car and bought a quart bottle of Magnum beer, which Cedric, Maurice and Jamel drank in the car. From there they went to Riceboro. According to Roberts, "Cedric was telling [me] where to go and Maurice was just showing me where it was." Eventually, Roberts drove to Hodges Grocery Store in Riceboro, where Jamel's life was changed forever.

Unbeknownst to him, Cedric and Maurice were planning to rob Mr. Hodges, and they were both armed with .25 caliber pistols. Maurice had an outstanding "bench warrant" for his arrest, and he needed money to get out of town. Roberts and Shawn were both aware of what Cedric and Maurice intended to do, but Jamel knew nothing. He was just along for the ride.

Roberts parked the car in the back behind Hodges Store. Cedric, Maurice, Shawn and Jamel got out and went into the store. It is not exactly known what happened inside the store, because there were no video cameras and no eyewitnesses. What *apparently* happened, however, is that Cedric, and possibly Maurice, pulled out their guns and demanded that Mr. Hodges give them money from the cash register. For some unknown reason, Cedric then began shooting at Mr. Hodges, and he was killed. It appears that Maurice may also have fired at least one shot at Mr. Hodges, although there is no conclusive proof of this.

What *is* known about the robbery and murder is this. The medical examiner concluded that Mr. Hodges was shot five times, of which one wound was fatal (severing the carotid artery), one wound was "potentially" serious (although it did not actually cause any injury), and three wounds were superficial. A ballistics expert concluded that two separate .25 caliber pistols were used, at least four shots were fired, and three of these shots were fired from the same gun. Two bullet fragments were recovered from Mr. Hodges' body, but neither of these bullets was fatal. Additionally, four .25 caliber shell casings and one additional bullet fragment were recovered by police from the crime scene. On the day after the robbery, a .25 caliber pistol was discovered by police in a search of Terry Roberts' car. According to the ballistics expert, the two bullet fragments recovered from Mr. Hodges' body and three of the shell casings found at the crime scene came from this gun. Despite diligent efforts by police to locate the other weapon, it was never found.

Mr. Hodges died quickly from his wounds. He was still alive when the robbery was first discovered and when emergency medical help arrived at the scene, but he died shortly thereafter without ever uttering a single word.

Apart from the medical and ballistics evidence presented above, there was no physical evidence of any kind indicating how this crime had occurred or who was responsible. No fingerprints, footprints, videotapes, photographs, blood samples, epithelial cells, hair samples, fabric traces, or any other type of physical evidence was found at the scene. A few bloody footprints were processed by the crime lab, but these all turned out to have been made by police and EMT technicians. Mr. Hodges' body was processed for "powder burns" but none were found, indicating that all the shots were fired from a distance greater than two feet.

As stated above, there were no eyewitnesses, and there was no way of determining who was responsible for what had happened. The only people who knew what had occurred were the perpetrators themselves, and they had no reason to talk to the police and incriminate themselves. Furthermore, if one or more of the perpetrators did talk to the police, how would anyone know whether he was telling the truth? The natural tendency of someone in that position is to deny responsibility and shift the blame to somebody else.

As it turned out, the police got a tremendous break. On the night of the robbery, Terry Roberts told his mother what had happened. Terry's father, Joe Roberts, then called the police. Terry and his father then went to the police station where Terry spoke with Chief Deputy Moran and Investigator Jim Gray. No record was kept regarding what Terry told the police at this time, but he was not arrested, which strongly indicates that he did not say anything incriminating.

The following day, the police returned to Roberts' house. By this time, they had become suspicious of Roberts' story, and they interrogated him for several hours. This time a tape recording and a transcript of the interrogation was made, although there were several times when the tape was conveniently turned off. At the same time, supposedly with the consent of Terry's father, the police searched Roberts' car, where a .25 caliber pistol was located under the front passenger seat.[1] Ballistics tests showed that this was one of the weapons used in the robbery.

From this point on, everything that is known about what happened in this case was based upon the testimony provided by Terry Roberts. Whether Roberts was telling the truth is unknown. What is known is that Roberts publicly admitted under oath that he "lied to the police the first couple of times that he spoke with them to protect himself and [his brother] Maurice."

---

1   Roberts was 21 at this time and lived with his parents, but he apparently owned the car that was searched. This did not become an issue during Jenkins' trial, but this search appears to have been unlawful because Terry's father lacked authority to consent to the search. If so, then the pistol recovered from Roberts' car (which appears to have been the murder weapon) could have been suppressed as the product of an unlawful search and seizure. Unfortunately, and this undoubtedly explains why this did not become an issue in Jenkins' trial, only Terry Roberts had standing to raise this issue, and he was cooperating with the police and had no motivation to complain.

Roberts told the police that he drove Cedric, Maurice, Jamel and Shawn to Hodges Grocery Store and remained in the car while the other four went into the store. A few minutes later, Maurice returned to the car and said, "Crank up, man, let's go. Cedric just shot that man in the head." When Cedric got back to the car, he said, "Yeah, I got him. I shot that cracker. I shot him in his head. Bang, bang, bang." Jamel also then said, "Yeah, yeah, yeah, I got him, bang, bang." At this time, according to Roberts, Cedric had a black .25 caliber pistol with a brown handle, and Jamel had .25 caliber chrome-plated pistol with a while handle. Roberts recognized the chrome-plated pistol because he saw Maurice with this gun about a week before the robbery.

When he got in the car, Cedric asked Roberts to drive to the bus station in Brunswick. After they got to Brunswick, Cedric gave Roberts some money and told him to get a room at the Sea Breeze Motel. They all then went into the motel, and Cedric distributed the proceeds of the robbery. Each person got about $150. They left the motel room shortly thereafter, and Roberts drove to the bus station, but it was closed. Cedric then asked Roberts to drive to the bus station in Savannah, where Cedric, Maurice and Jamel boarded a bus bound for Miami. Roberts later told the police that Cedric had relatives in Florida and that was where they were headed.

In his first recorded statement, Roberts told the police that Maurice was not involved in the robbery and that he never even went into the store. He insisted that Cedric and Jamel had guns and that they both admitted to Terry that they had shot Mr. Hodges.

Based upon the information provided by Roberts, the police were able to track Cedric, Maurice and Jamel to a motel outside of Miami. After summoning a swat team and a helicopter, Cedric, Maurice and Jamel were arrested at the hotel without incident. A search of the area was made for the second gun, but nothing was found. However, a food stamp was found in the motel room which the police traced back to Hodges Grocery.

After being arrested and advised of their rights, Georgia police questioned all three suspects in Florida. Cedric and Maurice gave detailed statements in which they eventually admitted their involvement in the robbery, although they attempted to minimize their guilt as much as possible. After being advised of his rights, Jamel refused to make any statement. However, according to a Florida police officer who transported Jamel back to Miami, Jamel supposedly told him, spontaneously and not in response to any questioning, "I only shot him once." Jamel denied under oath that he ever made such a statement.

After Cedric, Maurice and Jamel were returned to Georgia, the police again questioned Terry Roberts. They were concerned about Terry's prior statement because it conflicted significantly with what they had learned from Cedric and Maurice. For one thing, Roberts refused to say that Maurice had gone into the store during the robbery, but Maurice himself confessed that he did so. The police knew, therefore, that Terry was lying, and they told him so. Eventually, Terry was forced to admit that Maurice did go into the store, although he continued to say that it was Jamel who had the second gun and did the shooting.

In August of 1995, almost two years later, Jamel was tried for the murder and robbery of Mr. Hodges. The main witness for the prosecution was Terry Roberts. Jamel was represented by two court-appointed lawyers. Although Jamel had told his attorneys many times that he was not involved in the robbery, that he did not shoot Mr. Hodges, and that he was merely an innocent bystander, his attorneys refused to let him testify at the trial. The trial lasted a total of two days. Jamel was convicted and sentenced to life imprisonment without any possibility of parole. He was 19 years old at the time of the trial, and he remains in prison today, thirty years later.

Many mistakes and errors occurred during Jamel's trial, almost all of them extremely serious. After getting a new lawyer, Jamel brought a series of proceedings which attempted to get his conviction reversed. This included making a motion for a new trial in the Superior Court, appealing the conviction to the Georgia Supreme Court, filing a writ of habeas corpus in a federal district court in Augusta, and appealing the denial of that petition to the Eleventh Circuit Court of Appeals and the U.S. Supreme Court. He even filed a whole new lawsuit in federal court in Brooklyn seeking to have a 1996 amendment to the federal habeas corpus statute declared unconstitutional.

This book tells the extraordinary, previously untold story of what happened during Jamel's trial and appeals — and why I believe he was wrongfully convicted. I am the lawyer who represented him *pro bono* in his 1996 motion for a new trial and all subsequent appeals — a legal battle that spanned more than seven years. I know first-hand everything that occurred in those proceedings and why the justice system in Georgia failed Jamel so profoundly. As a former homicide prosecutor in Manhattan, a long-term trial lawyer for a prominent New York City law firm, a former Note and Comment Editor of the NYU Law Review, a summa cum laude graduate, and a member of the Order of the Coif, I offer an astute and insightful factual and legal analysis of exactly what happened during Jamel's trial and appeals.

Finally, let me say this: this is the ultimate whodunit. Although Jamel was found guilty by every court that reviewed his case, those decisions are not worth the paper they were written on. In this riveting and thought-provoking book, I discuss in great detail the evidence that was offered by the State in support of Jenkins' conviction. You can then put yourself in the minds of the jury and determine for yourself whether you think this evidence was sufficient to prove him guilty of murder beyond a reasonable doubt. Furthermore, I will also explain to you the applicable legal principles very carefully and clearly, and you can then decide for yourself whether you think the judges applied them correctly. In the end, it will be your task to determine whether you think Jamel is guilty, whether he received a fair trial, and whether he deserves to remain in prison. Thank you for being here. Let's begin.

CHAPTER 1

A HEINOUS MURDER IN RICEBORO, GEORGIA

On Friday, October 8, 1993, at approximately 6:40 p.m., Robert Franklin Hodges, the white owner and operator of Hodges Grocery Store in Riceboro, Georgia, was shot and killed during the commission of a robbery that occurred in his store. Approximately $850, a few food stamps, and some perfume was stolen. Hodges was struck by five separate bullets from two separate guns. Only one of the gunshots was fatal. Within a few days of the shooting, five young African-American males were arrested and charged with the robbery and murder.[2] This is the story of one of those

---

[2] The Hodges case is somewhat reminiscent of two other high profile murder cases that occurred in Georgia in the early 1970's, the "Marietta Seven" case (1971) and the "Alday Family murders" (1973). In the Marietta case, two white pathologists (Drs. Warren and Rosina Matthews) were shot and killed in their home in Cobb County, Georgia, during an apparent robbery. A white woman named Deborah Ann Kidd was arrested on an unrelated shoplifting charge and offered to trade information in exchange for immunity. She identified seven African-Americans in addition to herself as the perpetrators of the crime. Based on her testimony, James Creamer (the alleged shooter) was convicted of murder and sentenced to death. The other six individuals were also convicted of murder in five separate trials and sentenced to life imprisonment. The case was based primarily on questionable confessions and hearsay testimony. In 1975, after an investigation by the *Atlanta Constitution* and the FBI revealed numerous errors and serious improprieties, all seven defendants were exonerated. This case stands as one of the most notorious examples of wrongful convictions in Georgia history. In the other case, on May 14, 1973, in rural Seminole County near Donalsonville, Georgia, six members of the Alday family were brutally slain during a burglary at Jerry and Mary Alday's trailer. The attackers were escapees from a Maryland prison work camp. Four perpetrators were later apprehended, Carl Isaacs (19), Wayne Coleman (26), George Dungee (35), and Billy Isaacs (15), Carl's younger brother. Billy cooperated with the police and received a reduced sentence. Initially, Carl, Coleman and Dungee were all convicted of murder and sentenced to death. In 1985, the murder convictions were reversed by the Eleventh Circuit Court of Appeals due to prejudicial pretrial publicity and juror bias. The defendants were retried in 1988, and all three were again convicted of murder. Carl and Dundee were sentenced to death, and Coleman was sentenced to life. Dundee's death sentence was later commuted to life due to diminished mental capacity. Carl Isaacs remained on death row for thirty years before being executed by lethal injection in May of 2003. Billy Isaacs was released in the early 1990s and died in 2009. Dungee died in prison in 2006. Coleman is still incarcerated in Wilcox State Prison. He is currently 79 and has been in prison for 52 years. He is currently the longest serving inmate in Georgia. Jenkins is currently 49 and he has been in prison for 32 years. The Alday case is one of most notorious murder cases in Georgia history. It was depicted in the 1988 film *Murder One*.

young men, Clevon Jamel Jenkins, who is currently serving a life sentence in a Georgia prison without any possibility of ever being paroled for a crime he probably did not commit. At the time of his arrest, Jenkins was only seventeen years old, and he was the father of a daughter who was not yet born.

There were no eyewitnesses to the shooting, no videotapes of the robbery, no useful fingerprints found at the scene, and no identifiable footprints caked in blood on the floor. Four .25 caliber shell casings and one spent bullet were found at the scene, and two additional bullets were recovered from Mr. Hodges' body.

I did not know Mr. Hodges or his family, and I was not present when this robbery occurred. My only knowledge of this matter comes from the extensive record of the criminal trial that was brought against Mr. Jenkins by the State of Georgia and from his numerous appeals.

On October 9, 1993, one day after the robbery, a young, African-American male by the name of Terry Roberts was contacted by police officers and, after extensive questioning without benefit of an attorney and after giving numerous inconsistent and conflicting statements, he eventually implicated himself, Jenkins, Cedric Brown, Shawn Brown and Maurice Fleming as participants in the robbery. Also on October 9, a .25 caliber pistol was found by police inside an automobile that was owned and operated by Roberts. Ballistics tests would later determine that three of the shell casings found at the scene of the robbery and the two bullet fragments recovered from Mr. Hodges' body were all fired from this gun. The fourth shell casing and the spent bullet found at the scene were not fired from this gun, but from a different .25 caliber pistol that was never recovered.

During his lengthy questioning by police, Roberts indicated that he believed that Cedric Brown, Fleming and Jenkins were planning to go to Miami, Florida, where Brown had relatives. Further investigation by Georgia and Florida police revealed that the three suspects were probably staying at the Criss-Cross Motel in Opa-locka, Florida. A swat team and a helicopter were promptly dispatched to that location, and Brown, Fleming and Jenkins were arrested there without incident on October 12, 1993.

Following their arrest in Florida, the three suspects were advised of their constitutional rights under *Miranda v. Arizona* and questioned extensively by Georgia police. After waiving their right to remain silent, Brown and Fleming both gave detailed statements to the police in which they initially denied, but then eventually admitted, that they had robbed and murdered Mr. Hodges. Jenkins, on the other hand, refused to make any statement to the police, and he never indicated to them or anyone else that he had been involved in the robbery or murder of Mr. Hodges.

On December 9, 1993, Dupont K. Cheney, the District Attorney for Liberty County, Georgia, served notice that he intended to seek the death penalty in this case because the murder had occurred during the commission of a robbery.[3] On December 13, 1993, Cedric Brown, Shawn Brown, Fleming and Jenkins were all indicted for the murder and armed robbery of Mr. Hodges. Roberts was charged with the robbery in a separate indictment but, for reasons that will be discussed later, he was never charged with murder. However, an arrest warrant for Roberts for the murder of Mr. Hodges was issued by the Liberty County Superior Court on December 13, 1993, the very same day Jenkins, Fleming, Cedric Brown and Shawn Brown were indicted (1993 R. 6876).

Cedric was later determined to be mentally retarded and therefore, under applicable Supreme Court case law, he was not eligible for the death penalty. He pleaded guilty to murder and robbery on July 22, 1994, and was sentenced to two consecutive terms of life imprisonment. Shawn was under seventeen years of age at the time of the crimes in question and therefore, under applicable law, he too was ineligible for the death penalty. He pleaded guilty to murder and armed robbery on April 27, 1994, and was sentenced to imprisonment for a term of twenty years.[4]

---

3   Mr. Cheney died in Hinesville, Georgia, on February 18, 2006.
4   Although Cedric and Shawn were both sentenced to imprisonment, they would eventually become eligible for parole, and Shawn was in fact paroled in 1922. As of the date this book was first printed, Cedric remained incarcerated.

At the time of the robbery and murder, Roberts was 21, Cedric and Fleming were 19, Jenkins was 17, and Shawn was 16.

Mr. Hodges was a well-known, well-liked and prominent citizen of Riceboro, and both his murder and the subsequent arrest and prosecution of the perpetrators resulted in extensive publicity throughout Liberty County. The population of Riceboro was and is very small, only about 750 people in 1993 and even less than that today.[5] The city is less than forty miles from Savannah and is part of the Hinesville-Fort Stewart Standard Metropolitan Statistical Area. The county courthouse is located in Hinesville, Georgia.

The trial against Jenkins began on Tuesday, August 29, 1995, almost two years after the robbery was committed. The trial had been delayed by numerous pretrial proceedings, including a mandatory interim appeal to the Georgia Supreme Court. The first two days of the trial were occupied with the process of "jury selection" during which time the lawyers for the State and for Jenkins had the opportunity to question prospective jurors regarding their qualifications and potential biases. During these first two days, the presiding Judge, John R. Harvey,[6] maintained a very grueling trial schedule, beginning court at 8:30 a.m. and continuing until almost 11 p.m. After a jury of twelve members and two alternates had been selected, the actual trial began on Thursday, August 31, 1995. Two days later Jenkins was convicted of robbery and malice murder. Following a short trial before the same jury on the issue of punishment, on September 2, 1995, Jenkins was sentenced to life imprisonment without any possibility of parole on the murder charge. He was also sentenced by Judge Harvey to an additional consecutive life sentence on the robbery charge.

The trial was bifurcated into two phases, the "guilt" portion of the trial and the "penalty" portion. During the guilt phase of the trial, which

---

5 One of Riceboro's most prominent citizens is actor Ben Affleck, who purchased an 87-acre estate on Hampton Island in 2003 for $7.1 million. Ben and Jennifer Lopez had an elaborate wedding and reception there on August 20, 2022. The estate is technically in Riceboro, but it is sometimes said to be in Savannah. Ben has reportedly been trying to sell the estate for some time. Ben was not a resident of Riceboro at the time of the murder of Mr. Hodges.

6 Judge Harvey was a judge of the Superior Court of Georgia's Atlantic Judicial Circuit, which included Bryan, Evans, Liberty, Long, McIntosh and Tattnall Counties. Jenkins' trial took place in Liberty County. Judge Harvey died in Savannah, Georgia, on May 22, 2009.

only lasted for two days, evidence was presented by the State relating to defendant's guilt, and the jury was asked to render a verdict on the issue of whether the defendant should be found guilty of the crimes with which he was charged. Immediately after the guilt phase of the trial was completed, the sentencing phase began. During this phase, which lasted only a few hours, the defendant had the opportunity to offer mitigation evidence with respect to what sentence should be imposed.

Under applicable Georgia law, the determination of what sentence should be imposed was a decision that needed to be made by the jury. In this particular case, the jury had a choice of three possible options. They could sentence Jenkins to death, they could sentence him to life imprisonment without any possibility of parole, or they could sentence him to life imprisonment with a possibility of parole. In this case, the jury chose the middle option, life without any possibility of parole.

Jenkins was represented at the trial by two court-appointed attorneys, David C. Walker and Hal T. Peel., both of whom were well-regarded attorneys with substantial experience in criminal matters, including death penalty cases. Jenkins told Mr. Walker and Mr. Peel prior to the trial that he was not involved in the murder or robbery and that he wanted to take the stand and testify in his own defense. He was advised by his attorneys, however, not to testify. Furthermore, during the trial, he was explicitly told by his attorneys that the trial was "going well" and there was "no need" for him to testify. Based upon this recommendation, Jenkins decided not to testify.

The State called twenty-one witnesses during the guilt phase of the trial. Of this number, only three (Terry Roberts, Florida Police Officer James Smith, and Georgia prison inmate Kenneth McCall) provided evidence that actually incriminated Jenkins.[7] The other eighteen witnesses merely provided background information or other evidence that was necessary for the trial. For example, a medical examiner testified regarding

---

7   As will be discussed later, a fourth witness (Investigator Jim Gray) also provided testimony that incriminated Jenkins. However, this testimony was not based upon Mr. Gray's personal knowledge but upon inadmissible hearsay, and it should not have been allowed under applicable rules of evidence and federal constitutional law.

the cause of Mr. Hodges' death, and a ballistics expert testified regarding the two guns that were allegedly used in the robbery. However, none of the evidence provided by these eighteen witnesses implicated Jenkins in the robbery or the murder.

As noted above, pursuant to the advice of his court-appointed counsel, Jenkins did not testify at the trial. Furthermore, his attorneys did not call any witnesses to testify on Jenkins' behalf during the guilt phase of the trial,[8] nor did they offer any documents or other exhibits into evidence. Immediately after the prosecutors rested the State's case,[9] so too did Jenkins' trial attorneys. There were no Perry Mason or Ben Matlack moments here. A summary of the evidence presented by the State at the trial is set forth below.

The first witness called by the State was **William Bruce**. He testified that he operated an Amoco gasoline station next door to Hodges Grocery store in Riceboro (Tr. 1483)[10] and that on Friday, October 8, 1993, at approximately 6:40 p.m., he saw Frank Jones and Dewayne Paulk parked in front of Hodges' store (Tr. 1482-86).

The next witness called by the State was **Billy Strickland**. He testified that on October 8, at approximately 6:40 p.m., he went to Hodges' store and found Hodges lying on the floor bleeding (Tr. 1488-90). He called 911 and stayed at the scene until the ambulance and the police arrived (Tr. 1491-97).

The next witness called by the State was **Randy Garman**. He testified that he was a detective with the Liberty County Sheriff's Office (Tr. 1509); that on October 8, 1993, at 6:46 p.m., he received a 911 radio dispatch call and went to Hodges Grocery store (Tr. 1510); that when he arrived at the store he saw Hodges lying on the floor being attended to by emergency

---

8 Five witnesses testified for Jenkins during the penalty phase of the trial.
9 The case was presented by two prosecutors on behalf of the State: Dupont K. Cheney, the District Attorney for Georgia's Atlantic Judicial Circuit, and J. Thomas Durden, Jr., the Chief Assistant District Attorney for the Atlantic Judicial Circuit.
10 The abbreviation "Tr." refers to the transcript of the trial held from August 28 to September 2, 1995.

medical technicians (Tr. 1511-12); and that he secured the scene until additional detectives arrived (Tr. 1512-13).

The next witness called by the State was **Dwight Biechler**. He testified that he was an emergency medical technician (Tr. 1527-28); that on October 8, 1993, at 6:47 p.m., he received a call to respond to Hodges Grocery store (Tr. 1528); that he arrived at the store at 6:51 p.m. and found an elderly white male lying on his back in a large pool of blood inside the store (Tr. 1528-31); that the patient took two shallow breaths after he arrived but then stopped breathing (Tr. 1531); that he administered emergency medical assistance (Tr. 1531-34); that he and other EMS personnel transported the patient by ambulance to a different site for evacuation by helicopter (Tr. 1534-35); that the patient was pronounced dead at the evacuation site and returned back to the scene (Tr. 1535-37); and that the body was then transported to Liberty Memorial Hospital (Tr. 1537).

The next witness called by the State was **Joe Gregory**, who testified as an "expert crime scene analyst." He testified that he is a special agent with the Georgia Bureau of Investigation (Tr. 1561); that on October 8, 1993, at approximately 10:45 p.m., he arrived at Hodges Grocery store (Tr. 1563-64); that Mr. Hodges' body was not at the scene when he arrived (Tr. 1565); that he made a sketch (Tr. 1565-67) and took several photographs of the scene (Tr. 1568-81); that he found three spent shell casings and one projectile at the scene (Tr. 1581-84); that he processed the scene for fingerprints but found nothing of value (Tr. 1586); and that he processed the scene for footprints but found only footprints belonging to EMTs and police officers (Tr. 1592-94).

The next witness called by the State was **Gerald Hill**. He testified that he is a special agent with the Georgia Bureau of Investigation (Tr. 1600-01); that on October 9, 1993, at approximately 3:00 a.m., he arrived at Hodges Grocery store (Tr. 1602); that he found a shell casing inside the store (Tr. 1602-04); and that he took possession of the three shell casings and the projectile discovered by Agent Gregory and turned them over to Detective Davis (Tr. 1604-05).

The next witness called by the State was **Dennis Davis**. He testified that he is a Detective with the Liberty County Sheriff's Department (Tr. 1610); that on October 9, 1993, he received four shell casings and a projectile from Agent Hill and transported them to the State Crime Lab in Atlanta (Tr. 1610-11); and that on October 10, 1993, he received a .25 caliber pistol from Chief Deputy Keith Moran and transported it to the State Crime Lab in Atlanta (Tr. 1611-12).

The next witness called by the State was **Dr. Anthony Clark**, who testified as an expert medical examiner. Dr. Clark testified that he performed an autopsy on Mr. Hodges' body on October 9, 1993 (Tr. 1622); that various photographs were taken during the autopsy (Tr. 1623-24); that Mr. Hodges received *five* separate gunshot wounds to the right side of the face, the right side of the neck and the right shoulder (Tr. 1624); that two bullets were recovered from the body (Tr. 1630-31); that wound number *one* entered the right cheek area of the face, penetrated the cheekbone and entered the sinus cavity where a bullet was recovered (Tr. 1626-27); that wound number *two* entered the neck, nicked the jaw bone, went through the trachea, lacerated the left carotid artery, and exited the left side of the neck (Tr. 1627); that wound number *three* was a superficial wound which went in and out of Mr. Hodges' skin folds (Tr. 1628-29); that wound number *four* was also a superficial wound which only injured skin and soft tissue (Tr. 1629-30); that wound number *five* was also an insignificant injury which damaged only skin, fat and muscle, and did not affect any vital organs (Tr. 1630); that the bullet from wound number five wound up right inside the scapula in the shoulder and was recovered (Tr. 1630); that the *fatal* wound, in Dr. Clark's opinion, was the one that lacerated the carotid artery (Tr. 1628); that this wound caused rapid arterial bleeding which "squirts out and can go for quite a distance from the body, causing what we call arterial spray" (Tr. 1632); that the wound to the sinus cavity was "potentially fatal" since it could have caused injury to the brain (Tr. 1628) but Dr. Clark did not find any evidence of any injury to the brain (Tr. 1628); and that there was no evidence of powder burns, which indicated that the wounds were inflicted from beyond a distance of 18 to 24 inches (Tr. 1637-38).[11]

The next witness called by the State was **Terry Roberts**.[12] He testified that he was Maurice Fleming's half-brother (Tr. 1686); that he knew Cedric Brown, Shawn Brown and Clevon Jenkins (Tr. 1654, 1657); that on October 8, 1993, he drove Cedric, Shawn, Maurice and Jenkins to the vicinity of Hodges Grocery store (Tr. 1662-63); that prior to going to the store Cedric had said he planned to rob Hodges' store (Tr. 1665) and Jenkins said "yeah, he was ready to hold him up" (Tr. 1666); that Cedric, Shawn, Maurice and Jenkins got out of the car and went towards Hodges' store but came back shortly thereafter because there were people in the store (Tr. 1666); that Shawn then came back to the car and said the people in the store were gone (Tr. 1667); that Cedric, Shawn, Maurice and Jenkins then went back towards the store (Tr. 1667); that about ten minutes later they came back to the car and Maurice said "Crank up, man, let's go. Cedric shot that man in his head" (Tr. 1668); that Cedric, Shawn, Maurice and Jenkins then got in the car and Cedric said, "Yeah, I got him. I shot that cracker. I shot him in his head. Bang, bang, bang." (Tr. 1669); that Jenkins then said "Yeah, yeah, yeah, I got him, bang, bang" (Tr. 1669); that Cedric had a black .25 caliber gun with a brown handle and Jenkins had a .25 caliber chrome, nickel-plated gun with a white handle (Tr. 1670); that Roberts then drove the car away (Tr. 1672); that they went to the Sea Breeze Motel where they

---

11   The numbers which Dr. Clark attached to Mr. Hodges' wounds ("wound number 1," "wound number 2," etc.) were purely arbitrary for the purpose of discussion and did not indicate the order in which the wounds were inflicted.

12   Mr. Roberts suffered from some type of undiagnosed neurological disorder that affected his motor skills. Although he could drive a car without difficulty at the time of the robbery in October of 1993, by the time he testified at Jenkins' trial in September 1995 he needed to use crutches and a wheelchair and could no longer drive. No expert medical evidence with respect to this issue was presented by either side at Jenkins' trial. However, at the beginning of his testimony, in response to questioning by Assistant District Attorney Durden, Roberts testified, "I have a neurological problem, but I don't know what it is." Tr. 1654. Mr. Durden then stated, "Matter of fact, your doctors aren't exactly sure, but it appears to resemble multiple sclerosis or a type of multiple sclerosis, is that correct," to which Roberts replied, "Yes." Id. ADA Durden then asked, "but it does not affect your memory, does it?" to which Roberts replied, "No, sir." Id. To the best of my knowledge, Jenkins' attorneys never requested a physical or mental examination of Mr. Roberts prior to Jenkins' trial. Notably, Roberts died on February 16, 2005, at age 33.

rented a room (Tr. 1672-73); that Cedric then began counting out money and gave Roberts $150 (Tr. 1673); that Cedric also gave some money to Shawn, Maurice and Jenkins (Tr. 1673); that Roberts then drove to the bus station in Brunswick, but it was closed (Tr. 1675); that Cedric then asked Roberts to drive to the bus station in Savannah (Tr. 1675-76); that Roberts then drove to the bus station in Savannah (Tr. 1676); that Cedric, Maurice and Jenkins got out at the bus station (Tr. 1676) and Roberts and Shawn drove back to Hinesville (Tr. 1678); that Roberts later told his parents what had happened (Tr. 1680) and his father called the police (Tr. 1681); that Roberts then spoke with Investigator Jim Gray and Chief Deputy Keith Moran (Tr. 1681-82); that "the first couple of times that [he] talked with them [he] did not tell them the whole truth" (Tr. 1682) "because I was trying to look out for Maurice and myself" (Tr. 1682); that Roberts was indicted for his participation in the robbery (Tr. 1655); and that no one had made any promises to him about leniency in sentencing in return for his testimony (Tr. 1683).[13] Roberts also testified that about a week before October 8 Cedric had said, "We need to hit Bobby Hodges" (Tr. 1702), that Jenkins said "Yes, I'm with that. We can do that" (Tr. 1702); that Cedric said, "Yeah, and Terry, you can drive" (Tr. 1702); that Terry said, "No, I don't want no part of that" (Tr. 1702); that Cedric then said, "No, no, I'm just joking" (Tr. 1702); and that Terry thought they were joking (Tr. 1702). Roberts also testified that Maurice had told him that he needed to get out of town because there "was a bench warrant out on him" for an unrelated offense (Tr. 1658) and that Shawn also "had been arrested at the school" on the day of the robbery for an unrelated offense (Tr. 1660).[14]

The next witness called by the State was **Dewayne Paulk**. He testified that he was 14 years old (Tr. 1793); that on October 8, 1993, at about 6 or 7 p.m., he and his grandfather (Fred Jones) went to Hodges Grocery store

---

13   Roberts was originally charged with murdering Mr. Hodges, but the murder charge against him was dismissed by the District Attorney. Chief Deputy Moran testified at the trial that the reason the murder charge was dismissed was because no evidence was developed which showed that Roberts was aware of any plan to kill Mr. Hodges before it happened (Tr. 1840). For the reasons discussed in detail later, this testimony was improper and highly prejudicial.

14   A "bench warrant" is an arrest warrant issued by a court when a defendant fails to appear for a scheduled court date.

(Tr. 1704); that he saw Mr. Hodges in the store and he and his grandfather purchased some items from him (Tr. 1706); that when he left the store, he saw Shawn Brown standing outside the store (Tr. 1706-07); that he and his grandfather then drove to Midway (Tr. 1707); that before they got to Midway, he saw a fire truck, an ambulance and police heading away from Midway towards Riceboro (Tr. 1707-08); that he and his grandfather then went back to Riceboro to see what had happened (Tr. 1707-08); and that he saw the ambulance and police at Hodges' store (Tr. 1708).

The next witness called by the State was **Jim Gray**. He testified that he is an investigator with the District Attorney's Office (Tr. 1720); that he investigated the death of Bobby Hodges (Tr. 1721); that during the course of the investigation, he received information from various people, including information from unidentified "silent witnesses" (Tr. 1726); that based upon the information he received, he was able to identify Cedric Brown, Shawn Brown, Clevon Jenkins and Maurice Fleming as the participants in the robbery and the murder (Tr. 1727); that on October 10, 1993, at approximately 1:00 a.m., a search was made of Terry Roberts' vehicle and a .25 caliber weapon was found in the vehicle (Tr. 1727-28); that based on information he developed during the investigation he determined that Cedric, Maurice and Jenkins had gone to Opa-locka, Florida (Tr. 1729); and that based on information he developed during the investigation he determined that Roger Fleming, a cousin of Maurice, had reported that a Lorcin .25 caliber chrome-plated, pearl handled pistol had been stolen from his residence around the 12th of September, 1993 (Tr. 1733-35).

The next witness called by the State was **Roger Fleming**. He testified that he owned a .25 caliber Lorcin pistol which he kept in the bedroom of his house (Tr. 1739); that in September of 1993 his cousin, Maurice Fleming, had visited his house and went into the bedroom area (Tr. 1740); that the next day he noticed the pistol was missing (Tr. 1740); and that he reported it missing (Tr. 1741).

The next witness called by the State was **Bart Ingram**. He testified that he is a Special Agent with the Florida Department of Law Enforcement (Tr. 1742) and that on October 11, 1993, he was asked to assist in the apprehension of Cedric Brown, Maurice Fleming and Clevon Jenkins in Opa-locka, Florida (Tr. 1742-43). He testified about various efforts which he made to locate and arrest Cedric, Maurice and Jenkins (Tr. 1743-49) and that after arresting them, he advised them of their rights (Tr. 1752-55). Agent Ingram also testified that "information [was] developed as to the possible location of the other pistol" (Tr. 1756), that based on this information a search for a weapon was made in Florida (Tr. 1756-58), but that no weapon was found (Tr. 1758).

The next witness called by the State was **James Smith**. He testified that he is a police officer for the City of Opa-locka, Florida (Tr. 1774); that he was involved in arresting Cedric Brown, Fleming and Jenkins (Tr. 1774); that he transported Jenkins from the Opa-locka Police Department to Metro Dade Headquarters following his arrest (Tr. 1779); and that while being transported Jenkins "spontaneously" stated "I only shot him once" (Tr. 1780). On cross-examination, Smith stated that he told Jenkins, "Get your life together and tell the truth. Whatever happened, tell the truth" prior to this spontaneous statement being made by Jenkins (Tr. 1786).

The next witness called by the State was **Ramone Augusto**. He testified that he and his wife operated the Criss Cross Motel in Opa-locka, Florida (Tr. 1807); that the "defendants" (sic) were arrested at this motel (Tr. 1807); that after the defendants were arrested, a $1.00 food stamp was found in the room defendants had stayed at (Tr. 1810); and that he gave this stamp to Deputy Moran (Tr. 1810).

The next witness called by the State was **Keith Moran**. He testified that he was Chief Deputy of the Liberty County Sheriff's Department (Tr. 1814); that he was involved in investigating the murder of Mr. Hodges (Tr. 1815); that during the course of this investigation a .25 caliber pistol was recovered from the vehicle of Terry Roberts (Tr. 1818); that on October 13,

1993, he went to the Criss Cross Motel in Opa-locka, Florida (Tr. 1820); and that while at the Criss Cross Motel Mr. Augusto gave him a $1 food stamp (Tr. 1820).

Mr. Moran also testified regarding a statement which he took in October 1993 from an inmate at the Liberty County Jail named Kenneth McCall (Tr. 1822). Mr. Moran also testified that Terry Roberts was originally arrested for the murder of Mr. Hodges (Tr. 1840); that "no information was developed during the investigation to indicate that Mr. Roberts was aware of any plan to kill Mr. Hodges prior to the time it occurred" (Tr. 1840); and that, for this reason, the District Attorney decided to dismiss the murder charge against Mr. Roberts (Tr. 1841).

The next witness called by the State was **Cathy Hammock**. She testified that she was a vice-president of a computer service company which issues food stamps for Liberty County (Tr. 1829) and that, according to her company's books and records, State's Exhibit 38 (the food stamp found in the Criss Cross Motel) was issued to Carolyn Young of Riceboro on June 9, 1993 (Tr. 1830-31).

The next witness called by the State was **Carolyn Young**. She testified that she lives in Riceboro (Tr. 1835); that she receives food stamps (Tr. 1835); that in October of 1993 she did not travel to Opa-locka Florida and rent a motel (Tr. 1835); that she traded at Hodges Grocery store (Tr. 1836); that she usually used her food stamps within a couple of days after receiving them (Tr. 1837); and that she did not give food stamps to friends or trade them for money (Tr. 1835).

The next witness called by the State was **Kenneth McCall**. He testified that he was presently incarcerated at Macon Correctional Institution for a forgery conviction (Tr. 1843); that he was at the Liberty County Jail in October of 1993 when the defendants (sic) were brought back from Florida (Tr. 1843); that he was held in the same cell as Jenkins (Tr. 1843); that Jenkins told him that he shot "the old Cracker" twice (Tr. 1844); that Jenkins told him he threw the pistol out on the way to the bus station (Tr.

1845); that Jenkins told him he left the store after shooting Mr. Hodges (Tr. 1844); that Jenkins told him he heard three more shots after he left the store (Tr. 1844); that Jenkins told him "the other fellow took the money" (Tr. 1844); that "supposedly they got $800" (Tr. 1844-45); and that the District Attorney did not make any agreement with him or make any promises in return for his testimony (Tr. 1845). On cross-examination, Mr. McCall admitted that he was also in the same cell with Cedric Brown and Maurice Fleming and that he spoke with both of them also (Tr. 1855).

The next witness called by the State was **Charles D. Howard**. He testified that he was the Assistant District Attorney who handled the guilty plea entered by Kenneth McCall on the forgery charge (Tr. 1860-61); that at the time the guilty plea was entered he was not aware that Mr. McCall might be a witness in this case (Tr. 1861); that Mr. McCall did not request any special favors because he might be a witness in this case (Tr. 1861); and that two additional counts of forgery against Mr. McCall were dismissed because there was insufficient evidence to prosecute those counts (Tr. 1862).

The last witness called by the State was **Kelly Fite**, who testified as an expert firearms examiner. Mr. Fite testified that he was a firearms examiner for the GBI Crime Laboratory (Tr. 1866); that he examined the two bullets recovered from the body of Mr. Hodges, one bullet and four shell casings recovered from the crime scene, and the .25 caliber pistol recovered from Terry Roberts' vehicle (Tr. 1867); that the two bullets recovered from Mr. Hodges' body (State's Exhibits 29 and 30) were fired from the pistol recovered from Terry Roberts' vehicle (State's Exhibit 25) (Tr. 1868); that the bullet recovered from the floor of Mr. Hodges' store was not fired from State's Exhibit 25 but from a different .25 caliber pistol (Tr. 1870); that the weapon from which this projectile was fired was probably a .25 caliber Lorcin pistol (Tr. 1870); that three of the shell casings found at the scene (State's Exhibits 20, 21 and 24) were fired from State's Exhibit 25 (Tr. 1871); that the fourth shell casing found at the scene (State's Exhibit 19) was not fired from State's Exhibit 25 but from a different .25 caliber pistol (Tr. 1871); and that the weapon from which State's Exhibit 19 was fired was probably a .25 caliber Lorcin pistol (Tr. 1871-72).

As noted above, there were no eyewitnesses to the murder. Terry Roberts, who was himself *one of the alleged perpetrators of the robbery*, was the principal witness against Jenkins at the trial. Roberts was not physically present at the murder scene, however, and he did not see the crime committed. Besides the testimony of Terry Roberts, the only evidence connecting Jenkins to the crime were the two brief (and dubious) incriminating statements allegedly made by Jenkins after his arrest, one to a police officer in Florida (Officer James Smith) and the other to a cellmate at the Liberty County Jail (Kenneth McCall). Additionally, there was the improper testimony of Investigator Gray who testified that, based upon his investigation, including his conversations with so-called "silent witnesses," he was able to determine that Jenkins was one of the participants in the robbery and murder of Mr. Hodges (Tr. 1727).

Jenkins told his court-appointed lawyers that the statements made by Roberts, Smith and McCall were all false, that he never shot Mr. Hodges or participated in the robbery, that he never had a gun, and that he never made any incriminating statements to anyone. He also told his court appointed lawyers that he wanted to testify in his own defense, but they told him that the trial was "going well," and there was no need for him to testify.

Following completion of the testimony, the prosecutor and the defense attorneys had the opportunity to make "closing arguments" to the jury. Mr. Cheney, the district attorney prosecuting the case, took this opportunity to make an error-filled closing argument of which more will be said later. Jenkins' attorneys also had the opportunity to make closing arguments and they did so. However, since they never presented any evidence that contradicted the State's case, there was not very much they could point to during their summations to create a reasonable doubt regarding Jenkins' guilt.

Mr. Walker gave the final summation on Jenkins' behalf and he did a reasonably good job considering what he had to work with. He could have done a far better job, however, if he had permitted Jenkins to testify, if he and Mr. Peel had done a better job in cross-examining Terry Roberts, and if he had pointed out to the jury that Terry Roberts' testimony needed to be corroborated.

The main points of Walker's summation, all of which were true, were that Cedric Brown and Maurice were the "masterminds" of this robbery, that they had planned it because they needed money to get out of town because Maurice was wanted by the police for an outstanding bench warrant. Jenkins, on the other hand, was an outsider from New York who had no reason to participate in the robbery. Walker also emphasized that Roberts himself had testified that he had "lied the first couple of times" he spoke to the police in order to protect himself and his half-brother Maurice and that, for this reason, Roberts' testimony was simply not credible.

Despite Walker's arguments, it took very little time for the jury to find Jenkins guilty. The State then immediately began to present evidence in the "penalty phase" of the trial. This would determine whether Jenkins would be sentenced to death or be incarcerated for the rest of his life with or without possibility of parole.

Following completion of the penalty phase (which took less than four hours), Jenkins was immediately sentenced to life imprisonment without possibility of parole. He was 19 years old at that time. He remains in prison to this day.

As will be shown in detail in the following pages, there is considerable doubt regarding whether Jenkins was guilty. There is no doubt, however, that Jenkins did not receive a fair trial.

CHAPTER 2

A MUCH SAFER PLACE TO LIVE

Clevon Jamel Jenkins ("Jamel") was born in Brooklyn Jewish Hospital in Brooklyn, New York, on October 24, 1975. For most of his young life, he lived with his mother Dorothy and his father Cleveland in Bedford-Stuyvesant, Brooklyn, a place which his father described in court (during the penalty phase of Jamel's trial) as a "pretty rough neighborhood" and a bad place to live (Tr. 2066). In fact, his father went on to say, "down here (Hinesville, Georgia) is like heaven, compared with that (Bedford-Stuyvesant)." Tr. 2066.

Jamel's parents were both fine, hard-working, God-fearing people with full-time jobs. Cleveland worked as an inventory clerk for a building supply company in Brooklyn, and Dorothy worked as a legal secretary for a New York City law firm. In 1985, when Jamel was ten, his mother and father were divorced. Thereafter, Dorothy remarried, and Jamel lived for a short period of time with his mother and stepfather in Queens, New York. After two years, however, Dorothy and her son returned to Brooklyn. Following the divorce, Jamel remained in close contact with his father.

Jamel attended public schools in Brooklyn and Queens, graduating from grammar school in Queens and PS 231 Middle School in Brooklyn. PS 231 is a special needs education school. Jamel was not a particularly good student, and he had a relatively low IQ, but he never had any disciplinary problems in school or anywhere else.

When asked to describe her son during the penalty phase of the trial, Dorothy stated as follows:

> "Well, he's basically a good kid. I've never really had any problems. He's never disrespected any grown-ups or

anything. I've never had problems like that. And in our schools, we have open school where the parents can go and talk to the teachers for certain things, and the most I've ever heard from the teachers is like he would daydream in class sometimes. He wouldn't like, you know, be attentive, but he was never disrespectful or anything like that. And that was like from kindergarten to the present grade that he was in at that time, for me going back and forth to the school.

"And mostly all of the friends that he had I've practically knew them, and they came to the house. I met them, the girls and the boys. And, you know, I never had a problem like that. It's just so I guess, as he got older, he was a poor judge of character for the friends he picked at that point, being a teenager, whatever, but, other than that, I never had a problem with it. I never had a serious problem with him.

"He's never been in trouble with the law before. And in New York, like the southerners would say, 'oh, New York, that's bad. I mean he's bad, he's from New York.' [But] he's never even had a parking ticket or any kind of ticket or anything. He's never had any trouble with the law in New York.

"And I mean, I've lived in some pretty rough neighborhoods up there. I've been in a place, though I'm quite sure there may be some down here, call it Bed-Stuy. I mean, we call it Bed-Stuy there. If you've ever heard of that part of New York you will say, I mean that's a really bad place. But I've lived there, and he was there from the beginning, then we moved out to Queens. But I didn't have any problems with him at that point." Tr. 2047-48.

From a very early age, Jamel displayed a keen interest in, and a special talent for, music, particularly rap music. As his mother testified:

> "Jamel liked to write lyrics, like he likes rap music. That's like this new craze thing. But he was writing rap ballads ever since he was like — I call it rap ballads cause it's like it talks about love, but they put it in this rap sort of way you sing it. You're not like singing it out. He's been doing that ever since he was like about 11, cause he had a whole folder of music, you know."
>
> "At one point I wanted to put him in a school where it was just it did — it's like a school for talents. And they were supposed to submit them to the school in order for him to be entered, you know, into the school. But I didn't get to that point because he came down here for school."
>
> Tr. 2043.

This "special talent" was confirmed by Jamel's father. As Cleveland Jenkins testified in response to questioning by Mr. Walker:

Q.	"Are you familiar with Jamel's music making?
A.	Of course.
Q.	Has he sung for you?
A.	Well, he's sung for me a whole lot. He made — he gave me a few tapes and stuff.
Q.	He made some tapes?
Q.	Yeah. He made tapes and stuff. You know, demos and stuff. And he told me that he wanted to get into that — that field.
Q.	I know you're his father, but is he pretty good at that kind of thing?
A.	He's very good. I'm not saying that cause he's my son. He's very good.

Q.	Somebody thought he was good enough to make a demo tape?
A.	Yes
Q.	I don't guess he ever managed to work a record deal, though?
A.	No, not really. Not yet." Tr. 2066-67.

Since Jamel's mother and father both worked full-time jobs, and there was no one else at home, there was always a problem of what to do with Jamel when the school year ended in June. Jamel's grandmother, Essie Mae Bacon (Dorothy's mother), lived in Midway, Georgia, not far from Riceboro, and Jamel's grandfather (Fred Walthour) (Dorothy's father) lived in Aikens, South Carolina. From an early age, it was decided that the best thing to do was to let Jamel stay with his grandmother and/or his grandfather for the summer, and they were always glad to have him. This became especially important as Jamel got older, since both Jamel's mother and father thought that living on the "mean streets" of Brooklyn was not the best thing for him to do. They both agreed that Midway, Georgia, was a far "safer place" for Jamel to live, and one where he was unlikely to get into any kind of serious trouble.

In the Spring of 1993, when Jamel was seventeen, his father was able to secure a summer job for him at the building supply company where the father worked in Brooklyn. For this reason, Jamel did not go to Georgia to stay with his grandmother as usual. However, after only two weeks, the job fell through when the person that Jamel was replacing returned to work. When this happened, Jamel told his mother, "Mommy, I want to go to Grandma's," and she said, "Well, fine." Tr. 2045. Jamel then flew down to Hinesville and stayed with his grandmother. That was in June.

Ordinarily, Jamel would stay with his grandmother until the end of August and then return to Brooklyn for school. However, in August, Dorothy came down to Georgia for a family reunion, and Jamel told her that he wanted to stay in Midway with his grandmother and attend school there. As Dorothy testified:

> "I came down in August of '93 cause my family has a family reunion every two years. So, I came for the family reunion and he said he wanted to stay for school. So, I went over to the school, and I registered him for school and everything. And he was all set to stay, and he was down here since that time." Tr. 2046.

As will be disclosed in the next paragraph, Jamel had a special reason for staying in Midway besides living with his grandmother and attending school. But his mother Dorothy also thought that staying in Georgia was a good idea, since, as everyone knows, Brooklyn is a dangerous place and Georgia is much safer. And so, Mrs. Donaldson decided, very fatefully as it turned out, to let her son stay with his grandmother in Midway, Georgia.

On July 18, 1993, Jamel began dating Entwindle Williams, a nineteen-year old girl who lived "up the street" from Jamel's grandmother. They had known each other for several years, but at this time their relationship became more serious. Entwindle remembered the date exactly (Tr. 2973), so obviously Jamel must have made a good impression. Approximately nine months later, on April 29, 1994, Entwindle and Jamel gave birth to a baby girl, Shawnice Williams. The baby was born while Jamel was in prison, and she was sixteen months old at the time of Jamel's trial. Jamel was able to see Entwindle and Shawnice during prison visitations, but he was never able to touch or hold his daughter.

During the penalty phase of the trial, Jamel's mother (Dorothy Donaldson), father (Cleveland Jenkins), grandmother (Essie Mae Bacon), grandfather (Fred Walthour), and girlfriend (Entwindle Williams) all testified. By this time, Jamel had already been convicted by the jury of malice murder and armed robbery, and there was nothing they could say or do that would undo that result. The purpose of their testimony was solely to offer "mitigation evidence" to persuade the jury that Jamel was "worth saving" and should not be executed.

Obviously, Jamel's family loved him notwithstanding the horrendous crimes for which he had just been found guilty, and they continued to support him. Entwindle testified that she still intended to marry him. Tr. 2075. As she stated when questioned by Mr. Walker:

> Q. "What's your intentions towards Jamel?
> A. I intend to marry him still, regardless of if he gets convicted or no. I'm intending still to marry him.
> Q. Okay. Had y'all discussed this in the last year or so?
> A. Yes, we did.
> Q. And is that still your intention?
> A. Yes, it is.
> Q. Does he agree to that?
> A. Yes, he did." Tr. 2075.

Jamel's family fully understood that nothing they could say now would change the jury's verdict of conviction. Nevertheless, they all testified that they did not believe that it was possible that Jamel could have committed this heinous crime.

As Jamel's mother testified in response to questioning by the District Attorney:

> Q. "Mrs. Donaldson, you understand that this part of the proceeding is, of course, to determine the sentence to impose on your son?
> A. Yes.
> Q. And the purpose of your testimony is to mitigate, or to put into evidence mitigating circumstances?
> A. Yes
> Q. Well — what have you said that this jury ought to hear that's mitigating? That excuses him or [helps] understand what he did?

A.	Well, my whole family's sorry for what happened, including Jamel.
Q.	And so is the Hodges family.
A.	I truly — my heart goes out to them.
Q.	You know, a very, very respected man in that community's dead because of what your son did.
A.	I don't — if you want me to tell you how I really feel — what I really feel about this — I mean this is what they found, but in my heart, my son did not kill this mam. But this is what they're saying that he did, but he did not kill this man. My son did not kill Mr. Hodges.
Q.	Well, if he didn't do it an awful lot of people lied under oath on this witness stand.
A.	I'm telling — I truly believe that too.
Q.	So, what you are telling this jury, they're just wrong.
A.	I'm not saying they're wrong. In my heart, I know my son did not kill this man." Tr. 2049-50.

Jamel's father also testified in his son's defense, telling Mr. Cheney that what his son did was "make a mistake."

Q.	"But this was one hell of a mistake, if that's what it was, wasn't it, Mr. Jenkins? A man's dead because of this mistake. You understand that? Now, what mitigates that? What makes it less than what it really is? Anything?
A	Well, he made a mistake being with the wrong people at the wrong time. Just like they said on testimony, like they said earlier, he was just walking down the street with his girlfriend, his friends come up. He was at the wrong place at the wrong time. He made a bad judgment." Tr. 2071-72.

But perhaps Jamel's grandmother (Essie Mae Bacon) said it best when, in response to questioning by Mr. Peel, she testified as follows:

Q. "Ms. Bacon, how does your family feel about all this?

A. They are very remorseful, and my heart goes out to the Hodges family, because that was a store that I always stopped to when I go fishing. Me and my husband would always stop there because they had some good lunch meat and cheese. And I never passed that store, you know, without going in there. And he always treated me with respect. And I just — you know, I'm just sorry this all happened.

A. Ms. Bacon, I'll ask you what I asked Dorothy. Do you think that Jamel is — is somebody that is worth saving?

A. Yes, definitely he is. Jamel is worth saving. And I say to the jury, will you please spare my grandson's life, because I've sat here from day one and I heard all the testimony. And the testimonies really were given out of fear. My grandson didn't do that. And I know he didn't do it. So, I don't — y'all formed your opinion, but I know deep down in my heart that he did not do it. And justice will prevail one day. If we don't get justice here on earth, justice will be given in heaven. So please spare my grandson's life." Tr. 2054-55.

In addition to the testimony of these five family members, Jenkins' attorneys also presented into evidence, during the penalty phase of the trial, ten photographs that were taken at various times during Jamel's earlier life — when he celebrated his first birthday party with his mother and father in Brooklyn, when he graduated from grammar school in Queens, New York, when he was awarded a prize at Bible School, when he graduated from PS 231 in Brooklyn, when he celebrated Christmas with his parents in Brooklyn and the Fourth of July with his grandparents in Georgia, when he was singing rap music with his friends, a photograph of his girlfriend Entwindle and his daughter Shawnice and similar photos. Jamel's mother (Dorothy Donaldson) testified about these photographs in response to questions from Mr. Peel, explaining when they were taken, what they showed, and so forth.

During his cross-examination of Mrs. Donaldson, District Attorney Cheney, never one to miss an opportunity to act obnoxiously and callously, ridiculed Mrs. Donaldson's use of these photographs, and asked, sarcastically, "all the baby pictures in the world don't make things right for what happened, do they?" to which Mrs. Donaldson calmly and respectfully answered, "no." Tr. 2081.

Mr. Cheney then went one step further and loudly stated as follows:

> "I mean, we don't have a picture of him with a gun and coming out of the store. And we don't have that picture. And we don't have the picture of him laughing and talking about how he killed the old cracker, do we? We don't have a picture of that to show to the jury either. But you know there's a picture in the mind about those sorts of things." Tr. 2051.

This was completely improper cross-examination on Mr. Cheney's part since it was never intended as a question directed to Mrs. Donaldson, but solely as a self-serving inflammatory speech directed at the jury. Naturally, Jenkins' attorneys failed to object, either because they were too tired at this point to do so, or simply because they did not think it was wise to make an issue about this in front of the jury. Mrs. Donaldson, for her part, maintained her composure and sat by silently and respectfully, not wanting to anger the jury that would decide whether her son would live or die.

I fully understand the very difficult situation in which Mrs. Donaldson found herself, but, if it were me answering Mr. Cheney's questions, I would have responded a little differently:

"No, Mr. Cheney, we do not have those photographs, and that is the whole problem with this case. If you could show me a photograph of my son carrying a gun, or shooting Mr. Hodges, or talking about how he had killed "the old cracker," then maybe I could believe you when you say that he was involved in committing this heinous crime. But, as you say, you don't have those photographs, nor any other credible evidence that shows that Jamel robbed and killed Mr. Hodges. All you have is the untrustworthy, self-serving testimony of an unreliable accomplice who admitted many times that he lied to the police to protect himself and his brother Maurice, and who, by the way, was rewarded for his sketchy testimony by having the murder charge dismissed against him. And you also have the equally untrustworthy assertion of a convicted felon with a long criminal record who told the police exactly what they wanted to hear in order to obtain a "get-out-of-jail free" card for himself. And finally, you have the dubious testimony of an eager Florida police officer who likely made up the story about my son making a "spontaneous statement" because he knew that such evidence was needed in order to satisfy the legal requirement for corroboration of Terry Roberts' testimony. So, no Mr. Cheney, we do not have those photographs, but I sure wish we did, because that is the exactly the kind of evidence you needed to prove that my son was guilty of this crime. The evidence you had, in my mind and the minds of many others, was simply not sufficient. I know my son, and I know that he did not commit this crime."

I met Jamel several times during the course of my representation of him in connection with the numerous legal proceedings that will be discussed in this book. I cannot say, based upon these brief encounters, whether he committed the terrible crimes that are at issue here, or whether he was even capable of committing them. He was a large person, to be sure, weighing more than 240 pounds at only nineteen years of age, but he also appeared to be very gentle, and he loved music.

Mr. Hodges was not physically overcome by a larger person. He was shot with a single fatal bullet from a small caliber pistol, and the evidence appears to establish fairly conclusively that this fatal bullet was fired by Cedric Brown who, along with Maurice Fleming, needed money to "get out of town" and avoid being arrested by the police for other crimes they had committed. Jamel, on the other hand, had absolutely no reason to rob or kill Mr. Hodges, and he had never previously been in trouble with the law.

The biggest problem with Jenkins' case was that Mr. Hodges was shot with bullets fired from two different guns. The evidence established that only one of these bullets was fatal, and that that bullet was fired by Cedric, but it certainly complicated things that two different guns were used. Nobody knows for sure who fired the second gun, but the jury, by its verdict, unanimously concluded, supposedly by proof beyond a reasonable doubt, that it was Jamel. I cannot say with any degree of certainty whether this conclusion was right or wrong. What I can say with complete certainty, however, is that the legal process by which the jury reached this verdict was seriously flawed and irredeemably tainted by numerous errors, including egregious constitutional violations. This flawed process, and the significant legal errors that underpinned it, are what will be discussed in detail in the following pages of this book.

CHAPTER 3

MEET ATTORNEY ROBERT MICHAEL KELLY

My name is Robert Michael Kelly. I am an attorney licensed to practice law in the State of New York. For more than forty years, I was actively involved in the trial of criminal and civil cases, first as an Assistant District Attorney in the Manhattan District Attorney's Office and then as a trial lawyer with a prominent New York City law firm. I am retired now, living in North Carolina, and no longer engaged in the practice of law.

I first became involved in the criminal proceedings against Jenkins in 1996. By that time, he had already been convicted of robbery and murder and sentenced to life imprisonment without any possibility of parole. He was then in the process of making a motion for a new trial with the assistance of his two court-appointed Georgia lawyers, the same lawyers who had unsuccessfully defended him at the trial.

The reason I became involved in this case was because Jamel's mother, Dorothy Donaldson, worked as a legal secretary for White & Case, LLC, the New York City law firm for which I also worked as legal counsel. Dorothy had asked the corporate lawyer for whom she worked as a secretary to assist Jamel's court-appointed Georgia lawyers in preparing the motion for a new trial.

Understandably, the reason Dorothy had asked her boss to become involved in this case was because she believed that White & Case, an internationally prominent law firm with a strong civil litigation practice, would be able to discover flaws in the State's case that Jamel's court-appointed Georgia lawyers had overlooked.

Unfortunately, things do not work that way. A single practitioner, if he is a good lawyer, can be as capable, if not more so, than an entire firm of prestigious lawyers. This is especially so if the single practitioner is a skilled trial lawyer and the large firm is composed of corporate lawyers.

In this country, any lawyer who has passed the bar exam for his or her state and has been admitted to the bar can try a criminal case, regardless of whether he or she has any criminal trial experience.[15] I realize that everyone needs to start somewhere, but generally a capital murder case is not the best place to start.

If you have ever seen *My Cousin Vinny*, you will remember that Joe Pesci was extremely ineffective at the beginning of his cousin's trial. Gradually, as a result of repeated mistakes and some key assistance from his very attractive girlfriend, he "learns the ropes" and, somewhat miraculously, he becomes extremely effective when it matters most. But that was a movie. It was certainly entertaining, but it bears no relationship to what actually happens in real life.

Here, the lawyers from White & Case that Dorothy had asked to assist her were **corporate** lawyers who had no criminal trial experience. They spent many months researching and producing a lengthy memorandum of law which they intended to submit in support of Jamel's motion for a new trial. Throughout this lengthy period of time, they continued working with Jamel's two court-appointed Georgia trial lawyers. In the process, the deadline for filing the motion was repeatedly extended at the lawyers' request.

Eventually, White & Case's involvement in this matter came to the attention of Owen Pell, a partner at White & Case, who was at that time the head of the firm's Litigation Department. Mr. Pell strongly believed that it was inappropriate for corporate lawyers to be involved in this matter without any guidance and assistance from an experienced litigator. He then asked me to review the proposed memorandum and offer comments.

---

[15] That is not the case in the United Kingdom and most British Commonwealth countries where only licensed "barristers" are permitted to appear in court.

As requested, I then undertook to review the draft memorandum and offer comments. It was also necessary for me to review the trial transcript and examine the evidence that had been admitted at the trial. It was never my intention to become actively involved in this matter. As time went on, however, it became more and more necessary for me to do so.

After reviewing the proposed memorandum and the trial transcript, I quickly realized that the best possible arguments in support of Jamel's motion for a new trial were not being made. For one thing, the trial judge had failed to give a charge to the jury on the issue of "corroboration of accomplice testimony" which was clearly reversible error. For another, the case against Jamel included dubious hearsay evidence that was characterized as "silent witness" testimony, which violated Jamel's constitutional right to confront and cross-examine the witnesses against him. Thirdly, and most importantly, the performance of Jamel's court-appointed lawyers was clearly deficient, and this deprived him of his Sixth Amendment right to the effective assistance of counsel.

My first recommendation to the corporate lawyers who were representing Jamel was that they should immediately disassociate themselves from Jamel's court-appointed attorneys because, ultimately, it would become necessary to argue that they had been ineffective at trial. I also suggested numerous changes and additions to their proposed memorandum of law in support of the motion for a new trial. I had hoped, somewhat unrealistically, that this would be the end of my involvement in this case.

The corporate lawyers were extremely reluctant to disassociate themselves from Jamel's Georgia attorneys since, by this time, they had worked with them for more than nine months and they (the corporate lawyers) were comfortable with the quality of the Georgia lawyers' representation. Furthermore, the corporate lawyers were very hesitant to argue that the Georgia lawyers had been incompetent.

When Jamel finally filed his motion for a new trial on September 20, 1996 — more than a year after his conviction — he was jointly represented by Jamel's court-appointed Georgia lawyers and by White & Case. The accompanying memorandum of law that was filed in support of the motion was primarily drafted by me but, contrary to my recommendation, it did not include a claim for ineffective assistance of counsel.

The lead attorney from White & Case who represented Jamel in making this motion was the same corporate lawyer for whom Jamel's mother worked as a legal secretary. In addition to this corporate attorney, I deemed it necessary and appropriate for me to add my name as an attorney of record. By this time, it was becoming increasingly clear to me that I would have to become more actively involved in this matter than I had originally hoped.

After the Motion and accompanying Memorandum of Law were filed on September 20, 1996, the State of Georgia filed its Memorandum in Opposition to Jenkins' Motion. Thereafter, on November 29, 1996, I prepared and submitted a Reply Memorandum in support of the motion. A hearing on the Motion was then scheduled before Judge John Harvey of the Liberty County Superior Court on December 20, 1996.

By this time, it had become evident to me, as well as to the corporate lawyer with whom I had been working, that it would be necessary for me to take the lead in arguing Jamel's Motion for a new trial. It was also clear to me that the Motion for a new trial would need to be amended to add a claim that Jamel's court-appointed Georgia lawyers had been ineffective. This, of course, also meant that Jamel would need to sever his relationship with these lawyers.

On December 18, 1996, I traveled from New York to Hinseville, Georgia, to prepare for the hearing on the Motion for a new trial. The following day, I met with Jamel at the local jail to introduce myself and to discuss the case with him. He had been transferred to the jail from State prison so that he would be available to attend the hearing on December 20. After discussing the pending Motion with Jamel, he agreed to sever his relationship with his prior counsel and to raise the claim of ineffective assistance of counsel.

On December 20, I represented Jamel at the hearing before Judge Harvey. With Jamel's consent, Judge Harvey relieved Jamel's former attorneys as counsel of record and granted my application to appear on Jamel's behalf *pro hac vice* (for this case). This was necessary because I was not admitted as an attorney in the State of Georgia. Judge Harvey also agreed to appoint a local Georgia lawyer to assist me in representing Jamel on the Motion. This was necessary because Georgia procedural rules, like most states, require that a local lawyer appear as counsel of record in every case when out-of-state counsel is authorized to appear *pro hac vice*. Finally, Judge Harvey also granted my request for leave to amend the Motion for a new trial to add a claim of ineffective assistance of counsel and to submit a Supplemental Memorandum of Law addressing that issue.

On March 5, 1997, I submitted a Supplemental Memorandum of Law in support of the Motion for a new trial raising the issue of ineffective assistance of counsel. I also submitted an Affidavit containing additional evidence in support of the Motion. In due course, the State of Georgia submitted its Supplemental Memorandum in Opposition to the Amended Motion. Thereafter, an evidentiary hearing was held before Judge Harvey on March 14, 1997, at which time Jamel, his two court-appointed attorneys (David Walker and Hal Peel), and the District Attorney (Dupont Cheney) all testified. The details of this hearing will be discussed further in Chapter 4.

By this time, I was fully committed to representing Jamel in his effort to reverse his conviction and obtain a new trial. The corporate counsel from White & Case who had originally drafted a memorandum in support of the motion was no longer involved. And the local Georgia counsel who was appointed by Judge Harvey to assist me was not really a factor. He appeared at the hearing on March 14, and his name appeared on all the pleadings, but he had no active role.

Everything rested on me, and unfortunately for Jamel, that was not good enough. In more than forty years of practicing law, including extensive experience in trying homicide cases, I have never seen a greater travesty of justice than what occurred in this case. I firmly believed when I appeared before Judge Harvey on March 14, 1997, that he would probably overturn Jamel's conviction and grant him a new trial. I also believed that, if he failed to do so, the Georgia Supreme Court would surely do so. Little did I know then that I would spend the next seven years of my life pursuing this goal without success.

Over the course of those seven years, I appealed Jamel's conviction to the Georgia Supreme Court, the United States Supreme Court, the United States District Court for the Southern District of Georgia, the Eleventh Circuit U.S. Court of Appeals, the United States Supreme Court (again), the United States District Court for the Eastern District of New York, and the Second Circuit U.S. Court of Appeals. With the exception of the two proceedings before the U.S. Supreme Court — of which I have no criticism or complaint whatsoever — every one of these courts **failed miserably** in its duty to be fair and render impartial justice. As a result of these multiple failures, Jamel continues to rot in a Georgia prison for a crime he probably did not commit.

The purpose of this book is to describe in detail how all these courts (excepting the Supreme Court) utterly failed to discharge their duty to administer justice fairly, and why I believe that substantial doubt exists today — and has always existed — regarding Jamel's alleged involvement in the heinous crime at issue. Unfortunately, Jamel has already lost in our seriously flawed legal system. I hope that, by publishing this book, he may eventually win in the court of public opinion.

From time to time, I will be fairly harsh in criticizing the judges who were involved in making the various decisions that are discussed in this book. I believe that the reasons for such criticisms have been clearly stated and will be as obvious to you as they are to me. Nevertheless, in assessing these criticisms, it may be helpful for you to know a little bit about my background.

I was born in Brooklyn before the end of the last great war. I attended a Catholic elementary school in Brooklyn. I was then accepted to attend a prestigious public school in Brooklyn (Brooklyn Technical High School), but opted instead to attend a selective, all scholarship Catholic High School (Bishop Loughlin Memorial High School). In high school I was a member of the Honor Society, a member of student government, News Editor of the student newspaper, a member of the Latin Club, a frequent contributor to the Quarterly Literary Magazine, and a cum laude graduate.

After high school, I attended Fordham University in the Bronx where I majored in political science and sociology, with a strong minor in philosophy. When I graduated from high school, I was awarded three different scholarships, a New York State Regents Scholarship, a Mayor's Committee on Scholastic Achievement Scholarship, and a Fordham University Scholarship. While at Fordham, I was the News Editor and Editor-in-chief of the student newspaper (*The Fordham Ram*). I was also on the Dean's List. After Fordham, I attended the Maxwell Graduate School of Citizenship and Public Affairs at Syracuse University for a masters degree in political science.

After Syracuse, I attended New York University Law School in Washington Square. While at NYU, I was in the top five percent of my class, a Note and Comment Editor of the *NYU Law Review*, a member of the Order of the Coif, a John Norton Pomeroy Scholar, a winner of numerous *Corpus Juris Secundum* prizes, and a *cum laude* graduate. After my first year of Law School, I was awarded a full scholarship for my remaining two years.

After finishing Law School, I began working as an Assistant District Attorney with the New York County District Attorney's Office in Manhattan which, at that time, was headed by the legendary prosecutor

Frank S. Hogan.[16] Because of my law review experience, I was initially assigned to the Appeals Bureau where I assisted in preparing briefs for criminal appeals. I then spent six months on active duty with the United States Army. I was a member of the Army Reserve, serving as an interrogator for the 351st Psychological Operations Unit in the Bronx. While on active duty, I attended, and graduated with honor from, the U.S. Army Intelligence School at Fort Holabird, Maryland (since moved to Fort Huachuka, Arizona). I was honorably discharged from the army reserve in 1975 with the rank of Specialist 5th Class.

After serving in the army and after passing the New York State Bar Examination, I returned to the District Attorney's Office where I served for a year as an Assistant District Attorney prosecuting misdemeanor cases in the New York City Criminal Court. I was then selected to serve as an Assistant District Attorney in the Homicide Bureau prosecuting murder cases in NY State Supreme Court.[17] In the next three years, I tried more than twenty homicide and homicide-related cases.

After leaving the District Attorney's Office, I began working as an associate attorney for the New York City law firm of White & Case, LLP. I spent the first five months at W&C working in the Corporations Department and the next thirty-six years working as a trial lawyer in the Litigation Department. I was primarily involved in representing corporate clients in complex civil cases but, occasionally, due to my background, I became involved in representing clients in criminal cases.

After beginning my work at White & Case, I applied to, and was accepted by, New York University's Graduate School of Business. I then

---

16   Mr. Hogan served as District Attorney of New York County for 34 years (from 1941 to 1974). Prior to that time, he had served as Chief Assistant District Attorney for Tom Dewey, who later became governor of New York and a Republican candidate for President (losing to Harry Truman in 1948).

17   Contrary to its name, the Supreme Court is not the highest court in the State of New York. That honor goes to the New York Court of Appeals. The Supreme Court is the highest **trial** level court which hears felony criminal cases and the most significant civil cases. The recent criminal and civil cases that were brought against Donald Trump were both prosecuted in the New York County Supreme Court.

attended night classes at NYU for the next three years and was awarded an MBA degree with honors.

When I was first asked by Owen Pell to review the draft memorandum that had been prepared by the W&C corporate associates for the Jenkins case, I immediately recognized that significant errors had occurred during the trial due to my extensive experience in prosecuting murder cases in New York. For example, after reading the transcript of Jenkins' trial, I realized that the trial judge had failed to give the jury an instruction regarding the need for corroboration of accomplice testimony.[18] Neither the prosecutor, the defense attorneys, nor the trial judge had recognized this error until I pointed it out to them in the motion for a new trial.

Over the course of the seven years that I represented Jamel in his lengthy efforts to get his wrongful conviction overturned, I spent thousands of hours reading documents, analyzing cases and preparing briefs. All of this was done without any cost to Jamel. That was because I was representing him *pro bono publico* (for the public good). Actually, it was White & Case that was representing him *pro bono publico*. I was being paid my regular salary by the firm so there was really no cost to me. But there was a tremendous cost to White & Case. At that time, they were charging my time to clients at the rate of $700 or $800 per hour, so the cost in lost billings easily exceeded $1 million. I want to publicly thank White & Case for bearing this cost. I only wish my efforts had been more successful.

The trial of a criminal case is a fascinating and engrossing endeavor. Throughout history well-known stories have repeatedly been told of interesting cases, both real and imagined. From the trials of Socrates and Christ in ancient times, to those of Luther and Galileo in the middle ages, to more recent prosecutions of Lizzie Borden, Charlie Manson, Ted Bundy, O.J. Simpson, Bill Cosby, George Zimmerman, Derek Chauvin, Donald Trump and Sean "Diddy" Combs, criminal cases, especially murder cases, make good copy.

---

18 Terry Roberts was an accomplice in the robbery of Mr. Hodges, and therefore his testimony needed to be corroborated.

I dare to say there does not exist a single person in America, and probably not in the entire world, at least anyone over the age of six, who has never experienced the thrill of a criminal trial in some form, whether it be in a novel, a comic book, a newspaper, a movie, a play, a television program, or even in real life. Our society, and societies past, have been fascinated with legal dramas.

The litany of famous lawyers and crime scenes in literature rolls off the tongue quite easily: Cicero and the Cataline conspiracy, Portia in *The Merchant of Venice,* Sydney Carlton in *A Tale of Two Cities*, Radion Raskolnikov in *Crime and Punishment*, Dimitri Nekihlyudov in *Resurrection*, Henry Drummond and Matthew Harrison Brady in *Inherit The Wind,* Charles Laughton in *Witness for the Prosecution,* Atticus Finch in *To Kill A Mockingbird*, Jimmy Stewart in *Anatomy of a Murder*, Henry Fonda in *Twelve Angry Men*, Frank Galvin (Paul Newman) in *The Verdict*, Professor Kingsfield in *The Paper Chase*, Lt. Daniel Kaffee in *A Few Good Men,* Joe Pesci in *My Cousin Vinnie.*

And where would television be were there no lawyers? No Perry Mason, Horace Rumpole, Ben Matlock, Barnaby Jones, Ally McBeal, Jack McCoy, Denny Crane, Harmon Rabb, Mike McBride, Judge Judy, Jonathan Turley, Jeanine Pirro, Thomas Avenatti, Jeffrey Toobin.

And let's not forget the great lawyers and judges that changed history: Hammurabi, Moses, Solon, Cicero, Thomas More, Hugo Grotius, William Blackstone, Edward Coke, Andrew Hamilton, John Adams, John Marshall, Thomas Jefferson, Abe Lincoln, Clarence Darrow, Oliver Wendell Holmes, Louis Brandeis, Mahatmas Ghandi, Charles Hamilton Hudson, Earl Warren, Thurgood Marshall, James B. Donovan, Johnnie Cockran, Ruth Bader Ginsberg, David Boies, Rudy Giuliani, Alan Dershowitz, Ben Crump, Barack Obama, and countless others.

And yet, despite all this attention and exposure, or possibly because of it, the role of real lawyers in real cases is often underestimated and frequently misunderstood. As Henry David Thoreau once noted, albeit in another context, "The law will never make men free. It is men who have got to make the law free."

This is the work of everyone, of course, but, in the main, it is the work of lawyers and judges, and it is hard work indeed. The law is a demanding and exacting profession, and, unfortunately, not all lawyers and judges measure up to the task.

First, we have rules for everything — practice rules, procedural rules, evidentiary rules, ethical rules, conflict rules, statutes and substantive laws, administrative regulations, and constitutional provisions. These can be learned, of course — that is why people go to law school — but they cannot be mastered equally by everyone. Just as in baseball, basketball, or golf, some lawyers are stars, and others are not.

Second, and this covers a lot of ground, apart from knowledge of the law, successful lawyers must also possess a great variety of different skills, ranging from the ability to cogently and persuasively present evidence and legal arguments in court, to the ability to effectively cross examine witnesses at trial and in depositions, to the ability to research and analyze complex legal and factual issues in a logical manner, to the ability to evaluate and communicate well with witnesses, judges and prospective jurors and, finally, to the ability to recognize problems and solutions that others fail to see. Like Ralph Fiennes in *Taken*, or Tom Cruise in *Jack Reacher*, good trial lawyers must have "a unique set of skills."

If you ever saw *Runaway Jury* with John Cusack and Gene Hackman,[19] or *Bull* with Michael Weatherly, much was made of the role of "jury consultants" in modern complex litigation. These consultants are technical experts schooled in "the behavioral sciences" who assist trial lawyers, at great expense, in making tactical decisions regarding the trial, such as which jurors to exclude, what evidence to present, and what legal theories to emphasize or ignore.

---

19   The movie was based upon John Grisham's 1966 novel with the same name.

I have used jury consultants myself in several cases, and I know firsthand that their assistance can be, at times, extremely valuable. However, they are also very expensive and distracting. For these and other reasons, they are generally not used in typical run-of-the mill cases.

This is not to say, however, that the skills employed by jury consultants are unimportant in most trials. Quite the contrary, these skills are absolutely essential. The fact of the matter is that most trial lawyers, at least the successful ones, develop these skills innately as part of the litigation process. It has been thus from the early days of trial by jury and will doubtless continue to be so even in the age of artificial intelligence.

When I first began trial work in the Manhattan District Attorneys' Office, there was an extensive period of training for new lawyers. This consisted primarily of two parts: (i) a series of lectures and presentations by seasoned trial lawyers and (ii) a period of observation and analysis of actual trials. A large part of this training focused on the skills needed to select juries and present evidence at trial.

I fondly remember in my second year at NYU Law School I had a great professor of evidence named Irving Younger. He was far better than Professor Kingsford ever hoped to be, and he had a good personality to boot. Students in Irving's class were enraptured every day as he "took us to the woodshed" to explain key differences among relevancy, materiality and competence, or to explicate the arcane intricacies of the hearsay rule. The one word that naturally came to mind in describing Irving was charismatic.

This experience was decades before the invention of the internet and social media, and there was no such thing, technically speaking, at that time as "influencers" or "podcasts." Yet, Younger catapulted to rock star status in the legal profession by producing a series of videotapes on various legal topics, particularly evidence. His videotape entitled, "The Ten Commandments of Cross-Examination" was phenomenally successful, achieving cult status. And I had a front row seat, observing the great man every day in class.

Apart from being a great fan of Mr. Younger as a teacher, I mention him here to provide context for an important point. At some time after imparting his wisdom to the students at NYU, Younger decided to test his mettle as an actual litigator. He left NYU and eventually became a trial lawyer at Williams & Connolly, a top tier litigation firm based in Washington, D.C.[20]

Surely, if anyone would eclipse the enduring reputation of the great Clarence Darrow, it was Irving. I knew him personally (Irving not Clarence), and he was truly spectacular — in the classroom. In the real world, however, not so much. He was good, of course, but not nearly as good as his reputation. After three years as a litigator at Williams, he decided to return to the safer world of academia and do what he truly did best. Teach future lawyers.[21]

The point of this sidebar is to highlight, in my uniquely subtle fashion, that not all lawyers, and not all judges, are alike. For a variety of reasons, some are just better than others. I am sure this is true of doctors, plumbers, and other professions as well, but we are speaking here about lawyers. If the time ever comes when you or a loved-one needs a lawyer to represent you in a murder trial, I hope you find a good one.

Finally, it is important to note at the outset of this work that I have always believed, even from the first moment when I read the trial transcript, that Jenkins did not receive a fair trial. When I appeared before Judge Harvey on March 14, 1977, at the evidentiary hearing in support of his Motion for a new trial, I made the following statement to the Court:

---

20   Younger had briefly served as a trial lawyer with the Department of Justice prior to commencing his academic career. As an Assistant U.S. Attorney for the Southern District of New York he prosecuted Pete Seeger for contempt of Congress after Seeger refused to answer questions concerning his alleged Communist Party membership and activities. Seeger was convicted and sentenced to a year in prison, which was stayed pending appeal. The conviction was later reversed by the Second Circuit Court of Appeals on a pleading technicality. *See United States v. Seeger*, 303 F.2d 478 (2d Cir. 1962). In his autobiography, *Some of My Life*, which was published posthumously in 1991, Younger stated that he was not upset when Seeger's conviction was reversed.

21   Sadly, Irving died prematurely of pancreatic cancer in 1988 at age 55. He was truly one of the greats.

"First, Your Honor, I think, as I view the proceedings in this case, I think ultimately this is a case that is going to be reversed at some point. If not reversed here, I think it is going to have to be reversed at the Supreme Court level. I think that there were a number of errors that took place here that are going to require that to happen.

"As horrible a crime as this was, I don't think that takes away from the fact that my client, Jamel Jenkins, was entitled to a fair trial. I think in the heat of the moment when things were going on, a number of things happened that prevented him from getting a fair trial. And despite the fact that what happened here was a horrible situation, I don't think we should lose sight of the fact that my client should be entitled to a fair trial.

"Now, having said that, I think there are a couple of points that really are very critical in determining whether or not that fair trial took place. As I say, I think at some point, if not here then in an appellate court, it's going to be necessary that we have a retrial. I would hope that the Court will take these points very seriously and that, in its heart, it will look at this and determine whether or not it's convinced that Mr. Jenkins received a fair trial here. So, I think it is in everybody's interest that, since this is going to have to be reversed, it be reversed at this level. Because if we are going to have to have another trial, I think we should have it now when these events are more fresh in the minds of the witnesses than several years from now after the Supreme Court may have reversed it."

Transcript of the Hearing held on March 14, 1997, at pages 74-76.

Sadly, as discussed in the following chapters, Judge Harvey did not heed my advice.

CHAPTER 4

MOTION FOR A NEW TRIAL

By the time I had submitted the final Memorandum in Support of Jenkins' Motion for a new trial, I was firmly convinced that the Motion would surely be granted. The trial had been so bad, and so tainted by error, that no reasonable jurist could possibly fail to see that Jenkins had been wrongfully convicted.

If only this were so, this would be a much shorter book. People familiar with the antics of lawyers in literature know that the legal system in general, and legal practitioners in particular, are a disfavored lot. There are exceptions, of course, like Atticus Finch in *Mockingbord* and Syndey Carlton in *A Tale of Two Cities*, but for the most part we lawyers as a group have been disparaged and despised throughout history. There was a good reason Shakespeare wrote, "Let's kill all the lawyers" and the crowd cheered when the dinosaur in *Jurasic Park* ate the lawyer while he was sitting on a toilet. I strongly disagree with this, of course, but I understand the anger. I have witnessed lawyers and judges behaving badly more often than I care to admit.

And the lawyers, mostly judges, who you will encounter in this book are no better than the rest. In fact, for the most part, they are far worse. I don't think they consciously intended to be bad, they just never did what they needed to do to be good. They also never undertook to do what they were obligated to do by their sacred oaths of office. Even when faced with credible evidence of improprieties and persuasive arguments of wrongdoing, they simply buried their heads in the proverbial sand and never honestly considered the possibility that Jenkins might actually be innocent. Shame on them, and shame on me for never being able to convince them.

As noted above, on March 6, 1997, I filed an Amended Motion for a new trial which added a claim of ineffective assistance of counsel. Thereafter, on March 14, 1997, an evidentiary hearing was held in Hinesville, Georgia, with respect to this issue. Four witnesses testified at the hearing: Jenkins, his two court-appointed attorneys (Walker and Peel), and the honorable District Attorney of Georgia's Atlantic Judicial Circuit (Dupont K. Cheney). In addition, three exhibits were admitted into evidence.[22] This testimony is summarized below.

Mr. Jenkins testified that he did not shoot Mr. Hodges (Hr. 4)[23]; that he did not participate in the robbery of Mr. Hodges (Hr. 4); that he was present when Mr. Hodges was shot (Hr. 5) and saw Cedric Brown shoot Mr. Hodges (Hr. 5); that Maurice Fleming and Shawn Brown were also present when Mr. Hodges was shot (Hr. 5); that he did not have a gun when Mr. Hodges was shot (Hr. 5); that he did not know that Cedric Brown and Maurice were planning to rob Mr. Hodges (Hr. 6); that he never told Terry Roberts, Officer James Smith or Kenneth McCall that he had shot Mr. Hodges (Hr. 6): that David Walker and Hal Peel were his attorneys at the trial (Hr. 6); that he had told Mr. Walker and Mr. Peel repeatedly that he never shot Mr. Hodges (Hr. 6); that he had discussed with Mr. Walker and Mr. Peel the issue of whether he should testify at the trial and he told them that he wanted to testify (Hr. 7); that Mr. Walker and Mr. Peel recommended that he not testify (Hr. 7); that Mr. Walker and Mr. Peel also told him that the trial was "going well" (Hr. 7) and, therefore, there was "no need" for him to testify (Hr. 7), and that based upon Mr. Walker's and Mr. Peel's advice he decided not to testify (Hr. 7).

Mr. Walker testified that he and Mr. Peel represented Jenkins at the trial (Hr. 17); that Jenkins had told him prior to the trial that he did not shoot Mr. Hodges or participate in the robbery (Hr. 18 and 32); that Jenkins had told him prior to the trial that he never told Terry Roberts, Officer Smith or Kenneth McCall that he had shot Mr. Hodges (Hr. 32 and

---

22 Two other exhibits were attached to my affidavit dated March 5, 1997, which was submitted in support of the motion.
23 The abbreviation "Hr." refers to the transcript of the hearing held on March 14, 1997.

34); that Jenkins had also told him prior to trial that he wished to testify in his defense (Hr. 18); that Mr. Walker advised Jenkins not to testify (Hr. 19); that the reason he made this recommendation was because he did not think Jenkins would perform well under cross-examination and because he did not think that Jenkins had anything to say "which would help his defense" (Hr. 26). Mr. Walker also testified that he was aware that Terry Roberts, Officer Smith and Kenneth McCall had testified at the trial that Jenkins had admitted to them that he had shot Mr. Hodges (Hr. 33); that Jenkins had told him that these statements were untrue (Hr. 33); and that Mr. Walker and Mr. Peel had called no witnesses or presented any evidence in defense (Hr. 19).

Mr. Walker also testified that he was aware that Terry Roberts was an accomplice whose testimony required corroboration under Georgia law (Hr. 20) and that he had failed to request a jury instruction on the issue of corroboration or object to the court's charge on the ground that it failed to instruct the jury regarding the need for corroboration (Hr. 20). Mr. Walker also testified that he was aware that Terry Roberts had made several conflicting and inconsistent statements to the police prior to trial (Hr. 21) and that he did not use any of these statements to impeach Mr. Roberts at the trial (Hr. 22). Mr. Walker also testified that he was aware prior to the trial that Cedric Brown had been determined to be mentally retarded (Hr. 22) but that he did not introduce evidence of this fact during the trial (Hr. 22). Finally, Mr. Walker testified that the schedule of the trial was extremely grueling (Hr. 23); that he was "really tired" during the trial (Hr. 23); and that this may have affected his effectiveness as counsel (Hr. 23).

Mr. Peel testified that he and Mr. Walker represented Jenkins at the trial (Hr. 37); that Jenkins had told him prior to the trial that he did not shoot Mr. Hodges or participate in the robbery (Hr. 37); that Jenkins had told him prior to the trial that he never told Terry Roberts, Officer Smith or Kenneth McCall that he had shot Mr. Hodges (Hr. 37 and 39); that Jenkins had told him prior to trial that he wished to testify (Hr. 38); that he advised Jenkins not to testify (Hr. 38); and that the reason he made this recommendation was because he did not think Jenkins would perform well under cross-examination (Hr. 38).

Mr. Peel also testified that he was aware that Terry Roberts, Officer Smith and Kenneth McCall had testified at the trial that Jenkins had admitted to them that he had shot Mr. Hodges (Hr. 54); that Jenkins had told him that these statements were untrue (Hr. 54); and that Mr. Walker and Mr. Peel had called no witnesses or presented any evidence in defense (Hr. 54).

Mr. Peel also testified that he was aware that Terry Roberts was an accomplice whose testimony required corroboration under Georgia law (Hr. 39) and that he had failed to request a jury instruction on the issue of corroboration or object to the court's charge on the ground that it failed to instruct the jury regarding the need for corroboration (Hr. 40). Mr. Peel also testified that he was aware that Mr. Roberts had made several conflicting and inconsistent statements to the police prior to trial (Hr. 42); that he did not use these statements to impeach Mr. Roberts at the trial (Hr. 43); that this was not the result of a tactical decision but simply because "I just didn't consider using the statements" (Hr. 43). Mr. Peel also testified that the schedule of the trial was "a very exhausting pace" (Hr. 41) and "grueling" (Hr. 46); that he was "personally exhausted" (Hr. 41); and that this may have affected his effectiveness as counsel (Hr. 41).

Mr. Cheney testified that he was the District Attorney for the Atlantic Judicial District which included Liberty County (Hr. 59); that Kenneth McCall had testified for the State at Jenkins' trial (Hr. 60); that he (Mr. Cheney) had a policy that, whenever a prison inmate testifies favorably for the State in another case, he would write a letter to the State Board of Pardons and Paroles advising them of that fact and requesting leniency (Hr. 63); that after McCall testified against Jenkins in the present case Mr. Cheney did, in fact, write a letter to the Board of Pardons and Paroles on McCall's behalf (Hr. 63 and Movant's Exhibit 2) informing them that McCall had testified against Jenkins and that his "testimony was instrumental in obtaining a conviction" (Hr. 64 and Movant's Exhibit 2).

Mr. Cheney also testified that on October 28, 1996, he recommended to Judge Rahn that certain additional charges pending against Mr. McCall be dismissed (Hr. 59-60 and Movant's Exhibit 1) and that based, upon this recommendation, such charges were dismissed (Hr. 59-60 and Movant's Exhibit 1); that these charges were pending against Mr. McCall at the time McCall testified against Jenkins (Hr. 62); that no effort was made by him or by the District Attorney's office to determine whether these or any other charges were pending against Mr. McCall at the time he testified against Jenkins (Hr. 62) or to inform Jenkins' counsel of the pendency of these charges (Hr. 69) and that "I don't think I have any obligation to let [Jenkins' attorneys] know what the prior records of [the State's] witnesses are" (Hr. 69).

After the testimony at the hearing was concluded, the attorneys for both sides (me and the assistant district attorney) made brief arguments to the court highlighting why we thought the motion for a new trial should, or should not, be granted. These arguments were relatively brief because lengthy written memoranda had previously been submitted to the court describing our arguments in detail, with both legal and factual citations. The content of these arguments will be discussed in great detail below.

During the course of making my summary arguments in support of the Motion for a new trial, I pleaded with Judge Harvey to act now and not wait for some appellate court to act later. I argued that the numerous errors that had been committed during Jenkins' trial were so egregious that it would be unconscionable for the court not to grant him a new trial while the memories of the witnesses were still fresh.

One of the key legal arguments I had raised in support of Jenkins' Motion for a new trial — and this was set forth in great detail in the Memorandum of Law submitted in Support of the Motion — was that the Court had failed to give an instruction to the jury regarding the issue of corroboration of accomplice testimony. I will discuss this issue in greater detail below, but I mention it now to press a particular point.

After the evidentiary hearing which was held on March 14, 1997 had concluded and the legal arguments had been made, and as the parties were all preparing to leave the courthouse, me to New York, the other lawyers to their various offices in Hinseville, and Jenkins back to prison, Judge Harvey came over to me and privately stated, "I can't believe I failed to give a charge on corroboration." Obviously, he recognized, belatedly, that he had made a major mistake in conducting the trial, one that clearly could have changed the jury's verdict.

Unfortunately, however, he then added, "but I won't be the one to grant a new trial; I will let the Supreme Court [of Georgia] do that." I knew then and there we had lost, and that there was no way that anything I could ever say or do would make a difference.

Although I suspected as much, I did not actually know at this time that Judge Harvey would ultimately deny Jenkins' motion for a new trial. Perhaps, there was at least the possibility, however slight, that he might change his mind in the end after reading the papers. There is always hope.

I did ask myself, however, and I thought about this all the way back to New York, how could any person, especially an esteemed and trusted Superior Court Judge, not have the common decency to admit his mistake and do the right thing, especially when not doing the right thing would mean that a nineteen year boy might spend the rest of life in prison for a crime he did not do?

CHAPTER 5

ENUMERATION OF THE ERRORS

Jenkins asserted thirty grounds in support of his Motion for a new trial. Obviously, some of these grounds were stronger, more egregious, and more meritorious than others. However, to preserve all available grounds for appeal, it was necessary and appropriate to assert every plausible ground that could reasonably be raised. Furthermore, due process requires that the ***cumulative*** effect of ***all errors*** be considered in determining whether a defendant has received a fair trial. It would be wholly inappropriate, therefore, to consider some of these grounds in isolation from the others.

The thirty errors that Jenkins claimed tainted his trial are set forth in summary fashion below. Following this list, each ground will be separately discussed in greater detail. Unfortunately, there is no easy way to grasp the reasons Jenkins claimed he was deprived of a fair trial without understanding the basic legal principles involved.

1. At the conclusion of the trial, Judge Harvey failed to instruct the jury (i) that the testimony of Terry Roberts, an admitted accomplice in the robbery, needed to be sufficiently corroborated by other evidence and (ii) that it was the jury's obligation to determine whether sufficient corroborating evidence had been presented by the State.

2. Comments made by District Attorney Cheney, during his closing summation to the jury, regarding Jenkins' failure to present evidence at the trial rebutting the State's case were improper and prejudicial and violated Jenkins' Fifth Amendment privilege against self-incrimination.

3. The admission of hearsay evidence provided by unidentified "silent witnesses" during the testimony of Investigator Jim Gray was improper and prejudicial and violated Jenkins' Sixth Amendment right to confront and cross-examine the witnesses against him.

4. The testimony of prosecution witness Keith Moran was improper and misleading because it falsely implied to the jury that Terry Roberts, the State's principal witness, could not be charged with murdering Mr. Hodges.

5. District Attorney Cheney failed to correct the record regarding the false and misleading testimony presented by Keith Moran.

6. The testimony of prosecution witnesses Kenneth McCall and Charles Howard was improper and misleading because it falsely asserted that McCall would not receive any leniency from the State in return for his testimony.

7. District Attorney Cheney failed to correct the record regarding the false and misleading testimony presented by Kenneth McCall and Charles Howard.

8. Contrary to established principles of due process, District Attorney Cheney failed to provide Jenkins' attorneys with exculpatory *Brady* material relating to the credibility of Kenneth McCall.

9. The admission of additional hearsay (besides the "silent witness" evidence) during the testimony of investigator Jim Gray was improper and prejudicial.

10. The evidence presented at trial was insufficient to convict Jenkins of malice murder.

11. Judge Harvey's instruction to the jury regarding the issue of "malice murder" was erroneous and improper.

12. Judge Harvey's instruction to the jury regarding the issue of "parties to a crime" was erroneous and improper.
13. Judge Harvey's instruction to the jury regarding the issue of "conspiracy" was erroneous and improper.
14. The testimony of prosecution witness Terry Roberts was not sufficiently corroborated.
15. The admission of hearsay statements purportedly made by Jenkins' alleged co-conspirators was erroneous and improper.
16. Judge Harvey erred in failing to instruct the jury that the testimony of a co-conspirator regarding the issue of whether a conspiracy existed needed to be corroborated.
17. Judge Harvey made prejudicial remarks regarding the issue of whether a conspiracy existed which tainted the jury's verdict.
18. The admission of hearsay evidence regarding prior arrests of Jenkins' alleged co-conspirators was erroneous and improper.
19. Most of the testimony of prosecution witness Bart Ingram was irrelevant, misleading, inflammatory, and improper.
20. The admission of an incriminating statement allegedly made by Jenkins to a Florida police officer (James Smith) was erroneous and improper.
21. The prosecutor's closing argument during the guilt phase of the trial was improper and prejudicial.
22. The prosecutor's closing argument during the penalty phase of the trial was improper and prejudicial.
23. The prosecutors continuously and improperly engaged in "leading" the State's witnesses.
24. Judge Harvey erred in excluding relevant evidence offered by Jenkins' attorneys during the guilt phase of the trial.

25. Judge Harvey erred in excluding mitigation evidence offered by Jenkins' attorneys during the penalty phase of the trial.

26. Judge Harvey erred in refusing to answer the jury's question concerning when Jenkins would become eligible for parole if they sentenced him to life imprisonment.

27. Section 17-10-31.1(d) of the Georgia Code, which permitted the jury to impose a life sentence without any possibility of parole in this case, was unconstitutional.

28. Judge Harvey erred in sentencing Jenkins to an additional, consecutive term of life imprisonment on the robbery charge.

29. Jenkins was denied the effective assistance of counsel because of numerous significant errors that were made by his counsel during the trial.

30. Judge Harvey erred in denying Jenkins' motion for a change of venue.

1. ***Judge Harvey Failed to Instruct the Jury that the Testimony of Terry Roberts, an Admitted Accomplice, Needed to be Corroborated by Other Evidence***

It is settled law in Georgia, as in most other jurisdictions, that a criminal defendant cannot be convicted of a felony based solely on the testimony of an accomplice.[24] To support a conviction, the accomplice's testimony must be **corroborated** by other evidence. Furthermore, corroborating evidence must exist with respect to each essential element of the crimes at issue. The rationale for this rule is that an accomplice, as a participant in the crime, is inherently untrustworthy, and therefore what he says needs to be corroborated in order to be worthy of belief.

---

24   Section 24-4-8 of the Georgia Code *See, e.g., Bradford v. State,* 261 Ga. 833, 412 S.E.2d 534 (1992); *Harrison v. State,* 259 Ga. 486, 384 S.E.2d 643 (1989); *Hill v. State,* 235 Ga. 831, 225 S.E.2d 281 (1976); *West v. State,* 232 Ga. 861, 209 S.E.2d 195 (1974); *Allen v. State,* 215 Ga. 455, 111 S.E.2d 70 (1959); *Price v. State,* 208 Ga. 695, 69 S.E.2d 253 (1952).

This requirement is a fundamental principle of criminal procedure dating back hundreds of years.[25] Furthermore, it is explicitly **required by statute** (Section 24-4-8 of the Georgia Code). It cannot be ignored or disregarded by the prosecutor or the trial judge simply because they find it is convenient to do so. Any lawyer or judge who practices criminal law must be aware of this requirement, or he (or she) runs the risk of being deemed incompetent.

When I first read the transcript of Jenkins' trial, it immediately struck me that this critical issue of corroboration had never been addressed at Jenkins' trial. The prosecutor suggested at various times during his closing argument there was "corroborating evidence," but he never explained to the jury that there was a legal requirement for corroboration and that this legal requirement had been satisfied. It would appear, therefore, that District Attorney Cheney was clearly aware of the requirement of corroboration, but he did not object when Judge Harvey failed to instruct the jury on this critical issue.

Jenkins' defense attorneys, on the other hand, appear not to have been aware of the requirement. They never argued to the jury that the proof was deficient because it failed to show sufficient corroboration, they failed to request that Judge Harvey instruct the jury on the issue of corroboration, and they failed to object when Judge Harvey neglected to give a charge on this important issue. Actually, Jenkins' defense attorneys did not do very much of anything; they mostly sat by and let the prosecutors prove their case.

Finally, and most importantly, Judge Harvey, who presided at the trial and who had the legal obligation under both Georgia law and the federal constitution to provide adequate instructions to the jury, blatantly failed to instruct the jury regarding this important issue. Specifically, Judge

---

25 A person cannot be convicted of a crime unless the evidence presented at trial proves that he committed the crime **beyond a reasonable doubt**. If the only evidence showing the defendant's guilt consists of the testimony of another person who participated in the crime, then there is inherently a reasonable doubt because the accomplice may be lying. It makes no difference whether the accomplice is actually lying. The mere possibility that he may be lying requires that his (or her) testimony must be corroborated.

Harvey failed to explain to the jury: (i) that corroborating evidence was necessary in this case because Terry Roberts was an accomplice, (ii) what type and amount of evidence constitutes sufficient corroboration, and (iii) that it was necessary, in order to find Jenkins guilty of any of the crimes with which he had been charged (robbery and murder), for the jury to first determine whether sufficient corroborating evidence had been presented at the trial. No such instructions were given here, and this, **by itself**, was a fatal error **requiring** that Jenkins' conviction be reversed, and a new trial granted.

It must be clearly understood that the question of whether sufficient corroborating evidence had been admitted at the trial was an **issue of fact** that could **only** be determined by the jury **after receiving appropriate instructions**. As the Georgia Supreme Court ruled in Bradford v. State, 261 Ga. 833, 834, 412 S.E.2d 534, 535 (1992), "the sufficiency of the corroboration evidence is peculiarly a matter for the jury to determine."[26]

In this case, Terry Roberts, the State's principal witness, was unquestionably an accomplice in both the robbery and the murder of Mr. Hodges. This was established not only by Roberts' own testimony at the trial, but also by the fact that Roberts was actually indicted for the robbery. It was plainly evident, therefore, that Roberts' testimony needed to be corroborated. Yet, the jury never even considered this issue, because they were never told that they had to.

By the way, there was no valid reason why Roberts himself was not also charged with, and tried for, the murder of Mr. Hodges. Pursuant to the well-established legal doctrine of "felony-murder," any person who knowingly and voluntarily participates in the commission of a felony is criminally responsible for the death of any person who dies during the commission of the felony.[27] It does not even matter how the person died.

26　See also, West v. State, 232 Ga. 861, 209 S.E.2d 195 (1974); Caldwell v. State, 227 Ga. 703, 182 S.E.2d 789 (1971).
27　This doctrine is now specified by state statute, but it was originally part of English common law. It only applies to certain well-known egregious felonies, such as robbery, burglary, kidnapping, arson, and rape.

Whether the victim was intentionally or accidentally shot by one of the perpetrators, or whether he simply died of a heart attack, the felony murder doctrine still applies. Here, Roberts clearly participated in the robbery, and therefore he could have, and should have, been charged with felony murder for the death of Mr. Hodges.[28]

2. Comments Made by District Attorney Cheney During his Summation Regarding Jenkins' Failure to Present Evidence at the Trial Violated Jenkins' Fifth Amendment Privilege Against Self-Incrimination

It may seem logical to non-lawyers to allow prosecutors in criminal cases to argue to the jury, "well, if the defendant did not commit this crime, he should have taken the stand and told you so." Or this, "ladies and gentlemen, you have heard the testimony of three credible eyewitnesses who told you that the defendant committed this crime. That testimony has not been contradicted by the defendant in any way."

Although these statements may seem reasonable, they are clearly impermissible. The Fifth Amendment to the United States Constitution guarantees that defendants in criminal cases cannot be forced to testify or give evidence against themselves.[29] To protect this fundamental right, courts have consistently ruled that it is improper for the prosecutor in a criminal case to make **any comment** regarding a defendant's failure to testify. *See, e.g., Griffin v. California*, 380 U.S. 609 (1965).

For public policy reasons, what may seem logical and what is allowed by law are not always the same. In fact, many times they are directly opposite. I could give you many examples but just consider this. A perpetrator has just been caught red-handed committing an armed robbery of a

---

28 As will be discussed in more detail later, there were two reasons why Roberts was not charged with murder. First, District Attorney Cheney wanted Roberts to appear to be less culpable than Jenkins and therefore more credible and, second, he needed to reward Roberts for agreeing to testify for the State.

29 Technically, the Fifth Amendment only applies to cases brought in federal courts, but the United States Supreme court ruled many years ago that the same protections of the Fifth Amendment are available in state court prosecutions pursuant to the Due Process Clause of the Fourteenth Amendment. *Malloy v. Hogan*, 378 U.S. 1 (1964).

prominent NYC citizen in broad daylight on Fifth Avenue. After the perp is arrested and fingerprinted (and probably paroled), his "rap sheet" comes back and shows that he has previously been arrested for robbery seventeen times. The rap sheet also shows that he was convicted eight times and sentenced to a total of thirty-two years in prison. To be blunt and politically incorrect, the defendant is a "career criminal."

When the time finally comes for some young Assistant District Attorney to present the evidence in this latest case to a jury, may he offer evidence showing that the defendant was convicted of eight prior robberies?

As a matter of pure logic, any reasonable person would probably conclude that he should certainly be able to do so. The fact that the defendant committed similar crimes in the past is highly probative (tending to prove) that he probably committed this one as well. As a matter of public policy, however, the law provides otherwise. Unless there are special circumstances, proof of prior crimes is not admissible.[30]

The reason for this rule is **fairness**. If proof of prior crimes were admissible, such evidence would inherently prejudice the jury, and they might (and probably would) convict the defendant of the present crime based solely, or primarily, on the fact that he committed similar crimes in the past. It is possible, however, that the defendant did not commit this robbery. What the law requires is that the State prove, beyond a reasonable doubt, that the defendant committed **this robbery**, not that he has a general tendency to commit robbery.

The operative language that lawyers and judges use to describe this situation, and many others, is that "the probative value of the evidence is

---

30 This is the reason the rape conviction of movie mogul Harvey Weinstein was recently (and narrowly) reversed by the New York Court of Appeals. In that case, the trial judge had impermissibly allowed several women (none of whom was a victim of the crimes charged in the indictment) to testify that Weinstein had also molested them. See *People v. Weinstein,* 42 N.Y.3d 439 (2024). This same issue was also part of the reason why the rape conviction of Bill Cosby was also reversed. See *Commonwealth v. Cosby,* 252 A.3d 1092 (Pa. 2021). Prosecutors and trial judges often have difficulty resisting the temptation to offer inadmissible proof of other crimes to prove a defendant's guilt.

outweighed by its prejudice." Although the evidence is clearly relevant and probative, it is just too harmful to be allowed.

In this case, Jenkins' attorneys did not call any witnesses at his trial, nor did they offer any affirmative proof. Moreover, they unequivocally stated in the presence of the jury at the beginning of the trial that Jenkins would not call any witnesses (Tr. 1457). Nevertheless, the prosecutor repeatedly and improperly commented to the jury during his closing argument that Jenkins had failed to testify or present any evidence refuting the State's case. Thus, at page 1925 of the trial transcript, Mr. Cheney stated:

> "Each witness has testified. The defense, on each witness, has had the opportunity to present evidence and under cross-examination to refute the State's evidence. Is there any evidence that has been presented by **the defendant** that refutes what the State's evidence is?" (Tr. 1925) (emphasis added).

Shortly thereafter, the prosecutor added:

> "We have presented evidence as to this defendant's involvement, we have presented evidence **as to this defendant's statement**. Has the defense presented any evidence, any evidence, to refute the State's evidence? I think the answer to that is clearly no." (Tr. 1926) (emphasis added).

At this point Jenkins' attorneys properly objected to the prosecutor's comments and moved for a mistrial based upon the prejudicial statements (Tr. 1926). Judge Harvey, however, overruled the objection and denied the motion (Tr. 1928).

Even though he had been explicitly warned by the defense attorney's objection, the prosecutor doubled down and continued improperly commenting on Jenkins' failure to testify or present any evidence:

> "As I was saying before the objection was made, the State's contention is that **the defendant**, the defense in this case **has offered no evidence that would refute the testimony**

of the State's witnesses as they've testified in this case." (Tr. 1929) (emphasis added).

Shortly thereafter, the prosecutor continued:

"The second part of this State's evidence is **the admissions by the defendant**. . . . So there's three folks that have come into this courtroom, sat on this stand under oath and said, 'This man admitted to shooting Mr. Robert Franklin Hodges.' **And we contend that evidence has not been refuted in any way**." (Tr. 1938-39) (emphasis added).

These statements, whether considered singly or in combination, blatantly violated Jenkins' Fifth Amendment right against self-incrimination, and they were clearly prohibited by clearly established state and federal law.

First, the prosecutor's remarks were unquestionably of such a character that the jury would naturally and necessarily interpret them as comments on Jenkins' failure to testify. Second, as the prosecutor well knew, the only logical person Jenkins could possibly call as a defense witness was Jenkins himself. The prosecutor's actions, therefore, clearly violated Jenkins' constitutional right against self-incrimination.

Notably, this was not a case where the defendant had called one or more witnesses at the trial and the prosecutor argued that the testimony of the witnesses who testified on behalf of the defendant was insufficient to rebut the evidence presented by the State. Nor was this a case where the defendant had argued that the shooting was justified or accidental and then failed to offer any proof to substantiate these claims. In this case, Jenkins offered no affirmative proof whatsoever. He relied entirely upon the presumption of innocence and his Fifth Amendment privilege against self-incrimination, which he had an absolute right to do. The prosecutor, however, unconstitutionally infringed this right by making improper comments to the jury which unquestionably called the jury's attention to the fact that Jenkins did not testify.

As the United States Supreme Court explicitly stated in reversing a murder conviction in *Chapman v. California,* 386 U.S. 18, 25-26, 17 L. Ed.2d 705, 87 S. Ct. 824 (1967):

> "[T]he state prosecutor's argument . . . continuously and repeatedly impressed the jury that from the failure of petitioners to testify, to all intents and purposes, the inferences from the facts in evidence had to be drawn in favor of the State — in short that by their silence petitioners had served as irrefutable witnesses against themselves. . . . Under these circumstances, it is completely impossible for us to say that the State has demonstrated, beyond a reasonable doubt, that the prosecutor's comments . . . did not contribute to petitioners' convictions."

Similarly, it was impossible here for anyone to conclude, beyond a reasonable doubt, that the prosecutor's improper comments did not contribute to Jenkins' conviction. On the contrary, these erroneous statements provided sufficient grounds **by themselves** for reversing Jenkins' conviction and granting his Motion for a new trial.

3. ***Admission of Hearsay Evidence Provided by Unidentified "Silent Witnesses" Was Improper and Prejudicial and Violated Jenkins' Sixth Amendment Right to Confront and Cross-Examine the Witnesses Against Him***

Investigator Jim Gray was permitted to testify at the trial that he had received certain information from "silent witnesses" which caused him to believe that Jenkins was one of the perpetrators who murdered and robbed Mr. Hodges. (Tr. 1724-27). This was plain error and denied Jenkins his right to confront and cross-examine the witnesses against him. To compound the error, the prosecutor was permitted to repeat this testimony about the "silent witnesses" during his closing summation to the jury. (Tr. 1919). A criminal conviction based upon such egregious constitutional error should not be permitted to stand.

Under the Sixth and Fourteenth Amendments of the federal constitution, the accused in a criminal case has a constitutional right to confront and cross-examine all witnesses who testify against him. *Pointer v. Texas*, 380 U.S. 400, 13 L. Ed.2d 923, 85 S. Ct. 1065 (1965). This fundamental right is violated whenever a police officer (or anyone else) is permitted to testify about what he learned from "unidentified, anonymous witnesses." *Dutton v. Evans*, 400 U.S. 74, 27 L. Ed. 213, 91 S. Ct. 210 (1970); *California v. Green*, 399 U.S. 149, 26 L. Ed. 2d 489, 90 S. Ct. 1930 (1970). As the Eleventh Circuit U.S. Court of Appeals stated in setting aside a state criminal conviction in *Hutchins v. Wainright*, 715 F.2d 512, 515 (11th Cir. 1983), *cert. denied*, 465 U.S. 1071 (1984):

> "Reference to such a witness's statements, however, is inadmissible under the constitution. Here, the prosecutor gave in to the temptation to provide for the jury this inadmissible evidence. This violated the defendant's right to confront the anonymous, non-testifying witness."

It might be helpful to take a few minutes and try to explain the so-called "hearsay rule." This is somewhat complicated, but I think it is worth doing.

In a nutshell, hearsay consists of (i) an out-of-court statement, (ii) that is offered in court, (iii) to prove the truth, (iv) of what is stated in the statement. So, if Person A comes to court and tries to testify that Person B (his wife, for example) told him that "Person C shot Person D," this is hearsay (assuming that the reason the testimony is being offered is to show that Person C shot Person D). If the purpose of the testimony is merely to prove that Person B had the ability to speak, then it is not hearsay, since it is not being offered to prove the truth of what is contained in the statement. Of course, there would need to be a valid reason to prove that Person B had the ability to speak.

The general rule is that hearsay evidence is **not admissible**. However, there are numerous *exceptions* to the hearsay rule that allow the hearsay statement to be admitted. A key exception, for example, is an **admission** or a **statement against interest** by the declarant. So, if the driver of an automobile that has just been involved in an accident tells the other driver, "I am sorry, it was my fault," this constitutes an admission, and it will be admissible in a subsequent trial on liability even though it is hearsay. On the other hand, if the driver had said, "what were you doing, you dummy, I had the green light," this is not an admission, and it would not be admissible.

The rational for the hearsay rule is that hearsay statements are inherently self-serving and untrustworthy, and therefore they should be not admissible in a court of law because there is no way of ascertaining whether the person who made the out-of-court statement was telling the truth. The justification for the exceptions to the hearsay rule is that there is something special or unique about the circumstances in which the statement was made (such as an admission, or a "dying declaration" or a "business record") that provides sufficient indicia of truthfulness to justify an exception.

The hearsay rule is part of the law of evidence, which is generally a matter of state law. Although many states (including Georgia) now have statutory rules of evidence, the traditional rules of evidence developed as a matter of judge made common law over many centuries. When I practiced law in the state courts of New York, for example, the rules of evidence were primarily common law rules that were not governed by statute.[31] When I appeared in federal court, on the other hand, the evidentiary rules were governed by the Federal Rules of Evidence (which, in turn, were largely based upon the prior common law rules).

Although the hearsay rules are essentially matters of **state** law, the U.S. Supreme Court has determined, as a matter of **federal** law, that the federal constitution places certain limits on when hearsay can be used. Since the defendant in a criminal case has a **constitutional** right to confront and cross-examine witnesses under the Sixth Amendment, the hearsay rule

---

31   There were a few minor exceptions that were set forth in Article 45 of the New York Civil Practice Law and Rules.

cannot be used to circumvent this right. So, even though hearsay testimony may be admissible under state law, it is not admissible if it violates the defendant's right to confront and cross-examine witnesses under the Sixth Amendment.

Yet, that is exactly what happened here. Investigator Gray testified that he had received information from other witnesses (hearsay) which caused him to believe that Jenkins was one of the perpetrators who murdered and robbed Mr. Hodges. This was improper.

To make matters worse, Investigator Gray did not even identify who these "silent witnesses" were or, why, if they existed, they did not testify themselves. That is extraordinarily strange, and suspicious.

It appears to me that there were four different possibilities that could explain why these so-called silent witnesses were not called by the District Attorney to testify at Jenkins' trial, and none of them is good.

First, it is possible that the so-called silent witnesses never even existed and Investigator Gray just made the whole thing up. This seems to be extremely unlikely, but if this is what happened, then it was reprehensible and clearly reversible error.

Second, perhaps the silent witnesses did exist, but they were unavailable to testify at the trial, either because they had died or because they had moved away and could not be located. If this were true, it would still not permit the prosecutor to avoid the confrontation clause requirements of the Sixth Amendment by using hearsay. When a potential witness dies or cannot be located at the time of trial, the prosecutor is just out of luck.[32] He cannot avoid this unfortunate result by having a detective testify to what the missing witness previously told him.

---

32 There is an exception to this rule if the missing witness had previously testified under oath and was subject to cross-examination. Under these circumstances, the transcript of the prior testimony would be admissible. Obviously, that did not happen here. There is also the "dying declaration" exception to the hearsay rule. This is extremely limited and only applies when the victim of a homicide, with immediate knowledge of his impending death, makes a statement identifying his assailant. This also did not happen here. If a prosecutor fears that a witness may die prior to trial (because of age or illness, for example), he can always make a motion to "perpetuate" the witness' testimony. If the motion is granted, the witness will testify under oath and be subject to cross examination and thus satisfy both the hearsay rule and the confrontation clause requirements.

Third, the silent witness who Investigator Gray was referring to was actually Terry Roberts. This is certainly a possibility because Gray did, in fact, speak to Roberts during the investigation and he did get a great deal of information from him about who participated in the robbery. If this is what happened, however, it was completely improper, for several reasons. First, Gray's testimony concerning the information he got from Roberts was inadmissible because it was hearsay. Second, it would have constituted improper "bolstering" of Roberts' testimony. Roberts had already testified and, if the only thing that Gray was doing was repeating information he had previously gotten from Roberts, this was clearly improper. Third, and most importantly, the jury was not told and did not know the source of Gray's silent witness testimony. They were left with the impression that there were other witnesses besides those who testified at the trial who implicated Jenkins in the robbery and murder of Mr. Hodges.

Fourth — and this is probably the most likely and most pernicious explanation — the silent witnesses whom Investigator Gray was referring to were Cedric Brown, Shawn Brown and/or Maurice Fleming, the three other alleged perpetrators in the robbery and murder of Mr. Hodges. All three of these individuals were questioned by Georgia police at the time they were arrested, and all three gave detailed statements that were recorded by the police. Investigator Gray was present during these interrogations, and he had the opportunity to ask additional questions. If these were the witnesses whom Gray was referring to, then his testimony was completely reprehensible as well as inadmissible. The statements which these perpetrators gave to the police could not be admitted into evidence at Jenkins' trial because they constituted blatant hearsay.[33] And this hearsay problem could not be avoided by having Investigator Gray testify to what he learned from their statements.

---

33 These statements ***could*** have been admissible during the separate trials of Cedric Brown, Shawn Brown and Maurice Fleming because they constituted admissions as to each of these defendants. But they were not admissions with respect to Jenkins. Furthermore, even if they were somehow deemed to be admissible against Jenkins under state law, they still violated the confrontation clause of the Sixth Amendment.

If the District Attorney had wanted to provide testimony from Cedric, Shawn and/or Maurice at Jenkins' trial, the only proper way of doing so would have been to call them as witnesses. Cedric and Shawn had already pleaded guilty to Hodges' murder prior to Jenkins' trial, but it still would have been necessary for them to voluntarily waive their Fifth Amendment rights in order to testify. This was certainly possible, but it probably would have required that the prosecutor promise them something in return. Notably, Cedric had been listed as a potential prosecution witness, although the prosecutor ultimately decided not to call him at the trial (probably a wise decision). Maurice had not yet been tried at the time of Jenkins' trial so, obviously, he would have refused to testify. On the other hand, perhaps Maurice would have agreed to testify against Jenkins if the District Attorney promised to dismiss the murder charge against him like he did for Roberts.

Regardless of which of these four scenarios is correct, the District Attorney clearly violated Jenkins' rights (i) by surreptitiously introducing hearsay testimony contrary to his Sixth Amendment right to confront and cross-examine the witnesses against him and (ii) by deliberately creating the false impression in the minds of the jury that there were other witnesses, who did not testify at the trial, who also implicated Jenkins in the murder of Mr. Hodges. This was inexcusable and highly prejudicial.

4. *The Testimony of Prosecution Witness Keith Moran Was False and Misleading*

Keith Moran, the Chief Deputy of the Liberty County Sheriff's Department and the "chief investigator" on the case, testified that "when the investigation got completed [he had not] developed any information to indicate that Mr. Roberts was aware of any plan to kill Mr. Hodges, prior to the time that it occurred" (Tr. 1840) and this was the reason why the murder charge against Roberts was dismissed (Tr. 1841).[34] This testimony was false and misleading and highly prejudicial.

First, the obvious inference of Deputy Moran's testimony was that Terry Roberts could ***not*** be charged with Hodges' murder which, in turn, was intended to indicate to the jury that Roberts was more credible as a witness. Roberts was the State's single most important witness, and his credibility was absolutely critical. If, as the prosecutor claimed and as Roberts himself admitted, Roberts was a co-conspirator in the robbery with Cedric, Shawn, Maurice and Jenkins, then Roberts most certainly could have been charged with felony murder, ***even if he was unaware of any plan to kill Mr. Hodges***. Thus, Moran's testimony, which effectively said that Roberts could not be charged with murdering Mr. Hodges, was both false and intentionally misleading to the jury.

A second and even more pernicious inference which the jury could have drawn from Moran's testimony was that Moran must have received some information during the course of the investigation which indicated to him that Jenkins was aware of a plan to kill Mr. Hodges. As noted above, Moran testified that the reason the murder charge was dismissed against Roberts was because "when the investigation got completed [he had not] developed any information to indicate that Mr. Roberts was aware of any plan to kill Mr. Hodges, prior to the time that it occurred" (Tr. 1840-41). Obviously, Moran must have developed some evidence during the investigation which showed that Jenkins was aware of a plan to kill Mr. Hodges prior to the time that it occurred because the District Attorney did not dismiss the murder charge against him. Clearly, this was false and misleading testimony which should not have been allowed to go to the jury.

---

34   Roberts was originally arrested and charged with the murder and robbery of Mr. Hodges, but the murder charge against him was voluntarily and gratuitously dismissed by District Attorney Cheney prior to Jenkins' trial. At least this is what everyone, including me, was led to believe based upon Moran's testimony at Jenkins' trial. As it turns out, however, an arrest warrant for murder was issued for Roberts on December 13, 1993 (1993 R 6876), the very same day that Cedric, Shawn, Jenkins and Fleming were indicted for the robbery and murder of Mr. Hodges. This arrest warrant was pending against Roberts when he testified at Jenkins' trial, and it was not dismissed until July 20, 1996, after Roberts testified at Maurice's trial. So, when Moran testified that the murder charge against Roberts "had been dismissed," this was undeniably false because the arrest warrant against Roberts for the murder was still actively pending.

Finally, Moran's testimony was based upon the same type of inadmissible hearsay from anonymous, unidentified witnesses that infected the testimony of Mr. Gray. For the reasons discussed above, admission of such testimony constitutes reversible error because it deprived Jenkins of his Sixth amendment right to confront and cross-examine the witnesses against him.

As noted above, Deputy Moran explicitly testified during Jenkins' trial that Roberts "was originally arrested for the murder of Mr. Hodges" (Tr. 1840), but the District Attorney (Mr. Cheney) later decided to dismiss this charge (Tr. 1841) because "no information was developed during the investigation to indicate that Mr. Roberts was aware of any plan to kill Mr. Hodges prior to the time it occurred" (Tr. 1840). This testimony was utter nonsense, demonstrably false, and highly prejudicial.

First, for the reason just explained, there was never any need to develop evidence during the investigation, or at any other time, showing that Roberts was aware of any plan to kill Mr. Hodges prior to the time it occurred. Knowledge or intent to commit murder *is simply not a requirement for felony murder*.

On the contrary, the whole purpose of the felony murder doctrine is to dispense with the requirement of proving *mens rea* ("criminal intent"). By voluntarily participating in certain specified felonies (such as the armed robbery at issue here), each accomplice in the felony is legally deemed to be responsible for murder for any deaths that occur during the commission of the felony. There is no need to show malice, knowledge or intent. Furthermore, there is no need to show that the victim died as a result of an intentional or malicious act. Even if the victim died because he tripped and fell trying to escape the robbers, or if he had a heart attack opening the cash register, it would still constitute felony murder.

Second, Moran's testimony was deliberately one-sided and distorted. There was never any information developed during the investigation which indicated that Jenkins was aware of any plan to kill Mr. Hodges prior to the time it occurred either. Yet, the murder charge was not dismissed against him. Why were these two individuals treated so differently? Jenkins was prosecuted for murder while Roberts not.

Third, why was Deputy Moran even allowed to give this testimony in the first place? It was highly prejudicial and completely irrelevant. The prosecuting attorney (Mr. Cheney) must have known that it was improper to elicit the testimony,[35] Jenkins' defense attorneys should have objected (unfortunately they did not), and the judge should have acted **sua sponte** to disallow it.

Finally, Moran was not even a competent witness to provide the testimony in question.[36] The only person who could competently testify regarding the reason or reasons the murder charge against Roberts was dismissed was the District Attorney himself, and he chose not to do so. You could argue, of course, that the District Attorney told Detective Moran why he dismissed the indictment. This is true, of course, but that does not make the testimony any more admissible. Under these circumstances, the testimony constituted blatant inadmissible hearsay.

The foregoing statements are perhaps a little too cute on my part. Obviously, Mr. Cheney was no dummy. He knew perfectly well that the felony murder statute did not require that he prove that Roberts knew of any plan to kill Hodges before it occurred. Why, then, the subterfuge?

It does not surprise me, but it saddens me to say, that there were only two possible reasons the District Attorney wanted to dismiss the felony murder charge against Roberts. First, he feared that it would reflect badly on his star witness if he were charged with the very same murder that Jenkins was being charged with and that this, in turn, would make it more difficult to convince the jury to believe Roberts and convict Jenkins.

---

[35] Actually, Mr. Cheney knew exactly what he was doing and that what he was doing was improper, yet he intentionally went ahead and did it anyway because he wanted to present Roberts as a more credible witness.

[36] Moran was "incompetent" (as that term is used in the rules of evidence) because he had no personal knowledge regarding the reason or reasons the murder charge was dismissed against Roberts by the District Attorney.

Second, he needed to reward Roberts for agreeing to testify on behalf of the State.

Essentially, the District Attorney intentionally manipulated the law and the facts to bolster the testimony of his tainted star witness. As a former Assistant District Attorney myself, I find this conduct absolutely appalling. When I prosecuted cases in the Manhattan District Attorney's Office (1970 to 1975), I, and all the colleagues with whom I worked, felt a very strong obligation to act fairly and ethically. We were not there to win cases, we were there to ensure that justice was done. We would much rather lose a case against a guilty defendant than obtain a dubious conviction by unethical means. Obviously, that is not the fashion anymore, at least not in Liberty County, Georgia.

If this sounds like I am whining, get used to it. My entire purpose here is to complain. Indeed, my primary reason for writing this book is to demonstrate that the entire trial against Mr. Jenkins, and all of the many appeals that followed, was one long, continuous series of injustices. This was just the first.

5. *District Attorney Cheney Failed to Correct the Record Regarding the False and Misleading Testimony Presented by Deputy Moran*

When a witness for the State testifies falsely in a criminal case, the prosecutor is legally obligated to correct the error if he knows it is false. *Napue v. Illinois*, 360 U.S. 264, (1959); *Giglio v. United States*, 405 U.S. 150 (1972); *Moore v. Illinois*, 408 U.S. 786, (1972); *Tamplin v. State*, 235 Ga. 20, 218 S.E.2d 779 (1975). This is an affirmative obligation imposed on the district attorney by the Due Process Clause of Fourteenth Amendment. If the error is not corrected, a new trial is required. As the Georgia Supreme Court stated in *Tamplin v. State*, "where a witness for the state testifies falsely, and that testimony is known to be false by the district attorney's office, and that testimony is not corrected, a new trial must be granted." 235 Ga. at 22, 218 S.E.2d at 781.

In this case, Deputy Moran presented false and misleading testimony regarding the issue of whether Terry Roberts could have been charged with murder, yet the prosecutor did absolutely nothing to correct the error. Obviously, the prosecutor knew that the testimony was false because he was familiar with the felony murder doctrine, as shown by the fact that he had charged both Roberts and Jenkins with felony murder.

Furthermore, Deputy Moran's false and misleading testimony directly affected the credibility of the State's principal witness. This is precisely the type of situation in which a conviction must be reversed, and a new trial granted if the prosecutor fails to correct the false testimony. *See, e.g.*, *Napue v. Illinois*, 360 U.S. at 264.

6. *The Testimony of Prosecution Witnesses Kenneth McCall and Charles Howard Was Also False and Misleading*

In addition to the testimony of Deputy Moran, the testimony of Kenneth McCall and Charles Howard was also false and misleading. McCall was briefly a former cellmate of Jenkins at the Liberty County Jail. He testified that Jenkins had admitted to him that he shot Mr. Hodges (Tr. 1844), a statement which Jenkins denied (Hr. 6).

McCall was incarcerated in a Georgia state prison at the time of Jenkins' trial, and he testified that no deals or promises of leniency of any kind had been made to him by the prosecutor in return for his testimony (Tr. 1845). This was confirmed by the testimony of Mr. Howard, an Assistant District Attorney who prosecuted McCall for forgery (Tr. 1861-64). However, as Mr. Cheney later testified at the hearing in support of Jenkins' Motion for a new trial, he (the District Attorney) had a regular practice of writing letters to the State Board of Pardons and Paroles on behalf of any inmate who testifies favorably on behalf of the State (Hr. 63). Pursuant to this policy, almost immediately[37] after McCall testified against Jenkins at the trial, Mr. Cheney wrote a letter to the Board of Pardons

---

37   Jenkins' trial ended on Saturday, September 2, 1995. Mr. Cheney's letter to the Board of Pardons and Paroles was dated September 6, 1995, which was only two business days later.

and Paroles on McCall's behalf (Hr. 63 and Movant's Exhibit 2) informing them that McCall had testified against Jenkins and that his "testimony was instrumental in obtaining a conviction" (Hr. 64 and Movant's Exhibit 2). In light of the testimony which the State had elicited from McCall and Howard regarding the absence of any deals or promises of leniency, the District Attorney's practice of sending a letter to the Parole Board requesting leniency for anyone who testifies favorably on behalf of the State should have been disclosed to Jenkins' attorneys and to the jury.

Furthermore, Mr. Cheney also testified at the hearing with respect to Jenkins' Motion for a new trial that on October 28, 1995, in the case of *State v. Kenneth McCall*, Case No. 95-R-53, in the Superior Court of Tattnall County, he (Mr. Cheney) recommended to Judge Rahn that certain additional charges pending against Mr. McCall be dismissed (Hr. 59-60 and Movant's Exhibit 1) and that, based upon his recommendation, such additional charges were in fact dismissed (Hr. 59-60 and Movant's Exhibit 1). At that time Mr. Cheney stated to Judge Rahn as follows:

> "MR. CHENEY: Judge, this is the case that Van has got and that he and I had worked on for some time. This [referring to Mr. McCall] is the young man that testified on behalf of the State in the Hodges case. He had this case pending against him, scheduled to be released in '96, in June of '96, and we were [going to] recommend probation. Apparently, they decided to keep him for two more years. After I wrote a nice letter to the Pardon and Parole Board telling them what good he did for us, they wrote me back and said they really didn't care. As far as I'm concerned, the time's run on the trial demand, and this case has been disposed of by operation of law, and that suits me fine."
> (Movant's Exhibit 1).

These additional charges were pending against McCall at the time he testified against Jenkins at trial. (Hr. 62). However, no effort was made by the District Attorney's office to determine whether these or any other charges were pending against Mr. McCall at the time he testified, and no effort was made to inform Jenkins' attorneys of these additional charges against McCall. (Hr. 62)

7. ***The Prosecutor Failed to Correct the Record Regarding the False and Misleading Testimony Presented by Kenneth McCall and ADA Charles Howard***

Contrary to the testimony of Mr. McCall, as confirmed by the testimony of Mr. Howard, that no promises or deals of any kind had been made, it is clear that the District Attorney did, in fact, have a "deal" with McCall in exchange for his testimony: if McCall would testify favorably on behalf of the State against Jenkins, the District Attorney would write a "nice letter" to the State Board of Pardons and Paroles on McCall's behalf recommending leniency. Pursuant to this policy, shortly after McCall testified, Mr. Cheney did in fact write a nice letter to the Parole Board on McCall's behalf (Hr. 63 and Movant's Exhibit 2) informing them that McCall had testified against Jenkins and that his "testimony was instrumental in obtaining a conviction" (Hr. 64). Obviously, the purpose of this "nice letter" was to recommend leniency on McCall's behalf (as Mr. Cheney himself admitted in his October 28, 1995 statement to Judge Rahn).

Under these circumstances, the District Attorney had an affirmative obligation to correct the record created by the misleading testimony of Messrs. McCall and Howard, and his failure to do so constituted reversible error. McCall was one of the State's key witnesses, and his credibility was a critical issue. As noted above, this is precisely the type of situation in which a conviction must be reversed and a new trial granted. *See, e.g., Napue v. Illinois*, 360 U.S. at 264.

8. ***The Prosecutor Failed to Provide Jenkins' Attorneys with Exculpatory Brady Material Relating to the Credibility of Kenneth McCall***

As just noted, Mr. Cheney testified at the hearing in support of Jenkins' Motion for a new trial that his office had brought additional charges against Mr. McCall which were pending against him at the time McCall testified against Jenkins (Hr. 62). The existence of these additional charges was never disclosed to Jenkins' attorneys, even though they directly related to McCall's credibility. Mr. Cheney testified that he personally was not aware of these charges at the time McCall testified (Hr. 62), but he admitted that other attorneys in his office were aware of the charges (Hr. 62). Although Mr. McCall was put forth by the State as a credible witness, no effort was made by the District Attorney to determine whether these or other charges were pending against him at the time he testified against Jenkins (Hr. 62) or to inform Jenkins' counsel of any such charges (Hr. 69).

Under *Brady v. Maryland*, 373 U.S. 83 (1963), the District Attorney had an affirmative obligation to disclose all available exculpatory evidence. Evidence which casts doubt on the credibility of one of the State's principal witnesses certainly constitutes *Brady* material which should have been disclosed. McCall's credibility was a critical issue, and there is a reasonable probability that, had this evidence been disclosed to the defense, the result of the proceeding might have been different.[38] Accordingly, the State's failure to disclose this information was highly prejudicial and improper. *See, e.g., Waldrip v. State*, 267 Ga. 739, 482 S.E.2d 299, 311 (1997); *Rogers v. State*, 257 Ga. 590, 361 S.E.2d 814 (1987). As the Georgia Supreme Court noted in *Hines v. State*, 249 Ga. 257, 260, 290 S.E.2d 911, 914 (1982):

> "It is especially important in a case where a witness or an accomplice may have substantial reason to cooperate with the government that a defendant be permitted to search for an agreement between the government and the witness. Whether or not such a deal existed is not crucial. ***What counts is whether the witness may be shading his***

---

[38] McCall's testimony was extremely important because, if believed by the jury, it would have corroborated the testimony of Terry Roberts and Officer Smith. Since there were substantial questions raised regarding the credibility of both Roberts and Officer Smith, it is impossible to say how much weight, if any, the jury may have attached to McCall's testimony. It is possible, however, that McCall's testimony may have made the difference between conviction and acquittal.

testimony in an effort to please the prosecution. A desire to cooperate may be formed beneath the conscious level, in a manner not apparent even to the witness, but such a subtle desire to assist the state nevertheless may cloud perception" (citations and quotation makes omitted; emphasis added).

Similarly, McCall had ample reasons to *"shade his testimony in an effort to please the prosecutor,"* not only because of the expectation of possible leniency from the Parole Board if he gave favorable testimony for the State against Jenkins, but also because of the pendency of the additional charges which had been brought against him by the very same District Attorney for whom he was testifying.

It should also be noted that there were certain aspects of McCall's testimony (apart from the fact that he had been convicted of several felonies) that cast doubt upon his credibility. McCall testified at trial that Jenkins had told him while they were both together at the Liberty County Jail after Jenkins had been arrested that "he shot the old cracker twice." That is precisely the statement which, according to Roberts, had been made by Cedric, not by Jenkins. Cedric was also in the Liberty County Jail at the same time as McCall and Jenkins, and it is possible that McCall was confusing Cedric and Jenkins, either inadvertently or by unconscious design because it was advantageous for him to do so. It is also possible that McCall was deliberately "shad[ing] his testimony in an effort to please the prosecutor." Furthermore, McCall's testimony that Jenkins had said that he shot "the old cracker twice" is inconsistent with Officer Smith's testimony that Jenkins said, "he only shot him once."

9. *Admission of Hearsay Evidence During the Testimony of Investigator Jim Gray was Improper and Prejudicial*

In addition to his improper testimony regarding the anonymous "silent witnesses," almost the entirety of Investigator Gray's testimony was based upon and consisted of hearsay. The truth of the matter, as his testimony made perfectly clear, is that Mr. Gray did not have personal knowledge regarding any of the key facts he testified about.

The following excerpts illustrate the hearsay nature of Mr. Gray's testimony:

> Q. "When did y'all receive the first lead as to the identity of the perpetrators in this case?
> A. The investigation revealed that there was a witness across the street that saw some black males coming down the road and one of 'em was Cedric Brown. He knew him, going down the sidewalk, around the time the incident occurred. (Tr. 1724-25).
>
> * * * *
>
> Q. Did you talk with Joe Roberts and with his son, Terry?
> A. Yes, I did. (Tr. 1727).
>
> * * * *
>
> Q. And from the statement given to you by Terry Roberts, were you able to identify all of the participants . . .
> A. Yes, sir.
> Q. . . . in the robbery and in the murder?
> A. Yes, sir.
> Q. And who were they?
> A. It was Cedric Brown, Shawn Brown, Jamel Jenkins and Maurice Fleming. (Tr. 1727-28).
>
> * * * *
>
> Q. Shawn Brown, who had been identified as one of the suspects in the case, when was he picked up?
> A. The next morning, Sunday morning about 9:00.
> Q. Okay. And was he questioned?
> A. Yes, he was.
> Q. And did you develop certain information from his statement?
> A. That is correct. (Tr. 1728).

* * * *

Q. Based upon the information that — that had been developed from — from the two individuals, did you determine where Cedric Brown, Maurice Fleming and Clevon Jenkins might have gone?
A. Yes, sir.
Q. All right. And — And where was that that you had information they had fled to?
A. That they had went down to a relative, the Stacys in Opa-locka, Florida. (Tr. 1729)

* * * *

Q. Y'all, as your investigation progressed that day, did you become aware that two weapons had been used in this?
A. That is correct.
Q. Okay. And is this based on information you had received.
A. That's correct.
Q. Was there a description given to you as to the second weapon?
A. Yes, there was. (Tr. 1732)

* * * *

A. Terry Roberts described to you the other weapon?
A. Yes, he did.
Q. Okay. And what was that description?
A. It was a .25, it was silver, chrome in color white handles.
Q. Okay. And in — in your investigation did you find the possible source of that weapon?
A. Yes, I did.
Q. And what was that?
A. A Roger Fleming, from the Midway area.
Q. Okay. Who is Roger Fleming that is — is [he] related [to] these defendants?
A. He is the cousin of Maurice Fleming.

Q.	And did you talk with Roger Fleming?
A.	Yes, I did.
Q.	And did you — did you determine that he had filed a report of a theft of a weapon?
A.	Yes, I did.
Q.	What type of gun was that?
A.	It was a Lorcin, .25 caliber that was stolen out of his residence. (Tr. 1733-34).

The admission of such testimony was erroneous and prejudicial for three separate reasons. First, it constituted inadmissible hearsay. Mr. Gray did not have personal knowledge regarding any of the facts that he testified about. Since the testimony was also highly prejudicial, its admission denied Jenkins a fair trial.

Second, admission of this testimony violated Jenkins' right to confront and cross-examine the witnesses against him. *Dutton v. Evans*, 400 U.S. 74 (1970); *California v. Green*, 399 U.S. 149 (1969).

Third, allowing Mr. Gray to testify about facts concerning which he had no personal knowledge denied Jenkins due process of law in violation of the Fifth, Eighth and Fourteenth amendments. In effect, Mr. Gray was permitted to tell the jury that he "had conducted an investigation" and based upon this investigation he had concluded that Jenkins was guilty. This was clearly improper and prejudicial. It was solely for the jury to determine whether Jenkins was guilty **based upon competent and admissible testimony**. Mr. Gray's testimony was neither competent nor admissible. The plain and simple fact of the matter is that my ten year-old granddaughter, who was not even born until 2015, knew as much as about this case as Mr. Gray.

It should also be noted that it would make no difference whether some, or perhaps even all, of the persons with whom Mr. Gray had hearsay conversations also testified at the trial. Allowing Mr. Gray to repeat hearsay statements made to him by other witnesses (Terry Roberts and Roger

Fleming, for example) impermissibly bolstered the credibility of these statements. Even worse, allowing Mr. Gray to present these statements to the jury as though they were "facts" known by Mr. Gray to be true based upon his "investigation" was enormously prejudicial. Mr. Gray testified, for example, that he "was able to identify all of the participants in the robbery and in the murder" and "it was Cedric Brown, Shawn Brown, Jamel Jenkins and Maurice Fleming." (Tr. 1727-28). In actuality, Mr. Gray had no personal knowledge regarding whether Jenkins (or any of the others) participated in the robbery and in the murder of Mr. Hodges. He was merely (and impermissibly) repeating what had been told to him by others. Admission of such testimony was inherently prejudicial and denied Jenkins due process and a fair trial.

Although courts should always be careful in making evidentiary rulings, this is especially so in cases such as this where the defendant faced the death penalty and life without any possibility of parole. Indeed, the U. S. Supreme Court has ruled that in such cases, state evidentiary rules must give way to federal due process requirements. *Green v. Georgia*, 442 U.S. 95 (1979). Admission of extraneous prejudicial information such as that offered by Mr. Gray enhances the "risk of an unwarranted conviction. Such a risk cannot be tolerated in a case in which the defendant's life is at stake." *Beck v. Alabama*, 447 U.S. 625, 637 (1980). Because Jenkins' conviction was based upon such improper and highly prejudicial evidence, it should have been reversed. As the Georgia Supreme Court stated in *Render v. State*, 267 Ga. 848, 483 S.E.2d 570, 572 (1997), the defendant "is entitled to a new trial at which his guilt or innocence will be determined on the basis of admissible evidence, rather than 'rumor, gossip, and speculation.'"

10. *The Evidence Presented at Trial Was Insufficient to Convict Jenkins of Malice Murder*

The Due Process Clause of the Fourteenth Amendment protects a defendant in a criminal case against conviction except upon proof beyond a reasonable doubt ***of each and every element necessary to constitute the*** *crime with which he is charged*. *Jackson v. Virginia*, 443 U.S. 307 (1979); *Sandstrom v. Montana*, 442 U.S. 510 (1979); *Patterson v. New York*, 432 U.S. 197 (1977). As the Supreme Court emphatically stated in *In re Winship*, 397 U.S. 358, 364 (1970):

> "Lest there remain any doubt about the constitutional stature of the reasonable-doubt standard, we explicitly hold that the Due Process Clause protects the accused against conviction except upon proof beyond a reasonable doubt of every fact necessary to constitute the crime with which he is charged."

In determining whether the evidence in a state criminal trial reasonably supports a finding of guilt beyond a reasonable doubt, "the relevant question is whether, after viewing the evidence in the light most favorable to the prosecution, any rational trier of fact could have found the essential elements of the crime beyond a reasonable doubt." *Jackson v. Virginia*, 443 U.S. at 319.

Jenkins was convicted of **malice murder** under Section 16-5-1 of the Georgia Code. As defined in the statute, "a person commits the offense of [malice] murder when he unlawfully and with malice aforethought, either express or implied, causes the death of another human being." In order to convict Jenkins of malice murder, it was necessary for the State to prove, beyond a reasonable doubt, (1) that Jenkins caused the death of Robert Hodges and (2) that he intended to cause the death of Robert Hodges, *i.e.*, that he acted with "with malice aforethought." Both **intent to kill** and **malice** are essential elements of the crime of malice murder under Georgia law and both elements must be proven by the State beyond a reasonable doubt. *See e.g., Francis v. Franklin*, 471 U.S. 307, 320 (1985); *Stephens v. Kemp*, 846 F.2d 642 (11th Cir. 1988), *cert. denied*, 488 U.S. 872 (1988); *Lamb v. Jernigan*, 683 F.2d 1332 (11th Cir. 1982), *cert. denied*, 460 U.S. 1024 (1983); *Lattimore v. State*, 265 Ga. 102, 454 S.E.2d 474 (1995); *Parks v. State*, 254 Ga. 403, 330 S.E.2d 686 (1985). As the Georgia Supreme Court succinctly stated in *Lattimore*, "A person commits malice murder when he acts with the unlawful intention to kill without justification or mitigation." 265 Ga. at 105, 454 S.E.2d at 477.

Applying these principles to the facts of the present case, it is abundantly clear that the evidence submitted at trial was ***not*** sufficient to prove beyond a reasonable doubt that Jenkins was guilty of malice murder.[39]

A. The Evidence Was Not Sufficient to Convict Jenkins of Malice Murder Based on a Theory that He Personally Killed Mr. Hodges

There were three possible theories pursuant to which the jury could have convicted Jenkins of malice murder under the facts of this case. First, they could have found that Jenkins himself personally killed Mr. Hodges with malice aforethought. Unquestionably, there was insufficient evidence in the record to establish beyond a reasonable doubt that this happened. The medical evidence indicated that Hodges was shot four or five times[40] and that only one of these shots was fatal. The ballistics evidence established that Hodges was shot at least twice by Cedric Brown[41] and possibly

---

39   Even if Jenkins concedes for purposes of argument that there was sufficient evidence in the record to find him guilty of ***felony*** murder, that would not justify his conviction of ***malice*** murder. The State specifically chose to prosecute him for malice murder, and therefore it had the obligation to prove beyond a reasonable doubt all elements of that offense. Since the State failed to do so, Jenkins' conviction for malice murder should have been vacated. In addition, as discussed in greater detail below, the testimony of Terry Roberts was not sufficiently corroborated and therefore the evidence was not sufficient to convict Jenkins of felony murder either.

Furthermore, for some inexplicable reason, the jury never convicted Jenkins of felony murder. This was because the verdict sheet was never completed by the jury with respect to that charge. In the fog of the moment, this was apparently overlooked by everyone. Although the jury could obviously have convicted Jenkins of felony murder (as it could also have convicted Roberts of felony murder had he been charged), it failed to do so, and that omission cannot be corrected now.

40   Dr. Clark testified that there were five separate gunshot wounds, but only two bullets were recovered from the body. Since only four shell casings and one additional bullet were recovered from the scene, it is entirely possible that only four shots were fired, and two of Mr. Hodges' wounds were caused by the same bullet. Remember the "magic bullet" from the Kennedy assassination.

41   The ballistics evidence conclusively established that the two bullets recovered from Mr. Hodges' body were fired from the .25 caliber pistol recovered from the vehicle driven by Terry Roberts (Tr. 1868). According to the testimony of Mr. Roberts, this was the gun allegedly used by Cedric. (Tr. 1670).

as many as four or five times by Cedric.[42] The ballistics evidence also established that the additional shell casing and the additional bullet found at the scene were not fired from the gun allegedly used by Cedric (Tr. 1870-71). However, neither the ballistics evidence nor any other forensic evidence established that this bullet ever hit Mr. Hodges. There was **some** evidence (consisting primarily of the questionable testimony of Terry Roberts) that Jenkins also shot Mr. Hodges but this evidence was **insufficient** to establish beyond a reasonable doubt either that Jenkins killed Mr. Hodges or that he intended to kill him. Viewing the evidence most favorably to the prosecution, the most that can be said is that there was testimony and physical evidence which established that Jenkins **may** have fired at least one shot at Mr. Hodges. However, there was no evidence which established (i) that the shot fired by Jenkins actually hit Mr. Hodges, (ii) that the wound, if any, inflicted by Jenkins was fatal, or (iii) that Jenkins intended to kill Mr. Hodges. Accordingly, Jenkins' conviction of malice murder cannot be sustained on this basis.

B. The Evidence Was Not Sufficient to Convict Jenkins of Malice Murder Based on a Theory That He Conspired with Someone to Murder Mr. Hodges

A second theory under which Jenkins could conceivably have been convicted of malice murder was that he **conspired** with Cedric Brown and the others to murder Mr. Hodges. To find Jenkins guilty of malice murder under this theory, however, it would have been necessary for the prosecutor to prove beyond a reasonable doubt that Jenkins actually conspired with Cedric and the others to **murder** Mr. Hodges and not just to rob him.

---

42 The ballistics evidence conclusively established that three of the shell casings found at the scene were fired from the .25 caliber pistol recovered from the vehicle driven by Terry Roberts (Tr. 1871). Since this was the gun allegedly used by Cedric (Tr. 1670), it necessarily follows that Cedric must have fired at least three shots. The two bullets recovered from Mr. Hodges' body were also fired from the gun used by Cedric (Tr. 1868). Although it is likely that these two bullets came from the shell casings found at the scene, this was not necessarily so. It was impossible to determine from the evidence whether the two bullets found in the body came from the shell casings found at the scene. It is possible, therefore, that Cedric may have fired five shots.

No such evidence was presented and consequently the malice murder conviction cannot be sustained on this basis either.[43]

As Deputy Moran testified in explaining why the murder charge was dismissed against Terry Roberts (one of the alleged co-conspirators in the robbery), no information was developed during the investigation to indicate that Terry Roberts was aware of any plan to kill Mr. Hodges prior to the time it occurred (Tr. 1840). This was equally true with respect to Jenkins. There was simply no evidence which indicated that Jenkins conspired with anyone to kill Mr. Hodges or that he was aware of any plan to kill Mr. Hodges prior to the time it occurred. Accordingly, Jenkins' malice murder conviction cannot be sustained on this basis either.

C. The Evidence Was Not Sufficient to Convict Jenkins of Malice Murder Based on a Theory That He Aided and Abetted Cedric in Murdering Mr. Hodges

Finally, the third theory under which Jenkins could have been found guilty of malice murder was that he aided and abetted Cedric in killing Mr. Hodges. This was apparently the theory which the prosecutor believed to be applicable. To find Jenkins guilty of malice murder under this theory, however, it would still have been necessary for the prosecutor to prove that Jenkins actually intended that Mr. Hodges be killed, *i.e.*, that he personally acted "with malice aforethought." It would not be sufficient to find Jenkins guilty of malice murder merely to show that he aided and abetted Cedric in the commission of the robbery. Since there was no evidence in the record to establish beyond a reasonable doubt that Jenkins intended to kill Mr. Hodges, his conviction for malice murder cannot be sustained on this basis either.

---

[43] The State never claimed that Jenkins was part of a conspiracy to **murder** Mr. Hodges, only that he was part of a conspiracy to ***rob*** him. The only reason a conspiracy instruction was given to the jury was because the prosecutor sought to admit certain statements under the co-conspirator exception to the hearsay rule and therefore it was necessary for the jury to determine whether a conspiracy existed as a predicate for admitting these statements.

Viewing the evidence most favorably to the prosecution, the most that can be said is that Jenkins conspired with Cedric, Maurice, Shawn and Terry Roberts to **rob** Mr. Hodges and that during the course of this robbery Mr. Hodges was killed, most probably by Cedric. This may have been sufficient to find Jenkins guilty of felony murder, but it was not sufficient to convict him of malice murder. Although there was some evidence that Jenkins also shot at Mr. Hodges, this was insufficient to prove beyond a reasonable doubt either that he killed Mr. Hodges or that he intended to kill him. Under these circumstances, a reasonable juror would necessarily have a reasonable doubt as to whether Jenkins was guilty of malice murder. Accordingly, Jenkins' conviction for malice murder should have been vacated.

11. *Judge Harvey's Instruction Regarding the Issue of Malice Murder Was Erroneous and Improper*

When a trial court fails to instruct the jury properly regarding any required element of a crime, or when the effect of the instruction relieves the State of its burden of proof on any required element, the defendant is denied due process. *See, e.g., Francis v. Franklin*, 471 U.S. 307 (1985); *Sandstrom v. Montana*, 442 U.S. 510 (1979); *Henderson v. Kibbe*, 431 U.S. 145 (1977); *Hall v. Kelso*, 892 F.2d 1541 (11th Cir. 1990); *Stephens v. Kemp*, 846 F.2d 642 (11th Cir. 1988), *cert. denied*, 488 U.S. 872 (1988); *Parks v. State*, 254 Ga. 403, 330 S.E.2d 686 (1985). As the U.S. Supreme Court stated in *Patterson v. New York*, 432 U.S. 197, 215 (1977):

> "[A] State must prove every ingredient of an offense beyond a reasonable doubt, and . . . may not shift the burden to the defendant by presuming that ingredient upon proof of the other elements of the offense."

This is true even when the element in question is one of intent. *See, e.g., Francis v. Franklin*, 471 U.S. 307 (1985); *Sandstrom v. Montana*, 442 U.S. 510 (1979). As the U.S. Supreme Court held in *Mullaney v. Wilbur*, 421 U.S. 684, 702 (1975):

"[A]lthough intent is typically considered a fact peculiarly within the knowledge of the defendant, this does not . . . justify shifting the burden [of proof] to him."

Thus, the Supreme Court ruled in *Mullaney* that a state statute which required defendant to prove "heat of passion" by a preponderance of the evidence in order to reduce a murder charge to manslaughter was unconstitutional.

In the present case, Judge Harvey's instructions regarding the issues of malice, parties to a crime, and conspiracy violated these federal constitutional principles because they failed to explain to the jury that, in order to find Jenkins guilty of malice murder, the State had to prove beyond a reasonable doubt that Jenkins himself personally intended that Mr. Hodges be killed. These misleading instructions were highly prejudicial and required that Jenkins' conviction be vacated, and a new trial granted.

Judge Harvey instructed the jury on the issue of malice murder as follows:

"A person commits murder when he unlawfully and with malice aforethought, either express or implied, causes the death of another human being.

"Express malice is that deliberate intention unlawfully to take away the life of a fellow creature, which is manifested by external circumstances capable of proof.

"Malice may be implied where no considerable provocation appears and where all the circumstances of the killing show an abandoned and malignant heart.

"It will be for you, members of the jury, to decide whether or not the facts and circumstances of this case show malice.

"It will be noted in the definition of murder with malice aforethought either express or implied [sic]. As the Code section defines it, it is an essential ingredient and element of the offense of murder [sic]. The burden is on the State of Georgia to show malice under these rules beyond a reasonable doubt.

"Now, legal malice is not ill will or hatred. It is the unlawful intent to kill or take the life of a human being without any justification or excuse. It must exist at the time of the killing. It is not necessary for the unlawful intent to take the life of a fellow creature to exist for any length of time before the killing. In our law a person may form the intent to kill, do the killing instantly and regret the deed as soon as it is done." (Tr. 1984-85).[44]

The standard which must be applied to determine whether this instruction violated due process is to look at "the way in which a reasonable juror could have interpreted the [challenged] instruction." *Sandstrom v. Montana*, 442 U.S. at 514; *Francis v. Franklin*, 471 U.S. at 315. Accord, *Parks v. State*, 254 Ga. 403, 330 S.E.2d 686 (1985); *Johnson v. State*, 249 Ga. 621, 292 S.E.2d 696 (1982).

Judge Harvey's instruction on malice murder was erroneous as applied to the facts of this case for two separate reasons. First, it failed to make clear to the jury that they had to find **intent to kill** as a necessary element of the offense, as opposed to simply finding malice. As noted previously, both intent to kill and malice are essential elements of the crime of malice murder under Georgia law, and both elements must be proved beyond a reasonable doubt by the state. See e.g., *Francis v. Franklin*, 471 U.S. 307, 320 (1985); *Stephens v. Kemp*, 846 F.2d 642 (11th Cir. 1988), *cert. denied*, 488 U.S. 872 (1988); *Lamb v. Jernigan*, 683 F.2d 1332 (11th Cir. 1982), *cert. denied*, 460 U.S. 1024 (1983); *Lattimore v. State*, 265 Ga. 102, 454 S.E.2d 474 (1995); *Parks v. State*, 254 Ga. 403, 330 S.E.2d 686 (1985).

---

44 After beginning its deliberations, the jury requested further instructions from the court on malice murder. In response to this request, Judge Harvey simply repeated the confusing instruction given above. Tr. 2014-15.

Based upon the instruction as given, a reasonable juror may have believed it was sufficient to convict Jenkins of malice murder based solely upon a finding that he had "an abandoned and malignant heart." Furthermore, a reasonable juror may have concluded that Jenkins had "an abandoned and malignant heart" based solely upon the fact that he participated in the robbery. The net effect of Judge Harvey's instruction, therefore, was that the jury may have believed it was sufficient to find Jenkins guilty of malice murder simply because he participated in the robbery.[45] This was plain error, since it relieved the State of its burden of proof on the issue of intent to kill, one of the essential elements of the offense of malice murder.

A second flaw in Judge Harvey's instruction on malice murder was that it failed to make clear to the jury that the State had to prove, and the jury had to find, beyond a reasonable doubt, that Jenkins himself **personally** acted with the intent necessary to commit malice murder, *i.e.*, that he personally intended that Mr. Hodges be killed. Based upon the instruction as given, a juror may have reasonably believed that it was sufficient to convict Jenkins of malice murder based solely upon the fact that any one of the alleged participants (Cedric, for example) intended to kill Mr. Hodges. Judge Harvey's charge thus erroneously relieved the State of its burden of proof on the issue of intent to kill, one of the essential elements of the offense of malice murder.

Judge Harvey's failure to explain to the jury that it was necessary that they find that Jenkins **personally** acted with the intent necessary to commit malice murder was highly prejudicial and denied him due process. Furthermore, for the reasons discussed below, the effect of this error was compounded and exacerbated by the erroneous instructions which the court gave on the issues of parties to a crime and conspiracy.

---

45   Proof of Jenkins' participation in the robbery may have justified a conviction for **felony** murder. However, as noted above, the State chose to prosecute Jenkins for **intentional** murder and therefore it had the obligation to prove beyond a reasonable doubt all of the elements of that offense. Even if Jenkins participated in the robbery, therefore, this fact alone was not sufficient to find him guilty of malice murder.

12. *Judge Harvey's Instruction Regarding the Issue of "Parties to a Crime" Was Erroneous and Improper*

Judge Harvey instructed the jury with respect to the issue of "liability of parties to a crime" as follows:

> "Now, members of the jury, the Court instructs you that every person concerned in the commission of a crime is a party thereto and may be charged with and convicted of commission of the crime. A person is concerned in the commission of a crime only if he directly commits the crime or intentionally aids or abets in the commission of the crime.
>
> "I instruct you, members of the jury, that mere presence of a person at the scene of the commission of a crime at the time of its perpetration, without more, will not of itself authorize a jury to find the person who was merely present guilty of consenting or concurring in the commission of the crime, unless the evidence shows beyond a reasonable doubt that such person committed the alleged crime or that such person aided and abetted in the actual perpetration of the crime or participated in the criminal endeavor.
>
> "I further instruct you that mere association by one with other persons involved in the commission of a crime, without more, will not of itself authorize a jury to find such person guilty of consenting or concurring in the commission of the crime, unless the evidence shows beyond a reasonable doubt that such person aided and abetted in the actual perpetration of the crime or participated in the criminal behavior. (Tr. 1988-89).

This instruction was erroneous and improper as applied to the facts of this case for two separate reasons. First, it failed to explain to the jury that, in order to convict Jenkins of malice murder based upon the theory of party to a crime, the jury had to find, beyond a reasonable doubt, that Jenkins was in fact a party to the crime of **malice murder** (as opposed to felony murder or armed robbery). Under the instruction as given, the jury may have thought it was sufficient to convict Jenkins of malice murder if he was a party to any of the three crimes charged in the indictment.

A second problem with Judge Harvey's instruction on the issue of "parties to a crime" is that it failed to explain to the jury that, in order to find Jenkins guilty of malice murder as a party to that crime, it was necessary to find, beyond a reasonable doubt, that Jenkins personally intended that Mr. Hodges be killed. The instruction as given created the mistaken impression that Jenkins could be found guilty of malice murder if he "aided and abetted" Cedric in killing Mr. Hodges, even though Jenkins himself did not have the requisite intent necessary to commit malice murder. Such an instruction was plainly erroneous and improper and highly prejudicial. As the Georgia Supreme Court stated in reversing a malice murder conviction in *Lattimore v. State*:

> "[T]he charge given by the trial court erroneously authorized the jury to find appellant, as a party to the armed robbery, guilty of malice murder upon a finding that the person who shot and killed the robbery victim did so while acting with the intent to commit the armed robbery, *i.e.*, the intent necessary to commit felony murder." 265 Ga. at 105, 454 S.E.2d at 477.

13. *Judge Harvey's Instruction Regarding the Issue of Conspiracy was Erroneous and Improper*

Judge Harvey instructed the jury with respect to the issue conspiracy as follows:

> "I instruct you that a conspiracy is an unlawful agreement between two or more persons to do an unlawful

act, and the existence of a conspiracy may be established by proof of acts and conduct, as well as proof of an express agreement. ***Where persons associate themselves in an unlawful enterprise, any act done to further the unlawful enterprise by any party to the conspiracy is in legal contemplation the act of them all.*** However, each is responsible for the acts of the others only insofar as such acts are naturally or necessarily done to further the conspiracy.

"Whether or not a conspiracy existed in this case is a matter that you, the jury, must determine. Presence, companionship and conduct before and after the commission of the alleged offense may be considered by you, the jury, in determining whether or not such circumstances, if any, give rise to an inference of the existence of a conspiracy.

"***A person entering into a conspiracy already formed is a party to all acts done by the other conspirators before or after such entry in the furtherance of the criminal enterprise.*** If the existence of a conspiracy has been shown beyond a reasonable doubt by evidence other than by the declarations of any of the alleged co-conspirators, then any admissions or statements made by one or more of the conspirators during and in furtherance of the alleged conspiracy may be considered by you, the jury, against all of them. However, if you do not find that a conspiracy existed, any such evidence by alleged co-conspirators, if any, should be disregarded and given no consideration in your deliberations." (Tr. 1982-83; emphasis added).

This instruction was erroneous as applied to the facts of this case because it failed to explain to the jury how the law of conspiracy applied to the malice murder count of the indictment. As discussed above, the evidence submitted at trial was insufficient to prove beyond a reasonable doubt that Jenkins conspired with anyone to commit malice murder. Viewing the evidence most favorably to the prosecution, the most that can be said is that Jenkins may have conspired with Cedric, Maurice, Shawn, and/or Terry Roberts for the purpose of ***robbing*** Mr. Hodges.[46] There was no evidence, however, that Jenkins conspired with anyone to murder Mr. Hodges. However, Judge Harvey's ambiguous instruction regarding the law of conspiracy (Tr. 1982-83) created the mistaken impression that it was permissible for the jury to find Jenkins guilty of malice murder ***if he conspired with anyone for any purpose.***

The only reason the conspiracy charge was given in this case was because the prosecutor had sought to introduce evidence of incriminating hearsay statements purportedly made by Jenkins' alleged co-conspirators. The jury had to determine whether a conspiracy existed, and, if so, whether Jenkins was a member thereof, solely as a predicate for admission of these hearsay statements. There was never any claim by the prosecutor that Jenkins actually conspired with anyone to commit malice murder. However, Judge Harvey did not limit the effect of his conspiracy instruction to the issue of the admissibility of the co-conspirator statements. On the contrary, Judge Harvey clearly arstated that "***any act done to further the unlawful conspiracy by any party to the conspiracy is in legal consequence the act of them all.***" (Tr. 1982).

As a result of this erroneous instruction, the jury may have reasonably believed that they could convict Jenkins of malice murder based solely upon the fact that (i) Jenkins conspired with Cedric, Maurice, Shawn and Terry to rob Mr. Hodges and (ii) Cedric killed Mr. Hodges during the commission of the robbery. As noted above, Judge Harvey unequivocally told the jury that "any act done to further the unlawful conspiracy by any party to the conspiracy is in legal consequence the act of them all." If the jury believed that Jenkins conspired with Cedric to commit the robbery

---

46   As discussed below, Terry Roberts' testimony was not sufficiently corroborated, so the evidence was ***not*** sufficient to establish that Jenkins participated in a conspiracy to rob Mr. Hodges either.

and that Cedric killed Mr. Hodges during the course of the conspiracy, then it would have been logical, based upon the instruction given by Judge Harvey, for the jury to conclude that they could convict Jenkins of malice murder. The conspiracy instruction as given in this case, therefore, was erroneous and improper.

Judge Harvey's errors in charging the jury regarding the issues of malice, conspiracy and parties to a crime cannot be dismissed as "harmless error." As noted previously, the U.S. Supreme Court ruled in *Chapman v. California*, 386 U.S. 18 (1967) that "before a federal constitutional error can be held harmless, the court must be able to declare a belief that it was harmless **beyond a reasonable doubt**." 386 U.S. at 24 (emphasis added). In making this determination, the test is whether the error "might have contributed" to the conviction. *Id.* at 23. Moreover, the State has the burden "to prove beyond a reasonable doubt that the error complained of did not contribute to the verdict obtained." *Id.* at 24.

Cases applying the harmless error doctrine in the context of challenged jury instructions have established a two-prong test for determining when the error is harmless. First, where the instruction concerns an element of the crime which, because of the jury's verdict, is no longer at issue, the error will be deemed to be harmless. Thus, for example, when the instruction involves intent to kill in a murder case, and the defendant is only convicted of manslaughter, the error is harmless. *See, e.g., Hearn v. James*, 677 F.2d 841 (11th Cir. 1982). Second, where the erroneous instruction pertains to an element of the crime that is still at issue, the error can only be considered harmless if the evidence of guilt is so overwhelming that it is clear beyond a reasonable doubt that the erroneous instruction could not possibly have affected the jury's verdict. *See, e.g., Stephens v. Kemp*, 846 F.2d 642 (11th Cir. 1988), *cert. denied*, 488 U.S. 872 (1988); *Lamb v. Jernigan*, 683 F.2d 1332 (11th Cir. 1982), *cert. denied*, 460 U.S. 1024 (1983). *Accord, Yates v. Evatt*, 500 U.S. 391 (1991).

Applying these principles to the facts at issue here, the first part of the harmless error test is obviously inapplicable. Jenkins was convicted of malice murder and therefore the question of whether he intended to kill Mr. Hodges was very much at issue. With respect to the second part of the test, it cannot possibly be concluded beyond a reasonable doubt that the proof at trial was so overwhelming on the issue of whether Jenkins intended to kill Mr. Hodges that the erroneous jury instructions may not have affected the jury's verdict. On the contrary, as discussed above, the evidence presented at trial was insufficient to prove beyond a reasonable doubt that Jenkins intended to kill Mr. Hodges, even assuming there had been no error in the instructions. There is a reasonable possibility, therefore, that the erroneous instructions may have affected the jury's decision here, and the harmless error doctrine is thus inapplicable.

Francis v. Franklin, 471 U.S. 307 (1985), provides a good illustration of why the harmless error doctrine is not available here. Defendant in that case was a prisoner at the Cobb County jail when he was taken to a dentist's office for treatment. He grabbed a gun from one of the police officers guarding him and escaped, taking a hostage. During his escape, he knocked on someone's door trying to steal a car. When the person opened the door, defendant pointed the gun at him and demanded the keys to his car. The person slammed the door in defendant's face and defendant fired two shots, one of which went through the door and killed the victim. Defendant was tried and convicted of malice murder and kidnapping. After trial, he challenged the court's instructions with respect to intent, particularly an instruction which told the jury that "a person of sound mind and discretion is presumed to intend the natural and probable consequences of his acts." The Supreme Court held that this charge was erroneous because it impermissibly shifted the burden of proof to the defense. It affirmed a decision of the Eleventh Circuit which vacated the conviction and granted a new trial.

Obviously, there was sufficient evidence in the *Franklin* case from which the jury could have found malice. Defendant was a convicted felon who had escaped from custody at gunpoint, taken a hostage, and attempted to rob the victim at gunpoint. It was uncontested that defendant, and defendant alone, had fired two shots, one of which killed the victim. Yet, the Supreme Court held that the evidence regarding **intent to kill** was not sufficiently overwhelming as to be harmless. The Supreme Court also noted that the fact that the jury requested additional instructions on the element of malice "lends further substance to the court's conclusion that the evidence of intent was far from overwhelming in this case." 471 U.S. at 326.

Similarly, in the present case the evidence that Jenkins intended to kill Mr. Hodges was not overwhelming. In fact, it was non-existent. There was no testimony that Jenkins or any of his co-defendants planned to kill Mr. Hodges. The forensic evidence established that at least three shots were fired by Cedric Brown and that at least two of these hit Mr. Hodges. There was no forensic evidence which established that any shot was fired by Jenkins or that any shot fired by Jenkins hit Mr. Hodges. There was, of course, some evidence that Jenkins participated in the robbery, but this was not sufficient to establish that he intended to kill Mr. Hodges. Accordingly, for the reasons explained by the Supreme Court in *Franklin*, it cannot be said that the erroneous instructions given here were harmless. This is particularly so in view of the fact that the jury in *Jenkins* requested additional instructions on the element of malice. This, as the Court noted in *Franklin*, "lends further substance to the . . . conclusion that the evidence of intent was far from overwhelming in this case." 471 U.S. at 326.

14. *The Testimony of Terry Roberts Was Not Sufficiently Corroborated*

As noted above, a defendant in a criminal case may not be convicted of a felony based solely on the uncorroborated testimony of an accomplice. OCGA § 24-4-8. *See, e.g., Bradford v. State*, 261 Ga. 833, 412 S.E.2d 534 (1992); *Harrison v. State*, 259 Ga. 486, 384 S.E.2d 643 (1989); *Allen v. State*, 215 Ga. 455, 111 S.E.2d 70 (1959); *Price v. State*, 208 Ga. 695, 69 S.E.2d 253 (1952). Even where the testimony of the accomplice is corroborated regarding most of the details of the crime, that is not sufficient to justify conviction unless there is corroboration of the fact that the particular defendant on trial participated in the crime. *See, e.g., Hill v. State*, 235 Ga. 831, 225 S.E.2d 281 (1976); *West v. State*, 232 Ga. 861, 209 S.E.2d 195 (1974); *Castell v. State*, 250 Ga. 776, 301 S.E.2d 234 (1983); *Caldwell v. State*, 227 Ga. 703, 182 S.E.2d 789 (1971); *Hanson v. State*, 193 Ga. App. 246, 387 S.E.2d 441 (1989); *Hobbs v. State*, 142 Ga. App. 782, 237 S.E.2d 16 (1977); *Vaughn v. State*, 139 Ga. App. 565, 228 S.E.2d 741 (1976). As the Georgia Supreme Court stated in *Bradford v. State*:

> "The rule is well established that, to sustain a conviction in a felony case upon the testimony of an accomplice, there must be corroborating facts or circumstances, which, in themselves and independently of the testimony of the accomplice, directly connect the defendant with the crime, or lead to the inference that he is guilty, and [are] more than sufficient to merely cast on the defendant a grave suspicion of guilt." 261 Ga. at 834, 412 S.E.2d at 535.

The only evidence that corroborated Roberts' testimony that Jenkins participated in the murder and robbery of Mr. Hodges consisted of two brief incriminating statements allegedly made by Jenkins after he was arrested, one to Officer Smith of the Opa-locka police department and a second to Kenneth McCall, an inmate at the Liberty County Jail. Jenkins conceded that ordinarily such evidence would provide sufficient corroboration. In the particular circumstances of this case, however, the probative value of these statements was extremely questionable. With respect to the statement Jenkins allegedly made to Officer Smith, there was an unresolved issue as to whether this statement was obtained in violation of his Fifth Amendment privilege against self-incrimination (see Point 20, *infra*). With respect to the jailhouse statement allegedly made to Kenneth McCall, this was inherently suspect.[47] Furthermore, there were substantial questions regarding McCall's credibility (see Points 6, 7 and 8, *supra*). There was a genuine factual issue, therefore, as to whether sufficient evidence was introduced at trial to corroborate the testimony of Terry Roberts. However, neither Judge Harvey nor the jury ever focused on, or made any determination with respect to, the sufficiency of the corroboration evidence.

15. *Admission of Hearsay Statements Purportedly Made by Other Perpetrators Was Improper*

Terry Roberts was permitted to testify at trial about incriminating statements allegedly made to Roberts by Cedric Brown and Maurice Fleming (see Tr. 1659, 1666-69). The basis for admitting these statements was that Jenkins had allegedly conspired with Brown and Fleming to rob Mr. Hodges, and therefore the statements made by Cedric and Maurice to Roberts were admissible under the "co-conspirator exception" to the hearsay rule.[48]

Admission of these statements was erroneous and highly prejudicial for three reasons. First, Judge Harvey failed to determine whether a prima facie case of conspiracy had been proven sufficient to allow admission of the testimony. Second, even assuming that a prima facie case of conspiracy had been shown, Judge Harvey failed to consider whether the alleged

---

[47] As previously noted, it is noteworthy that McCall testified that Jenkins told him that he shot "the old cracker twice" (Tr. 1844). This is precisely the same phrase that Terry Roberts testified Cedric had used (Tr. 1669). McCall testified that he also spoke to Cedric in the Liberty County Jails and it is possible that he may have been confused or mistaken. Or perhaps he was consciously or subconsciously "shading his testimony in an effort to please the prosecutor." See the discussion of *Hines v. State*, 249 Ga. 257, 290 S.E.2d 911 (1982) in Point 8, *supra*.

[48] OCGA § 24-3-5 (Declarations of Conspirators) provides: "After the fact of conspiracy is proved, the declarations by any one of the conspirators during the pendency of the criminal project shall be admissible against all."

statements were sufficiently reliable to permit them to be admitted in a capital murder case. Third, even assuming that a prima facie case of conspiracy had been established, the statements would only be admissible if they were made "in furtherance" of the conspiracy. There was no showing that this latter condition was satisfied.

Before admitting statements under the co-conspirator exception to the hearsay rule, it is first necessary for the trial court to determine (i) whether a prima facie case of conspiracy has been shown, (ii) whether the person against whom the statements are offered was a member of the conspiracy, and (iii) whether the statements were made in furtherance of the conspiracy. As stated in *Roberts v. State*, 160 Ga. App. 717, 720, 288 S.E.2d 31, 33 (1981):

> "[B]efore the declarations of co-conspirators can be admitted as an exception to the hearsay rule, a prima facie case of conspiracy must be 'proved by evidence aliunde such declarations. . . .' The statutory exception to the hearsay rule of co-conspirator's declarations is inapplicable absent proof of a party's involvement in a conspiracy." (Citations omitted).[49]

This requirement was not satisfied here. Judge Harvey admitted the statements without making any preliminary determination of whether a prima facie case of conspiracy had been established (see Tr. 1667). Furthermore, for the reasons discussed in Point 1, *supra*, the testimony of an accomplice regarding the existence of a conspiracy must be corroborated. It was impossible, therefore, for the State to establish a prima facie case of conspiracy based solely upon the testimony of Terry Roberts. Judge Harvey failed to consider this requirement for corroboration, however, and

---

49 The term "aliunde" means "from another place or source." In the present context, it means that the existence of the conspiracy must be shown by evidence other than the testimony of one of the conspirators.

he admitted the statements based solely on the testimony of Mr. Roberts.[50] This was clearly improper. Before these statements could become admissible under the co-conspirator exception to the hearsay rule, additional evidence was necessary to corroborate the testimony of Mr. Roberts that a conspiracy actually existed and that Jenkins was a member thereof.

Even assuming that the existence of a conspiracy and Jenkins' participation therein had been established, the alleged statements lacked sufficient "indicia of reliability" to afford the trier of fact with an adequate basis for evaluating the truth of the statements. *See, e.g. Castell v. State*, 250 Ga. 776, 301 S.E.2d 234 (1983); *Timberlake v. State*, 158 Ga. App. 125, 279 S.E.2d 283 (1981); *Boswell v. State*, 158 Ga .App. 727, 282 S.E.2d 196 (1981); *Hardy v. State*, 245 Ga. 272, 277, 264 S.E.2d 209 (1980), *cert denied*, 454 U.S. 1114 (1981); *Mooney v. State*, 243 Ga. 373, 390, 254 S.E.2d 337, 349 (1979). As the Georgia Supreme Court stated in *Castell*, "[t]he thrust of *Dutton v. Evans, supra,* is that in cases involving a co-conspirator exception to the hearsay rule, the admission of the statement of a co-conspirator does not violate the confrontation clause ***if the statement and the circumstances surrounding it contain sufficient 'indicia or reliability.'***" 250 Ga. at 779, 301 S.E.2d at 340 (emphasis added). What constitutes sufficient "indicia of reliability" was explained in *Hardy* as follows:

> "The indicia of reliability required for admissibility are that the statements be non-narrative; that the declarant is shown by the evidence to know whereof he speaks; that the witness is not apt to be proceeding on faulty recollection; and that the circumstances show that the declarant had no apparent reason to lie to the witness." 245 Ga. at 277, 264 S.E.2d at 213.

---

50 Judge Harvey overruled the objection of Jenkins' attorneys to these statements while Mr. Roberts was still testifying on the ground that the co-conspirator exception to the hearsay rule was applicable. (See Tr. 1667). Eight witnesses had testified prior to that time, but none of these witnesses presented any evidence which established the existence of a conspiracy or linked Jenkins to the crime. Indeed, no evidence of any kind was presented prior to the testimony of Mr. Roberts which incriminated Jenkins in any way. Obviously, therefore, there was insufficient evidence in the record to establish the existence of a conspiracy apart from the testimony of Mr. Roberts.

See also Dutton v. Evans, 400 U.S. 74 (1970); *Mancusi v. Stubbs*, 408 U.S. 204, 213 (1972).

In the present case, the circumstances were such that there was grave doubt about the reliability of Roberts' testimony. The prosecutor himself elicited direct testimony that Roberts had lied the ***"first couple of times"*** he spoke to the police:

> Q. "Now, you know Mr. Gray, Investigator Gray. Is that right?
> A. Yes, sir.
> Q. And you know Chief Deputy Moran, right?
> A. Yes, sir.
> Q. Okay. Did they talk with you after you came down and met with — with the Sheriff's officers?
> A. Yes, sir.
> Q. You talked with — these gentlemen on more than one occasion, is that correct?
> A. Yes, sir.
> Q. Okay. The first — the first time, or **the first couple of times that you talked with them you did not tell them the whole truth, did you?**
> A. No, sir.
> Q. Okay. Why did you not tell them the whole truth the first couple of times you talked to 'em?
> A. **Because I was trying to look out for Maurice and myself.**" (Tr. 1681-82) (emphasis added).

The facts in this case made it clear that Roberts' testimony was inherently unreliable. As the prosecutor well knew, and as Roberts himself admitted at trial, Roberts had lied **several times** to the police about this case. This was because, as Roberts himself testified, "I was trying to look out for Maurice and myself." Under these circumstances, since there was substantial doubt as to whether Roberts was telling the truth, it was incumbent upon Judge Harvey to make a preliminary determination whether the co-conspirator exception should even be applicable to this case. Judge Harvey failed to make any such determination, and that was error.

Actually, Judge Harvey did not even focus on the issue of the admissibility of the co-conspirator statements until after both sides had rested, and Mr. Cheney stated, "I think the Court may need to rule [on the issue of] whether or not the State, through all its evidence has made a prima facie case of conspiracy so that that testimony would be admissible" (Tr. 1879). At this point Judge Harvey perfunctorily stated, "The Court will make a preliminary determination that there is sufficient evidence to establish that there is a conspiracy. But the ultimate determinate (sic) of that factor would have to be the jury..." (Tr. 1881). It is very clear from Judge Harvey's off-the-cuff remarks that he never even considered the question of whether there were any indicia of reliability for the statements. Accordingly, the admission of this evidence was improper and highly prejudicial.

16. *Judge Harvey Erred in Failing to Instruct the Jury that the Testimony of a Co-conspirator Regarding the Issue of Conspiracy Needed to be Corroborated*

As discussed in Point 1, *supra*, the sufficiency of evidence offered by the State to corroborate the testimony of an accomplice is a question of fact which must be decided by the jury under appropriate instructions. This corroboration requirement also applied to Roberts' testimony regarding the existence of a conspiracy. As the Georgia Supreme Court stated in *Caldwell v. State*, 227 Ga. 703, 707, 182 S.E.2d 789, 792 (1971), "[i]t is vital in establishing a conspiracy that the testimony of the corroborating accomplice connect the defendant with the offense and tend to show his guilt." Here, however, Judge Harvey erroneously failed to instruct the jury that corroboration was required.

As noted above, Judge Harvey's complete instruction to the jury on the issue of conspiracy in this case was as follows:

"I instruct you that a conspiracy is an unlawful agreement between two or more persons to do an unlawful act, and the existence of a conspiracy may be established by proof of acts and conduct, as well as proof of an express agreement. Where persons associate themselves in an unlawful enterprise any act done to further the unlawful enterprise by any party to the conspiracy is in legal contemplation the act of them all. However, each is responsible for the acts of the others only insofar as such acts are naturally or necessarily done to further the conspiracy.

"Whether or not a conspiracy existed in this case is a matter that you, the jury, must determine. Presence, companionship and conduct before and after the commission of the alleged offense may be considered by you, the jury, in determining whether or not such circumstances, if any, give rise to an inference of the existence of a conspiracy.

"A person entering into a conspiracy already formed is a party to all acts done by the other conspirators before or after such entry in the furtherance of the criminal enterprise. If the existence of a conspiracy has been shown beyond a reasonable doubt by evidence **other than by the declarations of any of the alleged co-conspirators**, then any admissions or statements made by one or more of the conspirators during and in furtherance of the alleged conspiracy may be considered by you, the jury against all of them. However, if you do not find that a conspiracy existed, any such evidence by alleged co-conspirators, if any, should be disregarded and given no consideration in your deliberations. (Tr. 1982-83) (emphasis added).

Although Judge Harvey instructed the jury that it could not consider any of the statements allegedly made by any of the co-conspirators in deciding whether a conspiracy existed, it failed to instruct them that the testimony of Terry Roberts himself regarding the existence of the conspiracy (and Jenkins' alleged participation in it) could not be considered unless it was sufficiently corroborated by other evidence This was plain error and highly prejudicial.

17. *Judge Harvey Made Prejudicial Remarks Regarding the Issue of Conspiracy Which Tainted the Jury's Verdict*

In overruling the objection of Jenkins' attorneys to the admission of the co-conspirator statements, Judge Harvey stated, **in the presence of the jury**, that the statements were admissible because of "the exception which allows a statement of a co-conspirator to be admitted." (Tr. 1667). In effect, therefore, Judge Harvey indicated to the jury that he believed that the evidence had shown the existence of a conspiracy. Since the question of whether a conspiracy existed was an issue that the jury themselves had to determine, this comment by the trial judge, in the presence of the jury, was highly prejudicial and denied Jenkins a fair trial.[51]

18. *The Admission of Hearsay Evidence Regarding Prior Arrests of Jenkins' Alleged Co-conspirators Was Improper*

During the testimony of Terry Roberts, the prosecutor elicited evidence, by means of hearsay statements, that Maurice and Shawn Brown, two of Jenkins' alleged co-conspirators, had previously been arrested for unrelated crimes. Thus, the prosecutor asked:

Q. "Did Maurice tell you why he needed to get out of town? He and/or Cedric?

A. Yes, sir. He told me that it was a bench warrant out on him.

Q. For some unrelated offense, is that right?

A. Yes, sir." (Tr. 1658).

---

51 Ordinarily, these types of evidentiary objections and rulings should be handled at a sidebar conference between the judge and the lawyers outside of the hearing of the jury.

The prosecutor also elicited testimony from Roberts that Cedric "asked me could I take his mother to the Police Station to pick up his brother, Shawn, because he — he had been arrested at the school that — that afternoon." (Tr. 1660).

According to the prosecutor's theory of the case, Maurice and Shawn were co-conspirators with Jenkins in planning the robbery of Mr. Hodges. Under these circumstances, evidence that Maurice and Shawn had previously been arrested for other crimes was extremely prejudicial because there was a substantial risk that the jury might draw adverse inferences against Jenkins from the fact that two of his associates and alleged co-conspirators had previously been arrested.

There was simply no justification for the prosecutor to elicit this harmful and gratuitous testimony other than to poison the minds of the jury and, therefore, it was improper.

19. *Most of the Testimony of Prosecution Witness Bart Ingram Was Irrelevant, Misleading and Inflammatory*

Bart Ingram, a Special Agent with the Florida Department of Law Enforcement, testified at great length regarding his efforts to locate and apprehend Cedric, Maurice and Jenkins in Florida. Most of this testimony was irrelevant, misleading, inflammatory, and based upon hearsay. Agent Ingram testified at length, for example, regarding various conversations he had with Jim Gray, Lucy Stacy, Terry Stacy and Agent Moran prior to apprehending the defendants (Tr. 1742-1746).[52] He also testified that "information [had been] developed as to the possible location of the other pistol [and] that an attempt was made to find it" (Tr. 1756), but the search was unsuccessful because it was "a difficult area to search" (Tr. 1756-58).

Admission of this testimony was improper and prejudicial. Although this error by itself might not require reversal of Jenkins' conviction, the

---

52 Lucy and Terry Stacy were relatives of Cedric who lived in Opa-locka, Florida. They did not testify at the trial.

cumulative effect of this error and all the other errors that have been enumerated required that a new trial be granted.

20. *Admission of an Incriminating Statement Allegedly Made by Jenkins to Officer Smith Was Erroneous*

Officer James Smith of the Opa-locka, Florida, Police Department, testified during the trial that Jenkins had stated to him, "I only shot him once." (Tr. 1776). This statement was determined to be admissible as a spontaneous, voluntary statement in a *Jackson Denno* hearing that was held prior to the trial,[53] and the trial court's finding on this issue was affirmed by the Georgia Supreme Court in an interim appeal prior to trial. *Jenkins v. State*, 265 Ga. 539, 458 S.E.2d 477 (1995).

Ordinarily, the fact that a defendant's statement had been held to be admissible by the Georgia Supreme Court in an interlocutory appeal prior to trial would preclude him from arguing at trial that the statement was inadmissible. This was a very unusual case, however. As Jenkins' counsel pointed out when he moved for a mistrial (Tr. 1791), the police officer's testimony on the issue of spontaneousness at trial was **inconsistent** with his testimony concerning this issue during the *Jackson-Denno* hearing held prior to the trial and indicated that Jenkins' alleged statement was not spontaneous but obtained in response to possible custodial interrogation. When Jenkins' counsel pointed out this inconsistency, Judge Harvey should have reopened the *Jackson-Denno* hearing to determine whether the statement was in fact made spontaneously or whether it was made in response to custodial interrogation. Since this was a capital murder case, due process and the procedural requirements of the Fifth, Eighth and Fourteenth amendments made it essential that Judge Harvey resolve any uncertainty regarding the admissibility of this critical piece of evidence.

Jenkins conceded that he had been advised of his constitutional right to remain silent prior to purportedly making the alleged incriminatory

---

[53] The purpose of a *Jackson-Denno* hearing is to determine whether a statement allegedly made by a defendant was obtained in violation of his Fifth Amendment rights, including his rights under the Supreme Court's decision in *Miranda v. Arizona*.

statement. However, there was a genuine question as to whether Jenkins knowingly and effectively ***waived*** his right to remain silent.[54] This issue was never considered either by Judge Harvey or by the Georgia Supreme Court because the basis upon which the statement was previously held to be admissible was that it was made ***spontaneously*** and not in response to custodial interrogation. As the District Attorney had stated in his Brief on the interim appeal, "The State does not contend that there had been an affirmative waiver of these rights by the defendant... ***The state's contention is that the statement made by Jenkins was spontaneous and not the result of custodial interrogation***." State's Brief on the Interim Appeal (December 4, 1994) at 5 (emphasis added).

The basis of the Georgia Supreme Court's prior decision allowing admission of the statement at trial was spontaneousness, not waiver. As the Court stated in its decision:

> "The evidence supports the trial court's finding that certain statements appellant made to an officer following his arrest were spontaneous and were not elicited by

---

[54] As the U.S. Supreme Court noted in *North Carolina v. Butler*, 441 U.S. 369, 373 (1979), generally "courts must presume that a defendant did not waive his rights" and "the prosecution's burden is great" in showing that the accused has in fact waived his rights. In *Moran v. Burbine*, 475 U.S. 412, 421 (1986), the Court held that the waiver inquiry has "two distinct dimensions": "First, the relinquishment of the right must have been voluntary in the sense that it was the product of a free and deliberate choice rather than intimidation, coercion, or deception. Second, the waiver must have been made with a full awareness of both the nature of the right being abandoned and the consequences of the decision to abandon it. Only if the 'totality of the circumstances' surrounding the interrogation' reveal both an uncoerced choice and the requisite level of comprehension may a court properly conclude that the *Miranda* rights have been waived." *Id.* at 422. See also *Self v. Collins*, 973 F.2d 1198, 1205 (5th Cir. 1992), *cert denied*, 507 U.S. 996 (1993); *United States v. McClure*, 786 F.2d 1286, 1288-89 (5th Cir. 1986). In *Reinhardt v. State*, 263 Ga. 113, 115, 428 S.E.2d 333, 335 (1993), the Court explained the test to be applied as follows: "The totality of the circumstances is determined through a consideration of nine factors: 1) age of the accused; 2) education of the accused; 3) knowledge of the accused as to both the substance of the charge and the nature of his right to consult an attorney and remain silent; 4) whether the accused is held incommunicado or allowed to consult with relatives, friends or an attorney; 5) whether the accused was interrogated before or after formal charges had been filed; 6) methods used in interrogation; 7) length of interrogation; 8) whether or not the accused refused to voluntarily give statements on prior occasions; and 9) whether the accused has repudiated an extra judicial statement at a later date." See also *Williams v. State*, 238 Ga. 298, 232 S.E. 2d 535 (1977). In the absence of an affirmative showing that defendant understood his *Miranda* rights and waived them knowingly, intelligently, and voluntarily, an alleged waiver must be found invalid. See *McDonald v. Lucas*, 677 F.2d 518 (5th Cir. 1982); *Cooper v. Griffin*, 455 F.2d 1142 (5th Cir. 1972).

custodial interrogation. Accordingly, we uphold the trial court's ruling that the statements are admissible at trial." 265 Ga. at 540, 458 S.E.2d at 478.

The testimony adduced at trial, however, indicated that there was a substantial question as to whether the alleged statement really was spontaneous. On cross-examination, Officer Smith testified that he had told Jenkins he should "get his life together and tell the truth. What ever happened tell the truth" (Tr. 1786) immediately prior to the time when Jenkins allegedly made the statement. This created a factual issue as to whether the statement was really spontaneous or whether it was made in response to custodial interrogation.

It should be noted in this regard that "interrogation" under *Miranda* refers "not only to express questioning, but also to any words or actions on the part of the police (other than those normally attendant to arrest and custody) that the police should know are reasonably likely to elicit an incriminating response from the suspect." *Rhode Island v. Innis*, 446 U.S. 291, 301 (1980). *Accord, Price v. State*, 160 Ga. App. 245, 249, 286 S.E.2d 744, 748 (1981) ("any practice that the police know is reasonably likely to evoke an incriminating response from the suspect amounts to interrogation").

Whether Jenkins' alleged statement here was elicited as a result of custodial interrogation was a factual issue that should have been considered further by the trial court. The fact that the Georgia Supreme Court had previously held the statement to be admissible as a "voluntary statement" was no longer controlling due to the change in circumstances. As Jenkins' attorney stated in support of his motion for a mistrial:

> "Judge, that is a very material difference, and it changes the whole fact situation and makes it very, very questionable as to whether or not this statement was made voluntarily and not in response to some type of, if not an actual question, some coercive conversation by the detective. It puts it in a whole different light. And in that event, we feel like

this statement was not voluntary and should have been suppressed. And that would have been the proper thing to take up on appeal, had we had that opportunity." Tr. 1792.

Under these circumstances, due process and the procedural requirements of the Fifth, Eighth and Fourteenth amendments required Judge Harvey to reopen the *Jackson-Denno* hearing to determine (i) whether the statement was made spontaneously or in response to custodial interrogation and (ii) if the statement was made in response to custodial interrogation, whether Jenkins **knowingly and effectively waived** his right to remain silent. Since the trial court failed to do this, admission of the statement was improper, and Jenkins' conviction should have been reversed.

21. Mr. Cheney's Closing Argument During the Guilt Phase of the Trial was Improper and Prejudicial

Although prosecuting attorneys are normally afforded wide latitude in making closing arguments to the jury, they must confine themselves to arguments that are supported by the evidence and to reasonable inferences which may be drawn therefrom, and they may not interject facts and arguments which are intended to mislead the jury and/or cause prejudice to the defendant. *See, e.g., Bell v. State*, 263 Ga. 776, 439 S.E.2d 480 (1994); *Conner v. State*, 251 Ga. 113, 303 S.E.2d 266 (1983), *cert. denied*, 464 U.S. 864 (1983); *Hall v. State*, 180 Ga. App. 881, 350 S.E.2d 801 (1986); *Brooks v. State*, 55 Ga. App. 227, 189 S.E. 852 (1937); *Brown v. State*, 57 Ga. App. 864; 197 S.E. 82 (1938); *Floyd v. State*, 143 Ga. 286, 289, 84 S.E. 971 (1915) ("the law condemns . . . the injection into the argument of extrinsic and prejudicial matters which have no basis in the evidence"). Nor may prosecutors attempt to obtain a verdict which is "impermissibly influenced by passion, prejudice, or any other arbitrary factor." *Conner v. State*, 251 Ga. at 123, 303 S.E.2d at 276. As stated in *Burns v. State*, 172 Ga. App. 645, 647, 324 S.E.2d 197, 198 (1984), "[t]he responsibility of a public prosecutor differs from that of the usual advocate; his duty is to seek justice, not merely to convict."

Improper argument by the prosecutor may constitute reversible error even in the absence of any objection. *See Todd v. State*, 261 Ga. 766, 410 S.E.2d 725 (1991), *cert. denied*, 506 U.S. 838 (1992); *Parks v. State*, 254 Ga. 403, 330 S.E.2d 686, 697 n.9 (1985); *Walker v. State*, 254 Ga. 149, 327 S.E.2d 475 (1985), *cert. denied*, 474 U.S. 865 (1985); *Prevatte v. State*, 233 Ga. 929, 214 S.E.2d 365 (1975). As provided in OCGA § 17-8-75, "[w]here counsel in the hearing of the jury make statements of prejudicial matters which are not in evidence, it is the duty of the court to interpose and prevent the same."

In the present case, Mr. Cheney's closing argument during the guilt phase of the trial was improper and prejudicial for ***four*** separate reasons. First, as discussed in detail in Point 2, *supra*, Mr. Cheney repeatedly told the jury that Jenkins had failed to testify and rebut the State's evidence, which was a flagrant violation of Jenkins' Fifth Amendment right to remain silent and rely upon his presumption of innocence. Furthermore, the prosecutor (i) misled the jury regarding applicable law and (ii) made statements that went beyond the scope of permissible argument and misrepresented the evidence to the jury. Finally, the prosecutor exceeded the scope of permissible argument by appealing to the jury's passions, emotions and biases.

A. The Prosecutor Misled the Jury Regarding Applicable Law

During his summation on the guilt phase of the trial, Mr. Cheney made statements which were misleading to the jury regarding the law applicable to the liability of "parties to a crime." Thus, the prosecutor advised the jury as follows:

> "[A]nybody that is a party to a crime in this State can be charged with and convicted of the offense. . . The terminology of that statute is that every person concerned in the commission of a crime — concerned in the commission of

a crime — is a party to that crime and may be charged with and convicted of that offense. Okay.

"And a person is a — is concerned in the commission of a crime if he either directly commits that crime **or if he intentionally aids and abets in the commission of that crime**. So any individual . . . that either directly commits that crime or aids and abets in the commission of it in any way, can be convicted of the crime. And that is critical when we look at all the acts that occurred and what some person did or what some other person did. . . .

"Now, the indictment in this case, which is a two-count indictment, which was read to you at the outset, and it charges four people, Shawn Jarrod Brown, Cedric Lewis Brown, Maurice Fleming and Clevon Jamel Jenkins first with the offense of murder. . . .

"In the indictment for armed robbery the same four individuals are charged with the commission of that crime. . . .

"Now, that's what the indictment says. . . . Now the question is, has the State, through its evidence, proved to you that Clevon Jamel Jenkins did these acts or was a party to the crime of doing these acts. He intentionally aided and abetted in the robbery, did he physically go up and grab the money and carry it out himself? The evidence generally says no.

"Do we have to prove that he physically picked up the money and carried it out himself? And the answer to that is clearly, no, **if he intentionally aided and abetted in the commission of the crime**. . . .

"In the murder case, if you find that he fired the fatal shot that killed Mr. Hodges, then certainly that shows that he is guilty of murder. If you find — or don't know for sure if he fired that fatal shot, and possibly the fatal shot was fired by Brown — you can still find that he is guilty of murder ***because he aided and abetted in the commission of the crime.*** (Tr. 1912-1915) (emphasis added).

These statements were misleading and highly prejudicial as applied to the facts of this case because Jenkins was charged with ***three separate crimes***: malice murder, felony murder and armed robbery. By arguing that Jenkins could be convicted of murder ***because he aided and abetted in the commission of the crime***, the prosecutor deliberately created the mistaken impression that Jenkins could be convicted of malice murder if he aided and abetted the commission of the robbery or the felony murder. This was plainly erroneous and highly prejudicial. Moreover, the damaging effect of these statements by the prosecutor was not cured by Judge Harvey's subsequent instruction regarding the liability of parties to a crime because, as discussed in Point 12, *supra*, Judge Harvey himself also failed to distinguish among the three crimes charged in the indictment in giving his instruction.

B. The Prosecutor Misrepresented Evidence During His Summation

Mr. Cheney also made statements during his summation on the guilt-innocence phase of the trial which went beyond the scope of permissible argument and misrepresented the evidence to the jury. This was erroneous and highly prejudicial. As noted above, attorneys must confine their arguments to facts which are supported by the evidence and to reasonable inferences which can be drawn therefrom. *See, e.g., Bell v. State*, 263 Ga. 776, 439 S.E.2d 480 (1994); *Conner v. State*, 251 Ga. 113, 303 S.E.2d 266 (1983), *cert. denied*, 464 U.S. 864 (1983).

1. Mr. Cheney told the jury during his summation on the guilt phase of the trial, "We know there were ***two fatal wounds***." (Tr. 1916). This was

not correct. Dr. Clark had clearly testified that only one of the five wounds was fatal. (Tr. 1628)

2. Mr. Cheney told the jury that Investigator Jim Gray had testified that during the investigation, the police "got certain information from this person, other information from that, **information came in from silent witnesses**, they began putting it together, they began talking to people, Terry Roberts came forward, gave them a statement that identified the conspirators or the individuals involved in this." (Tr. 1919). For the reasons previously discussed in Point 3, *supra*, the prosecutor's reference to information received from "silent witnesses" was improper and highly prejudicial.

3. Mr. Cheney stated that Kelly Fite, the State's firearms expert, testified that *"some"* of the spent shell casings found at the scene came from the gun which was not recovered and which was "most likely the weapon used by Jenkins in the commission of the crime." (Tr. 1921). This was purposefully misleading. Only four shell casings were found at the scene. Mr. Fite testified that all but one of these came from the gun that was allegedly used by Cedric Brown. (Tr. 1871). At most, therefore, only one of the shell casings could have come from the gun which was not recovered, and there was absolutely no evidence from Kelly Fite suggesting this "was most likely the weapon used by Jenkins in the commission of the crime."

4. Mr. Cheney stated that Terry Roberts "testified that two guns were used." (Tr. 1923). This was not correct. Terry Roberts merely testified that he *saw* two guns after the alleged robbery (Tr. 1670). He never stated that two guns were used, and he was not present in the store to see how many guns were used.

5. Mr. Cheney told the jury that "Detective Smith didn't know enough about the case to start questioning Jenkins" after he was arrested in Florida. (Tr. 1931). This was directly contrary to the testimony of Officer Smith himself, who had unequivocally testified in response to questioning by Mr. Cheney that he did have sufficient information about the case to question Jenkins:

Q: "Did you have enough information actually even to question him [Jenkins] concerning about what occurred?

A: Yes, I did." (Tr. 1775).

6. Mr. Cheney told the jury that "nobody was so close to Mr. Hodges when he was shot that they would have gotten blood splattered on them because there was no stippling marks at all on his face indicating that it was a contact or a close proximity wound" (Tr. 1937) and that "the bleeding that occurred on the floor was such that it did not occur initially." (Tr. 1937). This was directly contrary to the evidence. Dr. Clark had testified that when "you cut an artery and you've got a good heart action going, it squirts out and can go for quite a distance from the body, causing what we call arterial spray." (Tr. 1632).

Mr. Cheney's distortion of the evidence went well beyond the scope of latitude permitted in closing argument. He deliberately deceived the jury and invited them to convict Jenkins based upon a false view of the evidence. This was inexcusable. As the U.S. Supreme Court stated long ago:

> "[The prosecutor] is the representative not of an ordinary party to a controversy, but of a sovereignty . . . [W]hile he may strike hard blows, he is not at liberty to strike foul ones. It is as much his duty to refrain from improper methods calculated to produce a wrongful conviction as it is to use every legitimate means to bring about a just one." *Berger v. United States*, 295 U.S. 78, 88 (1935).

C. The Prosecutor Sought to Appeal to the Jury's Passions and Emotions

The prosecutor's summation during the guilt phase of the trial also exceeded the scope of permissible argument because it sought to inflame the jury's emotions. As Mr. Cheney stated:

"For $800 they killed Bobby Hodges; and, again, who do you see about that? Who does Athline see, who does Debbie see, who does the State see, who do the people of this county see? They see y'all. **It's y'all's job to say, 'The people in this county are not going to tolerate that type of deliberate, senseless violent act.' That's your job.** Nobody else's job. Nobody else can — can answer to these folks and to the other folks in the community for what's happened. *That's why you are here*."

. . . . [Y]ou have got to, as the conscience of the community, say, 'we're not gonna tolerate this sort of stuff . . .'"
(Tr. 1941)

This was highly improper because it clearly sought to elicit a verdict that was "impermissibly influenced by passion, prejudice, or other arbitrary factor." *See, e.g., Conner v. State*, 251 Ga. 113, 123, 303 S.E.2d 266, 276 (1983), *cert. denied*, 464 U.S. 864 (1983); *Walker v. State*, 254 Ga. 149, 327 S.E.2d 475, 484 (1985), *cert. denied*, 474 U.S. 865 (1985).

In *United States v. Young*, 470 U.S. 1, 17 (1985), the U.S. Supreme Court held that a prosecutor erred in urging a jury to "do its job." As the Court explained, "that kind of pressure, whether by the prosecutor or defense counsel, has no place in the administration of criminal justice." 470 U.S. at 18. As was aptly stated in *United States v. Mandelbaum*, 803 F.2d 42, 44 (1st Cir. 1986):

"In *United States v. Young*, 470 U.S. 1, 105 S. Ct. 1038, 84 L.Ed.2d 1 (1985), the Supreme Court found that a prosecutor had erred in urging a jury to "do its job." The Court said that, 'That kind of pressure, whether by the prosecutor or defense counsel, has no place in the administration of criminal justice, *see, e.g.*, ABA Standards for Criminal Justice . . . 3-5.8(c) and 4-7.8(c).' We see no difference between urging a jury to do its job and urging a jury to do its duty, and we find that the prosecutor erred in making such an exhortation. Cases are to be decided by a dispassionate review of the evidence admitted in court. There should be no suggestion that a jury has a duty to decide one way or the other; such an appeal is designed to stir passion and can only distract a jury from its actual duty: impartiality."

In the present case, Mr. Cheney's inappropriate statements not only impermissibly urged the jury to "do its job," but also threatened the jurors with condemnation by the community if they failed to "answer to these folks and to the other folks in this community for what's happened." (Tr. 1941). This is precisely the type of prosecutorial misconduct that is not allowed.

Mr. Cheney also sought to incense the jurors with arguments designed to play upon their local prejudices and biases. Riceboro was and still is a small community where residents pretty much know one another. Jenkins, on the other hand, as the evidence clearly established, was an outsider from New York. By characterizing the jury as "the conscience of this community" and by telling them "It's y'all's job to say, 'The people in this county are not going to tolerate that type of deliberate, senseless violent act'" (Tr. 1941), the prosecutor deliberately invited the jury to base their verdict on extraneous factors having nothing to do with the evidence. Clearly, these statements transgressed the law's requirement that the jury's verdict be a reasoned response based solely upon the evidence.

As discussed in Point 10, *supra*, the State's proof against Jenkins on the issue of malice murder was not especially overwhelming. There is a reasonable probability, therefore, that the misleading statements and other misconduct by the prosecutor noted herein may have adversely affected the outcome of the trial. Accordingly, Jenkins' conviction should have been vacated and a new trial granted.

22. *The Prosecutor's Closing Argument During the Penalty Phase of the Trial was also Improper and Prejudicial*

Mr. Durden began his summation on the penalty phase by dramatically telling the jury that Jenkins had said:

> "Bang, bang, Maurice, I got him for you. I got him for you, Man. Hey, they picked up somebody else for that — for that murder, for the armed robbery. We made it." (Tr. 2088).

The prosecutor made this factually flawed fantasy the central thrust of his emotionally charged appeal to the jury for sentencing. As Mr. Durden beseeched:

> "If you could only remember one thing and everything else were — were erased from your memory, you need only that one thing to complete your job here. Because that one act, that one incident, demonstrated to you by Terry Roberts, sums up what was going through that man's [Jenkins] head when he put those bullets in Mr. Hodges. That shows you the wanton disregard for what he — the value that he puts on human life. And in this situation the life of Bobby Hodges." (Tr. 2088).

Unfortunately for Jenkins, the "one thing" that Mr. Durden urged the jury to remember never happened. Jenkins never said, "Bang, bang, Maurice, I got him for you. I got him for you, Man." This was a gross distortion of the evidence. According to Terry Roberts, Jenkins had said, "Yeah, yeah, yeah, I got him, bang, bang" (Tr. 1669). However, there was no evidence that Jenkins, or anyone else, ever said, "Bang, bang, Maurice, I got him for you. I got him for you, Man."

There was also no evidence that Jenkins ever said, "Hey, they picked up somebody else for that — for that murder, for the armed robbery. We made it." This was also a gross distortion of the testimony. What Terry

Roberts had testified was that **Cedric Brown** had said, "Yeah, we made it man" (Tr. 1677), *not* Jenkins.[55]

Furthermore, Mr. Durden improperly sought to appeal to the jury's passions and emotions by imploring the jury to "please make sure, by your decision today, that you have done everything that the law entitles you to do to see that somewhere down the road another Athline Hodges, another Debbie, folks, see that nobody either in prison or out of prison will ever have to suffer at the hands of that man ever again." (Tr. 2095).

Prosecutors are not permitted to play so fast and loose with the truth, or to inflame the passions of the jury, especially when another man's life and liberty hangs in the balance. What Mr. Durden told the jury was untrue and improper. Since there is a reasonable probability that Mr. Durden's misconduct may have adversely affected the outcome of the sentencing phase, Jenkins' sentence should have been vacated and a new trial granted on the issue of penalty.

23. *The Prosecutors Continuously and Improperly Engaged in Leading the State's Witnesses*

A "leading question" is a question that suggests a particular answer and contains information that the examiner is merely looking to have confirmed by the witness. For example, if a prosecutor asks a witness, "Now, at the time when you saw him, the defendant had a gun in his hand, right?" that is an impermissible leading question.

Generally, leading questions are not allowed on direct examination.[56] They are only allowed on cross-examination, on preliminary matters during direct examination which do not result in any prejudice to

---

55   Furthermore, even if this statement was actually made by Cedric, it constituted hearsay which should not have been admitted into evidence.

56   The reason for this rule is to preserve the integrity of the fact-finding process and insure that what the witness states is based upon his or her own recollection of what occurred, and not upon suggestions or hints provided by the examining attorney.

the adverse party, or where due to other circumstances justice requires it. Georgia Code § 24-9-63.[57] None of these circumstances was present here.

Yet, throughout the entirety of Jenkins' trial, the prosecutors (Mr. Cheney and Mr. Durden) continuously and pervasively asked leading questions of the State's own witnesses. As the prosecutors well knew, this was erroneous and improper.

It is true, of course, that a trial judge has wide latitude and discretion in permitting leading questions. However, where this discretion has been abused and results in injury and prejudice to the adverse party, a new trial should be granted. See, e.g., *Blue Cross v. Whatley*, 180 Ga. App. 93, 348 S.E.2d 459 (1986); *Clary Appliance & Furniture Center, Inc. v. Butler*, 139 Ga. App. 233, 228 S.E.2d 211 (1976); *Hanson v. State*, 86 Ga. App. 313, 71 S.E.2d 720 (1952); *Peterson v. State*, 6 Ga. App. 491, 65 S.E. 311.

The following excerpt from the direct examination of Jim Gray (an investigator with the District Attorney's Office) illustrates the pattern of leading questions which was consistently used by the prosecutors[58] during the course of Jenkins' trial (the questioning here was conducted by District Attorney Cheney):

Q. "When did y'all receive the first lead as to the identity of the perpetrators in this case?

A. The investigation revealed that there was a witness across the street that saw some black males coming down the road and one of 'em was Cedric Brown. He knew him, going down the sidewalk, around the time the incident occurred.

Q. Okay. So — so, one possible suspect at that time was identified, is that correct?

---

57 Georgia enacted a new Code of Evidence in 2011 (effective January 1, 2013). The new provision dealing with leading questions is contained in Section 24-6-611. Although the wording is somewhat different, the substance is essentially the same as prior law.

58 As noted previously, the evidence against Jenkins was presented at the trial by two separate prosecutors, Mr. Cheney (the District Attorney) and his Chief Assistant District Attorney (Thomas Durden). Both of these distinguished attorneys engaged in leading the State's witnesses on numerous occasions.

A.   That's correct.

* * * *

Q.   Okay. The — Following the information developed from that witness as to at least one suspect in the case, did you later receive any information or — or any of the officers talk to the young man named Dewayne Paulk?

A.   That's correct.

* * * *

Q.   Okay. And — And that information that was developed from Mr. Paulk identified another possible suspect in the case?

A.   That is correct.

Q.   And who was that?

A.   Shawn Brown.

Q.   Okay. Without going into what — what information came in, did you later receive a silent witness call that was assist — some assistance to you?

A.   That is correct. Around 12:30 the next day. That'd been on Saturday.

Q.   Okay. Following this information that y'all began to develop in this case, were some search warrants issued by the Sheriff's Office.

A.   That's correct.

* * * *

Q.   Okay. Later in the evening, on - on Saturday, were your notified that a Mr. Joe Roberts had information for the investigators.

A.   Yes, sir.

Q.   Okay. By this time Chief Deputy Moran had returned and was involved with you in the investigation, is that correct?

A.   Yes, sir. We were together at that time.

* * * *

Q. And in fact, did you talk with Joe Roberts and with his son, Terry?
A. Yes, I did.

* * * *

Q. And from the statement given to you by Terry Roberts, were you able to identify all the participants . . .
A. Yes, sir.
Q. . . . in the robbery and in the murder?
A. Yes, sir.
A. And who were they?
Q. It was Cedric Brown, Shawn Brown, Jamel Jenkins and Maurice Fleming.
Q. Okay. Did you, in the — in the process of the investigation and in — talking with Terry Roberts, did y'all go to his residence and through his vehicle?
A. That's correct.

* * * *

Q. Okay. And was permission received from his father to — to make a search of the vehicle?
A. That's correct.
Q. And was one of the .25 caliber weapons recovered there from the vehicle. . .
A. That's correct." (Tr. 1725-1728).

    Ordinarily, the use of leading questions by a prosecutor would not, by itself, be a sufficient ground to require a new trial. However, where, as here, the misconduct was particularly egregious and where, as here, there were numerous other errors, the cumulative effect of these errors made it appropriate that a new trial be granted. This was especially true in a case such as this where the State sought to impose the death penalty and Jenkins was actually sentenced to a term of life without any possibility of parole.

24. Judge Harvey Erred in Excluding Relevant Evidence Offered by Jenkins' Attorneys During the Guilt Phase of the Trial

This was a capital murder case in which Jenkins faced the possibility of being sentenced to death or to life without possibility of parole. Under such circumstances, the U.S. Supreme Court has squarely held that state evidence rules must yield to federal constitutional requirements of due process. *See Skipper v. South Carolina*, 476 U.S. 1 (1986); *Eddings v. Oklahoma*, 455 U.S. 104 (1982); *Green v. Georgia*, 442 U.S. 95 (1979); *Lockett v. Ohio*, 438 U.S. 586 (1978); *Gardner v. Florida*, 430 U.S. 349 (1977). As established in these and similar cases, relevant, reliable evidence offered by a defendant in a capital murder case cannot be excluded merely because it is inadmissible under state evidence rules.

The facts in *Green v. Georgia* are analogous to what happened in Jenkins' case and mandated that a new trial should have been granted here. The defendant in *Green* sought to introduce hearsay evidence during the penalty phase of his trial that a co-conspirator had admitted to a third person that he (the co-conspirator) had killed the victim. The Georgia trial court excluded this evidence on the ground that it was hearsay. The U.S. Supreme Court ruled that exclusion of such evidence violated the Due Process Clause of the Fourteenth Amendment and deprived defendant of a fair trial. As the Court stated in its opinion:

> "Regardless of whether the proffered testimony comes within Georgia's hearsay rule, under the facts of this case its exclusion constituted a violation of the Due Process Clause of the Fourteenth Amendment. The excluded testimony was highly relevant to a critical issue in the punishment phase of the trial and substantial reasons existed to assume its reliability. . . . In these unique circumstances, 'the hearsay rule may not be applied mechanistically to defeat the ends of justice.'" 442 U.S. at 97 (citations omitted).

Similarly, in the present case, Jenkins' attorneys sought, unsuccessfully, to introduce evidence regarding the guilty plea entered by Cedric Brown, one of the alleged co-conspirators in the robbery. (Tr. 1841-42). This evidence was highly relevant, during both the guilt and the penalty phases of the trial, because Cedric was the person who, according to the evidence, planned the robbery and fired several shots that hit, and probably killed, Mr. Hodges. The fact that Cedric pleaded guilty, and especially any statements that he made in admitting his guilt, were highly relevant to the issue of whether Jenkins should be found guilty of malice murder. Yet, this evidence was excluded. (See Tr. 1841-42). The exclusion of this evidence was highly prejudicial and deprived Jenkins of due process of law in violation of the Fifth, Eighth and Fourteenth Amendments to the U.S. Constitution.

Furthermore, Jenkins' attorneys sought, unsuccessfully, to obtain discovery regarding Cedric's mental health file. This information was also highly relevant because Cedric was mentally retarded. According to the evidence, Cedric planned the robbery and fired several shots that hit, and probably killed, Mr. Hodges. In the trial court's instructions, the jury was told that Jenkins could be held responsible for any and all acts committed by Cedric. The fact that Cedric was mentally retarded was an important fact which the jury should have known before deciding whether and, if so, to what extent Jenkins should be held responsible for Cedric's actions. However, Cedric's mental health file was withheld from Jenkins' attorneys based upon a state evidentiary privilege. Since Cedric's mental condition was relevant and important evidence, withholding this information violated Jenkins' rights under the due process clause of the federal constitution.

25. *Judge Harvey Erred in Excluding Mitigation Evidence Offered by Jenkins' Attorneys During the Penalty Phase of the Trial*

As noted in Point 24, *supra*, Judge Harvey erred in excluding evidence regarding Cedric Brown's guilty plea which Jenkins' attorneys sought to introduce during the guilt portion of his trial. In addition, during the penalty phase, Jenkins' attorneys sought to admit evidence regarding the sentences which had been imposed on Cedric and Shawn Brown, Jenkins' alleged co-conspirators. (See Tr. 2030). This evidence was offered as a mitigation factor to be considered by the jury in deciding whether to sentence Jenkins to death, life without possibility of parole, or life.

Judge Harvey refused to allow Jenkins to introduce this evidence on the ground that it was "not relevant" (Tr. 2030-32). This was erroneous and highly prejudicial. The fact that other perpetrators of this crime, including the instigator and probable killer of Mr. Hodges, had received sentences less than death or life without possibility of parole was a significant mitigating factor which the jury was entitled to know and consider in determining what sentence would be appropriate for Jenkins. Exclusion of this evidence was highly prejudicial and deprived Jenkins of a fair trial on the issue of punishment.

Judge Harvey explained the basis for his reasoning as follows:

> "Disparity in sentencing in a death penalty case is for the [Georgia] Supreme to review it as compared to other sentences. It's not for the jury. That's a question that's done by statute for the Supreme Court, but not for the jury.
>
> "I mean, each case in a death penalty case has to stand or fall on the evidence of that particular case. And so, the only thing that would be relevant is what happened in this particular case. And the only thing that the jury can judge is based on the evidence in this case, not whatever the evidence was in the other cases." (Tr. 2031).

It is true that the jury's decision regarding the appropriate penalty to impose on Jenkins had to be based upon the "evidence" that was presented during "this case." That, however, was not a valid basis for excluding the mitigation evidence offered by Jenkins' attorneys. The very reason Jenkins' attorneys attempted to admit certified copies of the sentences imposed on the other defendants was precisely so that this information would constitute "evidence" in "this case" and be available for consideration by the jury.

It is also true that the issue of "disparity in sentence" is something which must be addressed by the Georgia Supreme Court in all cases in which the death penalty is imposed. Indeed, this was one of the factors cited by the U.S. Supreme Court in its decision upholding the constitutionality of Georgia's death penalty statute. *See Gregg v. Georgia*, 428 U.S. 153 (1976). However, the availability of this appellate review procedure as a safeguard against an inappropriate imposition of the death penalty does not mean that a defendant in a capital case is not entitled in the first instance to present evidence during the penalty phase of his trial regarding the sentence imposed on persons who are jointly liable with defendant for the crimes charged in the indictment.[59]

There is no concept more firmly rooted in our legal system than the principle that all persons should receive equal treatment under the law. Cedric Brown, the instigator and principal wrongdoer of the crimes for which Jenkins was indicted, was sentenced by Judge Harvey to life imprisonment. This was a highly relevant fact for the jury to know in deciding whether to sentence Jenkins to death, life without possibility of parole, or life.

There are many factors which can and should be considered in deciding what penalty is appropriate. The U.S. Supreme Court has made it very clear that defendants must be afforded wide latitude in offering mitigation evidence in death penalty cases. *See Skipper v. South Carolina*, 476 U.S. 1 (1986); *Eddings v. Oklahoma*, 455 U.S. 104 (1982); *Green v. Georgia*, 442 U.S. 95 (1979); *Lockett v. Ohio*, 438 U.S. 586 (1978).

---

59 In *Wilson v. State*, 250 Ga. 630, 300 S.E.2d 640 (1983), the Georgia Supreme Court held that it was permissible to exclude evidence offered by a defendant during the penalty phase of a murder trial regarding penalties imposed on other defendants in other cases. That case is distinguishable from the situation here, however, due to the absence of any connection between the case being tried and the sentences which defendant wanted to use as evidence. Here there is a close affinity between the two cases which makes the sentences directly relevant. The sentences which Jenkins wanted to offer as evidence were imposed on his alleged co-conspirators for their participation in the identical crimes that Jenkins himself was being tried for. The charges were alleged in one indictment and conceivably Jenkins and his co-defendants could have been tried together before the same jury.

The Supreme Court has also made it very clear that when juries are called upon to exercise their discretion in deciding what sentence to impose, they must be provided with all relevant information relating to this decision. *See Simmons v. South Carolina*, 512 U.S. 154 (1994); *Hicks v. Oklahoma*, 447 U.S. 343, 346 (1980); *Gregg v. Georgia*, 428 U.S. 153, 190 (1976). As the Georgia Supreme Court stated in *Fugate v. State*, 263 Ga. 260, 263, 431 S.E.2d 104, 108 (1993), "individual jurors must be allowed to consider whatever mitigating circumstances as are persuasive to each of them individually, thus giving the fullest play to the jury's consideration of mitigating circumstances."

Furthermore, as this same Court recognized in *Horton v. State*, 249 Ga. 871, 879, 295 S.E.2d 281, 289 (1982), *cert. denied*, 460 U.S. 1048 (1983), there is a difference between the question of whether a sentence is "disproportionate to the sentence imposed in a similar case" for purposes of appellate review and the question of "what sentence triers of the fact are willing to impose." Where, as here, a defendant in a death penalty case chooses to offer evidence regarding sentences imposed on persons who are jointly liable with him for the same crimes charged in the indictment, it is erroneous and prejudicial not to admit it. Accordingly, Jenkins' sentence of life without possibility of parole should have been vacated and a new trial granted on the issue of punishment.

26. Judge Harvey Erred in Failing to Answer the Jury's Question about when Jenkins Would Become Eligible for Parole if they Sentenced Him to Life Imprisonment

During its deliberations on the penalty phase of the trial, the jury asked when Jenkins would become eligible for parole if they sentenced him to life imprisonment (Tr. 2126). Jenkins' attorneys immediately requested that the jury be provided with the information it requested,[60] but Judge Harvey refused to do so, asserting that he did not have "the authority to

---

60   Jenkins' lawyer, Mr. Peel, reacted immediately to court's announcement of the query, urging "tell 'em, it's twenty years. That's what my understanding of the new guidelines is." (Tr. 2126).

tell 'em" (Tr. 2126). Judge Harvey's failure to inform the jury when Jenkins would become eligible for parole violated Section 17-10-31.1(d) of the Georgia Code and deprived Jenkins of a fair trial on the issue of punishment. It also violated federal constitutional requirements of the Fifth, Eighth and Fourteenth amendments.

A. Judge Harvey's Failure to Answer the Jury's Query Regarding When Jenkins Would Become Available for Parole Violated Georgia Statutory Law

Section 17-10-30.1 of the Georgia Code permits the jury in a capital murder case to impose a sentence of life without possibility of parole. Prior to the enactment of this statute in 1993, it was improper for counsel in any criminal case to argue that the defendant may become eligible for parole. Section 17-8-76, enacted in 1955, provided that "No attorney at law in a criminal case shall argue to or in the presence of the jury that a defendant, if convicted, may not be required to suffer the full penalty imposed by the court or jury because pardon, parole, or clemency of any nature may be granted."

When the statute creating the sentence of life without possibility of parole was enacted in 1993, the Georgia legislature explicitly recognized that it would now become necessary and appropriate to inform the jury regarding the possibility of parole. Accordingly, Section 17-10-31.1(d) expressly provided:

> "Notwithstanding any other provision of law, during the sentencing phase before a jury, counsel for the state and the accused may present argument and the trial judge may instruct the jury:
>
> (1) That "life without parole" means that the defendant shall be incarcerated for the remainder of his or her natural life and shall not be eligible for parole unless such

person is subsequently adjudicated to be innocent of the offense for which he or she was sentenced; and

(2) That "life imprisonment" means that the defendant will be incarcerated for the remainder of his or her natural life but will be eligible for parole during the term of such sentence."

Section 11 of the Act creating the sentence of life without parole provided that "[a]ll laws and parts of laws in conflict with this Act are repealed." Ga. L. 1993, p. 1654, section 11. The General Assembly thus clearly understood and intended that, in those cases in which the sentence of life without parole is available as an option, counsel can present arguments to the jury, and the court can provide instructions, regarding the availability of parole.

The relationship between Section 17-10-31.1(d) (which specifically permits argument and instructions to the jury regarding parole in capital murder cases) and Section 17-8-76 (which prohibits such arguments generally) was considered by the Georgia Supreme Court in *Jenkins v. State*, 265 Ga. 539, 458 S.E.2d 477 (1995), an interlocutory appeal decided in this very case. The Court held in that case that Section 17-8-76 has been superseded by Section 17-10-31.1(d) insofar as death penalty cases are concerned, and therefore it is now permissible for counsel and the court to advise the jury regarding the possibility of parole in cases in which the sentence of life without parole is an option. As the Supreme Court stated:

"OCGA § 17-10-31.1(d), by expressly authorizing argument to the jury on the issue of parole in the sentencing phase of death penalty trials, conflicts with OCGA § 17-8-76 (a), which imposes an absolute bar on such argument. The rule for construing statutes which may be in conflict is that the most recent legislative expression prevails. *Gunn v. Balkcom*, 228 Ga. 802, 804 (188 S.E.2d 500) (1972); *Simmons v. State*, 148 Ga. App. 317, 318 (251 S.E.2d 167)

(1978). OCGA § 17-1031.1 is the more recent legislative expression and its provisions thus prevail as to closing arguments made in the sentencing phase of death penalty cases." 265 Ga. at 540, 458 S.E.2d at 478.

Thus, Georgia's prior policy of not instructing a jury regarding the possibility of parole was not applicable to cases such as this in which the jury must decide whether to sentence a defendant to life or to life without possibility of parole. Furthermore, to the extent that a jury is called upon to make this determination, it needs to receive accurate information about parole options, including when the defendant will become eligible for parole under a life sentence. It would be illogical and arbitrary to require that a jury decide whether to sentence a defendant to life or to life without possibility of parole and yet refuse to answer their legitimate inquiry as to what life imprisonment actually means.

Judge Harvey's refusal to inform the jury when Jenkins would become eligible for parole was thus contrary to the Georgia sentencing statute. Section 17-10-31.1(d) was specifically intended to ensure that the jury receive accurate information about the possibility of parole and not sentence defendants arbitrarily based upon speculation or incorrect information. Where, as here, the sentencing jury specifically requested information about when defendant will become eligible for parole if they sentence him to life imprisonment, it was improper and contrary to the statute for the court to withhold such information. Accordingly, Jenkins' sentence of life without possibility of parole should have been vacated and a new trial granted on the issue of punishment.

B. Judge Harvey's Failure to Answer the Jury's Query Regarding When Jenkins Would Become Available for Parole Violated Federal Constitutional Law

Judge Harvey's failure to answer the jury's question about when Jenkins would become eligible for parole also violated federal constitutional requirements of the Fifth, Eighth and Fourteenth amendments. *See, e.g., Simmons v. South Carolina*, 512 U.S. 154 (1994); *Hicks v. Oklahoma*, 447 U.S. 343, 346 (1980); *Gregg v. Georgia*, 428 U.S. 153, 190 (1976); *Furman v. Georgia*, 408 U.S. 238 (1972).

These cases establish that when jurors are asked to determine what punishment should be imposed on a defendant in a criminal case, they must be provided with accurate information about the sentencing options. As the U.S. Supreme Court stated in *Gregg v. Georgia*, "accurate sentencing information is an indispensable prerequisite to a reasoned determination of whether a defendant shall live or die by a jury of people who may never before have made a sentencing decision." 428 U.S. at 190 (plurality opinion).

Most cases in which juries are asked to impose a sentence are death penalty cases. It is clear, however, that the due process clause of the Fourteenth Amendment applies equally to non-capital cases and requires that the sentencing body in a state criminal case have accurate information regarding available sentencing options.

Thus, in *Hicks v. Oklahoma*, 447 U.S. 343, 346 (1980), the Supreme Court invalidated a state criminal sentence where the defendant had been sentenced by a jury to a term of forty years. Defendant had been sentenced under the State's habitual offender statute which was later declared unconstitutional in an unrelated case. When defendant attacked his sentence, the State attempted to defend it on the ground that the jury could have sentenced defendant to a term of forty years even in the absence of any prior offenses and therefore the sentence as imposed was within the discretion of the jury. The Supreme Court rejected this argument and held that it violated due process for the jury to sentence defendant based upon a misunderstanding of the available sentencing alternatives. As the Court stated in that case:

> "It is argued that all that is involved in this case is the denial of a procedural right of exclusively state concern.

Where, however, a State has provided for the imposition of criminal punishment in the discretion of the trial jury . . . [t]he defendant in such a case has a substantial and legitimate expectation that he will be deprived of his liberty only to the extent determined by the jury in the exercise of its statutory discretion, and that liberty interest is one that the Fourteenth Amendment preserves against arbitrary deprivation by the State." 447 U.S. at 346 (citations omitted).

The Fifth Circuit U.S. Court of Appeals explained what is required to show a violation of this due process sentencing requirement in *Dupuy v. Butler*, 837 F.2d 699 (5th Cir. 1988), as follows:

"T[o] establish a valid *Hicks* claim, the state criminal defendant must show . . . that the sentencing authority lacked knowledge and understanding of the range of sentencing discretion under state law and . . . that there was a substantial possibility that prejudice was thereby caused." 837 F.2d at 703.

Prejudice is established "by showing that the sentencing authority was . . . ignorant of one or more less severe options" and that "a substantial possibility exists that the sentencer, if properly informed, would have chosen one of these less severe sentencing options." 837 F.2d at 703.

In *Simmons v. South Carolina*, the U.S. Supreme Court reversed a death penalty sentence because the trial judge had refused to answer the jury's question about whether the imposition of a life sentence carried with it the possibility of parole. The defendant in *Simmons* would not have been eligible for parole because of a prior felony conviction, and he requested that the court so instruct the jury. The trial judge refused to give such an instruction and then refused to answer the jury's question of whether the defendant would be eligible for parole if they sentenced him to life imprisonment.

The Supreme Court held that "due process requires that the sentencing jury be informed that the defendant is parole ineligible." 512 U.S. at 156. As explained in the Court's plurality opinion:

> "Because truthful information of parole ineligibility allows the defendant to 'deny or explain' the showing of future dangerousness, due process plainly requires that he be allowed to bring it to the jury's attention by way of argument by defense counsel or an instruction from the court." 512 U.S. at 169.

Justice Blackmun, writing the Court's plurality opinion (in which three other justices joined), noted that "it can hardly be questioned that most juries lack accurate information about the precise meaning of 'life imprisonment as defined by the States." 512 U.S. at 169. Justice O'Connor (joined by two other justices) concurred in the judgment and agreed that jurors cannot reasonably be expected to understand the meaning of "life imprisonment" as that term is used by the states. *Simmons*, 512 U.S. at 177 (O'Connor, J., concurring opinion).

The Court noted in *Simmons* that "[t]he actual duration of the defendant's prison sentence is indisputably relevant" in deciding what sentence to impose. 512 U.S. at 163 (plurality opinion). The Court then concluded that "[t]he trial court's refusal to apprise the jury of information so crucial to its sentencing determination . . . cannot be reconciled with our well-established precedents interpreting the Due Process Clause." 512 U.S. at 164.

Similarly, in the present case, it was a violation of Jenkins' due process rights to require the jury to choose between imposing a life sentence and a sentence of life without possibility of parole without explaining to the jury when Jenkins would become eligible for parole under a life sentence. This was particularly so in view of the fact that (i) the prosecutor had told the jury during summation that "the Judge will explain to you if [a life sentence] is your decision that at some point the defendant may be considered for parole, that is release, from prison" (Tr. 2093); (ii) the jury had specifically requested additional information about when Jenkins would become eligible for parole under a life sentence (Tr. 2126); and (iii) Jenkins' attorneys had explicitly requested that the jury be told when Jenkins would become eligible for parole (Tr. 2126).

Furthermore, the prosecutor had specifically argued during summation that the jury should consider Jenkins' "future dangerousness" in deciding whether to sentence Jenkins to death, life without possibility of parole, or life. (Tr. 2095).[61] Under these circumstances, it was a denial of due process of law to prohibit Jenkins' attorneys to respond to this argument by pointing out that he would not become eligible for parole for at least twenty years. *Simmons v. South Carolina*, 512 U.S. 154 (1994); *Gardner v. Florida*, 430 U.S. 349 (1977).

Accordingly, since Jenkins was deprived of his liberty without due process, the sentence of life without possibility of parole should have been vacated and a new trial granted on the issue of punishment.

27. Section 17-10-31.1(d) of the Georgia Code, Which Permitted the Jury to Impose a Sentence of Life Without Possibility of Parole in this Case, Is Unconstitutional

Georgia's death penalty statute was declared unconstitutional by the U.S. Supreme Court in *Furman v. Georgia*, 408 U.S. 238 (1972). The basis of the Court's decision was that the statute permitted juries to choose arbitrarily between the death penalty and life imprisonment without providing adequate standards for choosing between these two alternatives. Following the *Furman* decision, the statute was amended to limit imposition of the death penalty to cases in which certain statutorily defined aggravating circumstances were found to exist and other procedural safeguards were available. This amended statute was declared constitutional by the U.S. Supreme Court in *Gregg v. Georgia*, 428 U.S. 153 (1976).

---

61 Mr. Durden implored the jury to "please make sure, by your decision today, that you have done everything that the law entitles you to do to see that somewhere down the road another Athline Hodges, another Debbie, folks, see that nobody either in prison or out of prison will ever have to suffer at the hands of that man ever again." (Tr. 2095).

At the time when the death penalty statute was upheld in *Gregg*, jurors had only two options in capital cases: they could either impose the death penalty in those cases in which certain statutorily defined aggravating circumstances were found to exist or they could choose to not impose the death penalty, in which case the court was required to sentence the defendant to life imprisonment.

In 1993, two years before Jenkins' trial, the Georgia Assembly modified the statutory framework for imposing the death penalty by enacting Section 17-10-31.1. As noted in Point 26, *supra*, this statute now permits jurors in capital murder cases to impose a sentence of life imprisonment without any possibility of parole as an alternative to the death penalty.

Section 17-10-31.1 is unconstitutional because it incorporates the same flaws that the Supreme Court condemned in *Furman v. Georgia*. It authorizes jurors to impose a sentence of life without possibility of parole in precisely the same categories of cases in which jurors are authorized to impose the death penalty, yet it provides no guidance whatsoever as to when the death penalty is appropriate as opposed to life without possibility of parole. Since the statute now permits juries to choose arbitrarily between the death penalty and life without possibility of parole, it violates the principles established in *Furman v. Georgia*. Accordingly, Section 17-10-31.1 is unconstitutional and Jenkins' sentence of life without possibility of parole should have been vacated.

28. *Judge Harvey Erred in Sentencing Jenkins to an Additional, Consecutive Term of Life Imprisonment on the Robbery Charge*

The State argued in its opposition to Jenkins' Motion for a new trial that Jenkins could be convicted of malice murder based solely upon proof that he aided and abetted in the commission of the robbery. See State's Brief in Opposition to Appellant's Motion for a New Trial at 6-7, 8-10, 13, and 16-17.[62] I do not believe that this represented a correct statement of Georgia law. See Point 10, *supra*. However, in the event that the Georgia Supreme Court accepted the State's argument on this point, then Jenkins' conviction on the robbery charge would have merged into the conviction on the murder charge. *See Walker v. State*, 254 Ga. 149, 327 S.E.2d 475 (1985), *cert. denied*, 474 U.S. 865 (1985); *Stone v. State*, 253 Ga. 433, 321 S.E.2d 723 (1984); *Berry v. State*, 248 Ga. 430, 283 S.E.2d 888 (1981). Accordingly, Judge Harvey's imposition of an additional life sentence on the robbery charge was erroneous.

29. Jenkins Was Denied the Effective Assistance of Counsel in Violation of His Sixth Amendment Right to Counsel

As the United States Supreme Court firmly established in *Strickland v. Washington*, 466 U.S. 668 (1984), defendants in criminal cases are entitled to receive "effective assistance of counsel" at their trial and sentencing. This is required by the "assistance of counsel" clause of the Sixth Amendment to the United States Constitution. If a defendant is denied the effective assistance of counsel, then his conviction or sentence **must be set aside**.

The Supreme Court established a two-prong test for determining when counsel's assistance is so defective as to require reversal of the conviction. This standard was recognized by the Georgia Supreme Court in *Smith v. Francis*, 253 Ga. 782, 325 S.E.2d 362 (1985) and applied in such cases as *Johnson v. State*, 266 Ga. 380, 467 S.E.2d 542 (1996) and *Cochran v. State*, 262 Ga. 106, 414 S.E.2d 211 (1992).

To satisfy the *Strickland* standard, a defendant must first show that his or her counsel's performance was "deficient." 466 U.S. at 687. This requires a showing that counsel made "serious errors." Second, the defendant must

---

62 "[T]he jury was authorized to find Jenkins guilty of malice murder because he aided and abetted in the armed robbery." State Opposition Brief at 7. "Because Jenkins was a party to the crime of armed robbery, the State is only required to prove Jenkins intentionally aided and abetted Cedric Brown during the robbery." *Id.* at 13). "[T]he jury would be authorized to find Clevon Jamel Jenkins was a part of a conspiracy to rob Hodges Grocery and that a natural consequence of that robbery was Mr. Hodges' death. Assuming Cedric Brown was Mr. Hodges' killer, his intent to murder Mr. Hodges may be imputed to Clevon Jamel Jenkins, and Jenkins may be punished for that act." *Id.* at 16-17.

show that "the deficient performance prejudiced the defense." This requires a showing that "counsel's errors were so serious as to deprive the defendant of a fair trial, a trial whose result is reliable." *Id.*

Applying this standard to the trial at issue, it is clear that the performance of Jenkins' trial counsel was both "clearly deficient" and "highly prejudicial" within the meaning of *Strickland* and *Smith v. Francis*. Accordingly, his conviction and sentence should have been vacated and a new trial granted. This was so for numerous reasons.

1. **Jenkins' attorneys failed to request a jury instruction on the issue of corroboration of accomplice testimony and failed to object to Judge Harvey's charge which omitted such an instruction**

As discussed previously, Terry Roberts, the State's principal witness, was an accomplice in the robbery and murder of Mr. Hodges. This fact was clearly obvious to everyone, including Jenkins' trial attorneys, long before the trial ever began, since Roberts had been arrested and indicted for the robbery of Mr. Hodges along with Jenkins and the other defendants. Furthermore, Roberts admitted at Jenkins' trial that he had participated in the robbery (Tr. 1655) and he was even advised by Judge Harvey regarding his constitutional right not to testify (Tr. 1655-56). Furthermore, Roberts was represented by his own personal attorney (Gary Branan of Macon, Georgia) during his testimony (Tr. 1656).[63]

Despite the fact that Roberts was obviously an accomplice and that his testimony needed to be corroborated, Jenkins' trial counsel never requested Judge Harvey to instruct the jury on the issue of corroboration. Furthermore, they also failed to object to the charge as given by Judge Harvey even though it omitted any instruction on corroboration.

Under these circumstances, the failure of Jenkins' counsel to request a charge on the issue of corroboration and to object to the charge as given

---

[63] I do not know for sure, but I suspect there was probably one or more conversations between Mr. Branan and representatives of the District Attorney's office regarding Roberts' testimony prior to the trial.

by Judge Harvey was deficient, inexcusable and extremely prejudicial. This failure, by itself, was sufficient to find that Jenkins was denied the effective assistance of counsel since it unquestionably affected the outcome of the trial.

2. Jenkins' attorneys misled him regarding the probable outcome of the trial and advised him that he should not testify in his own defense

The question of whether a defendant in a criminal case should testify in his own defense is ordinarily a matter of trial strategy which should not be second-guessed with the benefit of hindsight. Under the particular facts and circumstances of this case, however, it was utterly unreasonable for Jenkins' attorneys to advise him not to testify in his own defense.

Jenkins was only 17 years old at the time this crime was allegedly committed, and he had never been arrested for anything before in his life. The principal evidence against him consisted of (i) the testimony of Terry Roberts, an admitted co-conspirator and acknowledged liar, and (ii) two witnesses (Officer Smith and Ken McCall) who testified that Jenkins had made brief incriminating statements to them.

As his attorneys knew full well, Jenkins had consistently denied that he participated in the robbery or shooting of Mr. Hodges. Although he admitted to being present at the scene, he insisted that he was merely a bystander and that he did not know that Cedric and Maurice intended to rob Mr. Hodges. (Hr. 18, 32, 37). He also denied that he ever had a gun, or that he had shot Mr. Hodges. Finally, he also denied that he ever made either of the incriminating statements alleged by Smith and McCall (Hr. 32, 34, 37, 39). Under these circumstances, it was absolutely essential for Jenkins to get his side of the story before the jury. This meant that he had to testify.

This was especially true if, as the State later claimed, it was permissible for the State to argue that Jenkins' failure to present any evidence to rebut the evidence offered by the State was a factor which the jury could properly consider in reaching its verdict.[64] The only way that Jenkins could get his side of the story before the jury was by testifying.

Furthermore, Jenkins' attorneys did not present any evidence which contradicted the evidence presented by the State, yet they advised him that the case was "going well" (Hr. 7) and that there was "no need" for him to testify (Hr. 7). Under the particular facts and circumstances of this case, it was clearly unreasonable and highly prejudicial for Jenkins' attorneys to advise him not to testify, and it was certainly unreasonable for them to advise him that the trial was going well, since clearly it was not going well.

3. **Jenkins' attorneys failed to object to the improper hearsay testimony provided by unidentified "silent witnesses"**

As discussed in Point 3, *supra*, Investigator Jim Gray testified for the State about information he had received from unidentified, anonymous "silent witnesses" which caused him to believe that Jenkins was one of the persons who murdered and robbed Mr. Hodges. (Tr. 1724-27). This evidence was clearly improper and highly prejudicial, and it should have been objected to. Not only was it hearsay, but also it violated Jenkins' constitutional right to confront and cross-examine the witnesses against him. See Point 3, *supra*. The failure of Jenkins' attorneys to object to this improper testimony was grossly erroneous and highly prejudicial.

4. **Jenkins' attorneys failed to object to other hearsay statements made by Investigator Gray**

In addition to the testimony regarding the "silent witnesses," the testimony of Investigator Gray consisted almost entirely of inadmissible hearsay. See Point 9, *supra*. Mr. Gray was permitted to testify about facts concerning which he obviously had no personal knowledge. Here again, this was erroneous because it constituted hearsay and because it violated Jenkins' right to confront and cross-examine the witnesses against him and

---

[64] Jenkins contended that the State went too far and violated his privilege against self-incrimination by making improper comments regarding his failure to testify. See Point 2, *supra*. If, however, it turns out that the State was able to comment on the Jenkins' failure to present any proof to rebut the prosecution's case, then this would have made it even more imperative that he take the stand and testify in his own defense.

deprived Jenkins of due process of law. See Point 9, *supra*. The failure of Jenkins' attorneys to object to this improper testimony was erroneous and prejudicial and deprived him of a fair trial.

5. **Jenkins' attorneys failed to object to the improper testimony provided by Bart Ingram**

Most of the testimony of Special Agent Bart Ingram was also improper and prejudicial. See Point 19, *supra*. The failure of Jenkins' attorneys to object to this improper testimony was also erroneous and highly prejudicial.

6. **Jenkins' attorneys failed to object to the conspiracy charge on the ground that it failed to inform the jury that a co-conspirator's testimony regarding the existence of a conspiracy must be corroborated**

Judge Harvey's instruction to the jury regarding its ability to consider as evidence statements allegedly made by Jenkins' alleged co-conspirators was erroneous because, among other things, it failed to inform the jury that a co-conspirator's testimony regarding the existence of a conspiracy needed to be corroborated. See Point 16, *supra*. Jenkins' trial attorneys should have objected to this charge and their failure to do so was erroneous and prejudicial.

7. **Jenkins' attorneys failed to object to improper testimony about other crimes**

Terry Roberts was permitted to testify that two of Jenkins' alleged co-conspirators had previously been arrested for unrelated crimes. Admission of this testimony was improper and highly prejudicial. See Point 18, *supra*. Jenkins' trial attorneys should have objected to this improper testimony and their failure to do so was erroneous and prejudicial.

8. **Jenkins' attorneys failed to object to the prosecutors' improper and pervasive use of leading questions**

The prosecutors continuously and pervasively asked leading questions of the State's own witnesses throughout the trial. See Point 23, *supra*. Such use of leading questions was particularly egregious and tainted the fairness and integrity of the entire fact-finding process. The failure of Jenkins' attorneys to object to this improper procedure was erroneous and prejudicial.

9. **Jenkins' attorneys failed to object to improper comments made by Mr. Cheney during his summation in the guilt phase of the trial**

The State's closing argument during the guilt phase of the trial was improper and highly prejudicial because the prosecutor (Mr. Cheney) misled the jury regarding applicable law, misrepresented evidence, and appealed to the jury's passions, emotions and biases. See Point 21, *supra*. Jenkins' attorneys should have objected to this improper conduct and their failure to do so was erroneous and prejudicial.[65]

10. **Jenkins' attorneys failed to object to errors made by Mr. Durden during his summation in the penalty phase of the trial**

The State's closing argument during the penalty phase of the trial was improper and prejudicial because the prosecutor (Mr. Durden) misrepresented evidence and deliberately sought to inflame the passions of the jury. See Point 22, *supra*. Jenkins' attorneys should have objected to this misconduct and their failure to do so was erroneous and prejudicial.

11. **Jenkins' attorneys failed to object to or correct the false testimony given by Deputy Moran**

Deputy Moran was permitted to testify, in response to questioning by Mr. Cheney, that Terry Roberts could not be charged with the murder of Mr. Hodges because there was no evidence "to indicate that Mr. Roberts was aware of any plan to kill Mr. Hodges, prior to the time that it occurred" (Tr. 1840) and that this was the reason why the murder charge

---

65 Mr. Cheney's closing argument was also improper for the additional reason that it impermissibly commented on the fact that Jenkins did not testify or offer any evidence which rebutted the State's case. However, Jenkins' attorney did object to this improper conduct.

was dismissed against Roberts by the District Attorney (Tr. 1841). As discussed in Point 4, *supra*, this testimony was false and misleading since, as a participant in the robbery, Roberts most certainly could have, and should have, been charged with felony murder.

This testimony was extremely prejudicial because Roberts' credibility was a critical issue. Yet, Jenkins' attorneys did nothing to impeach Deputy Moran or correct the record. Counsel should have objected to this entire line of testimony and asked the Court to instruct the jury that, as a party to the robbery, Roberts most certainly could be charged with felony murder. It was extremely important for the jury to know that the reason Roberts was not being charged with murder was because of a tactical decision made by the District Attorney, presumably because he wanted Roberts to testify for the State. In effect, Roberts was rewarded by the District Attorney for his false testimony against Jenkins.

12. Jenkins' attorneys failed to object to prejudicial remarks made by Judge Harvey regarding the issue of whether a conspiracy existed

During the testimony of Terry Roberts, Judge Harvey stated, in the presence of the jury, that certain hearsay statements made by Jenkins' alleged co-conspirators were admissible because of "the exception which allows a statement of a co-conspirator to be admitted." (Tr. 1667). As discussed in Point 17, *supra*, this statement was prejudicial because the question of whether a conspiracy had been established and whether the statements were admissible on this basis was an issue of fact which the jury had to determine. Jenkins' attorneys should have immediately requested Judge Harvey to instruct the jury to disregard the court's comments on this issue and to determine for themselves whether a conspiracy had been proved.

13. Jenkins' attorneys failed to object to the admission of co-conspirator statements on the ground that the State had failed to

prove, and the Court had failed to determine, whether a prima facie case of conspiracy existed

During the charge conference at the conclusion of the trial, Judge Harvey stated, in response to a request from the prosecutor, that he "will make a preliminary determination that there is sufficient evidence to establish that there is a conspiracy." (Tr. 1881). In making this statement, Judge Harvey apparently failed to consider the requirement that Roberts' testimony regarding the existence of a conspiracy needed to be corroborated. Instead, the court merely repeated the ruling it had made earlier in the trial during the testimony of Mr. Roberts. In effect, therefore, Judge Harvey admitted the statements without making a proper determination of whether a prima facie case of conspiracy had ever been established. Jenkins' attorneys should have objected to this ruling and requested the court to make a proper determination.

14. Jenkins' trial counsel failed to object to Judge Harvey's erroneous instructions on the issues of malice, parties to a crime, and conspiracy

For the reasons discussed in Points 11, 12 and 13, *supra*, Judge Harvey's instructions regarding the issues of malice, parties to a crime, and conspiracy were improper and misleading and deprived Jenkins of a fair trial. His attorneys should have objected to the charges as given and requested Judge Harvey to give proper instructions.

15. Jenkins' attorneys failed to impeach Terry Roberts with his prior inconsistent statements

Terry Roberts was the only witness at the trial who placed Jenkins at the scene of the crime. He was the State's principal witness, and his credibility was a critical issue. As Jenkins' attorneys well knew, Roberts had given at least three separate statements to the police shortly after the crime was committed.[66] These statements were grossly inconsistent with each other and with Roberts' testimony at the trial in several significant

---

66 Copies of two of these statements were attached as Exhibits A and B to the affidavit of Robert M. Kelly sworn to March 5, 1997, which was submitted in support of Jenkins' motion for a new trial.

respects. Although Roberts admitted during both direct and cross-examination that he had lied "the first couple of times he spoke to the police," he was never explicitly confronted by Jenkins' attorneys with his actual prior inconsistent statements. Consequently, the precise nature of Roberts' untruthful statements was never disclosed to the jury.

These statements made it perfectly clear that Terry Roberts had consistently lied about the facts of the crime in order to protect himself and his half-brother Maurice and, therefore, it was a flagrant error in judgment for Jenkins' attorney not to use the statements to cross-examine Roberts. Effective cross-examination using these statements could easily have raised substantial doubt in the minds of the jury about whether Roberts' testimony concerning Jenkins' involvement in the crime was credible, or whether, once again, Roberts was merely lying to protect himself and Maurice. Thus, even though Roberts himself had admitted that he had lied "the first couple of times" he spoke to the police, defense counsel's failure to impeach Roberts with his actual prior inconsistent statements was a significant deficiency which prejudiced the defense.[67]

16. Jenkins' attorneys failed to introduce evidence showing that Cedric Brown was mentally retarded

The evidence introduced at trial established that Cedric Brown fired at least three shots at Mr. Hodges. Cedric was mentally retarded,[68] but no evidence of this fact was ever put before the jury. The fact that Cedric was mentally retarded was an important fact for the jury to know because the State sought to hold Jenkins responsible for Cedric's actions and intent.[69] Had the jury known that Cedric was mentally retarded, this might have caused them to have a reasonable doubt as to whether the State had proven

---

67 Since Roberts testified at the trial, his prior inconsistent statements could have been admitted into evidence as **substantive evidence** under Georgia Law and not merely be used to impeach Roberts' testimony. See *Gibbons v. Georgia*, 248 Ga. 858 (1982). Thus, Jenkins' trial attorneys could have admitted these statements into evidence and actually read them to the jury.
68 The State was unable to seek the death penalty against Cedric Brown because of his diminished mental capacity. He pleaded guilty and received a life sentence.
69 In opposing Jenkins' motion for a new trial, the State claimed that Jenkins could be held liable for malice murder based upon Cedric Brown's intent to kill Mr. Hodges, which is "transferred" to Jenkins. See State's Brief in Opposition to Appellant's Motion for a New Trial at 15.

that Jenkins intended to kill Mr. Hodges. It was clearly deficient and prejudicial, therefore, for Jenkins' attorneys not to introduce evidence regarding Cedric's mental condition.

30. Judge Harvey Erred in Denying Jenkins' Motion for a Change of Venue

Prior to trial, Jenkins' attorneys moved for a change of venue based upon excessive and prejudicial pretrial publicity which prevented him from obtaining a fair trial in Liberty County. Judge Harvey reserved decision on this motion until after completion of the *voir dire*.[70] During the *voir dire*, a total of 104 prospective jurors were questioned, of which 22.64 percent were excused because of preconceived views, biases or prejudice that Jenkins was guilty (Tr. 1380). An additional 9.43 percent were excused on the ground they were family or friends of the parties (Tr. 1381). A total of 35.5 percent had to be excused because of bias, prejudice or relationship (Tr. 1381). Despite such evidence showing a strong likelihood of prejudice, Judge Harvey nevertheless refused to grant the motion for a change of venue. (Tr. 1388). Under the circumstances, the trial court's denial of Jenkins' motion for a change of venue was clearly erroneous and prejudicial and deprived him of a fair trial.

In *Jones v. State*, 261 Ga. 665, 409 S.E.2d 642 (1991), the Georgia Supreme Court ruled that Georgia trial courts are **required** to grant a defendant's motion for a change of a venue in all death penalty cases in which the defendant is able to make a substantive showing of the likelihood of prejudice by reason of extensive publicity. This mandatory rule was specifically adopted in order to replace the uncertain approach of *Berryhill v. State*, 249 Ga. 442, 291 S.E.2d 685 (1982) and earlier cases with a "better and surer rule." As stated in *Jones*:

> "The approach followed in *Berryhill* and our earlier cases concerning change of venue in death penalty cases is, we

---

70 As explained previously, the *voir dire* is the period of the trial, prior to the presentation of the evidence, where the lawyers have the opportunity to question prospective jurors regarding their qualifications and potential bias.

believe, too restrictive. Our inquiries have been laborious, and often yielded what might appear to be distinctions without differences. . . . We need a better and surer rule." 261 Ga. at 666, 409 S.E.2d at 643.

The rule which the Supreme Court adopted in *Jones* is that "trial courts **will** order a change of venue in death penalty trials in those cases in which the defendant can make a substantive showing of the likelihood of prejudice by reason of extensive publicity." 261 Ga. at 166, 409 S.E.2d at 643 (emphasis added). Since Jenkins did in fact make a substantive showing of the likelihood of prejudice, Judge Harvey's denial of his motion for a change of venue was improper and clearly erroneous. *See Jones v. State*, 261 Ga. 665, 409 S.E.2d 642 (1991); *Tyree v. State*, 262 Ga. 395, 418 S.E.2d (16) (1992).[71]

Judge Harvey's Ruling on the Motion

Notwithstanding the foregoing, lengthy list of significant errors that occurred during Jenkins' trial, Judge Harvey rejected all of Jenkins' arguments and denied the Motion for a new trial on May 6, 1997. The reasons given by Judge Harvey for denying the Motion, and the reasons why his reasons were wrong, are discussed fully in the next chapter.

---

71 Notably, nine months after Jenkins' trial was completed, the State tried Maurice Fleming for the same crimes that were at issue in Jenkins' trial. This time, however, Judge Harvey granted Fleming's motion for a change of venue and moved his trial to another county. Although Fleming was convicted, the jury only sentenced him to life imprisonment with a possibility of parole.

CHAPTER 6

JUDGE HARVEY DENIES THE MOTION

On May 6, 1977, almost two months after the hearing held on March 14, Judge Harvey issued a fourteen-page Order denying Jenkins' Motion for a new trial.[72] True to his word, Judge Harvey refused to reverse Jenkins' conviction due to his failure to instruct the jury properly regarding the issue of corroboration of accomplice testimony. Furthermore, Judge Harvey also refused to reverse the conviction based upon any of the other 29 grounds asserted by Jenkins in support of his Motion for a new trial. As Judge Harvey succinctly stated in his Order:

> *"As for each and every enumeration of error raised by the defendant [Jenkins] prior to raising the issue of ineffective assistance of counsel, the defendant's motion for a new trial is denied. As for the issue of ineffective assistance of counsel addressed in this order, the defendant's motion for a new trial is denied."*[73]

Although only fourteen pages long, the May 6 Order, like all of Gaul, was divided into three principal parts. The first part (two pages) consisted of "findings of fact on the issue of ineffective assistance of counsel." This was necessary to address the disputed issues of fact that had been raised

---

72   Judge Harvey's Order was not publicly reported in any official law reporter. Accordingly, a copy of the Order is reprinted in Appendix B.

73   Presumably, the reason Judge Harvey drew a distinction between "pre-ineffective assistance of counsel claims" and "post-ineffective assistance of counsel claims" was because Jenkins had submitted two separate memoranda in support of his Motion, the original September 19, 1996 Memorandum which contained 29 enumeration of errors (but not ineffective assistance of counsel) and the Supplemental Memorandum dated March 5, 1977, which raised the ineffective assistance of counsel claim. This distinction was completely arbitrary and unnecessary. The main point that should be noted, however, is that ***all*** of the grounds asserted by Jenkins in support of his Motion for a new trial were denied.

by the testimony and the documents presented at the March 14 evidentiary hearing.

The second part of the Order (12 pages) consisted of "conclusions of law regarding ineffective assistance of counsel." This addressed the eighteen errors that were identified by Jenkins as reasons why his trial counsel had been ineffective.

The third part of the Order was the single paragraph summary quoted above which denied the motion.

Significantly, Judge Harvey spent no time whatsoever discussing the 29 grounds that had originally been asserted by Jenkins in support of the Motion. On the contrary, he summarily dismissed them all with a single sentence. However, he did discuss some of these grounds tangentially as part of his discussion of the ineffective assistance of counsel claims.

A. "Findings of fact" Concerning the Ineffective Assistance of Counsel Claim

Based upon the evidence that was presented at the March 14 hearing, Judge Harvey made the following "findings of fact":

First, Judge Harvey found that "the defendant Jamel Jenkins testified at the hearing that he was present at the scene of the murder and armed robbery at Hodges Grocery along with Cedric Brown, Shawn Brown and Maurice Fleming (Hr. 4-16)," that "he [Jamel] stated that Cedric Brown fired the fatal shot and he only saw one gun (Hr. 5)," that "he also testified he was unaware of any plan to rob or murder Mr. Hodges (Hr. 6)," that "he did not have a gun and he was outside the store when Mr. Hodges was shot (Hr. 4-6)," and that "he told his trial counsel, David Walker and Hal Peel, this version of the robbery and murder, and they advised him not to testify at trial (Hr. 6 and 7)."[74] Order at 1.

Second, Judge Harvey also found that "the physical evidence presented at trial showed that two pistols were fired in Hodges Grocery (Trial

---

[74] The transcript references ("Hr. at __") relate to the hearing transcript cited by Judge Harvey in his Order. The notation "'Trial Tr." refers to the transcript of the trial.

Tr. 1582-83, 1602-05, 1610-13, 1818, 1865-72)," that "no evidence was presented at the Motion for a new trial hearing which showed that Jenkins' trial counsel forced or coerced him not to testify," and that "furthermore, at trial, Jenkins was questioned by the Court as to whether he wished to testify or remain silent (Trial Tr. at 1877)," and that "Jenkins replied that he decided not to testify" (Trial Tr. at 1877)." Order at 2.

Third, Judge Harvey also found that "Jenkins was represented [at the trial] by attorneys David Walker and Hal Peel," that "Mr. Walker has fourteen years of trial experience, seven years of which he served as an Assistant District Attorney (Hr. 24)," that "Mr. Peel has eight years of trial experience and has tried at least seven murder cases (Hr. 43-44), that "Mr. Walker and Mr. Peel spent over a year preparing for trial (Hr. 38), that "this preparation included reviewing the State's discovery, interviewing witnesses and conferring with a private investigator (Hr. 47)," that "Mr. Walker and Mr. Peel also met with Jenkins and discussed whether or not he should take the stand or remain silent (Hr. 18-19, 25-26, 37-38, 44-45), that "the ultimate decision to remain silent was made by Jenkins (Trial Tr. 1877), and that, "after speaking with Jenkins, Mr. Walker and Mr. Peel advised him not to take the stand because the information he had would not help their case, and they believed Jenkins would hurt the case if cross-examined by the prosecutor (Hr. 18-19, 25-26, 37-38, 44-45)." Order at 2.

Judge Harvey further found that Mr. Walker and Mr. Peel's "theory of the case was that Jenkins was merely present at the scene of the crime and that the principal wrongdoers were co-defendants Maurice Fleming and Cedric Brown (Hr. at 25, 34, 45)." Order at 2.

Judge Harvey further found that Mr. Walker and Mr. Peel "did not request a charge regarding corroboration of an accomplice's testimony" although they "did reserve exceptions to the Court's instructions (Hr. at 20)." Order at 2.

Finally, Judge Harvey found that "District Attorney Dupont Cheney testified that there was no offer of leniency made to State's witness Kenneth

McCall prior to his testimony at trial (Hr. 71)," that "at trial, Assistant District Attorney Charles Howard testified that prior to trial, he handled a guilty plea entered by McCall," but that "at the time he was unaware McCall had any information regarding Jenkins' case," and that "no deal or offer of leniency was made to McCall prior to trial." Order at 3.

Before discussing the legal issues, it is important to point out a few uncontested facts that Judge Harvey conveniently and deliberately omitted from his discussion of the factual findings.

With respect to Jenkins' failure to testify at trial, Jenkins testified at the hearing that Walker and Peel had explicitly told him during the trial that the trial "was going well" and therefore there was "no need" for him to testify. Notably, Walker and Peel were both present at the hearing when Jenkins made these statements and they did not deny, diminish or contradict Jenkins' testimony in any way. On the contrary, they confirmed in their own testimony at the hearing that, although Jenkins had told them that he wanted to testify, they advised him not to do so because they did not believe his testimony "would add anything of value."

These assertions at the hearing by Jenkins' former counsel were patently frivolous. As just noted, Walker and Peel's "theory of the case" was that Jenkins was a mere bystander, who did not participate in the robbery or murder and did not even know that a robbery was contemplated by Cedric and Maurice, or that they had guns. This was a nice theory (especially since it was true) but ***no evidence of any kind was introduced at the trial by Jenkins' attorneys to support this theory***.

On the contrary, the only evidence that was introduced at the trial was introduced by the prosecutors, and it clearly established that Jenkins was ***not*** a bystander. First and most importantly, Terry Roberts testified ***that Jenkins had a gun and was one of the actual shooters***. Second, there was the brief but highly prejudicial testimony of Officer Smith and Ken McCall who testified that Jenkins had admitted shooting Hodges to them.[75] Third, there was evidence that Jenkins had fled the scene and went to Florida where he was arrested in the company of Cedric and Maurice. And finally, there was forensic evidence which showed that Hodges had been shot with two different guns.

Frankly, my seven-year old grandson could have assessed this situation far better than Walker, Peel and Judge Harvey did. Under no circumstances could any reasonable person, let alone a reasonably competent attorney or judge, think that Jenkins' trial was "going well," and that was especially true in rural Georgia.

Contrary to what Walker and Peel said at the hearing — and to what Judge Harvey purportedly "***found***" as a "***fact***" — it would have been extremely helpful in Jenkins' defense for him to take the stand and testify under oath at his trial exactly as he did at the hearing in support of his Motion for a new trial: that he never had a gun, that he never shot or robbed Mr. Hodges, that he did not know that Cedric and Maurice planned to rob Mr. Hodges before it happened, or that they had guns, that he never told anyone that he shot Mr. Hodges, and that there was never any reason for him to do so because it was untrue.

Jenkins repeatedly told this to his attorneys, and he essentially begged them to let him testify, and yet, they continuously refused to permit him to do so, and, to make matters even worse, they affirmatively told him that the trial was "going well." This constituted utter malpractice and outright fraud. The only person for whom the trial was going well was the prosecutor. Maybe Walker and Peel forgot which side they were on.

In attempting to justify his decision, Judge Harvey noted that "the ultimate decision to remain silent was made by Jenkins" (Order at 2) and that "the Court questioned Jenkins at the trial as to whether he wished to testify or remain silent, and that Jenkins replied that he decided not to testify." (*Id*.). This was judicial sophistry at its absolute worst.

---

[75] Jenkins did not tell Officer Smith that he had shot **Mr. Hodges**. What he allegedly said was, "I only shot him once" without identifying who he allegedly shot. Similarly, Jenkins never told McCall that he shot Mr. Hodges. What he allegedly said was, "I shot the old cracker twice."

The whole purpose of relying on the **advice** of counsel is because lawyers are supposed to be skilled experts who are knowledgeable about trials and legal matters and, therefore, they can assist their clients to make better and more informed decisions. At the time of his trial, Jenkins was a nineteen-year-old uneducated and unsophisticated youth with a low IQ who had not finished high school. Obviously, he had no legal training of any kind, nor had he ever been in trouble with the law before, so he had no way of making an **informed decision** with respect to the critical issue of whether he should waive his right to testify. To characterize Jenkins' decision not to testify as anything other than a decision to follow the advice of his lawyers is utterly fatuous, and to rely upon this rationale as a basis for exonerating these very same lawyers from a claim of incompetence is close to lunacy.

Furthermore, to make matters worse, as if that were even possible, Jenkins had been explicitly told by his attorneys that the trial **"was going well"** and that **"there was no need for him to testify."** Both of these assertions were patently false. To the extent that Jenkins can be said to have "made the decision not to testify," therefore, his decision was based upon false information provided to him by his own lawyers. Under these circumstances, no reasonable person could possibly conclude that the decision not to testify was an informed voluntary decision made by Jenkins himself. Judge Harvey should have been ashamed of himself for even suggesting that it was.

Another "finding of fact" that Judge Harvey conveniently omitted from his Order was that Walker testified at the hearing that the schedule of the trial was extremely grueling (Hr. 23), that he was "really tired" during the trial (Hr. 23), and that this may have affected his effectiveness as counsel (Hr. 23).

Similarly, Peel also testified at the hearing that the schedule of the trial was "a very exhausting pace" (Hr. 41) and "grueling" (Hr. 46), that he was personally exhausted" (Hr. 41), and that this may have affected his effectiveness as counsel (Hr. 41).

This testimony from both of Jenkins' trial attorneys was uncontradicted and must be accepted as true. Yet, Judge Harvey apparently gave it no weight whatsoever in reaching his decision (probably because it reflected so poorly on him).

Another finding of fact which Judge Harvey conveniently omitted from his Order was that both Walker and Peel had testified during the hearing that they were aware of several detailed and inconsistent statements that Terry Roberts had given to the police prior to Jenkins' arrest, but they did not use these statements to impeach Roberts at the trial (Hr. 21-22 and 42-43). Mr. Peel (who conducted the actual cross-examination of Roberts) explicitly stated that the decision not to use these statements was not the result of any tactical decision on his part but simply because "I just didn't consider using the statements." (Hr. 43).

B. *"Conclusions of Law" Regarding the Ineffective Assistance of Counsel Claims*

As noted above, Judge Harvey did not explicitly rule on each of the numerous grounds that had been asserted by Jenkins in support of his Motion for a new trial. He just denied them summarily without any explanation. However, Judge Harvey did explicitly rule on the grounds asserted in support of the "ineffective assistance of counsel" claim.[76] These will now be discussed in detail.

1. Failure to Request a Jury Charge Regarding Corroboration of Accomplice Testimony

---

76 Obviously, there is a great deal of overlap between the individual errors and the ineffective assistance of counsel claim. For example, to the extent that Judge Harvey failed to charge the jury regarding corroboration, that is a separate and distinct error that tainted the trial by itself. However, to the extent that Jenkins' trial attorneys failed to correct that error, that is an example of why their representation of Jenkins at trial was ineffective. This was true with respect to most of the other errors as well.

Rather than confront the accomplice corroboration problem directly, Judge Harvey shamefully danced around this issue desperately trying to find some plausible excuse for not overturning Jenkins' conviction.[77]

First, Judge Harvey stated, "the fact the trial court did not instruct the jury as to corroboration of an accomplice's testimony is not grounds for a new trial *since trial counsel failed to make a written request for this charge.*" Order at 3 (emphasis added). This is not actually a correct statement of either Georgia or federal constitutional law since the "plain error" doctrine required Judge Harvey to give a correct charge to the jury regardless of whether Jenkins' lawyers requested it.

Nevertheless, two important things should be noted about Judge Harvey's erroneous self-serving statement. First, Judge Harvey blatantly attempted to shift responsibility for failing to give the corroboration charge from himself as the presiding judge to Jenkins' trial attorneys. Second, even if one assumed (incorrectly) that Judge Harvey was not obligated to give a corroboration charge unless Jenkins' attorneys first requested him to do so in writing, this makes it even clearer that Jenkins' attorneys were deficient (and therefore ineffective) here. They never requested a corroboration charge in a case where the State's entire case was based upon the testimony of an accomplice. What could they possibly have been thinking? Or maybe they weren't thinking because they were so exhausted.

The next thing that Judge Harvey stated in his Order was, "because the State did not rely wholly on the testimony of the accomplice Terry Roberts, the Court was not required to give this charge *absent a written request by trial counsel.*" Order at 3 (emphasis added). This was completely illogical, and it added nothing to the statement quoted above.

As to the first part, Judge Harvey implies, in making this misleading statement, that, if the State had relied solely on the testimony of the accomplice Terry Roberts, then the court would not be obligated to give a

---

77 It should be remembered that Judge Harvey had privately admitted to me following the hearing on March 14, "I can't believe I did not give a charge on corroboration here." He knew it was his responsibility to give the charge and that he blew it.

corroboration charge even if the defendant's attorneys had not submitted a written request. This is technically correct, but not for the reasons Judge Harvey suggested.

Georgia law requires, as a matter of substantive procedural law, that a criminal defendant **cannot** be convicted of a felony based solely on the evidence of an accomplice. If, as Judge Harvey suggested, the State had relied solely on the testimony of an accomplice, then there would be no need to give a corroboration charge because the case would have to be dismissed outright by the Judge for failure to comply with substantive law. Under these circumstances, the defendant would be entitled to a directed verdict of acquittal and there would be nothing for the jury to consider. Hence, of course, there would then be no need for a charge on corroboration.

As to the second part, Judge Harvey emphasized again how important it was for Jenkins' attorneys to have made a written request for a corroboration charge. And yet, as noted above, that did not happen here due to the incompetence of Jenkins' attorneys.

The next thing that Judge Harvey noted, in justifying his decision not to grant Jenkins a new trial, was that, even if it was erroneous not to give a corroboration charge, it was "harmless error" which did not affect the outcome of the trial because, in fact, there was sufficient evidence admitted at trial to corroborate the accomplice's testimony. As Judge Harvey stated in his Order:

> "Furthermore, the Court finds any error in the omission of this charge was harmless in light of the State's evidence at trial and the testimony that Jenkins admitted to two witnesses he shot the victim. He, along with two co-defendants fled to the State of Florida and the three were arrested in a motel room. A food stamp traced back to the Hodges Grocery was found in this motel room. Jenkins' admissions and the circumstances surrounding his arrest were established by the State apart from the testimony of

his accomplice and corroborated the accomplice's testimony." Order at 4 (citations omitted).

There is, of course, such a thing as the "harmless error" doctrine. It is extremely important and it will be discussed at much greater length later in this narrative. In a nutshell, the harmless error rule provides that, where an error or mistake has been committed during a criminal trial, **but it did not affect the outcome of the trial**, then the error can be ignored.

Obviously, criminal trials are complicated affairs requiring great skill and knowledge on the part of the participants. Inevitably, mistakes will happen, as they do in all activities of life. It would be completely unacceptable if every criminal trial had to be reversed simply because some minor error had occurred. To justify reversal of the conviction, therefore, the error at issue must be significant rather than trivial, and there must be a basis for believing that the error in question may have affected the outcome of the trial.

However, Judge Harvey's reliance on the "harmless error" doctrine here was indefensible and completely misplaced. Under no conceivable circumstances can what happened to Jenkins here be deemed to be "harmless." Jenkins was convicted of malice murder and sentenced to life imprisonment without possibility of parole by a jury that was never told that they had an obligation to consider whether Terry Roberts' testimony was sufficiently corroborated.

These facts speak for themselves. There was no reasonable basis for any jurist, including even Judge Harvey, to think that it was harmless to fail to give a charge on corroboration. It would be like asking a jury to decide whether a defendant committed murder without telling them what the elements of murder are, or without telling them what standard of proof needs to be satisfied.

Here, Judge Harvey tried to justify his failure to give a corroboration charge to the jury by arguing that sufficient evidence had been presented at Jenkins' trial to corroborate Terry Roberts' testimony. That may or may not be true,[78] but, even if so, it was completely irrelevant because the jury was never given a corroboration charge and, therefore, they never even considered the issue of whether sufficient corroboration evidence had been presented at the trial. Significantly, it was not Judge Harvey's prerogative to decide on his own whether the corroboration evidence was sufficient. That was exclusively the role of the jury after receiving adequate instructions. By failing to give adequate instructions, Judge Harvey prevented the jury from considering this essential issue and thereby deprived Jenkins of his right to trial by jury on this issue.

Finally, the U.S. Supreme Court has ruled, as a matter of federal constitutional law, that the harmless error doctrine cannot be relied on to excuse an error unless it is clearly established "beyond a reasonable doubt" that the error did not affect the outcome of the trial. *Chapman v. California*, 386 U.S. 18 24 (1967). Obviously, that standard could not possibly be satisfied here.

After this preliminary (and very faulty) analysis, Judge Harvey then turned to the question of whether Jenkins had been denied effective assistance of counsel due to his counsels' failure to request a jury charge on the issue of corroboration. Applying the Supreme Court's *Strictland* test, Judge Harvey correctly phrased the issue as follows: "[t]he question now turns to whether this omission by trial counsel amount[ed] to deficient performance, and whether this deficiency prejudiced the defendant." Order at 4. Judge Harvey then added, also correctly, "[b]efore the Court would be authorized to grant Jenkins' motion for [a] new trial, the defense must carry the burden of satisfying both prongs of the two-part test set forth in *Strickland*." Order at 4. The necessary and correct implication of this assertion is that, if Jenkins does carry his burden on these two prongs of the *Strickland* test, then the motion for a new trial **must** be granted.

---

78   I have consistently argued from the first time I became involved in this case that the corroboration evidence was **not** sufficient to support a conviction here, and that was one of the separately stated grounds for reversal.

Notably, Judge Harvey skipped over the first prong of the *Strickland* test, probably because he wished to avoid the unpleasantness of publicly humiliating Walker and Peel by ruling that their conduct had been deficient. However, that conclusion cannot possibly be avoided. Considering everything that Judge Harvey himself had already said about the necessity of Jenkins' attorneys making a written request for a charge on corroboration as a prerequisite for triggering his own obligation to give such a charge, it is evident and indisputable that their conduct was deficient under *Strickland*.

As to the second prong of the *Strickland* test, Judge Harvey then stated (incorrectly), "there was substantial evidence of Jenkins' guilt, and Terry Roberts' testimony was corroborated, therefore the defense has not met the second prong of the *Strictland* test by showing prejudice." Order at 4. After describing the "substantial evidence" he relied on to establish Jenkins' guilt, Judge Harvey then ruled as follows:

> "The Court concludes from the overwhelming evidence of guilt, excepting therefrom the testimony of Terry Roberts, there is no reasonable probability that a jury charge regarding corroboration of the accomplice's testimony **would have created a reasonable doubt** as to Jenkins' guilt. The Court further concludes that **the omission to instruct the jury on the necessity of corroboration of an accomplice's testimony was erroneous** but not clearly harmful as a matter of law and the jury instructions as given were sufficient for a proper determination by a jury of Jenkins' guilt or innocence and counsel's failure to request a charge that an accomplices [sic] testimony must be corroborated does not amount to ineffective assistance of counsel." Order at 7 (emphases added).

I do not wish to be unduly harsh on Judge Harvey (although he certainly deserves it), but this series of sentences is completely absurd. One wonders whether he failed logic in college or criminal procedure in law school, or possibly both, but, certainly, as an experienced Superior Court judge, he surely must have known that the purpose of a jury instruction on corroboration in a criminal case is not, as Judge Harvey indicated above, "to create a reasonable doubt" in the minds of the jury. No, the purpose of the charge is to inform the jury of the legal standards which they are required to apply in reaching their decision on the issue of whether reasonable doubt exists. If the jury had been properly informed that they had the legal obligation to determine whether sufficient evidence existed to corroborate Terry Roberts' testimony, they may very well have reached a different verdict. That **possibility** is sufficient under *Strictland* to require reversal. Jenkins' trial was so severely tainted by the failure to charge corroboration that it had to be reversed, and a new trial granted.

In effect, Judge Harvey usurped the function of the jury and ruled, "as a matter of law," that Jenkins was guilty. This was completely improper. Only the jury can make that determination, but they must be given adequate and correct instructions in order to do so. They were not given such instructions here and, as a result, Jenkins' conviction should have been reversed and a new trial granted.

Finally, one additional point needs to be made. Judge Harvey stated, in the quote from his Order which is set forth above, that there was "overwhelming evidence of guilt, **excepting therefrom the testimony of Terry Roberts**." Order at 7 (emphasis added). This was totally false and completely unworthy of a Superior Court Judge. If you exclude from evidence the testimony of Terry Roberts, there was **almost no evidence whatsoever** which established Jenkins' guilt, let alone overwhelming evidence.

The statements that Jenkins allegedly made to Officer Smith and Ken McCall *may* have been sufficient to corroborate Roberts' testimony, **but they certainly were not sufficient by themselves** to establish Jenkins' guilt. On the contrary, the statements were too vague and ambiguous to provide the type of evidence needed to convict anyone of capital murder.

Most significantly, neither of the two alleged statements identified **who** was allegedly shot, **when** he was allegedly shot, **where** he was allegedly shot, **why** he was allegedly shot, **how** he was allegedly shot, or whether the alleged shot caused any serious physical injury, let alone death. Furthermore, the statements, standing alone, did not exclude the possibility that whoever was shot was shot in self-defense or by accident. There was simply nothing to connect these statements to the murder of Mr. Hodges. According to Officer Smith, Jenkins allegedly said, "I only shot him once"; and according to McCall, Jenkins allegedly said, "I shot the old cracker twice." If this were all the prosecutor had for evidence, the case would quickly be dismissed by the trial judge (even Judge Harvey) as a matter of law for failure to prove a prima facie case. Furthermore, as was noted previously, there were also serious evidentiary problems with respect to the admission of these statements.

2. The Issue of the "Silent Witnesses"

Another ground for Jenkins' claim that he was denied effective assistance of counsel was the failure of his attorneys to object to the highly prejudicial testimony of Investigator Jim Gray about the so-called "silent witnesses" who allegedly implicated Jenkins in the robbery and murder of Mr. Hodges. The problem with this testimony, as previously explained, was that it violated Jenkins' constitutional right under the Sixth and Fourteenth Amendments of the U.S. Constitution to confront and cross-examine the witnesses against him.

Judge Harvey completely missed the point of the federal constitutional argument here and, apparently, he also misunderstood the hearsay argument. His entire discussion of this point in his Order denying the motion is as follows:

> "At trial, Investigator Jim Gray testified that he received a silent witness report, however, the content of this report was not published to the jury. The defendant

alleges this was improper hearsay, however the content of this report was not a part of Gray's testimony. Because the content of the report was not divulged, there was no grounds for a hearsay objection, thus counsel's failure to object does not amount to deficient performance.

"The Court further concludes that there is no reasonable probability an objection to this testimony would have created a reasonable doubt in the minds of the jury." Order at 7.

To refresh your recollection, Gray testified at trial that he was an investigator with the District Attorney's Office (Tr. 1720); that he had investigated Mr. Hodges' death (Tr. 1721); that during the course of this investigation, he had received information from various people, including information from unidentified "silent witnesses" (Tr. 1726); and that based upon the information he had received, he was able to identify Cedric Brown, Shawn Brown, Cleavon Jenkins and Maurice Fleming as the participants in the robbery and the murder of Mr. Hodges (Tr. 1727).

Contrary to Judge Harvey's assertion, this was unquestionably hearsay, and it was clearly prejudicial. Mr. Gray was not present when Mr. Hodges was murdered, and he had no personal knowledge regarding the identity of any of the participants in the robbery. His entire knowledge about the robbery and the murder, as he himself made clear in his testimony, was based upon information that was told to him by others, including the so-called unidentified "silent witnesses."

The notion that Gray's testimony did not constitute hearsay because some written report prepared by Mr. Gray regarding what the silent witnesses had told him was not admitted into evidence, or that the contents of such a report were not divulged to the jury, is absolutely preposterous. The jury heard directly from Mr. Gray what the silent witnesses told him, and this was what was impermissible.

Essentially, Mr. Gray was permitted to tell the Jury that he had conducted an investigation, that during the course of this investigation he had spoken to several people, whom he did not identify and who did not testify at trial, and that these so-called "silent witnesses" had told him that Jenkins was a participant in the murder and robbery of Mr. Hodges. This is precisely what the Sixth Amendment right to confront and cross examine the witness against you prohibits. If such silent witnesses actually existed, it was the obligation of the State to call **them** as witnesses at the trial and have **them** testify under oath and be subjected to cross-examination. To suggest otherwise, as Judge Harvey does in his Order, displays a profound misunderstanding of the Sixth Amendment right of confrontation.

Judge Harvey also stated in his Order, "[t]he Court further concludes that there is no reasonable probability an objection to this testimony would have created a reasonable doubt in the minds of the jury." Again, this is nonsense. Lawyers do not make objections to testimony, or at least they should not make such objections, for the purpose of "creating a reasonable doubt in the minds of the jury." Lawyers object to testimony because they believe the testimony is improper under the rules of evidence or other substantive law, and the objection is made to, and ruled on by, the presiding judge, not the jury.

Thus, the reason Walker and Peel should have objected to the testimony of Investigator Gray was because it was improper and inadmissible, and it should have been excluded by Judge Harvey. If, as now appears likely, Judge Harvey would have overruled the objection, this makes no difference because it was necessary to make the objection in order to preserve the issue as a basis for appeal. Either way, the conduct of Walker and Peel was deficient due to their failure to make the objection. Furthermore, since there is no practical way of assessing how much weight, if any, the jury may have assigned to this testimony, it cannot be said that the error was harmless.[79]

3. Failure to Object to Investigator Gray's Improper Testimony Regarding his Investigation (apart from the silent witness evidence)

One of the errors enumerated by Jenkins in support of his Motion for a new trial (and also listed as one of the reasons his counsel had been deficient) was the admission of hearsay and irrelevant evidence during the testimony of Investigator Gray (apart from the silent witness evidence) and counsel's failure to object to same. Judge Harvey rejected these arguments with the following explanation:

> "Jim Gray's testimony regarding information he received which resulted in Jenkins' arrest was admissible pursuant to [Georgia Code] § 24-3-2 and *Ivestor v. State*, 252 Ga. 333, 334-35 (313 S.E.2d 674) (1984). Because this testimony is admissible there is no deficiency in trial counsel's performance, and the defendant has not carried the burden required by the first prong of the *Strickland* test." Order at 8.

These statements by Judge Harvey were incorrect. Section 24-3-2 of the Georgia Evidence Code, as it existed at the time Jenkins' trial took place,[80] did not make Jim Gray's hearsay statements admissible. What it did was to clarify that "original statements" are not hearsay. As the statute provided:

---

79 The testimony of Investigator Gray was extremely harmful to Jenkins, perhaps even more so than the testimony of Terry Roberts. Roberts, McCall and Officer Smith all had significant credibility issues. But Gray was a trusted officer of the law who testified that, based on his detailed investigation, he had concluded that Jenkins robbed and killed Mr. Hodges. Gray had no basis for this testimony, it was wholly improper, yet it probably had a huge impact on the minds of the jury.

80 The Evidence Code in effect at the time of Jenkins' trial was originally enacted in 1863. Georgia enacted an entirely new Evidence Code in 2011 (effective January 1, 2013) which was modelled after the Federal Rules of Evidence. When the new Code was enacted, the prior Section 24-3-2 was repealed as unnecessary and obsolete.

> "When, in a legal investigation, information, conversations, letters and replies, and similar evidence are facts to explain conduct and ascertain motives, they shall be admitted in evidence not as hearsay but as original evidence."

As I explained at an earlier point in this book, a "hearsay statement" is an "out-of-court statement which is offered to prove the truth of the facts contained in the statement." If the statement is not offered to prove the truth of the facts contained in the statement but for some other proper purpose, then it is not hearsay. That is all that Section 24-3-2 of the prior Evidence Code purported to say. As was explained in an article in the Georgia State University Law Review at the time the new Evidence Code was enacted:

> "The term 'original evidence' [is] retired. Georgia's nineteenth century evidence statutes use the term 'original evidence' to refer to out-of-court statements that are offered for a non-hearsay purpose. Although current Georgia law is logically consistent with the federal definition of hearsay and the distinction between hearsay and non-hearsay use of out-of-court statements, Georgia has struggled with some of the arcane terminology in this area. Adopting the federal definition of hearsay introduces a more modern and descriptive vocabulary for distinguishing hearsay from non-hearsay. Such widely used and familiar terms as 'effect on the hearer' and 'verbal act' replace 'original evidence.' In the end, the goal is the same under the old and new rules: to distinguish the use of statements that depend upon the credibility of the out-of-court declarant (hearsay) from statements that are relevant for the mere fact that they were said (non-hearsay).[81]

---

[81] Paul S. Milich, "Georgia's New Evidence Code — An Overview," 28 Georgia State University Law Review 389 (2012).

It was incontrovertible that the out-of-court statements that Investigator Gray told the jury during his testimony were offered to prove the truth of the facts contained within the statements and thus they constituted inadmissible hearsay under both the old and the new Georgia Evidence Codes. Once again, Judge Harvey was simply mistaken.[82]

In addition to ruling that the hearsay statements offered during Jim Gray's testimony were admissible, Judge Harvey also ruled that, "[a]ny error in the admission of this evidence was harmless since Gray's testimony was cumulative of the testimony of other witnesses." Order at 8 (citing *Teague v. State*, 252 Ga. 534, 535, 314 S.E2d 910 (1984)).

Firstly, it was extremely ironic that Judge Harvey chose to rely on the *Teague* case since in that case the Georgia Supreme Court absolutely obliterated the interpretation of Section 24-3-2 that Judge Harvey was relying on to claim that the statements made by Investigator Gray were admissible. As the Georgia Supreme Court stated:

> "It will be seen that only in rare instances will the 'conduct' of an investigating officer need to be 'explained.' As in practically every case, the motive, intent, or state of mind of such an officer will not be 'matters concerning which the truth must be found.' At heart, a criminal prosecution is designed to find the truth of what a defendant did, and, on occasion, of why he did it. It is most unusual that a prosecution will properly concern itself with why an investigating officer did anything.
>
> "If the hearsay rule is to remain a part of our law, then OCGA **§ 24-3-2** (Code Ann § 38-302) must be contained within its proper limits. Otherwise, the repetition of the rote words 'to explain conduct' can become

---

82 *Ivestor v. State*, 252 Ga. 333, 334-35, 313 S.E.2d 674 (1984), the case which Judge Harvey cited in his Order is not contrary to this and does not support his position. The out-of-court statement that was admitted into evidence in that case was not offered to proof the truth of the facts contained within the statement and therefore it did not constitute hearsay.

imprimatur for the admission of rumor, gossip and speculation." 252 Ga. at 536.

The Georgia Supreme Court then explicitly ruled that the use of Section 24-3-2 to justify the admission of hearsay statements made to an investigator "for the limited purpose of explaining the officer's conduct in the continuing investigation of the robbery was error."

Lest anyone miss the point of what the Supreme Court was ruling, the Court emphatically stated as follows:

> "We have gone to some length to restate and reaffirm the rule [that Section 24-3-2 may not be used to justify the admission of hearsay statements made to investigating officers]. While the failure to apply that rule does not here result in reversal, violation in another case may be fatal to conviction, as in *Goodman v. State* [167 Ga. App. 378, 306 S.E.2d 417 (1963)]. **Prosecutors and trial judges would be well advised to walk wide of error in the proffer and admission of evidence under the provisions of OCGA § 24-3-2** (Code Ann § 38-302). 252 Ga. at 536 (emphasis added).

This case was decided by the Supreme Court in 1984, eleven years before Judge Harvey presided at Jenkins' trial. Apparently, District Attorney Cheney and Judge Harvey failed to get the memo.

The second thing that should be noted about Judge Harvey's decision on this issue is that the erroneous admission of the hearsay testimony offered by Investigator Gray cannot be considered harmless on the ground that it was merely "cumulative" of other testimony. First, not all of the testimony was cumulative, and secondly, and even more importantly, just because it was cumulative does not mean it was harmless. By having Investigator Gray testify to hearsay statements that were made to him by other witnesses (Terry Roberts, for example) the State was improperly bolstering the testimony of these witnesses. Furthermore, some of the hearsay statements that Investigator Gray was permitted to tell the jury about were told to him by individuals who never even testified at Jenkins' trial (Cedric Brown and Shawn Brown, for example). This was completely improper and grounds for reversal of Jenkins' conviction.

4. Failure to Object to Bart Ingram's Improper Testimony Regarding his Investigation

For the same reason that the admission of hearsay statements during the testimony of Investigator Gray was inadmissible and erroneous, so too was the admission of hearsay statements during the testimony of Bart Ingram. Furthermore, since this evidence was improper, Jenkins' attorneys should have objected to its admission. Their failure to do so was further evidence of their ineffectiveness as trial counsel.

Judge Harvey rejected this argument with the blanket assertion that "Agent Bart Ingram's testimony regarding the circumstances surrounding Jenkins' arrest was relevant and admissible" and "[t]herefore, counsel's failure to object to admissible evidence does not amount to deficient performance." Order at 8.

This conclusion appears to be based upon the same flawed interpretation of Section 24-3-2 that the Georgia Supreme Court condemned in *Teague*. Nowhere does Judge Harvey attempt to explain why he believes the circumstances surrounding Jenkins' arrest in Florida were relevant or why this would justify the admission of hearsay statements made to Mr. Ingram.

5. Failure to Object to Roberts' Testimony Regarding Prior Arrests and Bench Warrants for Maurice Fleming and Shawn Brown

Judge Harvey stated in his Order that "[t]he State's evidence showed that Cedric Brown and Maurice Fleming had pending bench warrants and needed money to flee the Liberty County Area (Trial Tr. 1658). This evidence was admissible and relevant to show the motive behind the murder and robbery (citing *Johnson v. State*, 260 Ga. 457, 458, 339 S.E.2d 888 (1990)).” Order at 9.[83]

There are several problems with this explanation. First, even if one assumes that the bench warrants were relevant for the reasons Judge Harvey stated, the purported evidence regarding the bench warrants was not properly admitted into evidence. The trial transcript which Judge Harvey references (p. 1658) contains the following testimony from Terry Roberts:

Q. Did Maurice tell you why he needed to get out of town? He and/or Cedric?

A. Yes sir. He told me that it was a bench warrant out on him.

Q. For some unrelated offense, it that right?

A. Yes, sir.

Sorry, Judge Harvey, but this is blatant, inadmissible hearsay, and it should have been objected to by Jenkins' attorneys.

Terry Roberts was asked by the prosecutor to testify about an out-of-court statement made by Maurice Fleming to prove the truth of what Maurice Fleming had told him. There is no exception to the hearsay rule that would permit this testimony to be admitted into evidence. If what the State intended to do was prove that there was an outstanding bench warrant issued for the arrest of Maurice Fleming, the proper procedure was for the State to call the Court Clerk as a witness and have the Clerk testify, based upon the official records of the Court, that a bench warrant had been issued and then have the bench warrant itself admitted into evidence.[84] It is

---

83 The facts stated by Judge Harvey here were incorrect. The evidence did not show, and Jenkins never claimed, that **Cedric Brown** had been arrested prior to the robbery of Mr. Hodges, or that there was an outstanding bench warrant for his arrest prior to the robbery. What the evidence showed, and what Jenkins complained about, was that Terry Roberts was permitted to testify (without objection) that **Shawn Brown** had been arrested prior to the robbery and that there was an outstanding bench warrant for the arrest of **Maurice Fleming** prior to the robbery. See Trial Tr. at 1658 and 1660. This mistake regarding who had prior arrests and outstanding bench warrants was not made by the Georgia Supreme Court in its opinion (see 268 Ga. at __, 491 S.E.2d at 58). However, for some reason it managed to reappear in Judge Nangle's decision. See 103 F. Supp.2d at 1377. It is possible that there was also a bench warrant outstanding for Cedric, but is not what Roberts testified and not what Jenkins claimed.

84 It would have been necessary to have the bench warrant itself admitted into evidence to satisfy the requirements of the "best evidence" rule.

not permissible to short circuit this procedure by having Roberts provide hearsay testimony about what he was told by Maurice Fleming, and Judge Harvey surely must have known that this was improper.

The second problem with this testimony was that it was highly prejudicial to Jenkins' defense, and therefore it should not have been admitted even if it was deemed to be marginally relevant and even if the prosecutor had followed the proper procedure. Jenkins did not have a bench warrant outstanding for him, he had not committed any prior crimes, and he had no need to get money to get out of town. The evidence that Maurice and Shawn, neither of whom was on trial in this case, had outstanding bench warrants and needed money to get out of town was inherently prejudicial to Jenkins. Furthermore, this evidence permitted the jury to infer that both Shawn and Maurice were career criminals, and this tainted Jenkins by association.

If the State had followed the proper procedure and called the Court Clerk as a witness for the purpose of proving there was an outstanding bench warrant for Maurice, this would have given Jenkins' attorneys an opportunity to object to both the relevance and the probative value of the proffered evidence. By using the illegal backdoor procedure of having Roberts testify to hearsay evidence,[85] the State denied Jenkins' attorneys the opportunity to do so.[86]

Judge Harvey's reliance on *Jackson v. State* to support his decision that Roberts' testimony was admissible here was completely misguided, since the facts in the two cases were completely different. In the *Jackson* case, the State had admitted into evidence the **defendant's** pretrial statement "which established that he used and sold drugs, that the victim [of a shooting] was his customer, and that the victim wanted to talk about drugs on the occasion of the shooting." 260 Ga. at 458. Under these circumstances, the Court ruled that this evidence was admissible to show

---

[85] At the time Jenkins' trial took place in 1995, the use of hearsay evidence was deemed to be "unlawful" under the Georgia rules of evidence. This characterization of hearsay evidence was changed by the new evidence code of 2011.
[86] Of course, whether Jenkins' attorneys would have made the objection is another matter.

a motive for the shooting even though it incidentally put the defendant's character in issue. As the Court stated:

> "The evidence that the appellant was a drug dealer, that he used drugs with and sold drugs to the victim, and that there was a dispute regarding drugs was clearly relevant to prove that appellant had a motive for killing the victim. Evidence that is relevant to an issue in the case is not rendered inadmissible by the fact that it incidentally puts the defendant's character in issue." 260 Ga. at 458.

Obviously, there were significant differences between this case and Jenkins' case. First, the statements that were admitted in *Jackson* were made by the *defendant* himself and were therefore admissible as admissions. The statements reported by Roberts, however, were not made by Jenkins, but by a third party (Fleming) who was not a defendant in this case. Second, in the *Jackson* case, the statements at issue related directly to the defendant's own character. In Jenkins' case, however, the statements related to the character of two other individuals who were not on trial. Third, in the *Jackson* case, the statements at issue provided a motive for the defendant to kill the victim. In Jenkins' case, the statements at issue did not provide a motive for Jenkins to participate in the crimes at issue.

For all of the forgoing reasons, the admission of Roberts' testimony regarding Maurice Fleming and Shawn Brown's outstanding bench warrants and prior arrests was improper, and it should have been objected to by Jenkins' attorneys.

6. Failure to Object to the Prosecutors' Persistent Use of Leading Questions

Judge Harvey justified the failure of Jenkins' attorneys to object to the prosecutors' persistent use of leading questions by noting that, "[t]rial counsel did not object to leading questions because most were designed to elicit basic information and because frequent objections would cause the jury to believe the defense was trying to hide information." Order at 9. However, if you refer back to the examples given in the prior chapter, it is easy to see that this is not correct. A portion of this testimony is reproduced below.

> Q. "When did y'all [Deputy Moran] receive the first lead as to the identity of the perpetrators in this case?
>
> A. The investigation revealed that there was a witness across the street that saw some black males coming down the road and one of 'em was Cedric Brown. He knew him, going down the sidewalk, around the time the incident occurred.
>
> Q. Okay. So — so, one possible suspect at that time was identified, is that correct?
>
> A. That's correct.
>
> * * * *
>
> Q. Okay. The — Following the information developed from that witness as to at least one suspect in the case, did you later receive any information or — or any of the officers talk to the young man named Dewayne Paulk?
>
> A. That's correct.
>
> * * * *
>
> Q. Okay. And — And that information that was developed from Mr. Paulk identified another possible suspect in the case?
>
> A. That is correct.
>
> Q. And who was that?
>
> A. Shawn Brown.
>
> Q. Okay. Without going into what — what information came in, did you later receive a silent witness call that was assist — some assistance to you?

A. That is correct. Around 12:30 the next day. That'd been on Saturday.
Q. Okay. Following this information that y'all began to develop in this case, were some search warrants issued by the Sheriff's Office.
A. That's correct.

* * * *

Q. Okay. Later in the evening, on - on Saturday, were your notified that a Mr. Joe Roberts had information for the investigators.
A. Yes, sir.
Q. Okay. By this time Chief Deputy Moran had returned and was involved with you in the investigation, is that correct?
A. Yes, sir. We were together at that time.

* * * *

Q. And in fact, did you talk with Joe Roberts and with his son, Terry?
A. Yes, I did.

* * * *

Q. And from the statement given to you by Terry Roberts, were you able to identify all the participants . . .
A. Yes, sir.
Q. . . . in the robbery and in the murder?
A. Yes, sir.
A. And who were they?
Q. It was Cedric Brown, Shawn Brown, Jamel Jenkins and Maurice Fleming.
Q. Okay. Did you, in the — in the process of the investigation and in — talking with Terry Roberts, did y'all go to his residence and through his vehicle?
A. That's correct.

* * * *

Q.	Okay. And was permission received from his father to — to make a search of the vehicle?
A.	That's correct.
Q.	And was one of the .25 caliber weapons recovered there from the vehicle. . .
A.	That's correct. (Tr. 1725-1728).

This is basically a long series of questions where the prosecutor provides the essential information, and the witness merely answers, "that's correct" or "yes, sir." That is the classic paradigm for leading the witness. And these questions do not refer to preliminary matters, but to the fundamental issues in the case and, as such, they should have been objected to as improper.

7. Failure to Object to the Misleading Testimony of Deputy Moran

As noted previously, Deputy Moran testified that the reason the murder charge had been dismissed against Roberts, an admitted accomplice in the robbery of Mr. Hodges, was because "no evidence had been developed that indicated that Roberts knew of any plan to murder Mr. Hodges before it occurred." This testimony was false and misleading because, as a participant in the robbery, Roberts could clearly be charged with murder regardless of whether he was aware of any plan to murder Mr. Hodges. Furthermore, since the murder charge was not dismissed against Jenkins, this testimony also implied to the jury that some evidence must have been developed that indicated that Jenkins was aware of a plan to kill Mr. Hodges before it occurred. Judge Harvey claimed that this testimony was proper for the following reason:

> "A review of the record reveals Moran found no indication that Roberts knew Cedric Brown, Fleming and Jenkins had planned to murder Bobby Hodges, and that the decision to dismiss the [murder charge] had been made

by the District Attorney's Office (Trial Tr. 1840-41). At no point did Moran state that Roberts could not be legally charged with murder (Trial Tr. 1840-41). Furthermore, the testimony was a legitimate response to trial counsel's strategy to show that the only reason the murder charge against Roberts was dismissed was in exchange for his testimony. Since Roberts' credibility had been attacked, it was proper for the State to show other mitigating circumstances which led to the dismissal of the murder warrant against Roberts." Order at 10.

There is nothing that is correct or appropriate about the foregoing statement, and I find it absolutely appalling that an esteemed jurist would make such a ludicrous statement in order to avoid confronting the possibility that Jenkins' trial may have actually been tainted by significant errors.

First, Judge Harvey's statement that "[a]t no point did Moran state that Roberts could not be legally charged with murder" is completely misleading. What Moran said, in effect, and what the jury surely understood him to say, was that Roberts was not charged with murder because he was not aware of any plan to murder Mr. Roberts prior to the time it occurred. And this certainly and deliberately implied to the jury that Roberts **could not be charged with murder** because he was not aware of any plan to murder Mr. Hodges prior to the time it occurred. Such evidence was indisputably false. As a participant in the robbery, Roberts most certainly could have been charged with murder and, in fact, he was charged originally with the murder prior to agreeing to testify on behalf of the State. It was only after the District Attorney realized that he needed Roberts to testify as his star witness that the murder charge against Roberts was dismissed.[87]

Second, Judge Harvey stated in the foregoing quote from his Order that there was "no indication that Roberts knew Cedric Brown, Fleming **and Jenkins** had planned to murder Bobby Hodges." Order at 10 (emphasis added). This statement was false to the extent it suggested that Jenkins had planned to murder Mr. Hodges. There was no such evidence in the record, and there was no factual basis for Judge Harvey to make such a reckless statement.

Third, Judge Harvey stated in his Order that "[s]ince Roberts' credibility had been attacked, it was proper for the State to show **other mitigating circumstances** which led to the dismissal of the murder warrant against Roberts." Order at 10 (emphasis added). As already explained, however, Roberts was legally responsible for the murder of Mr. Roberts solely as a result of his participation in the robbery. There was no need for him to be aware of any prior plan to kill Mr. Hodges. Accordingly, even if Roberts was unaware of a plan to kill Mr. Hodges prior to the murder, that would not constitute "a mitigating factor." This was exactly what the District Attorney wanted the jury to believe and exactly why the testimony was so misleading.

Fourth, there was no evidence in the record that Jenkins was aware of any plan to kill Mr. Hodges before it happened. Unlike Roberts, however, the murder charge against Jenkins was not dismissed by the District Attorney. Why not? A logical inference that could be drawn by the jury from Deputy Moran's misleading testimony was that Deputy Moran must have had some indication that Jenkins was aware of a plan to kill Mr.

---

[87] Actually, and unbeknownst to anyone at Jenkins' trial except, of course, Messrs. Cheney and Durden, the murder charge against Roberts was ***not*** totally dismissed. On December 13, 1993, the very same day Cedric, Shawn, Maurice and Jenkins were indicted, a warrant was issued by the Liberty County Superior Court for Roberts' arrest for the murder of Mr. Hodges (1993 R. 6876). This arrest warrant was not dismissed until July 20, 1996, after Roberts testified at the trial against Maurice. This was obviously a ploy to keep Roberts under the control of the District Attorney's office to insure his favorable testimony against Jenkins and Fleming. The DA did not want Roberts to be charged with Hodges' murder at the time of his testimony against Jenkins and Fleming (because that would undermine his credibility), but he also did not want Roberts to think that he was exempt from prosecution either. That seems a little devious to me, if not outright unethical.

Hodges before it occurred. Otherwise, the murder charge would have been dismissed against Jenkins also.

Finally, the testimony at issue was elicited from Deputy Moran by Mr. Cheney, the District Attorney himself. Mr. Cheney should have known better than to practice such an unethical stunt. Furthermore, the person who should have provided this testimony, if it was to be provided at all, should have been Mr. Cheney himself. He was the person who made the decision to dismiss the murder charge against Mr. Roberts, and he was the only person who could testify why this decision was made. To the extent that Deputy Moran was permitted to testify why the murder charge was dismissed against Mr. Roberts, it constituted inadmissible hearsay and should have been disregarded. If Mr. Cheney wanted to admit testimony on this issue into evidence, he should have testified himself and subjected himself to cross-examination on this issue.

8. Judge Harvey's Prejudicial Remarks Regarding the Issue of Conspiracy

Jenkins contended, during the Motion for a new trial, that a ruling by Judge Harvey regarding the issue of conspiracy in the presence of the jury was prejudicial because the question of whether a conspiracy existed was an issue which the jury ultimately had to determine for itself. Judge Harvey responded by saying that no error had occurred because he was merely ruling on an evidentiary objection made by Jenkins' attorneys. As Judge Harvey stated in his Order:

> "During Terry Roberts' testimony, a hearsay objection was made by trial counsel (Trial Tr. 1667). The Assistant District Attorney stated that "it's admissible as an exception to the hearsay rule on the — *that exception which allows a statement of a co-conspirator*.' The Court replied, 'It's hearsay but it's an exception, your objection is noted, but it's overruled.' (Trial Tr. 1667). During this

exchange, the Court did not say that a conspiracy existed but merely ruled on a point of law." Order at 10 (emphasis added).

It is true that Judge Harvey did not explicitly state that a conspiracy existed, but he agreed with the Assistant District Attorney's assertion that a conspiracy existed by overruling counsel's objection and stating, "it's hearsay, but it's an exception." In effect, therefore, Judge Harvey indicated to the jury that he believed that the evidence had shown the existence of a conspiracy. Since the question of whether a conspiracy existed was an issue which the jury had to determine, this comment by the trial judge, in the presence of the jury, was prejudicial and denied Jenkins a fair trial. This type of evidentiary objection and ruling should have been conducted at a sidebar conference between the judge and the lawyers out of the hearing of the jury.

Judge Harvey further stated in his Order, "Assuming arguendo this statement was prejudicial, it was cured by the Court's instruction that the State must prove the existence of a conspiracy beyond a reasonable doubt (Trial Tr. 1982-83)." Order at 10-11. Unfortunately, by the time this instruction was given, the damage had already been done. The jurors had already heard Judge Harvey admit evidence on the ground that a conspiracy existed, and it would be difficult, if not impossible, for them to erase this memory from their minds when the time came for them to decide whether a conspiracy existed.

9. Admission of the Hearsay Statements During the Testimony of Terry Roberts on the Basis of the Co-conspirator Exception to the Hearsay Rule was Erroneous

As just noted above, Terry Roberts was permitted to testify at trial about incriminating statements allegedly made to Roberts by Cedric Brown and Maurice Fleming. (See Tr. 1659, 1666-69). The basis for admitting these statements was that Jenkins had allegedly conspired with Brown and Fleming to commit the crimes charged in the indictment and therefore the statements made by Cedric and Maurice were admissible under the co-conspirator exception to the hearsay rule.[88] As noted above, Judge Harvey's comments in ruling on this issue within hearing of the jury was prejudicial because this was an issue the jury itself had to decide.

More fundamentally, Judge Harvey's ruling that these statements were admissible under the co-conspirator exception to the hearsay rule was also wrong. This was so for three reasons. First, Judge Harvey failed to determine whether a prima facie case of conspiracy had been proven sufficient to allow admission of the testimony. Second, even assuming that a prima facie case of conspiracy had been shown, Judge Harvey failed to consider whether the alleged statements were sufficiently reliable to permit them to be admitted in a capital murder case. Third, even if the co-conspirator exception to the hearsay rule was applicable, only statements made in furtherance of the conspiracy would have been admissible.

Judge Harvey's entire discussion of this issue in his Order was as follows:

> "The Court did at a later point in the trial rule that a prima facie case of conspiracy existed. (Trial Tr. 1989)....
>
> As set forth in the rational above, the Court did not err in finding a prima facie case that a conspiracy existed, thus trial counsel's performance was not deficient in not objecting. The Court further finds any error on trial counsel's part did not prejudice the defendant." Order at 11.

These brief and cursory assertions failed to consider any of the substantive objections Jenkins had made to the admission of this testimony. As Judge Harvey stated in his Order, he made the determination that a prima facie case of conspiracy existed "at a later point in the trial." Order at 11.

---

88   OCGA § 24-3-5 (Declarations of Conspirators) provides: "After the fact of conspiracy is proved, the declarations by any one of the conspirators during the pendency of the criminal project shall be admissible against all."

Actually, his decision was made at a much later point in the trial — after both sides had rested and the case was about to be submitted to the jury.

Before these statements could have been admitted under the co-conspirator exception to the hearsay rule, it would first have been necessary for Judge Harvey to determine (i) that a prima facie case of conspiracy had been shown from evidence other than Roberts' testimony, (ii) that Jenkins was a member of the conspiracy, and (iii) that the statements were made in furtherance of the conspiracy. As stated in the unrelated case of *Roberts v. State*, 160 Ga. App. 717, 720, 288 S.E.2d 31, 33 (1981):

> "[B]efore the declarations of co-conspirators can be admitted as an exception to the hearsay rule, a prima facie case of conspiracy must be 'proved by evidence aliunde such declarations. . . .' The statutory exception to the hearsay rule of co-conspirator's declarations is inapplicable absent proof of a party's involvement in a conspiracy." (Citations omitted).

These requirements were not satisfied here. Judge Harvey admitted the statements without making any determination of whether a prima facie case of conspiracy had been established. (See Tr. 1667). Furthermore, for the reasons discussed in Point 1, *supra*, the testimony of an accomplice regarding the existence of a conspiracy must be corroborated. It was impossible, therefore, for the State to establish a prima facie case of conspiracy based solely upon the testimony of Terry Roberts. Judge Harvey failed to consider this requirement for corroboration, however, and admitted the statements based solely on the testimony of Mr. Roberts.[89] This was clearly improper. For the statements to become admissible under the co-conspirator exception to the hearsay rule, additional evidence was necessary to

---

[89] Judge Harvey overruled the objection of Jenkins' attorneys to these statements while Mr. Roberts was testifying on the ground that the co-conspirator exception to the hearsay rule was applicable. (See Tr. 1667). Eight witnesses had testified prior to that time, but none of these witnesses had presented any evidence which linked Jenkins to the crime. Indeed, no evidence of any kind was presented prior to the testimony of Mr. Roberts which incriminated Jenkins in any way.

corroborate the testimony of Mr. Roberts that a conspiracy actually existed and that Jenkins was a member thereof.

Even assuming that the existence of a conspiracy and Jenkins' participation therein had been established, the alleged statements lacked sufficient "indicia of reliability" to afford the trier of fact with an adequate basis for evaluating the truth of the statements. *See, e.g. Castell v. State*, 250 Ga. 776, 301 S.E.2d 234 (1983); *Timberlake v. State*, 158 Ga. App. 125, 279 S.E.2d 283 (1981); *Boswell v. State*, 158 Ga. App. 727, 282 S.E.2d 196 (1981); *Hardy v. State*, 245 Ga. 272, 277, 264 S.E.2d 209 (1980), *cert denied*, 454 U.S. 1114 (1981); *Mooney v. State*, 243 Ga. 373, 390, 254 S.E.2d 337, 349 (1979). As the Georgia Supreme Court stated in *Castell*, "[t]he thrust of *Dutton v. Evans*, *supra*, is that in cases involving a co-conspirator exception to the hearsay rule, the admission of the statement of a co-conspirator does not violate the confrontation clause ***if the statement and the circumstances surrounding it contain sufficient 'indicia or reliability.'*** " 250 Ga. at 779, 301 S.E.2d at 340 (emphasis added). What constitutes sufficient "indicia of reliability" was explained in *Hardy* as follows:

> "The indicia of reliability required for admissibility are that the statements be non-narrative; that the declarant is shown by the evidence to know whereof he speaks; that the witness is not apt to be proceeding on faulty recollection; and that the circumstances show that the declarant had no apparent reason to lie to the witness." 245 Ga. at 277, 264 S.E.2d at 213.

See also *Dutton v. Evans*, 400 U.S. 74 (1970); *Mancusi v. Stubbs*, 408 U.S. 204, 213 (1972).

In the present case, the circumstances were such that there was grave doubt about the reliability of Roberts' testimony. The prosecutor himself elicited direct testimony that Roberts had lied the ***"first couple of times"*** he spoke to the police:

Q.	"Now, you know Mr. Gray, Investigator Gray. Is that right?
A.	Yes, sir.
Q.	And you know Chief Deputy Moran, right?
A.	Yes, sir.
Q.	Okay. Did they talk with you after you came down and met with — with the Sheriff's officers?
A.	Yes, sir.
Q.	You talked with — these gentlemen on more than one occasion, is that correct?
A.	Yes, sir.
Q.	Okay. The first — the first time, or **the first couple of times that you talked with them you did not tell them the whole truth, did you?**
A.	No, sir.
Q.	Okay. Why did you not tell them the whole truth the first couple of times you talked to 'em?
A.	**Because I was trying to look out for Maurice and myself.** (Tr. 1681-82) (emphasis added).

The facts in this case make it clear that Roberts' testimony was inherently unreliable. As the prosecutor well knew, and as Roberts himself admitted at trial, Roberts had lied several times to the police about this case. This was because, as Roberts himself testified, "I was trying to look out for Maurice and myself." Under these circumstances, since there was substantial doubt as to whether Roberts was telling the truth, it was incumbent upon Judge Harvey to make a preliminary determination whether the co-conspirator exception should even be applicable to this case. Judge Harvey failed to make any such determination, and this was error.

Actually, Judge Harvey did not even focus on the issue of the admissibility of the co-conspirator statements until after both sides had rested and Mr. Cheney stated, "I think the Court may need to rule [on the issue of] whether or not the State, through all its evidence has made a prima facie case of conspiracy so that testimony would be admissible." (Tr. 1879). At this point Judge Harvey perfunctorily stated, "[t]he Court will make a preliminary determination that there is sufficient evidence to establish that there is a conspiracy. But the ultimate determinate (sic) of that factor would have to be the jury . . ." (Tr. 1881). It is very clear from Judge Harvey's remarks that he never even considered the question of whether there were any indicia of reliability for the statements. Accordingly, the admission of this evidence was improper and highly prejudicial.

10. Failure to Object to Judge Harvey's Instructions Regarding the Issues of Malice, Parties to a Crime, and Conspiracy

For the reasons discussed previously, Judge Harvey's instructions regarding the issues of malice, parties to a crime and conspiracy were erroneous and should have been objected to. Judge Harvey's entire discussion of these issues was as follows:

> "Failure to object to **proper** instructions does not amount to ineffective assistance of counsel. . . . These instructions were proper and thus trial counsel's failure to request different instructions cannot form the basis for a claim of ineffective assistance of counsel." Order at 11 (emphasis added).

Obviously, failure to object to proper instructions can never provide a basis for a claim of ineffective assistance of counsel. What Jenkins had claimed, however, and what Judge Harvey failed to address, was that the instructions were not proper.

For a complete discussion of why Jenkins claimed that Judge Harvey's instructions regarding the issues of malice, parties to a crime and conspiracy were erroneous, see the discussion of these issues in Points 12, 13 and 14 of Chapter 4.

11. Failure to Impeach Terry Roberts with his Prior Inconsistent Statements

As noted previously, Terry Roberts, the State's primary witness against Jenkins and the only witness who actually connected Jenkins to the robbery and murder of Mr. Hodges, had given several prior inconsistent statements to the police. These statements, which were taped and transcribed, were extremely lengthy and provided numerous instances in which Roberts' prior statements were inconsistent with his trial testimony. These prior inconsistent statements were never used by Jenkins' attorneys to cross-examine and impeach Roberts at trial. This was gross negligence on the part of Jenkins' attorneys, and it cannot be defended as a matter of trial strategy. Yet, that is exactly what Judge Harvey attempted to do. As he stated in his Order:

> "The decision to impeach a witness is a matter of strategy which will not be second-guessed through hindsight. . . . The strategic decision of counsel not to impeach Roberts was a matter of trial strategy which does not amount to ineffective assistance of counsel. (Tr. 49. 50, 28, 29). Had trial counsel introduced the evidence, they would have lost opening and closing argument which both Mr. Walker and Mr. Peel felt was important (Tr. 49. 50, 28, 29).[90] Also, the fact that Roberts made inconsistent statements was brought out to the jury on direct and cross-examination and trial counsel made a strategic decision that this was sufficient to attack the witness's credibility. The Court finds that this strategic decision fell within the wide range

---

[90] The right to "open and close" closing arguments refers to the order in which attorneys may give closing arguments to the jury after the presentation of the evidence has been concluded. At the time of Jenkins' trial, this right was controlled by Section 17-8-71 of the Georgia Code, which provided as follows: "After the evidence is closed on both sides, the prosecuting attorney shall open and conclude the argument to the jury. If the defendant introduces no evidence, his counsel shall open and conclude the argument to the jury after the evidence on the part of the state is closed."

of reasonable professional conduct, and thus the defendant has not satisfied the first prong of the *Strickland* test.

The Court further finds that any error on trial counsel's part in this regard did not prejudice the defendant." Order at 12.

There were several flaws in Judge Harvey's analysis. ***First***, and most importantly, Hal Peel, the attorney who cross-examined Roberts at the trial, explicitly testified at the hearing in support of the Motion for a new trial, that ***he did not make a strategic decision not to cross-examine Roberts with his prior inconsistent statements***. His failure to use these statements was purely a matter of inadvertence. As Mr. Peel testified:

> Q. Now, are you aware of the fact that Terry Roberts had given very detailed statements to the police prior to the time he testified at the trial?
>
> A. Yes.
>
> Q. And did you at any time consider using these statements to impeach him during the trial?
>
> A. Well, the — the statements that he gave and the testimony that he gave at trial were such that — and he admitted — like I said before, he admitted lying to the police and he admitted the reason. The reason he did it was to protect himself and his brother because he was scared. I mean, he was frightened and scared and concerned about what had happened and he admitted lying. And I didn't know that I could impeach him any more by use of his statements than — than what he did by sitting on the stand and admitting that he lied to the police.
>
> Q. Well, did you make a tactical decision not to use the statements, or did you just not consider it?
>
> A. I just didn't consider using the statements." H. Tr. 42-43.

Based upon this sworn testimony of Mr. Peel, Judge Harvey's conclusion that the decision not to impeach Roberts with his prior inconsistent statements was a strategic decision consciously made by Jenkins' attorneys is patently false and is not supported by the evidence.

Second, the notion that Jenkins' attorneys made a strategic decision not to impeach Roberts with his prior inconsistent statements in order to retain the right to make opening and closing summations is completely frivolous. Merely using the prior inconsistent statements to **impeach** Roberts would not have affected their right to make opening and closing statements. That would only have been affected if they actually offered the prior inconsistent statements into evidence. As the Georgia Supreme Court made clear in *Smith v. State*, 272 Ga. 874, 536 S.E.2d 514 (2000):

> "[A] defendant who reads from a prior written inconsistent statement of a witness in order to impeach that witness is not, under the guise of cross-examination, presenting evidence to the jury that would otherwise have to be formally admitted. Accordingly . . . a defendant who cross-examines a witness by reading from the person's prior inconsistent statement is not introducing evidence . . . **and would not lose the right to open and close final arguments**." (emphasis added),

Third, even if Jenkins' attorneys would, in fact, have lost the right to make "opening and closing" summations by offering Roberts' prior inconsistent statements into evidence, that was a trade-off that would have been well worth making. The right to make an opening closing summation is pretty much worthless, especially if you have to sacrifice the opportunity to present exculpatory evidence in order to obtain it. If you read the initial closing statement that Hal Peel actually presented in this case, you will agree with me that it was totally ineffective and not worth foregoing the opportunity to offer helpful evidence. And, of course, just because the defense loses the opportunity to give "opening and closing" summations does not mean that it loses the right to give its principal closing statement; it merely means that you cannot give two. As a practical matter, however, there is no real advantage in giving two closing statements. One is usually sufficient and many times it is actually more effective.

Finally, I do not know what Judge Harvey was thinking, or what record he was reading, but there was no way to justify Mr. Peel's failure to impeach Roberts with his prior inconsistent statements in this case as a "strategic decision … within the range of professional conduct." Roberts was the principal and only witness who implicated Jenkins in the crimes at issue. His credibility was the most critical issue in the case. Even though he had admitted on direct examination that he "had lied the first couple of times that he spoke to the police," that was not sufficient. Time after time the police told Roberts in these statements that they did not believe that he was telling the truth and each time Roberts changed his story to tell the police exactly what they wanted to hear, all while minimizing the involvement of himself and Maurice and placing all the blame on Cedric and Jenkins. It was critical to confront Roberts with these numerous "flip flops" in his prior statements in order to demonstrate to the jury that Roberts was unworthy of belief and was probably not telling the truth at the trial.

12. Failure to Advise Jenkins to Testify in His Own Defense and Falsely Telling Jenkins that the Trial Was "Going Well"

One of the key arguments that Jenkins had made regarding why his trial attorneys had been ineffective was their advice to him that the trial was "going well" and, therefore, there was no need for him to testify in his own defense. Judge Harvey rejected this argument for two reasons: (i) that the decision not to testify was made by Jenkins himself and not by his attorneys and (ii) that "counsel's strategic decision to advise Jenkins to remain silent falls within the wide range of reasonable professional conduct." Order at 13.

Judge Harvey's entire analysis of this issue is set forth below:

> "The decision to testify or not by the accused lies with the accused, not trial counsel. Only the defendant makes the final decision to take the stand or remain silent. Thus, the fact trial counsel **did not persuade** the defendant to testify cannot be viewed as deficient performance. After the State's evidence was presented, the Court informed Jenkins that he had a right to testify or to remain silent and inquired of Jenkins what his desire was (Trail Tr. 1876-77). Jenkins replied, 'No, I made the decision myself.' (Trial Tr. 1877). The Court finds that trial counsel's strategic decision to advise Jenkins to remain silent falls within the wide range of reasonable professional conduct and does not amount to a deficiency in performance. Furthermore, the Court finds no evidence that trial counsel **forced or coerced** Jenkins to remain silent and that the decision was properly made by Jenkins." Order at 13 (case citations omitted; emphasis added).

This analysis by Judge Harvey was overly simplistic and utterly wrong. It is true, of course, that the defendant in a criminal case must ultimately decide whether he wishes to testify or not. But that does not mean that the advice which he receives from his attorney is unimportant or irrelevant in making this decision. On the contrary, counsel's advice is absolutely critical for the defendant to make an informed decision about whether to waive this fundamental right. Obviously, the average criminal defendant has little or no knowledge or expertise about criminal law and procedure and is not able to make an informed waiver of this right without first being informed about the consequences of such a waiver by a competent attorney. This was especially true for Jenkins who was only 19 years old at the time of his trial, he had a low IQ and had not even finished high school, and he had never had any prior experiences with the police or the courts.

Judge Harvey also stated that Jenkins' attorneys cannot be faulted because they "***did not persuade*** the defendant to testify." That was a complete mischaracterization of the issue. Jenkins was not claiming that his attorneys were ineffective because they did not persuade him to testify. What he was claiming, and what Judge Harvey certainly must have realized, was that his attorneys were ineffective because ***they persuaded him not to testify*** even though he repeatedly told them he wanted to testify. Furthermore, as explained previously, the fact that Jenkins had told his attorneys that he wanted to testify was fully supported by the testimony of both Mr. Walker and Mr. Peel at the hearing in support of the Motion for a new trial.

Judge Harvey further stated, "the Court finds no evidence that trial counsel ***forced or coerced*** Jenkins to remain silent." That was also a complete mischaracterization of the issue and an obvious red herring. Jenkins was not claiming that his attorneys forced or coerced him to remain silent, only that they strongly ***advised*** him to remain silent under circumstances where such advice was ***both unreasonable and incompetent***.

Actually, Jenkins' claim was a lot stronger than this. He was not merely claiming that his attorneys gave him bad advice, he was claiming that his attorneys affirmatively deceived and misled him by telling him that the trial was "going well" at a time when it should have been obvious to any reasonable attorney that the trial was definitely not going well.

Incredibly, Judge Harvey made absolutely no attempt to analyze whether, based upon the actual evidence that had been presented at trial, it was reasonable for Jenkins' attorneys to advise him not to testify. He just simply concluded, without any factual basis, that Jenkins' attorneys made a "strategic decision to advise Jenkins to remain silent" and that such a decision "falls within the wide range of reasonable professional conduct." Order at 13.

I will concede that, ordinarily, the decision about whether a defendant should testify at trial presents a strategic decision that his attorneys must decide based upon the unique circumstances of each individual case. For example, if the defendant has a prior criminal record, then usually he should not testify because evidence of his prior crimes can be used to impeach him at trial. Furthermore, if the prosecutor has a very weak case, then it may be advantageous for the defendant not to testify lest he provide the necessary evidence to bolster a weak case.

I will also concede that an attorney's advice to his client not to testify should not ordinarily be second-guessed with the benefit of hindsight. But this does not mean that uninformed and simple-minded deference should always be given to counsel's advice not to testify regardless of the circumstances. Where, as in Jenkins' case, a criminal conviction was clearly inevitable based upon the existing evidence, where the defendant's testimony would be helpful and plausible, where the defendant had no prior arrests, and where the defendant's testimony may provide the basis for creating reasonable doubt, then, under such circumstances, it was absolutely essential for the defendant to testify. And under such circumstances, it was objectively unreasonable for the defendant's attorneys to advise him not to testify.

That, of course, was the situation here. Roberts had testified that, not only was Jenkins involved in the robbery of Mr. Hodges, but also that Jenkins had admitted to shooting him. Roberts further testified that he saw Jenkins holding a gun which matched the description of the gun that was stolen from Roger Fleming prior to the robbery and which, according to the State's ballistics expert, was the same type of gun that was used in the robbery and murder of Mr. Hodges. Jenkins had fled from Georgia right after the robbery in the company of Cedric and Maurice, and all three were apprehended together a few days later in a motel in Florida. At the time of their arrest, a food stamp was found in this motel which was directly linked to Mr. Hodges store. In addition to the testimony of Terry Roberts, there was also the testimony of Officer Smith and Ken McCall who stated that Jenkins had admitted to them that he had shot somebody (although not necessarily Mr. Hodges). Additionally, there was also the testimony of Deputy Moran who testified (improperly) that he had spoken to "silent witnesses" during his investigation and that based upon the statements of the silent witnesses he had determined that Jenkins was one of the participants in the robbery and murder of Mr. Hodges. Finally, although not actual evidence in the trial against Jenkins, there had been a tremendous amount of pretrial publicity throughout Liberty County which identified Jenkins as one of the suspects in the robbery.

None of this evidence was contradicted in any way by any evidence that was introduced at Jenkins' trial. Although Roberts' credibility was seriously undermined by the fact that he admitted that he had lied the first couple of times that he spoke to the police, this, by itself, in my professional opinion, would not have been sufficient to prevent Jenkins from being convicted. On the contrary, based upon the available evidence, it was clearly inevitable that Jenkins would be convicted. There was no basis, therefore, for any reasonable attorney to think that the trial was "going well" for Jenkins.

In contrast to this evidence, Jenkins, if he had been permitted to testify, would have told the jury that he was not involved in the robbery or murder Mr. Hodges, that he was merely a bystander when the robbery occurred, that he had no reason to rob Mr. Hodges, that he did not know in advance that Cedric and Maurice planned to rob Mr. Hodges, that he did not have a gun or shoot Mr. Hodges, that he never told Officer Smith and Kenneth McCall that he shot anybody, and that the reason he went to Florida with Cedric and Maurice after the robbery was because he was scared. This evidence, if it had been introduced, may very well have caused some members of the jury, if not all, to have a reasonable doubt concerning whether Jenkins was involved in the robbery. This was especially so considering that it had already been established that Terry Roberts had lied to the police several times.

Under these circumstances, Judge Harvey's assertion that it was okay for Jenkins' attorneys to advise him that the trial was "going well" and there was no need for him to testify in his own defense was clearly erroneous and not supported by the evidence.

13. Failure to Introduce Evidence of Cedric Brown's Mental Retardation

The evidence introduced at the trial established that Cedric Brown had fired at least three shots at Mr. Hodges. Although Cedric was mentally retarded,[91] no evidence of this fact was ever put before the jury. The fact that Cedric was mentally retarded was an important fact for the jury to know because the State sought to hold Jenkins responsible for Cedric's actions and intent.[92] Had the jury known that Cedric was mentally retarded, that might have caused them to have a reasonable doubt as to whether the State had proved that Jenkins intended to kill Mr. Hodges. It was clearly deficient, therefore, for Jenkins' attorneys not to introduce evidence regarding Cedric's mental condition.

Judge Harvey rejected this argument on the ground that "[t]his decision not to offer this evidence was a matter of trial strategy and falls within the wide range of reasonable professional conduct." Order as 13. Judge Harvey further concluded, "the fact this evidence was not introduced at trial did not prejudice the defendant. There is not a reasonable probability that this omission caused the jury to find Jenkins guilty." Order at 14. One wonders how Judge Harvey could have possibly reached this conclusion. I am confident that he never spoke to any member of the jury on this issue and, therefore, he had no way of knowing what effect this evidence might have had in reaching their verdict.

Jenkins was charged with two separate counts of murder, **malice** murder and **felony** murder. Although the evidence was undoubtedly

---

91 The State was unable to seek the death penalty against Cedric Brown because of his diminished mental capacity. He pleaded guilty and received a life sentence.
92 In opposing Jenkins' motion for a new trial, the State claimed that he could be held liable for malice murder based upon Cedric Brown's intent to kill Mr. Hodges, which was "transferred" to Jenkins. See State's Brief in Opposition to Appellant's Motion for a New Trial at 15.

sufficient to find Jenkins guilty of felony murder,[93] surprisingly, he was never convicted of that crime. For some reason, the jury never returned a verdict on the felony murder charge. This was undoubtedly an oversight, but it had enormous consequences. Following his trial, Jenkins was **not** convicted of felony murder. The only murder charge that he was convicted of was ***malice*** murder.

In order to find Jenkins guilty of malice murder, the jury had to find, beyond a reasonable doubt, that Jenkins ***intended*** to kill Mr. Hodges. In fact, however, there was very little, if any, evidence in the record from which the jury could infer that Jenkins actually intended to kill Mr. Hodges. Certainly, he never told anyone that he intended to kill Mr. Hodges. Ordinarily, a person can be presumed to intend the natural and logical consequences of his acts, so that if a person shoots ***and kills*** someone, it can then be presumed that he intended to kill that person. Both the medical and the ballistics evidence here, however, clearly established that Jenkins did ***not*** kill Mr. Hodges. Only one fatal shot was fired and that was unquestionably fired by Cedric[94] Even if Jenkins did fire one or more shots at Mr. Hodges, they were not fatal shots, and they would not give rise to an inference or presumption that Jenkins intended to kill Mr. Hodges.

The prosecutor's theory of the case was that Jenkins could be held liable for malice murder, not because Jenkins intended to murder Mr. Hodges, but because Cedric intended to kill Mr. Hodges and Cedric's intent to kill Mr. Hodges "may be transferred to Jenkins because he intentionally aided and abetted [Cedric] during the robbery." As the District Attorney stated on page 15 of his Memorandum in Opposition to Jenkins' Motion for a New Trial:

> "So long as Cederic Brown intended to kill Mr. Hodges, that intent may be transferred to Jenkins because he intentionally aided and abetted Brown during the robbery."

---

93   Since Jenkins was found guilty of the robbery, the jury could easily have convicted him of felony murder. However, the jury failed to return a verdict on the felony murder charge.

94   The fact that Cedric fired the fatal would was established by overwhelming evidence.

First, as I pointed out in Jenkins' Reply Brief in Support of the Motion for a New Trial, the prosecutor's theory that Jenkins could have been held liable for malice murder based solely on his participation in the robbery was an incorrect statement of Georgia law. That only applies to felony murder. Since the State chose to prosecute Jenkins for malice murder, it had the obligation to prove, beyond a reasonable doubt, that Jenkins both intended to kill Mr. Hodges and that he acted with malice. *See, e.g. Francis v. Franklin*, 471 U.S. 307, 320 (1985); *Latimore v. State*, 265 Ga. 102 (1995); *Parks v. State*, 234 Ga. 403 (1986).

Second, if the prosecutor's theory of the case was that Jenkins could be held responsible for Cedric's intent to kill Mr. Hodges and be found guilty of malice murder on that basis, then it was extremely important for the jury to know that Cedric was mentally retarded. Under the law as established by the U.S. Supreme Court, Cedric himself could not be convicted of capital murder and sentenced to death because of his mental retardation. Why should Jenkins be put in a worse position than Cedric, the actual killer of Mr. Hodges and the only person who intended to kill him.

Once again, as was his usual practice, Judge Harvey displayed an unthinking and feckless knee-jerk reaction to a serious problem that required a little more critical analysis than he was willing or able to give.

14. Failure to Object to the Misleading Testimony of Kenneth McCall and Assistant District Attorney Charles Howard

Jenkins never claimed that his trial attorneys were deficient because they failed to object to Kenneth McCall's testimony on the ground that there was an undisclosed deal between McCall and the prosecutor. That was a strawman argument fabricated by Judge Harvey to justify his conclusion that "trial counsel's performance was not deficient because no objection was offered to McCall's testimony." See Order at 14.

What Jenkins actually complained about were three separate but related errors. **First**, that the testimony of prosecution witnesses Kenneth McCall and Charles Howard was false and misleading because it failed to disclose a secret arrangement between McCall and the District Attorney in return for his testimony against Jenkins. **Second**, that the prosecutor failed to correct the record regarding the misleading testimony presented by Kenneth McCall and Charles Howard. And **third**, that the prosecutor failed to provide Jenkins' attorneys with exculpatory *Brady* material relating to the credibility of Kenneth McCall. For a more complete discussion of these errors, see Points 5, 7 and 8 in Chapter 5.

Suffice it to say here that Judge Harvey never really addressed these issues, although he did rule, based solely on the self-serving and erroneous testimony of Mr. McCall at the trial, "[t]he Court finds that there was no deal with or offer of leniency to Kenneth McCall in exchange for his testimony at Jenkins' trial." Order at 14. In so ruling, Judge Harvey completely ignored the explicit testimony of District Attorney Cheney himself at the hearing in support of Jenkins' Motion for a new trial that he had a regular practice of writing nice letters to the State Board of Pardons and Paroles requesting leniency on behalf of inmates who testify favorably for the State (Hr. 63) and that, pursuant to this policy, immediately after McCall testified against Jenkins at trial, Mr. Cheney wrote such a letter to the Parole Board on McCall's behalf (Hr. 63 and Movant's Exhibit 2) informing them that McCall had testified against Jenkins and that his "testimony was instrumental in obtaining a conviction" (Hr. 64 and Movant's Exhibit 2).

It strains credulity beyond all reasonable limits to suggest that Mr. McCall was not made aware of this policy of requesting leniency on behalf of inmates who testify favorably on behalf of the State prior to the time he testified at Jenkins' trial. It necessarily follows, therefore, that Judge Harvey's conclusion that no promise of leniency was made to McCall in this case appears to be erroneous. Furthermore, the testimony which the State elicited from McCall and Howard during Jenkins' trial regarding the absence of any deals or promises of leniency made to McCall was obviously false. The District Attorney's practice of sending a letter to the Parole Board requesting leniency should have been disclosed to the jury because it directly related to the issue of McCall's credibility.

Under these circumstances, the prosecutor had an affirmative obligation to correct the record created by the misleading testimony of Messrs. McCall and Howard, and his failure to do so constituted reversible error. McCall was one of the State's key witnesses, and his credibility was a critical issue. As noted above, this is precisely the type of situation in which a conviction must be reversed and a new trial granted. *See, e.g., Napue v. Illinois*, 360 U.S. at 264.

Finally, Mr. Cheney also testified at the hearing with respect to Jenkins' motion for a new trial that on October 28, 1996, in the case of *State v. Kenneth McCall*, Case No. 95-R-53, in the Superior Court of Tattnall County, he recommended to Judge Rahn that certain additional charges pending against Mr. McCall be dismissed (Hr. 59-60 and Movant's Exhibit 1) and that based upon his recommendation such charges were dismissed (Hr. 59-60 and Movant's Exhibit 1). These additional charges were pending against McCall at the time he testified against Jenkins at trial. (Hr. 62). However, no effort was made by the District Attorney's office to determine whether these or any other charges were pending against Mr. McCall at the time he testified, and no effort was made to inform Jenkins' attorneys of these additional charges against McCall. (Hr. 62).

Under *Brady v. Maryland*, 373 U.S. 83 (1963), the District Attorney had an affirmative obligation to disclose all available exculpatory evidence. Evidence which casts doubt on the credibility of one of the State's principal witnesses certainly constitutes *Brady* material which should have been disclosed. McCall's credibility was a critical issue, and there is a reasonable probability that, had this evidence been disclosed to the defense, the result of the proceeding might have been different.[95] Accordingly, the State's failure to disclose this information was highly prejudicial and improper. *See, e.g.,* *Waldrip v. State*, 267 Ga. 739, 482 S.E.2d 299, 311 (1997); *Rogers v. State*, 257 Ga. 590, 361 S.E.2d 814 (1987). As the Georgia Supreme Court noted in *Hines v. State*, 249 Ga. 257, 260, 290 S.E.2d 911, 914 (1982):

> "It is especially important in a case where a witness or an accomplice may have substantial reason to cooperate with the government that a defendant be permitted to search for an agreement between the government and the witness. Whether or not such a deal existed is not crucial. ***What counts is whether the witness may be shading his testimony in an effort to please the prosecution. A desire to cooperate may be formed beneath the conscious level, in a manner not apparent even to the witness, but such a subtle desire to assist the state nevertheless may cloud perception***" (citations and quotation makes omitted).

Similarly, McCall had ample reasons to ***"shade his testimony in an effort to please the prosecutor"*** here, not only because of the expectation of possible leniency from the Parole Board if he gave favorable testimony against Jenkins, but also because of the pendency of additional charges which had been brought against him by the same District Attorney for whom he was testifying.

Unfortunately, Judge Harvey failed to address any of these important issues in his Order denying Jenkins' motion for a new trial.

---

[95] McCall's testimony was extremely important because, if believed by the jury, it would have corroborated the testimony of Terry Roberts and Officer Smith. Since there were substantial questions raised regarding the credibility of both Roberts and Officer Smith, it is impossible to say how much weight the jury may have attached to McCall's testimony. It is possible that McCall's testimony may have made the difference between conviction and acquittal.

CHAPTER 7

APPEAL TO THE GEORGIA SUPREME COURT

Following Judge Harvey's unfortunate and unjustified denial of Jenkins' Motion for a new trial, it became necessary for me to appeal that decision to a higher court. Accordingly, on June 2, 1997, I filed a timely Notice of Appeal. Because this was a capital murder case, the appeal went directly to the Georgia Supreme Court, bypassing Georgia's intermediate Court of Appeals.[96]

The grounds asserted in support of Jenkins' appeal to the Supreme Court were essentially the same as those asserted in support of his Motion for a new trial in the Liberty County Superior Court, with a few minor revisions. However, for the purpose of convenience, the actual "enumeration of errors" as set forth in Jenkins' Brief to the Supreme Court ("Appellant's Brief") are listed below.

ENUMERATION OF ERRORS

I. THE TRIAL COURT ERRED IN FAILING TO INSTRUCT THE JURY THAT THE TESTIMONY OF AN ACCOMPLICE NEEDS TO BE CORROBORATED.

---

96 The Court of Appeals is the intermediate appellate court of the State of Georgia. It consists of fifteen judges who are divided into five "divisions" with each division consisting of three judges. The Georgia Supreme Court presently has nine justices but, at the time of Jenkins' appeal in 1997, it only had seven justices. Both the Supreme Court and the Court of Appeals are located in Atlanta.

II. COMMENTS MADE BY THE PROSECUTOR DURING HIS SUMMATION REGARDING APPELLANT'S FAILURE TO PRESENT EVIDENCE WERE IMPROPER AND PREJUDICIAL AND VIOLATED APPELLANT'S FIFTH AMENDMENT PRIVILEGE AGAINST SELF-INCRIMINATION.

III. THE TRIAL COURT'S ADMISSION OF HEARSAY EVIDENCE PROVIDED BY UNIDENTIFIED "SILENT WITNESSES" WAS IMPROPER AND PREJUDICIAL AND VIOLATED APPELLANT'S SIXTH AMENDMENT RIGHT TO CONFRONT AND CROSS EXAMINE THE WITNESSES AGAINST HIM.

IV. THE TRIAL COURT ERRED IN EXCLUDING RELEVANT EVIDENCE OFFERED BY APPELLANT DURING THE PENALTY PHASE.

V. THE TESTIMONY OF PROSECUTION WITNESS KEITH MORAN WAS FALSE AND MISLEADING.

VI. THE DISTRICT ATTORNEY FAILED TO CORRECT THE RECORD REGARDING THE MISLEADING TESTIMONY PROVIDED BY KEITH MORAN.

VII. THE TESTIMONY OF PROSECUTION WITNESSES KENNETH McCALL AND CHARLES HOWARD WAS FALSE AND MISLEADING.

VIII. THE DISTRICT ATTORNEY FAILED TO CORRECT THE RECORD REGARDING THE MISLEADING TESTIMONY PROVIDED BY KENNETH McCALL AND CHARLES HOWARD.

IX. THE DISTRICT ATTORNEY FAILED TO PROVIDE APPELLANT'S ATTORNEYS WITH *BRADY* MATERIAL RELATING TO THE CREDIBILITY OF KENNETH McCALL.

X.	THE TRIAL COURT'S ADMISSION OF HEARSAY EVIDENCE DURING THE TESTIMONY OF INVESTIGATOR JIM GRAY WAS IMPROPER AND PREJUDICIAL.
XI.	THE PROOF SUBMITTED AT TRIAL WAS INSUFFICIENT TO CONVICT APPELLANT OF MALICE MURDER.
XII.	THE TRIAL COURT'S INSTRUCTION REGARDING THE ISSUE OF MALICE MURDER WAS IMPROPER.
XIII.	THE TRIAL COURT'S INSTRUCTION REGARDING THE ISSUE OF PARTIES TO A CRIME WAS IMPROPER.
XIV.	THE TRIAL COURT'S INSTRUCTION REGARDING THE ISSUE OF CONSPIRACY WAS IMPROPER.
XV.	THE TESTIMONY OF PROSECUTION WITNESS TERRY ROBERTS WAS NOT SUFFICIENTLY CORROBORATED.
XVI.	THE TRIAL COURT ERRED IN ADMITTING HEARSAY STATEMENTS ALLEGEDLY MADE BY CO-CONSPIRATORS OF APPELLANT.
XVII.	THE TRIAL COURT ERRED IN FAILING TO INSTRUCT THE JURY THAT THE TESTIMONY OF A CO-CONSPIRATOR REGARDING THE ISSUE OF CONSPIRACY NEEDS TO BE CORROBORATED.
XVIII.	THE TRIAL COURT MADE PREJUDICIAL REMARKS REGARDING THE ISSUE OF CONSPIRACY WHICH TAINTED THE JURY'S VERDICT.
XIX.	THE TRIAL COURT IMPROPERLY ADMITTED HEARSAY EVIDENCE REGARDING PRIOR ARRESTS OF APPELLANT'S ALLEGED CO-CONSPIRATORS.
XX.	MOST OF THE TESTIMONY OF PROSECUTION WITNESS BART INGRAM WAS IRRELEVANT, MISLEADING AND INFLAMMATORY.

XXI.	THE TRIAL COURT'S ADMISSION OF AN INCRIMINATING STATEMENT ALLEGEDLY MADE BY APPELLANT TO OFFICER SMITH WAS ERRONEOUS.
XXII.	THE PROSECUTOR'S CLOSING ARGUMENT DURING THE GUILT PHASE OF THE TRIAL WAS IMPROPER AND PREJUDICIAL.
XXIII.	THE PROSECUTOR'S CLOSING ARGUMENT DURING THE PENALTY PHASE OF THE TRIAL WAS IMPROPER AND PREJUDICIAL.
XXIV.	THE PROSECUTORS CONTINUOUSLY ENGAGED IN LEADING THE STATE'S WITNESSES.
XXV.	THE TRIAL COURT ERRED IN EXCLUDING MITIGATION EVIDENCE OFFERED BY APPELLANT DURING THE PENALTY PHASE.
XXVI.	THE TRIAL COURT ERRED IN FAILING TO INFORM THE JURY WHEN APPELLANT WOULD BECOME ELIGIBLE FOR PAROLE.
XXVII.	OCGA § 17-10-31.1(d), THE STATUTE WHICH PERMITTED THE JURY TO IMPOSE A SENTENCE OF LIFE WITHOUT POSSIBILITY OF PAROLE IN THIS CASE, IS UNCONSTITUTIONAL.
XXVIII.	THE TRIAL COURT ERRED IN SENTENCING APPELLANT TO AN ADDITIONAL, CONSECUTIVE TERM OF LIFE IMPRISONMENT ON THE ROBBERY CHARGE.
XXIX.	APPELLANT WAS DENIED EFFECTIVE ASSISTANCE OF COUNSEL.
XXX.	THE TRIAL COURT ERRED IN DENYING APPELLANT'S MOTION FOR A CHANGE OF VENUE.
XXXI.	THE TRIAL COURT ERRED IN DENYING APPELLANT'S MOTION FOR A NEW TRIAL.

Following the submission of briefs by myself on behalf of Jenkins and the Georgia Attorney General on behalf of the State,[97] the Supreme Court scheduled oral argument with respect to Jenkins' appeal for September 15, 1997. I was allowed fifteen minutes to persuade the Court regarding the merits of the myriad errors Jenkins was complaining about. Fortunately, being from New York, I speak very fast. The complete text of my oral argument before the Court is set forth below.

May it please the Court. My name is Robert Kelly. I am a pro bono attorney representing the appellant, Clevon Jenkins. With me, and also representing the appellant, is Robert Pirkle, who is a public defender in Liberty County. This is a capital murder case in which the appellant was convicted of malice murder and armed robbery. He was sentenced to life imprisonment without possibility of parole on the murder charge and to an additional consecutive term of life on the robbery count.

The crimes at issue occurred in Riceboro, in Liberty County, on October 8, 1993. The facts have been summarized in our brief, and therefore I won't take the time to repeat them here. Let me just say that, in addition to appellant, there were four other persons who were charged with committing the crime. Two of these people pleaded guilty and were sentenced to life imprisonment. A third was convicted after trial and sentenced to life imprisonment. The fourth is Terry Roberts, who was the principal witness against appellant at the trial. Roberts was originally charged with the murder, but the murder charge was dismissed against him when he agreed to testify for the State. Although the murder charge was dismissed, Roberts was still charged with the robbery.

Certainly, what happened here was a senseless and horrible crime. I did not know Mr. Hodges, but I am sure he was a fine and decent person, and there is no excuse for what happened to him. Nevertheless, as horrible as this crime was, that does not take away from the fact that appellant was entitled to a fair trial. For all the various reasons which we have

---

[97] Jenkins' initial brief was 108 pages long, and the Attorney General's Opposition Brief was 83 pages long. I also filed a Reply Brief that was 28 pages long.

listed in our enumeration of errors and in our brief, I do not believe that appellant received a fair trial here and, for this reason, we request that his conviction be vacated and reversed.

Appellant has enumerated thirty-one errors as the basis for this appeal. Both sides have filed very lengthy briefs which discuss each of these points in detail. Obviously, in the short period of time that I have available today, I will not attempt to discuss all of these points. If any member of the Court has a particular question which he or she would like me to discuss, please let me know, and I would be happy to respond. Otherwise, what I plan to do is to briefly discuss eight major points which I want to emphasize for the Court.

The first point I want to emphasize is the fact that the trial court never instructed the jury regarding the need for corroboration. Under Section 24-4-9 of the Georgia Code and applicable law, a defendant in a criminal case cannot be convicted of a felony based upon the uncorroborated testimony of an accomplice. The question of whether sufficient corroboration exists in any given case is an issue of fact for the jury to determine after receiving appropriate instructions. However, the jury here was never told they had to consider this issue. The important point to note here is that it was solely for the jury to determine whether there was sufficient evidence of corroboration. They never made that determination here because the judge failed to give them any instructions on this issue. As the trial judge himself later recognized, this was clearly erroneous.

The State argues that there was no error here because Jenkins' counsel never requested an instruction on corroboration and therefore it was waived. The law is clear, however, that a trial judge has an affirmative obligation to instruct the jury on all points of law which are raised by the evidence regardless of whether defense counsel requests an instruction or not. In this case, therefore, even if defense counsel did not request an instruction, the court was still obligated to instruct the jury on this issue.

The State also argues that, even if the court's failure to charge corroboration was erroneous, this does not require reversal of appellant's conviction because the error was harmless. This is simply not correct. Before this Court could apply the harmless error doctrine, it would first have to conclude that the error could not have contributed to the conviction. The problem here, however, is that we were not in the jury room and we have no way of knowing what evidence the jury found to be credible and what evidence it discarded. There was evidence submitted at trial which indicated that appellant had made two brief incriminating statements after he was arrested. If the jury believed these statements, then obviously this would have been sufficient corroboration. However, there were substantial questions raised at trial regarding the credibility of both of these statements. It is entirely possible that the jury disregarded both of these statements and convicted appellant based solely on the testimony of Terry Roberts. We simply have no way of knowing what evidence the jury used to reach its verdict. Under these circumstances, it is not possible to say that the trial court's failure to instruct the jury on the issue of corroboration was harmless.

The next issue which I want to emphasize for the Court's attention are the improper comments which the prosecutor made during his closing argument regarding appellant's failure to testify. As this Court ruled in Ranger v. State (249 Ga. 315) (1982), a criminal conviction must be reversed whenever the prosecutor makes a remark which is of such a character that the jury would naturally and necessarily take it to be a comment on the failure of the accused to testify.

The prosecutor's remarks in this case were unquestionably of such a character. [At this point, I read to the Court the four statements that Mr. Cheney made during his closing argument which improperly commented on Jenkins' failure to testify].

The defendant has no obligation to get on the stand and testify. The district attorney knew this, and it was clearly improper for him to make *this kind of a statement and the case law clearly holds that that kind of a statement is reversible error.*

It is also important to note in this regard that the evidence which the State asked appellant to rebut consisted primarily of statements which were allegedly made by the defendant himself. As explained in our brief, there was no way for defendant to rebut this testimony other than by taking the stand and testifying. As the prosecutor knew, therefore, the only logical person the appellant could possibly call as a defense witness was the appellant himself. Under these circumstances, it was a clear violation of the Fifth Amendment for the prosecutor to make the statements which he made.

The next issue I want to discuss is what has been called the "silent witness" testimony, which is appellant's third enumeration of error. One of the principal witnesses for the State was Jim Gray, an investigator who worked in the District Attorney's office. Mr. Gray was permitted to testify that he received information from anonymous, silent witnesses which caused him to believe that appellant was one of the persons who killed and robbed Mr. Hodges. It is hard for me to imagine any case that is more violative of a defendant's Sixth Amendment right to confront and cross-examine the witnesses against him than this.

The State argues that there was no error because the content of the communications with the silent witnesses was not disclosed. This is not correct. Mr. Gray was permitted to testify that he had conducted an investigation, that during the course of the investigation he spoke to various people, including the "silent witnesses" and that based upon the information he received, including the information he received from the silent witness, he had concluded that appellant killed and robbed Mr. Hodges. Obviously, the jury could infer from this testimony that the information which the silent witnesses told Mr. Gray incriminated the appellant. This clearly violated appellant's right, under both the federal and Georgia constitutions, to confront and cross-examine these witnesses.

Appellant's fourth enumeration of error was that certain evidence which appellant's counsel sought to offer at trial was improperly excluded. This evidence consisted of Cedric Brown's guilty plea as well as evidence relating to Cedric Brown's mental condition. This evidence was relevant for two reasons: first, Cedric was the person who planned the robbery and fired at least three shots at Mr. Hodges, including the fatal shot; second, Cedric was mentally retarded. Both the fact that Cedric pleaded guilty and the fact that he was mentally retarded were highly relevant to the issue of whether appellant should be held liable for malice murder.

Another error which appellant complains about relates to the testimony of Keith Moran. This includes appellant's fifth and sixth enumerations of error. Keith Moran was the Chief Deputy of the Liberty County Sheriff's Department. After Mr. Moran had completed his testimony, he was later recalled to the stand by the prosecutor for the sole purpose of testifying that the murder charge had been dismissed against Terry Roberts because Roberts could not have been charged with murder [At this point, I quoted from the trial transcript at pages 1640-41].

As explained in Appellant's Brief, there were at least five things that were wrong with this testimony. First, it falsely implied that Roberts could not be charged with murder. Second, it falsely implied that the DA dismissed the murder charge because Roberts could not be charged with murder. Third, it falsely implied that Roberts' cooperation with the State was not the reason the murder charge was dismissed. Fourth, it falsely implied that Moran had received information which indicated that appellant was aware of a plan to kill Mr. Hodges prior to the robbery. And finally, it falsely implied that Roberts' culpability for Mr. Hodges' murder was less than Appellant's.

As Georgia case law clearly establishes, and as the State concedes, whenever a witness for the State testifies falsely and the State knows that the testimony is false, the State has an obligation to correct the record. Here, the State deliberately tried to mislead the jury by presenting Moran's testimony. He was specifically recalled to the stand solely to present the testimony which I quoted earlier. This was clearly improper conduct on the part of the prosecutor. I will concede that certainly defendant's trial counsel should have done a better job cross-examining Moran on this issue and should not have let the State get away with this. Indeed, this is one of the grounds why we believe that Appellant was denied the effective assistance of counsel, However, the State itself had the affirmative obligation not to present misleading testimony, and it clearly violated that obligation here.

A similar error occurred in connection with the testimony of Kenneth McCall and Assistant District Attorney Charles Howard. This relates to Appellant's seventh, eighth and ninth enumerations of error.

Kenneth McCall was an inmate at the Liberty County Jail who claimed that Appellant made an incriminating statement to him. At the trial McCall testified that no promises or deals of any kind had been made in return for his testimony, and Mr. Howard, who was an Assistant District Attorney, was presented by the State to corroborate this. In fact, however, as shown by the evidence at the hearing in support of the Motion for a new trial, there was a deal made with McCall. In return for McCall's testimony, the District Attorney would write a letter to the State Parole Board recommending leniency. This was established by the evidence presented at the hearing in support of Appellant's Motion for a new trial, where Mr. Cheney, the District Attorney for the Atlantic Judicial Circuit, testified that he had a regular practice of writing letters on behalf of prisoners who testify favorably for the State. Indeed, almost immediately after Mr. McCall testified against Appellant at the trial, Mr. Cheney did in fact write a letter to the Parole Board on McCall's behalf. The fact that the District Attorney had this practice and intended to write this letter should have been disclosed to the jury. In the absence of such disclosure, McCall's testimony that he would not receive any benefit as a result of his testimony was false and misleading.

Furthermore, at the time when McCall testified against Appellant he had a new criminal charge pending against him which was brought by the very same prosecutor who was prosecuting Appellant. The existence of this pending charge was never disclosed to defendant's counsel or to the jury. For the reasons discussed in Appellant's Brief, the State's failure to disclose this information violated the State's obligation to disclose exculpatory evidence pursuant to Brady v. Maryland.

The next error which I want to bring to the Court's attention is the fact that Appellant was denied effective assistance of counsel. This is Appellant's 29th enumeration of error. There are at least sixteen different reasons why Appellant claims that his trial counsel was ineffective, and these reasons are discussed in detail in Appellant's brief. Many of these deficiencies relate to counsel's failure to object to errors that occurred at the trial which are covered by other specifications of error. However, there are two items in particular that I would like to call to the Court's attention in regard to the claim of ineffective assistance of counsel.

The first item is the fact that Appellant's trial counsel advised him not to testify. Not only did they advise Appellant not to testify, but they told him that the trial was "going well" and there was no need for him to testify. Under the facts and circumstances of this case, this was clearly a deficiency of counsel and not a matter of trial strategy.

Appellant was only 17 years old at the time when this crime took place and he had never been in trouble for anything before in his life. Although he admitted that he was present with Cedric Brown and Maurice Fleming at the time when the crime took place, he had consistently denied that he had anything to do with the robbery or with the murder. In fact, there was no logical reason why Appellant would have participated in this crime. Unlike Shawn and Maurice, who had outstanding bench warrants against them and needed money to get out of town, there was absolutely no reason why Appellant would rob or murder Mr. Hodges. He had consistently told his attorneys that he wanted to testify, but they told him that the case was "going well" and there was no need for him to testify.

Considering the evidence that was presented at trial, counsels' advice to Appellant not to testify was clearly a serious error in judgment and not a matter of strategy or tactics. As the district attorney repeatedly pointed out to the jury during his summation, no evidence of any kind was presented by the defense which refuted or contradicted the State's case, and there was absolutely no reason for Appellant's trial counsel to believe that Appellant would be acquitted unless he testified and told his side of what happened. On the other hand, if Appellant did testify, there was a very good possibility that he might have been acquitted. There was no rational basis for advising Appellant not to testify.

Another serious error committed by Appellant's trial counsel was their failure to impeach Terry Roberts with his prior inconsistent statements. As discussed in Appellant's Brief, Roberts had given two very detailed statements to the police prior to and after he was arrested. These statements were grossly inconsistent with his testimony at the trial. Effective cross-examination using these statements could have completely destroyed Roberts' credibility in the eyes of the jury. However, defendant's trial counsel never used the statements. Furthermore, Appellant's trial counsel testified at the hearing in support of the motion for a new trial that the failure to impeach Roberts with his prior inconsistent statements was the result of inadvertence, not a conscious tactical decision. Accordingly, their failure to use the statements cannot be justified on the grounds that it was a matter of trial strategy.

I should also point out in regard to Appellant's claim of ineffective assistance of counsel that the evidence presented at the hearing established that the trial schedule was extremely tiring and grueling and prevented counsel from being sharp and effective. During the first two days of the trial, the court started at 8:30 in the morning and went until 11 at night. Both Mr. Walker and Mr. Peel testified at the hearing that they were personally exhausted as a result of the trial schedule and that this may have affected their effectiveness as counsel.

The final point that I want to mention is that the trial court's instructions to the jury on the issues of malice, parties to the crime and conspiracy were erroneous. For several reasons that are discussed in our Brief, Appellant claims that these instructions were erroneous as applied to the facts of this case. These reasons are clearly set forth in our Brief and there is no need to repeat them here. However, there is one very significant point which I do wish to call to the Court's attention.

Appellant contends that the trial court's instructions on malice murder, parties to the crime and conspiracy were erroneous because they caused the jury to believe that Appellant could be convicted of malice murder based solely upon the fact that he participated in the robbery and without any proof that he intended to commit malice murder. The State admits that the court's charge would allow the jury to do this, but it argues that this is not erroneous because this is a correct statement of Georgia law.

The gist of the State's argument is that if a person agrees to commit a robbery and someone else commits a malice murder during the course of the robbery, all of the participants in the robbery are liable for malice murder based upon the notion of "transferred intent," which is to say that the intent of the actual killer is "transferred" to the other participants in the robbery regardless of whether they knew anything about the killing prior to the time it occurred. Appellant concedes that there a number of older Georgia cases which support this view. However, Appellant contends that these cases are no longer good law in light of the U.S. Supreme Courts's decision in such cases as Franklin v. Francis. To say that a person can be deemed to be guilty of malice murder simply because he agreed to participate in a robbery is precisely the same type of mandatory presumption which the Supreme Court ruled to be a violation of the Fourteenth Amendment due process clause in Francis v. Franklin.

Clearly, a person who agrees to participate in a robbery can be found guilty of felony murder for any murder that occurs during the robbery, but this is not true with regard to malice murder. Where, as here, the State chooses to prosecute a defendant for malice murder, it has the affirmative obligation to prove, beyond a reasonable doubt, that the person accused of the murder did in fact intend to commit murder. It is not permissible for the State to rely upon a legal presumption that anyone who participates in the robbery is deemed to have intended to commit murder. This was made clear by the U.S, Supreme Court in Franklin v. Francis.

Here, the State concedes in its Brief that the court's instructions would have allowed the jury to convict Appellant of malice murder based solely upon proof that he participated in the robbery. This was clearly erroneous and therefore the conviction must be reversed.

For all of the foregoing reasons, as well as for all of the additional reasons set forth in Appellant's Brief and Reply Brief, I respectfully request that this honorable Court vacate Appellant's conviction and remand this case to the Superior Court for further proceedings. Thank you.

Despite the obvious eloquence of my arguments, the Georgia Supreme Court was not persuaded. On October 6, 1997, the Court issued a ten-page, double-spaced, typewritten decision unanimously denying Jenkins' appeal in its entirety.[98] All thirty-one of the significant errors that had been so fulsomely and painstakingly briefed by myself and the State were summarily denied. To borrow a phrase from the world of literature, the Court's decision can best be characterized as "nasty, brutish and short."

I was extremely disappointed with the decision as, of course, was Jenkins. I am sure the justices honestly believed they were correctly applying both federal and Georgia law and that Jenkins' appeal lacked merit. The problem, however, perhaps due to the pressures of an onerous caseload and a paucity of time, was that the justices never really examined the issues critically and meticulously with an open mind. Essentially, they **assumed** that

---

98   The Court's Opinion and Decision is reported at 268 Ga. 468, 491 S.E.2d 54 (1997).

Jenkins was guilty because he had been found guilty by a jury, and then, whether consciously or unconsciously, they let this assumption unfairly influence their analysis of Jenkins' meritorious claims. In so doing, they neglected to appreciate that perhaps the only reason Jenkins had been found guilty in the first place was because he had been denied a fair trial. Had the justices taken the time, and made the effort, to analyze the issues more closely and more carefully, they would doubtless have realized that substantial doubt did indeed exist regarding Jenkins' guilt. Unfortunately, neither I nor Henry Fonda was in the robing room to show the justices the error of their ways.

There is a terrible flaw in human nature. People, even the most esteemed judges responsible for applying the law, have an innate tendency to believe that things are the way they are supposed to be simply because that is the way they are. They fail to comprehend that things may not be as they appear. Behavioral scientists call this the "status quo bias," an irrational form of cognitive dissonance. Unfortunately, this bias is often coupled with another cognitive flaw, "the confirmation bias," where people are predisposed to accept things that support their pre-existing views and reject those that do not.

Remember the movie *Twelve Angry Men*. Everyone in the jury room save one was readily disposed to convict an urban teenager of murder based upon their pre-existing misconceptions and the faulty premise that the State would never prosecute an innocent person. Despite the presumption of innocence and the heavy evidentiary burden of proving guilt beyond a reasonable doubt, jurors have a natural tendency to assume that people are guilty merely because they have been accused by the State. Taking this a step further, judges also have a natural tendency to assume that defendants are guilty merely because they have been found guilty by a jury, regardless of the fairness of the underlying trial. What is needed in both instances is a more diligent arbiter with an aporetic mind, a stalwart character like Henry Fonda who will take the time and expend the effort to examine the evidence carefully and critically, and then assess whether it truly is as compelling as originally claimed.[99]

This was especially true of what happened here. Despite the many warning signs that bespoke an urgent need for caution, the justices of the Supreme Court were perfectly content in **assuming** that every word spoken by Terry Roberts was gospel truth. They apparently never even considered the possibility that this may not have been so. Once you begin to ask, ***"is Roberts really telling the truth?"*** — and there are plenty of reasons for asking that question here — an entirely different picture emerges. Instead of a rock solid case built upon substantial evidence, the possibility emerges that the State's entire case against Jenkins rested on a flimsy house of cards, a stacked deck dealt by an interested and self-admitted liar. If any substantial portion of Roberts' testimony was false, and clearly some parts of it were, then the entire case against Jenkins crumbles because this creates a strong basis for having a reasonable doubt. The only problem for Jenkins was that neither Henry Fonda, nor someone like him, was sitting on the bench of the Georgia Supreme Court. I tried my best to explain these problems to the Court in my brief and in my oral argument, but obviously I failed.

Whether The Evidence Offered at Trial Was Sufficient to Convict Jenkins of Malice Murder

The most important point the Supreme Court justices made in explaining their decision was that, in their view, "the evidence was sufficient to find [Jenkins] guilty of both malice murder and armed robbery

---

99   Although *Twelve Angry Men* was a good movie, it was not good law. It is not permissible, and would actually constitute reversible error, for a member of the jury to conduct his own investigation of the facts.

beyond a reasonable doubt." 268 Ga. at __, 491 S.E.2d at 57.[100] This was extremely important not only because it signified that the justices believed that Jenkins was actually guilty of murdering Mr. Hodges, but also because such a belief would have necessarily and wholly tainted their views regarding the legal arguments Jenkins had raised regarding the fairness of his trial. Once you have concluded that a person is guilty of murder, it becomes difficult to set that decision aside for mere technicalities, even if the technicalities at issue are flagrant violations of basic constitutional rights.

Since this is such an important and pervasive issue, let me recite the entirety of what the Georgia Supreme Court thought the evidence offered at Jenkins' trial proved:

> "The jury was authorized to find that Terry Roberts drove [Jenkins], Cedric and Shawn Brown, and Maurice Fleming to Hodges Grocery Store on October 8, 1993. Roberts remained in the car and Shawn Brown kept lookout while [Jenkins], Cedric Brown, and Maurice Fleming robbed the store; [Jenkins] and Brown, armed with .25 caliber pistols, shot grocer Bobby Hodges five times in his face, neck and shoulder. One shot from one pistol inflicted a potentially fatal wound; a second shot, fired

---

[100] I want to thank Michael McArthur, the reference librarian at Duke University Law School, for assisting me in locating the "star pagination" cites for many of the cases cited in this book, particularly the Georgia cases. I had original copies of all relevant decisions, of course, but the copies I had did not contain the page references from the West Reporter system, which is the standard (and copyrighted) system for case citations in the U.S. Since I am now retired from legal practice, I do not have access to a fancy law library, nor online access to Westlaw or Lexis/Nexis. And what is available online generally to the public is woefully inadequate. I had thought that I could simply walk into any law school library in the country (or at least into one in the Research Triangle of North Carolina) and pull whatever books I needed off the shelf. Turns out, however, that law school libraries don't keep actual books anymore. Everything is online. I asked Michael how this could possibly be since Duke is a first-class law school renowned throughout the world for its scholarship, and his response was, "ask my Dean. He says we don't have enough space." Well Dean, I am asking you, isn't part of the purpose of a first-class law school like Duke to make books available to scholars like myself who need them for research? The reason for this lengthy footnote is to explain the absence of the jump cites from the Georgia Reporter. I had expected that these parallel cites would be contained in the copies of the decisions from the Southeastern Reporter which Michael provided to me, but they were not. Rather than bother Michael again, I am only providing the Southeastern cites. I assume this is not a problem since nobody uses the books any more anyway. And besides, the *Jenkins* decision is only eight pages long so the page references should not be too difficult to find.

from another pistol, severed the victim's carotid artery.[101] The men then left the grocery, reentered Robert's car and urged him to speed away. While in the car [Jenkins] and Cedric Brown made statements to Roberts that they had shot the victim, joking and laughing about the money, food stamps, and perfume they stole from the store. The victim was discovered minutes after the crime by other customers to the store; help was summoned, but the victim died shortly thereafter. [Jenkins], Cedric Brown and Fleming, after receiving their share of the robbery proceeds, fled to Florida. Authorities arrested the three men at a motel room outside Miami; a food stamp recovered from their hotel room was traced to a Riceboro citizen who shopped at Hodges Grocery. [Jenkins] told a Florida police officer, Bart Ingram,[102] that he only shot the victim once; [Jenkins] told McCall, a Georgia cellmate, that he shot the victim twice and was the first person to shoot him." 268 Ga. at __, 491 S.E.2d at 56-57.

At first blush, this is certainly a compelling story and, if true, it would clearly be sufficient evidence to convict Jenkins of murder, especially if, like Juror No. 7 in *Twelve Angry Men* (Jack Warden), you had something better you wanted to do that day or, if, like Juror No. 10 (Ed Begley, Sr.), you had a tendency to believe that minority youths are inherently untrustworthy, irresponsible and dangerous. Upon closer inspection, however, there were four fundamental problems with the Court's analysis. First, almost everything

---

101 This was not correct. Although the bullet that the Court describes as being "potentially fatal" (and which Dr. Clark described as "not causing any serious injury") was recovered from Mr. Hodges' body and matched to the gun that was recovered from Roberts' car, the other bullet (which Dr. Clark and the Court described as "fatal") was not recovered and could not be matched to any weapon. There was no proof, therefore, that Mr. Hodges was shot with bullets from two separate pistols. It is true that shell casings from two separate guns were found at the scene, but there was no physical evidence that Hodges was actually struck by any bullet from the second gun. It was entirely possible that all the bullets that struck Mr. Hodges came from the same gun.

102 This was factually incorrect for two separate reasons. First, it was Florida Police Officer **James Smith**, not Bart Ingram, who allegedly heard the statement. Second, what Jenkins allegedly said was, "I only shot him once." He did not, however, specify who he allegedly shot.

that the Court said "the jury was authorized to find" depended entirely upon the veracity and credibility of Terry Roberts. Second, there were reasonable grounds for believing that what Roberts said was untrue. Third, many of the "facts" as recited by the Court were not actually supported by the evidence. Fourth, finally, and most importantly, there were many reasons for believing that the jury's verdict resulted from an unfair trial.

Let us analyze the Supreme Court's summary of the evidence a little more closely.

First, there was no physical or forensic evidence of any kind that connected Jenkins (or any of the other defendants) to the murder scene. There were no fingerprints, no footprints, no DNA, no hair samples, no blood samples, no epithelial tissue, no video recordings, no photographs, no voice recordings, nada. Some ballistics evidence was found at the scene, but this was mostly inconclusive and certainly not sufficient to connect Jenkins to the crime.[103] There was a food stamp that was found in the Florida motel where Cedric, Maurice and Jenkins were apprehended, but this was not sufficient to connect Jenkins to the crime since it could have been (and probably was) brought to the motel by Cedric and/or by Maurice. So, essentially, there was no real evidence (as opposed to testimony) that connected Jenkins to the crimes at issue.

Second, apart from the brief statements allegedly made by Jenkins to Officer Smith and Kenneth McCall (which will be discussed in greater detail below), the only testimonial evidence that purportedly connected Jenkins to the robbery of Mr. Hodges was the questionable, self-serving testimony provided by Terry Roberts who was, to put it bluntly, an admitted liar who mostly wanted to protect himself and his half-brother Maurice

---

103   The ballistics evidence established that four shell casings (and three spent bullets) were found at the scene, that the bullets were fired from two different .25 caliber pistols, and that no powder burns were found on Mr. Hodges' body, meaning that the shots were probably fired from a distance greater than two feet away. The ballistics evidence also established that three of the shell casings (and two of the spent bullets) came from the pistol that was recovered from Terry Roberts' car. It was established by testimony, including the testimony of Terry Roberts, that this gun had been used by Cedric Brown. The other weapon that was allegedly used in the robbery was never recovered, although it was suspected to have belonged to Roger Fleming and to have been stolen from him by his cousin Maurice Fleming, one of the alleged participants in the robbery.

and place all of the blame on Cedric and Jenkins and who was highly motivated to give favorable testimony for the State in exchange for dismissal of the murder charge against him.

When Roberts was questioned by police shortly after the murder, he gave three different versions of what had happened. At first, he completely denied that he had any involvement in, or knowledge of, the robbery. This was known by the police to be false, so they continued questioning him for many hours until he finally gave the version of the facts that he subsequently testified to at trial. Along the way, Roberts kept changing his story several times because the police kept telling him that what he was saying was untrue.[104] Notably, and perhaps not so coincidentally, the "final" version, which the police and ultimately the District Attorney gladly accepted, put all the blame on Jenkins, less of the blame on Maurice, and none of the blame on Roberts.

Why should anyone accept Roberts' testimony at face value when he had such obvious motives to lie, and he had, in fact, lied multiple times when questioned by the police. This discrepancy alone, as Henry Fonda would certainly have pointed out, was a sufficient reason for doubting whether Jenkins was guilty.

Third, Roberts' testimony, even the final version that he gave at trial, made no sense. As the ballistics evidence showed, and as the Supreme Court was keen to point out in its decision, two guns were used in this robbery. The first was a 25. caliber pistol that was found in Terry Roberts' car. This pistol was traced back to Cedric Brown and was shown by ballistics evidence to be the likely murder weapon. The second gun was never found, although numerous searches were made by the police in various places trying to find it, including a search in and around the Florida motel where

---

104   By the time Roberts was questioned for the third time, the police had already arrested and taken statements from Cedric, Shawn and Maurice. They knew, therefore, that Roberts was lying because Maurice had already admitted his involvement in the robbery, but Roberts continued saying that Maurice was not involved. Perhaps, if Jenkins had given a statement denying his involvement, the police could have confronted Roberts with that statement also, and Roberts would have changed his story yet again. Unfortunately, Jenkins did not give any statement to the police, and the police had no interest in questioning Roberts further to find out what really occurred.

Cedric, Maurice and Jenkins were apprehended and where, according to some of the testimony, the second gun was reportedly discarded.

Roger Fleming, the cousin of Maurice Fleming, testified at the trial that he owned a .25 caliber Lorcin pistol which he kept in the bedroom of his house. He also testified that in September of 1993, about a month or so before the robbery, Maurice had visited his house and went into the bedroom area and the next day Roger discovered that his pistol was missing.

Presumably, this evidence was introduced at Jenkins' trial to show that Maurice probably stole Roger's pistol and that this was probably the second gun that was used in the robbery. These were mere inferences, however, and weak ones at that. Maurice never admitted that he stole the gun, and the theft of the gun was not confirmed by any other evidence. Kelly Fite, the State's ballistics expert, testified at trial that one or more of the shots fired during the robbery "probably came" from a .25 caliber Lorcin pistol. However, since the gun was never recovered, he was not certain of this.

Significantly, what this testimony proves is that Maurice, **not Jenkins**, was probably the person who had possession of the second gun. This, in turn, indicates that Roberts was likely lying when he testified that Jenkins had a gun and fired the first shot. Remember, Roberts originally told the police that Maurice was not involved in the robbery and did not even go into Hodges' store. It was only later, after Roberts was confronted by police with Maurice's contrary statement, that Roberts finally changed his story and admitted that Maurice was involved in the robbery.

Frankly, it defies logic to think that Maurice would have given this gun to Jenkins, or that Jenkins could have somehow taken it from Maurice. This was a huge hole in Roberts' testimony, and one that should have caused any reasonable juror (or Supreme Court justice) to doubt the truthfulness of Roberts' testimony. Pardon the pun, but this is literally the smoking gun that shows that Roberts was lying. Unfortunately, the people in power in Liberty County, Georgia, in 1995 were so intent on putting a black teenager in the electric chair that they didn't really care if they had the right one, and they overlooked this obvious hole in Roberts' testimony.

Fourth, Roberts admitted that he was a participant and accomplice in the robbery. The law presumes that accomplices like Roberts are inherently untrustworthy and that is why the testimony of an accomplice must be corroborated by other evidence. This corroboration requirement applies to each and every element of the crime, and it was not satisfied here.

Finally, and even more significantly, Jenkins testified at the Motion for a new trial and affirmatively denied, under oath, that he had anything to do with the robbery or murder of Mr. Hodges, that he ever had a gun, that he ever told Roberts that he had shot Mr. Hodges, or that he ever made the statements which he allegedly made to McCall and Officer Smith. Although this testimony was not before the jury due to the incompetence of Jenkins' trial attorneys, it was certainly part of the record before the Georgia Supreme Court, and it should have been considered by them in deciding whether, under all of the circumstances, Roberts was a credible witness and whether Jenkins' guilt had been proven beyond a reasonable doubt.

Denial of Jenkins' Motion for A Change of Venue

The next point noted by the Georgia Supreme Court was that "there is no manifest error in the trial court's denial of [Jenkins'] motion for a change of venue." 268 Ga. at __, 491 S.E.2d at 57. This motion was based upon the fact that there had been extensive pretrial publicity at the time of Hodges' murder and Jenkins' trial and that this may have "poisoned" the jury pool and made it impossible for Jenkins to get a fair trial in Liberty County.

The motion for a change of venue had been made before trial by Jenkins' court-appointed counsel, and it was based upon the fact that almost thirty percent of prospective jurors had to be excused for cause due to bias, prejudice, or prior relationship to the victim. I do not agree with the Georgia Supreme Court's decision on this point, but it was not one of the major grounds I was relying on in pursuing Jenkins' appeal. There is no need, therefore, to discuss this issue in detail here. However, I will return to this issue in Chapter 10, in discussing Jenkins' petition for a writ of habeas corpus in federal court.

It is interesting to note at this time, however, that, although Judge Harvey rejected Jenkins' motion for a change of venue, he granted a change of venue for Maurice Fleming's trial, which occurred nine months later. Both of these trials were based upon the same facts and essentially the same evidence, and the jury pools in both cases were identical. Yet, Judge Harvey saw fit to transfer Fleming's trial from Liberty County to Screven County. This did not make too much of a difference, however, because Fleming was also convicted of murder and robbery, and his conviction was also upheld by the Georgia Supreme Court.[105] Notably, however, the jury in Screven County only sentenced Fleming to life with a possibility of parole, so there was some benefit to the transfer.

Admission of the Improper Testimony of Inspector Gray, Deputy Moran, Kenneth McCall, Charles Howard, Terry Roberts, Bart Ingram and Officer James Smith

The next point made by the Georgia Supreme Court was that "we find no reversible error in the trial court's admission of testimony by Inspector Gray, Deputy Moran, Kenneth McCall, Charles Howard, Terry Roberts, Florida Department of Law Enforcement Special Agent Bart Ingram, or Officer James Smith." 268 Ga. at __, 491 S.E.2d at 57.

I strongly disagree with the Georgia Supreme Court's decision with respect to the improper testimony of these witnesses, but, here again, there is no need to discuss my reasons here. These issues will be revisited

---

105 The evidence against Fleming was actually stronger than the evidence against Jenkins because Fleming gave a detailed statement to the police admitting his guilt. Although the prosecutor claimed that Jenkins had made incriminating statements to Officer Smith and Ken McCall, these alleged statements (unlike Maurice's statement) were extremely brief, very ambiguous, and of questionable probative value.

in greater detail later in connection with Jenkins' motion for a writ of habeas corpus.

Improper Testimony of Inspector Gray and Detective Moran

With respect to the testimony of Inspector Gray, Jenkins claimed that this testimony was improper because it was based upon information which Gray purportedly received from so-called "silent witnesses" whom Gray had spoken to during his investigation. For this reason, it violated Jenkins' Sixth Amendment right to confront and cross-examine the witnesses against him. Unlike the denial of Jenkins' motion for a change of venue (which could be described as a minor and not unexpected error that only marginally affected Jenkins' ability to get a fair jury), the "silent witness" testimony was a major constitutional violation that clearly prevented him from getting a fair trial.

In addition to the "silent witness" testimony, Jenkens also claimed that the admission of other hearsay evidence during the testimony of Investigator Gray was improper and prejudicial. In fact, almost the entire testimony of Investigator Gray was based upon hearsay. As explained previously, this was improper because it improperly bolstered the testimony of other witnesses.

With respect to the "silent witness" testimony, the Georgia Supreme Court either completely misunderstood (unlikely) or completely ignored (more likely) the basis of my argument. The entire explanation for the Supreme Court's rejection of this point is as follows:

> "Gray's testimony that he investigated [Jenkins] based on information he received from an unnamed source did not constitute hearsay because Gray did not divulge the content of that information, see OCGA 24-3-1." 268 Ga. at __, 491 S.E.2d at 57.

This completely mischaracterized Gray's testimony and, furthermore, it was clearly wrong as a matter of law. What Gray actually stated at the trial was that "he had received information from various people, including information from unidentified 'silent witnesses'" (Tr. 1726) and that "based upon the information he received," he was able to identify Cedric Brown, Shawn Brown, Clevon Jenkins and Maurice Fleming as the participants in the robbery and the murder (Tr. 1727).

This testimony was far more substantive and far more pernicious than what the Supreme Court suggested. In effect, Gray was permitted to tell the jury that he had spoken to certain unidentified people in the course of his investigation and these unidentified people had told him that Jenkins was one of the participants in the robbery and murder of Mr. Hodges. Not only was this blatant hearsay, it was hearsay of the worst kind. The jury was led to believe that other witnesses existed besides Roberts who had identified Jenkins as a participant in the robbery. And, of course, Jenkins' attorneys had no opportunity to impeach or cross-examine these other witnesses. This is a clear violation of the Sixth Amendment, and yet the Georgia Supreme Court never even considered it.

The Supreme Court claimed that Gray's testimony regarding the silent witnesses "did not constitute hearsay because Gray did not divulge the content of that information." This is simply not true. Gray **did** divulge the content of the information because he said that **based on the information he received** he was able to determine that Jenkins was one of the participants. Obviously, the only possible conclusion the jury could infer from this testimony is that the silent witnesses told Gray that Jenkins was one of the participants.

The Court's citation of Section 24-3-1(a) of the Georgia Code is inexplicable and does not support their conclusion. That statute provides as follows:

> "Hearsay evidence is that which does not derive its value from the credit of the witness but rests mainly on the veracity and competency of other persons."

That was precisely the situation here. Gray's testimony that Jenkins was a participant in the robbery of Mr. Hodges was not based upon his own personal knowledge. On the contrary, it was based entirely "on the veracity and competency" of the silent witnesses, yet those witnesses were never even identified.

In addition to the testimony of the silent witnesses, Jenkins objected to other hearsay statements that were contained in the testimony of Investigator Gray. In effect, Gray's entire testimony was one long series of hearsay statements repeating what he had heard from other people during the course of his investigation. The Court rejected this argument stating as follows:

> "[T]he admission of Gray's testimony regarding the facts uncovered by his investigation, which were cumulative of properly admitted testimony, was **harmless error**." 268 Ga. at __, 491 S.E.2d at 57 (emphasis added).

At least the Court admitted it was *error*. However, it provided no analysis as to why it considered the error harmless.[106]

With respect to the testimony of Detective Moran — who improperly testified that Roberts was not prosecuted for murder because no evidence was "uncovered" during the investigation which showed that Roberts knew of any plan to kill Mr. Hodges before it happened — the Supreme Court stated as follows:

> "Moran's testimony that, based on the results of police investigation, Terry Roberts was not prosecuted for murder, **when read in context**, did not raise the inferences [Jenkins] claims rendered Moran's testimony false; accordingly, the prosecution was under no duty to correct the record in regard to Moran's testimony." 268 Ga. at __, 491 S.E.2d at 57 (emphasis added).

This analysis is grossly incomprehensible and clearly wrong. I have no idea what the Supreme Court contemplated when they said, "when read

---

[106] The Georgia practice of putting an "investigator" on the stand and having him testify to what he "discovered" during the course of his investigation is very pernicious and untrustworthy. I could never get away with such improper behavior when I was prosecuting homicide cases in New York, nor would I want to. The practice violates two fundamental principles of evidence: competence and hearsay. Competence requires that a witness have "personal knowledge" regarding the facts that he testifies about. Such knowledge requires sensory perception by the witness — things that the witness himself did, saw, heard, touched, smelled or tasted. It cannot be things that were told to him by others during an investigation. If an investigator has personal knowledge of things that happened during an investigation, for example, that he found shell casings at the scene of the crime, or that he saw the defendant running away, or that he took a photograph of the crime scene, then, obviously, he can testify regarding these things of which he has personal knowledge. But if the investigator interviewed fifteen people and his testimony is based upon what these people told him, this is improper. The witnesses who the investigator interviewed should themselves be called to the stand if they have relevant knowledge. An additional problem with this practice is that it improperly and unfairly "bolsters" the testimony of other witnesses. In the present case, for example, one of the possible sources of Gray's "silent witness" testimony was Terry Roberts. There was no other person whom Gray could have interviewed during his investigation who could possibly have implicated Jenkins in the robbery other than Roberts (and, of course, Cedric, Shawn and Maurice). If there had been some other witness, then surely the prosecutor would have called this mystery witness, particularly since it would have solved the accomplice corroboration problem. Yet, no such mystery witness was ever called. If the "silent witness" was Roberts, this was improper because Roberts had already testified personally at trial. By allowing Gray to essentially duplicate Roberts' testimony, this improperly bolstered Roberts' testimony. Furthermore, since Gray was a police investigator, his testimony was necessarily imbued with greater credibility in the minds of the jury. Yet, Gray, like Sergeant Schultz, actually knew nothing.

in context" (something they seem to say frequently), but there is no possible context in which Moran's testimony was not false.

Roberts was originally arrested for both the robbery and the murder of Mr. Hodges. As a participant in the robbery, he was unquestionably responsible for Mr. Hodges' murder under the **felony murder** doctrine regardless of whether he knew about any plan to kill Mr. Hodges before it occurred. There was never any need, at any time, for the prosecutor to prove that Roberts knew of any plan to kill Mr. Hodges prior to the robbery because intent is simply not a requirement of felony murder. District Attorney Cheney, who was no fool, obviously knew that intent was not required for felony murder and that is why Roberts was originally charged with murder. Yet, when it became necessary for the State to present Roberts as its star witness against Jenkins, the murder charge against Roberts was inexplicably dismissed.

The Supreme Court implies that Moran learned something during the course of his investigation which, "in context," justified dropping the murder charge against Roberts. This is unadulterated sophism. We all know exactly what Moran purportedly learned during his investigation because he told us, and what he purportedly learned was that "no evidence was developed to show that Roberts was aware of any plan to kill Mr. Roberts before it happened." Even if this true, however, it would not justify dismissing the murder charge against Roberts because evidence of intent is not necessary for felony murder. Furthermore, Roberts was initially charged with murder *after* Moran had already completed his investigation, so why then did the murder charge suddenly and magically disappear at a later date. Obviously, as they say in the cheap mystery novels, something more was afoot here, and what was afoot was that the District Attorney finally realized that he needed Roberts to testify as a witness for the State against Jenkins, and he did not want him doing so with a murder charge pending against him. And so, he dismissed the murder charge against Roberts, not because there was no evidence that Roberts knew of any plan to murder Mr. Hodges prior to the robbery, but merely because it was preferable for the prosecution that Roberts not be charged with murder when he testified against Jenkins. In effect, therefore, the District Attorney dismissed the murder charge against Roberts for his own convenience as a prosecutor and not as a result of any evidence (or lack thereof) that was discovered by Moran during his investigation.

Moran's statement that "no evidence was developed during the investigation to show that anyone intended to kill Mr. Hodges prior to the robbery" may have been true, but his subsequent statement that "this was the reason the murder charge against Robert was dismissed" was unquestionably false. Indeed, Moran's entire testimony on this issue was part of a grand charade deliberately orchestrated by Mr. Cheney.[107] There was no plausible basis, therefore, for the Supreme Court to conclude that Moran's testimony was not false and misleading.

The Supreme Court also stated, again without providing any discussion or analysis of any kind, that "Moran's testimony was not inadmissible on hearsay grounds." I am dumfounded by this statement since Moran's testimony about why the murder charge against Roberts was dismissed was obviously hearsay and no exceptions to the hearsay rule comes to mind that would have allowed its admission and none was cited by the Court. The only possible way that Moran could know why the murder charge was dismissed against Roberts was because Mr. Cheney told him, and this was obviously hearsay.

A second reason why Moran's testimony was false and misleading was because it falsely implied to the jury that Moran's investigation must have discovered some evidence that **Jenkins**, unlike Roberts, was aware of a plan to murder Mr. Hodges before the robbery occurred since the murder charge was not dismissed against Jenkins. If this were not so, then the

---

107   Significantly, Deputy Moran had already completed his initial testimony, but he was then explicitly "recalled" as a witness by Mr. Cheney sometime later to provide this "additional" testimony. Tr. at 1842-47. Apparently, Mr. Cheney dreamed up this strategy during lunch because he was concerned, based upon the cross-examination of Deputy Moran by Mr. Walker, that the jury might conclude that the reason the murder charge was dismissed against Roberts was to reward him for testifying against Jenkins.

murder charge would have been dismissed against Jenkins just like it was dismissed against Roberts.

In addition to the testimony of Inspector Gray and Deputy Moran, the Supreme Court also found no ***reversible error*** with respect to the testimony of Kenneth McCall, Charles Howard, Florida Special Agent Bart Ingram, or Officer James Smith. It is unclear from this statement whether the Count concluded (i) that there were, in fact, errors in the testimony of these witnesses, but the errors were not so serious as to require a reversal of Jenkins' conviction or (ii) that there were no errors in admitting the testimony. By explicitly using the term "reversible error" in its opinion, it would appear that the Court intended to signify the former. In any event, the Court provided no further discussion or analysis with respect to these witnesses.

Since the Supreme Court provided absolutely no explanation as to why these alleged errors were not reversible, there is no basis for further discussion here. However, these alleged errors will be discussed in greater detail in connection with Jenkins' petition for a writ of habeas corpus.

Whether Sufficient Evidence Was Presented to Corroborate the Testimony of Terry Roberts

The next issue considered by the Supreme Court was corroboration, not whether Judge Harvey's failure to give a corroboration charge to the jury was erroneous, but whether sufficient evidence had, in fact, been admitted during the trial to corroborate Roberts' testimony. Not surprisingly, the Court concluded that there was sufficient corroboration evidence. The Court's entire analysis of this issue was as follows: "[t]he record contains sufficient evidence to corroborate the testimony of Terry Roberts." 268 Ga. at __, 491 S.E.2d at 58. There was absolutely no discussion of what evidence the Court considered to be corroborative, nor was there any discussion of how this evidence could possibly be sufficient since the jury was never even told that it had an obligation to consider whether the testimony of Terry Roberts was corroborated by sufficient evidence. These issues will be discussed further in connection with Jenkins' petition for a writ of habeas corpus.

Consideration of the "Cumulative Error Doctrine"

The next issue considered by the Supreme Court was the cumulative error doctrine. Jenkins had argued that, even if the effect of the many individual errors committed during his trial were not sufficient by themselves to require reversal of his conviction and grant a new trial, the cumulative effect of these errors certainly was. The Supreme Court summarily dismissed this argument, succinctly stating, "Georgia does not recognize the cumulative error rule." 268 Ga. at __, 491 S.E.2d at 58.

The Court's refusal to apply the cumulative error doctrine to Jenkins' case presented an interesting situation. I knew, of course, prior to the time that Jenkins' appeal was argued, that, based upon existing precedents, Georgia did not recognize the cumulative error doctrine. I also knew, however, that federal courts required it. As the U.S. Court of Appeals for the Eleventh Circuit (which includes Georgia) stated in **United States v. Baker**, 432 F.3d 1189 (11th Cir. 2005):

> "The cumulative error doctrine provides that the aggregation of non-reversible errors can yield denial of the constitutional right to a fair trial, thereby necessitating a reversal of the conviction."[108]

During the oral argument of Jenkins' appeal, for which, as previously noted, I had only fifteen minutes to explain all the reasons why Jenkins' conviction should be reversed, the only comment or question from any of the justices (and I believe it was from Justice Hunstein, who eventually wrote the Court's opinion), was to point out to me that "Georgia does not recognize the cumulative error doctrine." My response to this statement was to say, "yes, but the federal constitution requires consideration of the

---

[108] I recognize that *Baker* was decided eight years after *Jenkins*, but there were many other federal cases recognizing the rule prior to *Jenkins*. I quote from *Baker* simply because it provides a nice summary of the rule.

cumulative error doctrine as a matter of due process, and Georgia courts are obligated to follow the federal constitution."

As the highest court in the State of Georgia, the Supreme Court had the authority to overrule its prior precedents regarding the cumulative error rule and follow the federal rule, which was constitutionally mandated. I recognized that this was a big ask, but it would have been the right thing to do. Unfortunately, the Court did not do what it should have done. It simply followed the old rule, which was constitutionally infirm.

In 2020, the Georgia Supreme Court decided the case of *State v. Lane*, 308 Ga. 10, 838 S.E.2d 808 (2020). The appellant in that case had been convicted of murder, but the trial judge set aside the conviction and granted a new trial because of the cumulative effect of several errors. The errors at issue were relatively minor in comparison to the significant errors that occurred during Jenkins' case, but the trial judge (unlike Judge Harvey) thought that the cumulative effect of the errors was sufficiently prejudicial to require a new trial. The State then appealed the trial court's use of the cumulative error rule, arguing that "Georgia does not recognize the cumulative error rule."

Unlike the Supreme Court in *Jenkins*, the Supreme Court in *Lane* did an extensive analysis of the reason why Georgia courts did not recognize the cumulative error rule. It then concluded, "the Georgia rule traces back to a civil case that could not have held anything about the proper standard for granting a new trial in a criminal case." 308 Ga. at __, 838 S.E.2d at 813. After discussing the history of the rule in Georgia, the Supreme Court then concluded that the rule made no sense and should be overruled. As the Court stated in its opinion:

> "[W]e consider whether to change our approach to cumulative error. Unable to identify any legal principle — let alone a compelling, reasoned explanation — behind our existing rule, and finding compelling case law from other jurisdictions endorsing cumulative error review, we

abandon this prior rule and hold that Georgia courts considering whether a criminal defendant is entitled to a new trial should consider collectively the prejudicial effect of trial court errors and any deficient performance by counsel — at least where those errors by the court and counsel involve evidentiary issues." 308 Ga. at __, 838 S.E.2d at 813.

Furthermore, the Supreme Court took the bold and highly unusual step of overruling **each and every** prior Georgia case, **explicitly including Jenkins**, that had refused to apply the cumulative error rule. As the Court stated in its opinion:

"We therefore overrule our prior decisions and those of the Court of Appeals that hold that the prejudicial effect of multiple trial errors may not be considered cumulatively in determining whether a criminal defendant is entitled to a new trial and disapprove any decisions with language to that effect; those cases are listed in the Appendix to this opinion." 308 Ga. at __, 838 S.E.2d at 815.

Significantly, Jenkins' case was one of the cases that was explicitly listed by the Supreme Court as being overruled. Unfortunately, it took the Court **twenty-three** years to do this. I had explicitly told them back in 1997 that the cumulative error rule was constitutionally required, but they refused to listen to me. Unfortunately, you can lead a judge to wisdom, but you can't make him think.

The interesting question, therefore, is what happens now? The Supreme Court explicitly ruled in 2020 that its 1997 decision upholding Jenkins' conviction was wrongly decided, and that the cumulative effect of the errors that had been committed during Jenkins' trial should have been considered in deciding whether to grant him a new trial. Although the Supreme Court took the unusual step of explicitly listing all prior cases in its decision that had been incorrectly decided, it did nothing to rectify the consequences of those prior mistakes. What it should have done was to grant a new hearing to every defendant, including Jenkins, who was still being incarcerated in a Georgia prison in order to decide whether their convictions should be reversed based upon the new rule.

That should have happened but, of course, it did not. Consequently, Jenkins remains incarcerated for a mistake the Georgia Supreme Court made in 1997. As the Supreme Court finally admitted in 2020, and as I told them in 1997, there was no legitimate reason for Georgia courts to ignore the cumulation error doctrine. Had it been applied to Jenkins' case in 1997, he probably would have been granted a new trial.[109]

Improper Comments Made by the Prosecutor Regarding Jenkins' Failure to Testify at Trial

The next issue considered by the Supreme Court was the propriety of the comments made by Mr. Cheney during his closing argument regarding Jenkins' failure to rebut the State's evidence. Jenkins claimed that these comments violated his Fifth Amendment privilege against self-incrimination. Needless to say, the Court rejected Jenkins' argument. As the Court stated in its opinion:

> "The prosecutor's closing argument, read in context, did not comment upon [Jenkins'] election not to testify but rather permissibly noted the failure of the defense to rebut the State's evidence. Contrary to [Jenkins'] contention this was not an instance in which [Jenkins] himself was the only potential witness the defense could have called." 268 Ga. at __, 491 S.E.2d at 58.

---

109 It seems clear to me that Jenkins' case was wrongfully decided and that application of the cumulative error rule should make this fact even clearer. Unfortunately, however, this does not necessarily mean that the Georgia Supreme Court, if given the chance, would automatically vacate Jenkins' conviction. The cumulative error doctrine only matters if there are errors to accumulate. And the Court ruled back in 1997 that no errors were committed during Jenkins' trial, at least no reversible errors. It is possible, therefore, that the Court might still affirm Jenkins' conviction today even though the cumulative error issue was wrongfully decided.

This was utter nonsense, on both counts. I do not know what "context" the Supreme Court was imagining, but any reasonable person, and certainly any reasonable juror, would naturally understand the prosecutor's comments to refer to the fact that Jenkins did not testify. Let's review the four offending statements made by Mr. Cheney:

A. *Impermissible statement number 1:*

"Each witness has testified. The defense, on each witness, has had the opportunity to present evidence and under cross-examination to refute the State's evidence. Is there any evidence that has been presented by **the defendant** that refutes what the State's evidence is?" (Tr. 1925) (emphasis added).

B. *Impermissible statement number 2:*

"We have presented evidence as to this defendant's involvement, we have presented evidence **as to this defendant's statement**. Has the defense presented any evidence, any evidence, to refute the State's evidence? I think the answer to that is clearly no." (Tr. 1926) (emphasis added).

C. *Impermissible statement number 3:*

"As I was saying before the objection was made, that the State's contention is that **the defendant**, the defense in this case **has offered no evidence that would refute the testimony of the State's witnesses** as they've testified in this case." (Tr. 1929) (emphasis added).

4. *Impermissible statement number 4:*

> "The second part of this State's evidence is **the admissions by the defendant**. . . . So there's three folks that have come into this courtroom, sat on this stand under oath and said, 'This man admitted to shooting Mr. Robert Franklin Hodges.' ***And we contend that evidence has not been refuted in any way***." (Tr. 1938-39) (emphasis added).

Notably, these four statements were made within a few minutes of each other. There was nothing innocent or inadvertent about them. Mr. Cheney, an experienced prosecutor, deliberately chose to violate Jenkins' Fifth Amendment right by repeatedly pointing out to the jury his failure to testify. Notably also, Jenkins' attorneys properly objected to Mr. Cheney's improper comments and moved for a mistrial based upon the prejudicial statements (Tr. 1926). Judge Harvey, however, overruled the objection and denied the motion (Tr. 1928).

It must be emphasized here that, contrary to the arguments made by Mr. Cheney, the defendant in a criminal case has no obligation of any kind to offer evidence which refutes the State's evidence. It is solely the State's obligation to offer sufficient evidence to prove that the defendant is guilty beyond a reasonable doubt. The State cannot, in any way, shift this burden to the defendant by arguing that the defendant needs to rebut its evidence.

The prosecutor's comments here were particularly egregious because the attorneys representing Jenkins offered no evidence of any kind in opposition to the State's evidence, as they had the absolute right to do. Furthermore, they unequivocally stated in the presence of the jury at the beginning of the trial that they would not call any witnesses. Under these circumstances, it was clearly improper and highly prejudicial for Mr. Cheney to comment on Jenkins' failure to testify or present any evidence in defense.

Finally, the Supreme Court mistakenly asserted that "this was not an instance in which [Jenkins] himself was the only potential witness the defense could have called." 268 Ga. at __, 491 S.E.2d at 58. With all due respect, I am certainly much more familiar with the facts and available evidence in this case than the justices of the Supreme Court were, and I can assure you that there were no other witnesses that Jenkins could have called. Jenkins' court-appointed trial attorneys obviously felt the same way because they did not call any witnesses.[110] Even if there had been other potential witnesses, however, that would not have excused or justified Cheney's outrageous comments.

Unfortunately, and undoubtedly unethically, the justices of the Georgia Supreme Court blatantly ignored the clear constitutional mandate of federal law and made up facts to justify their misguided decision.

Failure to Instruct the Jury Regarding Corroboration of Accomplice Testimony

The Supreme Court next considered the critical question of whether Judge Harvey's failure to instruct the jury regarding the need to corroborate the testimony of an accomplice constituted reversible error. Incredibly, the Court ruled that the failure to instruct the jury regarding corroboration in this case was not erroneous. As the Court stated in its opinion:

> "We find no error in the trial court's failure during the guilt-innocence phase to charge on corroboration of accomplices or co-conspirators. It is not error to fail to give a charge on corroboration of accomplices where the State relies on other evidence, including a defendant's confession, apart from the accomplice's testimony." 268 Ga. at __, 491 S.E.2d at 59.

It is astonishing to me how many times the justices of the Georgia Supreme Court were willing to ignore their own law to justify an erroneous decision to keep Jenkins in prison.

---

110 If the Supreme Court had knowledge of some person other than Jenkins who could have provided exculpatory evidence at his trial, then Jenkins' trial attorneys were even more incompetent than I thought because they never called this phantom witness to testify on Jenkins' behalf.

It will be remembered from Chapter 6 that Judge Harvey admitted in his decision denying Jenkins' Motion for a new trial that his failure to give a corroboration charge in this case was erroneous. He also admitted to me following the hearing in support of Jenkins' Motion for a new trial that his failure to charge corroboration was an inadvertent mistake which he "could not believe that he had made." Nevertheless, as noted in Chapter 4, he also admitted to me that he would not reverse Jenkins' conviction on this basis, and that "he would leave that up to the Supreme Court." Obviously, that was a fatal mistake because the Supreme Court itself was not up to the task.

In his written decision denying Jenkins' Motion for a new trial, Judge Harvey characterized this error as "harmless" and refused to grant a new trial on this basis. As discussed in Chapter 6, there was no reasonable basis for Judge Harvey to conclude that his failure to instruct the jury regarding the issue of corroboration was harmless, and therefore the Motion for a new trial should have been granted.

Although it did not say so, the Supreme Court probably realized that Judge Harvey's "harmless error" characterization was unsustainable. Accordingly, it either had to find another excuse for the trial court's failure to give a corroboration charge, or it had to reverse Jenkins' conviction. For some inexplicable reason, it chose the former option.

Let's analyze what the Supreme Court said. "It is not error to fail to give a charge on corroboration of accomplices where the State relies on other evidence . . . apart from the accomplice's testimony." Really? The whole purpose of a corroboration charge is to instruct the jury that it has to consider the sufficiency **of the other evidence offered by the State** to corroborate the accomplice's testimony. It is always necessary, therefore, for the State to offer other evidence when an accomplice testifies. If the State does not offer any other evidence to corroborate the accomplice's testimony, then the charge against the defendant must be dismissed **as a matter of law** for failure to comply with the requirement of substantive law that a criminal defendant cannot be convicted solely on the testimony of an accomplice.

The explanation offered by the Supreme Court in this case is utter nonsense, therefore, and would lead to the preposterous proposition that it would never be necessary for a trial court to give a charge on corroboration. On one hand, if the State fails to offer any other evidence, then the case is insufficient as a matter of law and must be dismissed by the judge. Under these circumstances, the case never goes to the jury, and there is no need to give them an instruction on corroboration. On the other hand, if the State does offer other evidence, then, according to this decision of the Supreme Court, there is also no need to charge corroboration. This is akin to running with the hare and hunting with the hounds.

Suffice it to say that the Court was incorrect. There are many times when trial court judges have to instruct the jury on the issue of corroboration *even where the State has offered other evidence.* Indeed, the whole purpose of the corroboration instruction is to inform the jury that they must weigh whether the other evidence that has been offered by the state is sufficient to corroborate the testimony of the accomplice. The Supreme Court's assertion to the contrary is just plain wrong.

What the Supreme Court probably intended to say, but did not, is that there are certain instances where independent evidence is offered by the State in addition to the testimony of an accomplice and this independent evidence, by itself, is sufficient to prove the defendant's guilt beyond a reasonable doubt without regard to the testimony of the accomplice. Under these limited circumstances, as a matter of law, it is not necessary to rely upon the testimony of the accomplice and therefore it is not necessary to give a charge on corroboration. For example, if there are three other witnesses (or even one other witness) who observed the robbery besides the accomplice, then it would not be necessary to give a charge on corroboration. The reason for this rule is that the testimony of the accomplice is not necessary to the State's case, and therefore there is no need to corroborate his testimony.

The problem in Jenkins' case, however, and the reason why the Supreme Court's decision was wrong, was that this limited exception did not apply. There was not sufficient independent evidence to convict Jenkins without Roberts' testimony, and therefore his testimony needed to be corroborated.

The only evidence which the State offered against Jenkins in this case besides the testimony of Terry Roberts were the two brief "admissions" which Jenkins allegedly made to inmate McCall and Officer Smith. In the statement to Officer Smith, Jenkins allegedly said, "I only shot him once." And in the statement to McCall, Jenkins allegedly said, "I shot the old cracker twice." These statements were not, under any circumstances, sufficient to convict Jenkins of the murder of Mr. Hodges without the testimony of Terry Roberts. Accordingly, Roberts' testimony had to be corroborated and therefore a jury charge on corroboration was absolutely essential.

The Georgia Supreme Court revisited this corroboration issue in a very similar case nine months after deciding Jenkins' case. This later case involved Maurice Fleming, the very same person who was allegedly involved in murdering Mr. Hodges on October 8, 1993. Fleming was tried separately from Jenkins, and he was convicted of felony murder and robbery on June 21, 1996. Unlike Jenkins, who was sentenced to life without possibility of parole, Fleming was sentenced to life with a possibility of parole. *Fleming v. State*, 269 Ga. 245, 497 S.E.2d 211 (1998).

I am not personally familiar with the evidence that was presented in Fleming's case but, based on statements made by the Supreme Court in denying Fleming's appeal, the evidence against Fleming appears to be very similar to the evidence presented against Jenkins. Once again, Terry Roberts was the main prosecution witness and there were no other witnesses who implicated Fleming in the crime. However, unlike Jenkins,

Fleming, after he was arrested, gave a more detailed statement to the police admitting his guilt.

As in Jenkins' case, the trial judge in Fleming's case (the Honorable John Harvey) failed to charge the jury regarding the issue of corroboration, even though Flemings' attorneys had explicitly requested such a charge. (I know this seems implausible, but it is entirely true). Nevertheless, the Supreme Court had no difficulty in affirming Fleming's conviction based essentially on the same theory it had applied to Jenkins, namely, that there was "other evidence" which corroborated Roberts' testimony and therefore a corroboration charge was unnecessary. Ironically, the majority opinion (written by Justice Hunstein, the same justice who wrote the opinion in **Jenkins**) explicitly relied on **Jenkins** in justifying the Court's decision in **Fleming**.

This time, however, there was a ***dissent***, a lone voice of reason. As Justice Benham correctly stated in his dissenting opinion, "the mere fact that there is other evidence which could serve as corroboration does not dispense with the need for the requested charge because the jury, as the exclusive judges of credulity, could have rejected the other evidence and convicted solely on the accomplice's testimony." 269 Ga. at 250, 497 S.E.2d at 215 (Benham dissenting).

Justice Benham also pointed out that the Court misinterpreted and misconstrued the key precedent on which it relied in **Jenkins** to justify its decision. As he said in his dissent:

> "The majority holds that there is no need for the charge [of corroboration] 'where the State relies on other evidence, including a defendant's confession, apart from the accomplice's testimony.' The case cited in **Jenkins** in support of that proposition was **Hall v. State**, 241 Ga. 252, 244 S.E.2d (1978), where this Court held that the charge was not required because 'there were other witnesses to the crime.' The majority opinion in this case [and in **Jenkins**]

broadens the scope of the evidence which obviates the need for the jury charge from 'other witnesses to the crime' to 'other evidence.'" 269 Ga. at 250-51, 497 S.E.2d at 215 (Benham dissenting).

Justice Benham further noted, "[t]he phrasing of the majority opinion's holding, **and the phrasing in Jenkins**, do violence to the statutory principle in aid of which the requested charge should be given." Finally, Justice Benham stated that "[b]ecause there was no testimony in this case other than the accomplice's which directly connected Fleming to the crime, I am convinced that the majority opinion is incorrect in finding no reversible error in the failure to charge." 269 Ga. at 251, 497 S.E.2d at 215 (Benham dissenting).

Unfortunately, Justice Benham was no more successful in convincing the majority of the Court in **Fleming** to apply Georgia law correctly than I was in **Jenkins**.[111] Apparently, notwithstanding the obvious flaws in their reasoning, they were hell-bent on upholding the conviction of a possibly innocent person based upon the uncorroborated testimony of an admitted liar. One can only ask, what were they thinking?[112]

---

111 Justice Benham believed there was a key difference between the **Fleming** case and the **Jenkins** case because in **Fleming** his attorneys explicitly asked the trial judge to give a charge on corroboration whereas Jenkins' attorneys did not. This is not correct, however, for two reasons. First, the failure to give a charge on corroboration constitutes **plain error** which is an appealable issue regardless of whether the defendant's attorneys requested a charge or made an objection. The trial judge has an affirmative obligation, as a matter of due process, to charge the jury correctly. Second, to the extent that Jenkins' attorneys failed to request a charge on corroboration, this constituted ineffective assistance of counsel. This, in turn, would require that same inquiry concerning whether the failure to charge corroboration adversely affected the outcome of the trial. Thus, either way, the conviction would have to be reversed regardless of whether the defendant's attorney failed to request the charge.

112 As it turns out, this was not the end of the story. As will be revealed in Chapter 17, the Georgia Supreme Court revisited this issue again in 2014 in the case of *Hamm v. State*, 294 Ga. 781, 756 S.E.2d 507, and this time the Court finally got it right. In the process, the Supreme Court explicitly overruled *Hall v. State*, *Jenkins v. State*, and *Fleming v. State*, holding that it was reversible error not to give the jury a charge on corroboration of accomplice testimony even where the state relies on "other evidence." Thus, in the final analysis, the decision upholding Jenkins' conviction was, in fact, reversed for failure to charge the jury on the issue of corroboration. In a tragic turn of events, Judge Harvey's indefensible decision to leave this issue up the Supreme Court turned out okay. Unfortunately, it took the Supreme Court 21 years to correct the error and, when they did, nobody noticed. Jenkins is still in jail, and justice arrived too late to matter.

Ineffective Assistance of Counsel

The final issue considered by the Georgia Supreme Court in Jenkins' case, and undoubtedly the most important issue he had raised, was whether Jenkins had been deprived of the effective assistance of counsel due to the numerous errors and mistakes that Jenkins' counsel had made while representing him at the trial, including especially their failure to request a charge on corroboration, their failure to object to the testimony of the "silent witnesses," their failure to impeach Roberts with his prior inconsistent statements, and their failure to have Jenkins testify at the trial despite his willingness and desire to do so. It may not surprise you to learn that the Supreme Court rejected all of Jenkins' arguments with respect to this issue.

The Court correctly began its legal analysis by focusing on the "two-prong" test established by the U.S. Supreme Court in *Strickland v. Washington* for ineffective assistance of counsel, namely, that "the defendant is required to show both that counsel's performance was deficient, and that the deficiency prejudiced the defense." 268 Ga. at __, 491 S.E.2d at 59. The Court also correctly noted that "[a]n error by counsel, even if professionally unreasonable, does not warrant setting aside the judgment of a criminal proceeding if the error had no effect on the judgment." *Id.* (quoting *Strickland*, 466 U.S. at 691).

Jenkins had identified sixteen separate grounds on which his trial attorneys' performance had been deficient, all of which have been previously discussed in detail, such as their failure to request a charge on corroboration and their failure to object to the "silent witness" testimony. The Court **summarily** disposed of **thirteen** of these grounds with the following **conclusory** statement:

> "We have already addressed and found to be without reversible error thirteen of the items in which counsel was claimed to be ineffective. Thus, [Jenkins] cannot establish

the second prong of the *Strickland* test as to those items."

268 Ga. at __, 491 S.E.2d at 59.[113]

The Court identified these thirteen grounds in a footnote as follows: (1) counsels' failure to object to the testimony of the "silent witnesses" during the testimony of Investigator Gray; (2) counsels' failure to object to Judge Harvey's erroneous jury instructions regarding the issues of malice murder, parties to a crime, and conspiracy; (3) counsels' failure to request a jury charge on the issue of corroboration and their failure to object to Judge Harvey's charge which omitted such an instruction; (4) counsels' failure to object to, or correct, the false and misleading testimony provided by Deputy Moran; (5) counsels' failure to object to hearsay during the testimony of Investigator Gray; (6) counsels' failure to object to hearsay and other improper testimony provided by Bart Ingram; (7) counsels' failure to object to the conspiracy charge on the ground that it failed to inform the jury that a co-conspirator's testimony regarding the existence of a conspiracy required corroboration; (8) counsels' failure to object to improper testimony about other crimes during the testimony of Terry Roberts; (9) counsels' failure to object to the prosecutors' improper use of leading questions; (10) counsels' failure to object to the improper comments made by the prosecutor (Mr. Cheney) during his summation during the guilt phase of the trial; (11) counsels' failure to object to improper comments made by the prosecutor (Mr. Durden) during his summation during the penalty phase of the trial; (12) counsels' failure to object to prejudicial remarks made by Judge Harvey regarding the existence of a conspiracy; and (13) counsels' failure to object to the admission of co-conspirator statements on

---

113   It is worth noting two interesting nuances in the Court's blanket assessment regarding this issue. First, the Court used the term ***reversible error***, implying that the errors complained about were indeed errors, but not serious enough to require reversal of Jenkins' conviction. In effect, the Court admitted that there were errors, but claimed that they were harmless (although the Court provided absolutely no rationale for reaching this conclusion). Second, the Court stated that Jenkins "cannot establish the ***second*** prong of the *Strickland* test as to these items." 268 Ga. at __, 491 S.E.2d at 59 (emphasis added). This clearly implies, of course, that Jenkins was able to establish the ***first*** prong of the *Strickland test*, which is to say that counsels' conduct was deficient. So, here again, the Court was relying on the notion that, ***even though the conduct of Jenkins' counsel was deficient***, the deficiencies did not affect the outcome of the trial. Given the nature of the numerous and substantial errors that Jenkins' counsel made, it is hard to see how this could be possible, and certainly the Court made no effort to explain why they thought it was so.

the ground that the State had failed to prove a prima facie case of a conspiracy. See 268 Ga. at __, 491 S.E.2d at 59, n.5. It would be a fair assessment of the Court's consideration of these important issues to say that the Court's analysis ranged from superficial to non-existent.

The three remaining grounds for Jenkins' claim that he had been denied the effective assistance of counsel were (1) counsels' failure to impeach Roberts with his prior inconsistent statements, (2) counsels' failure to introduce evidence showing that Cedric Brown was mentally retarded, and (3) counsels' refusal to permit Jenkins to testify at the trial.

With respect to the first two of these grounds, the Supreme Court, incredibly, accepted counsels' lame excuse (given at the hearing on the Motion for a new trial) that the reason they did not impeach Roberts with his prior inconsistent statements or introduce evidence of Brown's mental retardation was because they wanted to preserve the right to give the first opening statement. As the Court stated in its opinion:

> "Reviewing the transcript of the hearing on [Jenkins'] motion for a new trial in regard to the remaining three items, the record reveals that trial counsel's decision not to impeach Roberts with his prior inconsistent statements in order to retain open and concluding final arguments, and not to introduce the issue of Cedric Brown's mental retardation in order to avoid undermining the defense theory that Brown was the 'mastermind' of the crimes, were matters of trial strategy within the bounds of reasonable professional conduct." 268 Ga. at __, 491 S.E.2d at 59-60.

I do not know whether any of the justices who were members of Georgia's Supreme Court at this time ever defended a capital murder case, but this was absolute poppycock. Neither Abraham Lincoln nor Clarance Darrow, nor both together, could have given a sufficiently eloquent "opening" closing argument to justify foregoing the most effective cross-examination of Roberts that was possible, and that required use of Roberts' prior inconsistent statements to impeach him. And, for the record, neither David Walker nor Hal Peel was in any way comparable with either Abraham Lincoln or Clarence Darrow.

Terry Roberts was unquestionably the State's star witness. As a practical matter, he was their only witness, since he was the **only person** who could actually connect Jenkins to the crime. The other twenty witnesses who testified during the guilt phase of the trial were mostly window dressing. Sure, the State needed to produce a medical examiner to establish the cause of death, and the testimony of the ballistics expert was helpful to show that the gun purportedly **used by Cedric** matched the bullets found at the scene, but Roberts' testimony was the whole enchilada. He was the one who put Roberts at the scene, and he was the one who claimed that Jenkins shouted to him, as he got back in the car, "I shot him."

If Jenkins was to have any reasonable chance of being found not guilty, his attorneys needed to do two things. First, they needed to create significant doubt in the minds of the jurors regarding Roberts' credibility. And second, they needed to have Jenkins testify in his own defense and tell his side of the story. Unfortunately, they did neither.

Both prior to, and after, he was arrested, Roberts gave lengthy statements to the police regarding the events in question. He was questioned by the police for several hours on three separate occasions, and his statements were very inconsistent. Written copies of two of these statements were available and could have been used by a competent attorney to destroy Roberts' credibility on the stand. But Walker and Peel failed to do so. And then, to make matters worse, they tried to justify their failure to do so by saying that it was done **intentionally** in order to retain the right to "open and close" the summations to the jury. This was utterly unreasonable and indefensible, and I cannot believe that the Supreme Court actually claimed that "this was a matter of trial strategy and tactics within the bounds of reasonable professional conduct." Surrender is a form of strategy too, but it seldom wins wars, and it is never defended as being within the bounds of reasonable professional conduct.[114]

The same can also be said of Walker's and Peel's failure to introduce evidence regarding Cedric Brown's mental retardation This was not nearly as important as their failure to impeach Roberts with his prior inconsistent statements, but the notion that they intentionally refrained from doing so because they were afraid this might undermine their theory that Cedric Brown was the mastermind of the robbery is simply ludicrous. What Walker and Peel needed to do here was rise up and mount a defense. They failed to do so, and their dereliction cannot be defended as a matter of strategy.

The only evidence about the robbery came from the mouth of Terry Roberts, and he explicitly testified that Jenkins was one the shooters. He did not say anything about Cedric or Maurice being the masterminds of the robbery. It would have been much more important for Jenkins' defense for the jury to know that Cedric was mentally retarded, since this would make it much easier to argue that Jenkins did not know what Cedric intended to do and should not be held responsible for his actions.

With respect to the third ground of Jenkins' claim of ineffective assistance of counsel — counsel's failure to properly advise him whether he should testify at the trial — the Court stated as follows:

> "Likewise, trial counsel's strategy and tactics in advising [Jenkins] not to testify did not fall outside the wide range of reasonable professional conduct." 268 Ga. at __, 491 S.E.2d at 60.

---

114 The Supreme Court stated in footnote 6 of its Decision that, "[t]he trial transcript reveals the Roberts' prior inconsistent statements were before the jury, in that Roberts testified on direct that the first couple of times he spoke with the police he did not tell them the whole truth and acknowledged, during stringent cross-examination, that he 'lied' to the police in his earlier statements," 268 Ga. at __, 491 S.E.2d at 59, n.6. However, the fact that Roberts admitted that he lied is not the same thing as being pointedly and repeatedly confronted by his lies from his prior inconsistent statements, and the justices of the Georgia Supreme Court should have known better than to say that it did.

I get tired of saying this, but here again the Supreme Court's factual and legal analysis is totally indefensible. As the District Attorney correctly, but improperly, pointed out to the jury during his closing summation, the defense in this case did absolutely nothing to rebut or contradict the evidence that had been offered by the State to show that Jenkins committed the crimes at issue. No witnesses testified for the defense, no documents or exhibits were offered into evidence, no experts were called to contradict the State's medical and forensic evidence and, most importantly, the defendant himself did not testify. This was a gross mistake. The jury had no plausible basis for doubting the State's evidence unless Jenkins took the stand and provided some type of defense.

The State's evidence was not overwhelming, to be sure. Roberts was a very flawed witness who admitted on direct examination that he had lied to the police "the first couple of times" that he spoke to them. Furthermore, as an accomplice in the robbery, his testimony was inherently untrustworthy. But Roberts' testimony was partially and importantly corroborated by the testimony of Officer Smith and Ken McCall, both of whom testified that Jenkins had told them that he had shot somebody, either once or twice.[115] These brief incriminating statements were clearly inconsistent with each other and somewhat suspect, but, if believed, they certainly provided sufficient evidence for the jury to find that Jenkins probably shot Mr. Hodges. Furthermore, this testimony was confirmed by the ballistics evidence (which established that two guns had been used) and by the medical evidence (which established that Hodges had been shot four or five times, although only one of the wounds had been fatal). Based upon this forensic evidence, it was evident that somebody besides Cedric must have fired a shot at Mr. Hodges, and the testimony of Roberts, Smith and McCall strongly suggested to the jury that that person was Jenkins. Finally, it was indisputable that after the robbery Jenkins "fled" to Florida with Cedric

---

115 It must also be noted that Roberts' testimony was impermissibly bolstered by the improper testimony of Officer Gray who testified that, during his investigation, he had spoken to unidentified "silent witnesses" and that based upon this information he had determined that Jenkins was one of the perpetrators who had robbed and murdered Mr. Hodges.

and Maurice. Evidence of flight gives rise to a permissible inference of consciousness of guilt, so this was bad for Jenkins also.

On the other hand, Jenkins had a very credible story to tell, and he did so perfectly well at the hearing in support of the Motion for a new trial. He knew Cedric, Maurice and Roberts from living in the neighborhood, not very well, but well enough to get along with them. Jenkins had lived most of his life in New York City, but his mother had sent him to Georgia to live temporarily with his grandmother to prevent from him getting into trouble in New York. On the day of the robbery, and just before it occurred, he was walking along the street with his girlfriend when Cedric, Maurice and Roberts drove by in Roberts' car and Cedric told him to "get in the car." Jenkins had no idea where they were going or what they were planning to do; he just went along for the ride. When they wound up at Hodges Grocery and committed the robbery, Jenkins was totally shocked. He had no idea they were planning to do this, and he certainly had no idea that Cedric would shoot Mr. Hodges. Contrary to what Roberts had said, Jenkins never had a gun and he certainly never shot Mr. Hodges. He also never told Roberts, Officer Smith or Ken McCall that he did so. And the only reason that he went to Florida with Cedric and Maurice was because he was scared and he had no idea what else he could do. Jenkins was only seventeen years old at the time, he had never been in any kind of trouble with the police or at school. He was staying with his elderly grandmother in Midway, and he had no one to advise him what to do. It was a very unfortunate situation for him, but he was never in any way responsible for the robbery or death of Mr. Hodges.

As it turned out, nothing of Jenkins' side of the story was ever told to the jury because his attorneys advised him not to testify. Jenkins' always wanted to testify, and he had consistently told his attorneys prior to the trial that he was not involved in the robbery or the murder of Mr. Hodges, but they refused to let him testify. Furthermore, to make matters worse, Jenkins' attorneys explicitly told him that the trial was "going well" and there was "no need" for him to testify. All of this was confirmed by both

Walker and Peel when they testified at the hearing in support of the Motion for a new trial.

This brief recitation of the evidence (and potential evidence) leads to only two possible conclusions. First, if Jenkins does not testify at his trial, as actually happened here, he will certainly be convicted of robbery and murder and possibly sentenced to death. Second, if Jenkins does testify, as he always wanted to do, there was at least a good possibility that the jury might conclude that the evidence offered against him was not sufficient to find him guilty beyond a reasonable doubt. Under these circumstances, it was absolutely essential that Jankins testify and tell his side of the story. Furthermore, since Jenkins had no prior criminal record and had not committed any prior bad acts, there was very little downside risk to his testifying.

To suggest, as the Supreme Court did in its Decision, that "trial counsel's strategy and tactics in advising appellant not to testify did not fall outside the wide range of reasonable professional conduct" (268 Ga. at __, 491 S.E.2d at 50) is utterly indefensible. Even assuming that the level of legal expertise is far lower in Georgia than what I was used to in New York, this is still "a bridge too far", or, more precisely, "a bar too low." There are times when it is absolutely essential that a defendant testify in his own defense, and courts cannot shirk their responsibility to recognize this by uttering the lame shibboleth "well, that's just a matter or trials tactics." No, it is a matter of professional competence and negligence.

Finally, what must be added to the mix here is not only did Jenkins' attorneys advise him not to testify, they actually told him that the trial was "going well" and, therefore, there was no reason for him to testify. This was outright fraud and deceit. Obviously, Jenkins' attorneys had to know that the trial was not going well. It was completely irresponsible, therefore — as well as a breach of their fiduciary obligations as attorneys — for them to tell their client that the trial was going well when it wasn't. Under these circumstances, there was no possible way for Jenkins, a nineteen-year-old with no formal education, a low IQ, no prior run-ins with the law, and no legal education, to make an informed decision regarding the critical issue of whether he should testify at trial in his own defense. On the contrary, it was the legal and ethical obligation of his attorneys to advise him properly with respect to this critical issue, yet they failed to do so.

Under these circumstances, it was inexcusable for the Georgia Supreme Court to avoid addressing this issue. It may have been borderline defensible for the Court to say that advising Jenkins' not testify was a matter of trial strategy and tactics, but there is nothing that justifies outright fraud and deceit. Even in Georgia, such mendacious conduct surely falls outside the range of reasonable professional conduct.

For all of the foregoing reasons, the decision of the Georgia Supreme Court affirming Jenkins' conviction and denying his Motion for a new trial was clearly erroneous and improper. Actually, it was downright outrageous. As some used to say in certain corners of Brooklyn: "Woe be unto the false dispensers of justice, and the tarnished limousines they rode in on."

CHAPTER 8

PETITION TO THE U.S. SUPREME COURT

In 1821, in the well-known case of *Cohen v. Virginia*, 19 U.S. 264, the Supreme Court unanimously ruled that it had the power, under the U.S. Constitution, to review final decisions of state criminal proceedings that allegedly involved misapplication of federal law. This right is now governed by a federal statute that sets forth the Supreme Court's appellate jurisdiction. As that statute provides, "[f]inal judgments on decisions rendered by the highest court of a State . . . may be reviewed by writ of certiorari . . . where any title, right, privilege or immunity is specifically . . . claimed under the Constitution." 28 U.S.C. § 1257.

The good news here is that this statute creates a remedy pursuant to which the Supreme Court can review the validity of state criminal decisions such as the decision of the Georgia Supreme Court upholding the validity of Jenkins' murder conviction. The bad news is that this remedy is almost impossible to obtain because the Supreme Court has complete discretion over whether it will hear a particular case, and that discretion is rarely granted.

The procedure for obtaining Supreme Court review is to file a "petition for certiorari" requesting the Court to accept the case for review. Unfortunately, there are more than 9,000 petitions for certiorari filed with the Supreme Court every year, of which only about one percent (90 cases) are accepted for review.

Obviously, the Supreme Court has limited time in terms of how many cases it can hear each year since, for those few cases that are selected for review, a great deal of work is required to research and decide the issues.

For this reason, the Court is extremely selective in granting petitions for certiorari. Ultimately, and rightfully so, the Court only hears a few cases that it considers to be the most significant in terms of public policy and national importance.

I recognized, of course, that the probability that the Supreme Court would accept Jenkins' case for review was minimal, but I thought I owed it to him to try. As noted previously, his trial had been tainted by numerous constitutional violations that were flagrantly egregious. His case also presented some fairly novel issues of law, such as whether the court's failure to charge corroboration violated due process, whether the "silent witness" testimony as allowed by Georgia law violated the Confrontation Clause of the Sixth Amendment, and whether defense counsels' telling Jenkins that the case was going well when it obviously was not and then refusing the let him testify in his own defense violated his right to effective assistance of counsel under the Sixth Amendment. These are precisely the types of issues the Court is inclined to consider and, therefore, there was some hope that the Court might grant the petition here.

And so, the next step was for me to prepare and file a Petition for Certiorari asking the Supreme Court to accept Jenkins' case for review. I was already a member of the Supreme Court bar, so the unpleasantness that would later tarnish my relationship with Judge Nangle (see the next Chapter) was easily avoided. I am certain, however, that even if it had been necessary for me to apply *pro hac vice* to represent Jenkins in this case, the Supreme Court would have treated me far more favorably and with more respect than Judge Nangle did.

In order to challenge a state court criminal conviction in the Supreme Court, the Petition for Certiorari can only rely on **federal constitutional violations**. Errors occurring at the trial, even serious errors, are irrelevant if they only involve issues of **state** law. For example, the need to corroborate an accomplice's testimony, and the need to instruct the jury regarding the corroboration issue, are requirements of state law and, as such, they do not directly provide a basis for federal review. However, a criminal defendant is entitled to a fair trial as a matter of due process (a federal right) and he is entitled under the Sixth Amendment to have his case decided by a jury that has been properly instructed on all relevant issues. For this reason, what appears to be matters of state law may actually violate federal constitutional rights.

In addition to asserting claims based upon violations of federal constitutional law, it is also important to limit the Petition for Certiorari to only the most significant claims. This is not the time for a "kitchen sink" approach. On the other hand, it is difficult to predict in advance what issues will appeal to the justices (and their clerks) and therefore I was reluctant to leave out any issue that I felt was worthy of review by the Court.

Balancing these important and conflicting considerations, I decided to base Jenkins' Petition for Certiorari on seven grounds. The grounds are stated in the form of questions because the practice rules of the Supreme Court require a concise statement of the "questions presented" for review at the beginning of the Petition. The questions presented here were these:

1. Whether the decision of the Georgia Supreme Court, permitting the prosecutor in a capital murder case to argue to the jury that Petitioner [Jenkins] failed to present evidence to refute the State's case, violated Petitioner's privilege against self-incrimination?

2. Whether the decision of the Georgia Supreme Court, permitting the State to introduce hearsay evidence at Petitioner's murder trial from unidentified "silent witnesses," violated his constitutional right to confront and cross-examine the witnesses against him?

3. Whether the decision of the Georgia Supreme Court, permitting the State to exclude relevant, reliable evidence offered by Petitioner at his trial, deprived him of due process of law in violation of the Fifth and Fourteenth Amendments?

4. Whether the decision of the Georgia Supreme Court, permitting the State to convict Petitioner of malice murder without proof of criminal intent, deprived Petitioner of due process of law?

5. Whether the decision of the Georgia Supreme Court, affirming Petitioner's murder conviction, even though he was wrongfully and unjustifiably advised by his attorneys not to testify at trial violated Petitioner's constitutional right to effective assistance of counsel?

6. Whether the decision of the Georgia Supreme Court, affirming Petitioner's sentence of life imprisonment without possibility of parole, deprived Petitioner of due process of law and violated his right to trial by jury, where the sentencing jury had requested, but was denied access to, information regarding when Petitioner would become eligible for parole?

7. Whether the decision of the Georgia Supreme Court, holding that Georgia law does not permit the court to consider the effect of cumulative errors, deprived Petitioner of due process of law where the cumulative effect of such errors denied Petitioner a fair trial?

The Petition for Certiorari was filed with the Clerk of the Court on January 5, 1998, and docketed by the Clerk as Case No. 97-7617 on January 23, 1998. In addition to the statement of the "Questions Presented" for Review, the Petition contained six pages describing the facts of the case and thirty pages of legal arguments discussing why the writ of certiorari should be granted. I had also previously made an application to the Court to proceed *in forma pauperis*, which was granted without any unnecessary fanfare.

For a Petition for Certiorari to be granted, it is necessary that **four** of the Supreme Court Justices agree to grant the petition. This is a very high bar to meet, considering that it only takes five of the justices to reverse the decision of the court below.

Unfortunately, four of the Supreme Court justices did not agree that Jenkins' Petition should be granted.[116] On March 23, 1998, I was notified by the Clerk of the Court that Jenkins' Petition had been denied.

When the Supreme Court denied Jenkins' Petition for Certiorari, that marked the end of my lengthy efforts to appeal and vacate his wrongful conviction. No further procedural steps were available to directly challenge the conviction. Fortunately, however, federal law provided an additional remedy — the great writ of habeas corpus. Anyone who is wrongfully detained by a State in violation of federal law can challenge that detention by means of a writ of habeas corpus filed in a federal district court. This, then, became the next battle in Jenkins' long war to win back his freedom.

---

116   Deliberations of the Supreme Court regarding whether petitions for certiorari should be granted are not publicly reported, so it is unknown how many, in any, of the Supreme Court Justices would have granted Jenkins' Petition for Certiorari.

CHAPTER 9

MEET FEDERAL JUDGE JOHN NANGLE

John Francis Nangle ("Jack"), a long-time resident of St. Louis, Missouri, was appointed to the federal bench as a district court judge by President Nixon in 1973. He died on August 24, 2008, at the age of 86 in Savannah, Georgia. According to his paid obituary, published in the *Savannah Morning News*, he was an outstanding person, a good Methodist, and a role model to all who knew him. He was also as man of great humor, intellect, and fortitude, dedicated to public service and devoted to his family, his friends, and the sport of tennis.

I never met Jack, never spoke with him on the telephone, but, for reasons that will become obvious as this narrative proceeds, I came to dislike him intensely. I do not like to speak ill of the dead, but, in Jack's case, I will gladly make an exception.

As disappointing as Jenkins' defeat at the hands of the Georgia Supreme Court was — and, believe me, it was extremely disappointing, not just for me but especially for Jamel — there was the comforting thought that, in this great country of ours, there was always the remedy of habeas corpus, at least there was until Congress totally screwed everything up in 1996 with the passage of the Antiterrorism and Effective Death Penalty Act ("AEDPA").[117]

---

[117] Congress first granted federal courts the power to review state court criminal convictions for violations of federal law by means of habeas corpus in 1867. See Act of February 5, 1867, ch. 28, § 1, 14 U.S. Stat. 385, which provided that federal courts "shall have power to grant writs of habeas corpus in all cases where any person may be restrained of his or her liberties in violation of the constitution or of any treaty or law of the United States." This federal habeas corpus statute (now codified as 28 U.S.C. § 2254) has been amended several times in the intervening years, but the jurisdictional grant of authority to the federal district courts to review state court criminal convictions for violations of federal law remains essentially the same.

Lawyers, jurists, legal scholars, and even prisoners draw a distinction between what are called "direct appeals" and "collateral proceedings." A direct appeal is an appeal to a higher court, or higher courts if they are available, based upon errors, or claimed errors, that occurred in the lower court. Such an appeal can only be brought once, and it must be based upon errors that actually appear in the record of the proceeding appealed from. Once the highest appellate court available rules on the matter, it becomes "*res judicata*" (the matter has been judged) and thereafter no additional appeals are permitted.

Although further direct appeals of the original judgment are not permitted, it may be possible, under appropriate circumstances, to challenge the legality of the original judgment by instituting a new collateral proceeding, such as a petition for a writ of habeas corpus, or a writ or error coram nobis, and several others.

The most famous of these collateral proceedings is, of course, habeas corpus, sometimes referred to as the "great writ." There are other grounds for requesting habeas corpus, but the one most frequently relied on is that a person is being held in custody in violation of law.

Petitions for habeas corpus can, at times, be sought in state court, but the usual case, at least when attacking a state court criminal conviction that was upheld on direct appeal, is to institute the habeas proceeding in a federal district court. Essentially, the petitioner is claiming that his confinement in a state prison pursuant to a state court criminal conviction is unlawful because the state court conviction was obtained in violation of his federal rights under the U.S. Constitution. This means, of course, that federal habeas corpus proceedings can only be based on alleged violations of federal constitutional law.

The procedure for bringing a habeas proceeding in federal court, which has become the bane of federal district law clerks everywhere, is straightforward and simple. All that is necessary is to file a written petition with the clerk of the court setting forth the grounds for requesting the writ and certain other background information. It is not necessary that the petition be filed by an attorney, or that the petitioner even be represented by an attorney. On the contrary, most petitions for habeas corpus filed in federal courts are filed by incarcerated inmates based upon assistance they receive from other inmates or the prison library.

It is also not necessary that the petition be typewritten or printed. Many of these petitions are scribbled by prisoners in barely legible handwriting and the obligation sadly falls on the judge's law clerk to decipher as best as possible what the prisoner is claiming. On the other hand, the district court clerk's offices distribute preprinted blank forms that set forth all of the requirements for a petition for habeas, and all the prisoner, or in Jenkins' case, the prisoner's lawyer, needs to do is fill in the blanks.

The one formal requirement that a petition for habeas corpus must satisfy is that the petitioner must sign a declaration certifying under penalty of perjury that the statements contained in the petition are true.

Most petitions for habeas corpus are decided based solely on the pleadings and any related documents that may be filed with the pleadings. If there are any disputed issues of fact raised by the pleadings, an evidentiary hearing may be held, but that is neither usual nor required.

Following the United States Supreme Court's denial of Jenkins' petition for a writ of certiorari to review the lawfulness of the Georgia Supreme Court's decision affirming his conviction, it became necessary and appropriate for me to prepare a petition for habeas corpus on Jenkins' behalf, and I undertook to do so. In addition to the petition for habeas corpus, I also prepared a very lengthy memorandum of law for the district court which explained in great detail the facts of the case, the grounds for the petition, the relevant case law including applicable precedents, and a detailed discussion of why each of the errors alleged in the petition did not constitute harmless error.

Jenkins' Petition for a Writ of Habeas enumerated eighteen separate grounds for granting the petition. Each of these grounds, which will sound very familiar to the reader based upon the prior proceedings, alleged a separate violation of federal constitutional law. These grounds will be discussed in further detail below. The Petition, which did not contain any discussion of relevant case law, was twenty pages long; the Memorandum of Law accompanying the Petition, which did contain a detailed discussion of the applicable case law, was 112 pages long.

On July 11, 1998, I visited with Jamel at Telfair State Prison in Helena, Georgia. I discussed with him at that time the nature of the habeas proceeding, the legal grounds asserted in support of the petition, and the facts alleged in the petition. He reviewed the petition and signed the declaration in my presence.

Several days later, on July 16, 1998, I travelled to Augusta, Georgia, and filed the habeas petition with the Clerk of the Court for the United States District Court of the Southern District of Georgia. In addition to the petition, I also filed the accompanying memorandum of law, and an application to appear as Jenkins' attorney *pro hac vice* and an accompanying affidavit in support of that application.

As a left Georgia and travelled back to New York, I had a certain sense of satisfaction that things would be very different now, and that Jenkins would finally get the justice he deserved. Boy, was I wrong!

Sometime after July 21, 1998, I received a letter from Joseph A. Holwell III, the Deputy Clerk of the Court, informing me that Jenkins' case had been "assigned to the Honorable John B. Nangle, United States District Judge, sitting in Savannah." After looking up Judge Nangle's biography, I thought that this was probably good news because Judge Nangle was not a regular judge in Georgia. He was appointed as a federal district judge in St. Louis, Missouri, where he had served for many years, and he was only serving in Georgia now on special assignment.

In addition to informing me that Judge Nangle had been assigned to the case, Mr. Holwell also stated, "[i]f there is anything in the future that

I may [do to] assist you, please feel free to contact me. It was a pleasure meeting you." That was nice.

I did not hear anything further from the Court for several weeks. That was not unusual, of course, since, as everyone knows, these proceedings take time. I was flabbergasted, however, when I received two separate Orders from Judge Nangle dated August 20, 1998.

In the first Order, Judge Nangle denied my application to appear *pro hac vice* on behalf of Jenkins because Robert Pirkle, Esq, the local Georgia attorney who had worked with me as local counsel on the state court hearing and appeal, had failed to file an affidavit in support of my application.

That was certainly a little petty on Judge Nangle's part. A simple telephone call either to me or to Mr. Pirkle could easily have remedied this minor issue with little difficulty, but Judge Nangle preferred not to do so. Instead, he chose to draft a formal order, send it to me, and possibly deprive Jenkins of my services as an attorney. Apparently, it did not bother the eminent Judge Nangle that he may thereby be imperiling the liberty of a nineteen-year-old African-American male who may have been erroneously sentenced to prison for the rest of his life. I guess that it how things are done in St. Louis, or at least how they were done in 1998, before they discovered that black lives matter.

It was also somewhat disappointing that Mr. Holwell, the Deputy Court Clerk who had sent the very nice letter to me volunteering to do "anything in the future that might assist me," also failed to notify me that Mr. Pirkle had neglected to file his supporting affidavit. A simple "heads up" would have been nice before Judge Nangle took out his pen.

In the second Order, also dated August 20, 1998, Judge Nangle refused the allow the filing of the lengthy Memorandum of Law that I had submitted in support of Jenkins' petition because the memorandum exceeded the 25-page limit specified for such memoranda in the local rules of the Southern District of Georgia. It is true, of course, that the memorandum did exceed the parsimonious page limit of the local rules, and I knew this at the time I wrote it and filed it with the Court. However, I also understood that most judges would allow a lengthy memorandum to be filed even if it exceeded the limit of the local rules, especially since having such a memorandum would be very helpful to the court down the road.

As the reader can probably appreciate by now, this was fairly complicated stuff and complicated stuff takes time to explain, especially when the explanations need to be accompanied by lengthy case citations. Furthermore, the memorandum was not prepared for my benefit, but for the benefit of the Court. It would be extremely helpful to the law clerk who was assigned to research these issues (and possibly to Judge Nangle himself) to know exactly what legal precedents Jenkins was relying upon, and why he believed the harmless error doctrine was inapplicable to each of these issues.

I should also note that, although the memorandum was 112 pages, it could easily have been twice that length. I took great pains to state everything I needed to say as succinctly as possible.

As you can imagine, these two Orders were totally unexpected and extremely disconcerting. It did not give me any warm feelings about Judge Nangle's fairness if he could be so petty as to do what he did here. The bottom line, however, was that neither my appearance as an attorney nor my memorandum of law was in any way essential to Jenkins' petition for habeas corpus. They would be helpful, of course, but not essential. The Court, which is to say Judge Nangle himself, still had the obligation to decide the merits of Jenkins' petition that had been filed.

As this point, I thought my involvement with Jenkins' petition had come to an end. I would still advise him regarding any legal issues that might arise, of course, but I would no longer appear as his counsel of record.

To my great surprise, I subsequently received another Order from Judge Nangle which was even more disconcerting. This one, dated November 2, 1998, required Jenkins to "resubmit" his brief in compliance with the local rule within ten days, or his petition would be summarily dismissed. As Judge Nangle stated in this Order:

> "IT IS HEREBY ORDERED that **plaintiff** resubmit his brief in accordance with Local Rule 7.1 no later than ten (10) days from the date of this Order. Failure to comply will result is the dismissal of this **action** for want of prosecution pursuant to Local Rule 41.1(b)." (Emphasis added).

There were so many things wrong with this Order that I do not know where to begin. First, why was Judge Nangle sending this order to me? He previously denied my application to appear as Jenkins' attorney and, therefore, I could not file a revised memorandum even if I wanted to. He should have sent the Order directly to Jenkins who at this time was required to appear **pro se** due to Judge Nangle's prior order barring me from representing him.

Second, as previously noted, there is no legal requirement for a petitioner to file a memorandum of law in support of his (or her) petition for habeas corpus and, therefore, Judge Nangle had no plausible basis for requiring one here. And if one were to be written, who would write it: Jenkins, who had no legal training of any kind, or me, the lawyer who was not authorized to practice law before the Court?

Third, there was absolutely no legal basis for Judge Nangle to threaten to dismiss the petition for failure to file a memorandum. For a Judge who purported to be a stickler for following rules, he should have known that no rule of any kind existed that required the filing of a memorandum. Indeed, very few petitions for habeas corpus are ever accompanied by memoranda of law, and it would certainly have set a novel legal theory if such petitions could be dismissed summarily for failure to file a memorandum.

Fourth, Judge Nangle addressed his Order to the "plaintiff" and referred to the proceeding as an "action." By this time Judge Nangle had been serving as a federal district court judge for twenty-three years. He certainly should have known that a person who seeks a writ of habeas corpus is a "petitioner" not a "plaintiff" and the proceeding is a "special proceeding" not an "action."

It is painful to be so critical of Judge Nangle, but remember, this is the person who would ultimately decide, in his sole discretion, whether Jenkins would spend the rest of his life in prison. If he could not compose a simple one-paragraph order without making four major errors, how could he possibly rule on the complicated issues that were presented by Jenkins' petition? I was becoming extremely worried.

Although I knew that Jenkins had no legal obligation to "resubmit" the brief and that Judge Nangle had no legal authority to dismiss his petition for failure to do so, I thought at this point that discretion was the better part of valor, particularly in light of Judge Nangle's unexpected and misguided combativeness. Accordingly, I took the 112 page memorandum, gutted it to the bone, signed Jenkins' name as "Petitioner *Pro Se*," and sent a copy off to Augusta.

Two weeks later I got another Order from Judge Nangle, who apparently still did not realize that I was not authorized to represent Jenkins in this proceeding. In this Order, dated November 13, 1998, Judge Nangle did what he should have done in the first place. He ordered the Attorney General of the State of Georgia "to show cause why the relief requested [in the petition] should not be granted" and "to file all necessary documents, including the state trial transcript and the briefs in all prior appeals." Finally, Judge Nangle's ego had been satisfied, and the matter would proceed.

Before moving on to discuss the merits of the petition, I should briefly note here that Judge Nangle's boorish conduct regarding the filing of the memorandum and the application to appear *pro hac vice* was not the worst of Judge Nangle's behavior. Unfortunately, much more will need to be said about that later.

CHAPTER 10

PETITION FOR A WRIT OF HABEAS CORPUS

Following Judge Nangle's November 13, 1998 Order, the Attorney General of the State of Georgia filed its papers in opposition to Jenkins' Petition for a writ of habeas corpus. Two years later, on June 21, 2000, Judge Nangle finally issued a 57-page Order and Decision denying the Petition in its entirety. The reasoning of that decision, which was reported in the Federal Supplement Reporter, Series 2, beginning at 103 F. Supp. 2d 1350, will be discussed in detail below.

First, however, it is interesting to note that, throughout his 57-page decision, Judge Nangle made frequent and continuous references to the 112-page memorandum of law that he ordered ***not be filed*** due to its non-compliance with the Court's local rules. No mention was ever made by Judge Nangle of the redacted 25-page memorandum that he had ordered to be filed. It would appear, therefore, that, in the end, Judge Nangle finally recognized that his initial opposition to the memorandum I had prepared was ill advised.

It is not at all clear to me, however, how Judge Nangle could possibly have justified this turnabout to himself. In the end, he relied heavily upon an ***unfiled*** memorandum of law written by a ***person not authorized to practice law*** in the Southern District of Georgia to determine the fate of an inmate who was serving life in prison who was ***representing himself pro se***. There must be some local rule somewhere in the Southern District of Georgia that prohibits this.

The eighteen grounds that Jenkins asserted in his Petition for a writ of habeas corpus are set forth in summary form below:

1. Jenkins' state court conviction was obtained in violation of his Fifth Amendment privilege against self-incrimination due to improper comments made by Mr. Cheney during his closing argument to the jury.

2. Jenkins' state court conviction was obtained in violation of his Sixth Amendment right to confront and cross-examine the witnesses against him.

3. Jenkins' state court conviction was obtained in violation of due process of law because Judge Harvey's jury instructions regarding the issues of malice murder, parties to a crime, and conspiracy were constitutionally defective and relieved the State of its burden of proof.

4. Jenkins' state court conviction was obtained in violation of due process of law, equal protection of law and Jenkins' Sixth Amendment right to trial by jury because Judge Harvey failed to submit the issue of the sufficiency of the corroboration evidence to the jury for its determination.

5. Jenkins' state court conviction of malice murder was obtained in violation of due process of law because the proof submitted at trial was insufficient to convict him of that crime.

6. Jenkins' state court conviction was obtained in violation of due process of law because Judge Harvey improperly excluded relevant, reliable evidence offered by the petitioner during the guilt phase of the trial.

7. Jenkins' state court conviction was obtained in violation of due process of law because the testimony of three prosecution witnesses was known by the State to be false and misleading, yet the prosecutor did nothing to correct the record.

8. Jenkins' state court conviction was obtained in violation of due process of law because the State failed to provide Jenkins' attorneys with exculpatory *Brady* material.

9. Jenkins' state court conviction was obtained in violation of due process of law and his Sixth Amendment right to confront and cross-examine witnesses who testified against him due to the admission of hearsay evidence during the testimony of Investigator Gray.

10. Jenkins' state court conviction was obtained in violation of due process of law and his Sixth Amendment right to confront and cross-examine witnesses who testified against him due to the admission of hearsay statements made by alleged co-conspirators.

11. Jenkins' state court conviction was obtained in violation of due process of law and his Sixth Amendment right to trial by jury due to Judge Harvey's failure to instruct the jury that the testimony of a co-conspirator regarding the existence of a conspiracy needed to be corroborated.

12. Jenkins' state court conviction was obtained in violation of due process of law and his Fifth Amendment privilege against self-incrimination due to the admission of an involuntary confession.

13. Jenkins' state court conviction was obtained in violation of his Sixth Amendment right to receive effective assistance of counsel.

14. Jenkins' state court conviction was obtained in violation of due process of law because Judge Harvey improperly denied his motion for a change of venue.

15. Jenkins' sentence of life imprisonment without possibility of parole violated due process of law and his Sixth Amendment right to trial by jury because Judge Harvey refused to answer the jury's question regarding when Jenkins would become eligible for parole if they sentenced him to life imprisonment with a possibility of parole.

16. Jenkins' sentence of life imprisonment without possibility of parole violated due process of law because Judge Harvey

improperly excluded mitigation evidence offered by Jenkins during the penalty phase of the trial.

17. Jenkins' sentence of life imprisonment without possibility of parole violated due process of law because Section 17-10-31.3 of the Georgia Code, the Georgia statute which permits a jury to impose a sentence of life without possibility of parole, is unconstitutional.

18. Jenkins' state court conviction and sentence were obtained in violation of due process of law because the Georgia state courts refused to consider the cumulative effect of multiple errors committed during his trial.

Each of these grounds in support of Jenkins' Petition for a writ of habeas corpus was rejected by Judge Nangle. The reasons for his decision are discussed in detail below.

1. *Improper Comments Made by the Prosecutor Regarding Jenkins' Failure to Testify at the Trial (Ground 1)*

Judge Nangle recognized that "[t]he Supreme Court has clearly established that the prosecutor in a criminal case cannot comment on the accused's silence at trial and cannot ask the jury to draw adverse inferences from that silence." 103 F. Supp.2d at 1361. Judge Nangle also recognized that the Eleventh Circuit Court of Appeals "has held that prosecutorial statements are improper if they are 'manifestly intended' as a comment on the defendant's silence or if they 'would naturally and necessarily be understood by the jury' as a comment on his silence."[118] *Id*.

Notwithstanding his explicit recognition that this constitutional requirement was **clearly established by the Supreme Court**, Judge Nangle erroneously rejected Jenkins' argument that the comments made by the

---

118 Since the Southern District of Georgia is located within the Eleventh Circuit, decisions by that Court constitute binding precedent on the district court.

prosecutor here were improper and violated his Fifth Amendment privilege against self-incrimination.[119] As Judge Nangle stated in his decision:

> "[Jenkins] cites numerous circuit cases holding that the prosecutor may not comment on a defendant's failure to call witnesses if the only potential witness was the defendant himself" [citing four Court of Appeals cases cited by me in the 112-page memorandum that Judge Nangle previously rejected]. However, this legal rule has never been clearly established by the United States Supreme Court. Thus, under *Williams*, this rule of law cannot be the basis for habeas relief. *Williams*, 120 S. Ct. at 1523. Consequently, [Jenkins] has failed to show that the prosecutor's comments violated his Fifth Amendment rights to remain silent." 103 F. Supp.2d at 1361.

There were two fundamental flaws in this analysis. First, Jenkins' claim that the prosecutor's comments were improper was not based primarily or exclusively on the notion that Jenkins was the only potential witness who could have testified on his behalf. On the contrary, Jenkins' claim was based entirely on the Supreme Court's clearly established decision in *Griffin v. California* that the prosecutor in a criminal case is not permitted to comment on the accused's silence at trial and cannot ask the jury to draw adverse inferences from that silence. Judge Nangle, who explicitly recognized the correctness of this rule, nonetheless failed to follow this clear rule by creating a false "strawman" argument to avoid the consequences of the Supreme Court's clearly established precedent.

The second flaw in Judge Nangle's analysis was that it was based upon an erroneous interpretation of Section 2254(d)(1) of the Antiterrorism and Effective death Penalty Act of 1996 ("AEDPA"). Section 2254(d)(1) created a new standard of review to be applied by federal courts when reviewing state court criminal convictions under the federal habeas statute. That new standard provided that "[a]n application for a writ of habeas corpus . . . shall

---

119   The four improper comments made by the prosecutor are explicitly set forth in Chapter 5.

not be granted with respect to any claim that was adjudicated on the merits in State court proceedings unless the adjudication of the claim . . . resulted in a decision that was contrary to, or involved an unreasonable application of, clearly established Federal law, **as determined by the Supreme Court of the United States**." 28 U.S.C. § 2254 (emphasis added).

The key question here is what exactly is meant by the phrase "clearly established Federal law, as determined by the Supreme Court" or, more correctly stated, how has that phrase been interpreted by the Supreme Court. As interpreted and applied by Judge Nangle, there must exist a specific Supreme Court decision that is factually and legally identical to the case being brought by the petitioner. That would create an almost insurmountable burden to overcome because very few cases are actually decided by the Supreme Court. Fortunately, however, that is not the requirement. As the Supreme Court itself made clear in *Williams v. Taylor*, 529 U.S. 362 (2000), it is only necessary that the Supreme Court "has . . . **broken sufficient legal ground to establish an asked-for constitutional principle**." 529 U.S. at 381 (emphasis added). It is not necessary, therefore, that there be a Supreme Court decision that is directly identical to the claim being made by the petitioner.

Thus, if the Supreme Court "has not broken sufficient ground to establish an asked-for constitutional principle" then "the lower federal courts cannot themselves establish such a principle with clarity sufficient to satisfy the AEDPA bar." *Williams*, 529 U.S. at 381. However, if the Supreme Court **has** broken sufficient ground to establish a constitutional principle, then the decisions of the lower federal courts are relevant and may be cited for the purpose of defining the parameters of the core constitutional principle. As the Supreme Court stated in *Williams* (quoting from Justice O'Connor's concurring opinion in *Wright v. West*, 505 U.S. 277 (1992), an earlier pre-AEDPA decision):

> "[T]he maxim that federal courts should 'give great weight to the considered conclusions of a coequal state

judiciary' . . . does not mean that we have held in the past that federal courts must presume the correctness of a state court's legal conclusions on habeas, or that a state court's incorrect legal determination has ever been allowed to stand because it was reasonable. We have always held that federal courts, even on habeas, **have an independent obligation to say what the law is**.' 505 U.S. at 305 (opinion concurring in judgment). We are convinced that in the phrase, 'clearly established law,' Congress did not intend to modify that independent obligation." 529 U.S. at 383-84 (emphasis added).

In reaching its decision on how the new AEDPA requirement should be interpreted, the Supreme Court in *Williams* reached all the way back to *Marbury v. Madison*, 1 Cranch 137, 177 (1803), the landmark case that established judicial review in the first place. As Justice Stevens stated in the Court's majority opinion:

> "The inquiry mandated by the amendment relates to the way in which a federal habeas court exercises its duty to decide constitutional questions; the amendment does not alter the underlying grant of jurisdiction in § 2254(a). When federal judges exercise their federal question jurisdiction under the 'judicial Power' of Article III of the Constitution, it is 'emphatically the province and duty" of these judges to 'say what the law is.' *Marbury v. Madison*, 1 Cranch 137, 177 (1803). At the core of this power is the federal courts' independent responsibility — independent from its coequal branches in the Federal Government, and independent from the separate authority of the several States — to interpret federal law. A construction of AEDPA that would require the federal courts to cede this authority to the courts of the States would be inconsistent with the practice that federal judges have

traditionally followed in discharging their duties under Article III of the Constitution. If Congress had intended to require such an important change in the exercise of our jurisdiction, we believe it would have spoken with much greater clarity than is found in the text of AEDPA." 529 U.S. at 378-79.

In Jenkins' case, it was patently clear that the Supreme Court had firmly established the core constitutional principle at issue, namely, that it is a violation of a criminal defendant's Fifth Amendment privilege against self-incrimination for the prosecutor to comment on the defendant's failure to testify at trial. There was no justification, therefore, for Judge Nangle to refuse to consider this issue.

Furthermore, there was absolutely no justification for Judge Nangle to artificially narrow the issue to situations where "the only potential witness who could testify" was the defendant himself and then argue that this particular situation had never been addressed by the Supreme Court. This was pure sophistry and unworthy of a federal district judge. The Supreme Court's jurisprudence on the issue was clear and straightforward, and it should have been followed. The prosecutor's comments were clearly improper, and Jenkins' conviction should have been reversed.

Finally, there was no tenable reason for Judge Nangle to ignore the "numerous circuit court cases [cited in Jenkins' Memorandum] holding that the prosecutor may not comment on a defendant's failure to call witnesses if the only potential witness was the defendant himself" (see 103 F. Supp.2d at 1361) on the theory that, "this legal rule has never been clearly established by the United States Supreme Court. *Id*. On the contrary, the Supreme Court had clearly "broken sufficient legal ground to establish this asked-for constitutional principle" in such cases as *United States v. Robinson*, 485 U.S. 25 (1988) and *Griffin v. California*, 380 U.S. 609 (1965), cases which Judge Nangle himself cited in his Decision (see 103 F. Supp.2d at 1361). It was clearly improper, therefore, for Judge Nangle to refuse to follow the circuit cases here.

2. *Improper Admission of the "Silent Witness" Testimony (Ground 2)*

Jenkins complained that the admission of "silent witness" hearsay during the testimony of investigator Jim Gray violated his Sixth Amendment right to confront and cross-examine the witnesses against him. Judge Nangle clearly understood what Jenkins was complaining about, as shown from the following quote from his Decision:

> "Petitioner asserts that the trial court violated his Sixth Amendment right of confrontation by allowing Investigator Gray to testify as to hearsay from silent witnesses. **Gray testified that he received information from unidentified silent witnesses which caused him to believe petitioner was involved in the robbery and murder of Mr. Hodges.** Petitioner admits that the content of the statements made by the silent witnesses was never revealed to the jury but asserts that Gray's testimony was "'tantamount to a hearsay statement by these witnesses that petitioner was one of the perpetrators." 103 F. Supp.2d at 1361-62 (emphasis added).

Judge Nangle recognized that the Supreme Court has clearly established that the admission of hearsay statements *may* violate the Confrontation Clause of the Sixth Amendment, although he also noted (correctly) that "[t]he Supreme Court has clearly established that the Confrontation Clause **does not necessarily** prohibit the admission of hearsay statements against a criminal defendant." 103 F.Supp.2d at 1362 (emphasis added).

Judge Nangle also explicitly recognized that prior decisions of both the Eleventh and the Fifth Circuit U.S. Courts of Appeals (which are controlling precedents for the Southern District Court of Georgia) had clearly established that the admission of silent witness statements made to an investigating officer concerning the defendant's involvement in the crime at issue violated the Confrontation Clause.[120] As he stated in his Decision:

> "The Eleventh Circuit and the former Fifth Circuit have held that statements by an officer concerning information received during his investigation which amounts to substantive evidence of a defendant's guilt violates the Confrontation Clause. *Harris v. Wainright*, 760 F.2d 1148, 1151 (11th Cir. 1985) ('The district court correctly saw the issue as whether [the officer's] recital that he obtained information . . . was substantive evidence of petitioner's guilt, both because it bolstered [the identification testimony of other witnesses] and, . . . tended to connect defendant with the crime.'); *Hutchins v. Wainwright*, 715 F.2d 512, 515 (11th Cir. 1983) (holding that reference to the statements of an unidentified eyewitness who implicated petitioner in the crime is inadmissible under the Constitution); *Favre v. Henderson,* 464 F.2d 359, 362 (5th Cir. 1972) (holding that testimony of officer as to statements by confidential informers implicating petitioner in the crime is inadmissible hearsay)." 103 F. Supp.2d at 1362.

Rather than follow these clear and controlling precedents, Judge Nangle questioned the validity of Jenkins' claim by suggesting that it was not supported by clearly established federal law as established **by the Supreme Court**. As he stated in his Decision:

> "The Supreme Court has not, however, addressed the issue of whether statements from an officer that information received from unidentified witnesses, without stating

---

120   Since the Eleventh Circuit was previously part of the Fifth Circuit, decisions of the Fifth Circuit that were issued prior to the circuit split constitute binding precedent on the courts of the Eleventh Circuit, including the Southern District of Georgia.

the content of the information, are tantamount to hearsay." 103 F. Supp.2d at 1362.

Judge Nangle then engaged in a misguided factual analysis of the record to determine which of the statements that were made by Investigator Gray, based upon the hearsay statements he had received from the silent witnesses, actually implicated Jenkins. Based upon this analysis, he then concluded that, although some of the silent witness testimony implicated other co-conspirators (such as Cedric), the only silent witness testimony that implicated Jenkins were statements made to Investigator Gray by Terry Roberts. Judge Nangle then concluded that the admission of these hearsay statements was permissible under Georgia law because Roberts had testified at trial and was subject to cross-examination. As he stated in his decision.

> "The testimony which tended to implicate petitioner was testimony concerning statements made by Terry Roberts, a co-conspirator who testified at trial. Admission of hearsay statements by persons who later testify at trial does not violate the Confrontation Clause under the rationale of *Ohio v. Roberts*, 448 U.S. 56 (1987) and *California v. Green*, 399 U.S. 149 (1970)." 103 F. Supp.2d at 1362-64.

This analysis was incorrect. First, Judge Nangle completely disregarded the controlling decisions of the Eleventh and Fifth Circuit Courts of Appeals (noted above) which directly held that the admission of "silent witness" testimony from investigating officers is improper and violates the Confrontation Clause.

Second, even if the only statements made to Investigator Gray that implicated Jenkins were made by Roberts (and this was not nearly so clear as Judge Nangle suggested), it was still improper to admit them regardless of whether Roberts himself testified. This was so for three separate reasons. First, admission of Roberts' statements indirectly through the testimony of Investigator Gray constituted improper and impermissible **bolstering** of

Roberts' testimony. This is not permitted under the rules of evidence. As the Eleventh Circuit explained in *Harris v. Wainright*, 760 F.2d 1148, 1151 (11th Cir. 1985), "the district court correctly saw the issue as whether [the officer's] recital that he obtained information . . . was substantive evidence of petitioner's guilt, both because it bolstered [the identification testimony of other witnesses] and, . . . tended to connect defendant with the crime."

A second reason why the statements made to Investigator Gray by Roberts were inadmissible was because they constituted hearsay regardless of whether Roberts testified, and there was no exception to the hearsay rule that would justify their admission.

The third reason why Judge Nangle's analysis was faulty was because, even assuming that Judge Nangle correctly concluded that Investigator Gray's testimony was based solely on the testimony of Terry Roberts, the jury had no way of knowing this. What Investigator Gray stated, and what the jury heard, was that Gray spoke with **several** unidentified silent witnesses and that, based upon these conversations, he was able to determine that Jenkins was one of the participants in the murder and robbery of Mr. Hodges. Any way you slice it, this was impermissible hearsay that clearly violated Jenkins' fundamental right of confrontation.

Finally, as the Supreme Court clearly stated in *Idaho v. Wright*, a case that was decided after both *Ohio v. Roberts* and *California v. Green* (the two cases which Judge Nangle cited in his Decision), "[t]o be admissible under the Confrontation Clause, hearsay evidence used to convict a defendant must possess indicia of reliability **by virtue of its inherent trustworthiness**, not by reference to other evidence at the trial." 497 U.S. at 822 (emphasis added). There was no indication here that the hearsay statements made to Investigator Gray by Terry Roberts (or anyone else) were "inherently trustworthy" and no effort was made by Judge Nangle to justify why they should be admissible. This, of course, would be extremely difficult to do since Roberts had already admitted during his testimony at trial that he had lied to the police (including Investigator Gray) several times to protect himself and his brother Maurice.

For all of the forgoing reasons, Jenkins' objection to the "silent witness" hearsay testimony admitted during the testimony of Investigator Gray should have been sustained, and his conviction should have been reversed.

3. *Judge Harvey's Improper Jury Instructions Regarding Malice Murder, Parties to a Crime, and Conspiracy (Ground 3)*

Jenkins argued that Judge Harvey's instructions to the jury regarding the issues of malice murder, "parties to a crime," and conspiracy were improper because they relieved the State of its burden of proving that Jenkins intended to kill Mr. Hodges. Proof of intent to kill is a required element of the crime of malice murder, and the State had the burden of proving this element beyond a reasonable doubt. Judge Nangle clearly understood the nature of Jenkins' argument. As he stated in his Decision:

> "Petitioner asserts that the trial court violated his Fourteenth Amendment right to due process of law by issuing jury instructions on malice murder, parties to a crime and conspiracy which effectively relieved the State of its burden of proof on the essential elements of the offense. Petitioner asserts that the malice murder charge relieved the State of its burden on the element of intent to kill, as opposed to simply finding malice, and because it failed to require the jury to find the petitioner himself had the intent to kill. Petitioner also alleges that the parties to a crime charge relieved the State of its burden of proof by failing to explain that petitioner could only be convicted of malice murder under the party to a crime theory if the jury found beyond a reasonable doubt that petitioner was a party to the crime of malice murder. Further, the charge allegedly failed to require that petitioner personally intended that the victim be killed. Finally, petitioner

alleges that the conspiracy charge relieved the State of its burden of proof because it failed to explain how the conspiracy charge applied to the malice murder count." 103 F. Supp.2d at 1363-64.

Notably, Judge Nangle accurately summarized Jenkins' claims on this issue. It was notable also that Judge Nangle apparently agreed that, if Jenkins' claims were correct, then this would constitute a violation of clearly established federal law for purposes of the federal habeas statute. As Judge Nangle stated in his Decision:

> "The Supreme Court has clearly established that the Fourteenth Amendment 'prohibits the State from using evidentiary presumptions in a jury charge that have the effect of relieving the State of its burden of persuasion beyond a reasonable doubt of every essential element of a crime.'" 103 F. Supp.2d at 1364 (quoting from *Francis v. Franklin*, 471 U.S. 307, 311 (1985)).

What Judge Nangle did not agree with, however, was that Judge Harvey's instructions were as bad as Jenkins had claimed. According to Judge Nangle, the instructions, ***"when read in context,"*** (103 F. Supp.2d at 1365) (emphasis added), were okay. Apparently, the context that Judge Nangle was talking about was his 25 years of experience as a trial judge. The jury, on the other hand, only heard Judge Harvey's instructions orally for about 45 minutes.[121] They were evidently confused by the instructions and asked for clarification, but Judge Harvey merely repeated what he had previously told them. Tr. 2013-15.[122]

---

121 It never ceases to amaze me that we expect a jury composed of twelve ordinary citizens to apply complex legal principles after receiving a brief oral "instruction" from the trial judge. It took me three years of law school and many years of practice to comprehend what we expect the jury to master in an hour. And, don't forget, a person's life and liberty is hanging in the balance.

122 As Judge Harvey stated during the trial, "Mr. Foreman and members of the jury, it's my understanding that the jury would like the Court to re-instruct the jury on the definitions of both malice murder and felony murder. Is that correct? JURY FOREMAN: Yes, sir, Your Honor." Tr. 2013. Ironically, after repeating his prior instructions, Judge Harvey admitted on the record, "And once your request for the instructions were sent out to the Bailiff, I looked up the law to make sure." Tr. 2015. Not very comforting.

When a trial court fails to instruct the jury properly regarding any required element of a crime, or when the effect of the instruction relieves the State of its burden of proof on any required element, the defendant is denied due process. *See, e.g., Francis v. Franklin*, 471 U.S. 307 (1985); *Sandstrom v. Montana*, 442 U.S. 510 (1979); *Henderson v. Kibbe*, 431 U.S. 145 (1977); *Hall v. Kelso*, 892 F.2d 1541 (11th Cir. 1990); *Stephens v. Kemp*, 846 F.2d 642 (11th Cir. 1988), *cert. denied*, 488 U.S. 872 (1988); *Parks v. State*, 254 Ga. 403, 330 S.E.2d 686 (1985). As the U.S. Supreme Court stated in *Patterson v. New York*, 432 U.S. 197, 215 (1977):

> "[A] State must prove every ingredient of an offense beyond a reasonable doubt, and ... may not shift the burden to the defendant by presuming that ingredient upon proof of the other elements of the offense."

This is true even when the element in question is one of intent. *See, e.g., Francis v. Franklin*, 471 U.S. 307 (1985); *Sandstrom v. Montana*, 442 U.S. 510 (1979). As the U.S. Supreme Court held in *Mullaney v. Wilbur*, 421 U.S. 684, 702 (1975):

> "[A]lthough intent is typically considered a fact peculiarly within the knowledge of the defendant, this does not ... justify shifting the burden to him."

The Supreme Court explicitly ruled in *Mullaney* that a state statute which required defendant to prove "heat of passion" by a preponderance of the evidence in order to reduce a murder charge to manslaughter was unconstitutional.

In the present case, Judge Harvey's instructions regarding the issues of malice murder, parties to a crime, and conspiracy violated these federal constitutional principles because they failed to explain to the jury that, in order to find Jenkins guilty of malice murder, the State had to prove, beyond a reasonable doubt, that Jenkins himself personally intended that Mr. Hodges be killed. These misleading instructions were highly prejudicial and required that Jenkins' conviction be vacated, and a new trial granted.

Judge Harvey instructed the jury on the issue of malice murder as follows:

> "A person commits murder when he unlawfully and with malice aforethought, either express or implied, causes the death of another human being.
>
> Express malice is that deliberate intention unlawfully to take away the life of a fellow creature, which is manifested by external circumstances capable of proof.
>
> Malice may be implied where no considerable provocation appears and where all the circumstances of the killing show an abandoned and malignant heart.
>
> It will be for you, members of the jury, to decide whether or not the facts and circumstances of this case show malice.
>
> It will be noted in the definition of murder with malice aforethought, either express or implied, as the Code section defines it, it is an essential ingredient and element of the offense of murder [sic].[123] The burden is on the State of Georgia to show malice under these rules beyond a reasonable doubt.
>
> Now, legal malice is not ill will or hatred. It is the unlawful intent to kill or take the life of a human being without any justification or excuse. It must exist at the time of the killing. It is not necessary for the unlawful intent to take the life of a fellow creature to exist for any length of time before the killing. In our law a person may

---

123   This is quoted exactly as reported on page 1984 of the official trial transcript. It appears clear to me, however, that at least one or more words are missing from this sentence, although I have no idea what they were. Curiously, when Judge Nangle repeated the instruction at the jury's request, the instruction was given exactly the same way (see Tr. 2014).

form the intent to kill, do the killing instantly and regret the deed as soon as it is done." (Tr. 1984-85).[124]

The standard which must be applied to determine whether this instruction violated due process is to look at "the way in which a reasonable juror could have interpreted the [challenged] instruction." *Sandstrom v. Montana*, 442 U.S. at 514; *Francis v. Franklin*, 471 U.S. at 315. Accord, *Parks v. State*, 254 Ga. 403, 330 S.E.2d 686 (1985); *Johnson v. State*, 249 Ga. 621, 292 S.E.2d 696 (1982).

Judge Harvey's instruction on malice murder was erroneous as applied to the facts of this case for two separate reasons. First, it failed to make clear to the jury that they had to find **intent to kill** as a necessary element of the offense, as opposed to simply finding malice. As noted previously, both intent to kill and malice are essential elements of the crime of malice murder under Georgia law and both elements must be proved beyond a reasonable doubt by the state. *See e.g.*, *Francis v. Franklin*, 471 U.S. 307, 320 (1985); *Stephens v. Kemp*, 846 F.2d 642 (11th Cir. 1988), *cert. denied*, 488 U.S. 872 (1988); *Lamb v. Jernigan*, 683 F.2d 1332 (11th Cir. 1982), *cert. denied*, 460 U.S. 1024 (1983); *Lattimore v. State*, 265 Ga. 102, 454 S.E.2d 474 (1995); *Parks v. State*, 254 Ga. 403, 330 S.E.2d 686 (1985). Based upon the instruction as given, a reasonable juror may have believed it was sufficient to convict Jenkins of malice murder based solely upon a finding that he had "an abandoned and malignant heart." Furthermore, a reasonable juror may have also concluded that Jenkins had "an abandoned and malignant heart" based solely upon the fact that he participated in the robbery. The net effect of Judge Harvey's instruction, therefore, was that the jury may have believed it was sufficient to find Jenkins guilty of malice murder simply because he participated in the robbery.[125] This was plain

---

[124] After beginning its deliberations, the jury requested further instructions from the court on malice murder. In response to this request, Judge Harvey merely repeated the instruction given above. Tr. 2014-15.

[125] Proof of Jenkins' participation in the robbery may have justified a conviction for *felony* murder. However, as noted above, the State chose to prosecute Jenkins for *intentional* murder, and therefore it had the obligation to prove beyond a reasonable doubt all of the elements of that offense. Even if Jenkins participated in the robbery, therefore, that fact alone would not be sufficient to find him guilty of malice murder.

error, since it relieved the State of its burden of proof on the issue of intent to kill, one of the essential elements of the offense of malice murder.

A second flaw in Judge Harvey's instruction on malice murder was that it failed to make clear to the jury that the State had to prove, and the jury had to find, beyond a reasonable doubt, that Jenkins **personally** acted with the intent necessary to commit malice murder, *i.e.*, that he personally intended that Mr. Hodges be killed. Based upon the instruction as given, a juror may have reasonably believed that it was sufficient to convict Jenkins of malice murder based solely upon the fact that any one of the other alleged participants (Cedric, for example) intended to kill Mr. Hodges. For this reason also, Judge Harvey's charge erroneously relieved the State of its burden of proof on the issue of intent to kill, one of the essential elements of the offense of malice murder.

Judge Harvey's failure to explain to the jury that it was necessary that they find that Jenkins **personally** acted with the intent necessary to commit malice murder was highly prejudicial and denied defendant due process. Furthermore, for the reasons discussed in Points 13 and 14 *infra*, the effect of this error was compounded and exacerbated by the erroneous instructions which Judge Harvey gave on the issues of parties to a crime and conspiracy.

4.   *Sufficiency of the Corroboration Evidence and Failure to Instruct the Jury that Accomplice Testimony Needed to be Corroborated (Grounds 4 and 11)*

Judge Nangle explicitly recognized that Jenkins "alleges in ground four that the trial court violated petitioner's Sixth and Fourteenth Amendment rights by failing to submit the issue of the sufficiency of the corroboration evidence to the jury." 103 F. Supp.2d at 1367. Judge Nangle also explicitly recognized that Jenkins "further alleges in ground eleven that the trial court violated his Sixth Amendment rights by failing to charge the jury that accomplice testimony must be corroborated." *Id*. Finally, Judge Nangle also explicitly recognized that "Georgia law provides that a person may not be convicted of a felony based solely upon the uncorroborated testimony of an accomplice" and that "[t]he sufficiency of the corroboration testimony is a matter which must be determined by the jury." *Id.*

Notwithstanding all of these correct observations, Judge Nangle nevertheless refused to vacate Jenkins' conviction based upon the State's failure to comply with the corroboration requirement here. Why did this happen? It happened because Judge Nangle improperly gave undue deference to the erroneous decision of the Georgia Supreme Court regarding *state law* and thereby failed to apply his own independent judgment as to what was required by *federal constitutional law*.

This is admittedly a nuanced argument, so please follow carefully. The requirement of corroboration of accomplice testimony is solely a requirement of *state* law. If a state were to eliminate the corroboration requirement completely, that would not violate federal law (assuming the elimination did not involve some other federally protected right such as equal protection of the law). However, once a State creates a substantive right (such as the right to corroboration of an accomplice's testimony), then the enforcement of that right becomes a matter of due process of law, which is a federal right protected by the Fifth and Fourteenth Amendments. Judge Nangle clearly recognized this was so, since, as he stated in his decision, "[t]he Supreme Court has clearly established a constitutional right to have all factual issues necessary for a determination of guilt determined by a jury." 103 F. Supp.2d at 1367.

Where Judge Nangle erred, however, was in blindly following the decision of the Georgia Supreme Court without critically examining whether that decision violated *federal* law. As he stated in his decision:

> "Under Georgia law, the sufficiency of corroboration evidence would be such a factual issue [*i.e.*, one that triggers federal constitutional guarantees] if the State relies solely on the testimony of a single accomplice. The Georgia Supreme Court found that the State did not rely solely on

Terry Roberts' testimony in this case but also relied on defendant's statements admitting his participation in the crime. *Jenkins*, 491 S.E2d at 59. Petitioner asserts that this finding was erroneous **because the statements standing alone were not sufficient to establish petitioner's guilt**. Mem. Supp. Pet. Habeas Corpus at 46 (emphasis added). The Georgia Supreme Court, however, determined that these statements were sufficient under Georgia law to trigger the rule of *Hall v. State*. It is not the province of this Court to reexamine state-court determinations of state-law questions. Accordingly, the Court must defer to the state court's interpretation of state law. Because the State relied on evidence other than the accomplice's testimony, the trial court was not required to submit the sufficiency of the corroboration evidence to the jury and was therefore not required to charge the jury on corroboration." 103 F. Supp.2d at 1367.

In effect, therefore, Judge Nangle ruled that he was obligated to defer to the decision of the Georgia Supreme Court even if doing so meant that Jenkins could be convicted of murder based upon evidence which "standing alone w[as] not sufficient to establish petitioner's guilt." Obviously, that is not a correct application of ***federal*** law.

It should be noted here that in every case in which a federal district court has granted a writ of habeas corpus reversing a state court criminal conviction — and there are myriads of such cases — the conviction was undoubtedly previously upheld by the state's Supreme Court. If the standard of review in federal habeas cases required the level of deference suggested by Judge Nangle here, then few, if any, of these writs would have been granted. Judge Nangle was so focused on the right of the Georgia

Supreme Court to delineate the limits of Georgia law, that he failed to recognize that what the Georgia Supreme Court did violated federal law.[126]

5. *Sufficiency of the Evidence on the Issue of Malice Murder (Ground 5)*

Jenkins claimed that the evidence admitted at his trial was insufficient to permit the jury to find him guilty of malice murder. Judge Nangle conceded that "[t]he Supreme Court has clearly established that due process requires that no person shall [be] convicted except upon sufficient proof — defined as evidence necessary to convince a trier of fact beyond a reasonable doubt of the existence of every element of the offense." 103 F. Supp.2d at 1367 (citing *Jackson v. Virginia*, 443 U.S. 307, 316 (1979).

Judge Nangle correctly noted that "Georgia law on malice murder requires proof beyond a reasonable doubt that petitioner caused Hodges' death with malice aforethought. Malice consists of intent to kill and lack of provocation or justification." 103 F. Supp.2d at 1367. Judge Nangle also correctly noted that "[p]etitioner asserts that the evidence was insufficient to prove beyond a reasonable doubt that petitioner personally killed Mr. Hodges or that he aided and abetted Cedric Brown in the murder of Mr. Hodges." *Id.* at 1368. After analyzing the evidence, Judge Nangle then concluded that the evidence was sufficient to find Jenkins guilty of malice murder beyond a reasonable doubt. As he stated in his Decision:

---

126 It should also be noted that Jenkins' argument on this point was proven correct by later developments. As mentioned previously in Chapter 7, the Supreme Court of Georgia finally realized in *Lane v. State*, 294 Ga. 781, 756 S.E.2d 507 (2014) that its prior understanding of the accomplice corroboration rule as applied to Jenkins was fundamentally flawed. At that time, it **overruled** the *Jenkins* case and all similar cases. This error was obvious to me back in 1997, and it should have been obvious to Judge Nangle. As Justice O'Connor stated in her concurring opinion in *Wright v. West*, 505 U.S. 277, 305 (1992) and as the Court itself made clear in *Williams v. Taylor*, 529 U.S. 362, 383-84 (2000), "federal courts, even on habeas, **have an independent obligation to say what the law is**" (emphasis added). Instead of blindly accepting what the Georgia Supreme had said, Judge Nangle had an obligation **under federal constitutional law** to use his own independent judgment to determine whether what the Georgia Court did was correct. Had he done so, he would have realized that Judge Harvey's failure to give a charge on corroboration of accomplice testimony was erroneous and deprived Jenkins of a fair trial, notwithstanding what the Georgia Supreme Court had said.

"Viewing the evidence in the light most favorable to the prosecution, a reasonable jury could have found petitioner guilty of malice murder beyond a reasonable doubt. It was reasonable for the jury to infer from this testimony that petitioner shot Mr. Hodges at least once and that this shot was either the fatal shot or it enabled Cedric Brown to fire the fatal shot by wounding Mr. Hodges or otherwise impeding his escape. Accordingly, there was sufficient evidence to convict petitioner of malice murder, and the trial court did not violate petitioner's Fourteenth Amendment rights by submitting the case to the jury." 103 F. Supp.2d at 1368.

Contrary to Judge Nangle's assertion, I do not believe that his view represents a correct assessment of the evidence, or of the law.

First, let me say that the evidence was probably sufficient to find Jenkins guilty of ***felony murder***. If the jury believed that Jenkins was a participant in the robbery, then that fact alone would have been sufficient to find Jenkins guilty of felony murder, and there would be no need, for this particular charge, to prove that Jenkins actually killed Mr. Hodges or that he intended to cause his death. However, for some inexplicable reason, the jury never returned a verdict form on the felony murder charge, and therefore, as a matter of procedural law, even though Jenkins was found guilty of armed robbery, Jenkins was ***not*** found guilty of felony murder, nor could he be deemed guilty of felony murder *nunc pro tunc*.[127]

Second, the State deliberately chose to prosecute Jenkins for ***malice murder*** and, therefore, as a matter of law, the prosecutor had to prove, beyond a reasonable doubt, each and every element of that crime, including that Jenkins himself (i) personally caused the death of Mr. Hodges and (ii) personally intended to kill Mr. Hodges. Contrary to Judge Nangle's assertion, the evidence was not sufficient to establish either of these two elements.

---

127 *Nunc pro tunc* is a snobbish way of saying, "now for then."

Third, Judge Nangle correctly indicates that, in considering whether the evidence is sufficient to support the jury's verdict, it should be "view[ed] in the light most favorable to the prosecution" 103 F. Supp.2d at 1368. However, he goes much further than this. In his zeal to uphold the jury's verdict, Judge Nangle distorts the evidence. There was simply no evidence from which it could be reasonably inferred "that petitioner shot Mr. Hodges at least once *and that this shot was either the fatal shot or it enabled Cedric Brown to fire the fatal shot by wounding Mr. Hodges or otherwise impeding his escape.*" 103 F. Supp.2d at 1368 (emphasis added).

The entirety of the evidence on this issue was as follows: Dr. Clark, the medical examiner who performed the autopsy on Mr. Hodges' body, testified that there were *five* gunshot wounds to the body. However, *only one* of these wounds was fatal, severing the carotid artery and causing extensive bleeding. As Dr. Clark testified:

Q. "And is that wound a fatal wound?
A. Yes sir, I would — in all the five shots here, this is — would be considered the fatal wound because of its intersection of the left common carotid artery. A lot of blood flows through there and this person's gonna bleed out fairly rapidly after that, within several minutes after the gunshot wound." Tr. 1628

Dr. Clark testified that a *second* gunshot wound was *potentially fatal* although it did not, in fact, actually cause Mr. Hodges' death. In fact, this wound did not cause any direct injuries. As Dr. Clark testified:

"This gunshot wound is potentially fatal in the fact that even though it hit the arch at the right side of the face there's a lot of energy, or force, being put into the skull, which would injure the brain. . . . Even though there were no direct injuries, it's the type of thing that brings violent shaking inside, and that could potentially cause death in and of itself. But the lethal gunshot wound out of the five is the one to the neck [that severed the carotid artery]." Tr. at 1628.

Dr. Clark also testified that there were **three** other wounds, all of which were "superficial wounds" to soft tissue that caused no significant injury.

Finally, Dr. Clark testified that two bullet fragments were recovered from Mr. Hodges' body, although he could not say which bullet fragments caused, or were related to, any of the five wounds.

Kelly Fite, the State's firearms expert, testified that three bullet fragments and four shell casings were recovered at the scene. This includes the two bullet fragments that were recovered from Mr. Hodges' body plus an additional bullet fragment that was recovered from the crime scene floor. All four of the shell casings were recovered from the crime scene floor.

Mr. Fite testified that all three of the bullet fragments and all four of the shell casings were fired from a .25 caliber pistol, and that two separate .25 caliber pistols were used. Mr. Fite also testified that the two bullet fragments recovered from Mr. Hodges' body and three of the shell casings recovered from the floor were fired from the .25 caliber pistol that was recovered by the police from Terry Roberts' car (which was linked by testimony to Cedric Brown). Finally, Mr. Fite also testified that the markings on the third .25 caliber bullet fragment were consistent with having been fired from a Lorcin .25 caliber pistol (which was linked by testimony to the gun that had been stolen by Maurice from his cousin Roger). However, Mr. Fite admitted on cross-examination by Mr. Peel that this bullet fragment could have been fired by a different type of .25 caliber handgun.

> Q. "Mr. Fite, are there any other guns besides Lorcins that would give you the same rifling patterns and the same ejector markings and the same firing pin?
>
> A. There are — there's another brand of weapon called a Bryco, which gives similar type markings . . .

Q. Okay. Now, well, approximately how many different types of .25 caliber handguns are there?
A. There's probably 50 or 60 makes of .25s." Tr. 1873.

Although the prosecutor attempted to prove that a .25 caliber Lorcin pistol was used by Jenkins to shoot Mr. Hodges, that proof was inconclusive. First, no such weapon was ever recovered. Second, although Mr. Fite was able to say that two separate .25 caliber pistols were used, he was not able to say definitively that the second weapon was in fact a Lorcin. The only evidence linking a 25. caliber Lorcin to Jenkins was the testimony of Terry Roberts, who stated that he saw Jenkins holding a gun that matched the description of the Lorcin at the time of the robbery. However, Roberts also testified that it was Maurice Fleming who stole the Lorcin from his cousin and that Maurice had that gun prior to the robbery. There was no evidence explaining how this weapon would have been obtained by Jenkins from Maurice.

On the issue of intent, the prosecutor's evidence was exceedingly weak. As a former homicide prosecutor, I know from experience that there are two different ways of proving intent in murder cases. First, the defendant may have made a **statement** indicating that he intended to kill the victim. This is very rare, and it certainly did not happen here. There was no evidence in the record that Jenkins ever stated prior to, during, or after the robbery that he intended to kill Mr. Hodges.

The second and most common way of proving intent in a murder case is to present **circumstantial facts** from which the jury can reasonably **infer** that the defendant intended to kill the victim. As the judge will inevitably instruct the jury at the conclusion of the case, "a person can be presumed to intend the natural and logical consequences of his acts." Thus, where a perpetrator shoots or stabs the victim in a vital organ (such as the heart or the brain) and the victim dies as a result of the wound, it can reasonably be inferred that the perpetrator intended to kill the victim. Similarly, where the perpetrator shoots or stabs the victim multiple times resulting in serious injuries from which the victim dies, it can also reasonably be inferred that the perpetrator intended to kill the victim. However, if the perpetrator merely shoots or stabs the victim in the foot, and the victim nonetheless dies, no such intent can be inferred. Likewise, if the perpetrator shoots or stabs the victim but this only causes superficial or insignificant injury, no intent to kill may be inferred.

In the present case, there was no physical evidence which showed that Jenkins killed or caused serious physical injury to Mr. Hodges. There was testimonial evidence (from Roberts, McCall and Officer Smith) which claimed that Jenkins had admitted that he shot Mr. Hodges, but there is no way of determining from these alleged statements whether the shots, even if made by Jenkins, caused any serious physical injury to Mr. Hodges. Only one of the bullet wounds was fatal according to the medical examiner, and this appears from other evidence to have been fired by Cedric Brown. Three of the wounds were superficial which, even if they had been caused by Jenkins, would not give rise to an inference of an intent to kill. The fifth wound, which Dr. Clark described as a "potentially fatal" wound did not, in fact, cause any serious physical injury to Mr. Hodges. Thus, of the five bullets that were fired at Mr. Hodges, only one — the fatal one fired by Cedric — would permit an inference of intent to kill.

Judge Nangle never even discussed the issue of proof of intent in his Decision. As noted above, what he stated was that "[i]t was reasonable for the jury to infer from this testimony that petitioner shot Mr. Hodges *at least once* and that this shot was *either* the fatal shot *or it enabled Cedric Brown to fire the fatal shot by wounding Mr. Hodges or otherwise impeding his escape*. Accordingly, there was sufficient evidence to convict petitioner of malice murder . . ." 103 F. Supp.2d at 1368.

This was wishful thinking on Judge Nangle's part. There was absolutely no evidence in the record from which the jury could *reasonably* infer that Jenkins fired the fatal shot. And there was certainly no evidence in the record from which the jury could reasonably infer that Jenkins *enabled Cedric to fire the fatal shot*. Accordingly, there was insufficient evidence to prove either that Jenkins killed Mr. Hodges or that he intended to kill him, and Jenkins' motion for habeas relief on this issue should have been granted.

It is worth noting again that the District Attorney deliberately chose to prosecute Jenkins for the crime of malice murder and, in so doing, he deliberately and knowingly undertook the difficult obligation to prove, beyond a reasonable doubt, each element of that offense, including causation and intent to kill. It would have been far simpler, of course, for the State to prosecute Jenkins only for felony murder, which did not require proof that Jenkins intentionally killed Mr. Hodges.

Since proving malice murder is very difficult and proving felony murder is far simpler, why did the District Attorney choose to prosecute Jenkins for malice murder? I have never spoken to Mr. Cheney about this, of course, but the answer is patently obvious. Mr. Cheney, an elected official, wanted to seek the death penalty,[128] and he could not have done so unless he prosecuted Jenkins for malice murder.[129] Thus, although Mr. Cheney could easily have convicted Jenkins of felony murder and had him sentenced to life imprisonment, he chose the far more difficult path because he wanted to have him executed. Under these circumstances, it was certainly not unreasonable to hold the State to its stringent requirements of proving all the elements of malice murder beyond a reasonable doubt. The State failed to do so here, and judge Nangle shamelessly aided and abetted the State's dereliction of duty by inventing an unproven theory to justify the conviction.

For all of the foregoing reasons, Judge Nangle's decision with respect to this issue was clearly erroneous and improper.

---

128 Jenkins, Cedric Brown, Shawn Brown and Maurice Fleming, were jointly indicted on December 13, 1993. Mr. Cheney announced that he would seek the death penalty in this case shortly thereafter.

129 In order to seek the imposition of the death penalty, it was necessary for the State to prove, beyond a reasonable doubt, that the murder was accompanied by one or more statutory "aggravating circumstances." The aggravating circumstance alleged in this case was that the murder occurred during the commission of a robbery. It would not have been possible, therefore, for Mr. Cheney to seek the death penalty without charging Jenkins with malice murder.

6. *Exclusion of Relevant Evidence During the Guilt Phase of the Trial (Ground 6)*

Jenkins argued that Judge Harvey had improperly excluded relevant defense evidence during the guilt phase of his trial and that this violated his constitutional right to due process of law. Judge Nangle agreed that "[t]he Supreme Court has established that criminal defendants have a constitutional right to present a defense, including the right to offer testimony and evidence in their defense." 103 F. Supp.2d at 1368 (citing *Chambers v. Mississippi*, 410 U.S. 284, 302 (1973); *Webb v. Texas*, 409 U.S. 95, 98 (1972); *Washington v. Texas*, 388 U.S. 14, 18-19 (1967). However, Judge Nangle then noted that "the Supreme Court has never clearly established bright-line rules concerning particular types of evidence. Rather, the Supreme Court has established that the central issue is whether the state court's evidentiary rulings deprive the defendant of a fair trial under the facts and circumstances of the particular case." 103 F. Supp.2d at 1369 (citing *Chambers*, 410 U.S. at 303).

The evidence that Jenkins wanted to offer at his trial, and which Judge Harvey refused to let into evidence, consisted of (i) Cedric Brown's guilty plea to the robbery and murder of Mr. Hodges, (ii) statements made by Cedrice Brown during his plea hearing, and (iii) Cedric Brown's mental health file. Judge Nangle ruled that Judge Harvey's decision refusing to allow this evidence at trial could not form the basis for federal habeas relief because Jenkins "has failed to establish how the exclusion of Brown's guilty plea, statements at his plea hearing, and mental health file deprived petitioner of a fair trial." 103 F. Supp.2d at 1369.

Judge Nangle explained his reasoning on this issue as follows:

> "Because the evidence clearly indicates that two different shooters were involved in the murder, Brown's guilty plea alone does not exculpate petitioner. Furthermore, there is no evidence that Brown made any statements at his plea hearing tending to exonerate petitioner. Therefore, the

trial court's finding that this evidence was irrelevant did not deprive petitioner of a fair trial. Finally, the state court found that petitioner only sought Brown's mental health records for impeachment purposes and held that since Brown did not testify, petitioner's appeal on this issue was moot. Petitioner has failed to present clear and convincing evidence that this factual finding is incorrect. Accordingly, the Court finds that the trial court did not violate petitioner's right to due process of law by excluding the evidence from the guilt phase of the trial." 103 F. Supp.2d at 1369.

None of the foregoing statements made by Judge Nangle is correct. First, although the evidence indicated that two shooters were involved in the robbery, the evidence also indicated that only one shot was fatal. To the extent that Cedric Brown admitted he was the person responsible for firing this fatal shot, that most certainly would have been helpful to Jenkins' defense.

Second, Judge Nangle had no idea what statements Cedric may have made during his plea hearing, since neither these statements nor Cedric's plea hearing was part of the record of Jenkins' trial or of his federal habeas proceeding. Accordingly, Judge Nangle had no factual basis for assuming that Cedric Brown did not say anything during his plea hearing that might have been helpful to Jenkins' defense. Similarly, Judge Harvey also had no idea what statements Cedric made during his plea hearing; he merely ruled, as a matter of evidentiary law, that whatever statements Cedric may have made were irrelevant to the State's case against Jenkins. Without examining the particular statements at issue, however, this ruling was clearly erroneous. There may have been plenty that Cedric had said that was relevant to Jenkins' trial. Indeed, the District Attorney himself had originally planned to call Cedric as a witness in the case against Jenkins, but he ultimately decided not to do so. One wonders why he decided against calling Cedric. Was there something he was afraid Cedric might say that would be helpful for Jenkins' defense?

Third, although it is true that Jenkins' attorneys originally sought to obtain Cedric's mental health files for the purpose of impeaching him when he was called by the State as a witness, this does not mean that the files were not also relevant as substantive evidence. The fact that the "mastermind" of the robbery and the "principal shooter" of Mr. Hodges was mentally retarded was a relevant fact that should have been made known to the jury.

Fourth, the ruling by the Georgia Supreme Court that the issue concerning Cedric's mental health files was "moot" because Cedric did not testify at Jenkins trial was not a "factual finding" that had to be overcome by "clear and convincing evidence." It was a ruling of law, and an erroneous one at that. As such, it was not entitled to any deference by Judge Nangle.

Finally, and perhaps most importantly, it must be emphasized that this was a capital murder case in which the State sought to have Jenkins executed. In such cases, where the consequences of a mistaken verdict are so catastrophic, it is especially important to grant the defendant's attorneys wide latitude to determine for themselves what evidence they believe is relevant and helpful for establishing their defense. This is precisely what the Supreme Court mandated when it ruled that criminal defendants have a constitutional right to present a defense. It is unconscionable for state court judges to circumvent this fundamental right with dubious evidentiary rulings that limit important evidence on grounds of relevance.

For all of the foregoing reasons, Jenkins made a clear and compelling showing that Judge Harvey's "evidentiary rulings deprived [him] of a fair trial under the facts and circumstances of [this] particular case" (see 103 F. Supp.2d at 1369, quoting *Chambers*, 410 U.S. at 303) and, accordingly, Judge Nangle's decision on this issue was erroneous and improper.

7. ***False and Misleading Testimony by the State's Witnesses (Ground 7)***

Jenkins argued that three of the State's witnesses (Keith Moran, Kenneth McCall and Thomas Howard) presented false and misleading testimony at his trial which the State failed to correct and that this violated his constitutional right to a fair trial. Judge Nangle clearly understood the nature of Jenkins' argument. As he stated in his Decision:

> "Specifically, petitioner asserts that Moran's testimony falsely implied that Roberts could not be charged with murder, thus enhancing his credibility, and implied that petitioner was aware of a plot to kill Mr. Hodges prior to the robbery. Also, petitioner claims that McCall and Howard falsely testified that McCall received no deals or promises of leniency in exchange for his testimony." 103 F. Supp.2d at 1369.

Judge Nangle also agreed that Jenkins' claims, if true, amounted to a violation of due process. As he stated in his Decision:

> "The Supreme Court has clearly established that a conviction obtained via evidence, known by the State to be false, violates the Fourteenth Amendment. Falsehoods about the credibility of a witness also violate due process." 103 F. Supp.2d at 1369 (citing *Giglio v. United States*, 405 U.S. 150, 153-54 (1972) and *Napue v. Illinois*, 360 U.S. 264, 269 (1959).

Judge Nangle noted, however, that "a new trial is required only if the false testimony could in any reasonable likelihood have affected the judgment of the jury." 103 F. Supp.2d at 1369 (citing *Giglio*, 405 U.S. at 154; *Napue*, 360 U.S. at 271).

Applying these principles to the claims at issue, Judge Nangle concluded, based upon the decision of the Georgia Supreme Court, that Jenkins had failed to prove that Moran's testimony was false. As he stated in his decision:

"Petitioner asserts that Moran's testimony essentially stated that Terry Roberts could not be charged with the murder or felony murder of Mr. Hodges. He further alleges that the testimony implies that Moran's investigation must have developed some evidence that petitioner was aware of a plan to kill Mr. Hodges prior to the time it occurred [since, unlike Roberts, the murder charge against Jenkins was not dismissed by the District Attorney]. As the Georgia Supreme Court found, Moran's testimony, when read in context, neither stated nor implied any such thing. Petitioner has failed to present any clear and convincing evidence that this factual finding is incorrect. Accordingly, the court finds that Moran's testimony was not false, and petitioner's Fourteenth Amendment rights were not violated by the prosecution's failure to correct the testimony." 103 F. Supp.2d at 1369-70.

With all due respect to both Judge Nangle and the Georgia Supreme Court (which is very little), this statement, **when read in context**, was both erroneous and incongruous. Apart from boldly stating, "Moran's testimony, when read in context, neither stated nor implied any such thing," no attempt was made either by Judge Nangle or by the Georgia Supreme Court to explain the purpose or effect of this portion of Moran's testimony, or how it was likely perceived by the jury.

Moran testified, in response to questioning by the District Attorney, that Roberts had originally been charged with the murder of Mr. Hodges. He then testified, again in response to questioning by the District Attorney, that the murder charge against Roberts had been dismissed because no evidence was developed during the investigation that showed that Roberts was aware of any plan to kill Mr. Hodges prior to the robbery. Contrary to the assertions made by both Judge Nangle and the Georgia Supreme Court, the **only reasonable inference** that can be drawn from this testimony was that Roberts could not be charged with the murder of Mr. Hodges because he was not aware of any plan to murder Mr. Hodges before it occurred. This testimony was deliberately false and misleading. Even assuming that there was no evidence that Roberts was aware of any plan to kill Mr. Hodges prior to the robbery, he could still be charged with (and in fact he previously was charged with) *felony* murder, which does not require any evidence of intent to kill. The primary (and indeed the only) purpose of Moran's testimony on this issue was to falsely mislead the jury into believing that Roberts could not be charged with murder, and this was done solely (and improperly) to enhance Roberts' credibility. The District Attorney was obviously aware of the falsity of this testimony since he was the one who purposefully elicited the testimony.[130]

It is true, of course, that Moran did not explicitly state that Roberts could not be charged with felony murder in his testimony. But that omission was an integral part of the overall deception orchestrated by the District Attorney. Obviously, the District Attorney and Deputy Moran were both aware of the difference between malice murder and felony murder at the time when Moran testified. Yet, neither one made any attempt to clarify this difference in Moran's testimony. On the contrary, Moran simply stated that "the murder charge" against Roberts was dismissed because there was no evidence that he intended to kill Mr. Hodges. If the District Attorney and Deputy Moran misspoke, and what they really intended to say was that "the malice murder charge" was dismissed because they failed to uncover any evidence that Roberts was aware of any plan to kill Roberts before he was killed, this fails to explain why the felony murder charge was also dismissed. The only reasonable inference that can be drawn from this entire line of testimony is that the District Attorney and Deputy Moran deliberately chose to create in the minds of the jury the false impression that Roberts could not be charged with murder.

---

130 It should also be noted that Moran was explicitly recalled to the stand by the district attorney several hours after he had already completed his testimony. This was done for the sole purpose of eliciting this dubious testimony. Apparently, Mr. Cheney was concerned that the jury would conclude that the murder charge was dismissed to reward Roberts for his testimony, and he wanted to counter this argument by providing testimony that Roberts could not be charge with murder. This was a deliberate strategy adopted by Mr. Cheney. The only problem was that Moran's testimony was false, and Mr. Cheney knew it was false.

Similarly, and for the same reasons, Moran's testimony falsely and knowingly created the false impression that Jenkins must have been aware of a plan to kill Mr. Hodges prior to the time it occurred, since, unlike Roberts, the murder charge against him was not dismissed.

With respect to the testimony of Kenneth McCall and Charles Howard, Judge Nangle concluded that Jenkins' claim was unproven because (i) "there is no evidence in the record that McCall was ever told of the District Attorney's practice of writing a letter to the Pardons and Parole Board on behalf of inmates who testify on behalf of the state" and (ii) "[t]he Georgia Supreme Court found that the dismissal of the habitual violator charges was not part of a deal for McCall's testimony." 103 F. Supp.2d at 1370.

Even assuming that Mr. McCall was not explicitly told by the District Attorney of his practice of writing "nice letters" to the Board of Pardons and Parole recommending leniency for prison inmates who testify favorably on behalf of the State, this practice, which was obviously known to Mr. Cheney, should have been disclosed to the jury. The whole thrust of McCall's and ADA Howard's testimony was that no deals of any kind had been made with Mr. McCall in exchange for his testimony. But deals can be made tacitly as well as expressly. Under the circumstances of this case, it is unreasonable to conclude that Mr. McCall did not expect to receive leniency in exchange for his testimony against Jenkins. The blanket statement by McCall, as confirmed by the testimony of ADA Howard, that McCall would not receive any benefit in exchange for his testimony against Jenkins was actually false and should have been corrected by Mr. Cheney.

8. *Failure to Provide Brady Material (Ground 8)*

In *Brady v. Maryland*, 373 U.S. 83 (1963), the Supreme Court of the United States ruled that state prosecutors are constitutionally required to disclose to the defendant's attorneys all available exculpable evidence. Evidence is material under *Brady*, and the failure to disclose it justifies setting aside a state court conviction, if there is a reasonable probability that had the evidence been disclosed the result of the trial would have been different. *Kyles v. Whitley*, 514 U.S. 419 (1995).

Evidence which casts doubt on the credibility of one of the State's principal witnesses certainly constitutes *Brady* material which must be disclosed. As the Georgia Supreme Court, applying these federal constitutional requirements, noted in *Hines v. State*, 249 Ga. 257, 260 (1982):

> "It is especially important in a case where a witness or an accomplice may have substantial reason to cooperate with the government that a defendant be permitted to search for an agreement between the government and the witness. Whether or not such a deal existed is not crucial. **What counts is whether the witness may be shading his testimony in an effort to please the prosecution. A desire to cooperate may be formed beneath the conscious level, in a manner not apparent even to the witness, but such a subtle desire to assist the state nevertheless may cloud perception.**" (Emphasis added).

In the present case, Jenkins claimed in his petition for habeas corpus that the District Attorney had failed to disclose to Jenkins' attorneys that there were **additional** criminal charges pending against Kenneth McCall at the time he testified against Jenkins at the trial. Obviously, Jenkins' attorneys were aware that McCall had previously been charged with and convicted of one crime because McCall testified on his direct examination that, both at the time when Jenkins was arrested and at the time of the trial, he (McCall) was serving a sentence for forgery.[131] However, Mr. Cheney testified at the hearing in support of Jenkins' motion for a new trial that his Office had brought additional charges against Mr. McCall which were **pending at the time** McCall testified against Jenkins (Hr. 62). The existence of these charges was never disclosed to Jenkins' attorneys, even

---

131 McCall admitted during cross-examination by Mr. Peel that he had been convicted of several crimes, including "forgery, shoplifting, habitual violator. That's basically it." Tr. 1847. However, McCall did not disclose in response to Mr. Peel's question that he **currently** had **additional** charges pending against him that had not yet been resolved.

though they directly related to McCall's credibility. Mr. Cheney testified that he personally was not aware of the existence of these charges at the time McCall testified (Hr. 62), but he admitted that other attorneys in his office were aware of the charges (Hr. 62).

Mr. McCall was put forth by the State as a credible witness, but no effort was made by the District Attorney to determine whether other criminal charges were pending against him at the time he testified against Jenkins (Hr. 62) or to inform Jenkins' counsel of the existence of such additional charges (Hr. 69). This was because, as Mr. Cheney himself admitted, "I don't think I have any obligation to let [Jenkins' attorneys] know what the prior records of [the State's witnesses are." (Hr. 69).

This was not correct. McCall was a key witness for the State against Jenkins, and his credibility was a critical issue. Just like the prosecution witness in *Hines*, McCall had ample reasons to **"shade his testimony in an effort to please the prosecutor."** This resulted not only from the expectation of possible leniency from the Parole Board if he gave favorable testimony for the State against Jenkins, but also because of the pendency of additional charges which had been brought against him **by the very same** District Attorney for whom he was testifying. There is certainly at least a reasonable possibility that, if this evidence had been disclosed to the defense, the result of the proceeding might have been different.[132] Accordingly, the State's failure to disclose this information was highly prejudicial and improper and violated its obligations under *Brady*.

Judge Nangle admitted in his Decision that the existence of these additional charges was not disclosed to Jenkins' counsel, but he concluded that the State had no obligation to disclose them under B*rady* "because McCall's criminal record was a matter of public knowledge." 103 F. Supp.2d at 1371. With all due respect, I believe this is an incorrect interpretation of *Brady*. The State knew that McCall's credibility was a key issue in Jenkins'

---

132 McCall's testimony was important because, if believed by the jury, it corroborated, to some extent, the testimony of Terry Roberts and Officer Smith. Substantial questions existed regarding the credulity of both Roberts and Officer Smith and, therefore, it is impossible to say how much weight, if any, the jury may have attached to McCall's testimony.

trial and that he had additional charges pending against him at the time of the trial which were brought against him by the very same District Attorney for whom he was testifying. Furthermore, Mr. McCall did not disclose these additional charges when he was specifically asked by Mr. Peel, "what are all your other cases?" (Tr. 1847). Under these circumstances, the additional charges should have been disclosed.

9. *Improper Admission of Hearsay During the Testimony of Investigator Gray (Ground 9)*

In addition to the improper "silent witness" testimony (discussed in Point 2, *supra*), almost the entire testimony of Investigator Jim Gray was based upon, and consisted of, inadmissible hearsay. As Judge Nangle noted in his Decision:

> "Petitioner contends that the trial court violated his Sixth Amendment confrontation rights by admitting hearsay testimony by Investigator Gray concerning statements made by Terry Roberts, Shawn Brown and Roger Fleming. Further, petitioner asserts that the admission of these statements violated the Constitution even though Mr. Roberts and Mr. Fleming testified later at trial." 103 F. Supp.2d at 1372.

Jenkins claimed that this testimony was improper for three reasons. First, it constituted inadmissible hearsay. Mr. Gray did not have personal knowledge regarding any of the facts he testified about. On the contrary, everything that Mr. Gray testified about was based upon information that he received from others, primarily Roberts, Shawn Brown and Roger Fleming. Second, admission of this testimony violated Jenkins' right to confront and cross-examine the witnesses against him. Third, allowing Mr. Gray to testify about facts concerning which he had no personal knowledge denied Jenkins due process of law in violation of the Fifth, Eighth and Fourteenth Amendments. In effect, Mr. Gray was permitted to tell the jury that he "had conducted an investigation" and that, based upon this investigation, he had concluded that Jenkins was guilty. This was clearly improper and highly prejudicial. It was the jury's job to determine, based upon its evaluation of properly admissible evidence, whether Jenkins was guilty.

With respect to Gray's testimony that was based upon statements made to him by Roberts and Roger Fleming, Judge Nangle ruled that this was not improper "because hearsay statements made by persons who later testify at trial do not violate the Confrontation Clause." 103 F. Supp.2d at 1362-63 (citing *Ohio v. Roberts*, 448 U.S. at 65 and *California v. Green*, 399 U.S. at 162). Jenkins submits, however, that this was a misapplication of the Supreme Court's decisions in *Roberts* and *Green*. This was not a situation where Gray merely repeated statements that were told to him by Roberts and Fleming the accuracy of which could be checked by asking Roberts and Fleming whether they made the statements. This was a situation where Gray impermissibly testified that he himself had knowledge, based upon statements that had been told to him by others (including Roberts and Fleming), that Jenkins was one of the participants in the robbery and murder of Mr. Hodges.

Wholly apart from the confrontation issue, there were three additional problems with Gray's testimony. First, allowing Gray to repeat hearsay statements that were made to him by other witnesses (Terry Roberts and Roger Fleming) impermissibly bolstered the testimony of these witnesses. In effect, Mr. Gray was vouching for the reliability of statements made to him by others even though he himself had no personal knowledge regarding whether these statements were reliable.

Second, and even worse, allowing Mr. Gray to present these statements to the jury as though they were "facts" uncovered by him during his investigation, and known by him to be true, was improper and enormously prejudicial. Mr. Gray testified, for example, that he "was able to identify all of the participants in the robbery and in the murder" and "it was Cedric Brown, Shawn Brown, Clevon Jenkins and Maurice Fleming."

Tr. 1727-28. In actuality, however, Gary had no personal knowledge whatsoever regarding whether Jenkins participated in the robbery and in the murder. Admission of this testimony was thus inherently prejudicial and denied Jenkins his right to due process and a fair trial.

Third, the Georgia Supreme Court explicitly ruled that the admission of Gray's testimony was *erroneous*, but they ruled that the error was harmless. As the Supreme Court stated in its opinion, "the admission of Gray's testimony regarding the facts uncovered by his investigation . . . was harmless *error*." 268 Ga. at __, 491 S.E.2d at 57 (emphasis added). In fact, however, the Supreme Court had no reasonable basis for concluding that the error was harmless. Furthermore, in order to conclude that the error was harmless, the Supreme Court (as well as Judge Nangle) would need to find that the error was harmless *beyond a reasonable doubt*. No such finding was made here, and there was no reasonable basis for making such a finding.

With regard to the hearsay statements of Shawn Brown — who did not testify at the trial — Judge Nangle noted that "the Georgia Supreme Court found this testimony to be cumulative of properly admitted testimony" and then concluded that "[p]etitioner has failed to establish any actual prejudice that occurred as a result of the trial court's admission of hearsay statements that were wholly duplicative of the admissible testimony of Terry Roberts and other trial witnesses." 103 F. Supp.2d at 1372.

This explanation by Judge Nangle was erroneous and improper for two separate reasons. First, as just shown above, Gray's testimony — based upon the hearsay statements made to him by Roberts and Fleming — was *not* properly admitted. On the contrary, it plainly violated Jenkins' fundamental right to a fair trial. It is wholly improper, therefore, to attempt to bootstrap the improper admission of hearsay testimony by Investigator Gray based upon statements made to him by Shawn Brown by arguing that Brown's statements were merely cumulative of the improper hearsay statements made to Investigator Gray by Roberts and other witnesses. Second, if the statements made to Gray by Shawn Brown were truly cumulative, then they should have been excluded on grounds of relevance.

For all of the foregoing reasons, Judge Nangle's rejection of Jenkins' claim with respect to this issue was improper and erroneous.

10. *Improper Admission of Co-conspirator Statements (Ground 10)*

Terry Roberts was permitted to testify during Jenkins' trial regarding statements that had allegedly been made to him by Cedric Brown and Maurice Fleming. Mr. Walker immediately objected to this evidence on the ground that the statements were hearsay but, as noted previously, Judge Harvey overruled the objection on the ground that the statements were admissible "as statements made by a co-conspirator" (which is an exception to the hearsay rule).

Jenkins claimed in his habeas petition that this ruling by Judge Harvey was erroneous for two separate reasons. First, Judge Harvey failed to determine whether a prima facie case of conspiracy had been proven sufficient to allow admission of the statements under the exception to the hearsay rule. Second, even assuming that a prima facie case of conspiracy had been shown, Judge Harvey failed to consider whether the alleged statements were sufficiently reliable to permit them to be admitted in a capital murder case.

With respect to the first point, Judge Nangle stated as follows:

> "Petitioner's first argument is not one of constitutional law. Rather, it is an argument that the state court failed to follow state law by admitting the statements before making a finding that a prima facie case of conspiracy had been proven. Petitioner's reading of state law is erroneous. Georgia law allows the admission of testimony by co-conspirators before the conspiracy has been proven, provided its existence is ultimately shown at trial. Accordingly, the court did not err by admitting the testimony before

ruling on whether a prima facie case of conspiracy had been proven. Furthermore, the court did rule that a prima facie case of conspiracy was established, and [t]he Georgia Supreme Court found the facts supported the trial court's ruling. Petitioner has failed to present clear and convincing evidence that this factual finding was incorrect." 103 F. Supp.2d at 1373.

I will concede that Judge Nangle is correct in stating that, under Georgia law, the trial judge does not have to make a definitive ruling that a prima facie case of conspiracy exists before admitting co-conspirator statements at trial. However, the trial judge does have to make a definitive ruling at some time before the evidence is submitted to the jury. And contrary to Judge Nangle's ruling (as well as the ruling of the Georgia Supreme Court), I question whether Judge Harvey ever made a definitive ruling on this issue. I also question whether such a ruling, even if made, could possibly be correct based upon the admissible evidence in this case.

At the close of the evidence and prior to the summations of counsel, during what is known as the "charge conference," Judge Harvey asked Mr. Cheney, "[d]oes the State have any additional requests to charge?" Tr. 1878. Mr. Cheney stated that he had no requests for additional charges. However, he reminded Judge Harvey that he had never ruled on the conspiracy issue. As the District Attorney stated:

> "Let me bring one matter to the attention of the Court. At the time of the testimony of Terry Roberts, some of the testimony that was admitted included statements made by co-conspirators. The State's position is, and I think the Court may need to rule, is that whether or not the State, through all the evidence has made a prima facie case of conspiracy so that the testimony would be admissible.
>
> "The State's contention [is] that it has. We have shown, through testimony, that two weapons were used

in this case. We have shown through testimony, and this is other than Terry Roberts, through testimony that Shawn Brown is seen at the scene and was picked up and made a statement. We have shown, through testimony, that Cedric Brown had made a statement in the case.

"We've got three individuals together fleeing to the State of Florida and being arrested. And so based on the totality of the evidence, which included the statement of — or the testimony of Terry Roberts, the State's position is that we have shown more than — more than one person was involved in the action. I think it might be appropriate for the Court to make a determination of that at this time." Tr. 1878-79.

Judge Harvey then asked Jenkins' attorneys, "what do you wish to say in response to that? (Tr. 1879-80), to which Mr. Walker replied:

"My first thought is, what's gonna happen if the Court rules that the evidence is inadmissible? I mean the jury's heard it all.

"But I don't know that there's been a conspiracy shown here, Judge. If you take Roberts' testimony out of it, what you've got is — is two guns, but you don't have anything that shows who owns the gun. You've got the alleged statements by Jenkins to McCall and Smith, but that doesn't in any way say it was part of a conspiracy. And you've got the — the trip to Florida, which again, that in and of itself, is not a crime or any indication of a participation in a crime. So, I don't know that there's been a conspiracy shown here.

And, of course, the District Attorney certainly did not elect to indict them for conspiracy. So, I don't believe we've got a conspiracy shown here, Your Honor." Tr. 1880.

Despite Mr. Walker's objection and argument to the contrary, and without making any factual findings concerning what evidence he was relying on to show the existence of a conspiracy, Judge Harvey simply stated, "[t]he Court will make a preliminary determination that there is sufficient evidence to establish that there is a conspiracy." Tr. 1881.

Although Judge Nangle noted that Judge Harvey "did rule that a prima facie case of conspiracy was established" (103 F. Supp.2d at 1373) and that "[t]he Georgia Supreme Court found that the facts supported the trial court's ruling" (*Id.*), these rulings were not supported by the evidence.

Let's consider what evidence Mr. Cheney cited in support of his argument that a prima facie case of conspiracy had been shown.

First, he stated that the evidence showed that two guns were used in the robbery. This is true, but as Mr. Walker correctly pointed out to Judge Harvey, this does not in any way show either the existence of a conspiracy nor Jenkins' participation in a conspiracy.

Second, Mr. Cheney stated that Shawn Brown was seen by a witness in the vicinity of Hodges Grocery on the day of the robbery, and that Shawn Brown was "was picked up and made a statement." Here again, this evidence does not in any way establish either the existence of a conspiracy nor Jenkins' participation in a conspiracy. Furthermore, the evidence which showed that Shawn Brown "was picked up and made a statement" was completely improper and inadmissible.

Third, Mr. Cheney stated, "[w]e have shown, through testimony, that Cedric Brown had made a statement in the case." Here again, this evidence does not in any way establish either the existence of a conspiracy nor Jenkins' participation in a conspiracy. Furthermore, the evidence which showed that Cedric Brown "made a statement" was also improper and inadmissible.

Fourth, Mr. Cheney stated, "[w]e've got three individuals together fleeing to the State of Florida and being arrested." However, as Mr. Walker correctly pointed out to Judge Harvey, this does not in any way show either the existence of a conspiracy nor Jenkins' participation in a conspiracy.

Finally, Mr. Cheney stated, there is "the testimony of Terry Roberts." However, as Mr. Cheney well knew, it was necessary under Geogia law for the state to show the existence a conspiracy "apart from" the testimony of Mr. Roberts.

When the evidence cited by Mr. Cheney is examined in detail, it thus becomes clear that Judge Harvey's perfunctory ruling was ***not*** supported by sufficient evidence, and it should ***not*** have been sustained. A major problem, as Mr. Walker correctly pointed out, was "what's gonna happen if the Court rules that the evidence is inadmissible? I mean the jury's heard it all." Essentially and predictably, Judge Harvey had boxed himself into a quandary by not ruling on the conspiracy issue at the time when the co-conspirator statements were first offered by the District Attorney (and objected to by Mr. Walker). Either he ***had*** to rule now that a prima facie case of conspiracy had been proven, or he had to declare a mistrial (and start again from the beginning with a new trial). Obviously, Judge Harvey did not want to declare a mistrial, and so he made a bad ruling instead.

The second problem with the admission of the co-conspirator statements was that Judge Harvey failed to consider whether the alleged statements were ***sufficiently reliable*** to permit them to be admitted as an exception to the hearsay rule in a capital murder case. As the Eleventh Circuit Court of Appeals stated in *Horton v. Zant*, 941 F.2d 1449, 1465 (11th Cir. 1991), *cert. denied*, 503 U.S. 952 (1992), "[b]ecause the Georgia co-conspirator exception is so much broader than the traditional common law exception, this hearsay must be judged for reliability under the standards elaborated in *Dutton v. Evans*, [400 U.S. 74 (1970)]." And as the Georgia Supreme Court stated in *Castell v. State*, 250 Ga. 776 (1983), "[t]he thrust of *Dutton v. Evans* . . . is that in cases involving a co-conspirator exception to the hearsay rule, the admission of the statement of a co-conspirator does not violate the confrontation clause ***if the statement and the*** *circumstances surrounding it contain sufficient 'indicia of reliability.'"* 250 Ga. at 779 (emphasis added). What constitutes sufficient "indicia of reliability" was explained in *Hardy v. State*, 245 Ga. 272 (1980), *cert. denied*, 454 U.S. 1114 (1981), as follows:

> "The indicia of reliability required for admissibility are that the statements be non-narrative; that the declarant is shown by the evidence to know whereof he speaks; that the witness is not apt to be proceeding on faulty recollection; and that the circumstances show that the declarant had no apparent reason to lie to the witness." 245 Ga. at 277.

The evidence in Jenkins' case made it very clear that Roberts' testimony was inherently unreliable. As Judge Harvey well knew — because Roberts himself admitted so at trial — Roberts had lied **several times** to the police in this case. This was done, as Roberts himself conceded, because "I was trying to look out for Maurice and myself." Under these circumstances, there was clearly substantial doubt as to whether Roberts was telling the truth. It was therefore incumbent upon Judge Harvey to make a preliminary determination of **reliability** before applying the co-conspirator exception in this case. Judge Harvey failed to do so, and this was error.

As noted above, Judge Harvey did not even rule on the issue of the admissibility of the co-conspirator statements **until after both sides had already rested.** At that time the prosecutor stated, "I think the Court may need to rule [on the issue of] whether the State, through all its evidence, has made a prima facie case of conspiracy so that that testimony would be admissible." (Tr. 1878). At this point, Judge Harvey perfunctorily stated, "The Court will make a preliminary determination that there is sufficient evidence to establish that there is a conspiracy. But the ultimate determinate (sic) of the factor would have to be the jury. . ." (Tr. 1881). It is abundantly clear from Judge Harvey's offhand remarks that he never even considered the question of whether there were any "indicia of reliability" for the statements at issue.

Judge Nangle rejected Jenkins' arguments on this point for two reasons. First, Judge Nangle concluded that there was no reason for the ***trial judge*** (as opposed to an appellate court) to make a ruling on reliability and, second, that, in any event, the Georgia Supreme Court had found that sufficient indicia of reliability existed. As Judge Nangle stated in his Decision:

> "Petitioner provides no support for his assertion that the trial court must examine hearsay statements for indicia of reliability under *Dutton v. Evans*. Indeed, in *Dutton* itself there is no evidence that the ***trial court*** made a finding that 'indicia of reliability' existed. Rather, such a finding was made by the Supreme Court when it ruled that no confrontation violation occurred as a result of the admission of the hearsay statements. Consequently, the trial court's failure to address the existence of reliability was not error. The Georgia Supreme Court found that sufficient indicia of reliability existed, and petitioner has failed to establish that this finding was contrary to or was an unreasonable application of clearly established Supreme Court precedent." 103 F. Supp.2d at 1373 (emphasis added).

There are numerous flaws in Judge Nangle's statement. ***First***, Jenkins did, in fact, provide considerable "support for his assertion that the trial court must examine hearsay statements for indicia of reliability under *Dutton v. Evans*." See the court decisions in *Ohio v. Roberts, Horton v. Zant, Castell v. State,* and *Hardy v. State* discussed above. Judge Nangle simply ignored the cases cited by Jenkins, preferring to apply his own misguided interpretation of *Dutton v. Evans*.

Second, Judge Nangle's insinuation that a ***trial court*** has no obligation to comply with the constitutional requirements for admitting hearsay statements under *Dutton v. Evans*, because this is the responsibility of *appellate courts* is simply absurd. It is true, of course, that the trial court in *Dutton* did not make a ruling regarding the reliability of the statements at issue, but that is only because the Supreme Court had not yet established the requirement. Once the requirement became established, then it became necessary for trial courts in the future to comply with this requirement.[133]

Third, the notion that the Georgia Supreme Court had found adequate "indicia of reliability" for the hearsay statements at issue, and that this decision was entitled to deference by a federal court in a habeas proceeding, is complete nonsense. As shown above, the Georgia Supreme Court did not make a good faith effort to determine whether the statements at issue had sufficient indicia of reliability, but even if it did, Judge Nangle had an independent obligation under the Constitution to determine whether the decision of the Georgia Supreme Court was reasonably plausible based upon the actual evidence in Jenkins' case. Judge Nangle made no effort to do so, and that was wrong.

For all the foregoing reasons, Judge Nangle's rejection of Jenkins' claim with respect to this issue was erroneous and improper.

11. *Improper Admission of the Brief Incriminating Statement Allegedly Made by Jenkins to Officer Smith (Ground 12)*

Jenkins claimed at trial that there was an unresolved issue regarding whether the incriminating statement he allegedly had made to Officer

---

133 The *Dutton* decision was made by a highly fractured court, which ruled, in 5-4 decision, that the hearsay statement at issue (made, like in Jenkins' case, by an alleged co-conspirator who did not testify) did not violate the Confrontation Clause because there were sufficient "indicia of reliability" to allow the statement to be admitted as an exception to the hearsay rule. However, Justices Marshall, Black, Douglas and Brennan disagreed with this view and would have held that admission of the co-conspirator statement violated the Confrontation Clause, **even assuming that it was reliable**. As Justice Marshall stated in his dissenting opinion: "I am troubled by the fact that the plurality for reversal . . . shifts the ground and begins a hunt for whatever 'indicia of reliability' may cling to [the hearsay statement at issue] as told by [a different witness]. . . . If 'indicia of reliability' are so easy to come by and prove so much, then it is only reasonable to ask whether the Confrontation Clause has any vitality at all in protecting a criminal defendant against the use of extrajudicial statements and not exposed to a jury assessment of the declarant's demeanor at trial." 400 U.S. at 109, 91 S. Ct. at 230 (Marshall, J. dissenting). If these four justices were so outraged by the admission of the hearsay statement at issue in *Dutton* (which was not that prejudicial to the defendant in that case), they would have been absolutely apoplectic with what happened to Jenkins.

Smith ("I only shot him once") was the product of improper custodial interrogation which violated his Fifth Amendment right against self-incrimination. Prior to trial, Judge Harvey had held a *Jackson-Denno* hearing at which it was determined that the statement in question had been made **spontaneously** by Jenkins and not in response to any questioning by officer Smith. This ruling was subsequently upheld by the Georgia Supreme Court in an interim appeal prior to trial.

When Officer Smith testified at trial, however, he initially testified that, prior to the incriminating statement that was allegedly made by Jenkins, Officer Smith had told Jenkins that "he should get his life together and tell the truth. Whatever happened, tell the truth." Tr. 1786. Mr. Walker immediately objected to this testimony on the ground that it was inconsistent with Smith's prior testimony at the *Jackson-Denno* hearing that the statement had been made spontaneously. Walker demanded that Judge Harvey reopen the *Jackson-Denno* hearing to determine whether the statement was truly spontaneous or the product of custodial examination by Officer Smith. Judge Harvey refused to reopen the *Jackson-Denno* hearing and allowed the statement to be admitted. After further questioning on this issue by both Mr. Cheney and Mr. Walker, Officer Smith changed his testimony to say that the statement which he made to Jenkins about getting his life together and telling the truth came **after** Jenkins had already made the statement in question. Nevertheless, Officer Smith continued to say that he had had conversations with Jenkins prior to the statement at issue, although he did not recall specifically what he had said.

Jenkins claimed, both in his appeal to the Georgia Supreme Court and in his petition for habeas corpus, that Judge Harvey's refusal to reopen the *Jackson Denno* hearing to determine whether the statement in question had actually been the product of custodial interrogation (as opposed to a spontaneous declaration) was improper. Both the Georgia Supreme Court and Judge Nangle rejected this argument. As Judge Nangle stated in his Decision:

> "Reviewing Smith's trial testimony as a whole, it is obvious that Smith did not testify in the manner asserted by petitioner. *At one point during cross-examination, Smith appears to state that petitioner's statement was made after Smith's comments about getting his life together.* However, upon further questioning, Smith clearly indicated that petitioner's statement was made before any such comments by Smith." 103 F. Supp.2d at 1374 (emphasis added).

Judge Nangle also added that "[t[he Georgia Supreme Court also found that the totality of Officer Smith's testimony did not support petitioner's argument. . . . Accordingly, the Court finds that the trial court did not violate petitioner's Fifth Amendment rights by admitting the testimony of Officer Smith." 103 F. Supp.2d at 1374.

These decisions by Judge Nangle and the Georgia Supreme Court are highly questionable. First, it not only *appeared* from Officer Smith's testimony on cross-examination that Officer Smith had told Jenkins to "tell the truth and get his life together" *before* Jenkins made the statement in question, but that is exactly what Smith had actually said. It was only later, after realizing the significant problem this testimony created, that Smith *changed* his testimony to say that Jenkins' statement came first.

Second, despite changing his testimony about when he told Jenkins to "tell the truth," Smith continued to say that he was *talking* to Jenkins prior to, and at the time of, Jenkins' alleged incriminating statement, although notably Smith *did not recall* what he had said to Jenkins. There is a very fine line between talking to someone and questioning them, and both Judge Nangle and the Georgia Supreme Court were surprisingly indifferent regarding what Smith might have actually said to Jenkins to cause him to make the statement at issue.

Third, it seems extremely odd that Jenkins, who had steadfastly refused to speak to the police, suddenly and spontaneously made an incriminating statement to Officer Smith without any provocation or purpose, and just when such a statement was so desperately needed by the Georgia police to corroborate the testimony of Terry Roberts. As Isaac Asimov once famously said, "Gee, that's funny."[134] Or, as we lawyers frequently say, "*res ipsa loquitor*," which can be loosely translated as "the facts speak for themselves."

12. *Denial of Effective Assistance of Counsel (Ground 13)*

Jenkins claimed in his Petition for habeas corpus that he was deprived of the effective assistance of counsel for sixteen separate reasons. As Judge Nangle correctly noted in his Decision, "[t]he Supreme Court has clearly established that criminal defendants have a Sixth Amendment right to 'reasonably effective' legal assistance." 103 F. Supp.2d at 1374. As Judge Nangle also correctly noted in his Decision, "[t]o establish a violation of this Sixth Amendment right, the petitioner must show (1) that counsel's representation fell below an objective standard of reasonableness, and (2) that counsel's deficient performance prejudiced the defendant." *Id.* at 1374-75. Furthermore, "both parts of the test must be satisfied to show a violation of the Sixth Amendment." *Id.* at 1375.

In considering the sixteen separate grounds that Jenkins alleged violated his Sixth Amendment right, Judge Nangle stated that "[s]even of these alleged errors involve the failure to object to events at trial which this Court has already found did not violate petitioner's constitutional rights. Consequently, petitioner cannot establish that his attorney's failure

---

134 It has been widely reported that Asimov once said, "[t]he most exciting phrase to hear in science is not 'Eureka' (I found it!) but, 'Gee, that's funny . . .'" Despite diligent efforts by others to discover a definitive citation for this quote, none has ever been found, at least not in the official writings of Asimov.

to object to these events prejudiced his defense." 105 F. Supp.2d at 1375.[135] Although Judge Nangle claimed that these seven grounds had no constitutional merit, that decision itself was clearly erroneous for the reasons previously explained in this Chapter. Accordingly, Jenkins' counsels' failure to object to these seven errors did, in fact, amount to deficient performance on their part which did, in fact, prejudice Jenkins at his trial. Accordingly, notwithstanding Judge Nangle's blanket claim of irrelevance, these seven separate instances of incompetence did, in fact, support Jenkins' claim that he had been denied the effective assistance of counsel at his trial.

The **Eighth Ground** asserted in support of Jenkins' claim of ineffective assistance of counsel was that his trial lawyers had told him that the trial was "going well," that there was no need for him to testify, and that he should not testify. As Judge Nangle correctly noted in his Decision, "[p]etitioner claims his attorneys misled him regarding the probable outcome of the case and improperly advised him not to testify in his own defense." 103 F. Supp.2d at 1375. Judge Nangle rejected this claim for two reasons.

First, Judge Nangle asserted, incredibly, that "it was not obvious that the trial was going to result as it did." 103 F. Supp.2d at 1375-76. Amplifying this assertion, Judge Nangle stated as follows:

> "Viewing the trial as a whole, petitioner's counsel very effectively and thoroughly cross-examined the State's most important witness and managed to clearly present their alternate theory of how the robbery and murder occurred. Their failure to accurately predict which theory the jury would believe and their **concomitant optimism**

---

[135] The seven grounds which Judge Nangle excluded on this basis were the following: (1) failure to object to improper hearsay testimony by unidentified silent witnesses, (2) failure to object to erroneous jury instructions on the issues of malice, parties to a crime, and conspiracy, (3) failure to request an instruction on the issue of corroboration and failure to object to Judge Harvey's charge which omitted such an instruction, (4) failure to object to, or correct, the false testimony provided by Deputy Moran, (5) failure to object to hearsay during the testimony of Investigator Gray, (6) failure to object to Judge Harvey's conspiracy charge on the ground that it failed to inform the jury that a co-conspirator's testimony regarding the existence of a conspiracy must be corroborated, and (7) failure to object to the admission of co-conspirator statements on the ground that the State had failed to prove, and Judge Harvey had failed to determine, whether a prima facie case of conspiracy existed. See 103 F. Supp.2d at 1375, note 24.

when discussing the case with petitioner do not amount to ineffective assistance of counsel." 103 F. Supp.2d at 1375-76 (emphasis added).

This is complete nonsense and utterly unworthy of a federal judge with more than 25 years of experience on the bench. Actually, it was also unworthy of the first-year law clerk with no experience who probably drafted it.

First, Mr. Peel did not "effectively and thoroughly" cross-examine the State's principal witness (Terry Roberts). Not only was his cross-examination mediocre at best, but he totally failed to impeach Roberts with his detailed prior inconsistent statements, a failure which Peel admitted under oath was inadvertent and not the product of deliberate trial strategy. On the other hand, if Jenkins had taken the stand, as he consistently told his lawyers he wanted to, and testified that Roberts was lying when he said that Jenkins had a gun and stated that he had shot Mr. Hodges, that might have helped considerably in establishing Jenkins' defense.

Second, it is a complete fabrication to claim that an "alternate theory of how the robbery and murder occurred" was "clearly presented" by Jenkins' attorneys. The ***uncontradicted*** medical and ballistics evidence clearly established that Hodges was shot by four or five separate bullets fired from two separate guns. The ***uncontradicted*** testimony of Terry Roberts and Deputy Moran clearly established that Jenkins was one of the two people who shot Mr. Hodges, and this testimony was corroborated by the ***uncontradicted*** testimony of Officer Smith and Ken McCall. Furthermore, the ***uncontradicted*** testimony of Terry Roberts, Officer Smith and Kenneth McCall clearly established that Jenkins had made statements admitting his guilt. Finally, the ***uncontradicted*** evidence showed that Roberts had fled the scene of the robbery with Cedric and Maurice and was arrested shortly thereafter in Florida in possession of a food stamp that was stolen from Hodges' store. Nowhere in this story is there any evidence whatsoever of an "alternate theory of how the robbery and murder occurred." Other than cross-examining the State's witnesses (which was largely ineffective), no evidence of any kind was presented by Jenkins' attorneys to prove his innocence. On the other hand, if Jenkins had actually taken the stand and testified that he was not involved in the robbery, that he was entirely an unknowing and innocent bystander when the robbery and murder of Mr. Hodges occurred, that he did not know that Cedric and Maurice had planned to rob Mr. Hodges before it occurred, that he did not in any way participate in the robbery or murder, that he never had a gun, and that he never told Roberts, Officer Smith or Ken McCall that he had shot anybody, this might have helped considerably in establishing Jenkins' defense. As the case was actually tried, however, there was simply no evidence at all that supported "an alternate theory of how the robbery and murder occurred."[136]

Third, the assertion that Messrs. Walker and Peel, two experienced criminal defense attorneys, could not be expected to accurately predict what the jury was likely to do when considering the evidence that had been presented in this case is complete rubbish. That is like saying that Notre Dame is leading Navy 48 to 3 with four minutes left in the fourth quarter and suggesting that the outcome of the game is in still doubt. There may be some leeway for **concomitant optimism** on the part of diehard Navy fans at a football game, but the trial of a murder case is another matter. Criminal defense attorneys are expected, **as a matter of professional ethics and competence**, to be able to accurately and impartially evaluate the available evidence and advise their client accordingly. They are not permitted to hope, with unbounded optimism, that the jury may somehow accept fanciful arguments for which they have presented little or no evidence, and they

---

[136] Judge Nangle's assertion that "an alternate theory of how the robbery and murder occurred" was "clearly presented" by Jenkins' attorneys was based entirely upon statements that were made by Mr. Walker and Mr. Peel during their closing arguments to the jury. Unfortunately, these statements did not constitute "evidence" in the case, nor were they supported by any evidence in the case. It was preposterous, therefore, for Judge Nangle to say that this "alternate theory" was "clearly presented" to the jury. It was **argued** to the jury as a possibility, but the argument was not supported by *any* evidence, and therefore it had no chance of success. If Jenkins had testified, however, then the argument would have been supported by evidence and perhaps Jenkins might have been found not guilty.

are certainly not permitted to advise their client that a case is going well when it is obvious to any reasonably competent trial lawyer that it is not.

The second argument that Judge Nangle made in rejecting Jenkins' claim that Walker and Peel had acted improperly when they advised him not to testify was that "petitioner failed to establish that his attorneys' advice against testifying was anything other than reasonable trial strategy." 103 F. Supp.2d at 1376. As Judge Nangle stated in support of this position:

> "At the hearing in support of petitioner's motion for a new trial, his trial counsel testified that, after listening to petitioner's version of the robbery and murder, they did not hear anything that would help the defense and they were afraid petitioner might say something on cross-examination that would be detrimental to his defense." 103 F. Supp.2d at 1376.

Here again, what Judge Nangle asserted as a basis for condoning Walker and Peel's malfeasance was completely indefensible. Obviously, Walker and Peel tried to justify their own actions when they testified at the hearing in support of Jenkins' Motion for a new trial. Would you expect anything else? Would you expect them to admit, for example, that they completely messed up and that, as a result, a possibly innocent black man must now spend the rest of his life in prison for a crime he probably did not commit? Of course, not. Obviously, they said what they had to say to defend themselves from the charge of incompetence.

Judge Nangle's obligation, however, like the obligation of Judge Harvey before him, was not to blindly accept and parrot what Walker and Peel had stated at the hearing, but to critically examine and assess whether what they said was actually true and whether it provided a sufficient basis for advising Jenkins not to testify. When such an analysis is performed, it is obvious that what Walker and Peel said at the hearing was not only untrue, but completely unreasonable and indefensible.

It must be remembered that, from the time Jenkins was first arrested (about four days after the crime was committed) until the time he testified at the hearing in support of the Motion for a new trial (almost two years after the trial was completed), Jenkins never told anyone **except his attorneys** his version of what had happened. And his version of what had happened was very plausible, if not compelling. Indeed, it also had the advantage of probably being true. During this entire period, therefore, the only versions of what had happened that were available to the police and to the district attorney were the various versions given by Terry Roberts and the other defendants, and these versions all implicated Jenkins. It would have been very helpful, therefore, if Jenkins had come forward to the police as soon as he was arrested and told the police what actually happened, but he was advised by his attorneys not to do so. At the very least, however, it would have been very helpful if Jenkins was permitted to testify at his trial and tell the jury what happened, but, here again, he was advised by his attorneys not to do so. So, from the time this crime was first committed until well after Jenkins was already convicted, nobody ever heard Jenkins' account of what happened except Walker and Peel, and they refused to let him tell it to the police, the District Attorney, or the jury.

The explanation offered by Jenkins' attorneys — that he had nothing helpful to say — was just plain wrong. As Mr. Cheney (improperly) pointed out to the jury during his summation, there was no evidence of any kind that had been offered by the defense at the trial which contradicted the State's evidence that Jenkins had both shot Mr. Hodges and subsequently admitted to three different people that he had done so. Under these circumstances, it is absolutely ridiculous to suggest, as Judge Nangle did here, that it would not have been helpful for Jenkins to take the stand and deny these allegations. Not only would it have been helpful, it was absolutely essential.

Furthermore, the assertion that Jenkins "might say something on cross-examination that would be detrimental to his defense" is a complete red herring without any rationale basis. What could he possibly say on cross-examination that could make matters any worse than they already were? That he shot Lincoln and Kennedy, that he tried to overturn an election, that he stole classified documents from the White House? Of course not.[137]

Jenkins had a very simple and straightforward story to tell, so there was no reasonable risk that he would become confused on the stand. Furthermore, he had never had any prior problems with the law, so there was no risk that he could be impeached by the prosecutor with evidence of prior bad behavior. Finally, and perhaps most importantly, it was unquestionably the obligation of his attorneys to adequately prepare Jenkins to testify so that he would be as effective as possible and not say anything harmful during cross-examination. They cannot escape that responsibility by telling their client not to testify simply because it is more convenient for them that he do so. It was Jenkins' life and liberty that were at stake, and he absolutely needed to tell his story to the jury, and he needed Walker's and Peel's assistance when it counted most.

For all of the foregoing reasons, it was patently improper for Jenkins' attorneys to tell him that the trial was going well when clearly it was not, and to advise him there was "no need" to testify when obviously it was essential that he do so in order to provide some evidence of his innocence. Furthermore, it was clearly erroneous and improper for Judge Nangle to suggest that the actions of Jenkins' attorneys constituted "reasonable trial strategy."

The **Ninth Ground** asserted in support of Jenkins' claim of ineffective assistance of counsel was that his trial lawyers (specifically Mr. Peel) failed to impeach Terry Roberts, the primary witness against Jenkins at his trial, with his prior recorded and transcribed inconsistent statements. In rejecting this claim, Judge Nangle noted that "Roberts testified on direct and cross-examination that he lied to police *the first few times* he spoke to

---

137 The one thing that Jenkins could have said on cross-examination that might have hurt his case was that "he did not like Mr. Hodges, and he was glad he was dead." But there was no reason to believe that Jenkins would ever say any such thing. Furthermore, it was Walker's and Peel's professional responsibility to prepare Jenkins to testify and make sure that he did not say or do anything that would hurt the case.

them to protect himself and his cousin Maurice Fleming" (103 F. Supp.2d at 1376) (emphasis added),[138] and then he summarily dismissed Jenkins' claim of ineffective assistance of counsel by stating, "[t][here is no reasonable probability that introduction of Roberts' actual statements to the police would have damaged his credibility any more than the highly effective cross-examination [by Mr. Peel] did." *Id.* Judge Nangle then stated, "even if failure to introduce the actual statements was error, petitioner has failed to establish that this error prejudiced his defense in any way." *Id* (emphasis added).

These assertions by Judge Nangle were both factually erroneous and legally flawed. There was no plausible basis upon which Judge Nangle could possibly conclude, with any degree of certainty — as he was legally required to do in order to dismiss' Jenkins ineffective assistance of counsel claim[139]-- that "there [was] no reasonable probability" that impeaching Roberts with his prior inconsistent statements would have damaged his credibility "any more than the highly effective cross- examination [by Mr. Peel] did." This was so for numerous reasons.

First, it was a gross and unwarranted exaggeration to characterize Mr. Peel's cross-examination of Terry Roberts as "highly effective." To be kind, it was mediocre at best. However, even assuming that Peel's cross-examination had been absolutely stellar, that would not signify that it could not have been significantly improved by using Roberts' prior inconsistent statements to impeach him. On the contrary, it is a fundamental principle of trial practice that all witnesses, especially very important witnesses like Terry Roberts, should be impeached with their prior inconsistent statements whenever such statements are available. The fact that Mr. Peel failed to do so here was simply inexcusable, and Judge Nangle should have

---

138 Contrary to Judge Nangle's assertion, Maurice was Roberts' **half-brother**, not his cousin. The cousin was **Roger Fleming,** the person from whom Maurice allegedly stole the .25 caliber pistol that was allegedly used in the robbery but never recovered from the scene or anywhere else.
139 As the Supreme Court explicitly ruled in *Chapman v. California*, 386 U.S. 18, 24 (1967), "before a federal constitutional error can be held harmless the court must be able to declare that it was harmless **beyond a reasonable doubt**" (emphasis added).

known better than to try to justify Peel's omission by suggesting that use of the statements would not have made any difference.

Second, Judge Nangle seems to have assumed that using Roberts' prior inconsistent statements "for impeachment purposes" would have merely consisted of admitting the statements into evidence. That is totally incorrect. Armed with the prior inconsistent statements, a reasonably competent and skilled attorney would have sternly and skillfully confronted Roberts on the witness stand by questioning him extensively about each of the prior lies and falsehoods that he told to the police, the reasons for doing so, and pointedly ask Roberts why anyone should believe him now when he lied so easily and so frequently in the past. Elucidating each of these lies and falsehoods, a skilled questioner would have highlighted that Roberts continued to place all of the blame for the robbery and murder of Mr. Hodges on Jenkins and Cedric, and none of the blame on Roberts and his brother Maurice. Furthermore, Roberts should have been extensively questioned about the fact that it was Maurice, not Jenkins, who had stolen the .25 caliber Lorcin pistol from his cousin (Roger Fleming) and that it was Maurice, not Jenkins, who had the gun prior to the robbery. Using Roberts' lengthy prior inconsistent statements in this manner would have extended Roberts' cross-examination by several hours and would have created a far more accurate and lasting impression in the minds of the jurors that Roberts was not a person who could or should be believed, especially as the sole witness who implicated Jenkins in a capital murder case in which Roberts himself was involved. Frankly, but for the ill-advised decision of the DA, it could just as easily have been Jenkins who was testifying against Roberts for his role in the robbery and murder of Mr. Hodges.

Third, Judge Nangle justified his rejection of Jenkins' ineffective assistance of counsel claim by suggesting that Roberts' credibility had already been sufficiently impaired in the minds of the jury as a result of his own admission that he had lied several times to the police and, therefore, "there was no reasonable probability" that using Roberts' prior inconsistent statements would hurt his credibility any more. The simple answer to this spurious assertion is that Judge Nangle had no reasonable grounds for reaching this conclusion, and therefore it could not be used as basis for rejecting Jenkins' claim.

Contrary to Judge Nangle's convenient and self-serving assessment that Terry Roberts' credibility had already been sufficiently impaired, it should be noted that the jurors apparently disagreed, since they found Roberts' testimony sufficiently credible to quickly find Jenkins guilty of robbery and murder and sentence him to life imprisonment without any possibility of parole. Perhaps if Mr. Peel had impeached Roberts' credibility more effectively with his prior inconsistent statements, as any reasonably competent attorney would have done, the jurors might have had more cogent reasons for doubting Roberts' credibility and found Jenkins not guilty.

Furthermore, if Judge Nangle truly believed that Roberts' credibility was so utterly impaired that no further damage could have been achieved by impeaching him with his prior inconsistent statements, then Judge Nangle was legally obligated to vacate Jenkins' conviction on that basis alone. This necessarily follows from Judge Nangle's assessment that Roberts' was not a credible witness which, in turn, implies that the evidence against Jenkins was insufficient as a matter to law to support the verdict.

Finally, it is important to note that Judge Nangle did ***not*** rule that Mr. Peel's failure to impeach Roberts with his prior inconsistent statements constituted acceptable conduct. On the contrary, he deliberately avoided ruling on this issue. Instead, he **assumed** that Mr. Peel's conduct was deficient, but then he ruled that this deficiency did not affect the outcome of the trial. As he stated in his Decision, "even if failure to introduce the actual statements was *error*, petitioner has failed to establish that ***this error*** prejudiced his defense in any way." 103 F. Supp.2d at 1376 (emphasis added). As shown above, however, Jenkins very cogently did establish that Mr. Peel's failure to impeach Roberts with his prior inconsistent statements was prejudicial to his defense. In fact, it was one of the principal reasons why Jenkins was wrongfully convicted.

Accordingly, for all of the foregoing reasons, it was clearly improper for Mr. Peel to fail to impeach Roberts with his prior inconsistent statements, and it was clearly erroneous and improper for Judge Nangle to reject this ground for granting the requested writ of habeas corpus.

The **Tenth Ground** asserted in support of Jenkins' claim of ineffective assistance of counsel was that his trial lawyers failed to introduce evidence that Cedric Brown was mentally retarded. This was important because Cedric was the main perpetrator in planning and carrying out the robbery and murder of Mr. Hodges and, more importantly, because the State sought to hold Jenkins responsible for the malice murder of Mr. Hodges on the theory that Cedric intended to murder Mr. Hodges and Cedric's intent could be transferred to Jenkins under the doctrine of "transferred intent." Under these circumstances, it was important for the jury to know that Cedric was mentally retarded because this undermined the State's theory that Jenkins should be held accountable for what Cedric did.[140]

Judge Nangle rejected this claim of ineffective assistance of counsel on the ground that Jenkins' trial counsel's "theory of the case was that Cedric Brown, and to a lesser extent Maurice Fleming, were the masterminds behind the robbery and shooting" (103 F. Supp.2d at 1376) and that "introducing evidence that Cedric was mentally retarded would have severely undercut this argument" (*Id.* at 1377). Judge Nangle then concluded, "[b]ecause Jenkins has failed to establish that no competent counsel would have chosen to present this theory of the case, the Court finds that petitioner's trial counsel were not constitutionally ineffective in declining to introduce evidence that was inconsistent with this theory of the case." *Id.* at 1377.

There are three glaring problems with this analysis. First, Walker and Peel's so-called preferred "theory of the case" (that Cedric Brown was the

---

140 If Cedric himself cannot be held legally responsible for his actions due to mental retardation, how can it possibly make sense to hold Jenkins responsible for Cedric's actions.

"mastermind behind the robbery and shooting") would not have been any less effective if Cedric was shown to be mentally defective. In fact, it probably would have made more sense since that would explain why Cedric wanted to commit such a senseless and tragic act. So, Walker and Peel could still have advanced their preferred "theory of the case" even if it was shown that Cedric was mentally retarded.

Second, even if Walker and Peel's preferred "theory of the case" would have been "undercut" by showing that Cedric was mentally retarded, that is not a sufficient justification for failing to introduce important substantive evidence that could have benefitted Jenkins' defense. The jury may have been less inclined to hold Jenkins responsible for this senseless crime if they knew that Cedric was mentally retarded.

Third and most importantly, Walker's and Peel's preferred "theory of the case" was not particularly helpful as a defense for exonerating Jenkins. Even if Cedric were a highly intelligent master planner, that would not in any way diminish Jenkins' criminal responsibility if he knowingly and willingly participated in the robbery and murder of Mr. Hodges. What Walker's and Peel's preferred theory of the case should have been was that Jenkins was an innocent bystander who had absolutely no prior knowledge of, or involvement in, the robbery and murder of Mr. Hodges. If this had been their theory of the case, as it undoubtedly should have been, then there was no justification for failing to introduce evidence showing that Cedric was mentally retarded.

The ***Eleventh Ground*** asserted in support of Jenkins' claim of ineffective assistance of counsel was that his trial lawyers failed to object to hearsay and other improper testimony provided by Special Agent Bart Ingram of the Florida Department of Law Enforcement. Ingram testified at length regarding his efforts to locate and apprehend Cedric Brown, Maurice Fleming and Jenkins in Florida. Most of this testimony was irrelevant, misleading, inflammatory, and based upon hearsay.

Agent Ingram testified at length, for example, regarding conversations he had had with Jim Gray, Lucy Stacy, Terry Stacy and Agent Moran prior to apprehending the defendants (Tr. 1742-1746). He also testified that 'information [had been] developed as to the possible location of the other pistol [and] an attempt was made to find it" (Tr. 1756) but the search was unsuccessful because it was "a difficult area to search" (Tr. 1756-58). Admission of this testimony was improper and highly prejudicial. Jenkins' trial lawyers should have objected, and their failure to do so was grossly deficient and highly prejudicial.

Judge Nangle conceded that this testimony was probably improper, but he concluded that the error was harmless. As he stated, "[e]ven if counsel's failure to object . . . to this testimony could be considered error, petitioner has failed to show how this error prejudiced his defense." 103 F. Supp.2d at 1377. Judge Nangle further explained his reasoning by stating, "the bulk of Ingram's testimony merely established that petitioner was found in Florida with Cedric Brown and Maurice Fleming, a fact presented to the jury through the testimony of Terry Roberts, Detective James Smith and Ramone Augusto." *Id.* This was erroneous for three reasons.

First, if the circumstances regarding Jenkins' arrest in Florida had already been established through the testimony of Roberts, Smith and Mr. Augusto, then there was certainly no need for Ingram's additional testimony on this issue (which Judge Nangle admitted was improper). Second, the testimony of Roberts and Smith on this issue was also improper, so that cannot be used to buttress and bootstrap the improper testimony of Agent Ingram. Thirdly and most importantly, if what the prosecutor intended to accomplish by Ingram's testimony was to describe for the jury the circumstances of Jenkins' arrest, then the proper procedure for doing so was to put the arresting officer on the witness stand and have him testify succinctly and directly on that issue. There was no reason to muddy and embellish the record with the inflammatory and irrelevant hearsay testimony about conversations Ingram had with Jim Gray, Lucy Stacy, Terry Stacy and Agent Moran prior to apprehending the defendants.

With respect to Ingram's testimony about his unsuccessful search in Florida for the second gun, Judge Nangle stated, "Ingram's testimony concerning the search for the second gun did not implicate petitioner" since "Ingram specifically stated that no gun was found during the search of the abandoned house's yard and that he did not recall being informed of who allegedly disposed of the pistol." 103 F. Supp.2d at 1377. This completely misunderstands and mischaracterizes the harmful effect of Ingram's testimony on this issue.

As noted above, Ingram testified that "information [had been] developed as to the possible location of the other pistol [and] an attempt was made to find it" (Tr. 1756). This was very helpful to the State's case because it indicated to the jury that the second gun that was used to rob and murder Mr. Hodges was known to be present in Florida in the vicinity of where Jenkins had been arrested and that, although a search to find this gun was undertaken, it was unsuccessful because it was "a difficult area to search" (Tr. 1756-58). All of this testimony was based exclusively on speculation and improper hearsay, and it should not have been permitted. Agent Ingram himself had no personal knowledge regarding the existence or location of a supposed second gun, and he should not have been permitted to imply to the jury that he did.

Incredibly, clueless Judge Nangle claimed that this testimony was actually "beneficial" to Jenkins, since it "tends to highlight the weakest part of the prosecution's case: that the murder weapon allegedly used by petitioner was never found." 103 F. Supp.2d at 1377. It was true, of course, that the failure to produce a second gun, and even more importantly the failure to connect a second gun to Jenkins, was a significant hole in the prosecution's case. But what Judge Nangle completely failed to comprehend was that "fixing this hole" was the primary purpose of Ingram's improper testimony. By having Ingram testify (based entirely on speculation and hearsay) that the second gun used to kill Mr. Hodges was known to be present in Florida in the vicinity of where Jenkins was arrested, this tended to establish both the existence of the second gun and its connection to Jenkins. As Ingram testified in response to questioning by District Attorney Cheney:

    Q.   Was . . . information developed as to the possible location of the other pistol that some attempt was being made to find?

    A.   Yes, sir it was.

    Q.   Okay. And was a search made of a certain area based on that information?

    A.   Yes, sir it was.

    Q.   [I] ask you to look at what's been marked State's Exhibit 35 and see do you recognize that scene?

    A.   Yes, sir I do.

    Q.   And did you take that picture?

    A.   Yes, I did.

    Q.   Is this a picture of the area that was searched?

    A.   Yes, sir it is.

    Q.   Okay. State's Exhibit 36, [I] also ask you to look at that. Is that another photograph of the same scene?

    A.   Yes, it is.

    Q.   Okay. And did you take this photograph?

    A.   Yes, I did.

    Q.   This area that has been photographed, where is it and basically what kind of area is it?

    A.   That area is an abandoned home that is directly behind the Stacy residence, located at 15320 Northwest 33rd Avenue.

    Q.   Okay. And this was searched by several officers in an attempt to locate the weapon?

    A.   Yes, it was, on two different locations.

    Q.   What kind of area is it? Is it an easy area to search?

    A.   No. sir, it's very overgrown. The house has been abandoned, it looks like for well over a year. The weeds are up — up to the chest in many areas.

Q. Any chance to use a metal detector in the area that would locate the gun?
A. No, sir. There — the whole area is littered with different types of metal. Tin cans, that type of thing.
Q. Okay. Were y'all successful in locating the pistol in that area after the search?
A. No, sir, we were not." (Tr, at 1757-58).[141]

The entire thrust of this testimony was that Agent Ingram, and the other officers who assisted him, knew exactly where the second gun that was used to kill Mr. Hodges was located. In fact, they even took two photographs of the area. However, because there were too many weeds and tin cans in the area, they were never actually able to find the gun, since the area was "too difficult to search."

Judge Nangle falsely theorized that this testimony was favorable to Jenkins because the gun was not actually found, and therefore there was no reason for Jenkins attorneys to object to it. However, this view is completely mistaken. It is notable that this testimony was explicitly elicited by District Attorney Cheney, so he obviously thought that it was helpful to his case. And clearly it was. It established two things, both of which were highly prejudicial to Jenkins' defense. First, it established that the second gun that was used to kill Mr. Hodges had been brought down to Florida, presumably by Jenkins. Second, it established that this gun could not actually be recovered despite a diligent search because the area was "too difficult to search." But don't worry, we have two photographs of the area showing exactly where the gun was disposed of.

Contrary to Judge Nangle's overly nescient analysis, all of this evidence was entirely improper and highly prejudicial to Jenkins' defense. Accordingly, this entire line of testimony should have been objected to by Jenkins' trial lawyers, and it was erroneous and improper for Judge Nangle to conclude that their failure to do so did not constitute ineffective assistance of counsel.

---

141 Note that this entire series of questions consists of impermissible "leading questions."

The **Twelfth Ground** asserted in support of Jenkins' claim of ineffective assistance of counsel was that his trial lawyers failed to object to Roberts' testimony regarding other crimes that had been committed by his alleged co-conspirators Shawn Brown and Maurice Fleming. As Judge Nangle stated in his decision, "[p]etitioner alleges that his trial counsel were deficient in failing to object to direct examination testimony by Terry Roberts concerning other crimes with which Shawn Brown, Cedric Brown and Maurice Fleming had been charged." 103 F. Supp.2d at 1377.[142]

Judge Nangle admitted in his Decision that this occurred, but he nevertheless rejected Jenkins' claim that this amounted to an error or deficiency on the part of his trial counsel, since they used this information *(i.e.,* that Maurice and Cedric had outstanding bench warrants for prior crimes) "as an integral part of defense counsel's closing argument." 103 F. Supp.2d at 1377-78. Judge Nangle then noted, "[c]onsequently, the failure to object to this testimony was clearly part of petitioner's counsel's trial strategy." *Id.* at 1378. Finally, Judge Nangle noted, "[b]ecause petitioner has failed to establish that this strategy was unreasonable . . . the Court finds that petitioner's counsel were not deficient in failing to object to the testimony." *Id.*

Here again, Judge Nangle's circular reasoning regarding this issue was both logically and legally flawed. The reason evidence regarding prior crimes committed by Shawn and Maurice (and possibly Cedric) was highly prejudicial was because it tended to prove that these individuals were prone to criminal behavior which, in turn, tended to prove that they probably committed the robbery and murder at issue in the trial. Furthermore, the fact that Maurice had an outstanding bench warrant was apparently admitted to show that Maurice needed money to get out of town and therefore he had a motive for committing the robbery. However, if the District Attorney had attempted to admit such evidence directly *(i.e.,* that Shawn and Maurice had committed prior crimes and/or had outstanding bench

---

142 As noted previously, Jenkins did not claim that evidence of any prior crimes of Cedric Brown had been introduced, only that Maurice Fleming and Shawn Brown had other crimes. The record is unclear whether Cedric Brown may also have had a bench warrant outstanding against him. And the reason why the record is unclear is because both the prosecutor and Jenkins' defense attorneys did a poor job in clarifying Roberts' testimony on this issue.

warrants), he would have been prohibited from doing so because evidence of prior crimes is clearly inadmissible. What he could not do directly, he also should not have been permitted to do indirectly (by eliciting improper testimony from Terry Roberts).

This testimony was highly prejudicial to Jenkins because he was closely associated with Maurice and Shawn as an alleged co-conspirator in the robbery and murder of Mr. Hodges. If improper evidence of prior crimes committed by Shawn and Maurice were revealed to the jury, this would reflect badly on Jenkins also since the jury was likely to infer that Jenkins may also have committed prior crimes. Accordingly, Jenkins' trial counsel should have objected to this entire line of questioning, and they should have taken steps to insure that evidence of Shawn's and Maurice's prior crimes was not revealed to the jury. Furthermore, the notion that Maurice needed money to get out of town and this provided a motive for the robbery was also highly improper. Not only was it inadmissible hearsay, but Maurice was not even on trial. There was never any evidence suggesting that Jenkins needed money to get out of town, and therefore this testimony was completely irrelevant (and highly improper) as to him.

Instead of objecting to this testimony as they should have, Walker and Peel accepted the fact that Maurice had an outstanding bench warrant for an unrelated crime and even, as Judge Nangle correctly noted, referred to this fact in their closing summation. This was a mistake, however, not an effective "trial strategy." No reasonably competent lawyer would adopt a trial strategy that prejudices his own client by highlighting the fact that his alleged co-conspirators have prior criminal records and needed money to get out of town.

Judge Nangle argues that the fact that Jenkins' own counsel referred to Shawn's and Maurice's prior crimes in his summation provides a justification for not objecting to this evidence in the first place. But this is flawed circular reasoning. It was wrong for Jenkins' counsel not to object to this evidence in the first place, and it was equally wrong for them to refer to it during their summation. These two errors do not cancel each other out. On the contrary they magnify the harm.

Accordingly, it was an error for Jenkins' trial counsel not to object to this improper evidence, and it was error for Judge Nangle to reject Jenkins' claim that counsels' failure to object constituted ineffective assistance of counsel.

The ***Thirteenth Ground*** asserted in support of Jenkins' claim of ineffective assistance of counsel was that his trial lawyers failed to object to the prosecutors' persistent and improper use of leading questions during their direct examination of the State's witnesses. Judge Nangle rejected this claim for two separate reasons. First, ["t]he Georgia Supreme Court found 'no abuse of the trial court's discretion in regard to the prosecution's use of leading questions. Consequently, petitioner cannot establish that failure to object to these questions prejudiced his defense." 103 F. Supp.2d at 1378. Second, Judge Nangle noted that "petitioner has provided no Supreme Court precedent that failure to object to leading questions is constitutionally deficient behavior on the part of trial counsel. Accordingly, petitioner has failed to meet the requirements of *Williams*, and consequently, this allegation cannot form the basis of habeas relief." *Id.*

Needless to say, Judge Nangle was wrong on both counts. First, as to the decision of the Georgia Supreme Court, that Court did not say that it was okay for Jenkins' defense counsel to stand mute and let the prosecutor lead its witnesses without objection. What the Court said was that it found "no abuse **of the trial court's discretion** in regard to the prosecution's use of leading questions." That is a completely different question. If Jenkins' trial counsel had objected to the prosecutor's use of leading questions, it is likely that Judge Harvey would have sustained the objection and forced the prosecutor to ask proper questions. Thus, Jenkins was harmed by his counsels' **failure to object** to the prosecutor's use of leading questions, not by Judge Harvey's **failure to prohibit** the use of leading questions *sua sponte*.

Judge Nangle was also wrong with respect to his second reason. As previously explained in this Chapter, there is no requirement under Section 2254(d) of AEDPA and/or the Supreme Court's decision in *Williams* that a Supreme Court precedent must exist which precisely covers each claimed constitutional error in a federal habeas petition. All that is necessary is that a Supreme Court precedent exists which "breaks sufficient ground" for the claimed constitutional error. Here, it was crystal clear, as Judge Nangle himself admitted, that the Supreme Court "has clearly established that criminal defendants have a Sixth Amendment right to 'effective assistance' of counsel." 103 F.Supp.2d at 1374. Furthermore, as Judge Nangle himself also conceded, "[t]o establish a violation of this Sixth Amendment right," the only thing necessary is for petitioner to show "(1) that counsel's representation fell below an objective standard of reasonableness, and (2) that counsel's deficient performance prejudiced the defendant." *Id.* at 1374-75(quoting from *Strickland*). Finally, although not explicitly noted in Judge Nangle's Decision, it is also clear under *Strickland* that the adequacy or deficiency of counsel's performance must be evaluated based upon the "totality of the circumstances." This means that, if counsel committed more than one error, the **cumulative** effect of all of counsel's errors must be aggregated to determine whether the defendant was prejudiced. Thus, in Jenkins' case, even if counsel's failure to object to the prosecutor's use of leading questions was not, by itself, sufficient to conclude that his counsel's performance was deficient, this does not mean that this error should be completely disregarded. On the contrary, it should be aggregated with all the many other errors committed by Jenkins' counsel to determine whether their overall performance was deficient "under the totality of the circumstances."

Accordingly, for all of the foregoing reasons, Judge Nangle's rejection of Jenkins' claim that his counsel acted improperly in failing to object to the prosecutors' persistent use of leading questions was erroneously and improperly denied.

The ***Fourteenth*** and ***Fifteenth Grounds*** asserted in support of Jenkins' claim of ineffective assistance of counsel was that his trial lawyers failed to object to errors made during the prosecutors' summations during the guilt and penalty phases of the trial. As Judge Nangle stated, "[t]hese alleged errors include misleading the jury regarding the applicable law, misrepresenting evidence, and appealing to the jury's passions and emotions." 103 F. Supp.2d at 1378. Judge Nangle rejected this claim on the ground that, "[r]eading the prosecutor's summation in context, there is no error in his argument," and therefore "[b]ecause the prosecutor's comments were not error, petitioner can show no prejudice as a result of his counsel's failure to object to the comments." *Id.* at 1379.

Suffice it to say that, despite Judge Nangle's benign assessment of counsels' failure to object, I continue to believe, for the reasons previously stated, that the prosecutors' comments were manifestly improper and should have been objected to.[143]

The ***Sixteenth Ground*** asserted in support of Jenkins' claim of ineffective assistance of counsel was that his trial lawyers failed to object to prejudicial remarks made by Judge Harvey, in the presence of the jury, regarding the issue of whether a conspiracy existed. This situation arose during the testimony of Terry Roberts when Judge Harvey stated, in the presence of the jury, that certain hearsay statements made by Jenkins' alleged co-conspirators were admissible because of "the exception [to the hearsay rule] which allows a statement of a co-conspirator to be admitted." (Tr. 1667). This statement by the judge was very prejudicial because the question of whether a conspiracy had been established, and whether the statements were admissible on that basis, were issues of fact which the jury had to determine. Jenkins' trial counsel should have objected and requested Judge Harvey to instruct the jury to disregard the court's statements on this issue and to determine for themselves whether a conspiracy had been proven.

---

143 Mr. Walker did object to Mr. Cheney's improper comments regarding Jenkins' failure to testify (see Tr. at 1926), but he did not object to the other errors committed by Mr. Cheney.

Judge Nangle rejected this claim on the ground that "this was a ruling on an evidentiary objection raised by petitioner's counsel" and "[b]ecause there was no error by the trial court, counsel's failure to object did not prejudice the defense." 103 F. Supp.2d at 1379. The problem here is that Judge Nangle misapprehended the nature of Jenkins' claim. Jenkins was not claiming that it was improper for Judge Harvey to make a ruling on the issue of whether the hearsay statements were admissible; what he was claiming was that it was improper for him to make the ruling *in the presence of the jury*. The ruling should have been made at a sidebar conference out of the hearing of the jury.

Finally, as explained previously, under the Supreme Court's decision in *Strickland*, the prejudicial effect of all sixteen of these errors made by Jenkins' trial attorneys should have been aggregated and considered cumulatively to determine whether, under the totality of the circumstances, Jenkins was deprived of the effective assistance of counsel. Judge Nangle failed to do this, and therefore his decision on the issue of ineffective assistance of counsel was erroneous and improper for this reason also.

13.   *Denial of Jenkins' Motion for a Change of Venue (Ground 14)*

Jenkins argued, both in his appeal to the Georgia Supreme Court and in his petition for federal habeas relief, that Judge Harvey should have granted the pretrial request made by his attorneys to change the venue for the trial out of Liberty County due to profuse and prejudicial pretrial publicity and the possibility of inherent bias on the part of potential jurors due to the fact that the deceased was a prominent resident of Liberty County. Judge Harvey reserved decision on this request until after the *voir dire* of the potential jurors was completed.[144]

Once the *voir dire* was completed, the motion for a change of venue was renewed and there was considerable discussion on the record (Tr. at 1380-92) among Judge Harvey, defendants' attorneys and the District

---

144   The "*voir dire*" of the jury is the period of the trial prior to presentation of evidence when prospective jurors are questioned regarding their qualifications to serve as jurors, including whether they have any prejudices or biases.

Attorney. Mr. Walker noted, based upon the Court Clerk's statistical analysis of potential jurors who had been excused during the *voir dire*, that a sufficiently high number of potential jurors were excluded on the basis of "prior views, prejudice or bias" to warrant granting the motion. As he stated at that time:

> "Your Honor, looking at that [the statistical analysis] we feel that there is enough jurors excused that would allow the Court to grant our change of venue. Looking under the 'views' category on sheet number one, knowledge of facts of the case, person charged, automatically guilty, opinion, prejudice or bias resting on your mind, that's 22.64 percent.
>
> "Under relationships, friend of the family, related to the parties . . . [a]nd that is 9.44 percent of the friend of the family and that should be added into it, which brings it up to 31.77 percent . . . . And the related parties . . . [is] 3.77 percent, that brings it up to 35.54 [percent] that were excused because of bias, prejudice or knowledge.
>
> "And, Your Honor . . . we have several cases here where the [Georgia] Supreme Court reversed refusals or denials of a change of venue where anywhere from 20 to 27.4 percent [of prospective jurors] were excused for these same reasons. . . .
>
> "So, Your Honor, I believe that we've made our case out that there is a sufficient number of [potential] jurors that have expressed a bias or a knowledge of this case [so] that the defendant could not [get] a fair trial . . . The test is whether or not we have shown a substantial likelihood that the defendant cannot get a fair trial, and I believe that we have done that." Tr. 1380-82.

In response to Mr. Walker's statement, Judge Harvey stated as follows:

> "Well, the criteria that the Court has to apply is set forth in several recent cases and it's a two-pronged determination. Number one, the Court must consider whether the atmosphere in the community is so inherently prejudicial due to pre-trial publicity that the defendant cannot receive a fair trial in the community; and secondly, the Court must consider whether the defendant cannot receive a fair trial due to the prejudice of individual jurors." Tr. at 1382

The Clerk then noted that "these percentages [*i.e.*, the percentages that were cited by Mr. Walker] reflect the percentages of the category to the total number that were disqualified" [as opposed to the total number that were questioned], to which Mr. Cheney then noted, "This 22.64 percent is the disqualified, not the total number that were questioned. So your percentage is way down below the 22.64 percent, when you talk about the total number of jurors that were questioned."

In response to this, Mr. Walker noted that he did not agree with the statistical data that was being proposed by Mr. Cheney "because a good number of those jurors that were excused were not submitted to *voir dire*. These were people who had sick cousins, and nobody to babysit their young'uns, and this, that, and the other. We did not *voir dire* those. We simply decided we weren't gonna [keep them]." Tr. 1391. So, "we don't really accept his percentages on this." Tr. 1389.

Ultimately, Judge Harvey decided to deny the motion, stating:

> "The Court, after reviewing the statistical data's going to deny the motion for a change of venue. But in order to preserve the record in this case the Court is going to require that the court reporter mark these calculation sheets as an exhibit and the Court is also going to require that the court reporter mark the questionnaires of jurors number two through juror number 102 to be marked and

made an exhibit and part of the record in this case to be preserved as part of the record in the case." Tr. 1388-89.

Judge Nangle concluded that Judge Harvey's decision denying the motion for a change of venue was proper because Jenkins "has failed to establish that any pretrial publicity saturated the community in which the trial was held." 103 F. Supp.2d at 1379-80. In reaching this decision, Judge Nangle noted that the statistical data cited by Mr. Walker was flawed because it was calculated based upon the number of prospective jurors who had been disqualified and not upon the total number of jurors who had been questioned. As he stated in his Decision:

> "However, these percentages [*i.e.*, the ones cited by Mr. Walker and quoted above] are inaccurate. Petitioner calculated this percentage as the number excused for bias, prejudice or relationship divided by the total number excused. The correct procedure requires that the percentage be calculated as the number excused for bias, prejudice or relationship divided by the total number questioned." 103 F. Supp.2d at 1380.

I was not present in Liberty County during the time of Jenkins' trial, and therefore I have no personal knowledge regarding whether his motion for a change of venue should or should not have been granted. However, there are several flaws in Judge Nangle's somewhat simplistic analysis of this issue. First, Mr. Walker strongly disagreed with Mr. Cheney's view that the proper statistic was to divide the number of jurors excused for bias based upon the total number of jurors who were questioned. The reason for this, as he clearly explained during his argument on the motion, was that many of the potential jurors who were excused were never even questioned regarding the issue of whether they had any prejudices or biases. It would grossly distort the data, therefore, to include these people in the statistical analysis since there is no way of knowing whether they were actually biased. Judge Nangle (as well as the Georgia Supreme Court) failed to account for this problem. It is entirely possible, therefore, that the number of prospective jurors who had a bias, prejudice or interest in the case was much higher than the number assumed by Judge Nangle (and the Georgia Supreme Court).

Second, the statistical analysis of the challenges as recorded by the Court Clerk was based upon the total number of jurors who were excluded for cause, as opposed to the total number of potential jurors who were questioned. Presumably, the Court Clerk had a valid reason for compiling the data this way, and that reason was likely the same as the one cited by Mr. Walker, namely, that it made no sense to include witnesses who were dismissed for their own convenience in an analysis of witnesses who were excluded for cause.

Third, and most importantly, the statistical data that Judge Nangle (and the Georgia Supreme Court) was relying on is only one means of determining whether a motion for a change of venue should have been granted. As Judge Harvey himself correctly recognized when the motion was first made, "the Court must consider whether the atmosphere in the community is so inherently prejudicial due to pretrial publicity that the defendant cannot receive a fair trial in the community; and . . . whether the defendant cannot receive a fair trial due to the prejudice of individual jurors." Tr. 1383.

The total population of Liberty County in 1995 was approximately 57,000 people, including about 11,000 people who were living at Fort Stewart Army Base.[145] More than half of that population lived in the small city of Hinesville, the County seat and location of the courthouse. The robbery and murder of Mr. Hodges in 1993, the arrest of the various defendants shortly thereafter, and the trial of Mr. Jenkins in September of 1995 were all big news items in Hinesville and Liberty County. Unlike St. Louis, Baltimore, Detroit, Chicago and New Orleans — where the murder rate is so high people hardly notice anymore — most, if not all of the people living in Liberty County were painfully aware of Mr. Hodges' murder. As

---

145   According to the U.S. Census, the population was 52,745 in 1990 and 61,610 in 2000.

the presiding judge of the Liberty County Superior Court, Judge Harvey himself was well aware of this situation. It was his obligation, first and foremost, to insure that Jenkins got a fair trial. This was especially so since Jenkins' lawyers believed that it was impossible for him to get a fair trial in Liberty County.

Although Judge Harvey rejected Jenkins' request for a change of venue, ten months later, when the State began its trial against Maurice Fleming for exactly the same crimes that were at issue in Jenkins' trial, Judge Harvey granted Fleming's request for a change of venue and moved the case to Screven County, about seventy miles away. It strains credulity to believe that the local community prejudice and bias situation in Liberty County was any worse when Fleming was tried than when Jenkins was tried, especially since Jenkins' trial took place much closer in time to the actual murder. Despite the change of venue, Fleming was also convicted of robbery and malice murder. However, the jury only sentenced him to life imprisonment with a possibility of parole, so there may have been some benefit from the change of venue.

For all of the reasons stated above, I believe that Jenkins' motion for a change of venue should have been granted. Instead of focusing on the questionable statistical data regarding precisely how many prospective jurors were disqualified from serving on the jury based upon bias and prejudice, Judge Harvey should have focused more carefully on the question of whether Jenkins could actually get a fair trial in Liberty County under all of the circumstances of this case.

Although I believe that Jenkins' motion for a change of venue should have been granted, I do not believe that the Court's failure to grant this motion affected the outcome of the case, except possibly with respect to the issue of sentencing. Assuming Messrs. Walker and Peel represented Jenkins in the same ineffective manner as they did in Liberty County, the outcome of the trial would have been exactly the same regardless of which County the case was tried in.

14. *Failure to Answer the Jury's Question Regarding Parole Eligibility (Ground 15)*

During the penalty phase of Jenkins' trial, the jury had a choice of three possible sentences that it could impose: (i) death, (ii) life imprisonment without any possibility of parole, and (iii) life imprisonment with a possibility of parole. With respect to the sentence of life with a possibility of parole, Judge Harvey instructed the jury as follows:

> "You, the jury, may set the penalty to be imposed at life imprisonment. It is not required, and it is not necessary, that you find any extenuating or mitigating facts or circumstances in order for you to return a verdict setting the penalty to be imposed at life imprisonment. Whether or not you find any extenuating or mitigating circumstances, you are authorized to fix the penalty in this case at life imprisonment.
>
> * * * *
>
> "Under our law, life imprisonment means that the defendant will be sentenced to incarceration for the remainder of his natural life. However, **he will be eligible for parole during the term of that sentence**. If you decide to impose such a sentence of life imprisonment, you would return a verdict which reads: 'We, the jury, fix the penalty at life imprisonment.'" Tr. 2111-12 (emphasis added).

Judge Harvey concluded giving his instructions to the jury at 6:35 pm on Friday, September 1, 1995 (Tr. 2115). The jury then retired to the jury room. Five minutes later, at 6:40 pm, the jury returned to the jury box and informed Judge Harvey that they wished to recess for the evening and begin their deliberations the following morning. The trial was then recessed for the day at 6:45 pm (Tr. 2121).

The trial resumed at 8:30 am on Saturday, September 2 without the jury. Judge Harvey realized overnight that he had made an error in his charge and he held discussions with counsel about how best to correct the error. It was decided to recall the jury and give them a corrected instruction. This was done at 9:03 am. The jury then began their deliberations at 9:05 am. At 9:30 am, approximately twenty-five minutes after beginning their deliberations, the jury sent Judge Harvey a note requesting additional information about when Jenkins would become available for parole if they sentenced him to life with a possibility of parole (Tr. 2126).

This precipitated a heated discussion (on the record, but not in the presence of the jury) between Judge Harvey, the District Attorney, and Jenkins' lawyers about how to respond to the jury's request. See Tr. 2126-30. Mr. Peel immediately told Judge Harvey, "tell them it's 20 years, that's my understanding of the new guidelines." Tr. 2126. However, Mr. Cheney objected, stating "I don't think we can tell 'em." Tr. 2127. Judge Harvey agreed with Mr. Cheney, and he decided not to tell the jury anything beyond what they were previously told. Ultimately, it was decided to give the jury a written note stating as follows:

> "Beyond the instruction that the Court gave you that at some point he would be considered for parole if you impose a life sentence, the Court cannot provide you any additional instructions." Tr. 2129-30.

This note was delivered to the jury at 9:43 am (Tr. 2130). Twelve minutes later, at 9:55 am, the jury returned to the courtroom and delivered their verdict sentencing Jenkins to life imprisonment without any possibility of parole. The entire time that the jury spent deliberating was less than forty minutes, and most of that time seemed to be concerned with the question of when Jenkins would become eligible for parole if they sentenced him to life imprisonment with a possibility of parole.

Judge Nangle acknowledged in his Decision that the U.S. Supreme Court had ruled in *Simmons v. South Carolina*, 512 U.S. 154, 168-69 (1994), "that when the State relies in part on a defendant's future dangerousness [as it did in Jenkins' case], the defendant is entitled to have the jury informed if he is, in reality, ineligible for parole." Judge Nangle ruled, however, that this decision was inapplicable here because the jury had the option to sentence Jenkins to life imprisonment with the possibility of parole. As Judge Nangle stated in his Decision:

> "In the instant case, the jury was accurately informed that three sentencing options faced them: death, life without parole, and life with possibility of parole. The jury were informed that parole was available under the latter option, but were not informed exactly when said parole would be available. [Jenkins] has pointed to no clearly established Supreme Court precedent that would require the trial court to give the jury that information. . . . Accordingly, the Court will not grant habeas relief on this ground." 103 F. Supp.2d at 1381.

As usual, Judge Nangle was mistaken. In addition to *Simmons*, Jenkins had cited *Hicks v. Oklahoma*, 447 U.S. 343, 346 (1980). In that case, which did not involve the death penalty, the Supreme Court invalidated a state criminal sentence where the defendant had been sentenced by a jury to a term of forty years. Defendant had been sentenced under Oklahoma's habitual offender statute which was later declared unconstitutional in an unrelated case. When the defendant attacked his sentence, the State attempted to defend it on the ground that the jury could have sentenced defendant to a term of forty years even in the absence of any prior offenses, and therefore the sentence as imposed was within the discretion of the jury. The U.S. Supreme Court rejected this argument and held that it was a violation of due process of law to sentence defendant based upon a misunderstanding of available sentencing alternatives. As the Court stated:

> "It is argued that all that is involved in this case is the denial of a procedural right of exclusively State concern. Where, however, a State has provided for the imposition of criminal punishment in the discretion of the trial

jury . . . [t]he defendant in such a case has a substantial and legitimate expectation that he will be deprived of his liberty only to the extent determined by the jury in the exercise of its statutory discretion, and that liberty interest is one that the Fourteenth Amendment preserves against arbitrary deprivation by the State. 447 U.S. at 346 (citations omitted).

The Fifth Circuit Court of Appeals explained what is required to show a violation of this due process sentencing requirement in *Dupry v. Butler*, 837 F.2d 699 (5th Cir. 1988), stating as follows:

> "[T]o establish a valid *Hicks* claim, the state criminal defendant must show . . . that the sentencing authority lacked knowledge and understanding of the range of sentencing discretion under State law and . . . that there was a substantial possibility that prejudice was thereby caused. 837 F.2d at 703.

As the Court in *Dupry* made clear, prejudice is established "by showing that the sentencing authority was . . . ignorant of one or more less severe options" and that "a substantial possibility exists that the sentencer, if properly informed, would have chosen one of these less severe sentencing options. 837 F.2d at 703.

In *Simmons*, the Supreme Court's plurality opinion (in which four of the Justices concurred) explicitly noted that "it can hardly be questioned that most juries lack accurate information about the precise meaning of "life imprisonment" as defined by the States." 512 U.S. at 169. Justice O'Connor (joined by two other justices) concurred in the judgment and agreed that jurors cannot reasonably be expected to understand the meaning of "life imprisonment" as that term is used by the States. *Simmons*, 512 U.S. at 177 (O'Connor, J., concurring opinion). Thus, seven of the nine justices were in agreement on this point.

The Supreme Court's plurality opinion in *Simmons* also stated that "[t]he trial court's refusal to apprise the jury of information so crucial to its sentencing determination . . . cannot be reconciled with our well-established precedents interpreting the Due Process Clause." 512 U.S. at 164. Similarly, in the present case, it was a violation of Jenkins' due process rights to require the jury to choose between imposing a life sentence and a sentence of life without possibility of parole without explaining to the jury when Jenkins would become eligible for parole under a life sentence. This was particularly so in view of the fact that (i) the prosecutor had explicitly told the jury during his closing summation that "the Judge will explain to you if [a life sentence] is your decision that at some point the defendant may be considered for parole, that is, release from prison" (Tr. 2093), (ii) the jury had specifically requested additional information about when Jenkins would become eligible for parole under a life sentence (Tr. 2126), and (iii) Jenkins' attorney (Mr. Peel) had explicitly requested that the jury be told that Jenkins would become eligible for parole in twenty years. (Tr. 2126).

As noted previously, the jury spent a very small amount of time deliberating what sentence to impose (about 25 minutes prior to sending out the note and then an additional 12 minutes after receiving Judge Harvey's answer to their note). It would appear, therefore, that their primary concern was when Jenkins would become eligible for parole if they sentenced him to life with a possibility of parole. Under these circumstances, it was clearly a violation of due process to refuse to answer the jury's legitimate question about when Jenkins would become eligible for parole.

Accordingly, for all of the forgoing reasons, Judge Nangle's decision denying this ground of Jenkins' request for habeas relief was erroneous and improper.

15. *Refusal to Admit the Co-defendants' Sentences as Mitigation Evidence (Ground 16)*

The U.S. Supreme Court has clearly established that defendants must be afforded wide latitude in offering mitigation evidence in death penalty cases. *Skipper v. South Carolina*, 476 U.S. 1 (1986); *Eddings v. Oklahoma*, 455 U.S. 104 (1982); *Green v. Georgia*, 442 U.S. 95 (1979); *Lockett v. Ohio*, 438 U.S. 586 (1978). The Supreme Court has also made it very clear that whenever juries are called upon to exercise discretion in deciding what sentence to impose, they must be provided with all relevant information relating to that decision. *See Simmons v. South Carolina*, 512 U.S. 154 (1994); *Hicks v. Oklahoma*, 447 U.S. 343 (1980); *Gregg v. Georgia*, 428 U.S. 153, 190 (1994). As the Georgia Supreme Court stated in *Fugate v. State*, 263 Ga. 260, 263 (1993), "individual jurors must be allowed to consider whatever mitigating circumstances are persuasive to each of them individually, thus giving the fullest play to the jury's consideration of mitigation circumstances."

In the present case, during the penalty phase of the trial, Jenkins' attorneys attempted to introduce into evidence, on two separate occasions,[146] certified copies of court documents which showed that Cedric Brown and Shawn Brown had each been sentenced to life imprisonment **with a possibility of parole** for the very same crimes for which Jenkins had been convicted here.[147] Jenkins' attorneys argued that this evidence was relevant and admissible as "mitigation evidence" because the jury should be aware of any possibility of "disparity of sentencing" in considering what sentence to impose on Jenkins. As Mr. Peel stated in support of the evidence, "Well, Your Honor, it would be [relevant in showing] disparity of sentencing. I believe it would be relevant." Tr. 2030. Judge Harvey vigorously denied the request, stating: "That's the responsibility of the Supreme

---

146 The first attempt was made at the beginning of the penalty phase before any testimony had been presented. Tr. 2030-32. The second attempt was made after the testimony had been concluded. Tr. 2118. Both attempts were rejected by Judge Harvey on the ground that the proffered evidence was "irrelevant."

147 Cedric Brown and Shawn Brown were both permitted to plead guilty, and then they were each sentenced to life imprisonment **with** a possibility of parole. This was done because Cedric and Shawn were both ineligible to receive the death penalty or life without possibility of parole due to Cedric's mental retardation and Shawn's age.

Court under the law. . . But that's not the responsibility of the jury in this case." Tr. 2030. Both Mr. Walker and Mr. Peel strongly disagreed with Judge Harvey's ruling and continued to assert that the evidence was relevant. However, Judge Harvey stood firm, stating:

> "[D]isparity in sentencing in a death penalty case is for the Supreme Court to review as compared to other sentences. It's not for the jury. That's a question that's done by statute for the Supreme Court, but not for the jury.
>
> I mean, each case in a death penalty case, has to stand or fall on the evidence of that particular case. And so the only thing that would be relevant is what happened in this particular case. And the only thing that the jury can judge is based on the evidence in this case, not whatever the evidence was in the other case." Tr. 2031.

What Judge Harvey failed to grasp was that Jenkins' attorneys were explicitly trying to offer documentary evidence *in this case* which showed what sentences Cedric and Shawn had received. If admitted, the certified copies of the court records would have constituted **evidence in this case** that the jury could have considered in deciding what sentence to impose on Jenkins. The fact that two of the other participants in the robbery and murder of Mr. Hodges — including the so-called mastermind and principal shooter — were only sentenced to life imprisonment was highly relevant to the jury's determination.

It is true, of course, that the Georgia Supreme Court ultimately has the responsibility to determine **on appeal** whether the sentence imposed by the jury was appropriate. But that does not mean that the jury had no interest in this question. To suggest, as Judge Harvey explicitly stated, that the issue of imposing a disparate or inappropriate sentence "is not the responsibility of the jury in this case" (Tr. at 2030) is absolute nonsense. It was the jury, **and only the jury**, that had the legal responsibility to determine what sentence was appropriate and should be imposed. And, in assisting the jury to make this determination, defendants' attorneys should have been permitted to offer into evidence whatever mitigation evidence they thought was relevant. As the Supreme Court made clear in *Simmons*, whenever juries are called upon to exercise discretion in deciding what sentence to impose, they must be provided with all relevant information relating to this decision.

Judge Nangle rejected Jenkins' habeas claim on this issue on the narrow ground that Jenkens "has provided no Supreme Court authority for the proposition that evidence of co-defendants' sentences are constitutionally relevant mitigating evidence which must be presented to the jury during the penalty phase of a death penalty trial" and, "[a[ccordingly, the Georgia Supreme Court was not acting contrary to clearly established precedent when it ruled that such comparisons [of disparate sentences] are to be made by the appellate courts of Georgia and not by the jury." 103 F. Supp.2d at 1381.

As noted in several other places, this decision by Judge Nangle was based upon an incorrect interpretation of what a petitioner in a federal habeas proceeding is required to show. The Supreme Court's decisions in *Skipper*, *Eddings*, *Green*, *Lockett*, *Simmons* and *Hicks* were sufficiently specific to establish that what Judge Harvey did here was constitutionally infirm. Accordingly, Judge Nangle's decision on this issue was erroneous and improper.

16. *Constitutionality of Georgia's Life Without Possibility of Parole Statute (Ground 17)*

Jenkins argued that his sentence of life imprisonment without possibility of parole was improper and violated due process because the Georgia statute which authorized the imposition of this penalty failed to provide adequate standards to instruct the jury when it was appropriate to impose this sentence. As Judge Nangle stated in his Decision, "[p]etitioner argues in ground seventeen that the Georgia life without possibility of parole statute, O.C.G.A. § 17-10-31.1, is unconstitutional because it authorizes jurors to impose life without possibility of parole in the same categories of cases in which jurors are authorized to impose the death penalty." 103 F. Supp.2d at 1381.

To better understand this argument, it is necessary to review the Supreme Court's jurisprudence concerning the constitutionality of Georgia's death penalty statute. From the founding of the Republic in 1787 until 1972, imposition of the death penalty was always considered to be lawful and constitutional in the United States. This changed entirely in 1972 when the Supreme Court ruled in *Furman v. Georgia*, 408 U.S. 238 (1972) that Georgia's death penalty — as well as the death penalty in every other state — violated the Eighth Amendment's protection against "cruel and unusual punishment" because there were no statutory standards in place which delineated when the death penalty could and should be imposed. In effect, the Supreme Court ruled that the death penalty was unconstitutional because it was arbitrary.

Over the next few years, states, including Georgia, developed statutory standards which regulated when the death penalty could be imposed. These statutory standards essentially consisted of a list of "aggravating factors" that had to be found by a jury to be present in order to justify the imposition of the death penalty. If one or more of these aggravating factors was found to exist, then the jury was authorized, although not required, to impose the death penalty. In order for the jury to impose the death penalty, however, there had to be a "second trial" on the issue of punishment at which the State was obligated to prove the existence of one or more of the aggravating factors beyond a reasonable doubt and, at which, the defendant had the opportunity to present "mitigating evidence" in opposition to the death penalty. This statutory scheme was found to be constitutional by the Supreme Court in *Gregg v. Georgia*, 428 U.S. 153 (1976) and many states, including Georgia, were thereafter able to resume the ugly business of executing prisoners for certain enumerated capital crimes.

At the time when *Gregg* was decided, jurors had only two sentencing options in capital cases: they could either impose the death penalty in those cases in which certain statutorily defined aggravating factors were found to exist, or they could choose not to impose the death penalty, in which case the trial judge was required to sentence the defendant to life imprisonment. There was no option for either the jury or the trial judge to sentence the defendant to life without possibility of parole.

In 1993, the Georgia Assembly modified this statutory framework by enacting OCGA § 17-10-31.1, which permitted jurors to impose a new sentence of life imprisonment without possibility of parole as an alternative to the death penalty. In order for the jury to impose this new sentence, it was still necessary for the jury to find, beyond a reasonable doubt, that the State had proved the existence of one or more of the aggravating factors that justified the imposition of the death penalty. The problem with this new statutory scheme, however, is that no standards were provided to allow the jury to determine when it was appropriate to impose the death penalty versus when it was appropriate to sentence the defendant to life without possibility of parole. In effect, by enacting the alternative sentence of life without possibility of parole without providing any statutory standards governing when this sentence was appropriate, the Georgia Assembly reintroduced the same arbitrariness which the Supreme Court condemned in *Furman*.

Judge Nangle, like the Georgia Supreme Court before him, rejected Jenkins' argument that OCGA § 17-10-31.1 was unconstitutional on the ground that Georgia's death penalty statute had been upheld by the U.S. Supreme Court in *Gregg*. As Judge Nangle stated in his Decision, "the Supreme Court dismissed this very argument in *Gregg v. Georgia*." 103 F. Supp.2d at 1381.

This argument by Judge Nangle (and by the Georgia Supreme Court) was not correct. As just explained, Section 17-10-31.1 of the Georgia Code had not yet been enacted when *Gregg* was decided so it could not possibly have been considered by the Supreme Court in that case. By relying on

Gregg as the sole basis for his decision, Judge Nangle completely ignored Jenkins' argument as to why Section 17-10-31.1 was unconstitutional.

As explained above, the problem with Section 17-10-31.1 was that it reintroduced into Georgia death penalty law the very same ambiguity that the Supreme Court had found objectionable (and unconstitutional) in *Furman*. Instead of having one clear set of standards delineating when the death penalty could properly be imposed, the jury was now faced with two competing alternatives (death or life without possibility of parole) and no clearly articulated basis to choose which of these alternatives was more appropriate. The net result, therefore, was that the jury's decision regarding which penalty to impose was completely arbitrary. Not only is this a violation of the Eighth Amendment's prohibition against cruel and unusual punishment, it is also a violation of due process of law. Accordingly, Judge Nangle's decision that Section 17-10-31.1 was constitutional was improper.

17. *Denial of Cumulative Error Relief (Ground 18)*

Jenkins argued in his petition for a writ of habeas corpus, "that the Georgia courts' failure to recognize the cumulative error rule deprived him of due process of law" in violation of the Fourteenth Amendment. 103 F. Supp.2d at 1382 (quoting from Jenkins Mem. Supp. Pet. Habeas Corpus at 108-110). In support of this argument, Jenkins had cited numerous decisions of the federal Courts of Appeals (including decisions of the Eleventh

Circuit Court of Appeals) which had ruled that cumulative error analysis was constitutionally required.[148]

Judge Nangle summarily denied this argument on the ground that "there is no clearly established Supreme Court precedent requiring this rule" and, therefore, "the Court finds this ground insufficient to state a claim for habeas corpus relief." 103 F. Supp.2d at 1382. This was thus another instance in which Judge Nangle felt compelled by his erroneous interpretation of Section 2254(d) of AEDPA to deny Jenkins' request for habeas relief. In so doing, he ignored a clearly controlling decision of the Eleventh Circuit. He also failed to exercise his "independent obligation to say what federal law is."[149]

18. *Constitutionality of 28 U.S.C. § 2254(d) (Ground 19)*

Finally, Jenkins argued that Section 2254(d) of the Antiterrorism and Effective Death Penalty Act of 1996 was unconstitutional "because it limits federal courts' ability to interpret and apply federal law as that law is decided **by the Circuit Courts**." 103 F. Supp.2d at 1382 (quoting from

---

[148] It is manifestly clear to me — and to many of the federal Courts of Appeal that have considered this issue — that the cumulative error rule is constitutionally required by the due process clauses of the Fifth and Fourteenth Amendments. Yet, to this day, the United States Supreme Court has failed to rule on this issue, making it extremely difficult for petitioners like Jenkins to base habeas claims on this ground. The Supreme Court was presented with a great opportunity to rectify this problem in 2018 in the infamous case of *Texas v. Carty*, 543 S.W.3d 149 (Tex. Crim. App. 2018). Linda Carty, a dual citizen of the United Kingdom and the United States who resided in Texas, was convicted of murder in 2002 and sentenced to death. As a result of several collateral proceedings that she subsequently brought in both state and federal courts, it was determined that numerous errors had occurred during her trial, but none of them serious enough to warrant reversal of her conviction. On July 9, 2018, Carty filed a petition for certiorari with the U.S. Supreme Court requesting that her state court conviction be reversed based upon the cumulative error doctrine. Both the United Kingdom and the National Association of Criminal Defense Lawyers filed amicus curiae briefs requesting that the Court grant certiorari. However, on November 13, 2018, the petition for certiorari was denied. Ms. Carty remains incarcerated at the Texas Death Row facility awaiting execution by lethal injection. The case garnered a significant amount of publicity and television coverage, including several documentaries that were broadcast in the United Kingdom.

[149] As explained in Chapter 7, the Georgia Supreme Court finally ruled in 2020 that Georgia's consistent failure to apply the cumulative error rule was never a correct application of Georgia law. In so ruling, the Court reversed every prior Georgia case that had failed to consider the cumulate error rule, including Jenkins' case. I had explained to Judge Nangle back 1998 that the Georgia rule was unconstitutional because it failed to comply with federal constitutional requirements, but he simply failed to listen and do his duty. This entire problem might have been avoided twenty years earlier if Judge Nangle had a little more humility, a modicum of perspicacity, and a lot less hubris and intransigence.

Jenkins Mem. Supp. Pet. Habeas Corpus at 111) (emphasis added). It will be remembered that Section 2254(d) limited the authority of federal courts to grant writs of habeas corpus reversing state court criminal convictions to clearly established federal law **as determined by the United States Supreme Court**.

Quoting from and misapplying Justice Stevens' opinion in *Williams v. Taylor*, 529 U.S. 362 (2000), Judge Nangle rejected Jenkins' argument, stating as follows:

> "[A]s Justice Stevens noted in *Williams*, although this provision [section 2254(d)] limit[s] the source of doctrine on which a federal court may rely in addressing the application for a writ, it does not, however, purport to limit the federal courts' independent interpretative authority with respect to federal questions. Accordingly, the Court finds that 28 U.S.C. § 2254(d) is not unconstitutional." 103 F. Supp.2d at 1382.

The problem with Judge Nangle's analysis — whether consciously or unconsciously I cannot say — is that he said one thing but he actually did another. Although Judge Nangle stated in his decision that Section 2254(d) "does not purport to limit the federal courts' independent interpretative authority with respect to federal questions" (103 F. Supp.2d at 1382), Judge Nangle acted precisely as though it did. Throughout his opinion, Judge Nangle repeatedly states that certain principles of law that were decided by federal circuit courts cannot be relied on as a basis for Jenkins' request for habeas relief because those decisions were not decided by the Supreme Court. Thus, for example, in rejecting Jenkins' argument that improper comments made by the prosecutor regarding his failure to testify violated his Fifth Amendment privilege against self-incrimination, Judge Nangle explicitly stated:

> "Petitioner cites numerous circuit cases holding that the prosecutor may not comment on a defendant's failure

to call witnesses if the only potential witnesses was the defendant himself (citations omitted). However, this legal rule has never been clearly established by the United States Supreme Court. Thus, under *Williams*, this rule of law cannot be the basis for habeas relief." 103 F. Supp.2d at 1361.

This is a complete misapplication of the *Williams* decision. In *Williams* itself, the Supreme Court reversed a decision of the Fourth Circuit Court of Appeals which had refused to grant a writ of habeas corpus vacating a Virginia state court criminal conviction for similar grounds as that cited by Judge Nangle here, namely, that the rule relied on was not clearly established by the U.S. Supreme Court. However, as the Supreme Court clarified in *Williams*, all that is necessary is that the Supreme Court "has broken sufficient legal ground to establish an asked for constitutional principle." 529 U.S. at 381. Once that has occurred, then the exact parameters of the legal principle at issue can be explicated by decisions of the lower federal courts. As Judge Stevens made clear in *Williams*, "[w]e have always held that federal courts, even on habeas, have an independent obligation to say what the law is. We are convinced that in the phrase, 'clearly established law,' Congress did not intend to modify that independent obligation." 529 U.S. at 384.

In effect, what Judge Nangle did was to interpret Section 2254(d) one way for the purpose of considering its constitutionality (saying that Section 2254(d) does not limit the ability of lower federal courts to interpret federal law) and then he applied that section another way in deciding what judicial precedents Jenkins could cite in support of his habeas petition (saying that only Supreme Court precedents could be cited). As will be discussed later, this was precisely the reason why Jenkins commenced a declaratory judgment lawsuit in the Eastern District of New York, alleging that Section 2254(d) was both unconstitutional **on its face** and **as applied by Judge Nangle** in Jenkins' habeas proceeding. Unfortunately, as also discussed later, the EDNY and the Second Circuit Court of Appeals both concluded (erroneously) that federal courts did not have subject matter jurisdiction to decide this important issue.

To briefly summarize this very lengthy and complicated discussion, Judge Nangle's inept but well-organized Decision was totally wrong with respect to every issue he considered and discussed. In the final analysis, Jenkins' request for federal habeas relief should unquestionably have been granted, and his State court conviction and sentence should have been vacated and reversed.

CHAPTER 11

JUDGE NANGLE RETURNS TO THE STAGE

On July 17, 2000, Jenkins filed a timely Notice of Appeal from Judge Nangle's Order and Decision denying his Petition for a Writ of Habeas Corpus. Such an appeal would normally be heard by the United States Circuit Court of Appeals for the Eleventh Circuit in Atlanta, Georgia. Furthermore, under normal circumstances, the filing of the Notice of Appeal would divest the district court of jurisdiction over the matter, and all further proceedings would take place in the Court of Appeals.

Unfortunately, the recently enacted Antiterrorism and Effective Death Penalty Act of 1996 ("AEDPA") effectively changed all that. Under AEDPA, it was now necessary for Jenkins to obtain a ***certificate of appealability*** ("COA") from the district court before he could pursue an appeal. What was previously an automatic right to appeal was converted by AEDPA into a limited right to seek permission to appeal.

AEDPA contemplated that the district court judge who decided the petition for habeas corpus would be in the best position to issue (or refuse to issue) this Certificate, since he or she had just spent a considerable amount of time adjudicating the issues and therefore, presumably, he or she knew which issues, if any, provided plausible grounds for appeal. Thus, the district court judge had the discretion, in the first instance, to decide which issues, if any, could be appealed.

In the event that the petitioner was not satisfied with the appealability decision rendered by the district court judge, the petitioner was then permitted under AEDPA to make a request directly to the Court of

Appeals, either to grant a new COA, or to expand one previously granted by the district court.

Finally, under AEDPA it was **mandatory** for the district court judge who had decided the request for habeas corpus to rule on the issue of appealability after a Notice of Appeal was filed. There was no need for the petitioner to make a separate motion requesting a COA. The mere filing of the Notice of Appeal was sufficient to trigger the district judge's obligation to rule on the issues of appealability.

Pursuant to AEDPA, therefore, Judge Nangle was **required by law** to rule on the issue of appealability within a reasonable time after Jenkins filed his Notice of Appeal on July 17, 2000. That never happened, however.

On September 1, 2000, while waiting for Judge Nangle to rule on the issue of appealability, Jenkins filed a motion for permission to proceed on the appeal "*in forma pauperis*" (in the manner of a poor person). This was necessary to avoid the very expensive printing costs that would otherwise be incurred in pursuing the appeal.[150] By proceeding *in forma pauperis*, it would be permissible to proceed with typewritten briefs and photocopied copies of the record in lieu of having them printed (in multiple copies) by a commercial printer.

Remarkably, the motion to proceed *in forma pauperis* was promptly **granted** by Judge Nangle on September 6, 2000. This was the first and only time Judge Nangle ever ruled in Jenkins' favor in the entire history of the habeas proceeding. Unfortunately, as discussed below, this victory was short-lived.

On September 15, 2000, Thomas K. Kahn, the Clerk of the Eleventh Circuit Court of Appeals wrote a letter to Henry R. Crumley, the Clerk of the District Court, stating that Jenkins' Notice of Appeal and Judge Nangle's Order granting Jenkins permission to proceed *in forma pauperis* had been

---

150 The costs involved in pursuing the original motion in the district court were manageable, and therefore there was never any need to proceed *in forma pauperis* in the district court. The printing costs for an appeal, however, would have been extensive.

received and docketed, but noting that a ruling on the issue of appealability (as required by AEDPA) was lacking. As Mr. Kahn stated in this letter:

> "[A] ruling by your court on certificate of appealability is also required. **This appeal cannot proceed until this matter is resolved.** If there has been a ruling, or when there is a ruling, please promptly forward this office a copy of that order (emphasis added).

This gentle reminder should have been sufficient to spur Judge Nangle to issue a ruling on the issue of appealability, but it was not. Instead, he issued a new Order, **sua sponte**, revoking the Order of September 6 which had granted Jenkins permission to proceed *in forma pauperis*.

The rationale provided by Judge Nangle for issuing this new Order was that Jenkins had never made an application for a COA, which, of course, he had no obligation to do. As Judge Nangle stated in his September 18 Order:

> "On September 6, 2000, this Court issued an Order granting petitioner leave to appeal in forma pauperis (Doc 20). Since that time, it has come to the Court's attention that petitioner has not made an application for a certificate of appealability. If petitioner intended for his notice of appeal to serve as such an application, then it is inadequate because it makes no substantial showing of the denial of a constitutional right, as required by [AEDPA]. Therefore, this Court cannot issue a certificate of appealability at this time and must set aside its Order dated September 6, 2000 *nunc pro tunc*."

Apparently, this eminent jurist, honored in his obituary as "an outstanding person . . . and a role model to all who knew him," liked playing other games besides tennis. Unfortunately, this game was intended to deprive a 21-year-old black male of his liberty for the rest of his life. That probably should have been mentioned in Jack's obituary.

Once again, I just could not believe what had happened. How could any lawyer, especially a venerable United States district court judge, be so malevolent and prickish as to deny a litigant his right to appeal, especially when his liberty from life imprisonment was at stake.

My initial thought was to apply immediately to the Court of Appeals for the necessary certificate of appealability. As I thought more about it, however, I decided to give Judge Nangle the opportunity to redeem himself. After all, following our initial skirmish regarding the oversized memorandum that he had so childishly objected to, he did eventually allow Jenkins' petition for habeas to go forward and he did eventually recognize the utility of the memorandum. He erroneously denied the petition, of course, but at least he allowed it to proceed. Perhaps he just needed the same type of face-saving opportunity here.

And so, on September 28, 2000, I drafted a motion for a COA explaining in considerable detail the reasons why such a certificate was meritorious and should be granted. I was still not permitted to appear as Jenkins' attorney, however, due to Judge Nangle's prior order denying my application to appear *pro hac vice*. Accordingly, I signed Jenkins' name to the motion and filed it on his behalf.[151]

I was hopeful this would do the trick. No such luck. Even when faced with a well-reasoned motion explaining why a COA should be granted, Judge Nangle displayed once again what an absolute scalawag he was. Instead of considering the legal arguments advanced in the motion, he ruled that the motion was **untimely** because it failed to satisfy some imaginary deadline that Judge Nangle entirely dreamed up. As he stated in his October 23 Order refusing to grant a COA:

> "This Court denied [Jenkins'] petition for habeas corpus on June 21, 2000. [Jenkins] filed his application for a COA

---

[151] Although I was not authorized to appear **as an attorney** on Jenkins' behalf in the District Court for the Southern District of Georgia, I was authorized to act as his agent under both Georgia and New York law.

on September 28, 2000, well outside the 60-day limit of Federal Rule of Appellate Procedure 4(a)(1)."

This was completely wrong, and Judge Nangle, who by this time had been a federal district judge for 27 years, certainly must have known that it was completely wrong. Rule 4(a)(1) of the Federal Rules of Appellate Procedure ("FRAP") has absolutely nothing to do with the issuance of a COA in habeas corpus cases, which is governed by AEDPA, not by FRAP. The relevant text of Rule 4(a)(1) is as follows:

"Rule 4 — Appeal as of Right. When Taken

(a) Appeal in a Civil Case

(1) Time for filing a *Notice of Appeal*

(A) In a civil case . . . the *notice of appeal* required by Rule 3 must be filed with the district clerk within 30 days after entry of the judgment or order appealed from.

(B) The *notice of appeal* may be filed by any party within 60 days after entry of the judgment or order appealed from if one of the parties is:

(i) the United States,

(ii) a United States Agency,

(ii) a United States officer or employee sued in an official capacity, or

(iv) a current or former United States officer or employee sued in an individual capacity for an act or omission occurring in connection with duties performed on the Unted States' behalf . . . ." (emphasis added).

As can clearly be seen, this rule deals exclusively with the question of when a *notice of appeal* must be filed, not when a motion for a COA must be filed. And, as already noted above, Jenkins filed his Notice of Appeal on July 17, 2000, which was clearly within the time specified by FRAP Rule

4(a)(1). Once the Notice of Appeal was filed, Judge Nangle himself was **obligated** by ADEPA to rule on the issues of appealability. There was no need for Jenkins to make a motion for a COA, much less to do so within a certain time period.

Notably, in *Edwards v. United States*, 114 F.3d 1083 (1997), the Eleventh Circuit Court of Appeals had explicitly instructed all district courts within the Eleventh Circuit to treat a notice of appeal as an application for a COA and to act accordingly. As the Court stated in its opinion:

> "District courts **must** treat notices of appeal filed by petitioners following a denial of either a Section 2254 or a Section 2255 petition as applications for COAs" (emphasis added).[152]

This explicit directive of the Eleventh Circuit was reaffirmed by the Court of Appeals in *Jones v. United States*, 224 F.3d 1251, 1255 (11th Cir. 2000) just a few months before Judge Nangle issued his Order. As the Eleventh Circuit stated in *Jones*, "the COA process begins in the district court when the prisoner files **either a certificate of appeal or a request for a COA**" (emphasis added).

It is undeniable that Judge Nangle was aware of this directive from the Eleventh Circuit, since he actually mentioned the *Edwards* case in his October 23 Order denying Jenkins' motion for a COA as untimely. Why Judge Nangle thought he had the right to ignore an explicit directive from the higher court is perplexing, particularly since he had chastised me for failing to follow the local court rules of the Southern District of Georgia regarding the maximum length of legal memoranda.

Finally, not only did Judge Nangle apply the wrong statute, he applied the wrong statute **incorrectly**. Judge Nangle stated, "an application for a COA must be brought within the **60-day time limit** of Federal Rule of Appellate Procedure 4(a)(1) for it to be timely regardless of when or if a [notice of appeal] was filed." Order at 4 (emphasis added). Rule 4(a)(1)

---

152 The difference between a Section 2254 habeas petition and a Section 2255 habeas petition is that the former is for prisoners in state custody while the latter is for prisoners in federal custody.

of the Appellate Rules, of course, does **not** apply to requests for a COA, but, if it did, the time limit would be 30 days, not 60 days as cited by Judge Nangle.[153]

Once again, I was completely astounded by Judge Nangle's denial of Jenkins' motion for a COA, especially since it was based upon an erroneous application of several federal laws, and it was directly contrary to the explicit directive of the Eleventh Circuit that notices of appeal from habeas proceedings must be treated by the district courts as motions for a COA under AEDPA.

Although I was severely disappointed and perplexed by Judge Nangle's Order, I am a patient and reasonable person. I assumed that the Order must have resulted from a negligent failure to understand the applicable law, rather than a deliberate choice to violate it. Accordingly, I decided to make one final attempt to convince Judge Nangle that he was mistaken. On October 31, 2000 — eight days after the Order denying the motion for a COA as untimely — I moved for reconsideration of that Order. Actually, I merely prepared the papers. They were submitted by Jenkins as "petitioner *pro se*" since I was not permitted to represent him. As stated in the six-page memorandum in support of the motion for reconsideration, "the Court's order denying petitioner's motion for a certificate of appealability was based upon an erroneous interpretation of law." Three different reasons why this was so were specified and explained.

Unfortunately, Judge Nangle was unwilling to accept this proffered lifeline. He continued to adhere to his previous views, and he denied the motion for consideration in an Order dated November 7, 2000. Yet another attempt to get a new trial for a possibly wrongfully convicted person had been erroneously foreclosed by a powerful judge who appeared to be acting solely out of ignorance and malice. And, by the way, he sent the Order denying the motion for reconsideration to me, at my office in New York,

---

153 As can be seen from the explicit language of Rule 4(a)(1) quoted above, the 60-day time limit for filing a notice of appeal only applies to cases and proceedings against the United Staes. Jenkins' habeas proceeding was brought against the Warden of Telfair State Prison, an officer of the State of Georgia, and therefore he was required to file his notice of appeal within thirty days.

and not to Jenkins, who was representing himself *pro se*, due to Judge Nangle's prior order refusing to allow me to represent Jenkins *pro hac vice*.

CHAPTER 12

APPEAL TO THE ELEVENTH CIRCUIT U.S. COURT OF APPEALS

Obviously, as made crystal clear in the prior chapter, I was more than a little disappointed by Judge Nangle's obstinate refusal to issue a COA that would have permitted Jenkins to appeal to the United States Court of Appeals for the Eleventh Circuit.[154] I was not worried, however, because, under the explicit terms of AEDPA, it was still permissible for Jenkins to apply directly to the Court of Appeals for a COA.

And that is exactly what I did. On November 14, 2000, I made a motion on Jenkins' behalf for issuance of a COA by the Court of Appeals. This motion was a fairly extensive undertaking consisting of a five-page motion, a nineteen-page affidavit in support of the motion, and more than an inch of documents that were attached to the affidavit as exhibits. One of the attached exhibits was the original 112-page Memorandum in support of Jenkins' Petition for a writ of habeas corpus which Judge Nangle had found so offensive. The motion requested that the Court of Appeals issue a COA with respect to **all nineteen** of the errors that had been raised as grounds for relief in the petition for habeas corpus.

Having made this motion, I was fairly confident that the Court of Appeals (a respected Court with a good reputation) would grant the COA. It was, after all, unquestionably the right thing to do, at least it was in

---

154 For the purpose of appealing decisions of the district courts, the United States is divided into eleven different judicial circuits, with each circuit covering a number of different states. Originally, there were only ten circuits, but the Fifth Circuit became so large that it was divided into two separate circuits. Georgia is located in the Eleventh Circuit and the principal courthouse for the Eleventh Circuit is located in Atlanta. In addition to these eleven circuits, there is also a separate Court of Appeals for the District of Columbia (the D.C. Circuit).

almost all states outside of Georgia.[155] Once again, however, I was severely shocked and disappointed. On March 1, 2001, the Court of Appeals, in a two-page Order signed by Charles B. Wilson, United States Circuit Judge, granted Jenkins a COA limited to *a single issue only* and denied his request for a COA with respect to all other issues. The entirety of this Order stated as follows:

> "Appellant's motion for a certificate of appealability is GRANTED on the following issue only:
>
> > Whether the district court erred in denying appellant's claim that counsel was ineffective for misleading him regarding his right to testify in his own behalf.
>
> No certificate of appealability should issue on the remaining issues appellant raises, because he failed to make a substantial showing of the denial of a constitutional right, see 28 U.S.C. § 2253(c)(2)."

With all due respect to the learned Judge Wilson, there were two fundamental problems with this Order. First, as the United States Supreme Court had made perfectly clear, the question of whether a defendant in a criminal case has been denied the effective assistance of counsel must be evaluated in light of **all** of the facts and circumstances of the case, not just one or two of the most egregious errors. *Strickland v. United States*, 466 U.S. 335 (1963). As the Supreme Court stated in that case, "[t]he performance inquiry [regarding whether counsel's performance at trial was deficient] must be whether counsel's assistance was reasonable considering **all the circumstances.**" 466 U.S. at 688 (emphasis added).

Here, Jenkins had enumerated *fifteen* additional reasons why his trial counsels' performance had been deficient besides the issue of whether they had misled him concerning his right to testify in his own defense.

---

155 Technically speaking, the Eleventh Circuit Court of Appeals is a *federal* court, not a Georgia court. But the courthouse for the Eleventh Circuit is located in Atlanta, and I guess there must be something in the water down there that prevents judges from thinking clearly.

Many of these additional reasons were extremely important, such as counsels' failure to request a jury charge regarding the key issue of corroboration of an accomplice's testimony, counsels' failure to object to the so-called "silent witness" testimony, and counsels' failure to impeach Terry Roberts with his prior inconsistent statements. Under these circumstances, it was completely improper and downright negligent for Judge Wilson to limit the COA to a single ground regarding whether Jenkins' trial counsel had been deficient. All sixteen of the grounds asserted by Jenkins needed to be considered.

The second problem with Judge Wilson's Order was that it completely eliminated almost all of the issues that Jenkins had raised as meritorious grounds for his appeal. Jenkins had asserted, in his petition for habeas corpus, and in his motion for a COA, that his Georgia murder conviction was invalid because of **eighteen** constitutional violations that occurred during his trial in addition to the ineffective assistance of counsel claim. Judge Wilson stated in his Order refusing to grant a COA with respect to these additional grounds that Jenkins "failed to make a substantial showing of the denial of a constitutional right" with respect to these issues.

Here again, with all due respect to Judge Wilson, the affidavit and the copious exhibits that were attached thereto did, in fact, "make a substantial showing of the denial of a constitutional right" with respect to these additional issues. Indeed, the nineteen-page affidavit explicitly explained why Jenkins had been denied his constitutional rights with respect to each of the nineteen grounds that had been asserted in the petition for habeas corpus and the motion for issuance of a COA. The plain and simple fact of the matter was that Judge Wilson applied the wrong standard in determining whether Jenkins had made a "substantial showing of the denial of a constitutional right."

It would have been nice, of course, if Judge Nangle had granted the petition for habeas corpus, since that would clearly have demonstrated that "a substantial showing of the denial of a constitutional right" had been made. But if Judge Nangle had granted the petition, then there would not be any need for Jenkins to appeal. Clearly, it cannot be necessary to show a likelihood of success on the merits in order to bring an appeal, since that is a standard that can never be satisfied.

Any time there is an appeal in a habeas proceeding, it is precisely because the district court judge did not agree with the petitioner's assertion that he had been denied a constitutional right. Otherwise, the petition would have been granted. But the fact that Judge Nangle did not believe that any of Jenkins' constitutional rights had been violated did not mean that Jenkins failed to make a "substantial showing" that his constitutional rights had been violated. An experienced criminal trial attorney with thirty years of experience had submitted an affidavit in which he averred **under oath** that he believed that Jenkins' constitutional rights had been violated, and he explained in considerable detail precisely why in the affidavit. Furthermore, a detailed memorandum of law had been submitted along with the affidavit which explained precisely how and why Jenkins' constitutional right had been violated. If this was not sufficient to make a "substantial showing," I cannot possibly imagine what Judge Wilson would have deemed to be sufficient.

Unfortunately, Judge Wilson made his ruling, and there was nothing I could do about it.[156] On one hand, I thought that this might be a good development, since it probably signaled that the Court of Appeals intended to reverse Jenkins' conviction on this single ground alone. Why else would they ignore the Supreme Court's decision in *Strickland* and limit Jenkins' appeal on the ineffective assistance of counsel claim to a single error? On the other hand, if the Court of Appeals was not signaling that it intended to reverse Jenkins' conviction on this ground, then it was very bad news indeed.

---

156 As will be discussed in Chapter 13, I also instituted an entirely new lawsuit in Brookyln, New York, which alleged that Judge Nangle and the Eleventh Circuit had unconstitutionally applied Sections 2254(d) and 2254(c) of AEDPA.

The next step was to pursue the limited appeal that was permitted to Jenkins under the COA as granted. On April 3, 2000, I served and filed a copy of Appellant's Record Excerpts and the Brief for Appellant. As required by the COA, the Brief for Appellant was limited to the single issue of whether Jenkins' "counsel was ineffective for misadvising him regarding his right to testify in his own behalf." As stated in the Brief for Appellant, the "issue presented for review" was as follows:

> "Whether Appellant was deprived of his constitutional right to effective assistance of counsel due to the fact that he was misled by his counsel regarding the likely outcome of the trial and wrongfully and unjustifiably advised by his attorneys not to testify at trial?"

Although Jenkins' Brief was promptly filed on April 3, 2000, the case was delayed extensively before getting to the Court of Appeals for decision. On July 18, 2000, Henry R. Crumley, Jr., the Deputy Clerk of the District Court for the Southern District of Georgia, certified that the record was complete for appeal. On May 7, 2001, after several requests for enlargement of time to file his brief, Thomas E. Byrd, the Warden of Telfair State Prison, represented by the Attorney General of the State of Georgia, finally served and filed his Brief for Appellee. On May 23, 2001, Jenkins served and filed his Reply Brief for Appellant. I also requested that the matter be orally argued before the Court. The State of Georgia opposed oral argument, and the request for oral argument was denied by the Court.

On August 10, 2001, a three-judge panel of the Court of Appeals issued a seven-page decision unanimously denying Jenkins' appeal.[157] The Court concluded that the performance of Jenkins' attorneys at the trial had been "reasonable" and, therefore, there was no basis for concluding that they had been "ineffective." Accordingly, since they found that Jenkins had

---

[157] The various Circuit Courts of Appeals are normally composed of about twenty judges for each circuit, although some are larger and some are smaller. However, individual appeals are decided by "panels" of three judges on a rotating basis. If necessary and appropriate, a request can be made by a party for a rehearing *en banc*, meaning that all the circuit judges participate. However, this is rarely granted.

failed to show that his counsel had been ineffective — and since that was the only ground that Jenkins had been allowed to pursue on appeal — the Court of Appeals affirmed the decision of Judge Nangle denying his petition for habeas corpus.[158]

Needless to say, I strongly disagreed with this decision, and I will attempt to explain to you why I believe their decision was wrong. I made these same arguments to the judges of the Court of Appeals and failed, but maybe you will consider my perspective with a more open mind.

As a preliminary matter, let me repeat that the Court of Appeals only heard one possible ground as to why Jenkins' trial attorneys had been ineffective, and they completely ignored many other grounds due to the stringent limitations that had been placed on Jenkins' appeal by the COA. Even with respect to this one ground, however, I believe that the decision of the Court of Appeals was dead wrong.

The Judges of the Court of Appeals clearly understood what Jenkins' argument was. As they stated in their decision:

> "Jenkins argues that, because the theory of the case was that he was a mere bystander, it was imperative that he testify because his counsel did not present any evidence to support that theory. He also argues that counsel misled him about the probable outcome of the trial by telling him before he made the decision not to testify that it was going well and that he need not testify. This erroneous information, he argues, prevented him from making an informed decision when he chose to waive his right to testify in his own defense." Decision at 2.

In fairness to the Court of Appeals, this is a very accurate summary of what Jenkins was complaining about. Let me emphasize some of the key facts that the Court itself noted here: (i) Jenkins claimed "that he was

---

[158] For some reason (perhaps embarrassment), the decision of the Court was explicitly marked "DO NOT PUBLISH" and therefore the decision was not officially reported in the Federal Reporter. A copy of the Decision is reprinted in Appendix C.

a mere bystander"; (ii) Jenkins' lawyers "did not present any evidence to support that theory"; (iii) Jenkins' lawyers "misled him about the probable outcome of the trial and told him that the trial was going well and there was no need for him to testify"; and (iv) "this erroneous information prevented him from making an informed decision when he chose to waive his right to testify in his own defense." How the Court ever got from this restatement of the issues to saying that Jenkins' trial lawyers acted reasonably is another matter. It seems incomprehensible to me.

In assessing whether Jenkins' counsel had acted reasonably, the Court noted that, at the evidentiary hearing in support of the motion for a new trial, counsel "testified that they advised Jenkins not to testify because his flat denial of the charges did not add anything to his plea of not guilty." Decision at 5. It is true that counsel said this at the hearing, but that does not make their actions "reasonable."

On the contrary, it shows how completely unreasonable their conduct was. When Jenkins testified at the hearing, he did a whole lot more than simply say "not guilty." He denied, under oath, that he had anything to do with the robbery, that he ever shot Mr. Hodges, that he ever told anyone that he had shot Mr. Hodges, that he ever had a gun, and that he never knew anything about the robbery before it happened. This was extremely important testimony for the jury to hear if Jenkins expected them to believe that he was merely a bystander and not a participant in the robbery. And, by the way, it was the *only* evidence that could be presented to show that Jenkins was a mere bystander, and therefore it was essential.

The assertion of Jenkins' counsel — and the acceptance of this assertion by the judges of the Court of Appeals — that this testimony "did not add anything to his plea of not guilty" is just plain wrong, and I cannot comprehend how any reasonable lawyer or jurist would ever say such a foolish thing. Furthermore, as the eminent judges of the Court of Appeals either knew or should have known, the "pleadings" in a case, including a plea of "not guilty," do *not* constitute *evidence* in the case. As Judge

Harvey explicitly and properly instructed the jury prior to their deliberations, "Neither is the plea of not guilty to be considered as evidence." Tr. at 1973. On the other hand, if Jenkins had testified, his testimony would most certainly have constituted valuable evidence. It is indisputable, therefore, that Jenkins' sworn testimony regarding these issues would have "added" a great deal beyond his plea of not guilty.

In further support of the "reasonableness" of trial counsels' decision not to let Jenkins testify, the decision of the Court of Appeals noted as follows:

> "Additionally, they were afraid of what the prosecutor might elicit on cross-examination and at the evidentiary hearing, that fear proved well-founded. Jenkins testified at the hearing that he was outside of Hodges' store at the time of the murder. He also testified that he saw one of the other accused men shoot Hodges. However, on cross-examination, when asked where he was standing so that he could see the shooting, Jenkins could not remember. He also could not explain why there were bullets from two different guns found in the victim's body when he maintained that he only saw one person shooting. Finally, his explanation of why three people testified that he had stated that he shot the victim was merely that they were lying. In short, Jenkins added little to his defense in his testimony, and in fact the cross-examination succeeding in discrediting his story." Decision at 6.

So, the Court identified three "key facts" which it believed showed that Jenkins' attorneys were reasonable in not letting him testify because they were afraid of what he might say: (i) "he could not remember where he was standing" when he saw the shooting, (ii) he could not explain why there were bullets from two different guns found in the victim's body[159]

---

159 Actually, this was false. According to the medical examiner and the ballistics expert, the two bullets found in Mr. Hodges' body were from the same gun.

if he only saw one person shooting, and (iii) "his explanation of why three people testified that he shot the victim was merely that they were lying." The Court characterized this testimony as "discrediting." However, the Court's specious analysis of this testimony was gravely flawed and totally unpersuasive.

First, I have examined and cross-examined thousands of witnesses at numerous trials and depositions over the years, and I can assure you that it is not at all unusual for witnesses not to remember certain facts, like where they were standing when something happened. And this is especially true when the witness is being asked about the event three and a half years after it occurred. In no sense, is there anything "discrediting" about this. I sincerely doubt that any of the learned judges who authored this decision could tell you what they themselves were doing three months prior to reaching this decision, let alone three years before.

Second, witnesses can only testify, and should only testify, about what they actually see, hear and can recall. The fact that Jenkins only saw one person shoot Mr. Hodges does not mean that some other person (Maurice, for example) did not also shoot Mr. Hodges; it merely means that Jenkins did not see this other person shoot Mr. Hodges. Furthermore, the fact that Jenkins only saw one person shoot Mr. Hodges does not, in any way, indicate that his testimony was either false or unbelievable. The only reason we now know, after the fact, that two guns were used was because a ballistics expert said that bullets from two different guns were found at the scene, although in fact only one gun was recovered. And the fact that Jenkins "did not recall" exactly where he was standing when he saw the shooting does not indicate that he did not see the shooting, but only that he does not recall where he was standing when he saw the shooting.

Rather than being "discrediting," as the judges of the Court of Appeals falsely argued, Jenkins' testimony bore all the hallmarks of what knowledgeable trial lawyers call "badges of truth" (and what epistemologists sometimes call "criteria of truth"). Unlike Terry Roberts, Jenkins did not tailor his testimony to fit a certain expected narrative. Obviously, Jenkins knew that the ballistics evidence showed that two separate guns were used. He could easily have testified that he saw Maurice shoot Mr. Hodges. But that was not true, and so he did not say it. He could also have invented an answer and told Mr. Durden exactly "where he was standing" when he saw the shooting, but this also would not have been true because, in fact, Jenkins did not recall where he was standing.

Finally, the fact that Jenkins' only explanation for why three people had testified that he had told them that he shot Mr. Hodges was that "they were lying" is not an unreasonable answer. He knew their testimony was false because he knew that he never made these statements. Since he knew he never made the statements, his only explanation was that they must be lying. What is unreasonable about this? Would you expect him to say that Roberts was lying because he wanted to protect his brother Maurice, or that Officer Smith was lying because the police needed something to corroborate Roberts' story, or that McCall was lying because he was getting a "get out of jail free" card from the DA? These things may have been true, but Jenkins did not know that, so he could not testify about them. But he did know that he never made the statements and therefore these people must be lying. For a federal appellate court to characterize Jenkins testimony on these issues as "discrediting" is preposterous.

Notably, I was present when Jenkins testified at the hearing in support of his Motion for new a new trial and I can assure you there was nothing "discrediting" about his testimony or his cross-examination. And there was certainly nothing that happened, or could have happened, that would have justified his lawyers' decision to advise him not to testify in his own defense at the trial.

I find simply incredible (and despicable) the lengths to which some judges will go to defend the indefensible. The plain and simple fact of the matter is that Jenkins had absolutely no chance of avoiding a murder conviction unless he testified in his own defense. And frankly, he had nothing to lose by testifying. He was already facing the death penalty, and his conviction was all but certain given the uncontradicted evidence that had been presented against him. He needed to do something to give the jury a basis for finding reasonable doubt. And the only thing that he could do to accomplish this was to testify and tell his side of what happened, which was, as he testified at the hearing in support of a new trial, that he was merely a bystander, that he did not do what he was accused of doing, and that he did not say what Roberts, Smith and McCall claimed that he said. And, by the way, this was exactly the same story that he had consistently told his attorneys from the time he was first arrested, as his lawyers themselves confirmed **under oath** at the hearing in support of a new trial.

The second issue that the Court of Appeals had to deal with in its decision was Jenkins' claim that his lawyers had **misled** him when they told him that the trial was going well and that there was no need for him to testify. Predictably, the Court dealt with this issue just as glibly as they did with the first issue. As the Court stated in its decision:

> "Similarly, Jenkins' claim that counsel's assessment that the trial was going well, and that he did not need to testify, constituted ineffective assistance is meritless. We give great deference to counsel's choices and make every effort 'to eliminate the distorting effects of hindsight, to reconstruct the circumstances of counsel's challenged conduct, and to evaluate the conduct from counsel's prospective at the time' (quoting *Strickland*). Here, Jenkins benefits from hindsight that counsel could not have enjoyed at the time of trial.[160] Both Peel and Walker had a great deal of experience in criminal trials. Peel was the public defender for several counties and had practiced for over eight years and Walker had been an assistant district attorney for seven

---

160 The notion that "Jenkins benefits from hindsight that counsel could not have enjoyed at the time of trial" is particularly egregious and offensive considering that Jenkins has spent the past thirty years of his life in prison, while Mr. Walker and Mr. Peel probably enjoyed a steak dinner on the day Jenkins' sentence was imposed. Do the judges ever read their own decisions?

years. It is reasonable to assume that they would have had a good idea of whether a trial appeared to be going well and the fact that their assessment was incorrect, without any contemporary evidence that it was wrong, is not enough to conclude that their advice fell below the range expected of competent counsel." Decision at 6-7.

I am sorry, but this is unmitigated lunacy. The Court seemed to be more concerned with protecting Mr. Walker and Mr. Peel's feelings and sensibilities than with the critical question of whether Jenkins had been denied a fundamental right that may have wrongfully caused him to be imprisoned for the rest of his life.

I met Mr. Walker and Mr. Peel, and they are both good and honorable men, and fine lawyers, but that does not mean they are incapable of making mistakes. Mr. Walker and Mr. Peel both testified at the motion for a new trial that the schedule of the trial imposed by Judge Harvey was extremely grueling and tiring, and that this may have adversely affected their performance. Whatever the reason, Mr. Walker and Mr. Peel certainly made mistakes, and the Court of Appeals utterly failed to recognize this. On the contrary, the Court overlooked and condoned their ineptitude and thereby imposed even greater harm on Mr. Jenkins.

Four additional points should be noted. **First**, in assessing whether the performance of Mr. Walker and Mr. Peel was deficient, the Court of Appeals restricted its analysis to the *single* issue of whether their advice that Jenkins not testify was an error. In so doing, the Court completely ignored the *fifteen* other grounds that Jenkins had complained about, such as counsels' failure to request a jury charge on corroboration, their failure to object to the "silent witness" testimony of Investigator Gray, their failure to impeach Terry Roberts with his prior inconsistent statements, and so forth. If these additional grounds had been considered — as they should have been under the U.S. Supreme Court's explicit directive in

Strickland — it would have been far more difficult for the Court of Appeals to justify counsels' deficient performance.

Second, the Court of Appeals explicitly recognized in its decision that Jenkins had claimed that his trial lawyers affirmatively **misled** him by telling him that the trial was going well when it should have been obvious to any skilled lawyer that it was not going well. As the Court stated in its recitation of the facts:

> "He [Jenkins] also argues that counsel **misled** him about the probable outcome of the trial by telling him before he made his decision not to testify that it was going well and that he need not testify. This **erroneous information**, he argues, **prevented him from making an informed decision** when he chose to waive his right to testify in his own defense." Decision at 2 (emphasis added).

In assessing whether counsels' performance was deficient, the Court of Appeals seems to have forgotten this very important point (which the Court itself explicitly recognized in its decision) that Jenkins claimed that he was **deceived** by his lawyers. The Court only considered the question of whether it was **reasonable** for Walker and Peel to advise Jenkins not to testify. The Court concluded that this advice was reasonable "because they did not think that it would help his case and they were afraid that he might say something on cross-examination that would be damaging."[161] Decision at 2-3. As explained above, this assessment (both by Jenkins' lawyers and by the Court of Appeals) was actually **unreasonable**. But, be that as it may, there is a vast difference between saying that counsel **deceived** Jenkins and saying that counsel merely gave him bad advice that turned out not to be true.

---

161 The only thing that Jenkins could possibly have said that would have made matters worse was that "he never liked Mr. Hodges, and he was glad he was dead." Of course, there was no reason to believe that Jenkins would ever say such a thing. Furthermore, and more importantly, it was the lawyers' responsibility to prepare Jenkins to testify and make sure that he does not say anything harmful in his testimony. They cannot shift responsibility to Jenkins for their own failure in preparing him to testify.

Third, the Court of Appeals, as well as all the other courts that have considered this issue, attempted to excuse counsels' malfeasance for advising Jenkins not to testify by noting that it was Jenkins himself who made the decision not to testify. As the Court of Appeals stated in its decision, "[t]his erroneous decision, [Jenkins] argues, prevented him from making an informed decision **when he chose to waive his right to testify in his own defense.**" Decision at 2 (emphasis added).

It is true, of course, that Jenkins ***purportedly*** waived his right to testify in his own defense at trial. In fact, Judge Harvey made a major ritual of having Jenkins state on the record that he voluntarily intended to waive his right to testify at the trial. The reality, however, was that Jenkins only did this because he was told to do so by his trial attorneys, whose experience and expertise he was relying on to make an informed decision. As the Court of Appeals was quick to note in its decision:

> "Both Peel and Walker had a great deal of experience in criminal trials: Peel was the public defender for several counties and had practiced for over eight years and Walker had been an assistant district attorney for seven years." Decision at 7.

Jenkins, on the other hand, was a 19 year-old high school drop-out with a very low IQ and no legal experience of any kind. He could barely write a grammatically correct sentence, let alone define what a waiver is. For those who may not know, a waiver is a ***voluntary*** and ***informed*** abandonment of a known legal right. There was no way that Jenkins' purported waiver was either voluntary or informed. He was merely following his lawyers' advice, which he had a constitutional right to do. Unfortunately, his lawyers' advice was both deficient and fraudulent. For the Court of Appeals to endorse counsels' fraudulent behavior and try to shift responsibility for making the decision not to testify from Jenkins' lawyers to Jenkins himself was misguided and unconscionable.

Finally, as you may remember from the very beginning of this Chapter, the judge of the Eleventh Circuit Court of Appeals who granted Jenkins his very limited certificate of appealability was Charles B. Wilson. I was very surprised and disappointed to learn, when the three-judge panel that was scheduled to hear Jenkins' appeal was announced, that Judge Wilson was ***not*** one of the judges assigned to hear the case.[162] This means that the three Circuit Judges who actually heard Jenkins' appeal were probably completely unaware of the prior sordid history with respect to the drastic limitations that were improperly imposed on Jenkins' appeal.

It was extremely prejudicial and improper for the Eleventh Circuit Court of Appeals to refuse to grant Jenkins a COA with respect to most of the issues he wanted to appeal and to limit his appeal to the single issue of whether his lawyers had misled him regarding his right to testify in his own defense. However, even if one considers this single issue alone, Jenkins was clearly deprived of his Sixth Amendment right of effective assistance of counsel, and this clearly deprived him of a fair trial. It is never acceptable, even in Georgia, for lawyers to lie to their clients about important matters affecting their rights, and it is certainly unacceptable for lawyers to deceive their clients in order to induce them to waive their constitutional right to testify. This should have been an easy slam dunk for the Eleventh Circuit. The decision of Judge Nangle should have been quickly reversed, Jenkins' petition for habeas corpus should have been happily granted, and his state court conviction should have been completely vacated and reversed. However, like the once great Fred Snodgrass in the 1912 World Series, the Eleventh Circuit inexplicably dropped an easy fly ball.

---

162   The three judges who were assigned were Chief Judge Anderson and Circuit Judges Tjoflat and Black.

CHAPTER 13

PETITIONS FOR REHEARING AND CERTIORARI

After the Eleventh Circuit Court of Appeals affirmed the dismissal of Jenkins' Petition for a writ of habeas corpus, I knew the battle was over and that both Jamel and I had lost, him more so than I. There were still a few legal proceedings I could pursue, but they were all longshots and unlikely to prevail.

The first of these procedures was to file a petition with the Court of Appeals requesting a rehearing of the case by the panel that originally heard the appeal and a rehearing *en banc* by the entire Court. The latter is a request to have all the judges who are members of the Eleventh Circuit consider the case and not just the three judges who originally heard the appeal. Such motions are rarely granted, and that is exactly what happened here.

On August 30, 2001, I filed a fifteen-page petition on Jenkins' behalf requesting that the Court of Appeals rehear Jenkins' appeal or, alternatively, that the full Court consider the case *en banc*. Four separate arguments were raised in support of this petition. The first argument was that the Panel that originally heard the appeal had incorrectly applied the Supreme Court's decisions in *Strickland v. Washington* and *Williams v. Taylor*. These are the two leading cases of the Supreme Court setting forth the requirements for determining when a defendant in a criminal case has been denied the effective assistance of counsel.

The second argument asserted in the Petition for rehearing was that the Court had erred in limiting Jenkins' ineffective assistance of counsel claim to a single issue when he had, in fact, claimed that his trial counsel made numerous errors. As noted in the Petition for Rehearing, this was contrary to the Supreme Court's explicit directive in *Strickland* that "[t]he performance inquiry must be whether counsel's assistance was reasonable ***considering all the circumstances***." 466 U.S. at 688 (emphasis added).

The third argument raised in the Petition for rehearing was that the Court had erred in failing to consider the effect of cumulative error. As noted in the Petition, Jenkins had argued in his State court appeal that the cumulative effect of the multiple errors he complained of had denied him due process of law. The Georgia Supreme Court refused to consider this argument, stating that "Georgia does not recognize the cumulative error rule." 268 Ga. at 471, 491 S.E.2d 58. In seeking habeas relief, Jenkins noted that the refusal of the Georgia courts to consider the effect of cumulative error was contrary to clearly established federal constitutional law. Judge Nangle refused to consider this argument, however, stating, "there is no clearly established Supreme Court precedent requiring this rule." 103 F. Supp 2d at 1382. The Panel that heard Jenkins' appeal also failed to consider the effect of cumulative error because the limited COA that was granted by Judge Wilson did not include this issue. However, cumulative error was one of the meritorious grounds for which Jenkins had sought a COA, and it should have been granted. The refusal of the District Court and of the Court of Appeals to issue a COA on this issue constituted constitutional error that deprived Jenkins of due process of law.

The fourth argument stated in the Petition for rehearing was that the Court had erred in limiting Jenkins' appeal to a single ground — ineffective assistance of counsel — when he had in fact raised numerous other meritorious issues for appeal.

Unfortunately, the Eleventh Circuit was unwilling to reconsider any of these matters. On December 27, 2001,[163] the Court of Appeals denied Jenkins' request for reargument. As the Court stated in its brief Order:

"The Petition(s) for Rehearing are DENIED and no member of this panel nor other Judge in regular service on

---

163 Not my best Christmas present.

the Court having requested that the Court be polled on rehearing *en banc* (Rule 35, Federal Rules of Appellate Procedure, Rule 35-5), the Suggestion(s) of Rehearing *En Banc* are DENIED."

The next and final step was to file a petition for certiorari with the U.S. Supreme Court requesting that that Court review the decision of the Eleventh Circuit. And so, on March 25, 2002, I filed a forty-page Petition for Certiorari with the Clerk of the Supreme Court on Jenkins' behalf. The Petition requested that the Supreme Court grant certiorari to address the following questions:

1. Whether petitioner, who did not present any evidence at trial and relied on the presumption of innocence, was denied due process of law and deprived of his constitutional privilege against self-incrimination because the prosecutor repeatedly commented to the jury that petitioner had failed to present any evidence to refute the State's case?

2. Whether petitioner was deprived of his constitutional right to confront and cross-examine the witnesses against him because the prosecutor was permitted to introduce hearsay evidence at trial from unidentified "silent witnesses"?

3. Whether petitioner, who had consistently told his lawyers that he was merely a bystander at the scene of the crime and that he wanted to testify at trial, was denied effective assistance of counsel, due process and his constitutional right to testify, because he was deceived by his lawyers regarding the progress and likely outcome of the trial and was wrongfully induced by them not to testify?

4. Whether the Court of Appeals erred by limiting its consideration of petitioner's ineffective assistance of counsel claim to one issue when, in fact, petitioner had asserted that his counsel's performance was deficient for fifteen additional reasons?

5. Whether petitioner was denied due process of law because the courts below refused to consider whether the cumulative effect of numerous errors deprived him of a fair trial?

6. Whether petitioner was denied due process and his statutory right to appeal because the courts below refused to issue a certificate of appealability with respect to numerous issues for which he made the requisite showing under 28 U.S.C. § 2253(c) that he had been denied a constitutional right?

7. Whether petitioner's sentence of life imprisonment without possibility of parole deprived him of due process of law and violated his right to trial by jury, where the sentencing jury had requested, but was denied access to, information regarding when petitioner would become eligible for parole if they sentenced him to life with a possibility of parole?

In addition to enumerating the questions presented for review, the Petition contained a very lengthy discussion of the legal issues presented by each of these questions and why the Supreme Court should accept Jenkins' case for review. I was, as always, hopeful that the Court would grant the Petition for Certiorari and finally right that wrongs that had been done. Unfortunately, that was not to be.

On May 28, 2002, I was informed by the Clerk of the Supreme Court that the Court had just issued an order denying Jenkins' Petition for Certiorari. Unfortunately, this was the end of the road. No further legal recourse was available. The long and complex journey that had begun on September 20, 1996, with Jamel's initial motion for a new trial had finally come to a sad and devastating end.

There was, however, one further "Hail Mary pass" I could pursue. This will be discussed in the next two chapters

CHAPTER 14

A WHOLE NEW LAWSUIT IN BROOKLYN

Following the devastating debacle in attempting to get the federal courts in Georgia to issue a certificate of appealability that would have allowed Jenkins to obtain a meaningful appeal of the outrageous denial of his Petition for a writ of habeas corpus, I thought it necessary and prudent to make one final attempt to test the constitutionality of the Antiterrorism and Effective Death Penalty Act of 1996 ("AEDPA").

It was this terrible statute, as appallingly applied by the federal courts in Jenkins' habeas proceeding, that prevented him (i) from appealing Judge Nangle's awful decision to the Court of Appeals and (ii) from obtaining habeas relief from Judge Nangle. As you will remember, the Eleventh Circuit drastically limited Jenkins' certificate of appealability to a ***single ground*** (out of ***sixteen***) with respect to the issue of why Jenkins' trial counsel had been ineffective. Additionally, the certificate of appealability, as granted by the Court of Appeals, unfairly omitted ***eighteen*** meritorious grounds for Jenkins' appeal. Furthermore, as you may recall, Judge Nangle relied extensively on Section 2254(c) of AEDPA to say that the federal constitutional law that Jenkins was relying on in support of his habeas petition had not been explicitly promulgated by the Supreme Court.

As noted previously, my initial reaction to the Eleventh Circuit's ruling on the issue of appealability was one of shock. I could not believe they had limited Jenkins to a single ground for claiming that his trial counsel had been ineffective, while simultaneously neglecting all the other reasons his counsel had been deficient, as well as ignoring all the other serious errors that infected his trial.

I could not sit by and take the chance that the Circuit Court might deny Jenkins' appeal on such an unfairly truncated appeal. I felt I had to do **something** to ensure that Jenkins could **somehow** obtain **meaningful appellate review** of **all** the issues he had raised in his Petition for a writ of habeas corpus and not just the single issue of whether his trial attorneys had been ineffective because they told him not to testify. And so, once again, I plodded on, a solitary voice against the ineluctable current, fighting futilely against the callous torpidity of the heartless criminal justice leviathan and the soulless charlatans who so arrogantly control it.

I decided to commence an entirely new proceeding on Jenkins' behalf seeking a declaratory judgment that two provisions of AEDPA were unconstitutional as applied to Jenkins in his habeas corpus proceeding. I recognized, of course, that if I filed this new lawsuit in Georgia, it would undoubtedly be doomed from the beginning, since the new proceeding would probably be assigned to Judge Nangle as a "related case." I did not need a soothsayer to know where he stood on this issue.

Accordingly, I decided to commence the new lawsuit in Brooklyn, the place where Jenkins was born and had lived for most of his short life prior to moving temporarily to Georgia to stay with his grandmother. There are, of course, strict rules that limit where federal lawsuits can be brought. One of the key limitations is the **venue** rule, which requires that cases against the federal government may only be brought in judicial districts where (i) the defendant resides, (ii) "where a substantial portion of the events or omissions giving rise to the claim occurred," or (iii) **where the plaintiff resides**. Residence for this purpose means "domicile," which is a technical legal term signifying the place where a person **intends to make his home**. A person can have many residences, but only one domicile.

The Court in which I decided to file this new lawsuit was the United States District Court for the Eastern District of New York ("EDNY"). This is an extremely large and busy Court, but it only serves four counties in New York State: Brooklyn, Queens, Nassau and Suffolk (Long Island). I was already a member of the EDNY bar, so this would not pose any problems like the ones created by Judge Nangle. More importantly, despite his incarceration in Georgia, Jenkins remained a domiciliary of the State of New York and a resident of Brooklyn, so venue in the EDNY was proper.

Accordingly, on March 13, 2001 — twelve days after the Eleventh Circuit had issued its limited certificate of appealability — I filed a seven-page civil complaint on Jenkins' behalf against the United States of America in the EDNY. Although very short, the complaint alleged three very important claims for relief against the federal government.

The first claim alleged that the provision of AEDPA (28 U.S.C. § 2254(d)) which created a new standard of review of state court decisions under the federal habeas corpus statute was unconstitutional **as applied** to Jenkins in his habeas proceeding. As interpreted and applied by Judge Nangle, this statutory provision precluded Jenkins from obtaining federal habeas relief unless the precise ground alleged by him in his habeas petition had been previously determined to be unlawful by the United States Supreme Court. The new Brooklyn lawsuit alleged that this interpretation of Section 2254(d) violated the Habeas Clause, the Separation of Powers clause, and the Due Process Clause of the federal Constitution.

The second claim alleged that the provision of AEDPA (28 U.S.C. § 2254(c)) which imposed the requirement for obtaining a certificate of appealability as a condition precedent for an appeal from the denial of a petition for habeas corpus was unconstitutional **on its face** because it deprived Jenkins and all other unsuccessful habeas petitioners of their fundamental right to appeal in violation of the Due Process Clause of the federal Constitution.

The third claim alleged that the provision of AEDPA (28 U.S.C. § 2254(c)) which imposed the requirement for obtaining a certificate of appealability in order to appeal from the denial of a petition for habeas corpus was unconstitutional **as applied** to Jenkins because it deprived him of his right to appeal in violation of the Due Process Clause of the federal Constitution.

After the new case was filed and docketed, it was assigned to Judge Nicholas G. Garaufis of the EDNY. It was also assigned to Assistant U.S. Attorneys Peter Alfred Norling and Ceci Scott of the U.S. Attorney's Office for the EDNY.

At the time when the new case was filed, the Eleventh Circuit Court of Appeals had not yet heard the limited appeal which it had permitted Jenkins to pursue. It was possible, therefore, that the Eleventh Circuit could reverse the decision of Judge Nangle and grant Jenkins a new trial. If that were to happen, then the new Brooklyn case would become moot.

Accordingly, on May 11, 2001, I entered into a stipulation with Peter Norling of the U.S. Attorney's Office extending the time in which the United States had to respond to Jenkins' complaint until thirty days after the Eleventh Circuit issued its decision in the pending proceeding. This stipulation was amended on September 17, 2001, to include a possible appeal to the Supreme Court from the Eleventh Circuit's decision. These stipulations were approved and "so ordered" by Judge Garaufis. As a result of these stipulations, Judge Garaufis issued an order on October 30, 2001, closing the case administratively without prejudice to its being reopened at a subsequent time if conditions warranted.

On June 4, 2002 — following the denial of Jenkins' appeal by the Eleventh Circuit — I wrote a letter to Judge Garaufis requesting that the Brooklyn case be reopened and restored to the Court's active calendar. Judge Garaufis granted this request by order dated June 7, 2002.

On June 20, 2002, a status conference was held before Judge Garaufis to discuss how the matter should proceed. Ceci Scott, the Assistant U.S. Attorney representing the government, indicated that the government intended to make a motion to dismiss. She was granted until July 26, 2002 to file her motion.

On or before July 26, 2002, the government filed its motion to dismiss and an accompanying Memorandum of Law. In due course, (i) Jenkins filed a Memorandum of Law and an Affidavit in opposition to the government's motion to dismiss, (ii) the government filed a Reply Memorandum in further support of its motion to dismiss, and (iii) Jenkins filed a Rebuttal Memorandum in further opposition to the motion to dismiss.

Initially, the government asserted three grounds for dismissal of Jenkins' complaint: (i) that venue was improper in the EDNY, (ii) that Jenkins' claims were barred by the legal doctrine of "res judicata"[164] and (iii) that Jenkins' challenges to Section 2253 "failed to state claims upon which relief can be granted." Additionally and alternatively, the government argued that the EDNY case should be transferred to the Southern District of Georgia. Each of these claims was addressed in Jenkins' Memorandum in opposition to the motion.

First, with respect to venue, Jenkins pointed out that venue was proper in the EDNY because he continued to be a domiciliary of the State of New York at all relevant times. He was a resident and domiciliary of New York at the time of his arrest in Florida, and he continued to be a domiciliary of New York notwithstanding his incarceration in Georgia.[165] Federal law in both the Second (which includes New York) and the Eleventh (which includes Georgia) Circuits was clear at the time the Brooklyn lawsuit was

---

164 Res judicata is a legal doctrine that provides that, once a claim has been decided in court, it cannot be relitigated or challenged in a subsequent action involving the same parties.

165 In what can only be characterized as a "red herring" "I am trying to be too cute" argument, the government's lawyer noted that Jenkins had only stated in his memorandum in opposition to the motion to dismiss that Jenkins was a "domiciliary of New York" and not that he was a resident of the EDNY. As the government stated, "[Jenkins] has not indicated the town or county of New York where he allegedly resided. This omission is problematic whether he means that he lived in New York City or New York State, since even New York City is located in more than one federal district." Defendant's Memorandum at 7. As clever as this argument may appear to be, it was totally frivolous and misleading. The Complaint — the only pleading at issue — was only seven pages long and it very clearly and explicitly alleged that "[Jenkins] **resides in** and is a domiciliary of this District" (emphasis added). Complaint, ¶ 5. I know the government's lawyer read the Complaint because she made numerous references to it in her memorandum. Apparently, however, she skipped over one this key allegation of the Complaint. By the way, the reason I stated that Jenkins was a "domiciliary of New York" was to emphasize that he was not a domiciliary of Georgia. Ordinarily, when speaking of a person's domicile for legal purposes, the relevant entity is the State in which that person resides, not the village, town, city, or judicial district.

commenced that involuntary imprisonment does not change a person's residence or domicile for purpose of venue or jurisdiction.

With respect to the government's second argument — that Jenkins' claims were barred by the doctrine of *res judicata* — there were several fatal flaws in this argument. One of the requirements for the doctrine of res judicata to apply is that both proceedings at issue must involve the **same parties**. That requirement was not satisfied here. The proceeding in the EDNY was against the United States, whereas the habeas proceeding in Georgia was against the Warden of Telfair State Prison, a public officer of the state of Georgia.

A second and even more significant flaw in the government's res judicata argument was that the habeas proceeding and the EDNY lawsuit **did not involve the same claims**, which is an essential requirement for res judicata to apply. As the Second Circuit Court of Appeals had explicitly explained in *Prime Management Co. v. Streinegger*, 904 F.2d 811, 816 (2d Cir. 1990), in determining whether two causes of action are the same for purposes of res judicata, the court examines whether "the same transaction or connected series of transactions is at issue, whether the same evidence is needed to support both claims, and whether the facts essential to the second were present in the first." That standard was clearly not satisfied here.

The claim at issue in the habeas proceeding was whether Jenkins' state court conviction and sentence violated federal constitutional law. Jenkins had asserted eighteen separate grounds why he believed that his state court conviction and sentence violated federal law. In ruling on these claims, it was necessary for the Georgia District Court to examine what transpired at Jenkins' **state court trial**. The relevant "set of operative facts" was thus the evidence and proceedings that supported Jenkins' state court conviction and whether those proceedings complied with the requirements of federal constitutional law. None of the eighteen grounds cited by Jenkins in support of his habeas petition involved any of the claims that were asserted in the EDNY lawsuit, and there was no reason for the Georgia district court to consider any of the claims alleged in the Brooklyn case.

As the government explicitly recognized in its Memorandum in support of the motion to dismiss, the claims alleged by Jenkins in the EDNY lawsuit were as follows:

> "Specifically, he claims that: (1) the Georgia district court, in evaluating his habeas claims, applied 28 U.S.C. § 2254(d) in an unconstitutional manner by reading the section to require [Jenkins] to show that the U.S. Supreme Court had previously ruled on each issue raised, thereby precluding application of the Georgia district court's independent judgment to interpret and apply federal constitutional law; (2) Section 2253(c), which sets forth the standard a habeas petitioner must meet to appeal the denial of his petition, unconstitutionally deprives unsuccessful petitioners of their right to appeal; and (3) Section 2253(c) was unconstitutionally applied to deprive him of his right to appeal." Memorandum at 4-5.

First, it should be noted that the government's lawyers correctly and succinctly summarized in their memorandum exactly what Jenkins' claims were in the EDNY lawsuit, so obviously they understood at that time what claims were being asserted. It was only later, after they began arguing lack of justiciability, that they began confusing the issues in the EDNY lawsuit with the issues raised in the habeas petition.

Second, even as characterized by the government, it was clear that none of the three claims asserted by Jenkins in the EDNY lawsuit was at issue in the proceedings before the Georgia district court or the Eleventh Circuit Court of Appeals. Moreover, the claims in both cases arose from a completely different set of operative facts and they involved different evidence. The facts and evidence relevant for purposes of the habeas proceeding were those relating to Jenkins' state court conviction and sentence; the facts and evidence relevant for the EDNY lawsuit were whether Sections 2253(c) and 2253(d) were unconstitutional as applied by the Georgia district court and the Eleventh Circuit Court of Appeals.

Accordingly, since the habeas proceeding and the EDNY lawsuit involved different claims and different parties, since the two proceedings arose out of a different set of operative facts and involved different evidence, and since the Georgia courts had never adjudicated the claims at issue in the EDNY lawsuit, the doctrine of res judicata was simply not applicable.

The third argument raised by the government in support of its motion to dismiss was that the two claims asserted by Jenkins regarding Section 2253(c) — the section that limited his right to appeal the denial of his habeas petition — "failed to state a claim upon which relief can be granted" because "there is no federal right to appeal." Memorandum at 10.

The first thing that should be noted is that the government did ***not*** argue that Jenkins' claim with respect to Section 2254(c) failed to state a claim upon which relief could be granted. Accordingly, it would have been inappropriate to dismiss Jenkins' entire complaint even if the government lawyers were correct about Section 2253(c) (which, as shown below, they were not).

The second thing that needs to be noted is that the government was ***not*** correct about Section 2253(c). Relying on *United States v. Matista*, 932 F.2d 1055 (2d Cir. 1991) and *Felker v. Turpin*, 518 U.S. 651 (1996), the government argued that Jenkins' Second and Third Claims should be dismissed because "there is no constitutional right to appeal," and therefore Jenkins' allegations with respect to Section 2253(c) failed to state a claim. This argument was invalid for two separate reasons.

First, Jenkins' Second and Third Claims did ***not*** depend upon the existence of a ***constitutional*** right to appeal. There were several Supreme Court decisions at the time the government's motion to dismiss was made that had explicitly found ***constitutional*** violations in connection with the exercise of a right to appeal, ***even though the basis for the right to appeal***

was statutory rather than constitutional. Thus, for example, in *Griffin v. Illinois*, 351 U.S. 12 (1956), the Supreme Court, relying on both the Due Process and the Equal Protection clauses of the Fourteenth Amendment, ruled that it was unconstitutional for a state to require appellants to furnish a bill of exceptions as a prerequisite for prosecuting an appeal, since this might discriminate against appellants who cannot afford to obtain a transcript. The Court stated, "[i]t is true that a State is not required by the Federal Constitution to provide appellate courts or a right of appellate review at all [citing *McKane v. Durston*, 153 U.S. 684, 687-88 (1894)], [b]ut that is not to say that a State that does grant appellate review can do so in a way that discriminates against some convicted defendants on account of their poverty." *Id.* at 590.

Justice Harlan, who dissented in *Griffin*, also agreed that a statutory right to appeal is protected by the federal Due Process Clause:

> "[T]he fact that appeals are not constitutionally required does not mean that a State is free of constitutional restraint in establishing the terms upon which appeals will be allowed. . . . Rather the constitutional right under the Due Process Clause is simply the right not to be denied an appeal for arbitrary or capricious reasons." 351 U.S. at 599 (dissenting opinion).

Similarly, in *Douglas v. California*, 372 U.S. 353 (1963), the Supreme Court ruled that it was unconstitutional for California to establish an appellate procedure whereby, before appointing counsel to represent indigent defendants on appeal, the appellate court "examined the record" to determine whether the appeal had sufficient merit to warrant appointment of counsel. As in *Griffin*, the basis for the appellate right in *Douglas* was statutory. Nevertheless, the Court ruled that the limitation that the state had placed on defendant's right to appeal violated the Due Process and Equal Protection clauses of the Fourteenth Amendment.

The Supreme Court had also ruled that a criminal defendant has a constitutional right to effective assistance of counsel **on appeal**. *See Smith v. Robbins*, 528 U.S. 259 (2000); *Evitts v. Lucy*, 469 U.S. 387 (1985). As noted in *Martinez v. Court of Appeal*, 528 U.S. 152, 155, (2000), the right to counsel on appeal stems from the due process and equal protection clauses of the Fourteenth Amendment . . ."

Thus, even assuming that there is no **constitutional** right to appeal, this does not mean that a **statutory** right of appeal is not subject to constitutional limitations. In Jenkins' case, it is indisputable that he had a statutory right to appeal the denial of his habeas petition. The Second Count of the EDNY complaint alleged that he was unconstitutionally deprived of this right due to the impermissible limitations imposed by 28 U.S.C. § 2253(c). Complaint, ¶¶ 34-37. The Third Count alleged that Jenkins was unconstitutionally deprived of his right to appeal due to the impermissible way in which 28 U.S.C. § 2253(c) was applied to him by the government (namely, the Eleventh Circuit Court of Appeals). These allegations were clearly sufficient to state a claim for the relief requested.

Second, Jenkins also disputed the government's broad assertion that there was no constitutional right to appeal. Jenkins conceded that numerous cases existed which **said** there was no such right, including, for example, *Griffin, Douglas, Abney v. United States*, 431 U.S. 651 (1977) and *United States v. Matista*, 932 F.2d 1055 (2d Cir. 1991). Such statements, however, were merely **dicta**.[166] Significantly, no case in the past hundred years had ever actually **ruled** that there is no constitutional right to appeal. This should not be surprising since the right to appeal is so universally recognized by statute that there has been neither the need nor the opportunity to establish a constitutional right.

The leading case for the proposition that there is no constitutional right to appeal was *McKane v. Durston*, 153 U.S. 684 (1894). This is the case

---

166 The term *dicta* refers to statements made in a court's opinion that were unnecessary for the court's decision in the case at hand and, therefore, should not have any precedential value in future cases involving different facts.

that was cited by the Supreme Court in *Abney*, which in turn was cited by the Second Circuit in *Matista*. Actually, *McKane* itself did not involve a right to appeal but merely whether a convicted defendant is entitled to bail pending appeal. McKane was convicted of a felony in New York and sentenced to six years imprisonment. Under New York law, he had a statutory right to appeal, but he was not entitled to bail as a matter of right pending appeal. McKane argued that the absence of bail violated his rights under federal constitutional law. In denying this request, the Supreme Court stated "whether an appeal should be allowed and, if so, under what circumstances, or on what conditions, are matters for each state to determine for itself." *Id.* at 688. As the Court further explained:

> "An appeal from a judgment of conviction is not a matter of absolute right, independently of constitutional or statutory provisions allowing such appeal. A review by an appellate court of the final judgment in a criminal case, however grave the offense of which the accused is convicted, was not at common law, and is not now, a necessary element of due process of law. It is wholly within the discretion of the state to allow or not to allow such a review . . . It is therefore clear that the right to appeal may be accorded by the state to the accused upon such terms as in its wisdom may be deemed proper." *Id.* at 687.

McKane was decided in 1894. Obviously, current views of what is required by the Due Process Clause have changed dramatically since then. At the time *McKane* was decided, for example, there was no constitutional right to counsel (*see Gideon v. Wainwright*, 372 U.S. 335 (1963)), no privilege against self-incrimination (*see Malloy v. Hogan*, 378 U.S. 1 (1964)), no right to confront and cross-examine witnesses (*see California v. Green*, 399 U.S. 149 (1969)), no right to exclude illegally-seized evidence (*see Mapp v. Ohio*, 372 U.S. 335 (1961)), no right to trial by jury (*see Duncan v. Louisiana*, 391 U.S. 145 (1968)), no right to be informed of exculpatory evidence (*see Brady v. Maryland*, 373 U.S. 83 (1963)), and no right to be free from double jeopardy (*see Benton v. Maryland*, 395 U.S. 784 (1969)). As a result of the vast expansion of due process rights since 1894, the need for appellate review has become essential. Thus, despite *McKane*'s oft-repeated dicta, it seems extremely unlikely that the Supreme Court, or any other federal court, would rule today that a state could completely eliminate the right to appeal.

None of the cases cited by the government in their Memorandum in support of the motion to dismiss actually ruled that there was no constitutional right to appeal. *Matista* merely held that a defendant who became a fugitive during trial waived his right to appeal. *Abney* held that a pre-trial order denying a motion to dismiss an indictment on double jeopardy grounds constituted an appealable order. And *Felker v. Turpin*, 518 U.S. 651 (1996) held that the "gatekeeping mechanism" contained in 28 U.S.C. § 2244(b)(3) for second or successive habeas applications was constitutional. There was no valid basis, therefore, for the government's argument that Jenkins did not have a constitutional right to appeal.

It should also be noted that the statutory provision that was at issue in *Felker* (28 U.S.C. § 2244(b)(3)) is significantly different from the one that was at issue here in Jenkins' EDNY case. Section 2244 provides for "finality" of habeas decisions by requiring (i) that second or successive habeas applications which raise the same claim that was presented in the earlier petition must be dismissed (§ 2244(b)(1)) and (ii) that second or successive petitions which purport to raise new claims must first be approved for filing by a three-judge panel of the Court of Appeals (§ 2244(b)(1)). The Supreme Court ruled in *Felker* that these "gatekeeping" provisions did not violate the "suspension clause" (Article I, § 9) because they "constitute a modified res judicata rule, a restraint on what is called in habeas corpus practice 'abuse of the writ.'" 518 U.S. at 664.

In contrast to *Felker*, the statutory provision at issue in Jenkins' case was 28 U.S.C. § 2253(c), which applied to appeals from a petitioner's **first** habeas petition. Obviously, the principles of res judicata relied on by the

Supreme Court in deciding *Felker* have no application to initial habeas petitions and thus *Felker* was completely irrelevant.[167]

In addition to arguing that Jenkins' complaint should be dismissed for the three reasons discussed above, the government also argued that, if the motion to dismiss were not granted, then the case should be transferred to the Southern District of Georgia. In support of this motion, the government cited 28 U.S.C. § 1404(a) which provides as follows:

> "For the convenience of parties and witnesses, in the interest of justice, a district court may transfer any civil action to any other district or division where it might have been brought."

In moving for a change of venue, "the party requesting transfer bears the burden of establishing, by a clear and convincing showing, the propriety of transfer." *Arrow Electronics, Inc. v. Ducommun, Inc.*, 724 F. Supp. 264, 265 (S.D.N.Y. 1989); *Factors Etc., Inc. v. Boxcar Enterprises Inc.*, 579 F.2d 215, 218 (2d Cir. 1978), *cert. denied*, 440 U.S. 908 (1979) ("the burden is on . . . the moving party to establish that there should be a change of venue"); *Wine Markets International, Inc. v. Bass*, 939 F. Supp. 178 (E.D.N.Y. 1996) ("[t]he movant bears the burden of clearly establishing that the motion should be granted"). "This burden," as Judge Haight observed in *Manufacturers Hanover Trust Co. v. Palmer Video Corp.*, 798 F. Supp. 161, 164 (S.D.N.Y. 1992), "is an onerous one."

The law is also clear that "plaintiff's choice of forum will not be disturbed unless the movant shows that the balance of convenience and justice weighs heavily in favor of transfer." *Somerville v. Major Exploration, Inc.*, 576 F. Supp. 902, 908 (S.D.N.Y. 1983). *See Piper Aircraft Co. v. Reyno*,

---

167   In addition to this difference based upon res judicata, the gatekeeping mechanism of Section 2244(b)(1) also differs procedurally from the COA mechanism of Section 2254(d). For second or successive habeas petitions, Section 2244(b)(1) provides for initial screening by a three judge panel of the Court of Appeals. Section 2254(d), in contrast, provides for screening by only a single judge. Moreover, the judge who screens for appealablity is not even a member of the panel that hears the appeal. Thus, the statute affords greater protection for a habeas petitioner who wants to file a second or successive petition than for one who wants to appeal from the denial of his initial petition.

454 U.S. 235, 255 (1981) ("there is ordinarily a strong presumption in favor of the plaintiff's choice of forum, which may be overcome only when the private and public interest factors clearly point towards trial in the alternative forum"); *Snyder v. Madera Broadcasting, Inc.*, 872 F. Supp. 1191, 1199 (E.D.N.Y. 1995) ("the plaintiff's selection should not be disturbed unless the balance of the several factors is strongly in favor of the defendant").

The government did not, and could not possibly, meet this burden here because the requested transfer failed to satisfy the requirement of Section 1404(a), that the proposed change of venue must serve "the convenience of parties and witnesses" or be "in the interest of justice." As explained in *In Re Eastern District Repetitive Stress Injury Litigation*, 850 F. Supp. 188, 194 (E.D.N.Y. 1994), "defendants must establish both (1) that the actions could have been brought in the proposed transferee district and (2) that transfer serves the convenience of parties and witnesses or is in the interest of justice." The government here failed to satisfy the second requirement, and thus the request for a change of venue had to be denied.[168]

Apart from the threshold question of determining whether the case could have been brought in the district to which transfer is proposed, courts generally consider the following factors is deciding whether to grant a motion for a change of venue: "(1) the place where the operative facts occurred; (2) the convenience of the parties; (3) the convenience of witnesses; (4) the relative ease of access to sources of proof; (5) the availability of process to compel the attendance of unwilling witnesses; (6) the plaintiff's choice of forum; (7) the forum's familiarity with the governing law; and (8) trial efficiency and the interests of justice." *APA Excelsior III L.P. v. Premiere Technologies, Inc.*, 49 F. Supp.2d 664, 667 (S.D.N.Y. 1999); *see also, Wine Markets*, 939 F. Supp. at 181; *Snyder*, 872 F. Supp. at 1199. The burden is on the moving party to establish that there should be a change of venue, *Factors Etc.*, 579 F.2d at 218, and balancing the factors is generally left to the sound discretion of the district court. *Filmline Cross-Country Productions, Inc. v. United Artists Corp.*, 865 F.2d 515, 520 (2d Cir. 1989). In

---

168   Moreover, the government failed to provide any evidentiary support for the requested transfer.

the present case, analysis of these factors clearly showed that New York was a more appropriate forum than the Southern District of Georgia.

The government cited three factors to support its motion for transfer: (1) "the facts underlying this action — the trial and the legal proceedings that followed it — all occurred in Georgia"; (2) "witnesses and other evidence are within easy reach in the Southern District of Georgia and are difficult to access from this District"; and (3) "[Jenkins] seems to have chosen this forum simply because he believes it is more likely than the Georgia district court to yield a ruling in his favor." Def. Mem. at 11-12. None of these arguments had any merit.

1. *Plaintiff's Choice of Forum*

Jenkins "chose" to commence his lawsuit in the EDNY for three legitimate reasons. First, and most importantly, this is where he resided for federal venue purposes and therefore under 28 U.S.C. §§ 1391(b) and 1402(a), this was a proper district for commencing the lawsuit. Second, this is the District where his family resided and where he was able to obtain the services of counsel willing to represent him on a *pro bono* basis. Third, the hostility demonstrated by the federal judges in Georgia to Jenkins' prior habeas proceeding indicated that he was far more likely to get a fair consideration of his claims in the EDNY than in Georgia. These were significant factors that clearly justified Jenkins' choice of venue.

2. *Convenience of the Parties*

The EDNY was clearly more convenient for the parties than the Southern District of Georgia. Not only was Jenkins' family located here, but also he was able to obtain the services, on a *pro bono* basis, of experienced trial counsel who resided in New York and was a member of the bar of this District. It would be significantly less convenient for counsel to represent plaintiff if the case were transferred to Georgia, especially since at least one of the judges in the Southern District of Georgia had already shown a reluctance to allowing New York lawyers to represent clients in that district on a *pro hac vice* basis.

The only defendant in this case was the United States, and it was currently being represented by the United States Attorney's Office for the EDNY. Obviously, the EDNY was more convenient for the government's present counsel than the Southern District of Georgia, and there was no reason why Georgia would be any more convenient for the United States than New York. Indeed, the clear public policy underlying Section 1402(a) is that suits against the United States should always be brought in the district where the plaintiff resides. There was no basis, therefore, for believing that Georgia would be more convenient for the parties than New York.

3. Location of Witnesses and Evidence

Resolution of this action would not have been any more convenient in Georgia than in New York. Jenkins' claims did not require either any pretrial discovery nor a trial, and therefore the location of witnesses and documents was irrelevant. The only relevant evidence consisted of public court records which could be admitted by affidavit or judicial notice.

4. The "Operative Facts" at Issue Here Did Not Arise Out of Plaintiff's Trial in Georgia

The government argued that "the facts underlying this action — the trial and the legal proceedings that followed it — all occurred in Georgia" (Def. Mem. at 11) and that "if [Jenkins'] constitutional claims were found to have merit . . . the court so finding would then have to consider aspects of his trial and representation by trial counsel" (*Id.* at 8). Neither of these assertions was correct.

The basis of Jenkins' claims in the EDNY action was that 28 U.S.C. § 2253(c) is unconstitutional **on its face** (Second Claim) and that 28 U.S.C. §§ 2253(c) and 2254(d) were unconstitutional **as applied** by the Georgia district court and the Eleventh Circuit Court of Appeals (First and Third

Claims). Resolution of these claims did not in any way depend upon the proceedings that occurred at Jenkins' state court trial, and therefore there would be no reason for the Court deciding these claims to consider what happened during Jenkins' state court trial. It would only be necessary to examine the constitutionality of the two statutory provisions at issue. There was no reason, therefore, why venue in Georgia would be any more convenient than New York based upon the "operative facts" at issue.

5. *Relative Ease of Access to Sources of Proof*

The only evidence that would be necessary to adjudicate Jenkins' claims in the EDNY lawsuit were official court and legislative records which could easily be submitted by affidavit and of which the EDNY Court could take judicial notice. There was no reason, therefore, why venue in Georgia would be any more convenient based upon the relative ease of access to sources of proof.

6. *Availability of Process to Compel Attendance of Unwilling Witnesses*

This factor was also irrelevant here. No witnesses were necessary and therefore there was no need for court process to compel attendance of unwilling witnesses.

7. *Forum Court's Familiarity with Governing Law*

The governing law at issue in Jenkins' Brooklyn lawsuit was federal constitutional and statutory law. Obviously, Judge Garaufis was very familiar with same and there was thus no reason to defer to the Southern District of Georgia with respect to application of federal law.

8. *Trial Efficiency and the Interests of Justice*

As previously noted, resolution of Jenkins' claims in the Brooklyn lawsuit would not require a trial because there were no disputed facts that needed to be determined. Promptly after the government's motion to dismiss was resolved, both parties could move for summary judgment on the basis of documentary evidence. Accordingly, there was no reason to believe that this matter could be handled any more efficiently in Georgia than in New York. This was particularly true since Judge Garaufis had already gained some familiarity with this matter as a result of the present motions, whereas the court in Georgia has no knowledge of Jenkins' claims.

The interests of justice would also be better served by retaining this matter in the EDNY. This was so for three reasons. First, plaintiff is represented by experienced *pro bono* counsel who is admitted to practice in the EDNY. When this same counsel requested permission to appear *pro hac vice* for Jenkins in the habeas proceeding in Georgia, his application was denied.

Second, the United States was also presently represented in this action by experienced counsel admitted to practice in this District. If the matter were transferred to Georgia, in all likelihood it would become necessary for the Department of Justice to assign new counsel to represent the government, which would result in unnecessary expense and delay.

Third, two of Jenkins' claims allege that the federal habeas statute was unconstitutionally applied by the Georgia district court and the Eleventh Circuit. Consequently, these courts were "interested parties" that should not be involved in adjudicating the claims at issue.

Evaluating all of these factors in the aggregate, the balance of convenience and justice clearly weighed very heavily against transfer. Thus, even assuming hypothetically that the EDNY action could be transferred to Georgia, there was no plausible reason why Jenkins' choice of forum should be disturbed.

On October 7, 2002, the government filed its so-called "Reply Memorandum" in support of its motion to dismiss Jenkins' complaint. This was a truly extraordinary document. Rather than defend the three previous grounds that had been asserted in its original memorandum as bases for dismissing the Complaint, the government now raised an entirely new argument in support of its motion.

Notably, the government completely and explicitly withdrew the res judicata argument. As it stated in a footnote on page 1 of its Reply Memorandum, "[t]he government hereby withdraws its res judicata argument."

Unfortunately, the government was not quite as straightforward with respect to the venue argument. Although its attorneys clearly recognized that its venue argument was in serious trouble due to the points that had been raised in Jenkins' Opposition memorandum, the government refused to withdraw the venue argument completely. Instead, the government sheepishly tried to defend its venue argument with a single paragraph of its Reply Memorandum which cited no case law, utterly failed to respond to Jenkins' arguments, and explicitly ignored controlling Second Circuit case law. The better part of valor here would have been for the government to simply concede the point, but they were just unwilling to do so, even though they apparently recognized that their venue argument lacked merit.

The more important part of the Reply Memorandum, however, was the entirely new ground that the government raised in support of the motion to dismiss, namely, **lack of subject matter jurisdiction**. Obviously, in order to decide a case, a court needs have to have subject matter jurisdiction, and this is especially true of federal courts whose jurisdiction is governed by Article III of the Constitution and by Title 28 of the United States Code.

The question of whether federal jurisdiction exists is normally a fairly simple question, but there are certain complicating issues that arise from the constitutional mandate in Article III that the judicial power of the

United States only extends to "actual cases and controversies." The Supreme Court has interpreted this mandate to limit subject matter jurisdiction in the federal courts to cases in which there are **actual parties** with **adverse interests** that are *"ripe"* (ready for judicial resolution) and not *"moot"* (already resolved by other circumstances). The case must also be suitable for judicial resolution by a court of law by applying settled principles of law. Cases that do not meet these requirements are said to be "***non-justiciable***." For example, if one person sues another for conduct that he claims is immoral, that is non-justiciable because courts do not have the power to determine what is moral. Similarly, courts do not have the power to decide political questions. Finally, sometimes there are situations where federal courts do have subject matter jurisdiction, but they voluntarily decide to "abstain" from exercising that jurisdiction due to countervailing policy considerations.

There are three common situations in which federal district courts have subject matter jurisdiction in civil cases. The first of these is called "federal question" jurisdiction, and it is governed by 28 U.S.C § 1331, which provides, "[t]he district courts shall have original jurisdiction of all civil actions arising under the Constitution, laws or treaties of the United States."

The second common situation when federal courts have subject matter jurisdiction in civil cases is called "diversity jurisdiction," and it is governed by 28 U.S.C. § 1332, which provides, "[t]he district courts shall have original jurisdiction of all civil actions where the matter in controversy exceeds $75,000 . . . and is between (1) citizens of different States, (2) citizens of a State and citizens or subjects of a foreign state . . . (3) citizens of different States and in which citizens or subjects of a foreign state are additional parties, and (4) a foreign state . . . as plaintiff and citizens of a State or of different States."

A third, but less common, situation when federal courts have subject matter jurisdiction in civil cases is called "admiralty jurisdiction" and it is governed by 28 U.S.C. § 1333, which provides, "[t]he district courts shall have original jurisdiction, exclusive of the courts of the States, of (1) any civil case of admiralty or maritime jurisdiction . . . and (2) any prize brought into the United States and all proceedings for the condemnation of property taken as a prize."

Obviously, the type of subject matter jurisdiction that was at issue in Jenkins' lawsuit against the United States in the EDNY lawsuit was *federal question* jurisdiction. The Complaint alleged that two federal statutes (28 U.S.C. § 2253(c) and 28 U.S.C. § 2254(d)) violated various provisions of the federal Constitution. It is hard to imagine a more quintessential case of federal question jurisdiction than this. To the extent that the government was arguing that Jenkins' Complaint should be dismissed due to a lack of subject matter jurisdiction, they were obviously not arguing that the lawsuit failed to satisfy the requirements of 28 U.S.C. § 1331.

One of the subjects that students used to study in law school (I do not think anyone studies it any more) is called Remedies.[169] This has to do with the kinds of relief a person bringing a lawsuit can obtain from a court to remedy the harm that was caused by the defendant's wrongful conduct. The most common form of remedy is **money damages**. With this remedy, the court awards the plaintiff a certain amount of money to compensate him or her for the injury, and the defendant is then required to pay this amount to the plaintiff. However, there are many other remedies that can be awarded by the court. For example, the court can issue an ***injunction*** or a ***writ of mandamus*** which are orders directing that the defendant perform or refrain from performing a certain action or series of actions. A court can also issue a judgment calling for ***specific performance*** of a contract, ***rescission*** or ***reformation*** of a deed or contract, ***eviction*** from a tenancy, ***ejectment*** from realty, a judgment of ***divorce*** or ***annulment*** of a marriage, and many other things. All these remedies, and many others, are centuries-old deriving from the English common law.

---

169 Unfortunately, the law school curriculum in the modern era is cluttered with a myriad of non-essential electives and there is not enough time for essentials. When knowledge of fundamentals is neglected, the profession and clients suffer.

In addition to the remedies that were created by the English common law, there are certain other remedies that were created more recently by statute. Workers compensation, for example, is a statutory remedy that was created to mitigate the problems of recovering money damages from employers in civil tort cases. The same is true for no-fault insurance and other statutory compensation programs.

One of the remedies that was ***not*** available under English common law, and which ***was*** not generally available in either state or federal courts, was the notion of a ***declaratory judgment***. A declaratory judgment is an order (judgment) issued by a court which merely ***declares*** what the rights of the parties are. The court does not award any money, it does not issue an injunction, it does not order specific performance, it does not evict, annul, or eject anybody, it merely makes a declaration of the parties' rights. But this declaration of rights can be extremely useful. Once a court issues a judgment declaring that a state or federal statute is unconstitutional, then the state or federal agency cannot enforce that statute against you without violating the judgment, which can then be enforced by other, more coercive, remedies. Similarly, if a court issues a judgment declaring a contract void, then the litigants are discharged from any obligation to perform under the contract. Obviously, the situations in which this remedy can be extremely useful and effective are endless.

A recurring problem with declaratory judgments, however, is that they seem to be somewhat inconsistent with the "case or controversy" requirement of the Constitution. If the only thing that the court is being asked to do is to "declare the rights of the parties," that sounds similar to an "advisory opinion" which courts are forbidden to grant. On the other hand, if the plaintiff is asking for money, or an injunction, or an eviction, then obviously there is a real controversy. Either the plaintiff is entitled to the relief he has requested under applicable law or he is not. But if the only remedy that the plaintiff requests is a declaration of rights, that sounds a little more sketchy.

This was the problem that Congress and the federal courts faced in 1934. At that time Congress passed the Federal Declaratory Judgment Act of 1934 (now codified as 28 U.S.C. § 2201). This statute provided that, "***in cases of actual controversy***," federal courts could "declare rights and other legal relations of any interested party petitioning for such declaration , ***whether or not further relief is or could be prayed***" (emphasis added). As the Report of the United States Senate accompanying this legislation stated:

> "The declaratory judgment differs in no essential respect from any other judgment except that it is not followed by a decree for damages, injunction, specific performance or other immediately coercive decree. It declares conclusively and finally the rights of the parties in litigation over a contested issue, a form of relief which often suffices to settle controversies and fully administer justice."[170]

The federal Declaratory Judgment Act was unanimously upheld as constitutional by the United States Supreme Court in 1937,[171] and it has been used and applied frequently by federal courts ever since. The fact that a declaratory judgment may be issued "whether or not further relief is or could be granted" clearly shows (i) that a request for declarative relief is an ***alternative remedy*** to all other remedies that could have been requested and (ii) that the issue of whether a declaratory judgment should be granted does not depend upon whether the court could have granted any other relief.

Rule 57 of the Federal Rules of Civil Procedure explicitly provides that "[t]hese rules govern the procedure for obtaining a declaratory judgment under 28 U.S.C.§ 2201." The Notes of the Advisory Committee on the Federal Rules (1937) stated as follows:

> "A declaratory judgment is appropriate when it will terminate the controversy giving rise to the proceeding. Inasmuch as it often involves only an issue of law on

---

170 Senate Report No. 1005, 73d Congress, 2d Session (1934).
171 See *Aetna Life Insurance Company v. Haworth*, 300 U.S. 227 (1937).

undisputed or relatively undisputed facts, it operates frequently as a summary proceeding, justifying docketing the case for early hearing as on motion . . . ."

The Advisory Committee Notes further stated that the "controversy" at issue in the declaratory judgment action "must necessarily be 'of a justiciable nature, thus excluding an advisory decree **upon a hypothetical state of facts**'" (citing *Ashwander v. Tennessee Valley Authority*, 297 U.S. 288, 325 (1936) (emphasis added). As the Committee further noted:

"The existence or nonexistence of any right, duty, power, liability, privilege, disability or immunity, or of any fact upon which such legal relations depend, or of a status, may be declared. The petitioner must have a practical interest in the declaration sought and all parties having an interest therein or adversely affected must be made parties or be cited."

Finally, the Advisory Committee also stated:

"When declaratory relief will not be effective in settling the controversy, the court may decline to grant it. **But the fact that another remedy would be equally effective affords no ground for declining declaratory relief**" (emphasis added).

The complaint for declaratory relief which Jenkins filed in the EDNY satisfied all of these jurisdictional requirements and, therefore, it should have been promptly considered by the court. However, the government, it its so-called Reply Memorandum, did everything possible to confuse the legal issues that were involved in Jenkins' declaratory judgment action with the legal issues that were involved in his criminal trial in the State of Georgia. It then argued, incorrectly and somewhat dishonestly, that Jenkins' request for declarative relief was ***"non-justiciable"*** because a declaratory judgment from the EDNY would not have any effect on Jenkins' criminal conviction.

This was true, of course, but it was also totally irrelevant. Jenkins was not asking the EDNY to do anything about his criminal conviction in Georgia. The only relief that Jenkins was asking — and the government clearly recognized this in its opening memorandum — was a declaration that two provisions of AEDPA, a federal statute that prevented him from obtaining effective habeas corpus relief, be declared unconstitutional as applied to him by the Southern District of Georgia and the Eleventh Circuit Court of Appeals. This was unquestionably a justiciable issue that could have been addressed by the EDNY.

It should be emphasized here that Jenkins was injured by two **separate** and **distinct** harms. First, he was subjected to a criminal trial by the State of Georgia that was severely tainted by numerous errors, both of Georgia law and of federal constitutional law. Second, he was deprived of his federal constitutional right of habeas corpus by **Congress** (in enacting AEDPA) and by the **federal courts** in Georgia (Judge Nangle and the Eleventh Circuit) who incorrectly applied AEDPA. Obviously, if Jenkins had never been wrongfully convicted by the state court, there would never have been any need for him to seek habeas relief in the federal courts. But this does not permit Congress and the federal courts to disregard the constitutional limits that govern applications for habeas relief in the federal courts.

What happened to Jenkins was somewhat akin to what happened to President Garfied in 1881. Garfield was shot by Charles J. Guiteau on July 2, but he did not die until September 18. Initially, it was thought that the gunshot wound was very serious, and that Garfield would not last the night.[172] However, he recovered from the gunshot wound, and he seemed to be doing fine. When he died on September 18, it was due to sepsis, not the gunshot wound. Most historians and medical experts believe that Garfield could have easily survived if he had received better, more competent

---

172 Garfield was shot twice. The first was a superficial would that did not cause any serious injury and the other was a shot in the back that was more serious but missed all vital organs.

medical care. Nevertheless, Guiteau was convicted of murder and hanged on June 30, 1882. None of the doctors were hanged.

Like Garfield, Jenkins was injured here by two separate parties, each acting separately. First, he was harmed by the state courts of Georgia who violated and ignored numerous state and federal laws designed to protect criminal defendants. Second, he was deprived of his fundamental right of habeas corpus — a right explicitly guaranteed by Article I, Section 9, of the Constitution — by Congress (in enacting AEDPA) and by the federal courts who applied AEDPA unconstitutionally.

The first thing that should be noted about the government's Reply Memorandum is that it completely mischaracterized and misrepresented the basis of Jenkins' claim for declaratory relief. As the government stated:

> "Notably, the Eleventh Circuit has ruled, based on a full record, that [Jenkins'] habeas petition lacked merit. Now, inexplicably, [Jenkins] demands that this Court question and rule in opposition to that court's informed judgment. [Jenkins'] complaint should accordingly be dismissed."

With apologies to Elizabeth Barrett Browning, "how many errors can government lawyers make in a single sentence, let me count the ways." First, the Eleventh Circuit most definitely did ***not*** rule that Jenkins' habeas petition lacked merit ***based upon a full record***. As explicitly pointed out in the Complaint and in Jenkins' Memorandum in opposition to the motion, the Eleventh Circuit's consideration of Jenkins habeas petition was ***drastically limited*** due to its failure to issue a proper certificate of appealability. Instead of a full record, the Eleventh Circuit failed to consider ***seventeen*** of the eighteen grounds Jenkins had asserted in support of his habeas petition. And with respect to the single ground which the Eleventh Circuit did deign to consider (ineffective assistance of counsel), the Eleventh Circuit failed to consider ***fifteen*** of the sixteen grounds Jenkins had claimed to show that his counsels' performance had been deficient. To suggest, therefore, that the Eleventh Circuit denied Jenkins' habeas petition "based upon a full record" is outright deceitful and fraudulent.

Second, the government's lawyers asserted that Jenkins "demands that this Court rule in opposition to that court's informed judgment." This was also clearly incorrect, and the government lawyers knew it was incorrect. What Jenkins was asking the EDNY Court to do was to rule on the issue of whether two provisions of AEDPA were unconstitutional, both on their face and as applied to Jenkins. Contrary to the government's assertion, these issues were never considered by the Eleventh Circuit and therefore there was no way a decision of the EDNY would "question" or be "in opposition to" the judgment of the Eleventh Circuit.

Third, the government's lawyers stated that the decision of the Eleventh Circuit was "informed." As already explained, however, the decision of the Eleventh Circuit was completely misinformed. They neglected to consider seventeen of the grounds that Jenkens had raised in support of his habeas petition and fifteen of the grounds he had asserted in support of his claim of ineffective assistance of counsel.

Fourth, the government's lawyers stated that Jenkins' request for declaratory relief was "inexplicable." This was also untrue. The basis for Jenkins' request for declaratory relief was very clearly explained both in the Complaint and in the Memorandum in opposition to the government's motion to dismiss. And, as noted previously, the government's lawyers themselves had a very good grasp of Jenkins' claims in their original Memorandum which sought to have the Complaint dismissed on the frivolous grounds of improper venue and res judicata. It was only after the government's lawyers dreamed up the dubious issue of "non-justiciability," that the grounds for Jenkins' Complaint suddenly became "inexplicable" to them.

Finally, the government's lawyers summarily stated that Jenkins' complaint "should accordingly be dismissed." According to what? The government's series of false and fraudulent statements regarding the nature of

Jenkins' claims did not, in any way, provide a justification for dismissing his Complaint.

The fact that the government's lawyers had found it necessary to mischaracterize and misrepresent the true nature of Jenkins' Complaint is very telling. They obviously realized that their frivolous arguments would be completely unavailing if they accurately delineated the true nature of Jenkins' claims, and therefore they needed to create a convenient "straw-man" which they could then attack with deceitful arguments. This hardly seems worthy of government lawyers, or of any lawyer for that matter, but I guess that is how things are done these days.

The government raised the following three new arguments in its Reply Memorandum in support of its motion to dismiss Jenkins' Complaint: (i) that the Declaratory Judgment Act ("DJA") did not provide a basis for jurisdiction over Jenkins' Complaint and therefore the Court lacked subject matter jurisdiction, (ii) that the United States could not be sued under then DJA due to sovereign immunity, and (iii) that Jenkins lacked standing to assert the claims at issue because they did not present an actual "case" or "controversy" within the meaning of Article III of the Constitution.

All of these arguments were invalid as a matter of law. However, since the government raised these claims for the first time in its Reply Memoradum,[173] it was first necessary for me to obtain permission from Judge Garaufis to submit a Rebuttal Memorandum. Such permission was sought and granted.

The government's first argument — that "the DJA did not provide a basis for jurisdiction over Jenkins' Complaint and therefore the Court lacked subject matter jurisdiction" — was totally bogus. The DJA ***never*** provides a basis for jurisdiction ***for anyone*** at any time; it merely provides a remedy.

---

173 The government's lawyers recognized, in a footnote, the impropriety of raising new grounds for dismissal in a reply memorandum, but they excused their tardiness on the ground that "[c]hallenges to a court's subject matter jurisdiction can be raised at any time in the course of litigation" and, therefore, "it did not therefore waive the defense." Reply Mem. 2, note 1. It is true, of course, that subject matter jurisdiction cannot be waived, but a "lack of standing" defense can be waived.

The statutory basis for subject matter jurisdiction over Jenkins' Complaint, as was clearly alleged in the Complaint, was Section 1331 of the United States Code. As noted previously, that Section provides that "[t]he district courts shall have original jurisdiction of all civil actions arising under the Constitution, laws or treaties of the United States." Jenkins' Complaint was a civil action arising under the Constitution and laws of the United States, and therefore subject matter jurisdiction was clearly proper. There was absolutely no reason to look to the DJA for jurisdiction because that statute has nothing to do with jurisdiction.

In support of its argument that the DJA did not provide a basis for subject matter jurisdiction, the government's lawyers cited a series of irrelevant cases which had previously held that an action for declaratory relief was improper in certain circumstances (Reply Mem at 2-4). All of these cases can be grouped into two broad categories.

First, there were several cases (such as *United States v King*, 395 U.S. 1 (1969) and *Yeskel v. United States*, 31 F. Supp. 956 (D. N.J. 1940) which had held that federal district courts do not have subject matter jurisdiction to issue declaratory judgments against the United States. I will admit that, at first blush, these cases surely sound pretty good for the government. The problem, however, as any competent lawyer should have realized,[174] is that these cases were completely **overruled** by statute in 1976 when Congress amended the Administrative Procedure Act (5 U.S.C § 551 et seq.) to waive the defense of sovereign immunity. As amended, Section 702 of the Administrative Procedure Act has been broadly interpreted as a general waiver of sovereign immunity for **all** cases in which the United States is sued in federal district courts for declaratory or injunctive relief.[175]

---

174 It is an ethical violation for a lawyer, even a government lawyer, to cite a legal precedent to the court which he or she knows has been overruled. There is also a corresponding ethical obligation to verify that cases cited have not been overruled.

175 Section 702 of the Administrative Procedure Act did **not** expand the subject matter jurisdiction of the Court of Claims (now the U.S. Claims Court) (nor did the Federal Courts Improvements Act of 1982). As a result, there are still some situations in which the Claims Court does not have subject matter jurisdiction to issue equitable relief. *See Placeway Construction Co. v. United States*, 920 F.2d 903 (Fed. Cir. 1990). Obviously, that situation was not relevant to Jenkins' case in the EDNY, since Jenkins' Complaint was pending in a **district court**, which did have general subject matter jurisdiction to issue equitable relief against the United States.

The second and more extensive category of cases cited by the government in support of its motion to dismiss consisted of cases (such as *Benson v. State Board of Parole and Probation*, 384 F.2d. 238 (9th Cir. 1967), *Grajewski v. United States*, 368 F.2d 533 (8th Cir. 1966) and *Forsythe v. Ohio*, 333 F2d 678 (6th Cir. 1964), in which the plaintiff (usually a prison inmate acting *pro se*) attempted to use the declaratory judgment remedy as a **substitute** for a writ of habeas corpus, a writ of error coram nobis, or a motion to correct or vacate his sentence. In all of these cases, the relief requested related directly to the validity of the conviction or sentence at issue. Under these circumstances, courts have generally (and quite properly) ruled that it is improper to bring a declaratory judgment action to circumvent the procedural requirements of habeas corpus, coram nobis, or a motion to vacate or correct a sentence. None of these cases was relevant to Jenkins' lawsuit in the EDNY, since Jenkins was not challenging the validity of his conviction, sentence or confinement. What he was challenging was the validity of two federal statutes that imposed unconstitutional limitations on his right to obtain federal habeas review. Accordingly, the cases that the government cited with respect to the validity of seeking declaratory relief as an alternative to habeas relief were completely irrelevant.

Finally, even if Jenkins' claim were deemed to be a request for habeas relief (which it clearly was not), this would still not deprive the EDNY of **subject matter** jurisdiction. The Supreme Court made this clear in *Braden v. 30th Judicial Circuit Court*, 410 U.S. 484 (1973), where the Court ruled that a federal district court in Kentucky had jurisdiction to hear a habeas claim brought by a prisoner who was confined in a state prison in Alabama. The significance of *Braden* was succinctly summarized in *Chatman-Bay v. Thornberg*, 864 F.2d 804, 811 (D.C. Cir. 1988), one of the cases cited by the government in its memorandum:

> Braden's teaching [is] that habeas jurisdiction is **not** limited to the district where the individual is incarcerated. That is to say, by virtue of *Braden*'s holding, **it can no longer be maintained that a federal court outside the district**

of incarceration lacks subject matter jurisdiction over a habeas claim (emphasis added).

The government's final argument regarding the issue of justiciability was that Jenkins lacked **standing** to bring his lawsuit in federal court because his Complaint against the government did not allege an actual "case of controversy" within the meaning of Article III of the Constitution. In support of this astonishing argument, the government cited the Supreme Court's decision in *Steel Co. v. Citizens for a Better Environment*, 523 U.S. 83, 102 (1998), where the Court stated as follows:

> "The irreducible constitutional minimum of standing contains three requirements. First and foremost, there must be alleged (and ultimately proved) an injury in fact — a harm suffered by the plaintiff that is concrete and actual or imminent, not conjectural or hypothetical. Second, there must be causation — a fairly traceable connection between the plaintiff's injury and the complained-of conduct of the defendant. And third, there must be redressability — a likelihood that the requested relief will address the alleged injury. This triad of injury in fact, causation, and redressability constitutes the core of Article III's case or controversy requirement, and the party invoking
>
> federal jurisdiction bears the burden of establishing its existence."

The government argued that Jenkins failed to satisfy two prongs of this triad, **causation** and **redressability**. Apparently, the government conceded that Jenkins had shown that he had suffered harm, although it did not specify what harm it thought Jenkins was complaining about. With respect to the issue of **causation**, the government argued as follows:

> "As to causation, [Jenkins'] lawsuit is against the United States, which had nothing to do with the underlying state conviction and was not — and could not have

been — named as a defendant in the subsequent habeas proceeding. Rather, [Jenkins] was first prosecuted by the state of Georgia and, after his conviction became final in the Georgia courts, he filed a petition pursuant to 28 U.S.C. § 2254, naming the state agent responsible for his incarceration. Thus, the party that has caused his injury is the state of Georgia, not the United States." Gov Reply Mem in Supp of Motion to Dismiss at 6.

This is complete and utter nonsense, and the government's lawyers should have known (and undoubtedly did know) better.

First, the *injury* that Jenkins complained about in the EDNY lawsuit — which was clearly articulated in his Complaint and which the government's lawyers clearly understood in their initial Memorandum — had nothing to do with the underlying state court conviction in Georgia. On the contrary, the injury alleged in the Complaint related solely to the unconstitutional effect of Sections 2253(c) and 2254(d) of AEDPA, which had severely limited his ability to obtain effective habeas corpus review in the federal courts.

Second, the injury that Jenkins complained about here was clearly *caused* by *the United States*, not by the state of Georgia. Congress enacted the legislation at issue, and Judge Nangle and the Judges of the Eleventh Circuit Court of Appeals unconstitutionally applied it. It was as a direct result of the actions *of the United States*, therefore, that none of the eighteen constitutional errors Jenkins cited as grounds for habeas relief was ever properly considered by the *federal courts* in Georgia. The state courts in Georgia did a lot that was bad, of course, but this was not one of them.

Third, contrary to the government's argument, the United States was correctly named as the proper defendant in the EDNY lawsuit because the United States was the party that caused the injury.

With respect to the issue of *redressability*, the government argued as follows:

"[Jenkins] cannot show that a decision in his favor would be likely to redress his alleged injury. *Were [Jenkins] to prevail on the merits of his lawsuit, he would obtain from this Court a declaratory judgment asserting that 28 U.S C. § 2253(c) is unconstitutional on its face and that Sections 2253(c) and 2254(d) were unconstitutionally applied in his habeas proceeding.* Such a declaratory judgment would have no direct effect on the Eleventh Circuit's decision affirming the denial on his habeas petition. *Although it could be cited as persuasive authority for the Georgia district court to reopen his habeas proceeding*, it is not necessarily likely that this court would agree to do so. Moreover, even if the court did re-open the proceedings, it is not more likely than unlikely that it would conclude that this court had correctly decided the constitutional issues. Nor can we assume that the Eleventh Circuit would agree with a ruling of the Georgia district court in [Jenkins'] favor. The large number of proceedings — each with uncertain outcomes — that would have to take place before the judgment of this court could be said to have redressed Jenkins' injury renders it an attenuated remedy at best" (emphasis added). Gov Reply Mem at 6-7.[176]

Here again, the government's argument is utter nonsense. In the 1830s, there was a terrible problem in this country regarding the callous and inhumane treatment of Native Americans in the southern states. In 1830 Congress passed, and President Jackson signed into law, an Act known as the "Indian Removal Act" which provided for forcible removal

---

176 The government also added, "[i]t may be that [Jenkins] hopes to appeal these issues all the way to the Supreme Court. With a Supreme Court ruling in his favor, he would then have a stronger basis to re-open his habeas proceeding and overturn the Eleventh Circuit's decision. However, this, too, is a speculative theory of redressability on which the ground standing, given that the Supreme Court would be as likely as not to rule against him. Reply Memorandum at 7.

of Native Americans to lands west of the Mississippi. This led, of course, to the unspeakable "trail of tears."

At this same time, Georgia passed a series of laws, including certain criminal laws, that were violative of Native American rights as previously recognized by U.S. treaties and laws. The constitutionality of these Georgia laws was explicitly considered by the Supreme Court in **Worcester v. Georgia**, 31 U.S. 515 (1830). In an opinion written by the great Chief Justice John Marshall, the Supreme Court declared these Georgia laws to be unconstitutional. The Supreme Court's decision had no effect, however, because Georgia simply ignored the Court's ruling and President Jackson, who was a strong proponent of the Indian Removal Act, refused to take any steps to enforce it. Although this may be entirely apocryphal, Jackson reportedly said, "John Marshall has made his decision, now let him enforce it!" If President Eisenhower had done the same thing following *Brown v. Board of Education*, we might still have segregation in this country.

Based upon the government's fallacious theory of redressability, one could argue that the Supreme Court's decision in **Worcester** was "non-justiciable" because it was not, and could not, be enforced because the responsible civil authorities were unwilling to enforce it. By the same token, one could also argue that the Supreme Court's decision in *Brown v. Board of Education* (or any other case for that matter) was also non-justiciable because it, too, might not be enforced.[177] This is utter nonsense. Once a court has issued its judgment, it has done everything necessary to render a justiciable decision. Just because the effectiveness of the court's decision ultimately depends on the willingness of others to honor and enforce it does not make the court's decision "non-justiciable." This is true in every case, and it was true also in Jenkins' case.

What was absolutely remarkable about the government's lawyers' argument on redressability is how accurately and succinctly they stated

---

[177] Like Georgia in 1830, Arkansas in 1957 refused to enforce the Supreme Court's desegregation order. Unlike Jackson, however, Eisenhower sent federal troops into Little Rock to enforce the order.

what a summary judgment could do to benefit Jenkins in this case. As they stated, *"Were [Jenkins[to prevail on the merits of his lawsuit, he would obtain from this Court a declaratory judgment asserting that 28 U.S C. § 2253(c) is unconstitutional on its face and that Sections 2253(c) and 2254(d) were unconstitutionally applied in his habeas proceeding."* Reply Memorandum at 6 (emphasis added). *Yes, yes, yes, this is exactly what Jenkins was requesting and exactly what Judge Garaufis had the legal authority to do*. If Judge Garaufis issued such a judgment, this would have provided Jenkins with all the relief that he requested and all the relief that he needed. If others were unwilling to recognize the validity of this judgment, he could then enforce the judgment by other means.

The government then went on to argue, however, that such relief would not be sufficient because *"[s]uch a declaratory judgment would have no direct effect on the Eleventh Circuit's decision affirming the denial of his habeas petition."* Reply Memoradum at 6 (emphasis added). This was utterly false and erroneous.

A declaratory judgment, like any other judgment, is a *judgment,* a legal document that finally and forever defines the rights of the parties. In this case, as the government's own attorneys clearly recognized and stated, the judgment would have ruled *that 28 U.S C. § 2253(c) is unconstitutional on its face and that Sections 2253(c) and 2254(d) were unconstitutionally applied [by the Eleventh Circuit] in his habeas proceeding."* Reply Memorandum at 6 (emphasis added). Such a judgment would not be a mere opinion of another court that the Eleventh Circuit was free to accept or reject as it chose. It would be a binding legal judgment against the United States that the Eleventh Circuit would be legally obligated to honor and enforce.

The government explicitly conceded that such a declaratory judgement, if granted, "could be cited as persuasive authority for the Georgia district court to reopen the habeas proceeding" (Reply Memorandum at 6), but then it incongruously argued that "it is not necessarily likely that the court would agree to do." *Id*. This argument clearly shows that the government's attorneys failed to understand the difference between a ***judgment*** and an ***opinion***. According to the precedential rules of **stare decisis**, courts in one federal circuit (say the Eleventh Circuit) are not obligated to follow the ***opinions*** of courts in another circuit (say the Second Circuit). But this is not so with respect to ***judgments.*** Once a judgment has been issued by a federal court in one district, it must be recognized and enforced by all other federal courts regardless of what circuit they are located in.

It may very well be, in fact it was probably likely, that Jenkins would not have been able to obtain a judgment on the merits declaring Sections 2253(c) and 2254(d) to be unconstitutional. But that is completely irrelevant. He was prevented from getting his day in court on a false premise — that such a judgment, if issued, would be ineffective.

Jenkins' Rebuttal Memorandum in opposition to the government's motion to dismiss was served on the defendant and filed with the Court on October 29, 2002. No further proceedings were had in the case, and the motion was submitted to Judge Garaufis for decision. On June 9, 2003, Judge Garaufis issued a five-page Memorandum and Order granting the government's motion and dismissing Jenkins' Complaint for lack of subject matter jurisdiction.[178]

Most of Judge Garaufis' five-page Memorandum was used to recite the factual and procedural history of the case. Discussion of the legal issues involved was barely more than a single page. Essentially, Judge Garaufis accepted the government's argument for dismissal, hook, line and sinker. As he stated in his Memorandum and Order:

> "An actual controversy does not exist in this case because it is not likely that a decision in [Jenkins'] favor will provide him with the relief he seeks. According to [Jenkins], his injury is 'the fact that he was denied the opportunity to obtain meaningful habeas relief due to

---
[178] Judge Garaufis' Decision was not published in the Federal Supplement. A copy of the Decision is reprinted in Appendix D.

certain alleged constitutional infirmities in AEDPA'. . . . To redress this injury, this court's declaratory judgment would have to make it likely that [Jenkins] will be granted meaningful habeas relief. Jenkins argues that '[i]f these limitations are declared unconstitutional by this Court, then [Jenkins] would be entitled to seek further habeas relief.' That argument is simply not correct.

"A declaration by this court that section 2253(c) is facially unconstitutional, and that sections 2254(d) and 2253(c) were unconstitutionally applied to [Jenkins'] habeas petition, can, at best, be used by [Jenkins] as persuasive authority in attempting to convince the Georgia district court to reopen the habeas proceeding. Consequently, a declaration by this court concerning the constitutionality of [Jenkins'] claims would have no effect on [Jenkins'] *entitlement* to seek further habeas review. Accordingly, this court is without subject matter jurisdiction over [Jenkins'] claims." Memorandum and Order at 4-5 (emphasis in original).

I hate to say this about Judge Garaufis, who I personally know to be a learned and honorable man, but this reasoning is pure poppycock. As I explained in detail above with respect to the government's argument regarding redressability, a *judgment* from the EDNY declaring Sections 2253(c) and 2254(d) unconstitutional, either on their face or as applied in Jenkins' habeas proceeding, would have as much legal effect as any other declaratory judgment ever has. It would not be, as Judge Garaufis incorrectly stated (quoting *in haec verba* from the government's Reply Memorandum), "persuasive authority in attempting to convince the Georgia district court to reopen the habeas proceeding." (Garaufis Decision at 4, Government's Reply Memorandum at 6). On the contrary, it would be a binding *judgment* that the Georgia district court and the Eleventh Circuit Court of Appeals would be legally obligated to accept (unless, like President Jackson, they decided to ignore the rule of law).

Judge Garaufis, in effect, ruled that a judgment of a federal court declaring a federal statute unconstitutional has no effect. This would come as a great surprise to John Marshall who, in 1803, declared that Section 13 of the Judiciary Act of 1789 was unconstitutional and thereby established the principle of judicial review.[179] It would also come as a great surprise to the Justices who declared in 1954 that various statutes that had been passed by Congress following the Civil War that required segregated public schools in the District of Columbia were unconstitutional,[180] to the Justices who declared in 1997 that certain provisions of the Brady Handgun Violence Prevention Act were unconstitutional,[181] to the Justices who declared in 2010 that certain provisions of the Bipartisan Campaign Reform Act of 2002 were unconstitutional,[182] to the Justices who declared in 2013 that Section 3 of the Defense of Marriage Act was unconstitutional,[183] and to the justices who declared in 2020 that certain provisions of the Telephone Consumer Protection Act were unconstitutional.[184]

Since 1803, more than two hundred federal statutes have been declared unconstitutional, in whole or in part, by the Supreme Court,[185] and undoubtedly many more have been declared unconstitutional by the lower federal courts. Only a handful of these cases involved declaratory judgments, but that is immaterial. A declaration that a statute is unconstitutional has the same legal effect whether the requested relief is in the form of a declaration of rights, a request for an injunction, a request for mandamus, rescission or reformation of a contract, reversal of a criminal conviction, annulment of a civil forfeiture, or any other possible remedy.

---

179 See *Marbury v. Madison*, 5 U.S. 137 (1803).
180 See *Bolling v. Sharp*, 347 U.S. 497 (1954).
181 See *Printz v. United States*, 521 U.S. 898 (1997).
182 See *Citizens United v. Federal Elections Commission*, 558 U.S. 310 (2010)
183 See *United States v. Windsor*, 570 U.S. 744 (2013).
184 *Barr v. American Ass'n of Political Consultants, Inc*, 591 U.S. __, 140 S. Ct. 2335, 207 L.Ed.2 784 (2020).
185 For a complete list of these cases, see "Table of Laws Held Unconstitutional in Whole or in Part by the Supreme Court," published on the website of *Constitution Annotated*, published by the Congressional Research Service (2023).

None of these cases would have been possible if the theory of justiciability proposed by the government and accepted by Judge Garaufis in Jenkins' case were correct.

The flaw in Judge Garaufis' reasoning was that he, like the government's attorneys, failed to recognize the key difference between a ***judgment***, which is legally binding between the ***parties***, and a judicial opinion, which is a document in which a judge explains the basis for his reasoning in deciding a particular case and which other courts can look to for guidance in deciding similar cases. In the latter situation, the other courts are free to accept or reject the reasoning of the first court. In the case of a judgment, however, there is no such leeway. All courts have to accept and enforce a judgment.

Contrary to what Judge Garaufis said in his decision, therefore, if he had issued a summary judgment in Jenkins' favor, this would have been binding on the courts in Georgia.

Following the issuance of Judge Garaufis' Memorandum and Order dated June 10, 2003, a judgment was entered on July 7, 2003, by the Clerk of the EDNY dismissing Jenkins' Complaint for lack of subject matter jurisdiction. Once again, I had failed to obtain any relief from the courts on Jenkins' behalf, and once again I had the distinct feeling that yet another court had acted improperly and contrary to law.

CHAPTER 15

APPEAL TO THE SECOND CIRCUIT U.S. COURT OF APPEALS

After Judge Garaufis issued his terrible decision, I knew I had to head to a different court for relief. The only good thing was that the commute to the Courthouse was getting shorter. At that time, my offices were located in midtown Manhattan, a stone's throw from Times Square. So, I had been travelling, in order of appearance, to Hinesville, Georgia, for Judge Harvey, to Atlanta, Georgia, for the Georgia Supreme Court, to Augusta, Georgia, for Judge Nangle, back to Atlanta, for the Eleventh Circuit Court of Appeals, to downtown Brooklyn, for Judge Garaufis, and now to downtown Manhattan, for the Second Circuit U.S. Court of Appeals. I do not count my two trips to the U.S. Supreme Court in this itinerary because all of the legwork for those two appeals was done by Federal Express. I would have loved to go to Washington to argue Jenkins' case personally before the Supreme Court but, unfortunately, both of his petitions for certiorari were denied.

On August 5, 2003, I filed a timely Notice of Appeal from the judgment of the EDNY dismissing Jenkins' Complaint. This began the process for having an appeal heard by the Second Circuit Court of Appeals. On January 8, 2004, the Clerk of the Second Circuit entered a Scheduling Order which provided that the Record on Appeal needed to be filed by December 29, 2003, that Appellant's Brief was due by January 5, 2004, that Appellee's Brief was due by February 4, 2004, and that oral argument before the Court would be heard prior to March 22, 2004. After all the paperwork was filed, oral argument actually took place on June 8, 2004. Following oral argument, the case was submitted to the Court for decision.

On October 15, 2004, the Court of Appeals unanimously affirmed the decision of Judge Garaufis dismissing Jenkins' complaint. The decision is reported at 386 F.3d 415 (2d Cir. 2004).

Like the decision of the district court, the decision of the Second Circuit was relatively short (five pages) and it mirrored the same flawed reasoning that had been articulated by Judge Garaufis. Thus, the decision explicitly stated:

> "The real dispute here is between Jenkins and his custodian — whoever that may be in the Georgia state prison system. *See* 28 U.S.C. § 2242 ('Application for a writ of habeas corpus shall . . . name the person who has custody over [petitioner] and by virtue of what claim or authority…'). The declaration Jenkins seeks will not secure him 'effective' habeas review; that can only be had in a habeas proceeding." 386 F.3d at 418.

To make this erroneous point even clearer, the Second Circuit also stated as follows:

> "Jenkins' dispute here is with the State of Georgia, which is holding him in jail. One reason Jenkins' claim is non-redressible is that the United States cannot release him. Though the United States has litigated this suit, the United States and Jenkins are not the adverse parties in this dispute, with no case or controversy for Article III purposes. '[T]o achieve the status of a case or controversy, a dispute must exist between two parties having adverse legal interests. *S. Jackson & Sun*, 24 F.3d at 431." 386 F.3d at 419 (footnote).

Up until this point, I had always thought that the Second Circuit Court of Appeals was the preeminent Circuit Court in the nation. After reading this decision, however, I began to have serious doubts. Obviously, this was not their finest hour.

It is necessary for me to state here once again, that Jenkins' dispute in the EDNY action ***was most definitely not against the State of Georgia.*** The State of Georgia did not enact Sections 2253(c) and 2254(d) of AEDPA. Congress did that and Congress, of course, is a part of the United States. The State of Georgia also did not apply Sections 2253(c) and 2254(d) unconstitutionally in Jenkins' habeas proceeding. The District Court for the Southern District of Georgia and the Eleventh Circuit Court of Appeals did that, and both of these entities are instrumentalities of the United States. So, Jenkins' complaint against the United States was unquestionably brought against the proper party because it was these instrumentalities of the United States — and only these instrumentalities of the United States — that had caused Jenkins' injury. Contrary to what the Second Circuit stated in its decision, therefore, the State of Georgia had absolutely nothing to do with the injuries that Jenkins was complaining about in the present proceeding.

The Second Circuit stated in its opinion, "[t]hough the United States has litigated this suit, the United States and Jenkins are not the adverse parties in this dispute." This seems to imply that Jenkins named the wrong defendant in his lawsuit, and that the real party in interest was Georgia, and that the United States made a grave mistake in "litigating this suit." None of this was true. The United States was represented by competent counsel and they never argued, nor could they, that the United States was the wrong defendant. This argument would have been ludicrous, and I think that even Judge Garaufis would have rejected it. How it could have been suggested here by the judges of the Second Circuit as a basis for dismissing Jenkins' complaint is unfathomable. But, just to be clear, the United States was unquestionably the proper party because it was the party that caused the injuries that Jenkins complained of.

Furthermore, the gravamen of Jenkins' complaint was that two provisions of federal statutory law were either unconstitutional on their face or unconstitutionally applied to Jenkins' habeas petition. The State of Georgia had neither a legitimate interest in nor standing to defend these federal statutes from constitutional attack. That was the role of the United States government as represented by the United States Attorney's Office.

It is clear from the excepts from the Second Circuit decision quoted above, that the panel of the Court that issued the decision had confused the remedy of declaratory judgment under 28 U.S.C. § 2201 with the remedy of habeas corpus under 28 U.S.C. § 2246. These are completely separate remedies, they serve completely different purposes, they are governed by different federal statutes, and they have different substantive and procedural requirements.

Jenkins was not seeking a declaratory judgment to collaterally attack his state court conviction. There was no need, therefore, as the Second Circuit suggested, for him to "name the person who has custody over [petitioner] and by virtue of what claim or authority." 386 F.3d at 418. On the contrary, that would have been completely inappropriate, since the Warden of Telfair State Prison (the place where Jenkins was then incarcerated in Georgia) had nothing to do with the claims at issue.

The Second Circuit made the following incongruous statement in its decision:

> "Jenkins made an (unsuccessful) facial challenge to the constitutionality of § 2254(d) in his initial habeas petition. See *Jenkins*, 103 F. Supp. 2d at 1382. **It is not clear why** he did not raise then the constitutional issues he asks us to consider now . . ." 386 F.3d at 418 (emphasis added).

The fact that the Second Circuit included this ridiculous assertion in its analysis of why Jenkins' complaint should be dismissed illustrates how truly clueless they were regarding the nature of Jenkins' claims. It is true, of course, that Jenkins had raised an unsuccessful *facial challenge* to Section 2254(d) in his habeas petition before Judge Nangle. He did so because anyone, myself included, could plainly see that Section 2254(d), on its face, unconstitutionally purported to limit the ability of federal judges to "to say what the law is" in habeas cases "to clearly established federal law **as** *determined by the Supreme Court of the United States.*" This language was narrowly interpreted by the Supreme Court in *Williams v. Taylor*, 529 U.S. 362 (2000) to require only that the Supreme Court "has broken sufficient ground" on a particular issue rather than has "clearly established" the relevant law. I thought at the time, and I continue to believe, that *Williams* was wrongly decided and that it should have declared AEDPA unconstitutional on this basis. This was why I included the facial challenge to Section 2254(d) in the habeas petition. As discussed in Point 18 of Chapter 10, Judge Nangle properly denied this ground in Jenkins' habeas petition based on the *Williams* decision.[186]

The fact that Jenkins was able to assert a facial challenge to Section 2254(d) in his habeas petition did not imply or indicate that he could also raise in that petition the three claims that he asserted in the EDNY lawsuit, namely, that Section 2254(d) was unconstitutional *as applied* by Judge Harvey and that Section 2253(c) was unconstitutional *on its face* and *as applied* by the Eleventh Circuit. The obvious reason why these claims could *not* have been asserted in the habeas petition is because **they had not yet occurred**. It was only after Judge Nangle issued his erroneous decision, and only after he and the Eleventh Circuit refused to issue a certificate of appealability, that Jenkins' constitutional claims under Sections 2253(c) and 2254(d) accrued. Obviously, it would not have been possible, therefore, for Jenkins to complain in his habeas petition about something that had not yet occurred and had not yet caused him any injury.

Finally, the Second Circuit made the same mistake as Judge Garaufis regarding the binding effect of a *judgment* issued by the EDNY. As the Court stated in its decision:

> "Because Jenkins must bring any future habeas petition (successive or otherwise) in Georgia . . . a declaration of the Eastern District of New York or of this Court

---

[186] I should note that I never expected that Judge Nangle would overrule or distinguish *Williams* and declare Section 2254(d) unconstitutional. I was merely preserving this issue for appeal to a higher court.

would not govern those proceedings, or have any binding or authoritative effect. The district courts of Georgia are bound to apply Eleventh Circuit law, as would the Circuit court itself. The proposed decree cannot end the controversy; it would be merely commentary on the validity of a statutory scheme that will govern a habeas proceeding in another jurisdiction. The courts of this Circuit are without jurisdiction to grant such relief." 386 F.3d at 418-19

It is true that a ***judgment*** of the EDNY would not ***govern*** any further proceedings in Georgia or elsewhere. Judgments ***never*** govern proceedings anywhere because they are not, and are not intended to be, statements of law. What judgments are, instead, are binding and effective adjudications of the rights of the parties who are subject to the judgment and, as such, they are binding and effective everywhere, including Georgia.

It is also true that any further proceedings in the federal courts in Georgia — whether civil actions for injunctive or mandamus relief pursuant to 28 U.S.C. § 1331 or habeas proceedings pursuant to 28 U.S.C. § 2554 — would be governed by federal law as applied by the courts of the Eleventh Circuit, but this does not mean that the courts in that Circuit have discretion to ignore ***judgments*** that have been issued by federal courts in other Circuits. To do so would be a clear violation of the federal Declaratory Judgment Act. Just as federal courts have to give "full faith and credit" to state court judgments from other states, so too they have to give "full faith and credit" to federal judgments from other Circuits.

For all of the foregoing reasons, the decision of the Second Circuit affirming Judge Garaufis' decision dismissing Jenkins' complaint for declaratory relief was a bad decision, the last in a long series of bad decisions that prevented Jenkins from obtaining a fair hearing on the many constitutional violations that tainted his conviction.

On October 15, 2004, Roseann B. MacKechnie, the Clerk of the U.S. Court of Appeals for the Second Circuit, entered a judgment affirming the dismissal of Jenkins' EDNY case in accordance with the decision of the Court of Appeals. As stated in this judgment, "it is hereby ORDERED, ADJUDGED and DECREED that the judgment of said District Court be and hereby is AFFIRMED in accordance with the opinion of the Court." I guess nothing ever gets more final than that.

After the Second Circuit denied Jenkins' appeal, my initial reaction was to file yet another petition for certiorari with the U.S. Supreme Court. Upon further reflection, I concluded that such a petition was extremely unlikely to be granted, and therefore not worth pursuing. There is a difference between dogged persistence in the face of unfavorable odds and futilely pursuing of a goal that cannot possibly be attained.

As a result, my seven-year effort to free Jenkins from unlawful incarceration had failed. The assertion I had previously made to Judge Harvey at that very first hearing on March 14, 1997, that Jenkins' conviction was improper and would be reversed "by some court at some time" turned out not to be true. I had done my best to make this happen, of course, but unfortunately, my best efforts were not good enough. On the other hand, I cannot think of anything else that I could have done, or anything else that I could have done better or differently. At the end of the day, my only explanation, as Mr. Bumble so eloquently noted in *Oliver Twist*, is that the "the law is an ass."

CHAPTER 16

COMPARING THE FOUR DECISIONS THAT DENIED JENKINS HIS LIBERTY

Every judge who was asked to vacate Jenkins' conviction on the ground that his trial had been unfair and improper refused to do so. However, they often did so for different reasons. A brief comparison of the reasons given by each court on each ground is set forth below.

1. *Improper comments made by the prosecutor regarding Jenkins' failure to testify at his trial and refute the State's evidence*

A. Surprisingly, Judge Harvey never explicitly ruled on the issue of whether District Attorney Cheney had improperly commented to the jury regarding Jenkins' failure to testify and present evidence. Instead, he simply stated, "[a]s for each and every enumeration of error raised by the defendant prior to raising the issue of ineffective assistance of counsel, the defendant's motion for a new trial is denied." Order at 14.[187]

B. The Georgia Supreme Court ruled, inexplicably, that "the prosecutor's closing argument, [when] read in context, did not comment upon appellant's election not to testify but rather permissibly noted the failure

---

[187] For some inexplicable reason, Judge Harvey never discussed *any* of the numerous grounds Jenkins had raised in support of his motion for a new trial other than the "ineffective assistance of counsel" claim. Although there was some overlap between some of these other grounds and the ineffective assistance of counsel claim, they were not the same, and in many cases, they were completely different. Thus, for example, the prosecutor's egregious comments regarding Jenkins' failure to testify was never asserted as a basis for Jenkins' ineffective assistance of counsel claim and, as a result, it was never considered by Judge Harvey. One wonders whether he even grasped how significant this major constitutional violation was to Jenkins' motion, since he dismissed it so carelessly and perfunctorily. By the way, the reason Cheney's comments were not included in the ineffective assistance of counsel claim was because even Mr. Walker realized how improper these comments were, and he objected.

of the defense to rebut the State's evidence." 268 Ga. at ___, 491 S.E.2d at 58. This missed the entire thrust of the U.S. Supreme Court's authoritative rulings that the defendant in a criminal case never has any obligation to rebut the State's case; he can sit mute, present no evidence, and rely entirely upon his presumption of innocence. It is entirely the State's burden to present evidence proving the defendant's guilt, and this burden never shifts to the defendant. Accordingly, it was a clear violation of Jenkins' Fifth Amendment privilege against self-incrimination for District Attorney Cheney to suggest otherwise, and it was an unfathomable error of judgment for the Georgia Supreme Court to fail to recognize this and reverse Jenkins' conviction.

C. Judge Nangle blindly accepted the reasoning of the Georgia Supreme Court and ruled that Mr. Cheney's comments were permissible. As he stated in his decision, "[r]eading the comments at issue here in context, it is clear that they were aimed at the defense's failure to produce evidence rather than at petitioner's failure to testify." 103 F. Supp.2d at 1361. The fallacy here, of course, is that Jenkins had no obligation to produce evidence rebutting the State's case. On the contrary, he was entitled to present no defense and rely entirely upon his presumption of innocence.

D. The Eleventh Circuit Court of Appeals failed to consider this issue because it was not included in the limited certificate of appealability ("COA") granted by Judge Wilson.

2. *Improper admission of hearsay testimony from "silent witnesses" during the testimony of Investigator Gray*

A. Judge Harvey never explicitly ruled whether the admission of hearsay testimony from "silent witnesses" violated Jenkins' Sixth Amendment right to confront and cross-examine the witnesses against him. He simply denied the motion without discussing this issue. See Order at 14.

B. The Georgia Supreme Court ruled that "Gray's testimony that he investigated appellant based on information he received from an unnamed source did not constitute hearsay because Gray did not divulge the content of that information." 268 Ga. at ___, 491 S.E.2d at 57. This was pure sophistry. Gray had testified that he was able, based upon the information he had received, to determine that Jenkins was one of the perpetrators who murdered and robbed Mr. Hodges. This was, as Jenkins had argued, "clearly tantamount to divulging the content of the information he received" and it was preposterous for the Georgia Supreme Court to insinuate otherwise.

C. Judge Nangle recognized that prior decisions of the federal courts "have held that statements by an officer concerning information received during his investigation which amount to substantive evidence of a defendant's guilt violates the Confrontation Clause." 103 F. Supp.2d at 1362. Nevertheless, Judge Nangle somehow managed to conclude that "Investigator Gray's testimony about information received from silent witnesses did not serve to implicate petitioner in this crime." *Id.* at 1362.

D. The Eleventh Circuit failed to consider this issue because it was not included in the limited COA granted by Judge Wilson.

3. *Jenkins' claim that he was denied effective assistance of counsel at his trial*

A. Despite the numerous egregious errors and deficiencies identified by Jenkins in his ineffective assistance of counsel claim, Judge Harvey determined that Jenkins' attorneys acted "reasonably" and "professionally" at all times, and that their conduct was not "deficient" within the meaning of *Srickland v. Washington*, 446 U.S. 668, 687 (1984). Judge Harvey also concluded that counsels' performance did not adversely affect the outcome of the trial.

B. The Georgia Supreme Court agreed with Judge Harvey's assessment that Jenkins' trial counsel acted reasonably and professionally at all times, and that there was no basis for finding that their conduct had been deficient. 268 Ga. at ___, 491 S.E.2d at 59-60.

C. Judge Nangle also agreed with the conclusion of Judge Harvey and the Georgia Supreme Court that Jenkins' trial counsel had acted reasonably and professionally, and that there was no basis for finding that their conduct had been deficient. See 103 F. Supp.2d at 1374-79.

D. The Eleventh Circuit Court of Appeals ruled that Jenkins' claim that his "counsel's assessment that the trial was going well, and that he did not need to testify, constituted ineffective assistance of counsel is meritless" (Decision at 5) because "[w]e give great deference to counsel's choices and make every effort to eliminate the distorting effects of hindsight, to reconstruct the circumstances of counsel's conduct, and to evaluate the conduct from counsel's perspective at the time." *Id.*

The Eleventh Circuit reached this conclusion notwithstanding the fact that Jenkins had explicitly alleged in his enumeration of error that his attorneys' assertion that the trial was "going well" was ***false and misleading*** and that, accordingly, his waiver of his right to testify had been obtained ***by deceit***.

Furthermore, contrary to authoritative rulings of the U.S. Supreme Court that the appropriateness of counsel's conduct must be evaluated in light of "the totality of the circumstances," the Eleventh Circuit failed to consider the effect of *fifteen* additional grounds that Jenkins had asserted regarding why his trial counsels' performance had been deficient.

4. *Failure to charge the jury regarding the Issue of corroboration of accomplice testimony*

A. Judge Harvey explicitly ruled that it was ***erroneous*** for him not to have charged the jury regarding the issue of corroboration (see Decision at 7). However, he refused to vacate Jenkins' conviction on this ground, ruling instead that his failure to charge the jury on the issue of corroboration constituted "harmless error." *Id.*

In order to reach this conclusion, Judge Harvey would have had to find, ***beyond a reasonable doubt***, that his failure to charge the jury concerning the issue of corroboration could not ***possibly*** have affected the outcome of the trial. *See Chapman v. California*, 386 U.S. 18 (1067) (discussed previously in Chapter 5). Since the jury here never even considered the issue of corroboration, it was impossible for anyone (including Judge Harvey) to say whether the failure to give a corroboration charge had any effect on the jury's verdict, let alone be able to conclude beyond a reasonable doubt that it had no effect. Accordingly, Judge Harvey's decision on this issue was clearly erroneous.

B. The Georgia Supreme Court did not explicitly say so, but they apparently realized that Judge Harvey's "harmless error" defense was improper and could not be justified. Accordingly, instead of relying on harmless error, the Supreme Court ruled that there was no need for Judge Harvey to give a corroboration charge in this case because the State had relied on "other evidence" besides the accomplice's testimony to establish Jenkins' guilt. 268 Ga. at ___, 491 S.E.2d at 59.

This undoubtedly came as a complete surprise to Judge Harvey (who presided at the trial) because he previously ruled that his failure to charge corroboration was erroneous. It also must have come as a complete surprise to District Attorney Cheney because he spent a considerable amount of time during his closing summation arguing that the testimony of Terry Roberts had been sufficiently corroborated. Obviously, there would have been no reason for him to do so if he thought corroboration was unnecessary. Contrary to the conclusion of the Georgia Supreme Court, therefore, both the trial judge who presided at the trial and the District Attorney who prosecuted the case both believed that corroboration was required.

. The obvious problem with the Georgia Supreme Court's decision regarding this issue is that this was clearly ***not*** a case in which the State had relied — or could possibly rely — on other evidence ***besides the testimony of the alleged accomplice*** to establish Jenkins' guilt. There was some "other evidence," of course,[188] but this other evidence was not sufficient ***by***

---

188 This "other evidence" consisted entirely of the two brief (and dubious) statements Jenkins allegedly made to Officer Smith and Kenneth McCall.

itself to establish Jenkins' guilt. It may have been sufficient to ***corroborate*** Roberts' testimony, but it was manifestly insufficient to find Jenkins guilty. Accordingly, a corroboration charge was essential, and the decision of the Georgia Supreme Court saying otherwise was clearly erroneous.[189]

C. Judge Nangle, in denying Jenkins' motion for a writ of habeas corpus, did not independently consider the issue of whether it was improper, under the circumstances of this case, for Judge Harvey to have failed to instruct the jury on the issue of corroboration. Instead, he blindly ***deferred*** to the judgment of the Georgia Supreme Court and ruled, "[b]ecause the state relied on evidence other than the accomplice's testimony, the trial court was not required to submit the sufficiency of corroboration to the jury and was therefore not required to charge the jury on corroboration." 103 F. Supp.2d at 1367.

This was clearly erroneous. Judge Nangle was clearly aware that Jenkins had argued that "the statements [of Officer Smith and McCall] standing alone were not sufficient to establish [his] guilt." *Id*. Under these circumstances, Judge Nangle had an independent obligation under federal constitutional law to critically examine whether the factual assertions made by the Georgia Supreme Court were supported by the evidence. He failed to do so, and that was clearly erroneous on his part.

D. The Eleventh Circuit failed to consider this issue because it was not included in the limited COA granted by Judge Wilson.

5. *Jenkins' claim that the evidence admitted at his trial was insufficient to convict him of malice murder*

A. Judge Harvey never explicitly ruled on the issue of whether the evidence admitted at trial was sufficient to convict Jenkins of malice murder. It is not even clear from his decision whether he understood that this

---

189 As will be discussed further in the following chapter, the Georgia Supreme Court ultimately came to this very same conclusion in *Hamm v. State*, 294 Ga. 781, 756 S.E.2d 507 (2014), which overruled its prior decision in Jenkins' case. Unfortunately, this epiphany came sixteen years too late for Jenkins.

issue had been raised. Nevertheless, as noted above, Judge Harvey stated in his decision that, "[a]s for each and every enumeration of error raised by the defendant prior to raising the issue of ineffective assistance of counsel, the defendant's motion for a new trial is denied." Order at 14.

B. The Georgia Supreme Court, after briefly summarizing (in a single paragraph) what they believed the evidence showed, ruled "[w]e find this evidence sufficient to enable a rational trier of fact to find appellant guilty of both malice murder and armed robbery beyond a reasonable doubt." 268 Ga. at __, 491 S.E.2d at 57.

C. Judge Nangle accepted the reasoning of the Georgia Supreme Court and ruled, "[v]iewing this evidence in the light most favorable to the prosecution, a reasonable jury could have found petitioner guilty of malice murder beyond a reasonable doubt." 103 F. Supp.2d at 1368.

D. The Eleventh Circuit failed to consider this issue because it was not included in the limited COA granted by Judge Wilson.

6. *Jenkins' claim that Judge Harvey's instructions regarding the issues of malice murder, parties to a crime, and conspiracy were improper*

A. Judge Harvey did not directly rule on the issue of whether his instructions concerning the issues of malice murder, parties to a crime, and conspiracy were improper. However, he did rule, in his consideration of Jenkins' ineffective assistance of counsel claim, that the instructions were proper, and therefore there was no reason for Jenkins' trial counsel to object to them. Decision at 11.

B. The Georgia Supreme Court tersely ruled, "[w]e find no error in the trial court's charges on malice murder, parties to a crime, and conspiracy." 268 Ga. at __, 491 S.E.2d at 59.

C. Unlike the Georgia Supreme Court, Judge Nangle presented a lengthy discussion of this issue. However, he ultimately agreed with the

Georgia Supreme Court that the charges were proper and did not violate Jenkins' Fourteenth Amendment right to due process. 103 F. Supp.2d at 1363-67.

D. The Eleventh Circuit failed to consider this issue because it was not included in the limited COA granted by Judge Wilson.

7. *Failure to consider the effect of "cumulative error"*

A. Judge Harvey did not explicitly consider the issue of whether Jenkins had been denied a fair trial due to the cumulative effect of the numerous errors that occurred during his trial. However, he necessarily rejected this argument by implication since he denied Jenkins' motion for a new trial. See Decision at 14.

B. The Georgia Supreme Court explicitly considered the issue of cumulative error, but their consideration of this issue consisted of the terse statement, "contrary to appellant's position, Georgia does not recognize the cumulative error rule." 268 Ga. at __, 491 S.E.2d at 58 (citing *Polk v. State*, 225 Ga. App. 257, 483 S.E.2d 687 (1997)).

As noted elsewhere in this narrative, on February 10, 2020 — more than 22 years after Jenkins' conviction had been affirmed — the Georgia Supreme Court explicitly and unanimously ruled in *State v. Lane*, 308 Ga. 10, 838 S.E.2d 808 (2020), that all of its prior jurisprudence regarding the issue of cumulative error had been wrong. Furthermore, in an Appendix to the *Lane* decision, the Court explicitly stated, "[w]e overrule our prior decisions and those of the Court of Appeals that hold that the prejudicial effect of multiple trial court errors may not be considered cumulatively in determining whether a criminal defendant is entitled to a new trial. We also disapprove any decisions with language to that effect." The Court then identified in the Appendix a long list of cases that were overruled, including the very decision at issue here which upheld Jenkins' conviction.

C. Judge Nangle did not rule on the issue of whether consideration of the effect of cumulative error was required by federal constitutional law as Jenkins had argued in his habeas petition. Instead, he ruled that Jenkins could not raise this issue because of his misguided and erroneous interpretation of the limits placed on federal habeas relief by Section 2254(d) of AEDPA. As Judge Nangle stated in his decision, "[b]ecause there is no clearly established Supreme Court precedent requiring this rule, petitioner has failed to meet the requirements of *Williams*, and the Court finds this ground insufficient to state a claim for habeas corpus relief." 103 F. Supp.2d at 1382.[190]

D. The Eleventh Circuit failed to consider this issue because it was not included in the limited COA granted by Judge Wilson.

8. *False and misleading testimony of Deputy Moran regarding dismissal of the murder charge against Terry Roberts*

A. Judge Harvey did not explicitly consider the issue of whether the testimony of Deputy Moran regarding dismissal of the murder charge against Terry Roberts was false and misleading and whether Jenkins was denied due process due to the failure of District Attorney Cheney to correct this false testimony. However, he necessarily rejected this argument by implication since he denied Jenkins' motion for a new trial. See Decision at 14.

B. The Georgia Supreme Court ruled, "Moran's testimony that, based on the results of police investigation, Terry Roberts was not prosecuted for murder, when read in context, did not raise the inferences appellant claims rendered Moran's testimony false; accordingly, the prosecution was under no duty to correct the record in regard to Moran's testimony." 268 Ga. at __, 491 S.E.2d at 57.

It is truly sad to note the depth to which the members of the Georgia Supreme Court sank to uphold such a bad decision. There is no plausible

---

190 Contrast this view with Judge Nangle's contrary assertion in Point 20, *infra*, that Section 2254(d) does not "limit the federal courts' independent authority with respect to federal questions." 103 F. Supp.2d at 1382.

way any reasonable judge or lawyer (or first year law student) could possibly conclude that the murder charge against Roberts was dismissed based upon "the results of police investigation." Roberts admitted under oath at the trial (and before) that he participated in the robbery of Bobby Hodges and, accordingly, he was guilty of Hodges' murder by operation of law under the felony murder doctrine. The Court's assertion that the murder charge was dismissed based upon "the results of police investigation" was itself patently false and misleading.

C. Judge Nangle, in an embarrassing feat of verbal legerdemain, defended the bad decision of the Georgia Supreme Court. On one hand, Judge Nangle conceded that "[p]etitioner asserts that Deputy Moran essentially stated that Terry Roberts could not be charged with the murder or felony murder of Mr. Hodges." 103 F. Supp.2d at 1369 (citing Mem. Supp. Pet. Habeas Corpus at 55).[191] On the other hand, Judge Nangle stated, "[a]s the Georgia Supreme Court found, Moran's testimony, when read in context, neither stated nor implied any such thing." *Id.*

Roberts was originally charged with felony murder. Moran testified that this charge was dismissed because "no evidence was developed to show that Roberts knew of any plan to kill Mr. Hodges before it happened." How does this testimony not falsely imply that Roberts could not be charged with felony murder?

D. The Eleventh Circuit failed to consider this issue because it was not included in the limited COA granted by Judge Wilson.

9. *Jenkins' claim that the testimony of Kenneth McCall and ADA Charles Howard was false and misleading because it falsely implied that Mr. McCall had not been promised any leniency in exchange for his testimony*

---

191 By the way, this was the infamous Memorandum of Law that Judge Nangle refused to accept for filing due to its excessive length.

A. Judge Harvey ruled, "[t]he Court finds that there was no deal with or offer of leniency to Kenneth McCall in exchange for his testimony" and "[t]herefore, trial counsel's performance was not deficient because no objection was offered to McCall's testimony." Decision at 14.

Contrary to Judge Harvey's ruling, Jenkins never claimed that his counsel was deficient for failing to object to McCall's testimony. What Jenkins had claimed was that the **prosecutors** acted improperly because the testimony of Kenneth McCall and ADA Charles Howard was false and misleading, yet the prosecutors failed to correct the record. See Jenkins' Enumeration of Errors, Points VII and VIII.

B. Unlike Judge Harvey, the Georgia Supreme Court clearly recognized that Jenkins was claiming that he had been denied a fair trial because the testimony of McCall and ADA Howard was false and misleading and because the prosecutors failed to correct the record. However, the Georgia Supreme Court ruled that, in their opinion, the testimony of McCall and Howard was not false and misleading. As they explained in their opinion:

> "We do not agree with appellant that the testimonies of McCall (appellant's former cellmate) and Howard (who prosecuted McCall on forgery charges) that McCall was promised no deals in exchange for his testimony must be deemed false and misleading merely because habitual violator charges against McCall in another county, which were pending at trial, were dismissed months later; our review of the evidence in the record as to the handling of the habitual violator charges does not support appellant's assertion. Thus, the prosecutor was under no duty to correct the record in regard to this testimony." 268 Ga. at __, 491 S.E.2d at 57-58.[192]

---

[192] The Supreme Court conveniently omitted to mention that, prior to the dismissal of these additional charges, District Attorney Cheney sent a "nice letter" to the Georgia Parole Board recommending leniency on McCall's behalf due to his helpful testimony for the State in the Jenkins trial.

C. Judge Nangle noted that, "[t]he Georgia Supreme Court found that the dismissal of the habitual violator charges was not part of a deal for McCall's testimony" and then ruled, "[p]etitioner has provided no clear and convincing evidence that this factual finding is incorrect." 103 F. Supp.2d at 1370.

With respect to the "nice letter" that District Attorney Cheney wrote to the Georgia Parole Board on McCall's behalf (which the Georgia Supreme Court completely failed to mention), Judge Nangle asserted, "[p]etitioner's entire argument is based on the timing of the testimony vis-à-vis the mailing of the letter to the parole board. Mem. Supp. Pet. Habeas Corpus at 56 n.26 and accompanying text. Timing alone is not enough for the Court to conclude that an agreement for testimony existed." 103 F. Supp.2d at 1369, n.15.[193]

Furthermore, Judge Nangle argued, with absolutely no factual basis for believing this might apply to McCall, "when the alleged promise offers marginal benefit to the witness, it is doubtful that such a promise would motivate a reluctant witness to tailor his testimony to please the prosecutor." 103 F. Supp.2d at 1369, n.15. Based upon this dubious theory, Judge Nangle then concluded, "[c]onsequently, even if McCall had been told of the District Attorney's intention to write a "nice letter" to the pardon and parole board, such a promise would not be the type required to be disclosed under *Giglio* and *Napue*." *Id.* Somewhere in his long judicial career, someone should have informed Judge Nangle that judicial opinions, especially judicial opinions denying significant habeas petitions, should not be based on mere "wishful thinking."

D. The Eleventh Circuit failed to consider this issue because it was not included in the limited COA granted by Judge Wilson.

---

193 In addition to the so-called timing argument, Jenkins also argued that any finding that no promise of leniency had been made "would be contrary to the evidence presented at the hearing in support of petitioner's motion for a new trial." See Petitioner's Memorandum in Support of the Petition for Habeas Corpus at 56, note 26.

10. *Jenkins' claim that the District Attorney failed to provide his counsel with exculpatory Brady material relating to the testimony of Kenneth McCall*

Pursuant to *Brady v. Maryland*, 373 U.S. 83 (1963), the prosecutor in a criminal case has an affirmative obligation to disclose exculpatory evidence to the defendant's attorney prior to trial, including any evidence known by the prosecutor which could be used to impeach the credibility of the state's witnesses at trial. In this case, Jenkins claimed that the existence of additional criminal charges that were pending against Kenneth McCall at the time when he testified against Jenkins at his trial constituted *Brady* material which should have been disclosed but was not.

A. Judge Harvey did not explicitly rule on this issue. However, he rejected the argument by implication since he denied Jenkins' motion for a new trial. See Decision at 14.

B. The Georgia Supreme Court rejected Jenkins' *Brady* claim "because the charges against McCall were a matter of public record, appellant had the services of a private investigator, and McCall on direct examination stated he had other cases against him and enumerated the habitual violator case when queried about other cases on cross-examination." 268 Ga. at 58, 491 S.E.2d at 58. However, McCall did not disclose the existence of the additional cases that were ***pending*** against him at the time he testified at Jenkins' trial. Furthermore, even if Jenkins' attorneys could have discovered the existence of these charges by making a diligent search of public arrest records (and it is dubious whether they could have done so), it was not their obligation under *Brady* to do so. The prosecutor had an independent obligation under *Brady* to disclose all exculpatory material, including material which could be used to impeach the State's witnesses.

C. Judge Nangle rejected Jenkins' *Brady* claim on the same ground, concluding that, "[t]he Georgia Supreme Court held that because the charges were a matter of public record and because McCall admitted the existence of the habitual violator charges on cross examination, no *Brady* violation existed" (103 F. Supp.2d at 1371). He then noted, "[p]etitioner has not shown that this *finding* was an unreasonable application of relevant Supreme Court precedent." *Id*. (emphasis added).

The so-called "finding" that the Georgia Supreme Court made on this issue was not a finding of *fact* but a conclusion of *law*. Judge Nangle, as a duly appointed federal judge deciding a habeas petition, had an independent obligation to determine whether the legal conclusion of the Georgia Supreme Court on this issue violated federal constitutional law.

D. The Eleventh Circuit failed to consider this issue because it was not included in the limited COA granted by Judge Wilson.

11. *Jenkins' claim that Judge Harvey excluded relevant evidence during the guilt phase of the trial*

Jenkins claimed that the trial court had violated his right to due process of law by improperly excluding evidence during the guilt phase of his trial. Specifically, Jenkins claimed that the Court's exclusion of Cedric Brown's guilty plea and statements he made at the plea hearing, as well as Brown's mental health file, denied him the right to present reliable material evidence in his defense.

A. Judge Harvey did not explicitly consider the issue of whether evidence regarding Cedric Brown's guilty plea and mental health file was properly excluded from the trial. However, he ruled that defense counsels' failure to offer Cedric Brown's mental health files did not amount to ineffective assistance of counsel because "[t]he decision not to offer this evidence was a matter of strategy and falls within the wide range of reasonable professional conduct." Decision at 13.

B. The Georgia Supreme Court ruled that exclusion of Cedric Brown's guilty plea "was correct under the well-recognized rule of *Neal v. State*, 160 Ga. App. 834, 288 S.E.2d 241 (1982), which had previously ruled that '[t]he legal relevance of a co-defendant's guilt or innocence is nonexistent in the trial of the other co-defendant (except in the nonapplicable instance of a charged conspiracy)' (citing *Gray v. State,* 13 Ga. App. 374, 79 S.E.2d 223) (1980))." 268 Ga. at __, 491 S.E.2d at 57.

There were two problems with this reasoning. First, the District Attorney explicitly argued that Cedric Brown (as well as Maurice Fleming, Shawn Brown and Terry Roberts) were co-conspirators with Jenkins, and therefore the stated rationale of *Neal v. State* was clearly inapplicable. Second, and more importantly, the U.S. Supreme Court has clearly ruled that defendants in capital murder cases must be given wide latitude in presenting whatever they consider to be relevant evidence and cannot be prevented from doing so by state evidence rules. *See, e.g., Chambers v. Mississippi,* 410 U.S. 284 (1973); *Skipper v. South Carolina,* 476 U.S. 1 (1986).

With respect to the issue of Cedric Brown's mental health records, the Georgia Supreme Court ruled that "[a]ppellant sought these records for impeachment purposes; because Brown did not testify, this argument is moot." 268 Ga. at __, 491 S.E.2d at 58, n.3. The fact that Jenkins originally sought to obtain these records for purposes of impeaching Brown does not mean that the records were not also relevant for the purpose of determining Jenkins' guilt and/or potential punishment.

C. Judge Nangle recognized that "[t]he Supreme Court has established that criminal defendants have a constitutional right to present a defense, including the right to offer testimony and evidence in their defense" (103 F. Supp.2d at 1368) and that "the central issue is whether the state court's evidentiary rulings deprive the defendant of a fair trial under the facts and circumstances of the particular case." *Id.* Judge Nangle then concluded that Judge Harvey did not violate Jenkins' right to due process by excluding the evidence at issue here. *Id.*

D. The Eleventh Circuit failed to consider this issue because it was not included in the limited COA granted by Judge Wilson.

12. *Improper admission of hearsay evidence during the testimony of Investigator Jim Gray*

A. Judge Harvey did not explicitly rule on the issue. However, he rejected the argument by implication since he denied Jenkins' motion for a new trial. See Decision at 14.

B. The Georgia Supreme Court ruled that the admission of this testimony was erroneous, but it concluded that the error was "harmless." As the Court stated in its opinion, "the admission of Gray's testimony regarding the facts uncovered by his investigation, which were cumulative of properly admitted testimony, was harmless error." 268 Ga. at __, 491 S.E.2d at 57.

C. As noted above, Judge Nangle ruled that the admission of hearsay evidence during the testimony of Investigator Gray which he received from "silent witnesses" did not violate Jenkins' Sixth Amendment right to confront and cross-examine the witnesses against him. 103 F. Supp.2d at 1362-63. However, Judge Nangle did not make any separate ruling regarding the admission of other hearsay evidence admitted during the testimony of Investigator Gray.

D. The Eleventh Circuit failed to consider this issue because it was not included in the limited COA granted by Judge Wilson.

13. *Improper admission of hearsay statements made by Jenkins' alleged co-conspirators*

Jenkins had argued that Judge Harvey's evidentiary ruling admitting hearsay statements made by Jenkins' alleged co-conspirators was erroneous for four separate reasons. First, Judge Harvey failed to make a proper ruling, supported by sufficient evidence apart from the testimony of Terry Roberts, that a conspiracy existed. Second, he failed to make a finding that the testimony of Terry Roberts regarding the putative hearsay statements was sufficiently reliable to allow them to be admissible under the co-conspirator rule. Third, he publicly stated, in the presence of the jury, that a conspiracy existed, which prejudiced the ability of the jury to reach an unbiased independent decision on this issue. And fourth, he failed to instruct the jury that the testimony of a co-conspirator (Roberts) regarding whether a conspiracy existed needed to be corroborated.

A. Judge Harvey did not explicitly rule on these issues apart from Jenkins' claim that he had been denied the effective assistance of counsel. With respect to that issue, Judge Harvey ruled, "there was no error in the court's ruling on an evidentiary issue [and] thus there was no reason for trial counsel to object." Decision at 10. Judge Harvey also stated, "the Court did not state that a conspiracy existed, but merely ruled on a point of law." Id. He then added, "[a]ssuming arguendo this statement was prejudicial, it was cured by the Court's instruction that the State must prove the existence of a conspiracy beyond a reasonable doubt." Id. (citing Trial Tr. 1982, 1983).

B. The Georgia Supreme Court summarily stated, "we find no error in the trial court's finding after the State presented its evidence that a prima facie case of conspiracy to rob Hodges Grocery Store existed; and the record contains sufficient indicia of reliability under *Dutton v. Evans*, 400 U.S. 74, 88-89 (91 S. Ct. 210, 27 L. Ed. 2d 213 (1970) (plurality opinion) to authorize the admission of Roberts' testimony made by appellant's co-conspirators in the concealment phase of the conspiracy." 268 Ga. at __, 491 S.E.2d at 58. The Georgia Supreme Court did not specify what the "sufficient indicia of reliability" consisted of.

C. Judge Nangle concluded that, "[t]he Georgia Supreme Court found that the facts supported the trial court's ruling. *Jenkins II*, 491 S.E.2d at 58. Petitioner has failed to present clear and convincing evidence that this factual finding was incorrect." 103 F. Supp.2d at 1373.

Judge Nangle further concluded that "the trial court's failure to address the existence of indicia of reliability was not error. The Georgia Supreme Court found that sufficient indicia of reliability existed, and petitioner has failed to establish that this finding was contrary to or was an unreasonable application of clearly established Supreme Court precedent."

Id. Apparently, Judge Nangle was not the least bit curious regarding what these indicia of reliability might be, since neither he nor the Georgia Supreme Court made any effort to enumerate them, and Roberts was, of course, both an admitted liar and an admitted murderer and thief.

D. The Eleventh Circuit failed to consider this issue because it was not included in the limited COA granted by Judge Wilson.

14. *Improper admission of the incriminating statement allegedly made by Jenkins to Officer Smith*

Jenkins claimed that admission into evidence of the brief incriminating statement he allegedly made to Officer Smith following his arrest in Florida ("I only shot him once') was improper because there was an unresolved issue regarding whether this statement was obtained in violation of his Fifth Amendment right to remain silent.

A. Judge Harvey did not explicitly rule on this issue. However, he rejected the argument by implication since he denied Jenkins' motion for a new trial. See Decision at 14.

B. The Georgia Supreme Court concluded, "[t]he trial court's pre-trial ruling on the admissibility of appellant's **spontaneous** statement to Detective Smith was affirmed by this Court in *Jenkins v. State*, 265 Ga. 539, 458 S.E.2d 477 (1995) and our review of Detective Smith's entire testimony at trial fails to establish any clear error in that pre-trial ruling." 268 Ga. at __, 491 S.E.2d at 58 (emphasis added).[194]

C. Judge Nangle concluded, "[r]eviewing Smith's testimony as a whole . . . . Smith clearly indicated that petitioner's statement was made

---

[194] As the Georgia Supreme Court noted in its Opinion, the admissibility of this statement was previously upheld by the Supreme Court in a pretrial interim appeal on the ground that the statement was made **spontaneously** to Officer Smith and not as a result of **custodial interrogation**. However, Jenkins claimed that Officer Smith's testimony at trial showed that the statement was ***not*** made spontaneously but as a result of questioning by Officer Smith and therefore Judge Harvey needed to make a finding about whether the statement was unlawfully obtained in violation of Jenkins' Fifth Amendment rights. The Supreme Court rejected this argument stating, "our review of Detective Smith's entire testimony at trial fails to establish any clear error in that pre-trial ruling." 268 Ga. at __, 491 S.E.2d at 58.

before any such comments by Smith." 103 F. Supp.2d at 1374 (emphasis added). However, Judge Nangle explicitly recognized in his decision that "[a]t one point during cross-examination, Smith appears to state that petitioner's statement was made ***after*** Smith's comments about getting his life together." *Id.* (emphasis added). Needless to say, this was an extremely important discrepancy, since, if the statement was made after Smith told Jenkins "to get his life together," then it would not have been spontaneous.

D. The Eleventh Circuit failed to consider this issue because it was not included in the limited COA granted by Judge Wilson.

15. *Improper exclusion of mitigation evidence which Jenkins offered during the penalty phase of the trial*

During the penalty phase of the trial, Jenkins' counsel had sought to introduce evidence which showed that Cedric Brown and Shawn Brown (who had pled guilty prior to Jenkins' trial) were both sentenced to life imprisonment with a possibility of parole. This evidence was offered as a mitigation factor to be considered by the jury in deciding whether to sentence Jenkins to death, life without possibility of parole, or life with a possibility of parole. Judge Harvey refused to allow this evidence to be admitted on the ground that it was "not relevant" to the jury's decision of what sentence should be imposed on Jenkins. Trial Tr. 2030-32. In Jenkins' motion for a new trial, and in his appeal to the Georgia Supreme Court, Jenkins argued that this ruling by Judge Harvey was improper and denied him a fair trial on the issue of punishment.

A. Judge Harvey did not explicitly rule on this issue in his Order denying Jenkins' motion for a new trial. However, he obviously rejected the argument by implication since he denied the motion. See Decision at 14.

B. The Georgia Supreme Court ruled, "[w]e find no error in the exclusion of this evidence at the penalty phase as Brown's guilty plea had no relevance to appellant's character, prior record or the circumstances of the offense, and it is for this Court, not the jury, to determine whether a defendant's sentence is excessive or disproportionate to the sentence imposed on others." 268 Ga. at __, 491 S.E.2d at 58.

C. Judge Nangle recognized that "the [U.S.] Supreme Court has clearly established that the Constitution requires that the sentencing jury in a capital case not be precluded from considering 'any aspect of a defendant's character or record and any of the circumstances of the offense that the defendant proffers as a basis for a sentence less than death.'" 103 F. Supp.2d at 1381 (quoting *Lockett v. Ohio*, 438 U.S. 586, 604, 57 L. Ed. 2d 973, 98 S. Ct. 2954 (1978)). However, Judge Nangle then ruled, "[p]etitioner has provided no Supreme Court authority for the proposition that evidence of co-defendants' sentences are constitutionally relevant mitigating evidence which must be presented to the jury during the penalty phase of a death penalty trial." *Id.* Additionally, Judge Nangle then concluded, "[a]ccordingly, the Georgia Supreme Court was not acting contrary to clearly established Supreme Court precedent when it ruled that such comparisons are to be made by the appellate courts of Georgia and not the jury." *Id.* And yet, as Judge Nangle failed to note, under Georgia law, it is the jury, not "the appellate courts of Georgia," that are charged with the responsibility of determining, in the first instance, what sentence should be imposed as appropriate in death penalty cases. Thus, under the U.S. Supreme Court's decisions in *Lockett v. Ohio* and similar cases, the jury is entitled to consider all mitigating evidence offered by defendant's counsel including, when available, what sentences were imposed on the defendant's co-conspirators in the same case and for the same conduct.

D. The Eleventh Circuit failed to consider this issue because it was not included in the limited COA granted by Judge Wilson.

16. *Failure to answer the jury's question regarding parole eligibility*

During its deliberations on the penalty phase of the trial, the jury asked Judge Harvey for clarification regarding when Jenkins would become eligible for parole if they imposed a life sentence with possibility of parole. Jenkins' trial counsel requested that Judge Harvey answer the jury's question, but he refused to do so. Shortly thereafter, the jury imposed a sentence of life without any possibility of parole. Jenkins claimed in his motion for a new trial and/or new sentence, that this failure to advise the jury when Jenkins would become available for parole amounted to a violation of due process of law.

A. Judge Harvey did not explicitly rule on this issue. However, he rejected the argument by implication since he denied Jenkins' motion for a new trial. See Decision at 14.

B. The Georgia Supreme Court succinctly ruled, "[t]he trial court's failure during the penalty phase to charge on parole eligibility was not error." 268 Ga. at __, 491 S.E.2d at 59.[195]

C. Judge Nangle clearly recognized the problem Jenkins was complaining about, but he nevertheless ruled, "[p]laintiff has pointed to no clearly established Supreme Court precedent that would require the trial court to give the jury that information. . . . Accordingly, the Court will not grant habeas corpus relief on this ground." 103 F. Supp.2d at 1381.

D. The Eleventh Circuit failed to consider this issue because it was not included in the limited COA granted by Judge Wilson.

17. *Constitutionality of the Georgia statute (OCGA § 17-10-31.1) which permitted the jury to impose a life sentence without any possibility of parole*

A. Judge Harvey did not explicitly rule on this issue. However, he rejected the argument by implication since he denied Jenkins' motion for a new trial. See Decision at 14.

---

195 Jenkins never claimed that Judge Harvey had an obligation to *charge* the jury on the issue of parole eligibility. What he claimed was that it was a violation of due process of law for Judge Harvey to refuse to answer the jury's legitimate question of when Jenkins would become eligible for parole if they sentenced him to a term of life imprisonment with a possibility of parole.

B. The Georgia Supreme Court first noted, "under OCGA § 17-10-31.1 a jury cannot impose a sentence of life without parole without including a finding of at least one statutory aggravating circumstance as defined in OCGA § 17-10-30(b) . . ." 268 Ga. __, 491 S.E.2d 60. Based upon this requirement, the Court then concluded, "we reject appellant's argument for the same reasons OCGA § 17-10-30 has been found constitutional." *Id.* (citing *Gregg v. Georgia*, 428 U.S. 153, 96 S. Ct. 2909, 49 L.E.2d 262 (1976)).

This, of course, missed the entire point of Jenkins' argument. In *Furman v. Georgia*, 408 U.S. 238 (1972), the U.S. Supreme Court had ruled that Georgia's prior death penalty statute was unconstitutional because it failed to provide specific statutory standards which a jury could apply to determine when a death sentence is appropriate, and therefore it was impermissibly arbitrary. In response to that decision, the Georgia Legislature adopted the "aggravating circumstances" standards. This was then relied upon by the U.S. Supreme Court in *Gregg* to uphold the constitutionality of Georgia's revised death penalty statute.

In 1993, more than fifteen years after the *Gregg* decision, the Georgia Legislature amended the death penalty statute to provide the additional, alternative sentence of life imprisonment without any possibility of parole. However, the new statute did not provide any separate or different standards which the jury could look to and apply to determine when the new penalty of life without parole is appropriate, as opposed to the death penalty. According to the statute, the same aggravating factors that justified imposition of the death penalty also justified imposition of a sentence of life without parole. This reintroduced the same problem of arbitrariness which the Supreme Court had condemned in *Furman*. This was the reason Jenkins argued that OCGA § 17-10-31.1 was unconstitutional, but this argument was completely misconstrued by the Georgia Supreme Court.

C. Judge Nangle appeared to properly comprehend the thrust of Jenkins' argument on this point. As he stated in his decision, "[p]etitioner argues in ground seventeen that the Georgia life without possibility of parole statute, OCGA § 17-10-31.1, is unconstitutional because it authorizes jurors to impose life without parole in the same category of cases in which jurors are authorized to impose the death penalty." 103 F. Supp.2d at 1381. However, he then resorted to some unfounded sleight of hand to try to defend the statute.

First, he argued that "the Supreme Court dismissed this very argument in *Gregg v. Georgia*, 428 U.S. 153, 49 L. Ed. 2d 859, 96 S. Ct. 2909 (1976)." 103 F. Supp.2d at 1381. No, this was not correct. Although the Supreme Court did uphold Georgia's death penalty statute in *Gregg*, the additional question of whether Georgia's "life sentence without possibility parole" was valid was never considered in *Gregg* for the simple reason that this alternative penalty had not yet been enacted.

Second, Judge Nangle asserted, quoting from the Supreme Court's decision in *Gregg*, "petitioner next argues that the requirements of *Furman* are not met here because the jury has the power to decline to impose the death penalty even if it finds that one or more statutory aggravating circumstances are present in the case. This contention misinterprets *Furman*. Moreover, it ignores the role of the Supreme Court of Georgia which reviews each death sentence to determine whether it is proportional to other sentences imposed for similar crimes." 103 F. Supp.2d at 1381. Here again, Judge Nangle resorts to misdirection.

The core problem which the Supreme Court focused on in *Furman* was **arbitrariness**. If one jury is authorized to sentence a defendant to death based upon one of more of the aggravating factors set forth in OCGA § 17-10-30(b), but another jury is authorized to sentence a different defendant to life without possibility of parole for exactly the same conduct with exactly the same aggravating factors, then the sentences imposed on these and similar defendants become wholly arbitrary. Contrary to Judge Nangle's contention to the contrary, this is exactly what the Supreme Court found to be unlawful in *Furman*.

Finally, Judge Nangle stated that Jenkins' argument "ignores the role of the Supreme Court of Georgia which reviews each death sentence to determine whether it is proportional to other sentences imposed for similar crimes." 103 F. Supp.2d at 1382. While it is true that the Georgia Supreme Court has the ability the review the proportionality of sentences on appeal, this is not a substitute for a proper jury verdict in the first instance.

Furthermore, as a practical matter, the Georgia Supreme Court rarely, if ever, exercises its discretion to overturn a jury's sentence on the ground that it is disproportionate. To the best of my knowledge, the last time the Georgia Supreme Court set aside a jury's verdict on the ground of lack of proportionality was in 1977 in the very unusual case of *Ward v. State*, 239 Ga. 205, 236 S.E.2d 365 (1977). In that case the defendant had been tried previously for murder and was sentenced to life imprisonment. After that conviction was reversed on appeal, he was tried again, and this time he was sentenced to death. Instead of vacating this sentence on constitutional grounds (violation of due process and double jeopardy), the Georgia Supreme Court set aside the sentence on the ground of proportionality. This was not really a proportionality case, therefore, because under the peculiar circumstances of this case, the death sentence was actually unconstitutional. And significantly, in the almost fifty years since *Ward* was decided, the Georgia Supreme Court has never set aside a jury verdict on the ground of lack of proportionality.

D. The Eleventh Circuit failed to consider this issue because it was not included in the limited COA granted by Judge Wilson.

18. *Improper denial of Jenkins' pretrial motion for a change of venue*

Prior to the commencement of his trial, Jenkins' counsel had moved for a change of venue on the ground that it would be impossible for him to obtain a fair trial in Liberty County due to extensive pretrial publicity and jury bias. Judge Harvey deferred deciding this motion until after a jury was already empaneled, and then he denied the motion. Jenkins then argued in his motion for a new trial, and in his appeal to the Georgia Supreme Court, that this ruling was erroneous and denied him the opportunity to have a fair trial.

A. Judge Harvey did not explicitly rule on this issue in his Order denying Jenkins' motion for a new trial. However, he obviously rejected the argument by implication since he denied the motion. See Decision at 14.

B. The Georgia Supreme Court ruled that "there [was] no ***manifest*** error in the trial court's denial of appellant's motion for a change of venue" (268 Ga. __, 491 S.E.2d at 57) (emphasis added) because "appellant [failed] to utilize the correct procedure for calculating the percentage of jurors excused for cause resulting from pretrial publicity." Id.

However, as Jenkins had pointed out, both at the time when the motion for a change of venue was first considered and when the motion for a new trial was made, there was an actual factual dispute between the prosecutors and Jenkins' attorneys regarding how the number of jurors "excused for cause" should properly be calculated. Jenkins' trial attorneys relied upon a calculation made by the ***court clerk*** on this issue, which seems to me to be a very reasonable procedure. However, the prosecutor argued that a different calculation should be used. Judge Harvey agreed with the proposal made by the prosecutor and, ultimately, so did the Georgia Supreme Court. However, the Georgia Supreme Court never discussed the existence of this factual dispute, nor explained why the calculation made by the court clerk should not have been used. Instead, the Georgia Supreme Court fatuously asserted, "appellant [failed] to use the correct procedure." 268 Ga. __, 491 S.E.2d at 57.

C. Judge Nangle accepted the calculation of "jurors excused for cause" that was used by Judge Harvey and the Georgia Supreme Court and then ruled, "in light of these calculations, petitioner has failed to establish that the trial court's denial of the motion for a change of venue and the Georgia Supreme Court's decision upholding that denial are an unreasonable application of clearly established federal law." 103 F. Supp.2d at 1380.

D. The Eleventh Circuit failed to consider this issue because it was not included in the limited COA granted by Judge Wilson.

19. *Unlawful imposition of an additional, consecutive life sentence on the robbery conviction*

Jenkins was convicted by the jury of **malice murder** and **armed robbery**. He was not, however, convicted of **felony murder**. As noted previously, this appears to have been an inadvertent oversight by the jury.[196] In the heat of the moment, after the jury's verdict on the malice murder count was announced, no one in the courtroom — neither Judge Harvey, the court clerk, nor District Attorney Cheney — noticed that the jury had failed to return a verdict on the felony murder charge. As a result, Jenkins was **not** convicted of felony murder. One could argue, of course, that this makes absolutely no difference, since he was subsequently sentenced by the jury to life without any possibility of parole on the malice murder charge, and no one, not even a healthy 19-year-old teenager from Brooklyn could possibly serve a sentence longer than his natural life.

However, after the jury sentenced Jenkins to life without possibility of parole on the malice murder charge, Judge Harvey then sentenced him to an additional, **consecutive** life sentence on the armed robbery charge. Trial Tr. 2133. As Jenkins argued in his motion for a new trial, and in his appeal to the Georgia Supreme Court, this was improper because the armed robbery charge was used by the jury as the sole aggravating factor to justify the imposition of the sentence of life without possibility of parole on the malice murder charge. Trial Tr. 2131.

---

196   If the jury had determined that Jenkins was guilty of robbing Mr. Hodges, then they could certainly have convicted him of felony murder, since Mr. Hodges was killed during the commission of the robbery and no further evidence was needed. However, due to an administrative error, Jenkins was not convicted by the jury of felony murder.

Under Georgia law, where an armed robbery charge is used as the sole statutory aggravating factor to support an enhanced sentence for malice murder, the defendant cannot be separately sentenced to an additional sentence on the armed robbery charge because the armed robbery charge should be merged into the murder conviction for sentencing purposes. This is necessary to prevent double punishment for the same conduct, a concern under both constitutional double jeopardy protections and Georgia's sentencing guidelines. *See, Hulett v. State, 296 Ga. 49, 766 S.E. 2d 1 (2014); Ford v. State, 257 Ga. 461, 360 S.E.2d 258 (1987).*

A. Judge Harvey did not explicitly rule on this issue in his Order denying Jenkins' motion for a new trial. However, he necessarily rejected the argument by implication since he denied the motion. See Decision at 14.

B. The Georgia Supreme Court ruled, "[w]e find no merit in appellant's contention that the trial court erred in entering a life sentence on the armed robbery conviction." 268 Ga. __, 491 S.E.2d at 57.

Jenkins did not raise this issue as a ground for attacking his conviction in his federal habeas petition for two reasons. First, it did not address the merits of the murder conviction, and therefore it could not provide a basis for granting the relief he was seeking. Second, although based on double jeopardy grounds, the merger doctrine is primarily a matter of state law. Accordingly, neither Judge Nangle nor the Eleventh Circuit Court of Appeals had any need to consider this issue.

20. *Constitutionality of 28 U.S.C. § 2254(d)*

As noted previously, when Congress adopted the Antiterrorism and Effective Death Penalty Act of 1996 (AEDPA), it provided, in what became 28 U.S.C. § 2254(d), that "an application for a writ of habeas on behalf of a person in custody pursuant to the judgment of a State court shall not be granted . . . unless the adjudication of the claim . . . resulted in a decision that was contrary to, or involved an unreasonable application of, clearly established federal law, as determined by the Supreme Court of the United States . . ."

Obviously, this federal statute was not relevant to Jenkins' motion for a new trial and his state court appeal, and therefore this issue was not raised before Judge Harvey or the Supreme Court of Georgia. However, Jenkins did argue in his habeas petition that Section 2254(d) was unconstitutional because it unduly limited the ability of federal district and circuit court judges to apply federal constitutional law in habeas cases.

A. Judge Nangle rejected Jenkins' argument on this point, stating that Section 2254(d) "does not purport to limit the federal court's independent interpretative authority with respect to federal questions." 103 F. Supp.2d at 1382 (purporting to quote Justice Stevens' opinion in *Williams*). Although Judge Nangle **stated** that Section 2254(d) did not limit his ability to apply federal constitutional law to decisions of the U.S. Supreme Court, he acted throughout his decision as though it did, stating repeatedly that Jenkins' arguments lacked merit because there was no decision of the U.S. Supreme Court directly on point. In the process, he consistently ignored decisions of the Fifth and Eleventh Circuit Courts of Appeals that directly supported Jenkins' arguments.

B. The Eleventh Circuit failed to consider this issue because it was not included in the limited COA granted by Judge Wilson.

CHAPTER 17

SOME SIGNIFICANT CHANGES IN THE LAW SINCE 1995

A lot has changed in the legal landscape since Jenkins was convicted and sentenced in 1995. A few of the more notable changes are discussed below.

1. *Abolition of the Death Penalty for Minors*

In 2005, ten years after Jamel's trial, the U.S. Supreme Court ruled in *Roper v. Simpson*, 543 U.S. 351 (2005) that the death penalty could not be imposed on anyone who was under the age of 18 at the time the crime was committed. The Court ruled that imposing the death penalty in such cases violated the "cruel and unusual punishment" clause of the Eighth Amendment.

In addition to declaring the death penalty for minors unconstitutional, the Court also invalidated the pending death sentences of 73 individuals who had been sentenced to death for various crimes committed when they were younger than 18. The vast majority of these inmates were located in Texas (29) and Alabama (13). No other state (including Georga) had more than five juveniles on death row. Unfortunately, the Supreme Court was unable to restore life to the 22 juvenile offenders who had been executed between 1976 (the year the constitutionality of the death penalty was resumed) and 2005 (the year *Roper* was decided).

Jenkins, of course, was facing the death penalty at his trial even though he was only seventeen years old when the crime was allegedly committed. Fortunately, he was not sentenced to death and executed prior to the Court's *Roper* decision. If Jenkins' trial took place today (or at any time after 2005), the death penalty would not be an available option.

When Jenkins was convicted, the sentencing jury had three options to choose from: death, life without any possibility of parole, and life with a possibility of parole. The jury chose to impose the middle option, which, in all probably, represented a "Goldilocks" compromise, neither too harsh nor too lenient in the jury's eyes. If the death penalty had not been available as an option, it is far less likely that Jenkins would have been sentenced to life without any possibility of parole and thus, in all likelihood, he would have been released on parole by now. Unfortunately, at age 49, he still faces continued incarceration for the rest of his life.

2. *Abolition of Mandatory Life Sentences Without Parole for Minors*

In addition to declaring capital punishment for minors unconstitutional, in *Miller v. Alabama*, 567 U.S. 460 (2012), the U.S. Supreme Court ruled that mandatory life sentences without any possibility of parole also could not be imposed on anyone who was under the age of 18 at the time when the crime was committed. Here again, the Court ruled that imposition of such sentences on anyone under the age of 18 at the time when the crime was committed violated the "cruel and unusual punishment" clause of the Eighth Amendment.

In *Montgomery v. Louisiana*, 577 U.S. 190 (2016), the Supreme Court ruled that its *Miller* decision had to be applied retroactively, meaning that "mandatory life without parole" sentences imposed on juveniles prior to the *Miller* decision had to be vacated and the defendants had to be resentenced. Since the *Miller* decision, 33 states and the District of Columbia have changed their laws for people under eighteen who were convicted of homicide, mostly by banning life without parole for people under eighteen, but also by eliminating life without parole for felony murder or revising penalties that were struck down by *Grahm v. Florida*, 560 U.S. 48 (2010) (which prohibited mandatory life without parole sentences for juveniles in certain non-homicide cases).[197]

Jenkins, of course, faced a "life without possibility of parole" sentence at his trial and, indeed, the jury actually sentenced him to life without any possibility of parole. The problem for Jenkins, however, was that his sentence was not **mandatory** and therefore, technically speaking, it did not fall within the protection of *Miller*, since the jury had the option of choosing between a life sentence with parole and a life sentence without any possibility of parole.

Nevertheless, the basis for, and the reasoning of, the *Miller* decision applies equally to Jenkins. As the Supreme Court explained in its decision:

> "*Roper* held that the Eighth Amendment bars capital punishment for children, and *Graham* concluded that the Amendment also prohibits a sentence of life without the possibility of parole for a child who committed a non-homicide offense....
>
> *Roper* and *Graham* establish that children are constitutionally different from adults for purposes of sentencing. Because juveniles have diminished culpability and greater prospects for reform, we explained, 'they are less deserving of the most severe punishments.' *Graham*, 560 U.S. at 68. These cases relied on three significant gaps between juveniles and adults. First, children have a lack of maturity and an underdeveloped sense of responsibility', 'leading to recklessness, impulsivity, and heedless risk-taking.' *Roper*, 543 U.S. at 569. Second, children are 'more vulnerable ... to negative influences and outside pressures,' including from their family and peers; they have limited 'control over their own environment' and lack the ability to extricate themselves from horrific, crime producing settings.

---

197 See "Juvenile Life Without Parole: An Overview," written by Josh Rovner, Director of Youth Justice at the Sentencing Project, Washington, D.C. (2023) (page 3) at sentencingproject.org.

Ibid. And third, a child's character is not as 'well formed' as an adult's; his traits are 'less fixed' and his actions less likely to be 'evidence of irretrievable depravity.' *Id.* at 570." 567 U.S. at 470-71.

The sound and salient considerations cited by the Supreme Court in *Miller* apply equally to Jenkins. When one considers generally the purposes of incarceration, especially the rehabilitative purpose of incarceration, there is no rational or valid reason why anyone who committed a crime (even murder) as a juvenile should ever be deemed at the outset of his confinement so irretrievably beyond the point of rehabilitation that a sentence of life imprisonment without any possibility of parole is appropriate.[198] Indeed, if you can remember all the way back to Chapter 2, this is essentially what Jamel's father, Cleveland Jenkins, meant when he testified that Jamel had made a mistake, a terrible mistake to be sure, but not a valid reason for taking his life or even for sentencing him to life without any possibility of parole. If it turns out that Jamel cannot be rehabilitated, then he would remain in prison for the remainder of his life under a life sentence. On the other hand, if it turns out that he can be rehabilitated, there is no sound and valid reason why he should never become eligible for parole. Such a sentence is purely vindictive and not justified by sound penal policy or due process.

Surprisingly, the Georgia Supreme Court **unanimously** came to this same realization in 2016. In *Veal v. State*, 298 Ga. 691, 784 S.E.2d 403 (2016), decided a few months after *Montgomery*, the Georgia Supreme Court vacated a life without parole sentence ("LWOP") that had been imposed on an individual who was only 17 years old at the time of the murder. The sentencing judge had held a separate hearing on the issue of what punishment should be imposed in which he had explicitly considered the defendant's age, but did not consider the particular question or make a

---

198 It is sadly ironic and very telling that a person who was once deemed to be so "incorrigibly dangerous" and "irredeemable" at nineteen years of age that it was appropriate to sentence him to life imprisonment without any possibility of parole is now, thirty two years later, being held in a minimum security facility (the Augusta Transition Center) which is usually reserved for model inmates who can be trusted to safeguard and protect the safety of others.

specific finding on the issue of whether the defendant "was irreparably corrupt or permanently incorrigible" so as to make a sentence of life without possibility of parole appropriate. As the Court stated in its opinion:

> "The trial court did not, however, make any sort of distinct determination on the record that Appellant is irreparably corrupt or permanently incorrigible, as necessary to put him in the narrow class of juvenile murderers for whom an LWOP sentence is proportional under the Eighth Amendment as interpreted in *Miller* and refined in *Montgomery*." 298 Ga. at __, 784 S.E.2d at 413.

This was true, of course, for Jenkins also. Neither Judge Harvey nor the jury that sentenced Jenkins ever made "any sort of distinct determination on the record that [Jenkins] is irreparably corrupt or permanently incorrigible, as necessary to put him in the narrow class of juvenile murderers for whom an LWOP sentence is proportional under the Eighth Amendment." *Veal*, 298 Ga. at __, 784 S.E.2d at 413. Accordingly, Jenkins' sentence of life without possibility of parole was unconstitutional under the Eighth Amendment as recognized and applied by the Georgia Supreme Court. Unfortunately, nothing was ever done to rectify this situation, and Jenkins remains in prison under an questionable sentence of life without parole.

3. *Decision of the Georgia Supreme Court in Moore v. State*

Remarkably, there is yet another reason why Jenkins' sentence of life without possibility of parole is improper and void. In *Moore v. State*, 293 Ga. 705, 749 S.E.2d 660 (2013), the Georgia Supreme Court ruled, based upon the U.S. Supreme Court's decision in *Roper*, that it is not permissible, **under Georgia law**, to impose a penalty of life without possibility of parole on a person who was under eighteen years of age at the time the crime was committed. This was not based upon any alleged violation of the Eighth Amendment's "cruel and unusual punishments" clause, but upon a statutory interpretation of Georgia's death penalty law.

In December 2000, Marcus Moore, age 17, was indicted for two counts of malice murder and other crimes that occurred in Richmond County, Georgia. After a bifurcated trial, Moore was convicted by the jury of all crimes. Rather than proceed to a trial on the issue of punishment, Moore elected to avoid the death penalty by pleading guilty in return for a reduced punishment of life without possibility of parole. As part of this plea bargain, Moore agreed to waive all rights to appeal and all post-conviction review of his convictions and sentences.

In 2010, ten years after he was sentenced and five years after the Supreme Court's *Roper* decision, Moore filed a motion in state court seeking to have his sentence vacated on the ground of illegality and voidness. Moore's theory of the case was that, since the U.S. Supreme Court had declared the death penalty unlawful for criminal defendants who were under eighteen at the time of the crime, he was ineligible **under Georgia law** to receive a sentence of life without parole.

The first question the Georgia Supreme Court had to resolve was whether Moore had waived his right to assert this defense when he entered into the plea agreement in 2000. As noted above, Moore had agreed "to waive his rights to appeal and all post-conviction review of his convictions and sentences." 293 Ga. at __, 749 S.E.2d at 661. The Court concluded that waiver was not an issue because "a defendant who knowingly entered into a plea agreement and accepts the benefit of that bargain does not waive or 'bargain away' the right to challenge **an illegal and void sentence**." *Id*. at __, 749 S.E.2d at 661 (emphasis added).

Turning then to the merits of Moore's challenge, the Court concluded that Moore was correct in asserting that his sentence was improper. The Court began its analysis by noting that, "[a]t the time Moore was sentenced in 2001, OCGA § 17-10-32.1 [the Georgia death penalty statute] provided that . . . [n]o person shall be sentenced to life without parole unless such person could have received the death penalty under the laws of this state as such laws have been interpreted by the United States Supreme Court and the Supreme Court of Georgia. Ga. L. 1993, p. 1654, § 9 (not codified)." 293 Ga. at __, 749 S.E.2d at 662.

The Court then noted, "[i]t is clear from the language of the statute that in 2001 the State could seek a sentence of life without possibility of parole *only in those cases where the State could, consistent with state and federal laws, impose a sentence of death.*" 293 Ga. at __, 749 S.E.2d at 662 (emphasis added).

The "fly in this ointment" (Ecclesiastes 10:1) is that *Roper* made it impossible for any court in the U.S. to impose the death penalty on any person who was under 18 when the crime was committed. Therefore, under Georgia law, Moore could not be sentenced to life without possibility of parole because, as a result of *Roper* (which had to be applied retroactively), he could not be sentenced to death. As the Court cogently stated in its decision:

> "*Roper*, which eliminated the death penalty as a sentencing option available to the state in its prosecution of juvenile offenders, obviously does not on its face address whether in 2001 a juvenile offender could have been legally sentenced to life without parole under OCGA § 17-10-32.1. Its holdings, however, retroactively applicable as a new rule of substantive law, prohibit[ed] a category of punishment for a class of defendants because of their status, and we find that when applied retroactively to the state sentencing scheme in place at the time of Moore's sentencing, it rendered Moore ineligible to receive a sentence of death under OCGA § 17-10-32.1. Because, as determined by this Court, authority to seek a death sentence was a prerequisite for imposition of a sentence of life without parole under OCGA § 17-10-32,1, and because after proper retroactive application of *Roper* the State could not consistent with federal law seek the death penalty against Moore

due to his age, ***Moore could not legally be sentenced to life without parole under OCGA § 17-10-32.1***." 293 Ga. at __, 749 S.E.2d at 662 (emphasis added).

What was decided by the Supreme Court in *Moore* about the invalidity of Moore's sentence of life without possibility of parole applies equally with respect to Jenkins. When Jenkins was tried in 1995, it was lawful and permissible for the State to seek both the death penalty and a sentence of life without parole. After *Roper* was decided in 2005, it became unlawful to sentence Jenkins to death. This was a moot point, of course, since Jenkins had not been sentenced to death. However, under federal constitutional law, the *Roper* decision was required to be applied retroactively to all prior cases. Because *Roper* had to be applied retroactively, Jenkins was ineligible to receive the death penalty when he was sentenced in 1995. Furthermore, since Jenkins was not eligible to receive the death penalty in 1995 due to *Roper*, he was also ineligible to receive a sentence of life without possibility of parole because, as the Georgia Supreme Court clearly ruled in Moore, "[n]o person shall be sentenced to life without parole unless such person could have received the death penalty under the laws of this state as such laws have been interpreted by the United States Supreme Court and the Supreme Court of Georgia." 293 Ga. at __, 749 S.E.2d at 662 (quoting Ga. L. 1993, p. 1654, § 9 (not codified).

The bottom line is that, since October 7, 2013, Jenkins' current sentence of life without possibility of parole has been illegal and void.[199] And yet, sadly, he remains in prison.[200]

4.   *Adoption By Georgia of the Cumulative Error Doctrine*

---

[199]   Robin Cook, a news reporter for the *Atlanta Journal-Constitution*, correctly noted that Jenkins needed to be resentenced as a result of the *Moore* decision in an article published on December 8, 2013, entitled "Court ruling means some inmates serving life without parole to be re-sentenced." Unfortunately for Jenkins, there was never any follow-up by anybody.

[200]   As previously discussed, Jenkins was also sentenced to a second, consecutive life sentence on the robbery charge (which Jenkins claims was improper). Some judge in Liberty County needs to sort this out and resentence Jenkins to a proper and appropriate sentence.

One of the grounds that Jenkins had asserted in support of his Motion for a new trial, and in support of his Petition for habeas corpus, was that the cumulative effect of all the many errors that occurred during his trial had deprived him of due process of law in violation of the fourteenth Amendment. The Georgia Supreme Court summarily denied this claim on the ground that "Georgia does not recognize the cumulative error doctrine" and Judge Nangle, who, as a federal district judge, should have looked to federal constitutional law rather than Georgia law, also denied Jenkins' claim for the same reason.

As noted earlier, in 2020, in the case of *State v. Lane,* 308 Ga. 10, 838 S.E.2d 808, the Georgia Supreme Court, after undertaking an extensive analysis of its prior case law, finally recognized that all of its prior decisions (including Jenkins' case) had been wrongly decided. The Court explicitly ruled that application of the cumulative error doctrine is legally required. Furthermore, the Court explicitly overruled each and every prior Georgia case (including both Jenkins' case and Maurice Fleming's case) that had refused to apply the cumulative error rule.

Although the Georgia Supreme Court took the unusual step of explicitly overruling all prior cases that had refused to apply the cumulative error doctrine (including Jenkins' case), it did nothing to rectify the consequences of its prior mistakes. What it should have done was grant a new hearing to every defendant, including Jenkins, who was still incarcerated in a Georgia prison in order to decide whether their convictions should be reversed based upon the new rule. That should have happened but, regrettably, it did not.[201]

5. *Modification of Georgia law requiring trial judges to instruct the jury regarding corroboration of accomplice testimony*

---

201 Unfortunately, the fact that the Georgia Supreme Court has belatedly recognized the validity of the cumulative error rule does not automatically mean that Jenkins' conviction needs to be reversed. It will still be necessary for some court to find that one or more errors were committed during Jenkins' trial which, either singly or cumulatively, deprived him of a fair trial.

One of the major errors that occurred during Jenkins' trial was Judge Harvey's failure to instruct the jury regarding the necessity for corroboration of accomplice testimony. Terry Roberts was unquestionably an accomplice during the robbery of Bobby Hodges and therefore his testimony needed to be corroborated.

This corroboration issue was important here for two separate reasons. First, since a finding of corroboration is a substantive requirement of Georgia law, and since the jury was never even told about this requirement, Roberts' conviction violated due process of law. Judge Harvey had an affirmative obligation to instruct the jury regarding every issue necessary for the jury's determination of guilt, including the issue of corroboration, and he failed to do so.

Second, competent trial counsel have an affirmative obligation to their client to ensure that the trial judge's instructions to the jury are proper and correct. In this case, Jenkins' trial counsel should have requested a charge on corroboration of accomplice testimony and, second, they should have objected to Judge Harvey's instructions because they failed to include such a charge. Jenkins' counsel did neither here, and that was clearly an error of deficient performance on their part within the meaning of *Williams v. Strickland*. As Jenkins had argued in his appeal to the Georgia Supreme Court, and in his petition for habeas corpus, his counsels' failure to request a charge on corroboration amounted to ineffective assistance of counsel.

Judge Harvey clearly recognized that his failure to charge corroboration was erroneous, but he refused to reverse Jenkins' conviction on this basis on the very dubious theory that the error was "harmless." Furthermore, Judge Harvey ruled that "[t]he fact the trial court did not instruct the jury as to the corroboration of an accomplice's testimony is not grounds for a new trial since trial counsel failed to make a written request for this this charge" (citing, *inter alia*, *Hall v. State*, 163 Ga. App. 515, 295 S.E.2d 194 (1983). Decision at 3.

It is true that, at the time when Jenkins' motion for a new trial was denied by Judge Harvey, *Hall v. State* and similar cases appeared to indicate that there was no need for the trial judge to give a charge on corroboration unless specifically requested by defendant's counsel. That was always a dubious rule since it violated the "plain error" doctrine, and it was clearly in conflict with prior Georgia case law. In 2014, in *Hamm v. State*, 294 Ga. 781, 756 S.E.2d 507, the Georgia Supreme Court finally corrected this anomaly and explicitly ruled that a corroboration charge is required **even where the state relies on other evidence.**

As the Supreme Court stated in its opinion, "[a]ccordingly, we now overrule *Hall v. State* and its progeny, to the extent these cases hold that it is not error for a trial court to refuse to give a requested instruction on accomplice corroboration so long as the State relies in part on other evidence connecting the defendant to the crime. In so doing, we reaffirm the pre-*Hall* Court of Appeals line of cases holding that the failure to give such an instruction when it is requested, is error." 294 Ga. at ___, 756 S.E.2d at 512.[202]

Two of the cases which the Georgia Supreme Court explicitly referred to as being overruled in *Hamm* were *Jenkins v. State*, 268 Ga. 468, 491 S.E.2d 54 (1997) and *Fleming v. State*, 241 Ga. 245, 497 S.E.2d 211 (1998).

Thus, the Georgia Supreme Court's 1997 decision affirming Jenkins' conviction for the murder of Bobby Hodges has been subsequently overruled as erroneous **by two separate decisions** of the Georgia Supreme Court: (i) *Hamm v. State* in 2014 for failure to apply the correct rule for charging the jury regarding the issue of corroboration of accomplice

---

202   It is sadly ironic to note that the Court's opinion in *Hamm* was written by Justice Hunstein, the very same justice who authored the Court's opinions in both *Jenkins* and *Fleming*. (Justice Hunstein served on the Court for 26 years). In *Hamm*, Justice Hunstein strongly criticized the reasoning of *Hall v. State*, the decision she herself had relied on in affirming the murder convictions in both *Jenkins* and *Fleming*. As Mary Blakely aptly noted, "[t]he truth invariably arrives several years after you need it."

testimony and (ii) *State v. Lane* in 2020 for failure to apply the cumulative error doctrine correctly.[203]

Furthermore, Jenkins' sentence of life without possibility of parole has also been declared unlawful and void **by two other decisions** of the Georgia Supreme Court: (1) *Moore v. State*, 293 Ga. 705, 749 S.E.2d 660 (2013) which held, in effect, that a penalty of life without possibility of parole cannot lawfully be imposed on a juvenile who was under 18 at the time of the crime and (2) *Veal v. State*, 298 Ga. 691, 784 S.E.2d 403 (Ga. 2016) which held that a sentence of life without possibility of parole cannot lawfully be imposed on a juvenile who was under 18 at the time of the crime absent a specific finding that the defendant "was irreparably corrupt or permanently incorrigible" so as to make a sentence of life without possibility of parole appropriate

Inexplicably, despite the unambiguous language of the Georgia Supreme Court's opinions overruling its prior cases affirming the convictions of Jenkins and Maurice Fleming, both of these black men still remain imprisoned in Georgia in violation of due process of law. This is an abomination. As Martin Luther King, Jr., aptly stated, "Injustice anywhere is a threat to justice everywhere."

6. *Amendment of Rule 11 of the Federal Habeas Rules for Section 2254 Cases*

Attentive readers of this narrative will recall the terrible and scandalous debacle that ensued when Jenkins tried to appeal Judge Nangle's decision denying his federal habeas petition to the Eleventh Circuit Court of Appeals. Despite filing a timely Notice of Appeal and making numerous unnecessary motions in the District Court, Judge Nangle steadfastly and erroneously refused to grant him a certificate of appealability, and he

---

203 The decision of the Georgia Supreme Court affirming the conviction of Maurice Fleming for the murder and robbery of Bobby Hodges was also explicitly overruled by the Georgia Supreme Court in *Hamm* for failure to charge the jury correctly on the issue of corroboration of accomplice testimony.

ultimately ruled that Jenkins' request for a COA was time-barred by some imaginary statute of limitations that Judge Nangle himself invented.

Under federal habeas law as it existed at the time Jenkins filed his Notice of Appeal, Judge Nangle was legally obligated either to issue a COA or to state the reasons why a COA should not be issued. Unfortunately, Judge Nangle did not see things that way, and nothing I could do was ever able to persuade him otherwise.

In 2009, Rule 11 of the Federal Rules Governing Section 2254 Cases in the United States District Courts (the Section under which Jenkins' habeas petition was brought) was amended to explicitly provide that district court judges *must* rule on the issue of appealability without any specific request from the petitioner. As that Rule now provides:

> (a) **Certificate of Appealability**. The district court *must* issue or deny a certificate of appealability when it enters a final order adverse to the applicant. Before entering the final order, the court may direct the parties to submit arguments on whether a certificate should issue. If the court issues a certificate, the court must state the specific issue or issues that satisfy the showing required by 28 U.S.C. § 2253(c)(2). If the court denies a certificate, the parties may not appeal the denial but may seek a certificate from the court of appeals under Federal Rule of Appellate Procedure 22."

We all know what a stickler Judge Nangle was for following "the rules," so it is possible that he might have ruled differently on the issue of appealability if this new Rule had been in place when Jenkins' habeas petition was denied. On the other hand, I would have been shocked if Judge Nangle actually granted Jenkins a certificate of appealability so, in the long run, it probably made no difference.

7. *Recognition by the U.S. Supreme Court that the Lower Federal Courts Have Been Consistently Misapplying the Requirements for Obtaining a COA in Section 2254 Habeas Cases*

After Judge Nangle refused to grant a Certificate of Appealability, Jenkins' then requested a COA directly from the Eleventh Circuit Court of Appeals. As discussed in Chapter 11, however, Jenkins fared no better with the learned judges of that tribunal. Ultimately, Judge Wilson of the Eleventh Circuit did grant Jenkins a COA, but it was so severely restricted in terms of what he was allowed to appeal that it was essentially worthless. As discussed in Chapters 14 and 15, this was the reason Jenkins filed his lawsuit for a declaratory judgment in the U.S. District Court for the Eastern District and New York.

In 2017, in the case of *Buck v. Davis*, 580 U.S. 100 (2017), the U.S. Supreme Court finally appeared to recognize that the lower federal courts have frequently applied the wrong standard in denying certificates of appealability in Section 2254 cases. As the Court stated in that opinion:

> "The COA inquiry, we have emphasized, is not coextensive with a merits analysis. At the COA stage, the only question is whether the applicant has shown that 'jurists of reason could disagree with the district court's resolution of his constitutional claims or that jurists could conclude the issues presented are adequate to deserve encouragement to proceed further' (quoting from *Miller-El v. Cockrell*, 537 U.S. at 327). This threshold question should be decided *without* 'full consideration of the factual or legal bases adduced in support of the claims." *Id*. at 336 (emphasis added).
>
> "[W]hen a court of appeals properly applies the COA standard and determines that a prisoner's claim is not even debatable, that necessarily means that the prisoner has failed to show that his claim is meritorious. But

the converse is not true. That a prisoner has failed to make the ultimate showing that his claim is meritorious does not logically mean he failed to make a preliminary showing that his claim was debatable. Thus, when a reviewing court (like the Fifth Circuit here) inverts the statutory order of operations and 'first decides the merits of an appeal . . . then justifies its denial of a COA based on its adjudication of the merits,' **it has placed too heavy a burden on the prisoner at the COA stage**." 580 U.S. at 115-16 (emphasis added).

Apparently, that was exactly what happened in Jenkins' cases. The Eleventh Circuit judge who reviewed his application for a COA expected too much. He expected Jenkins to prove the **merits** of his claims in order to obtain a COA when, in reality, under the applicable Supreme Court precedents, all he had to prove was that there was a reasonable basis for disagreeing with the district court's decision.[204]

Frankly, I view this as a problem of the Supreme Court's own making. That Court had a golden opportunity in *Slack v. McDaniel*, 529 U.S.

---

204 In many ways what happened to Jenkins was far worse than what happened to Buck. There was never any doubt that Buck had committed the murder at issue; the only question was whether he had received a fair trial **on the issue of punishment**. As discussed throughout this book, Jenkins received neither a fair trial on the issue of guilt, nor on the issue of punishment, nor did he receive a fair opportunity for appeal. Furthermore, Jenkins filed two unsuccessful petitions for certiorari with the US Supreme Court. The second of these petitions raised exactly the same question that was later raised by Buck, namely, that the Court of Appeals had applied the wrong standard under AEDPA for granting a certificate of appealability. Fortunately for Buck, the Supreme Court granted Buck's petition, vacated his sentence, and ordered a new trial on the issue of punishment. Why was Buck treat differently from Jenkins? I don't know but I suspect it was because Buck had been sentenced to death, while Jenkins was only sentenced to life without any possibility of parole. Courts, especially the Supreme Court, have a definite tendency to take death penalty cases more seriously. Apparently, it is okay for a state to send someone wrongfully to prison for the rest of his or her life, so long as it doesn't try to execute them. What Robin M. Maher, a capital murder case defender and lecturer at George Washington University Law School, noted after Buck's sentence was reversed by the Supreme Court applies equally to Jenkins: "this case is emblematic of much that is wrong with the death penalty: racial discrimination, incompetent defense counsel, prosecutorial misconduct, the exaltation of procedure over fairness, and the priority placed on achieving "finality" instead of justice." R. Maher, "Buck v. Davis, Fulfilling the Promise of Justice," *On the Docket*, George Washington University Law Review, February 26, 2017. After Buck's death penalty was vacated by the Supreme Court and the case was remanded to Texas, he accepted a plea bargain where the death penalty was dropped, and he was sentenced to life imprisonment plus two concurrent sixty-year terms for two additional attempted murder counts. He will become eligible for parole in 2035, while Jenkins will still be serving life without parole.

473 (2000), to rule that 28 U.S.C. § 2253(c)(2) unconstitutionally infringed upon the power of federal courts to interpret and apply federal law, especially federal constitutional law. They failed to do so, however, and, in trying to defend the statute, they adopted a standard of review that is impossible to apply, especially by lower federal courts that already feel overburdened by state prisoner habeas cases and don't want to hear them in the first place. As was recently noted in an article published in the admittedly partisan *Prison Legal News*:

> "After 25 years, the Antiterrorism and Effective Death Penalty Act has been a total success in ensuring that the vast majority of prisoners are unable to seek a review on the merits of their constitutional claims related to criminal convictions. It has neither sped up the death penalty nor stopped terrorism, but it has helped to keep a lot of non-death sentenced prisoners who have nothing to do with 'terrorism' locked in cages. Indeed, the death penalty wait time doubled and the worst terrorist attack in U.S. history occurred after the AEDPA. Congress' rush to pass AEDPA put a severe, but short term, burden on the courts to interpret its shoddy language, negating any effect the AEDPA had on reducing habeas petitions by prisoners — its intended goal. Still, the courts continue to uphold AEDPA as necessary for a fair criminal justice system. As the saying goes, "You can't make this stuff up.""[205]

Before I became involved in Jenkins' various appeals,[206] I never would have imagined how completely dysfunctional the federal habeas corpus

---

205 Dale Chappel, "25 Years of the AEDPA: Where do we Stand?" published in *Prison Legal News*, June 1, 2021.
206 It is impossible to overstate the significance of the procedural roadblocks that Jenkins faced in attempting to obtain a COA to review Judge Nangle's decision. As discussed in detail in Chapters 11 and 14, these roadblocks prevented Jenkins from obtaining effective habeas review of the many constitutional errors that tainted his state court criminal conviction. This was not what Congress intended when it passed the habeas statute, nor when it passed AEDPA in 1996

remedy had become as a result of Congress' rushed and ill-advised passage of AEDPA in 1996 and the Supreme Court's ill-advised decisions to uphold that statute in *Williams v. Taylor*, 529 U.S. 362 (2000) and *Slack v. McDaniel*, 529 U.SW. 473 (2000). As I noted in Chapter 8, children in high school, myself included, learn about how the constitutional right to obtain federal court review of improper state court criminal convictions was established in *Cohen v. Virginia*. But that right does not mean very much if you cannot obtain appellate court review of an improper district court decision denying habeas relief, and that is exactly what happened to Jenkins here because of AEDPA. One can only hope that the Supreme Court's decision in *Buck v. Davis* marked a turning point in the long road to returning sanity for federal habeas proceedings, but I remain very skeptical.

8. *Adoption by Georgia of a New Code of Evidence*

At the time of Jenkins' trial, Georgia's rules of evidence were governed by a statute that had first been adopted in 1863. That statute had been amended many times over the years, of course, but it was still very archaic in 1995. In 2010, Georgia finally repealed the old statute and enacted an entirely new and more modern Code of Evidence, which became effective on January 1, 2012. The new code was modelled after the Federal Rules of Evidence, which were first adopted in 1975. Some of Georgia's old evidence rules were retained, but many were not. Many of the rules that were changed related to the definition and admissibility of hearsay evidence, which was a particularly troublesome issue in Jenkins' trial. Georgia completely repealed its old hearsay rules in its new Code of Evidence and replaced them with the more modern rules contained in the Federal Rules of Evidence.

It would be impossible for me to say whether the outcome of Jenkins' trial would have been significantly affected if the new code of evidence had been in place when his trial took place. However, as discussed throughout this book there were numerous key issues that depended on the rules of evidence, including the admission of the silence witness testimony during the testimony of Investigator Gray, the admission of hearsay testimony during the testimony of Deputy Moran, and so forth. It is likely that some of this evidence might have been more readily excluded if the new rules of evidence had been in place.

CHAPTER 18

AN APPLICATION FOR CLEMENCY OR PAROLE

In November of 2017, years after I had retired from the practice of law and moved to North Carolina, I was contacted by a partner of White & Case concerning the Jenkins matter. He informed me that Dorothy Donaldson, Jamel's mother, had hired a lawyer in Georgia to make an application for clemency or parole on behalf of her son. He requested that I write a letter on Jamel's behalf in support of the application. I told him, absolutely, I would be happy to do so. A copy of the draft of the letter which I submitted in response to this request is set forth below.

RMK Draft 11/7/17

TO WHOM IT MAY CONCERN

Re Clevon Jamel Jenkins

My name is Robert M. Kelly. I submit this letter in support of the application for clemency or parole filed by Clevon Jamel Jenkins (hereafter "Petitioner").

My Background and Experience

From January 1972 through December 31, 2010, I served as an attorney admitted to practice in the state of New York. In addition to all state and federal courts in New York, I was admitted to practice before the Supreme Court of the United States, the United States Court of Appeals for the Second Circuit, and the United States Court of Appeals for the Eleventh Circuit. I was also admitted *pro hac vice* before the Supreme

Court of Georgia and the Superior Court of Liberty County, Georgia, in connection with the criminal proceedings involving Petitioner.

I graduated with distinction from New York University Law School in 1971. While in law school, I was Note and Comment Editor of the NYU Law Review, a John Norton Pomeroy Scholar, and a member of the Order of the Coif. Following law school, I served more than four years as an Assistant District Attorney in New York County, New York, including three years as a member of the District Attorney's Homicide Bureau. As an Assistant District Attorney, I prosecuted numerous felony cases including more than a dozen homicide cases.

After leaving the New York County District Attorney's Office, I worked for more than thirty years as a trial lawyer for White & Case, LLP, a prominent New York City and international law firm. Most of my work during this period involved civil litigation, although I also occasionally performed criminal work on behalf of *pro bono* clients, including Petitioner herein.

My Relationship with Petitioner

I began representing Petitioner in the Summer of 1996. At that time, he had already been convicted of first-degree murder and robbery following a two-day jury trial in Liberty County, Georgia. After the merits trial, Petitioner was sentenced to life imprisonment without possibility of parole following a one-day penalty trial. Petitioner was represented at the merits and penalty trials by two court-appointed attorneys.

I became involved in representing Petitioner at the request of his mother who worked at that time (and for many years before) as a legal secretary for White & Case. At that time, and for many years before, Petitioner and his mother both lived in Brooklyn, New York. When the crime was allegedly committed (October 8, 1993), Petitioner was only 17 years old, and he had an IQ that was barely above the mental retardation level. He had no prior criminal record of any kind, he had never been arrested before, and he had never previously been involved in any trouble with the law. He was basically a good person who attended school and was deeply involved in music. Ironically, his mother, a hard-working and decent person, had recently sent Petitioner to stay with his grandmother in rural Georgia, believing that this would provide a better and safer environment for her teenage son than the mean streets of Brooklyn.

My Representation of Petitioner

My representation of Petitioner initially consisted of preparing for and filing a motion for a new trial based upon numerous errors that had occurred during Petitioner's merits and penalty trials. In preparing for this motion, I had extensive discussions with Petitioner regarding the facts of the case, and I also interviewed Petitioner's two court-appointed trial counsel. I also, of course, reviewed the complete transcript of the trial and all prior proceedings.

In connection with the motion for a new trial, I requested and represented Petitioner at an evidentiary hearing at which Petitioner and several other witnesses testified, including Petitioner's two court-appointed counsel and the District Attorney. This was the first time that Petitioner testified and explained that he was not involved in the murder or robbery. Based upon the advice of counsel, Petitioner had not previously made any statements to the police and, therefore, they did not know that Petitioner claimed to be wholly innocent of this heinous crime. After the hearing, and following the submission of extensive written memoranda, on May 6, 1997, Judge Harvey of the Liberty County Superior Court issued a written opinion denying Petitioner's motion for a new trial.

I then filed and argued a direct appeal before the Supreme Court of Georgia. Following oral argument, on October 6, 1997, the Supreme Court issued a written opinion unanimously affirming Petitioner's conviction and sentence. *Jenkins v. State*, 268 Ga. 468, 491 S.E.2d 54 (1997). I then filed a petition for certiorari with the United States Supreme Court which was denied on March 23, 1998. *Jenkins v. Georgia*, 523 U.S. 1029 (1998).

On July 16, 1998, I filed a petition for habeas corpus in the United States District Court for the Southern District of Georgia. The petition enumerated 18 separate and district constitutional errors that had occurred during Petitioner's trial, including claims that Petitioner was denied his Fifth Amendment right against self-incrimination, his Sixth Amendment right to confront and cross-examine witnesses against him, his Sixth Amendment right to effective assistance of counsel, and his Sixth Amendment right to trial by jury. The habeas corpus petition also alleged various violations of due process of law, including failure to disclose exculpatory *Brady* material, failure to provide proper jury instructions, admission of improper and prejudicial evidence, and exclusion of exculpatory defense evidence.

Based upon my experience as a prosecutor in New York City, as well as my many years of experience as a private trial attorney, I believe that each of the grounds alleged in support of the petition for habeas corpus was substantial and meritorious. However, after considering the alleged errors for approximately 18 months, and without ever scheduling oral argument or holding an evidentiary hearing, on June 21, 2000, Judge Nangle issued a written opinion denying the petition for habeas corpus *in toto*. *Jenkins v. Byrd*, 103 F. Supp.2d 1350 (S.D. Ga. 2000).

On July 18, 2000, I filed a timely notice of appeal to the Eleventh Circuit U.S. Court of Appeals. Unfortunately, due to a provision of the recently enacted Antiterrorism and Effective Death Penalty Act (28 U.S.C. § 2254), it became necessary for Petitioner to obtain a certificate of appealability from the district court to perfect his appeal. Without providing any reasonable explanation or excuse, Judge Nangle summarily refused to grant Petitioner leave to appeal.

I then filed a motion for issuance of a certificate of appealability with the Eleventh Circuit itself. The motion enumerated 18 federal constitutional errors that had occurred during Petitioner's merits and sentencing trials. One of the errors asserted was ineffective assistance of counsel, for which 16 separate grounds were enumerated.

On March 1, 2001, the Eleventh Circuit Court of Appeals granted Petitioner leave to appeal. However, the certificate of appealability was severely limited to a single claim (ineffective assistance of counsel), and this claim was itself severely limited to a single ground (improperly advising Petitioner not to testify).[207] Thus, the overwhelming majority of the meritorious grounds asserted for Petitioner's appeal were never considered by the Court of Appeals. Furthermore, the single Circuit Judge who had granted Petitioner leave to appeal was not even a member of the panel that ultimately heard the appeal.

I originally thought that, when the Court of Appeals limited its order granting the appeal to the single issue of ineffective assistance of counsel, this was because it had already determined that it would reverse Petitioner's conviction on that basis. Sad to say, I was mistaken. On August 10, 2001, without ever scheduling oral argument, the Eleventh Circuit denied Petitioner's severely truncated appeal.[208] Petitioner's motion for rehearing was denied on December 27, 2001.

Thereafter, I filed another petition for certiorari with the United States Supreme Court asking that Court to reverse the decision of the Eleventh Circuit. This petition was denied by the Supreme Court on May 28, 2002. *Jenkins v. Byrd*, 535 U.S. 1104 (2002).

On March 13, 2001, ten days after the Eleventh Circuit issued its severely truncated certificate of appealability, I filed a civil action on Petitioner's behalf in the U.S. District Court for the Eastern District of New York (located in Brooklyn, New York). This complaint asked the court to declare unconstitutional the portion of the Antiterrorism and Effective

---

207 Limiting Petitioner's ineffective assistance of counsel claim to a single ground (instead of the 16 alleged) was particularly incomprehensible because determination of an ineffective assistance of counsel claim must be evaluated based upon the **totality** of the circumstances of the case. Such a determination is impossible where, as here, the Court arbitrarily limits Petitioner's claim to a single error made by counsel and ignores 15 others.
208 The decision of the Court of Appeals was based upon an unpublished opinion reported in 273 F.3d 397 (Table No. 00-17348) (2001).

Death Penalty Act which, as applied herein, prevented Petitioner from appealing the denial of his petition for habeas corpus without first obtaining a certificate of appealability.

The United States initially moved to dismiss this new action for improper venue because Petitioner was incarcerated in Georgia. The district court denied this motion because, despite his incarceration in Georgia, Petitioner continued to be a domiciliary of Brooklyn and therefore venue in Brooklyn was proper.

The United States then moved to dismiss the action for lack of subject matter jurisdiction arguing that the issue before the court was non-justiciable. In a memorandum decision and order dated June 9, 2003, the district court accepted the government's argument, ruling that "a declaration by this court concerning the constitutionality of plaintiff's claims would have no effect on plaintiff's *entitlement* to seek further habeas review" (unpublished slip opinion at 5) (emphasis in original). This seems to me to be clearly erroneous since, if the requirement that Petitioner obtain a certificate of appealability were held to be unconstitutional, then Petitioner would certainly have been entitled to full appellate review of his claims.

Thereafter, on August 5, 2003, I filed an appeal to the Second Circuit U.S. Court of Appeals. On October 15, 2004, the Second Circuit issued its decision denying Petitioner's appeal. *Jenkins v. United States*, 386 F.3d 415 (2d Cir. 2004).

Throughout my lengthy representation of Petitioner, I have always believed two things: first, that he did not receive a fair trial and, second, that at some point some court would recognize this and reverse the conviction. As I stated to Judge Harvey at the conclusion of the March 14, 1997 hearing in support of Petitioner's motion for a new trial:

> *As horrible a crime as this is, I don't think that takes away from the fact that my client, Jamel Jenkins, was entitled to a fair trial. I don't believe that he received a fair trial. I think in the heat of the moment, when things were going*

on, a number of things happened that prevented him from getting a fair trial. And despite the fact that what happened here was a very horrible situation, I don't think we should lose sight of the fact that my client, Jamel Jenkins, should be entitled to a fair trial.

Now, having said that, I think there are a couple of points that really are very critical in determining whether or not that fair trial took place. As I say, I think at some point, if not here then in an appellate court, it's going to be necessary that we have a retrial. I would hope that the Court takes these points very seriously and that, in its heart, looks at this and determines whether or not it's convinced that Mr. Jenkins received a fair trial. So I think it's in everybody's interest that this is going to have to be reversed but it [it will be better] if it is reversed at this level. Because if we're going to have another trial, I think we should have it now when these events are more fresh in the minds of the witnesses than several years from now after the supreme court may have reversed it. Hearing Held Before Judge Harvey on March 14, 1997 at 75-76.

Unfortunately, after seven long years of motions and appeals, I was ultimately unable to persuade any court to seriously consider the many substantial errors that had infected Petitioner's trial.

My Belief That Petitioner May Actually Be Innocent

As a former assistant district attorney experienced in prosecuting murder cases, I truly believe that Petitioner was wrongfully convicted here and that he may actually be wholly innocent of the heinous crimes with which he was charged. Although the underlying evidence admitted at trial was nominally sufficient to support a conviction, upon closer examination it was highly suspect and very unconvincing. Unfortunately, no one — not the police, not the district attorney, not petitioner's court-appointed trial counsel, not the trial judge, not the judges of the Georgia Supreme Court, and especially not Judge Nangle — ever took the time to seriously evaluate whether the numerous and substantial errors that infected Petitioner's trial prevented him from receiving a fair trial. They all simply assumed that Petitioner was guilty because he never offered any evidence that caused them to question this premise.

This was primarily the fault of Petitioner's court-appointed counsel — who failed to provide a competent and effective defense and who inexplicably refused to let him testify — but there was also plenty of fault on the part of other parties as well. Judge Harvey, for example, admitted to me following the hearing on the motion for a new trial that he "could not believe" he had failed to charge the jury with respect to the need for corroboration of accomplice testimony. He also told me, however, that he would not reverse Petitioner's conviction on this basis, and that he would "leave this up to the Supreme Court."

Apparently concerned about the cost this capital case was having on his budget, Judge Harvey also insisted on pursuing an extremely aggressive trial schedule which may have contributed to the many errors that occurred during trial. It's hard to be effective when you are falling asleep.

Judge Nangle, the federal district judge who was assigned to hear Petitioner's petition for habeas corpus, refused to grant me permission to represent Petitioner *pro hac vice*[209] and struck from the record a lengthy

---

209 Judge Nangle denied my application to appear *pro hac vice* because Robert F. Pirkle, Esq., a local Georgia attorney who had agreed to serve as local counsel (and who had previously served as local counsel throughout the state court proceedings) failed to file a necessary affidavit agreeing to serve as local counsel with the clerk of the court. However, neither Judge Nangle nor the clerk of the court ever notified me or Mr. Pirkle of this omission, which could easily have been corrected. Instead, Judge Nangle mailed me an order denying my application.

memorandum of law I had submitted on Petitioner's behalf.[210] As noted above, he also refused to grant Petitioner leave to appeal his decision to the Court of Appeals. One can only surmise what he was thinking, but obviously it was not concern for whether Petitioner had received a fair trial.

As noted above, the Eleventh Circuit Court of Appeals inexplicably and severely limited the grounds for Petitioner's appeal. One can only wonder what the Court of Appeals might have done had they had the opportunity to consider the full record.

Finally, the prosecuting attorney here made numerous errors that seriously tainted the reliability of the jury's verdict, including improperly commenting on Petitioner's failure to testify, failure to provide *Brady* material, affirmative misrepresentations regarding why the state's principal witness was not charged with murder, and affirmative misrepresentations regarding promises of leniency made to another key witness.

---

210 The memorandum of law was 112 pages and clearly exceeded the page limit for briefs provided by Local Rule 7.1. However, this was a very unusual and complicated case, and the memorandum was intended to be helpful to the Court in understanding Petitioner's claims. Of course, there is no need to submit a memorandum in support of a petition for habeas, nor is there any need for petitioner to be represented by counsel. It was the court's obligation to decide the petition based upon the grounds alleged therein. Since the court had already denied my application to appear *pro hac vice* and had struck the brief I submitted in support thereof, I simply relied on the Petition that Petitioner had already signed and submitted. Approximately six weeks later, however, Judge Nangle mailed to me at my New York City office an order demanding that "plaintiff (sic) resubmit his brief in accordance with Local Rule 7.1 no later than ten (10) days from the date of this Order" and further stating that "[f]ailure to comply [with this order] will result in the dismissal of this action (sic) for want of prosecution pursuant to Local Rule 41.1(b)" (Order of Judge Nangle dated November 2, 1998). I was completely dumbfounded. Not only was I not authorized to represent Petitioner due to the judge's denial of my application to appear *pro hac vice*, but also there is absolutely no requirement that a habeas corpus petitioner needs to submit a brief in support of his petition. Yet, here, Judge Nangle explicitly threatened in writing to dismiss Petitioner's petition not on the merits but solely because an attorney who was not even authorized to appear on his behalf had failed to file a brief that was not required by any applicable order or rule, and all of this was done without ever granting me the courtesy of any notice. Needless to say, I immediately filed a new brief on Petitioner's behalf which was limited to the required 25 pages and which was, therefore, virtually useless. A year and a half later, when Judge Nangle finally issued his opinion denying the petition, he quoted extensively from the 112 page memorandum that he had previously struck from the record and which was written by an attorney who was not permitted to represent Petitioner. What can one say?

Basis for My Belief That Petitioner May Actually Be Innocent

The record in this case is voluminous and relatively complex. It is not possible, therefore, to easily summarize the basis for my belief that Petitioner was wrongfully convicted and may actually be innocent. However, I will highlight the key facts as follows:

1. On October 8, 1993, Robert Hodges, the white owner of a convenience store in Riceboro, Georgia, was shot and killed during the commission of a robbery at his store. He was shot five times with bullets from two different guns (both .25 caliber pistols). Only one of the shots was fatal.

2. Four African-American teenagers were subsequently arrested and charged with this crime: Cedric Brown, Shawn Brown, Maurice Fleming, and Petitioner. Each of these defendants was charged with two counts: murder and armed robbery. A fifth defendant (Terry Roberts) was also charged with robbery but not with murder.

3. ***It is undisputed that all five of these individuals were present when Mr. Hodges was robbed and killed. What was disputed is what role, if any, each of the defendants played in the robbery.***

4. Cedric Brown, who admitted that he shot Mr. Hodges several times during the robbery, was 19 years old at the time of the crime and was mentally retarded. Because he was mentally retarded, he was not eligible for the death penalty. He was permitted to plead guilty and was sentenced to two terms of life imprisonment.

5. Shawn Brown, who was only 16 at the time of the robbery, also pleaded guilty and was sentenced to one term of life and one term of twenty years.

6. Maurice Fleming, who was 19 at the time of the robbery, was separately tried, found guilty of murder and robbery, and sentenced

to life. This meant that Maurice was eligible for parole after serving approximately twelve years.

7. Petitioner, who was only 17 at the time of the robbery, was separately tried, found guilty of murder and robbery and sentenced to life without possibility of parole.[211] Since he was arrested on October 12, 1993, he has already served more than 24 years in prison.

8. Terry Roberts, **an admitted accomplice in the robbery**, was the main witness against Petitioner at his trial. Roberts was 21 years old at the time of the robbery and was the half-brother of Maurice Fleming, one of the other participants. As a reward for testifying against Petitioner, Roberts was not charged with the murder and he served only a limited amount of time in prison.

9. Thus, of the five individuals who were allegedly involved in the commission of this heinous crime, **Petitioner received the harshest sentence by far**. Yet, his alleged involvement was probably the least, **and quite possibly completely innocent**. Unlike Cedric, Shawn and Roberts — all of whom admitted their involvement in the robbery — **Petitioner has always claimed that he was an innocent bystander**. However, due to the advice and incompetence of his court-appointed trial counsel, he was never given the opportunity to tell his side of the story at trial. The first and only time Petitioner told his side of the story was during the hearing on the motion for a new trial when he testified that he had nothing to do with the robbery.

10. Petitioner's trial (not including jury selection) began on August 29, 1995. After only two days of testimony, he was convicted of malice murder and robbery on September 1, 1993. Because the state was seeking the death penalty, a second penalty trial began immediately before the same jury. After only one day of

---

211 He was also sentenced to an additional consecutive term of life on the robbery charge.

testimony, the jury imposed a penalty of life without possibility of parole.

11. Twenty-one witnesses testified at Petitioner's trial. Most of these witnesses provided non-critical background information. With one notable exception (explained further below), **there were no eyewitnesses to the crime**. Furthermore, **there was no physical or forensic evidence that connected Petitioner to the crime**.

12. The primary evidence against Petitioner was the testimony of Terry Roberts, **an admitted participant in the crime**. Although Roberts' testimony was highly incriminating, **it was also highly dubious**. Furthermore, although Roberts was an admitted accomplice in the crime, the trial judge failed to charge the jury on the need for corroboration of Roberts' testimony. **Judge Harvey admitted to me later that this was a mistake and that he had intended to charge corroboration**.

13. Roberts testified that he drove Cedric, Maurice, Shawn and Petitioner to Mr. Hodges' store on the day of the robbery, that prior to going to the store Cedric had told him that he planned to rob Mr. Hodges, that Petitioner also said, "yeah, he was ready to hold him up," that Cedric, Maurice, Shawn and Petitioner went into the store and came back about ten minutes later, that Maurice then said, "Crank up, man, let's go. Cedric shot that man in the head, that Cedric, Shawn, Maurice and Petitioner then got in the car and Cedric said, "Yeah, I got him. I shot that cracker. I shot him in the head. Bang, bang, bang," that Petitioner then said, "Yeah, yeah, yeah, I got him, bang, bang," that Cedric had a black .25 caliber pistol with a brown handle and that Petitioner had a .25 caliber chrome-plated pistol with a white handle, that Roberts then drove the car away, that they went to a hotel where Cedric gave some money to each of the other defendants (including Roberts), and that Roberts then drove Cedric, Maurice,

Shawn and Petitioner to the bus station in Savannah. Roberts also testified that, after getting home, he told his parents what had happened and that his father then called the police.

14. Roberts was questioned by the police on October 9, 1993, the day after the robbery. At first, **Roberts denied any involvement in the robbery**. However, after lengthy and persistent questioning by the police, **Roberts changed his story several times** and eventually implicated himself and the other four defendants. Notably, Roberts gave several different versions of what had happened before eventually giving the version that he testified to at trial. As Roberts testified on direct examination, *"the first couple of times I spoke with them [the police] I did not tell them the whole truth"* *"because I was trying to look out for Maurice and myself."* As noted above, Maurice was Roberts' half-brother and therefore Roberts had a significant incentive to place blame on Petitioner instead of Maurice.

15. On October 9, 1993, a search was made of the vehicle driven by Roberts and a .25 caliber pistol was found in the car. Ballistics evidence presented at trial established that the two bullets recovered from Mr. Hodges' body (and three of four shell casings recovered at the scene) were fired from this gun. No evidence was presented at Petitioner's trial regarding who owned or used this gun, but it was undisputed that this gun was used by Cedric.

16. In addition to the gun used by Cedric, another .25 caliber shell casing (but no bullet) was recovered at the scene. A ballistics expert testified that this shell casing probably came from a .25 caliber Lorcin pistol. This second pistol was never recovered by the police, and **there was no forensic evidence of any kind connecting Petitioner to this gun**. However, as noted above, Roberts testified that Petitioner had a .25 caliber chrome-plated gun with a white handle at the time of the robbery.

17. One of the witnesses who testified at trial was Roger Fleming, who was Maurice Fleming's first cousin. Roger testified that he owned a .25 caliber Lorcin pistol which he kept in the bedroom of his house, that in September 1993 **his cousin Maurice visited his home and went into the bedroom area, and that the next day Roger noticed the pistol was missing,** and that he reported it was missing.

18. The inference of Roger Fleming's testimony is that Maurice Fleming took Roger's pistol, and that this was possibly the second gun used in the robbery. Even assuming this was true, however, the most logical inference is that **Maurice had the gun at the time of the robbery not Petitioner**. It defies logic to think that Maurice stole the gun from his cousin and then gave it to Petitioner. **No evidence of any kind was presented at trial (or at any other time) that could plausibly explain how or why Petitioner came into possession of this gun (which belonged to Roger and was presumably stolen by Maurice).** Unfortunately, no one involved in Petitioner's trial ever thought this was odd.

19. When Roberts testified against Petitioner at trial, he was charged with robbery and was obviously an accomplice in the crime. As an accomplice, his testimony needed to be corroborated under Georgia law to support a conviction. However, **the trial judge failed to instruct the jury regarding the requirement for corroboration**. As a result, **the jury never considered whether sufficient corroboration evidence existed to support conviction.** This error by itself should have been sufficient to reverse Petitioner's conviction. Alas, that did not happen.

20. On March 14, 1997, immediately following the hearing on the motion for a new trial, Judge Harvey told me that he "could not believe" that he had failed to give the required charge on corroboration. However, he also told me at that time **that he would not**

reverse Petitioner's conviction on this ground and that he would "leave this up to the [Georgia] Supreme Court."[212] In his ruling on the motion for a new trial, Judge Harvey explicitly stated that *"the omission to instruct the jury on the necessity of corroboration of an accomplice's testimony was erroneous."* Decision at 7. However, he concluded it was "not clearly harmful as a matter of law." *Id.* at 7. That, however, was a decision that should have been made by the jury.

21. Not only was the issue of corroboration completely omitted from Petitioner's trial, but *Roberts' involvement in the underlying crime was purposefully and erroneously minimized by the prosecution*. Roberts had originally been charged with murder, as he should have been under Georgia's felony murder law. However, prior to the time Roberts testified as the prosecution's main witness at Petitioner's trial, this murder charge was dismissed by the State. Deputy Keith Moran testified that "no information was developed during the investigation to indicate that Roberts was aware of any plan to kill Mr. Hodges prior to the time it occurred," and therefore the District Attorney decided to dismiss the murder charge against Roberts. *This testimony was highly prejudicial for several reasons.* First, Roberts had admitted his role as a participant in the robbery and thus he was indisputably liable for felony murder regardless of whether he was aware of any plan to kill Mr. Hodges prior to the robbery. Second, Deputy Moran's testimony wrongfully implied that there must have been evidence that Petitioner knew of a plan to kill Mr. Hodges prior

---

212 Ultimately, the Georgia Supreme Court ruled that, under the circumstances of this case, it was not necessary to charge corroboration because "[i]t is not error to fail to give a charge of corroboration of accomplices where the State relies upon other evidence, including a defendant's confession, apart from the accomplice's testimony." However, Petitioner here never made a "confession" and it was clearly inappropriate for the Supreme Court to rely on this exception to the usual rule. Furthermore, even if the decision of the Supreme Court was technically correct, it was plainly inappropriate (think Kafka or Dickens) for the Supreme Court to rely on such a hyper-technicality to incarcerate a teenager for the remainder of his natural life. Frankly, if the corroboration charge had been given here, there was a good possibility that the jury would have concluded that the corroboration evidence submitted here was insufficient.

to the robbery since, unlike Roberts, his murder charge was not dismissed. Third, **the District Attorney intentionally and impermissibly bolstered the testimony of his star witness by wrongfully implying that he was not responsible for Hodges's murder.**

22. Petitioner allegedly made two brief incriminating statements that constituted key evidence at his trial. First, after being arrested in Florida, he allegedly spontaneously told a Florida police officer, "I only shot him once." Second, after Petitioner was returned to Georgia, he allegedly made incriminating statements to a cellmate (Kenneth McCall) including that he shot "the old Cracker" twice. This evidence was undoubtedly sufficient to corroborate Roberts' testimony that Petitioner had shot Mr. Hodges, **but it was also highly convenient and suspicious**.

23. Dupont Cheney, the District Attorney for Georgia's Atlantic Judicial District, testified during Petitioner's motion for a new trial that, after Petitioner had been convicted and pursuant to his regular practice for cooperating witnesses, he wrote a letter on McCall's behalf requesting that all charges pending against him be dismissed and that, based upon this recommendation, all charges against McCall were in fact dismissed. **This promise of leniency was not disclosed at Petitioner's trial.** On the contrary, an Assistant District Attorney (Charles Howard) explicitly testified at Petitioner's trial (immediately after McCall had testified) that "Mr. McCall did not request any special favors because he might be a witness in this case" and that two additional charges pending against Mr. McCall were dismissed because there was insufficient evidence to prosecute these charges. **This was misleading at best, if not outright false.** At the very least, the jury that convicted Petitioner should have been informed about District Attorney Cheney's regular policy of granting leniency to witnesses like McCall who testify for the State since obviously this undermined his credibility.

24. Petitioner's alleged statement to the Florida police officer that "he only shot him once" is also highly suspicious, not only in light of its utter brevity and lack of detail but, more importantly, in light of the fact that ***Petitioner consistently told his attorneys that he was not involved in the robbery.*** It would not be illogical to suggest that this "statement" was conveniently invented to satisfy the known need to corroborate Robert's testimony.

25. Petitioner explicitly testified at the motion for a new trial that he did not make either of the statements allegedly claimed by the Florida police officer or cellmate McCall. He would have made a similar denial at trial, but he was not afforded the opportunity to do so because of the incompetent advice he received from his court-appointed counsel.

26. As just noted, ***Petitioner consistently told his attorneys that he was not involved in the robbery and that he was merely an innocent bystander***. He also told his attorneys that he wanted to testify at trial. Both of these assertions were clearly confirmed by Petitioner's court-appointed attorneys (David C. Walker and Hal T. Peel) when they testified at Petitioner's hearing for a new trial. However, ***Petitioner did not testify at trial because his court appointed attorneys advised him not to do so***.

27. Not only did Petitioner's attorneys refuse to let him testify, ***they affirmatively misled him regarding the progress and likely outcome of the trial***, telling him that ***the trial was "going good" and that there was "no need" for him testify. Clearly, these statements were patently false.*** Obviously, Petitioner's trial was not going well. One witness (Roberts) explicitly testified that Petitioner had shot and robbed Mr. Hodges, and two additional witnesses (the Florida police officer and the cellmate snitch) had testified that Petitioner admitted that he had shot someone. This testimony was virtually uncontradicted and unimpeached (even

though evidence existed which could have been used to contradict and impeach it). Under these circumstances, it was absolutely essential that Petitioner had to testify in order to establish his defense. Yet, his lawyers refused to let him do so. On the contrary, they explicitly told him there was no need for him to testify because the trial was going well. It was not surprising, therefore, that the jury found him guilty. They were simply not given any other choice.

28. Both of Petitioner's court-appointed attorneys (Messrs. Walker and Peel) confirmed at the motion for a new trial that they had explicitly advised Petitioner not to testify, explaining that (i) they did not think Petitioner would perform well under cross-examination and (ii) **they did not think that Petitioner had anything to say which would help his defense**. This was clearly erroneous and prevented Petitioner from getting a fair trial. Obviously, **it was absolutely essential for Petitioner to testify and tell the jury that he was an innocent bystander and that he was not involved in the robbery**. There was no other way to get this evidence before the jury except by having Petitioner testify. Although Petitioner was not a great witness due to his low IQ, he was credible and he had never previously been arrested so he was not subject to impeachment on that basis.

29. Although Petitioner did not testify at trial or present any affirmative evidence in his defense, **the prosecuting attorney repeatedly argued to the jury during summation that the defendant failed to present any evidence to refute the State's case**. This was clearly improper and violated Petitioner's Fifth Amendment privilege against self-incrimination.

30. A police investigator (James Grey) was permitted to testify **that he had received information from certain unidentified "silent witnesses" which caused him to believe that Petitioner was one**

of the perpetrators of the crime at issue. Furthermore, the prosecutor later repeated this testimony during his summation to the jury. ***Admission of this so-called "silent witness" testimony was highly prejudicial and violated Petitioner's right to confront and cross-examine the witnesses against him.***

31. In addition to the testimony about "silent witnesses," ***almost the entire testimony of Investigator Gray was based upon inadmissible hearsay.*** In effect, Mr. Gray was permitted to testify that he had conducted an investigation and that based upon this investigation he had concluded that Petitioner was guilty. This was erroneous and highly prejudicial. Mr. Gray had no personal knowledge of any of the facts or conclusions he was permitted to testify about.

32. During Roberts' testimony, the prosecutor elicited testimony, by means of hearsay statements, that Maurice and Shawn had previously been arrested for unrelated crimes, that Maurice had an outstanding bench warrant, and that this was the reason Maurice needed money to get out of town. This was highly prejudicial and improper.

33. The trial schedule that Judge Harvey insisted on maintaining was extremely lengthy (more than 12 hours a day during voir dire) and excessively exhausting. Both of Petitioner's court-appointed counsel testified during the motion for a new trial that the trial schedule was "extremely grueling," that they were "really tired," and that this "may have affected their effectiveness" as counsel.

According to Petitioner, on the day of the crime, he was innocently walking along the street when four young men whom he barely knew invited him to take a ride in their car. Unbeknownst to Petitioner, two of these individuals had prior arrests and one had an outstanding warrant. Also unbeknownst to Petitioner, these four individuals intended to rob Hodges's convenience store in order to get money to leave town. Also unbeknownst to Petitioner, two of these individuals (Cedric and Maurice) had loaded handguns. A few minutes later, with Petitioner now riding in the car, Cedric, Maurice, Shawn and Roberts drove to Hodges's convenience store and robbed him of approximately $850. In the course of the robbery, Cedric and Maurice shot Hodges with two separate guns and Hodges died from his injuries.

Petitioner's version of the facts was directly supported by his testimony at the motion for a new trial, and it was confirmed in key respects by the testimony of his court-appointed counsel. It was also indirectly supported by the evidence which showed that Maurice (and not Petitioner) had access to the second gun. Although Petitioner's testimony was contradicted by the testimony of Terry Roberts, Roberts' testimony was utterly unreliable. By his own admission, he was a willing participant in the robbery who had lied "several times" to the police in order to protect himself and his half-brother Maurice. The fact that the state was willing to rely on such unreliable testimony in seeking the death penalty for Petitioner is grossly inexcusable and totally perplexing.

Accordingly, for all of the foregoing reasons, I strongly recommend that Petitioner be granted clemency or parole.

Respectively submitted,

Robert M. Kelly

Attorney at Law

After this draft letter was submitted to the attorney who was representing Jamel in his application for clemency or parole, I had the opportunity to speak to her about the application. She indicated that the letter which I wrote could not be submitted to the Board of Parole because I was suggesting that Jenkins may be innocent, and they would not consider that important. They wanted Jamel to say that he was sorry for what he had done. I said, why should he say he is sorry if he is completely innocent. She thanked me for the letter and said it would be extremely helpful as background information but that she could not submit it to the Board as written.

I never heard again from anyone regarding the outcome of the application, or even if it was actually made. The one thing I do know is that Jamel is still confined in a Georgia prison.

It has now been more than thirty years since Jamel was wrongfully convicted and yet, apparently, no one but his mother and I seem to care. My one remaining hope is that perhaps this book will finally shine a light on this terrible miscarriage of justice.

CHAPTER 19

WHY DID I FAIL?

It is entirely possible that I am not as good a lawyer as I think I am, and the reason I failed was due to my own incompetence or misguided overreach. It is also entirely possible that Jenkins was actually guilty and no lawyer, regardless of how competent or clever he or she was, could ever have gotten his conviction reversed. These are possibilities, of course, but I do not believe they are the reason I failed.

The reason I failed was because others, who had the responsibility to do so, never took the time to consider the **possibility** that Jenkins **might actually be innocent**, and they never made the effort to ascertain whether the numerous errors that allegedly occurred during his trial may have actually prevented him from getting a fair trial. They **assumed** that Jenkins was guilty because he had been arrested by the police and found guilty by a jury. And they **assumed** that the guilty verdict was correct because there was **some** evidence which, if believed, was sufficient to justify such a verdict. Because they assumed both that Jenkins was guilty and that his guilt had been established by sufficient evidence, they convinced themselves that the plethora of significant errors that infected his trial could be dismissed as **harmless**. Otherwise, they would have had to grant him a new trial, and that was something they obviously did not wish to do.[213] I have no evidence to substantiate this, but there is also the distinct possibility, however slight, that Jenkins' race may have been a contributing factor. If Jenkins had been a white teenager from a more respectable family, it is likely that the judges who considered his case might have been a little more

---

[213] I do not know how things are normally done in Georgia, but I must say that I have seen numerous cases in New York where criminal defendants have been granted a new trial for far less serious errors than those that occurred during Jenkins' trial and also where the consequences of an unfair trial were far less serious than they were for him who, at age 19, was sentenced to life imprisonment without any possibility of parole.

skeptical of the skimpy evidence and a little less forgiving of the egregious errors. And, of course, Jenkins' poverty did not help either. Money may not be able to buy happiness, but it can certainly buy better lawyers.

Let us now revisit the evidence. As noted previously, there was **no physical evidence** of any kind that connected Jenkins to the crime. No fingerprints, no ballistics evidence, no surveillance tapes, no photographs, no trace evidence of any kind. When he was apprehended, Jenkins was not in possession of any of Mr. Hodges' property or of anything else that could connect him to the crime.[214] A diligent search was made by the police in several different locations (including where Jenkins was arrested in Florida) for the second gun that was allegedly used in the robbery, but no second gun was ever found. There was testimonial evidence that indicated that Maurice had access to a gun which he had stolen from his cousin, but there was no physical evidence connecting this gun to the crime, and there was certainly no physical evidence connecting this gun to Jenkins.

Unlike all the other defendants (Cedric, Maurice, Roberts and Shawn), Jenkins never made any detailed statement to the police after he was apprehended. In retrospect, other than getting into Roberts' car when Cedric told him to do so, this was probably his biggest mistake. He should have told the police immediately that he was not involved in the crime. But he had already been arrested, and he was told by the police that anything he said could and would be used against him. He was also told by the police that a lawyer would be appointed for him. Under these circumstances, it was perfectly reasonable for Jenkins not to make any statement to the police. In fact, that is exactly what a lawyer would have advised him to do. Some time later, after a lawyer (Hal Walker) had been appointed by Judge Harvey to represent him, Jenkins told his lawyer his side of what happened, but the lawyer never told Jenkins' side of the story to the police or the

---

214 There was a food stamp that was found in the motel room in Florida where Jenkins was arrested. However, Cedric Brown and Maurice Fleming were also staying at this motel, and there was no evidence that directly connected this food stamp to Jenkins.

District Attorney, nor advised Jenkins to speak to the police.[215] Incredibly, even at the trial, Jenkins' lawyers refused to allow him to testify and tell his side of what had happened.

In addition to the fact that there was no physical evidence connecting Jenkins to the crime and that he had never made any detailed statements to the police, there were no eyewitnesses to the crime. The **only** evidence connecting Jenkins to the crime was the testimony of Terry Roberts, an undisputed participant in the robbery who admitted under oath at Jenkins' trial that he had lied **several times** to the police in order to protect himself and his half-brother Maurice. Furthermore, although Roberts had originally been charged by the District Attorney for the murder of Mr. Hodges, the murder charge against him was conveniently dropped by the District Attorney prior to Jenkins' trial. Obviously, this was done to reward Roberts for agreeing to testify favorably for the State and to make it appear to the jury that Roberts was less culpable than Jenkins. Roberts may have agreed to rob Mr. Hodges, but at least he was not a murderer.[216]

Roberts testified that he drove Cedric, Maurice, Shawn and Jenkins to Hodges' Grocery Store on the day of the murder and then waited in the car as the other four went into the store. He claimed that he did not leave the car and that he did not see what happened inside the store. He also claimed that when the others came back a few minutes later, Cedric stated that he "shot the old cracker" and that Jenkins also said that he shot him. Roberts also claimed that he saw Jenkins holding a gun, the same gun which he said Maurice Fleming had stolen from his cousin.

---

215 In fairness to Mr. Walker, it probably would have been pointless at this time for Jenkins to make a statement to the police or the District Attorney, since Jenkins had already been indicted and it was unlikely that any statement made by him to the police at this time would have changed that result, especially since Jenkins had no other evidence to verify his side of the story. I have seen cases where it does make sense for an indicted defendant to make a voluntary statement to the district attorney prior to trial, but this was probably not one of them. Having met Mr. Cheney, I seriously doubt that it would have made any difference.

216 Actually, Roberts was still a murderer. As previously explained, Roberts was clearly guilty of Mr. Hodges' murder under the felony murder doctrine. The only reason the murder charge was dismissed by the District Attorney was to gain a tactical advantage by portraying Roberts as less culpable and therefore more credible than Jenkins.

Although not overwhelming, this evidence was certainly sufficient to find Jenkins guilty of murder *if it was credible, if it was not contradicted or impeached by other evidence*, and *if it was found by the jury to have been corroborated by other evidence.* The problem, however, was that Roberts' testimony was not very credible, it could easily have been contradicted and impeached by available evidence, and the jury was never even asked to consider whether Roberts' testimony was corroborated by other evidence.

Roberts first came to the attention of the police shortly after the murder was committed when he told his parents that he had been in the vicinity of Hodges' Grocery Store at the time of the robbery. Roberts' father then called the police. Roberts himself did not call the police; it was his father who called the police. Roberts and his father then went to the police station, where Roberts was questioned. There is no written record or recording regarding what Roberts told the police at this time but, significantly, he was not arrested. This strongly implies that Roberts did not say anything that implicated himself in the robbery at that time.

The following day Roberts was questioned again by the police for several hours, and a tape and a transcript of this questioning was made and is available.[217] Roberts' car was also searched and the gun that was used by Cedric in the robbery was found inside his car. It is clear from the extensive questioning that the police did not believe that Roberts was telling them the truth, and they kept pressuring him to revise his story. As a result of this pressure and continued questioning, Roberts eventually told the police what they wanted to hear. Unfortunately, he put all the blame on Cedric and Jenkins, and none of the blame on Maurice or himself. As noted previously, Maurice is Roberts' half-brother, and Roberts explicitly testified at Jenkins' trial that he had lied to the police "the first couple of times" because he was trying to protect himself **and Maurice.**

---

217   Although a tape and transcript of Roberts' questioning at this time exists, there were times when the recording device was deliberately turned off by the police, and therefore it is impossible to know for sure exactly what occurred at these times.

A few days later, Cedric, Maurice and Jenkins were arrested in Florida, and they were questioned in Florida by Georgia police. Jenkins declined to make any statement, but Cedric and Maurice both made detailed statements that were recorded and transcribed. Cedric and Maurice both admitted that they were involved in the murder and robbery of Mr. Hodges, although they tried to minimize their involvement as much as possible. After obtaining these statements from Cedric and Maurice, the police went back to Roberts and confronted him yet again with numerous inconsistencies in his story. They specifically told Roberts that Marice "has admitted that he was involved in the robbery, so why are you saying that he never went into the store?" Eventually, Roberts changed his story several more times. He finally admitted that he was aware of Cedric's plan to rob Mr. Hodges before it happened, and that Maurice went into the store. He also admitted that he received money from Cedric from the proceeds of the robbery, although he had denied this previously. He also continued to say that Jenkins had admitted to him that he shot Mr. Hodges.[218]

Roberts' admission at trial that he had lied to the police "the first couple of times" he had spoken to them, and that he did this to protect himself and Maurice, was clearly damaging to Roberts' credibility, both the fact that he had lied several times and the fact that he did this to protect his half-brother Maurice. This admission, however, was elicited **by the prosecutor** during Roberts' direct testimony. The reason for doing this, obviously, was to minimize its damaging effect in the minds of the jury. One of the things lawyers are taught both in law school and at continuing legal education programs is how to conduct direct and cross-examination effectively. And one of the key techniques is to minimize any weaknesses

---

218 It is impossible to say whether this was a factor here, but there is substantial scientific, legal, and sociological evidence supporting the idea that criminal defendants, especially young black males, are more susceptible to police suggestion and coercion during prolonged interrogations. *See. e.g.*, Malloy, Shulman and Cauffman, "Interrogations, Confessions, Guilty Pleas Among Serious Adolescent Offenders," 38 *Law and Human Behavior*, pp. 181-93 (2013); Kassin, Drizin, et al., "Police Induced Confessions: Risk Factors and Recommendations," 34 Law and Human Behavior, pp. 3-38 (2009); Kassin, "False Confessions: Causes, Consequences, and Implications for Reform," Annual Review of Law and Social Science, Vol. 4, Issue 4, pp. 249-253 (2008). According to the Innocence Project website, more than 25 percent of wrongful convictions overturned by DNA evidence involve false confessions. One of the most notorious examples of a false confession induced by coercive and suggestive police questioning occurred in New York City in 1964, a few years before I arrived at the Manhattan District Attorney's Office. George Whitmore, Jr., a young black teenager living in Brooklyn was brought in for questioning about an attempted rape. After more than 22 hours of questioning, without a lawyer, he confessed to murdering Janice Wylie (21) and Emily Hoffert (23) in Manhattan in August of 1963 as well as two other crimes. The Wylie-Hoffert murders became front page news in New York as the "career girl murders." Unlike the bungling and incompetent prosecutors in Jenkins' case, Mel Glass, a homicide prosecutor in the Manhattan DA's Office, became very skeptical about Whitmore's confession ("it just didn't seem right") and he undertook his own independent investigation, which eventually concluded that Whitmore was wholly innocent and had been induced into confessing by coercive police tactics. When Glass and his investigators discovered that the actual murderer was Richard Robles, he dismissed the indictment against Whitmore, who had been held in jail for 1,216 days (from April of 1964 until July of 1966). This case was cited by the U.S. Supreme Court in *Miranda v. Arizona*, 384 U.S. 436 (1966), as a notorious example of the dangers of police interrogation (see footnote 24) ("Interrogation procedures may even give rise to a false confession. The most recent conspicuous example occurred in New York, in 1964, when a Negro of limited intelligence confessed to two brutal murders and a rape which he had not committed. When this was discovered, the prosecutor was reported as saying: 'Call it want you want — brainwashing, hypnosis, fright. They made him give an untrue confession. The only thing I don't believe is that Whitmore was beaten.' *N.Y. Times*, Jan 28, 1965, p. 1, col. 5." A dramatic inside account of the Whitmore case was presented by Robert K. Tanenbaum, another homicide prosecutor in the Manhattan DA's Office, in his riveting book, *Echoes of My Soul* (2013). I personally knew both Mr. Glass and Mr. Tanenbaum from my days in the DA's Office, and they were both fine lawyers, honorable men, and staunch defenders of justice.

that your witness may have by drawing this out on direct examination in a way that is least likely to hurt your witness' credibility.

Incredibly and inexplicably, Jenkins' trial lawyers did very little to attack Roberts' credibility on cross-examination. He was the State's **key witness**, yet Jenkins' lawyers were content that he had readily admitted that he had lied on direct examination, and they failed to confront Roberts with the details of his prior inconsistent statements. What they should have done was raise their voice, pound the table, become indignant, and demand to know exactly what lies Roberts had told the police, and why he had told them. And every time Roberts gave an answer to these questions, they should have immediately followed up with even more questions about his lies (and perhaps even more pounding of the table). The goal here was to impress upon the jurors as strongly as possible that Roberts was not a person who could or should be believed or trusted.

What was even more egregious on the part of Jenkins' trial lawyers was that they failed to use the written transcripts of the detailed statements Roberts had given to the police when he was arrested and a few days thereafter. These statements were filled with prior inconsistent statements which clearly showed that Roberts was **consistently and persistently** changing his story in an effort to placate the police. In the hands of a skilled cross-examiner, these statements should have been sufficient to destroy Roberts' credibility in the minds of the jury.[219] At the very least, it should have been sufficient to raise a reasonable doubt regarding whether Roberts was telling the truth this time, or whether he was still trying to protect Maurice.

And, of course, the fact that Judge Harvey erroneously failed to inform the jury that Roberts' testimony needed to be corroborated by other evidence cannot be overlooked. And the details that needed to be corroborated were the specific details that supposedly connected Jenkins to the crime. It was not enough to show that a robbery took place, or that

---

219 As noted previously, Roberts' prior inconsistent statements could have been admitted into evidence as ***substantive evidence*** under Georgia Law and not merely be used to impeach his testimony. See *Gibbons v. Georgia*, 248 Ga. 858 (1982).

two guns were used, or that Jenkins went to Florida and was arrested there in the company of Cedric and Maurice in a motel room where a food stamp which was used at Hodges Store was found. What had to be corroborated was that Jenkins himself had a gun and shot Mr. Hodges. There is absolutely no way of knowing now whether the evidence was sufficient to corroborate Roberts' testimony because the jury was never asked to make this determination.

It should also be emphasized that the gun Jenkins allegedly used (according to Roberts) was previously in the possession of Maurice, who had apparently stolen it from his cousin Roger three weeks earlier. Furthermore, Roberts explicitly testified at Jenkins' trial that he had seen Maurice shooting this gun with Cedric earlier during the day when the robbery occurred. Why would Maurice have given this gun to Jenkins? It made no sense.

It is also worth noting, as Roberts testified, that Maurice "needed money to get out of town" because he had an outstanding arrest warrant. This was probably the reason Cedric and Maurice planned to rob Mr. Hodges — because Maurice needed money to get out of town. Obviously, Maurice had committed at least one prior crime, since there was an outstanding bench warrant for his arrest. Jenkins, on the other hand, had never previously been in any kind trouble with the law. According to all of the statements that had been given to the police by Cedric, Maurice and Roberts, Jenkins was "just walking along the street with his girlfriend" when Cedric told him to "get in the car." It is entirely possible, therefore, perhaps even likely, that Jenkins had no idea where they were going or why they were going there.

Finally, although Jenkins did not testify at his trial, he did testify at the hearing in support of his Motion for a new trial. This was the first and only time that he ever gave his side of the story to anyone other than his lawyers. He testified at the hearing that he was just an innocent bystander at the scene of the robbery, that he never participated in the robbery or the murder, that he never had a gun, that he never shot Mr. Hodges, that he never made any of the incriminating statements that Roberts, Officer Smith and cellmate Ken McCall claimed he had made, and that he never knew that Cedric planned to rob Mr. Hodges. Jenkins was subjected to cross-examination by an assistant district attorney at this hearing which, contrary to the false assertions made by the Georgia Supreme Court, had no significant effect at undermining his credibility.

Jenkins' testimony at the hearing was not available at the trial, of course, but it was part of the record for all subsequent proceedings discussed in this book — the Motion for a new trial before Judge Harvey, the appeal to the Georgia Supreme Court, the Petition for habeas corpus before Judge Nangle, and the truncated appeal to the Eleventh Circuit Court of Appeals. Evidently, and for no apparent reason, none of the judges involved in these proceedings ever considered giving any weight to what Jenkins had testified to, preferring instead to accept the testimony of an admitted accomplice in the robbery who had explicitly conceded that he had lied "several times" in order to protect himself and his half-brother Maurice and who was highly motivated to give false testimony against Jenkins by Mr. Cheney's promise to dismiss the murder charge against him.

Under all of these circumstances, I believe that Roberts' testimony was extremely dubious and highly unreliable, especially when it was being used as the primary evidence to sentence a 19 year-old black man to death or to prison for the rest of his life. If I had been a member of the jury, I certainly would have had a reasonable doubt about whether Jenkins was guilty due to the fact I could not be sure that Roberts was telling the truth. And remember, the prosecution had to prove that Jenkins was guilty **beyond a reasonable doubt**. The inherent unreliability of Roberts' testimony was a prima facie cause for reasonable doubt.

In addition to the testimony of Terry Roberts, there were two other items of evidence that need to be discussed. These were the so-called "admissions" that Jenkins allegedly made to Officer Smith of the Opa-locka,

Florida, Police Department and to Kenneth McCall, a fellow inmate at the Liberty County Jail. Here again, these admissions, if made, would have been sufficient to corroborate Roberts' testimony, and therefore they do provide an explanation why all the judges who have been involved in these proceedings may have been reluctant to grant Jenkins' motion for a new trial. They looked at this evidence superficially and they said, "well, he admitted that he shot Mr. Hodges to three different people, obviously he must be guilty." And then they said, "well, if he is guilty, there is no good reason to reverse his conviction just because a few of his constitutional rights were violated." This is understandable, of course, but also reprehensible.

I have no way of knowing whether Jenkins made these admissions or not. Maybe he did and, if so, maybe he did kill Mr. Hodges. But I have serious doubts that he made the statements.

As mentioned in Chapter 3, beginning in 1970 I worked in the New York County District Attorney's Office for almost five years, including one year in the Criminal Courts Bureau and more than three years in the Homicide Bureau. Although I do not recall this ever happening when I worked with detectives as a member of the Homicide Bureau, there were numerous instances when I suspected that police officers may have been lying when I worked in the Criminal Courts Bureau. This was particularly true with respect to suppression hearings in narcotics cases.[220] It always astounded me that the testimony of the officers always sounded the same, as though they were reading from a script prepared by a Hollywood screenwriter. "I observed the defendant walking down the street and saw him take a glassine packet out of his pocket and throw it on the ground, whereupon I immediately gave chase and apprehended the suspect without ever losing sight of the packet which I thereupon retrieved from the ground and turned over to the police laboratory for analysis." It may have happened this way once, or even twice, but hundreds of times? I don't think so. The

---

220 Pursuant to the Supreme Court's decision in *Mapp v. Ohio*, 367 U.S. 643 (1961), evidence that is illegally seized by the police in violation of the probable cause requirements of the Fourth Amendment may not be used as evidence at trial. The purpose of a pretrial suppression hearing is to determine whether the evidence was properly seized and may be used at trial.

officers were obviously shading their testimony to make it comply with the requirements of establishing probable cause for making an arrest and conducting a search, and thereby avoid having the evidence suppressed and the case dismissed. Believe me, it happens.

While I was working in the District Attorney's Office, Mayor John Lindsay appointed a five-member "Commission to Investigate Alleged Police Corruption" which later became known as the "Knapp Commission" after its Chairman Whitman Knapp. This came about largely as a result of the public revelations of corruption made by Police Officer Frank Serpico and Sergeant David Durk. After a two-year investigation, the Knapp Commission ultimately concluded that there was "systematic corruption" in the New York City Police Department, and it made numerous recommendations for changes.

I do not intend to single out New York City for criticism, but this was where I worked and where corruption was evident to me. I am sure, however, that with a little research, I could find similar problems in many other police departments throughout the country, both in the past and presently. One recent example is the Karen Read murder case where improprieties on the part of the Boston Police, the Canton Police, and the State Police were alleged (and apparently verified). And remember that Michael Horowitz, the Inspector General of the U.S. Department of Justice, concluded that an FBI lawyer intentionally lied in an application that was used to get a FISA warrant against Carter Page. Horowitz also found 17 "basic and fundamental" errors were made by the FBI across four separate warrant applications to the FISA Court

The point of these anecdotes is simply to illustrate that all police officers, like all accomplices, do not always tell the truth. I am sure the vast majority of police officers are honest and truthful, but certainly not all. And sometimes, even good officers find it necessary to put a little varnish on the truth, especially if they think it may be necessary to help their case.

I am not saying that Officer Smith was untruthful when he claimed that Jenkins had told him, "I only shot him once" or when he claimed that Jenkins had made the statement "spontaneously." What I am saying, however, is that there is room for doubt. Jenkins vociferously denied making the statement, and he had steadfastly refused to make any other statements to any other officer at any other time. It was awfully convenient that Jenkins just happened to make this one "spontaneous" statement to Officer Smith, considering that the Georgia police knew that they needed some additional evidence to corroborate Roberts' testimony, or they would not be able to make a case against Jenkins. Furthermore, Officer Smith originally testified on cross-examination that he had told Jenkins "to get his life together" and "tell the truth" **before** Jenkins made the statement. If this was true, then the statement was not really as spontaneous as Officer Smith had first claimed.

The same uncertainty also exists with respect to the testimony of Kenneth McCall, the inmate at the Liberty County Jail, who claimed that Jenkins had told him, "I shot the old cracker twice." **First**, the District Attorney was obviously looking for someone who could corroborate Roberts' testimony, and that is why they affirmatively sought out McCall's testimony.[221] They evidently promised him something in return for his testimony and thereby incentivized him to lie. Indeed, after McCall testified for the State at Jenkins' trial, two additional charges that were pending against him were dismissed by the District Attorney and Mr. Cheney also wrote a "nice letter" on McCall's behalf to the Board of Pardons and Paroles. So, McCall clearly profited from his testimony. Whether that was sufficient motivation to cause him to "shade his testimony" in favor of the prosecution, I cannot say.

Second, at the time that McCall was in the cell with Jenkins, he was also in the same cell with Cedric and Maurice. Roberts explicitly testified

---

221 This is an old prosecutor trick of which I am very familiar from my days in the New York County District Attorney's Office. Always interview the cellmates of defendants for possible incriminating evidence. Of course, the cellmate always expects to get something in return for his testimony. I should also note that sometimes an appropriate cellmate is "planted" by the prosecutor for the specific purpose of attempting to elicit an incriminating statement. I have no way of knowing whether that happened here, but it is possible.

at trial (and stated in his pretrial statements to the police) that Cedric had said, "I shot the old cracker twice." No evidence was ever presented at trial (and none is known to me) that Jenkins ever used this term. It is possible, therefore, that it was **Cedric** and not **Jenkins** who had made this statement to McCall.

Third, the statements that Jenkins allegedly made to Smith and McCall are inconsistent with each another. Smith claimed that Jenkins said, "I only shot him once," but McCall claimed that Jenkins said, "I shot the old cracker twice." One would think that if Jenkins had actually made the statements at issue, he would know exactly how many times he had shot whoever it was he shot.

Fourth, and this is very important, the evidence suggests that it was **Maurice**, not Jenkins, who actually had possession of the second gun. If Jenkins did not even have a gun, why would he be admitting to anybody that he had shot somebody?

And *finally*, it must be remembered that Jenkins explicitly denied under oath that he had a gun, that he shot Mr. Hodges, or that he made these alleged statements to Smith and McCall. He may have been untruthful when he said this, but there is no reason to believe that he was any less truthful than either Smith or McCall, both of whom had good reasons to lie.

When evaluated in this light, the fact that the jury found Jenkins guilty of murder becomes far less compelling than it might otherwise seem. And this becomes even truer when you factor in the numerous significant errors that the various judges and courts failed to consider which obviously tainted the jury's verdict.

Would the jury have found Jenkins guilty if they were properly instructed by Judge Harvey that Roberts was an accomplice in the robbery and therefore his testimony needed to be corroborated by sufficient additional evidence? Nobody knows — this was an issue the jury alone had to decide, and they were never asked to do so.

Would the jury have found Jenkins guilty if Mr. Cheney had not repeatedly and improperly told the jury that Jenkins had failed to testify or provide any evidence which rebutted the State's case? Nobody knows. Only the members of the jury could tell us whether this affected their verdict.

Would the jury have found Jenkins guilty if Investigator Jim Gray had not been permitted to testify about the "silent witnesses" who reportedly implicated Jenkins in the robbery? Here again, nobody knows. Only the jury could tell us.

Would the jury have found Jenkins guilty if his lawyers had permitted him to testify as he requested? Once again, nobody knows. That was a decision that had to be made by the jury, but they were never given the opportunity.

Would the jury have found Jenkins guilty if his lawyers had done a better job impeaching the credibility of Terry Roberts? Nobody knows, but I suspect this would have made it much more difficult for the jury to believe Roberts' testimony.

Finally, would the jury have found Jenkins guilty if his lawyers had not made all the other mistakes and errors described in Jenkins many appeals? Here again, nobody knows, not even the jury.

Obviously, the point I am trying to hammer home here is that it was wrong for Judge Harvey and Judge Nangle and the Geogia Supreme Court and the Eleventh Circuit Court of Appeals to simply presume that Jenkins was guilty merely because he had been found guilty by a jury. The evidence was not nearly as strong as it seemed, and the trial was significantly contaminated by numerous reversible errors. Under these circumstances, it was incumbent on these judges and these courts to scrutinize the evidence more carefully and then critically evaluate whether the many errors that Jerkins complained about could have adversely affected the jury's verdict. They failed to do that, and that is why I failed.

Furthermore, all the judges and courts that considered Jenkins' appeal erroneously refused to consider the **cumulative effect** of the many errors that occurred during his trial. Notably, the Georgia Supreme Court explicitly (and somewhat boastfully) stated during oral argument, and in its written decision, that Georgia "does not recognize the cumulative error doctrine." This was so even though I had strenuously argued to the Court that application of the cumulative error doctrine was constitutionally required by federal law. Later, when Judge Nangle considered Jenkins' habeas petition, he simply parroted the ruling of the Georgia Supreme Court and reiterated the shibboleth, "Georgia does not follow the cumulative error rule." And the Eleventh Circuit never even considered this issue because it was not part of the limited certificate of appealability that has been so parsimoniously granted by Judge Wilson. Accordingly, none of these courts ever really considered whether Jenkins' right to a fair trial had been impermissibly violated by Georgia's failure to apply the cumulative error rule.

Significantly, as previously noted, the Georgia Supreme Court explicitly ruled ***in 2020*** that all its prior decisions regarding the cumulative error doctrine had been ***wrongly decided*** and that, yes, of course, Georgia law requires consideration of the effect of cumulative errors in criminal cases. *State v. Lane*, 308 Ga. 10, 838 S.E.2d 808 (2020). The Court at that time took the highly unusual step of overruling every prior case that had refused to apply the cumulative error rule, including both Jenkins' and Fleming's cases. Thus, the decision of the Georgia Supreme Court which had affirmed Jenkins' conviction in 1997 has now been explicitly overruled by the same Court due to the court's failure to apply the cumulative error doctrine. This is nice to know, but it comes 23 years too late. The fact that the Georgia Supreme Court has now explicitly acknowledged that it wrongfully failed to consider cumulative error claim in 1997 raises, at least in my mind, an irrefutable presumption that Jenkins' murder conviction is invalid and should be reversed

Furthermore, as if more were needed to set Jenkins free, the Georgia Supreme Court has also explicitly abrogated its prior dubious rule that a corroboration charge regarding accomplice testimony need not be given where the State presents "other evidence." *Hamm v. State*, 294 Ga. 781, 756 S.E.2d 507 (2014). That case explicitly overruled *Hall v. State*, 241 Ga. 252, 244 S.E.2d 833 (1978), which was the precedent that the Georgia Supreme Court had relied on in affirming Jenkins' and Fleming's convictions. *Hamm* also explicitly overruled the decisions affirming Jenkins' and Fleming's convictions. *See* 294 Ga. at __ 756 S.E. at 512, notes 5 and 7. As the Georgia Supreme Court explained in *Hamm*, "the mere fact that there is other evidence which could serve as corroboration does not dispense with the need for the requested charge because the jury, as the exclusive judges of credibility, could have rejected the other evidence and convicted solely on the accomplice's testimony." 295 Ga. at ___, 756 S.E.2d at 512 (quoting from Chief Justice Benham's dissent in *Fleming*). That is exactly what I told the Georgia Supreme Court back in 1997. Unfortunately, it took them seventeen years to realize I was right.

To summarize, two of the pivotal arguments that I made on Jenkins' behalf back in 1996 (in the motion for a new trial before Judge Harvey), in 1997 (in the appeal to the Georgia Supreme Court), and in 1998 (in the petition for habeas corpus) — namely, (i) that Judge Harvey failed to charge the jury on the issue of corroboration of accomplice testimony and (ii) that Judge Harvey failed to apply the cumulative error doctrine — have since been determined by the Georgia Supreme Court to have been wrongly decided.

Furthermore, these two errors were not even the worst mistakes that occurred during Jenkins' trial. In my view, the following errors were even more egregious: (i) allowing Investigator Gray to testify, based upon hearsay conversations he had with unidentified "silent witnesses," that he had concluded that Jenkins was one the perpetrators who robbed and murdered Mr. Hodges; (ii) allowing Jenkins' attorneys to falsely tell him that the trial was "going well" and there was "no need" for him to testify; (iii) allowing District Attorney Cheney to point out to the jury during summation that Jenkins had failed to testify and had failed to present any evidence which rebutted the State's case; (iv) concluding that the failure of

Jenkins' attorneys to impeach Terry Roberts with his prior inconsistent statements constituted reasonable professional conduct, (v) allowing Keith Moran to testify that the murder charge against Terry Roberts was dismissed because there was no evidence that he was aware of any plan to kill Mr. Hedges before it happened and (vi) Judge Harvey's failure to inform the jury when Jenkins would become eligible for parole if they sentenced him to life imprisonment.

Furthermore, as previously noted, Jenkins was sentenced to life imprisonment without possibility of parole in 1995, and he has now served more than thirty years in prison. And yet, in 2013 (in *Moore v. State*, 293 Ga. 705, 749 S.E.2d 660) and in 2016 (in *Veal v. State*, 298 Ga. 691, 784 S.E.2d 403), the Georgia Supreme Court ruled that such a sentence is unlawful and void.

Was Jenkins guilty of murdering Mr. Hodges? Frankly, I do not know. But I know for certain that he did not get a fair trial, nor a fair appeal. I also know for certain that there was significant evidence indicating that Jenkins was actually innocent. And I also know for certain that the sentence the court imposed on Jamel in 1995 is now unlawful and void.

So, why did I fail? Frankly, I don't know, but the reason I wrote this book was to try to accomplish with the written word what I was unable to accomplish with my lawyering skills: justice for Jamel.

Ladies and gentlemen, you have now heard all the evidence. You have also heard me discuss the applicable law. What do you think?

Is Jamel guilty?

Did he receive a fair trial?

Should he remain in prison?

CHAPTER 20

WHAT HAPPENED TO JENKINS' ALLEGED CO-CONSPIRATORS?

Jenkins was arrested in Opa-locka, Florida, on October 12, 1993, and charged with the robbery and murder of Bobby Hodges. At that time, he was only 17 years old. Following the trial that has been extensively discussed in this book, he was sentenced on September 2, 1995, to life imprisonment without possibility of parole. He was also sentenced to serve an additional *consecutive* term of life imprisonment on the robbery charge. He has been incarcerated in Georgia since 1993 and is currently being held at the Augusta Transition Center, a minimum-security facility in Augusta, Georgia. Barring some unforeseen circumstance, he will remain incarcerated for the remainder of his natural life.

Four other individuals — all young black males — were also arrested and indicted for the robbery and murder of Mr. Hodges. These four individuals were Cedric Lewis Brown, Shawn Jarrod Brown, Maurice Fleming, and Terry Tyrell Roberts.

Cedric Brown

Cedric was 19 years old at the time of the robbery, and he was determined to be "mentally retarded." Because of this mental disability, he was not eligible to receive the death penalty. On August 17, 1994, he pleaded guilty to murder and armed robbery, and he was sentenced to two consecutive terms of life imprisonment. He is currently being held at Wilcox State Prison in Abbeville, Georgia. He will, at some point, become eligible for parole.

Maurice Fleming

Maurice was also 19 years old at the time of the robbery. After a change of venue, he was tried before a jury (and Judge Harvey) in Screven County, Georgia, and found guilty of felony murder and armed robbery on June 21, 1996. The jury imposed a sentence of life imprisonment with the possibility of parole on June 22, 1996.

The principal witness against Fleming at trial was his half-brother Terry Roberts, the same person who testified against Jenkins at his trial. Notably, Fleming was not convicted of malice murder. Like Jenkins, Fleming faced three sentencing options (death, life without possibility of parole, or life with a possibility of parole). The jury returned a sentence of life imprisonment with a possibility of parole. Since Fleming was not convicted of malice murder, the trial judge, as required by Georgia law, merged the armed robbery charge into the felony murder conviction.

Like Jenkins, Fleming filed a motion for a new trial on July 22, 1996, asserting that numerous errors had occurred during his trial. This motion was amended on March 26, 1997, and denied by Judge Harvey on June 10, 1997. The denial of the motion was affirmed by the Georgia Supreme Court on March 16, 1998. *Fleming v. State*, 269 Ga. 245, 497 S.E.2d 211 (1998).

For the reasons discussed previously, Fleming's conviction has been overruled **twice** by the Georgia Supreme Court. First, in *Hamm v. State*, 294 Ga. 781, 756 S.E.2d 507 (2014), for failure to properly apply the accomplice corroboration rule and, second, in *State v. Lane*, 308 Ga. 10, 838 S.E.2d 808 (2020), for failure to properly apply the cumulative error doctrine. Despite these developments, Maurice also remains incarcerated. Although eligible for parole, he has never been granted parole. He remains incarcerated at Telfair State Prison in Helena, Georgia.

Shawn Brown

Shawn Brown was only 16 years old at the time of the robbery. Due to his age, he was not eligible to receive the death penalty. He pleaded guilty to armed robbery and murder on April 27, 1993, and was sentenced to imprisonment for a term of twenty years. According to the inmate records database of the Georgia Department of Corrections, he was convicted of an additional unspecified crime and sentenced to an additional term of five years. Thereafter, he was either released or paroled on August 3, 2022.

Terry Roberts

Terry Roberts was 21 years old at the time of the robbery. Roberts was originally charged with both the murder and the armed robbery of Mr. Hodges, but the murder charge was reportedly dismissed by District Attorney Cheney prior to Roberts' testimony against Jenkins. Although the murder charge was dismissed, Roberts continued to be charged with armed robbery, as he should have, since he admitted under oath that he participated in the robbery.

In addition to testifying against Jenkins, Roberts was also the State's principal witness in the trial against his half-brother Maurice Fleming, which occurred in June of 1996. As noted above, Fleming was convicted by the jury of armed robbery and felony murder on June 21, 1996, and sentenced by the jury to life imprisonment with the possibility of parole.

There is no indication in any publicly available records that Roberts was ever incarcerated in state prison for the robbery.[222] According to the Clerk's Office of the Liberty County Superior Court, Roberts pleaded guilty to armed robbery on October 30, 1996, and was sentenced to a term of fifteen years, with ten years of the sentence to be served in prison followed by five years of probation.[223] Obviously, if Roberts was sentenced to ten years of imprisonment, that sentence would have had to be served in a Georgia State Prison. However, according to the Georgia Department of Corrections, Roberts was never incarcerated in any Georgia state prison.

---

[222] After his arrest in October of 1993, Roberts was probably held at the Liberty County Jail. Since he was cooperating with the District Attorney's Office, he was probably granted parole.

[223] I personally spoke with the Court Clerk's Office on June 11, 2025, and obtained this information. To the best of my knowledge, there is no publicly available database which contains this information.

Furthermore, according to the Liberty County Clerk's Office, Roberts was never indicted for the murder of Mr. Hodges, only for the robbery. However, an ***arrest warrant*** was issued for Roberts for the murder of Mr. Hodges on December 13, 1993 (1993 R 6876). Notably, this was the very same date that Jenkins, Fleming, Cedric Brown and Shawn Brown were indicted for Hodges' murder.

Apparently, District Attorney Cheney did not want to have a murder indictment pending against the State's star witness, but he also did not want Roberts to believe that he was no longer subject to prosecution for the murder charge. Accordingly, Cheney procured the issuance of an arrest warrant for murder against Roberts in order to insure that Roberts testified favorably for the State in the cases against Jenkins and Fleming. Significantly, this arrest warrant was not dismissed until ***July 20, 1996***, which was exactly one month after Roberts completed his testimony against Fleming.

This new information casts further doubt on the veracity of the testimony of Deputy Keith Moran and the clear impropriety of the conduct of District Attorney Cheney. It will be remembered from prior discussions that Moran testified at Jenkins' trial that the murder charge against Terry Roberts was "dismissed" because "the results of Moran's investigation did not uncover any evidence that Roberts knew about any plan to kill Mr. Hodges before it occurred." This testimony was false and misleading for the reasons previously discussed in this text. However, it now appears to be false for the additional reason that the murder charge against Roberts was not actually dismissed until July 20, 1996, which was more than ten months after Roberts and Moran testified at Jenkins' trial. Obviously, Deputy Moran and District Attorney Cheney knew about the existence of this arrest warrant against Roberts for murder at the time when both Roberts and Moran testified at Jenkins' trial and therefore, ***ipso facto***, Moran's testimony was false. Despite what Moran had stated under oath in his testimony, the murder charge against Roberts was not actually dismissed until July 20, 1996.

Finally, according to information which I received from the Clerk's Office of the Liberty County Probate Court, Terry Roberts died on February 16, 2005. My understanding (based upon Roberts' testimony at Jenkins' trial) (see Tr. at 1654) is that he suffered from a debilitating neurological disease, and that he eventually died from this illness. I do not know whether Roberts ever served any time in jail following his testimony against Fleming in June of 1996.

APPENDIX A

LIST OF THE CASES AND PROCEEDINGS FILED ON BEHALF OF MR. JENKINS

1. Motion for a New Trial before Judge Harvey (Denied May 9, 1997) *State v. Jenkins*, Liberty County Superior Court, Georgia (unreported) Judge Harvey's Decision is reprinted in Appendix B

2. Appeal to the Georgia Supreme Court (Denied October 6, 1997) *Jenkins v. State*, 268 Ga. 468, 491 S.E 2d 54 (1997)

3. Petition for Certiorari to the United States Supreme Court (Denied March 23, 1998) *Jenkins v. Georgia*, 523 U.S.1029, 118 S. Ct. 1318, 140 L.Ed.2d 481 (1998)

4. Petition for Habeas Corpus, Southern District of Georgia (Denied June 21, 2000)
Jenkins v. Bird, 103 F. Supp.2d 1350 (S.D. Ga. 2000)

5. Appeal to the Eleventh Circuit U.S. Court of Appeals (Denied August 10, 2001)
Jenkins v. Bird, 273 F.3d 397 (11th Cir. 2001) (*per curiam* unpublished decision)
The Eleventh Circuit's Decision is reprinted in Appendix C

6. Petition for Rehearing or Rehearing *En Banc* (Denied December 27, 2001)
Jenkins v. Bird, ___ F.3d ___ (11th Cir. 2001) (*per curiam*)

7. Petition for Certiorari to the United States Supreme Court (Denied May 28, 2002)

Jenkins v. Georgia, 535 U.S. 1104, 122 S. Ct. 2309, 152 L.Ed.2d 1064 (2002)

8. Complaint for Declaratory Judgment, Eastern District of N.Y. (Dismissed June 9, 2003)

   Jenkins v. United States, 01-CV-1545 (NGG) (EDNY) (2003) (unreported)

   Judge Garaufis' Decision is reprinted in Appendix D

9. Appeal to the Second Circuit U.S. Court of Appeals (Denied October 15, 2004)

   Jenkins v. United States, 386 U.S. F.3d 415 (2004)

APPENDIX B

DECISION OF JUDGE HARVEY DENYING JENKINS' MOTION FOR A NEW TRIAL

IN THE SUPERIOR COURT OF LIBERTY COUNTY
STATE OF GEORGIA

STATE OF GEORGIA

VS.

CLEVON J. JENKINS

CASE NUMBER
93-R-6877

ORDER

The defendant, Jamel Jenkins, was tried before a Liberty County jury and convicted of the malice murder and armed robbery of Mr. Bobby Hodges. The jury sentenced the defendant to serve a life sentence without the possibility of parole. On September 20, 1996, the defendant filed a motion for a new trial alleging the general grounds[224] and eighteen additional enumerations of error. On March 6, 1997, the defendant filed an amended motion for a new trial alleging his trial counsel was ineffective. On March 14, 1997, an evidentiary hearing was held to address the issue of ineffective assistance of defendant's counsel.

---

224 By "the general grounds," Judge Harvey means that defendant was arguing that the jury's verdict was unsupported by the evidence and/or that the evidence was so weak or conflicting that the verdict is unjust or unfair. See OCGA §§ 5-5-20 and 5-5-21. (Footnote added by author).

FINDINGS OF FACT ON THE ISSUE OF INEFFECTIVE ASSISTANCE OF COUNSEL

At the motion for a new trial hearing, the defendant Jamel Jenkins testified that he was present at the scene of the murder and armed robbery at Hodges' Grocery along with Cedric Brown, Shawn Brown and Maurice Fleming. (Tr. 4-16).[225] Jenkins stated Cedric Brown fired the fatal shot and he only saw one gun. (Tr. 5). He also testified that he was unaware of any plan to rob or murder Mr. Hodges. (Tr. 6). Jenkins stated he did not have a gun and he was outside the door when Mr. Hodges was shot. (Tr. 4-6). Jenkins testified he told his trial counsel, David Walker and Hal Peel, this version of the robbery and murder and they advised him not to testify. (Tr. 6 and 7). The physical evidence presented at trial showed that two pistols were fired in Hodges' Grocery (Trial Tr. 1582-1583, 1602-1605, 1610-1613, 1818, 1865-1872). No evidence was presented at the motion for a new trial hearing which showed that Jenkins' counsel forced or coerced him not to testify. Furthermore, at trial, Jenkins was questioned by the Court as to whether he wished to testify or remain silent. (Trial Tr. at 1877). Jenkins replied that he decided not to testify. (Trial Tr. at 1877).

At trial, Jenkins was represented by Attorneys David Walker and Hal Peel. Mr. Walker has fourteen years of trial experience, seven years of which he served as an Assistant District Attorney. (Tr. 24). Mr. Peel has eight years of trial experience and has tried at least seven murder cases. (Tr. 43, 44). Mr. Walker and Mr. Peel spent over a year preparing for trial. (Tr. 39). The preparation included reviewing the state's discovery, interviewing witnesses and conferring with a private investigator. (Tr. 47). Mr. Walker and Mr. Peel also met with Jenkins and discussed whether or not he should take the stand or remain silent. (Tr. 37, 38, 44, 45, 25, 26, 18, 19). The ultimate decision to remain silent was made by Jenkins. (Trial Tr. 1877). After speaking with Jenkins, Mr. Walker and Mr. Peel advised him not to take the stand because the information he had would not help their case, and they

---

[225] "Tr." refers to the transcript of the hearing held on March 14, 1997. (Footnote added by author).

believed Jenkins would hurt their case if cross-examined by the prosecutor. (Tr. 37, 38, 44, 45, 25, 26, 18, 19).

Trial counsel's theory of the case was that Jenkins was merely present at the scene of the crime and that the principal wrongdoers were co-defendants Maurice Fleming and Cedric Brown. (Tr. 25, 34, 45).

At trial, defendant's trial counsel did not request a charge regarding corroboration of an accomplice's testimony. However, trial counsel did reserve exceptions to the Court's instructions (Tr. 20).

The District Attorney Dupont Cheney testified that there was no offer of leniency made to the State's witness Kenneth McCall prior to his testimony at trial. (Tr. 71). At trial, Assistant District Attorney Charles Howard testified that prior to trial, he handled a guilty plea entered by McCall, however at that time, he was unaware McCall had any information regarding Jenkins' case. The Court finds that no deal or offer of leniency was made to McCall prior to trial.

CONCLUSIONS OF LAW REGARDING INEFFECTIVE ASSISTANCE OF COUNSEL

To establish a claim of ineffective assistance of counsel, a defendant must show that counsel's performance was deficient and that the deficient performance prejudiced the defendant. Strickland v. Washington, 466 U.S. 558, 687 (104 SC 2052) (80 LE2d 674) (1984). When a defendant challenges a conviction, the question is whether there is a reasonable probability that, absent the errors, the fact finder would have had a reasonable doubt respecting guilt. Id. at 695. Furthermore, "there is a strong presumption that counsel's conduct falls within the wide range of reasonable professional conduct, and that all significant decisions were made in the exercise of reasonable professional judgment," Brown v. State, 257 Ga. 277, 278 (357 SE.2d 590) (1987). With these principals (sic) in mind, none of the defendant's alleged errors by his trial counsel are cause for a new trial.

The evidence of Jenkins' guilt was substantial and Terry Roberts' testimony was corroborated, therefore any error caused by trial counsel's failure to request a charge regarding corroboration of an accomplice's testimony is not grounds for a new trial.[226]

The fact the trial court did not instruct the jury as to corroboration of an accomplice's testimony is not grounds for a new trial since trial counsel failed to make a written request for this charge.[227] Thorton v. State, 264 Ga. 563, 578 (23i) (sic) (449 SE 2d 98) (1994), Hall v. State, 163 Ga. App. 515, 516 (295 SE2d 194) (1983), Workman v. State, 137 Ga. App. 746, 747 (224 SE.2d 757) (1976). Because the State did not rely wholly on the testimony of the accomplice Terry Roberts, the Court was not required to give this charge absent a written request by trial counsel. Smith v. Lane, 154 Ga. App. 741, 742 (270 SE2d 5) (1980), McDaniel v. State, 158 Ga. App. 320 (279 SE2d 762) (1981). Furthermore, the Court finds any error in the omission of this charge was harmless in light of the State's evidence at trial and the testimony that Jenkins admitted to two witnesses he shot the victim. He, along with two co-defendants fled to the State of Florida and the three were arrested in a motel room. A food stamp traced back to Hodges Grocery was found in this motel room. (Trial Tr. 1777-1781, 1843-1845, 1774-1781, 1806-1811, 1829-1831, 1834-1840). Jenkins' admissions and the circumstances surrounding his arrest were established by the State apart from the testimony of the accomplice and corroborated the accomplice's testimony. See generally Bowley v. State, 261 Ga. 278, 281 (404 SE2d 97) (1991).

The question now turns to whether this omission by trial counsel amounted to deficient performance, and whether this deficiency prejudiced

---

226 Judge Harvey's use of the adjective "substantial" in this subtitle is perplexing, since surely he knew that "substantial evidence" is insufficient to convict anyone of a minor crime, let alone murder. A more appropriate adjective would have been "overwhelming," but I guess even Judge Harvey knew that the evidence here was not overwhelming. (Footnote added by author).

227 This sentence implies that the court's failure to give a corroboration charge would have been grounds for a new trial *if* Jenkins' counsel had made a written request for such a charge. Notably, counsel's failure to request such a charge was one of the reasons Jenkins claimed his counsel was ineffective. (Footnote added by author).

the defendant. Strictland v. Washington, 446 U.S. 668, 687 (104 SC 2052) (80 LE2d 674) (1984). Present Georgia law exempts the defendant through his attorney in criminal cases from the strict requirements imposed on litigants in civil cases to preserve an issue on the giving or the failure to give instructions to the jury. This does not relieve defendant through counsel from the necessity of requesting instructions except in those circumstances where the omission is clearly harmful and erroneous as a matter of law in that it fails to provide the jury with the proper guidelines for determining guilt or innocence. Jefferson v. State, 191 Ga. App. 306, 307 (381 SE2d 564) (1989). Before the Court would be authorized to grant Jenkins' motion for a new trial, the defense must carry the burden of satisfying both prongs of the two-part test set forth in Strickland at 687. Bowley v. State, 261 Ga. 678, 280 (404 SE2d 97) (1991).

There was substantial evidence of Jenkins' guilt, and Terry Roberts' testimony was corroborated, therefore the defense has not met the second prong of the Strickland test by showing prejudice. "Where a defendant raises an ineffective assistance of counsel claim based on counsel's failure to except to a certain charge or to preserve the right to do so on appeal, the defendant must show that the charges in question were erroneous, and if proper charges had been given, there is a reasonable probability that the result to the trial would have been different." Peavy v. State, 262 Ga. 782, 783 (425 SE2d 654) (1993), Wadley v. State, 258 Ga. 465, 466 (369 SE2d 734) (1988). In light of the State's evidence and the fact that Terry Roberts' testimony was corroborated, there has not been a sufficient showing of prejudice. Terry Roberts testified that Jamel Jenkins was a part of the planning and execution of the robbery and murder at Hodges Grocery. He also testified that Jenkins ran from Hodges Grocery with a chrome .25 caliber pistol in his waistband and stated "Yeah, yeah, yeah, I got him, bang, bang." (Trial Tr. 1669-1670).[228] After the robbery and murder, Roberts, Jenkins, Cedric Brown, Shawn Brown and Maurice Fleming went to a motel and

---

228 Roberts also testified that he lied to the police "the first couple of times I spoke to them" in order to protect himself and his half-brother Maurice. (Footnote added by author).

divided the proceeds of the robbery. (Trial Tr. 1673). Roberts then drove to the bus station in Savannah, Georgia, where Fleming, Jenkins and Cedric Brown boarded a bus bound for Miami, Florida. (Trial Tr. 1673). Roberts' testimony was corroborated by other witnesses and the physical evidence gathered at the crime scene.

1. Detective (sic) James Smith testified that Jenkins stated, "I only shot him once" and expressed concern about the electric chair. (Trial Tr. 1780). This occurred in Miami shortly after Jenkins' arrest. (Trial Tr. 1780).

2. Kenneth McCall, Jenkins' cellmate at the Liberty County Jail, testified Jenkins bragged about killing Mr. Hodges, and receiving proceeds from the robbery. (Trial Tr. 1844).

3. A ballistics expert confirmed Roberts' testimony that two .25 caliber pistols were used, and Roberts led Chief Deputy Moran to one of those pistols which was left in his car.[229] (Trial Tr. 1866, 1867, 1818).

4. Roberts testified that Maurice Fleming provided Jenkins with a chrome pearl handled .25 caliber pistol.[230] (Trial Tr. 1670-1673). Maurice's cousin, Roger Fleming, testified that his Lorcin .25 caliber chrome, pearl handled pistol was missing after Maurice visited his house. (Trial Tr. 1738-1740). A ballistics expert confirmed that a Lorcin .25 caliber pistol fired at least one bullet and one casing found at Hodges Grocery. (Trial Tr. 1866-1867).

5. Roberts testified that Jenkins and Cedric drank a one-quart bottle of Magnum beer moments before the robbery while parked on Jones

---

229 Deputy Moran did **not** testify that Roberts "led [him] to one of these pistols which was left in his car." What Deputy Moran testified was that "a search was made" [of Roberts' car] and a pistol was found "under the front passenger seat of Terry's car." (Trial Tr. 1818). The implication that Roberts **led** Deputy Moran to the pistol was false. (Footnote added by author).

230 This is inaccurate and misleading. What Roberts said was that "about a week or two before the incident, the Hodges incident . . . Maurice gave it (the chrome-plated pistol) to Jamel when they were shooting at the cans." (Trial Tr. 1671). At that time, Roberts "took it [the gun] in the house and I handed it back to Maurice." (Trial Tr. 1671). Roberts "did not see that gun anymore from that day until the day of the robbery." (Trial Tr. 1671). Although Roberts testified that he saw Jenkins with the gun on the day of the robbery (Trial Tr. 1671), he did not explain how Jenkins obtained the gun, and he certainly did not say that Maurice provided the gun to Jenkins. (Footnote added by author).

Road. (Trial Tr. 1662). Investigator Jim Gray recovered the bottle on Jones Road.[231] (Trial Tr. 1732).

6. Roberts testified that the proceeds of the robbery consisted partly of food stamps. (Trial Tr. 1668). He also testified that after the robbery, he drove Jenkins, Fleming and Cedric Brown to the bus station in Savannah where they boarded a bus bound for Miami. Agent Bart Ingram and Detective James Smith testified that they arrested Jenkins, Fleming and Cedric Brown at a motel in Opa-Locka, Florida, which is a few miles from Miami. (Trial Tr. 1774-1781, 1742-1758). A food stamp was found in the motel room which was traced back to Carolyn Roberts, a resident of Riceboro, Georgia, who shops at Hodges Grocery.[232] (Trial Tr. 1806-1811, 1829-1831, 1834-1840). The fact that Jenkins fled to Florida with Cedric Brown and Fleming and proceeds from the robbery were found in his motel room corroborate Roberts' testimony.[233] Parkerson v State, 265 Ga. 438, 439 (457 SE2d 667) (1995), Bradford v. State, 262 Ga. 512, 513 (421 SE2d 523) (1992).

7. Finally, Roberts testified that Shawn Brown acted as a lookout moments before the robbery while Cedric Brown, Jenkins and Fleming waited near Roberts' car. (Trial Tr. 1665-1667). Shawn stated there were three people in the store. (Trial Tr. 1666).[234] The testimony of Dewayne Paulk confirmed that three people were in the store at that time: himself, his grandfather and Mr. Hodges. (Trial Tr. 1703-1709). He also testified he saw Shawn Brown in the store at this time. (Trial Tr. 1703-1709).

---

231 Curiously, no evidence was ever presented at trial regarding whether this bottle had ever been tested for fingerprints. (Footnote added by author).
232 This appears to be some type of Freudian slip. The witness' name was actually Carolyn Young, not Carolyn Roberts. (Footnote added by author).
233 The fact that a food stamp was found in a Florida hotel room were Cedric, Fleming and Jenkins were arrested only corroborates Roberts' testimony that food stamps were taken in the robbery and that Cedric, Fleming and Jenkens went to Florida. It does not corroborate Roberts' testimony that Jenkins **participated** in the murder and robbery, which was the key part of Roberts' testimony that needed to be corroborated. (Footnote added by author).
234 Shawn did not testify at the trial. The transcript page cited by Judge Harvey refers to the testimony of Terry Roberts, who claimed that Shawn had told him that there were three people in the store. Obviously, this was improper hearsay. (Footnote added by author).

Given the substantial amount of evidence indicating Jenkins' guilt, there is a reasonable probability that the jury would have found Jenkins guilty even if the Court had instructed the jury on corroboration of an accomplice's testimony.[235] Jamel Jenkins admitted to Terry Roberts, Detective James Smith and Kenneth McCall that he shot Bobby Hodges.[236] His accomplice Terry Roberts testified about Jenkins' participation throughout the planning and execution of the crime. Finally, Jenkins was arrested at a motel in Opa-Locka, Florida, with Fleming and Cedric Brown and proceeds of the robbery were found in their motel room. This Court concludes from the overwhelming evidence of guilt, excepting therefrom the testimony of Terry Roberts, there is no reasonable probability that a jury charge regarding corroboration of the accomplice's testimony would have created a reasonable doubt as to Jenkins' guilt. The Court further concludes that the omission to instruct the jury on the necessity of corroboration of an accomplice's testimony was erroneous but not clearly harmful as a matter of law and the jury instructions as given were sufficient for a proper determination of Jenkins' guilt or innocence and counsel's failure to request a charge that an accomplice's testimony must be corroborated does not amount to ineffective assistance of counsel.

Defendant's trial counsel's failure to object to testimony regarding a silent witness report did not amount to ineffective assistance of counsel.

At trial, Investigator Jim Gray testified that he received a silent witness report, however, the content of this report was not published to the jury. The defendant alleges this was improper hearsay, however, the content of the report was not a part of Gray's testimony. (Trial Tr. 1726). Because the content of the report was not divulged, there was no grounds for a hearsay objection, thus trial counsel's failure to object does not amount to

---

235 This is not the correct standard for application of the "harmless" error doctrine. The correct standard is that it must be established *"beyond a reasonable doubt"* that the error did not affect the outcome of the trial. *Chapman v. California*, 386 U.S. 18 (1967). (Footnote added by author).

236 Jenkins did not admit to Smith and McCall that he had shot Bobby Hodges. What he allegedly admitted was that he had shot some unspecified person. (Footnote added by author).

deficient performance. Strictland v. Washington, 446 U.S. 668, 687 (104 SC 2052) (80 LE2d 674) (1984).

The Court concludes further that there is no reasonable probability an objection to this testimony would have created a reasonable doubt in the minds of the jury. Id. at 687.

Defendant's trial counsel's failure to object to Jim Gray's testimony regarding his investigation did not amount to ineffective assistance of counsel.

Jim Gray's testimony regarding information he received which resulted in Jenkins' arrest was admissible pursuant to O.C.G.A. § 24-3-2 and Ivestor v State, 252 Ga. 333, 334, 335 (313 SE2d 674) (1984). Because this testimony was admissible there is no deficiency in trial counsel's performance, and the defendant has not carried the burden required by the first prong of the Strickland test. Strictland v. Washington, 446 U.S. 668, 687 (104 SC 2052) (80 LE2d 674) (1984). Any error in the admission of this evidence was harmless since Gray's testimony was cumulative of the testimony of other witnesses. Teague v. State, 252 Ga. 534, 535 (314 SE2d 910) (1984).

The Court further finds there is no reasonable probability any error on trial counsel's part in not objecting to this testimony prevented the jury from finding a reasonable doubt as to Jenkins' guilt. Strickland at 687.

Defendant's trial counsel's failure to object to Bart Ingram's testimony did not amount to ineffective assistance of counsel.

Agent Bart Ingram's testimony regarding the circumstances surrounding Jenkins' arrest in Florida was relevant and admissible. (Trial Tr. 1743-1768). DeCastro v. State, 221 Ga. App. 83, 85 (470 SE2d 748) (1996). Therefore, counsel's failure to object to admissible evidence does not amount to deficient performance. Strickland at 687.

The Court further finds there is no reasonable probability this failure to object caused prejudice to the defendant. Strickland at 687.

Trial counsel's failure to object to testimony that Maurice Fleming and Cedric Brown had bench warrants against them does not amount to ineffective assistance of counsel.

The State's evidence showed that Cedric Brown and Maurice Fleming had pending bench warrants and needed money to flee the Liberty County area.[237] (Trial Tr. 1658). This evidence was admissible and relevant to show the motive behind the murder and armed robbery.[238] Johnson v. State, 260 Ga. 457, 458, (396 SE2d 888) (1990). Because this evidence was admissible, counsel's failure to object does not amount to deficient performance thus the first prong of the Strickland Test has not been met. Furthermore, defendant's trial counsel's theory of the case that Cedric Brown and Maurice Fleming were the principal actors during the crime is furthered by a showing that they had prior criminal dealings. (Tr. 25, 34, 45). A strategical decision to allow the introduction of this evidence cannot form the basis for a claim of ineffective assistance of counsel. Van Alstine v. State, 263 Ga. 1 (426 SE2d 360) (1993).

Although there was evidence that Cedric Brown and Maurice Fleming had pending bench warrants, no mention was made of any criminal record of Jenkins. Thus, even if trial counsel's performance was deficient, there has been no showing of prejudice to the defendant. Strictland v. Washington, 446 U.S. 668, 687 (104 SC 2052) (80 LE2d 674) (1984).

Trial counsel's failure to object to leading questions did not amount to deficient performance, nor did the use of leading questions prejudice defendant.

---

237 This was incorrect. The evidence showed that **Maurice Fleming** had an outstanding bench warrant and needed money to get out of town. (Trial Tr. 1659, testimony of Terry Roberts). The evidence also showed that **Shawn Brown** had been arrested at school on the same day as the robbery. (Trial Tr. 1660, testimony of Terry Roberts). There was no evidence, however, that **Cedric Brown** had been arrested, or that he had an outstanding bench warrant. (Footnote added by author).

238 This evidence was ***not*** admissible at Jenkins' trial on this basis. It might have been admissible at Maurice Fleming's trial since it showed that Maurice had a motive to commit the robbery. However, it did not show that Jenkins had a motive to commit the robbery, and therefore it was not admissible ***against Jenkins*** on this basis. (Footnote added by author).

Trial counsel did not object to leading questions because most were designed to elicit basic information and because frequent objections could cause the jury to believe the defense was trying to hide information. (Tr. 29, 30, 50). If the prosecutor asked a leading question harmful to the defense's case, trial counsel would object. (Tr. 50). This strategic decision by trial counsel does not lead to a conclusion that their performance was deficient, and falls within the wide range of professional conduct. Brown v. State, 257 Ga. 277, 278 (357 SE2d 590) (1987).

There has been no showing of prejudice and there is no reasonable probability that the jury's verdict was influenced by the use of leading questions. Strictland v. Washington, 446 U.S. 668, 687 (104 SC 2052) (80 LE2d 674) (1984).

Trial counsel's decision not to object to the testimony of Keith Moran does not support a claim of ineffective assistance of counsel.

Defendant claims that his trial counsel was ineffective since they did not object to Keith Moran's testimony regarding the dismissal of the murder warrant against Terry Roberts. The defendant contends Moran misrepresented to the jury that the State could not charge Roberts with murder. A review of the record reveals Moran found no indication that Roberts knew Cedric Brown, Fleming and Jenkins had planned to murder Bobby Hodges, and that the decision to dismiss the warrant had been made by the District Attorney's office. (Trial Tr. 1840-1841). At no point did Moran state Roberts could not be legally charged with murder. (Trial Tr. 1840-1841). Furthermore, this testimony was a legitimate response to trial counsel's strategy to show that the only reason the murder charge against Roberts was dismissed was in exchange for his testimony. (Trial Tr. 1686-1688, 1698-1700). Since Roberts' credibility had been attacked, it was proper for the State to show other mitigating circumstances which led to the dismissal of the murder warrant against Roberts.[239]

Moran's testimony was not deceptive in regard to law, therefore, trial counsel's failure to object did not amount to deficient performance. Strickland at 687. Furthermore, there is no reasonable probability this testimony affected the jury's verdict, and thus no showing of prejudice. Strickland at 687.

There was no error in the court's ruling on an evidentiary issue thus there was no reason for trial counsel to object.

During Terry Roberts' testimony, a hearsay objection was made by trial counsel. (Trial Tr. 1667). The Assistant District Attorney stated that "it's admissible as an exception to the hearsay rule on the - that exception which allows a statement of a co-conspirator." The Court replied, "It's hearsay, but it's an exception, your objection is noted, but it's overruled." (Trial Tr. 1667). During this exchange, the Court did not state that a conspiracy existed, but merely ruled on a point of law. Assuming arguendo this statement was prejudicial, it was cured by the Court's instruction that the State must prove the existence of a conspiracy beyond a reasonable doubt. (Trial Tr. 1982, 1983). It was further cured by the Court's instruction that "anything I did or said during the trial of this case was not intended to and does not in any way hint or suggest to you jurors what your verdict should be." (Trial Tr. 1989). (The Court did at a later point in the trial rule that a prima facie case of a conspiracy existed, however this was done outside the jury's presence). (Trial Tr. 1878, 1881).

The Court did not state that a conspiracy had been proven, thus there was no reason for trial counsel to object, and no deficiency in their performance. Strictland v. Washington, 446 U.S. 668, 687 (104 SC 2052) (80 LE2d 674) (1984). Furthermore, the instructions given by the Court

---

239 The only reason the murder charge against Roberts was dismissed **was** in exchange for his testimony, and the fact that Roberts was not aware of any plan to murder Mr. Hodges before it happened was not, in any way, a "mitigating circumstance" to felony murder, so these excuses by Judge Harvey were not very well thought out. (Footnote added by author).

prevented any prejudice to the defendant. Strictland v. Washington, 446 U.S. 668, 687 (104 SC 2052) (80 LE2d 674) (1984).

There was no reason for trial counsel to object to the Court's finding a prima facie case that a conspiracy existed, therefore counsel's performance was not deficient

As set forth in the rationale above, the Court did not err in finding a prima facie case that a conspiracy existed, thus trial counsel's performance was not deficient in not objecting. Strictland v. Washington, 446 U.S. 668, 687 (104 SC 2052) (80 LE2d 674) (1984).

The Court further finds that any error on trial counsel's part did not prejudice the defendant. Id. at 687.

Defendant's trial counsel did not err in failing to object to nor in failing to request different instructions regarding the issues of malice, parties to a crime and conspiracy.

Failure to object to proper instruction does not amount to ineffective assistance of counsel. Hayes v. State, 262 Ga. 881, 882, 883 (426 SE2d 886) (1993). These instructions were proper and thus trial counsel's failure to request different instructions cannot form the basis for a claim of ineffective assistance of counsel. Id. at 881. Trial counsel did reserve any exceptions, thus there is no showing of deficient performance.

The Court further finds any error on trial counsel's part in not requesting different instructions did not prejudice the defendant.

Trial counsel's decision not to impeach Terry Roberts with prior inconsistent statements was a matter of trial strategy which does not amount to ineffective assistance of counsel

"Counsel's assistance was not ineffective where he failed to impeach a witness with a prior inconsistent statement in order to retain the right to open and close." Victorine v. State, 264 Ga. 580, 582, 583 (449 SE2d 91) (1994). The decision to impeach a witness is a matter of strategy which will not be second guessed through hindsight. This Constitutional right to assistance of counsel insures "not errorless counsel and not counsel judged ineffective by hindsight, but counsel reasonably liable to render, and rendering reasonably effective assistance." Van Alstine v. State, 263 Ga. 1,4,5 (426 SE2d 360) (1993). The strategic decision by trial counsel not to impeach Roberts was a matter of trial strategy which does not amount to ineffective assistance of counsel. (Tr. 49, 50, 28, 29). Had trial counsel introduced the evidence, they would have lost opening and closing argument which both Mr. Walker and Mr. Peel felt was important. (Tr. 49, 50, 28, 29). Also, the fact Roberts made inconsistent statements was brought out to the jury on direct and cross examination and trial counsel made a strategic decision that this was sufficient to attack the witness's credibility. (Trial Tr. 1653-1701). The Court finds that this strategic decision fell within the wide range of reasonable professional conduct, and thus the defendant has not satisfied the first prong of the Strickland test. Strictland v. Washington, 446 U.S. 668, 687 (104 SC 2052) (80 LE2d 674) (1984).

The Court further finds any error on trial counsel's part in this regard did not prejudice the defendant. Strictland v. Washington, 446 U.S. 668, 687 (104 SC 2052) (80 LE2d 674) (1984).

Whether a defendant elects to testify or not is a decision left to him, therefore counsel's performance cannot be deficient if he does not persuade the defendant to testify.

"The decision to testify or not by the accused lies with the accused, not trial counsel." Van Alstine v. State, 263 Ga. 1 (426 SE2d 360) (1993). Only the defendant makes the final decision to take the stand or remain silent. Thus, the fact trial counsel did not persuade the defendant to testify cannot be viewed as deficient performance. Strictland v. Washington, 446 U.S. 668, 687 (104 SC 2052) (80 LE2d 674) (1984). After the State's evidence was presented, the Court informed Jenkins that he had a right to testify or to remain silent and inquired of Jenkins what his desire was. (Trial Tr. 1876, 1877). Jenkins replied, "No, I made the decision myself." (Trial Tr. 1877). The Court finds that counsel's strategic decision to advise Jenkins to remain silent falls within the wide range of reasonable professional conduct, and does not amount to a deficiency in performance. Furthermore, the Court finds no evidence that trial counsel forced or coerced Jenkins to remain silent and that the decision was properly made by Jenkins.

Trial counsel's decision not to introduce evidence of Cedric Brown's mental retardation does not support a claim of ineffective assistance of counsel.

Prior to trial, trial counsel sought privileged psychological reports regarding Cedric Brown's mental retardation. Trial counsel requested this information for the limited purpose of impeaching Cedric Brown should he take the stand. (Tr. 26, 27, 48). Brown did not take the stand, thus trial counsel had no use for this information. (Tr. 48). The defense alleges trial counsel's performance was deficient since Cedric Brown's mental evaluations were not offered into evidence. This decision not to offer this evidence was a matter of strategy and falls within the wide range of reasonable professional conduct. Trial counsel's theory was that Jenkins was merely present at the scene of the crime and that Cedric Brown was the leader and principal wrongdoer. (Tr. 28). Trial counsel felt that showing Brown was retarded could lead the jury to believe Jenkins was involved in the planning and execution of the crime. (Tr. 26, 27, 49).[240] The decision not to tender this evidence was a tactical decision which does not amount to deficient performance of trial counsel. Strictland v. Washington, 446 U.S. 668, 687 (104 SC 2052) (80 LE2d 674) (1984). The Court further finds that the fact that this evidence was not introduced did not prejudice the defendant.[241] There is not a reasonable probability that this caused the jury to find Jenkins guilty.

NO "DEAL" EXISTED BETWEEN THE STATE AND KENNETH McCALL IN EXCHANGE FOR HIS TESTIMONY

Kenneth McCall entered a guilty plea to one count of forgery on a Liberty County case prior to testifying in this case. Assistant District Attorney Charles Howard testified he negotiated the plea and at the time had no knowledge that McCall would be called as a witness in this case. (Trial Tr. 1860-1864). The Court finds that there was no deal with or offer of leniency to Kenneth McCall in exchange for his testimony at Jenkins' trial. Therefore, trial counsel's performance was not deficient because no objection was offered to McCall's testimony.[242]

---

240 Judge Harvey implies (citing pages 26, 27 and 49 of the March 14 hearing transcript) that Jenkins' trial counsel made a deliberate strategic decision not to introduce Cedric Brown's mental health records because doing so might undercut their theory that Cedric was the master planner of the robbery. That, however, is not what the evidence showed. Mr. Walker was explicitly asked by Assistant District Attorney Pittman at the March 14 hearing, why he "did not tender into evidence during the guilt phase of the trial the mental evaluations and the mental state of Cedric Brown?" (Tr. 27), to which Mr. Walker explicitly stated, "I don't remember what — why the decision was made that way." Tr. at 27. It was Mr. Pittman who then suggested, by his questioning, the theory espoused by Judge Harvey, but that was not what Mr. Walker had testified. Furthermore, there was nothing in the testimony of Mr. Peel either that suggested that Jenkins' trial counsel had made a conscious strategic decision not to introduce Brown's mental health files. See Tr. 47-49. Peel testified that he had sought the records to impeach Cedric Brown in case he testified, but since he did not testify, "I didn't need it." Tr. 48. Here again, there is no evidence that Mr. Peel made a strategic decision not to introduce Cedric's mental health files during the guilt portion of Jenkins' trial because he thought it might undermine their theory of the case. The fact is, neither Walker nor Peel explained why they failed to introduce this important evidence during Jenkins' trial. (Footnote added by author).

241 Judge Harvey states many times throughout his decision that he finds no evidence that the actions of Jenkins' trial counsel "prejudiced the defendant." I do not know what Judge Harvey considered prejudicial, but Jenkens was convicted of malice murder and sentenced to life imprisonment without any possibility of parole which seems awfully "prejudicial" to me. (Footnote added by author).

242 Jenkins never claimed that his trial counsel had been deficient with respect to the testimony of Kenneth McCall. What Jenkins claimed was that this testimony was false and misleading and should have been corrected by the prosecutor. (Footnote added by author).

ORDER

As for each and every enumeration of error raised by the defendant prior to the issue of ineffective assistance of counsel, the defendant's motion for a new trial is denied. As for the issue of ineffective assistance of counsel addressed in this order, the defendant's motion for a new trial is denied.

SO ORDER[ed] this the 6th day of May, 1997

/s/_____John R. Harvey

JOHN R. HARVEY, JUDGE

LIBERTY COUNTY SUPERIOR COURT

ATLANTIC JUDICIAL CIRCUIT

APPENDIX C

DECISION OF THE ELEVENTH CIRCUIT DENYING JENKINS' HABEAS APPEAL

[DO NOT PUBLISH]

IN THE UNITED STATES COURT OF APPEALS
FOR THE ELEVENTH CIRCUIT

No 00-13748
Non-Argument Calendar

D.C. Docket No. 98-00167-CV-4

CLEVON JAMEL JENKINS,   Petitioner-Appellant,

Versus

THOMAS E. BYRD, Warden,   Respondent-Appellee.

Appeal from the United States District Court
for the Southern District of Georgia

(August 10, 2001)

Before ANDERSON, Chief Judge, TJOFLAT and BLACK, Circuit Judges.

PER CURIAM:

Clevon Jamel Jenkins appeals the district court's denial of his petition for writ of habeas corpus pursuant to 28 U.S.C. § 2254. We affirm.

On appeal, Jenkins is limited to one issue because this court issued a certificate of appealability on only the issue of whether his trial counsel rendered ineffective assistance when they counseled him not to testify in his own defense. Jenkins argues that because the theory of the case was that he was a mere bystander, it was imperative that he testify because his counsel did not present any evidence to support that theory. He also argues that counsel misled him about the probable outcome of the trial by telling him before he made his decision not to testify that it was going well and that he need not testify. This erroneous information, he argues, prevented him from making an informed decision when he chose to waive his right to testify in his own defense.

Jenkins and three others were arrested for the murder and robbery of Robert Hodges. A fourth person was charged with only the robbery and he provided damaging testimony against Jenkins at trial. Jenkins was tried separately before a jury and represented by Hal Peel and David Walker. At trial, three people testified that Jenkins had admitted to shooting the victim. Walker and Peel did not call any witnesses or present any evidence so that they could retain their opening and closing arguments. Walker and Peel portrayed Jenkins as the outsider among the defendants because the others were related and he was from New York, and suggested that the others were attempting to pin the crimes on Jenkins to save their relatives. They advised Jenkins not to testify because they did not think it would help his case, and they were afraid that he might say something on cross-examination that would be damaging. When asked by the trial judge whether he wanted to testify, Jenkins replied that he did not and that he had reached this decision without the advice of counsel.[243]

The jury found Jenkins guilty of malice murder and armed robbery. After a separate penalty phase where the prosecution sought the death penalty, the jury sentenced Jenkins to life imprisonment without possibility of parole on the murder charge. The judge sentenced Jenkins to an additional life sentence, to be served consecutively.

Jenkins retained new counsel and moved for a new trial. Among many arguments, he raised the instant claim of ineffective assistance of counsel for advising him to waive his right to testify. The trial judge held an evidentiary hearing and then denied the motion. Jenkins appealed to the Supreme Court of Georgia, which upheld the conviction and sentence. See Jenkins v. State, 268 Ga. 468, 481 S.E.2d 54 (1997). After the United States Supreme Court denied his petition for a writ of certiorari, see Jenkins v. Georgia, 523 U.S. 1029, 118 S. Ct. 1318 (1998), Jenkins filed this petition for writ of habeas corpus in the district court. The district court denied the petition without holding a new evidentiary hearing or receiving any new evidence. Although the district court would not issue a certificate of appealability, this court issued one on the single issue of whether counsel rendered ineffective assistance.

Because Jenkins filed his federal habeas petition after the April 24, 1996, effective date of the Antiterrorism and Effective Death Penalty Act ("AEDPA"), AEDPA's review provisions apply. See McIntyre v. Williams, 216 F.3d 1254, 1256 (11th Cir. 2000). Under 28 U.S.C. §§ 2254(d)(1), "we can only reverse if we conclude that the state court's decision was contrary to, or involved an objectively unreasonable application of, the governing Federal law set forth by Supreme Court cases. If we cannot so conclude, we must affirm." McIntyre, 216 F.3d at 1257; see also 28 U.S.C. §§ 2254(d)(1).

---

243 This gratuitous factual assertion by the Court of Appeals was demonstrably **false**. Jenkins never claimed or stated that he did not rely on his counsels' advice in deciding to waive his right to testify. What he stated, in response to questioning by Judge Harvey at the trial, was that "I made the decision [not to testify] myself." Trial Tr. at 1877. That is a completely different issue from the question of whether he relied on counsels' advice in deciding not to testify. [Footnote added by author].

A state court decision involves an unreasonable application of Supreme Court precedent "if the state court identifies the correct governing legal rule from [Supreme Court] cases but unreasonably applies it to the facts of the particular state prisoner's case." Williams v. Taylor, 529 U.S. 362, 120 S. Ct. 1495, 1520 (2000). In addition, a state court decision involves an unreasonable application of Supreme Court precedent "if the state court either unreasonably extends a legal principle from [Supreme Court] precedent to a new context where it should not apply or unreasonably refuses to extend that principle to a new context where it should apply." Id.

In order to succeed with a challenge based on ineffective assistance of counsel, a petitioner has to satisfy a two-part test. First, the petitioner must show that counsel's performance was deficient. See Strickland v. Washington, 466 U.S. 668, 687, 104 S. Ct. 2052, 2064 (1984). This means that the petitioner must show that the representation provided by counsel was outside the "wide range of competent assistance" and he must also overcome the presumption of competence. Id. at 690, 104 S. Ct. at 2066. In analyzing counsel's competence, the court must apply a "heavy measure of deference to counsel's judgments." Id. at 691, 104 S. Ct. at 2066. Second, the petitioner must show that the performance prejudiced the defense, so that the result of the trial is not reliable. See id. To satisfy this test, the defendant "must show that there is a reasonable probability that, but for counsel's unprofessional errors, the result of the proceeding would have been different." Id. at 694, 104 S. Ct. at 2068. Furthermore, "[a] reasonable probability is a probability sufficient to undermine confidence in the outcome." Id. Because both parts of the test must be satisfied in order to show a violation of the Sixth Amendment, the court need not address the performance prong if the defendant cannot meet the prejudice prong, see id., or vice versa.

We cannot conclude that the state court unreasonably applied the law of ineffective assistance of counsel when it found that Peel and Walker provided effective assistance. At the evidentiary hearing, counsel testified that they advised Jenkins not to testify because his flat denial of the charges did not add anything to his plea of not guilty.[244] Additionally, they were afraid of what the prosecutor might elicit on cross-examination and at the evidentiary hearing, that fear proved well-founded. Jenkins testified at the hearing that he was outside of Hodges' store at the time of the murder. He also testified that he saw one of the other accused men shoot Hodges. However, on cross-examination, when asked where he was standing so that he could see the shooting, Jenkins could not remember. He also could not explain why there were bullets from two different guns found in the victim's body when he maintained that he only saw one person shooting.[245] Finally, his explanation of why three people testified that he had stated that he shot the victim was merely that they were lying. In short, Jenkins added little to his defense in his testimony, and in fact, the cross-examination succeeded in discrediting his story. Finally, counsel did subject all of the state's witnesses to cross-examination so that the testimony Jenkins deems damaging did not go into evidence unchallenged.[246]

Similarly, Jenkins' claim that counsel's assessment that the trial was going well, and that he did not need to testify constituted ineffective assistance is meritless. We give great deference to counsel's choices and make every effort "to eliminate the distorting effects of hindsight, to reconstruct the circumstances of counsel's challenged conduct, and to evaluate the

---

244 It is incomprehensible to me that three judges of the Eleventh Circuit Court of Appeals, including its Chief Justice, could proffer this bogus argument. Surely, they must have known that Jenkins' not guilty plea did not constitute evidence. Indeed, Judge Harvey explicitly and properly instructed the jury prior to its deliberations, "I caution you that an indictment is not evidence, nor is the mere fact that a grand jury has returned an indictment constitute any evidence or inference of guilt. **Neither is the plea of not guilty to be considered as evidence**." Trial Tr. 1973 (emphasis added). To suggest, as the Court did, that Jenkins' sworn testimony under oath that he did not participate in this crime but was merely a bystander, that he did not have a gun and did not shoot Mr. Hodges, and that he did not make any of the incriminating statements alleged by Roberts, Smith and McCall, would not "add anything" to his defense is preposterous. [Footnote added by author].

245 This statement by the Court of Appeals was false. The ballistics and medical evidence clearly established that the two bullets recovered from Mr. Hodges' body came from a single gun. [Footnote added by author].

246 It is ironic and unfortunate that the Court of Appeals chose to rely on this argument in supporting its decision, considering that Jenkins had specifically argued that his counsels' cross-examination of the witnesses at trial had been deficient for numerous reasons, including especially their failure to impeach Terry Roberts with his prior inconsistent statements. Unfortunately, the Court of Appeals was unaware of these alleged deficiencies due to the limited nature of the certificate of appealability that had been previously granted by Judge Wilson. [Footnote added by author].

conduct from counsel's perspective at the time." Strickland, 466 U.S. at 689, 104 S. Ct. at 2065. Here, Jenkins benefits from hindsight that counsel could not have enjoyed at the time of the trial.[247] Both Peel and Walker had a great deal of experience in criminal trials: Peel was the public defender for several counties and had practiced for over eight years and Walker had been an assistant district attorney for seven years. It is reasonable to believe that they would have had a good idea of whether a trial appeared to be going well and the fact that their assessment was incorrect, without any contemporary evidence that the assessment was wrong, is not enough for us to conclude that their advice fell below the range expected of competent counsel.

The district court's denial of Jenkins' petition for writ of habeas corpus is AFFIRMED.[248]

---

247 To suggest, as the Court of Appeals does here, that "Jenkins benefits from hindsight that counsel could not have enjoyed at the time of the trial" is a blatant example of "putting one's head in the sand." During his summation to the jury after the close of the evidence, District Attorney Cheney accurately (and unlawfully) pointed out to the jury — not just once but four times — that Jenkins had not presented *any evidence* which refuted the State's case. Hindsight was not at issue here. It was obvious from the get-go to anyone with half a brain that Jenkins would be convicted based upon the uncontroverted evidence that had been presented by the State. There was no possible way any competent attorney could think that this case was "going well" for Jenkins and that there was "no need" for his to testify. {Footnote added by author].

248 The parties' requests for argument are denied [footnote in original].

APPENDIX D

DECISION OF JUDGE GARAUFIS DISMISSING THE DECLARATORY JUDGMENT COMPLAINT

UNITED STATES DISTRICT COURT
EASTERN DISTRICT OF NEW YORK

X _____

CLEVON JAMEL JENKINS,

Plaintiff,

v.

UNITED STATES OF AMERICA,

Defendant.

MEMORANDUM AND ORDER

01-CV-1545 (NGG)

X _____

GARAUFIS, United States District Judge.

Clevon Jamel Jenkins ("plaintiff") brings this action against the United States of America ("defendant"), asking this court to declare that United States District Court Judge John F. Nagle's (sic)[249] application of 28 U.S.C. § 2254(d) and § 2253(c) to his habeas corpus petition was unconstitutional. Additionally, plaintiff asks this court to declare that 28 U.S.C. § 2253(c), on its face, is unconstitutional. The defendant, represented by the

---

249   His name was "Nangle." Footnote added by author.

Office of the United States Attorney for the Eastern District of New York, has moved to dismiss the complaint on several grounds. For the reasons set forth below, the defendant's motion to dismiss for lack of subject matter jurisdiction is granted.

Factual Background

In September 1995, plaintiff was convicted of murder and armed robbery in the Superior Court of Liberty County, Georgia. (Complaint ("Compl.") ¶ 9.) Plaintiff was sentenced to consecutive terms of life imprisonment. (Id.) After exhausting his state court remedies, plaintiff filed a petition for a writ of habeas corpus in the United States District Court for the Southern District of Georgia before Judge Nagle (sic). (Id. ¶ 12-13.) In his petition, plaintiff alleged that the state court committed at least nineteen federal constitutional violations. (Id.) In a decision dated June 21, 2000, Judge Nagle (sic) denied the petition. (Jenkins v. Byrd, 103 F. Supp. 2d 1350 (S.D. Ga. 2000.)) Judge Nagle's (sic) decision was based, in part, on his interpretation of case law construing § 2254(d)'s limitation to granting habeas corpus relief to persons incarcerated pursuant to state court judgments. (Id.)

On July 17, 2000, plaintiff filed a notice of appeal with the Court of Appeals for the Eleventh Circuit. (Compl. ¶ 16.) On September 1, 2000, plaintiff moved in the district court for leave to prosecute the appeal in forma pauperis. This motion was granted. (Id. ¶ 17.) However, the district court did not issue a Certificate of Appealability ("COA").[250] On September 22, 2000, the district court vacated its order granting plaintiff's motion to proceed in forma pauperis, on the ground that no COA had been issued. (Id. ¶ 19.) Plaintiff subsequently moved for a COA and the district court denied that motion as untimely. (Id. ¶ 21.) On November 14, 2000, plaintiff moved in the Court of Appeals for a COA. (Id. ¶ 24) The motion was granted, but only to consider the issue of ineffective assistance of counsel.

---

250 28 U.S.C. § 2253(c) requires a petitioner to obtain a COA prior to appealing a denial of a § 2254 petition. [Footnote in original].

(Id. ¶ 25.) Regarding the remaining issues raised by the plaintiff, the court held that "he failed to make a substantial showing of the denial of a constitutional right." (Affidavit of Robert M. Kelly, Exhibit E.)

Plaintiff filed this action in March 2001. Plaintiff asks this court to declare that (i) Judge Nagle's (sic) application of 28 U.S.C. § 2254(d) and § 2253(c) was unconstitutional; and (ii) that 28 U.S.C. § 2253(c), on its face, is unconstitutional.

Defendant's Motion to Dismiss

The defendant filed a motion to dismiss the complaint based upon the following grounds: (i) lack of venue; (ii) plaintiff's cause of action is barred by the doctrine of res judicata; and (iii) for failure to state a claim for which relief can be granted. In the alternative, defendant moved to transfer this case to the United States District Court for the Southern District of Georgia and for plaintiff to make a more definite statement of his claims. (See generally, Memorandum in Support of Defendant's Motion to Dismiss.) In its Reply Memorandum of Law, the defendant withdrew its res judicata argument. Additionally, it claimed, for the first time, that this court lacks subject matter jurisdiction over this action for the following reasons: (i) plaintiff may not use the Declaratory Judgment Action to review denial of his habeas petition; and (ii) plaintiff lacks standing to bring this lawsuit.[251]

For the reasons set forth below, defendant's motion is granted.

Discussion

The defendant moves to dismiss plaintiff's cause of action for lack of subject matter jurisdiction. "A party seeking a declaratory judgment bears the burden of proving that the district court has jurisdiction." E.R Squibb & Sons, Inc. v. Lloyd's & Cos., 241 F.3d 154, 177 (2d Cir. 2001) (citations omitted). Jurisdiction in a declaratory judgment action exists only if there

---

251 Although the defendant had not raised this ground for dismissal in its initial Memorandum of law, lack of subject-matter jurisdiction can be raised at any point during litigation. See Bender v. Williamsport Area School Dist., 475 U.S. 534, 541 (1986). [Footnote in original].

is an "actual controversy." 28 U.S.C. § 2201(a). An "actual controversy" has been defined as one that is "real and substantial . . . admitting of specific relief through a decree of a conclusive character, as distinguished from an opinion advising what the law would be on a hypothetical state of facts.'" Olin Corp. v. Consolidated Aluminum Corp., 5 F.3d 10, 17 (2d Cir 1993) (quoting Aetna Life Ins. Co. v. Haworth, 300 U.S. 227, 341 (1937)). Where "the remedy sought is a mere declaration of law without implications for practical enforcement upon the parties, the case is properly dismissed." Browning Debenture Holders' Comm. v. Dasa Corp., 524 F.2d 811, 817 (2d Cir. 1975). See also, S. Jackson & Son v. Coffee, Sugar & Cocoa Exch., 24 F.3d 427, 431 (2d Cir. 1994).

An actual controversy does not exist in this case because it is not likely that a decision in plaintiff's favor will provide him with the relief he seeks. According to plaintiff, his injury is "the fact that he was denied the opportunity to obtain meaningful habeas relief due to certain alleged constitutional infirmities in AEDPA." (Plaintiff's Rebuttal Memorandum of Law ("Rebut. Mem.") at 10.) To redress this injury, this court's declaratory judgment would have to make it likely that plaintiff will be granted "meaningful habeas relief." Plaintiff argues that "[i]f these limitations are declared unconstitutional by the Court, then plaintiff would be entitled to seek further habeas relief." (Id. at 11.) That argument is simply not correct.

A declaration by this court that section 2253(c) is facially unconstitutional, and that sections 2254(d) and 2253(c) were unconstitutionally applied to plaintiff's habeas petition, can, at best, be used by plaintiff as persuasive authority in attempting to convince the Georgia district court to reopen the habeas proceeding.[252] Consequently, a declaration by this court concerning the constitutionality of plaintiff's claims would have no effect on plaintiff's entitlement to seek further habeas review. Accordingly, this court is without subject matter jurisdiction over plaintiff's claims.

---

252 Indeed, pursuant to 28 U.S.C. § 2244(b)(3), plaintiff will have to seek permission from the Eleventh Circuit to file another habeas petition. In light of the fact that the Eleventh Circuit already concluded that "petitioner failed to make a showing of the denial of a constitutional right" it is not likely that it will grant a request for another habeas petition. [Footnote in original].

Conclusion

For the reasons set forth above, plaintiff's claim is dismissed for lack of subject matter jurisdiction.

Dated: June 9, 2003

Brooklyn, N.Y.

/s/ __Nicholas G. Garaufis

Nicholas G. Garaufis

United States District Judge

AUTHOR BIOGRAPHY

Robert Michael Kelly is a *summa cum laude* graduate of both the NYU School of Law and the NYU Graduate School of Business (now Stern). At NYU Law, he served as Note and Comment Editor of the *NYU Law Review*, was named a John Norton Pomeroy Scholar, and was inducted into the Order of the Coif. At Stern, he was selected for membership in Beta Gamma Sigma, the national business honor society. He earned his undergraduate degree in political science and philosophy from Fordham University, where he was News Editor and Editor-in-Chief of *The Fordham Ram*, a member of the Dean's List, and a recipient of both a New York State Regents Scholarship and a New York City Mayor's Committee on Scholastic Achievement Scholarship.

After graduating from law school, Kelly studied at the U.S. Army Intelligence School at Fort Holabird, Maryland, graduating with honors, and served as an interrogator in the U.S. Army Reserve for five years, attaining the rank of Specialist Fifth Class before receiving an honorable discharge in 1973.

Kelly began his legal career in the Manhattan District Attorney's Office in 1970, where he spent five years prosecuting more than twenty homicide and homicide-related cases. He then spent over three decades as a senior trial lawyer at a prominent New York City and international law firm, focusing on complex civil litigation and filing more than a dozen petitions for certiorari with the U.S. Supreme Court. While at this firm, Mr. Kelly spent a significant portion of his time working on *pro bono* projects for indigent clients and was awarded the firm's first ever "*Pro Bono* Service Award."

In his debut book, *State of Georgia versus Clevon Jamel Jenkins*, Kelly delivers a scathing indictment of the American criminal justice system — not as a prosecutor, but as a *pro bono* advocate for a wrongfully convicted black teenager. This riveting and meticulously researched work provides a comprehensive and scholarly analysis of an error-filled and badly decided case that has haunted the author for over two decades.

Now retired from legal practice, Kelly lives in central North Carolina with his wife, Margaret. He enjoys writing, studying, traveling, playing piano and violin, taking exercise classes at his local senior center, and following the marvelous adventures of his seven beloved grandchildren.